**TOP NOTCH 3**

# Teacher's Edition
## and Lesson Planner

Joan Saslow ■ Allen Ascher

with Silvia Carolina Tiberio

PEARSON
Longman

Includes
Teacher's Resource Disk
with printable activities

**Top Notch: English for Today's World**    **3**
Teacher's Edition and Lesson Planner

Pearson Education, 10 Bank Street, White Plains, NY 10606

Editorial director: Pamela Fishman
Senior development editors: Maretta Callahan, Peter Benson, Trish Lattanzio
Vice president, director of design and production: Rhea Banker
Director of electronic production: Aliza Greenblatt
Managing editor: Mike Kemper
Senior production editor: Sasha Kintzler
Art director: Ann France
Senior manufacturing buyer: Dave Dickey
Photo research: Aerin Csigay
Digital layout specialist: Warren Fischbach
Text composition: The Mazer Corp.
Text font: 11/12 Palatino
Cover photograph: "From Above," by Rhea Banker. Copyright © 2005 Rhea Banker.

ISBN: 0-13-110640-6

**Photo credits:** All original photography by David Mager. Page 2 (Sydney) Peter Adams/Getty Images, (Cambridge) Steve Vidler/SuperStock, (London) Gail M. Shumway/Bruce Coleman, Inc., (Auckland) Rex A. Butcher/Bruce Coleman, Inc., (Edinburgh) Ken Sherman/Bruce Coleman, Inc., (San Francisco) Claver Carroll/PhotoLibrary.com, (Cape Town) Hein von Horsten/Gallo Images/Corbis, (New York) Jochen Tack/Peter Arnold, Inc., (Toronto) SuperStock; p. 5 (middle) Tom & Dee Ann McCarthy/Corbis; p. 7 (top) Russ Lappa, (bottom) Dave King/Dorling Kindersley; p. 9 Will & Deni McIntyre/Getty Images; p. 10 Elpida Memory, Inc.; p. 12 Royalty-Free/Corbis; p. 13 Angelo Cavalli/Getty Images; p. 14 (top) Dorling Kindersley, (left) Bob Daemmrich/The Image Works, (middle) Frozen Images/ The Image Works, (right) Adam Woolfitt/Woodfin Camp & Associates; p. 17 Garry Gay/Mira.com; p. 19 (left to right) Will & Deni McIntyre/Photo Researchers, Inc., Maxine Hall/Corbis, Custom Medical Stock Photo, Inc., Lew Lause/SuperStock, Lester Lefkowitz/Corbis; p. 20 (top to bottom) Digital Vision Ltd./SuperStock, Sylvia Johnson/Woodfin Camp & Associates, Phil Schermeister/Corbis, Barbara P. Williams/Bruce Coleman Inc., Charles Gupton/Corbis, Paul Barton/Corbis; p. 22 (ragweed) Getty Images, (bacteria) David Spears/Corbis; p. 23 Royalty-Free/Corbis; p. 26 Arnulf Husmo/Getty Images; p. 29 Getty Images; p. 31 (left to right) Xerox Corporation, George Hall/Corbis, Michael Newman/PhotoEdit, Michelle D. Bridwell/PhotoEdit; p. 34 (caterer) Stewart Cohen/Getty Images, (DJ) Jeff Greenberg/The Image Works; p. 38 (top to bottom) V.O. Press/PhotoEdit, C Squared Studios/Getty Images, Olympus America Inc., Siede Preis/Getty Images, Siede Preis/Getty Images; p. 44 Benelux Press/Index Stock Imagery; p. 45 Steve Gorton/Dorling Kindersley; p. 46 (left) DPA/The Image Works, (right) Bettmann/Corbis; p. 47 (left) Steve Gorton/Dorling Kindersley, (right) Dorling Kindersley; p. 50 (background) Nancy R. Cohen/Getty Images, (top left) Russell Gordon/Odyssey, (top right) Hong Suk-young and Son Kwan-soo, (middle left) Steve Vidler/SuperStock, (middle right) Tony Freeman/PhotoEdit, (bottom left) Stephanie Maze/Woodfin Camp & Associates, (bottom right) AP Wide World Photos; p. 51 John Paul Endress; p. 52 (background) SuperStock, (cake) Michael Newman/PhotoEdit, (fireworks) SuperStock, (parades) Chip East/Corbis, (picnics) Michael Newman/PhotoEdit, (pray) Zafer Kizilkaya/Coral Planet, (gifts) Ryan McVay/Getty Images, (dead) Doug Martin/Photo Researchers, Inc., (costumes) Philip Gould/Corbis; p. 54 Steve Shott/Dorling Kindersley; p. 55 Stephen Hayward/Dorling Kindersley; p. 56 (top) Richard Powers/Corbis, (left) Mark Downey/Lucid Images, (right) Pablo Corral/Corbis; p. 57 Prentice Hall School Division; p. 58 (left) Elyse Lewin/Getty Images, (middle) Stockbyte/SuperStock, (right) Darama/Corbis; p. 62 (left) Bettmann/Corbis, (top right) The Granger Collection, New York, (bottom) The Manila Times; p. 65 David Young-Wolff/PhotoEdit; p. 66 South Florida Sun-Sentinel. Reprinted with permission; p. 68 (all) Dorling Kindersley; p. 69 (all) Dorling Kindersley; p. 70 (top) Corbis, (bottom) Michael S. Yamashita/Corbis; p. 75 Henryk T. Kaiser/Index Stock Imagery; p. 79 (home) Ira Montgomery/Getty Images, (others) Dorling Kindersley; p. 80 (Spider-Man) Marvel; p. 86 (background) Philip Harvey/SuperStock, (wagon wheel) Carl & Ann Purcell/Corbis, (two-wheeled carts) Bettmann/Corbis, (horse-drawn) The Art Archive/ Bibliotheque des Arts Decoratifs Paris/Dagli Orti, (potter's wheel) Blair Seitz/Photo Researchers, Inc., (auto) Ron Kimball/Ron Kimball Stock. All rights reserved; p. 87 (inset) Fadek Timothy/Corbis Sygma, (bottom) Science & Society Picture Library; p. 89 (camera) courtesy Canon USA, (monitor) IBM Corporation, (scanner) Michael Newman/PhotoEdit, (phone) SuperStock, (palmtop) Ryan McVay/Getty Images; p. 93 Dorling Kindersley; p. 94 (top left) North Wind Picture Archives, (top right) Science & Society Picture Library, (bottom) Inc., Martin Paul Ltd./Index Stock Imagery; p. 95 (left to right) Alinari/Art Resource, NY, Hulton Archive/ Getty Images, Ray Ellis/Photo Researchers, Inc., Brown Brothers; p. 98 Reuters/Corbis; p. 104 NASA/Corbis; p. 111 Buddy Mays/Corbis; p. 113 (snake) Breck P. Kent/Animals Animals/Earth Scenes, (scorpion) Austin J. Stevens/Animals Animals/Earth Scenes, (shark) Brandon Cole/naturepl.com, (jellyfish) O.S.F./Animals Animals/Earth Scenes, (mosquito) Timothy Fadek/Corbis Sygma; p. 115 Robert Harding World Imagery/Getty Images; p. 116 (mountainous) Douglas Mason/Woodfin Camp & Associates, (hilly) David Weintraub/Photo Researchers, Inc., (flat) Jim Steinberg/Photo Researchers, Inc., (lush) K. H. Hanel/Panoramic Images/NGSImages.com, (arid) Jeff Foott/Bruce Coleman Inc., (forest) Jim Steinberg/Photo Researchers, Inc., (jungle) Gregory G. Dimijian/Photo Researchers, Inc., (canyon) T. Gervis/Robert Harding Picture Library, (island) Don Hebert/Getty Images, (valley) John Lamb/Getty Images; p. 117 (Galapagos) Alison Wright/Corbis, (Tahiti) N. DeVore III/Bruce Coleman, Inc., (Zambia) Hans Reinhard/Bruce Coleman, Inc., (Alaska) True North Images/www.agefotostock.com, (Tibet) Glen Allison/Getty Images, (bottom) Dorling Kindersley; p. 118 (background) Richard T. Nowitz/Corbis, (middle) Stephen Saks/Lonely Planet Images/Photo 20-20, (right top to bottom) SuperStock, Neil Duncan/ PhotoLibrary.com, Mark Edwards/Peter Arnold, Inc., K. Ammann/Bruce Coleman Inc.; p. 119 (top) Dave G. Houser/Corbis, (middle) Ingo Arndt/naturepl.com (bottom).

**Illustration credits:** Steve Attoe, pp. 28, 92, 112; Kevin Brown / Top, p. 121; Sue Carlson, pp. 110, 114, 115, 120; Mark Collins, pp. 83, 92; Chris Gash, pp. 61, 97; Brian Hughes, pp. 27, 67; Stephen Hutchings, p. 82; Andy Myer, pp. 41, 102; Tom Newsom, pp. 25, 49, 73, 109; Dusan Petricic, pp. 17, 18, 24, 42, 43, 120; Gail Piazza, p. 16; Realia / Kirchoff Wohlberg, pp. 22, 26, 45, 46, 76; Robert Saunders, pp. 37, 85; Arvis Stewart, p. 86; Anne Veltfort, p. 35.

Printed in the United States of America
5 6 7 8 9 10–QWD–10 09 08

# Contents

# *Top Notch* unit walk-through

UNIT 8

# Inventions and Technology

UNIT GOALS

1. Describe an innovation
2. Accept responsibility for a mistake
3. Evaluate inventions
4. Discuss the impact of key inventions in history

**A TOPIC PREVIEW.** Do you consider the wheel to be the most important mechanical invention in history? What other modern uses of the wheel can you name?

logs used as wheels

a wooden wagon wheel

two-wheeled carts

a horse-drawn chariot

a potter's wheel

**B DISCUSSION.**

1. What difficulties did people have before the in
2. How did the wheel change the lives of people

86 UNIT 8

**UNIT GOALS.** Clearly state the communication goals of the unit.

**TOPIC PREVIEW.** Previews the content of the unit and accesses prior knowledge.

**LANGUAGE SUPPORT.** Illustrations and photos define new language and ensure comprehensibility.

**SOUND BITES.** Previews the language of the unit and provides exposure to "+1" natural language for observation.

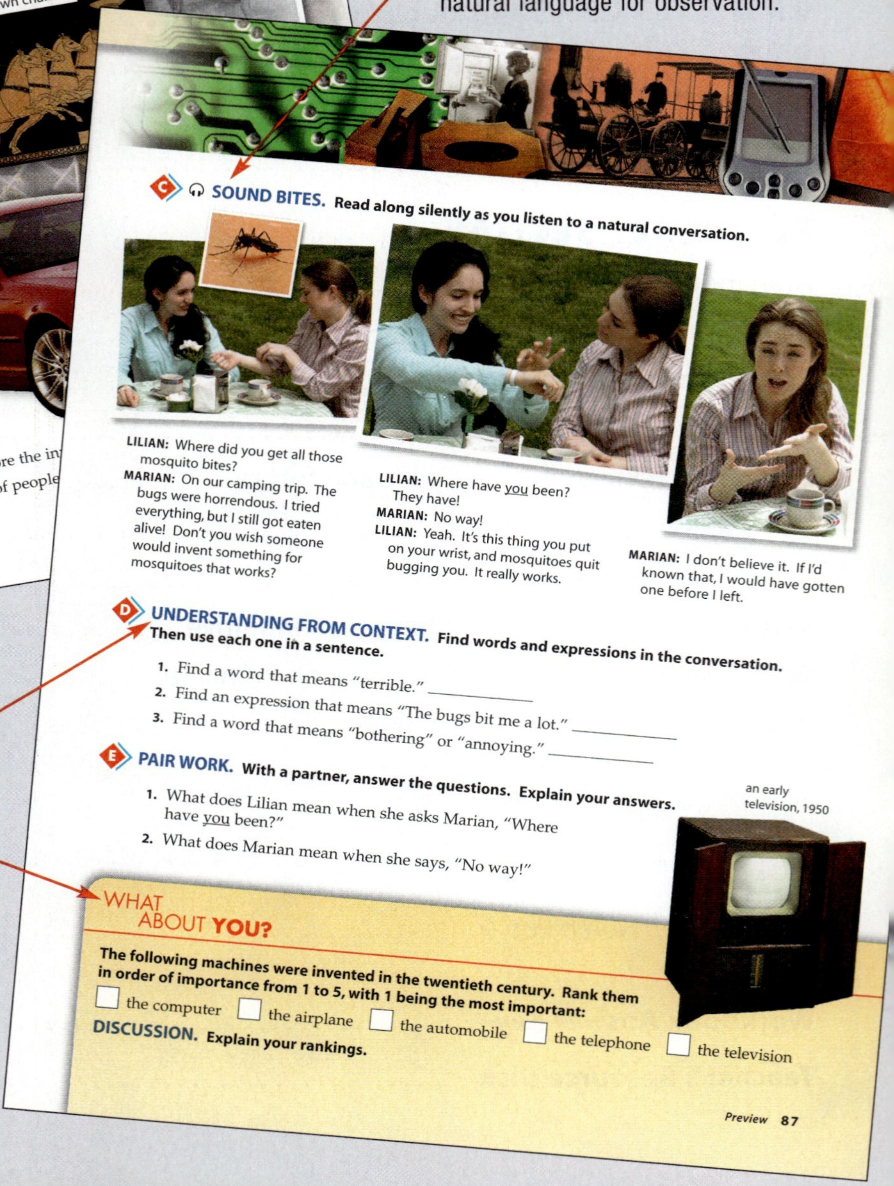

**C SOUND BITES.** Read along silently as you listen to a natural conversation.

**LILIAN:** Where did you get all those mosquito bites?
**MARIAN:** On our camping trip. The bugs were horrendous. I tried everything, but I still got eaten alive! Don't you wish someone would invent something for mosquitoes that works?

**LILIAN:** Where have you been? They have!
**MARIAN:** No way!
**LILIAN:** Yeah. It's this thing you put on your wrist, and mosquitoes quit bugging you. It really works.

**MARIAN:** I don't believe it. If I'd known that, I would have gotten one before I left.

**D UNDERSTANDING FROM CONTEXT.** Find words and expressions in the conversation. Then use each one in a sentence.

1. Find a word that means "terrible." ____________
2. Find an expression that means "The bugs bit me a lot." ____________
3. Find a word that means "bothering" or "annoying." ____________

**E PAIR WORK.** With a partner, answer the questions. Explain your answers.

1. What does Lilian mean when she asks Marian, "Where have you been?"
2. What does Marian mean when she says, "No way!"

an early television, 1950

WHAT ABOUT YOU?

The following machines were invented in the twentieth century. Rank them in order of importance from 1 to 5, with 1 being the most important:

☐ the computer ☐ the airplane ☐ the automobile ☐ the telephone ☐ the television

**DISCUSSION.** Explain your rankings.

Preview 87

**UNDERSTANDING MEANING FROM CONTEXT.** Students learn an essential skill for comprehension of unfamiliar language.

**WHAT ABOUT YOU?** Confirms students' understanding, provides language support, and readies students for the unit.

**CONVERSATION MODEL.** Transferable conversation models make social language memorable. Photos support meaning and provide a stimulus for additional oral work.

**VOCABULARY.** Vocabulary presentations always define meaning and provide easy reference for study.

---

### Discuss a New Product

🎧 **CONVERSATION MODEL** Read and listen.

**A:** I need a new coffee maker. Do you think I should get the Brew Rite? It's on sale at TechnoMart.
**B:** That depends. How much are they selling it for?
**A:** $75.
**B:** Definitely. That's a great price. If I needed a coffee maker, I'd buy one too. It's top of the line.

🎧 Rhythm and intonation practice

🎧 **VOCABULARY.** Describing manufactured products. Listen and practice.

| Uses new technology | Offers high quality | Uses new ideas |
|---|---|---|
| high-tech | high-end | innovative |
| state-of-the-art | top-of-the-line | revolutionary |
| cutting-edge | first-rate | novel |

**GRAMMAR.** Factual and unreal conditional sentences: review

**Present factual conditionals:** Use the simple present tense in both clauses.
If you **make** a lot of coffee, you **need** a good coffee maker.

**Future factual conditionals:** Use the simple present tense in the *if* clause. Use the future with **will** or **be going to** in the result clause.
If they **sell** the Brew Rite for as low a price as the Coffee King, they**'ll sell** a lot of them.

**Present unreal conditionals:** Use the simple past tense or **was / were** in the *if* clause. Use **would** in the result clause.
If I **were** you, I **wouldn't buy** it. (unreal condition: I am not you.)
If Teletex **had** a cutting-edge digital camera phone, they **would sell** more. (unreal condition: Teletex doesn't have one.)

**BE CAREFUL!** Don't use a future form in the **if** clause.
If I buy it, I'll be happy. **NOT** If I will buy it, I'll be happy.

Don't use **would** in the **if** clause.
If they knew the best brand, they would get it. **NOT** If they would know the best brand, they would get it.

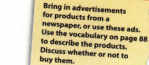

GRAMMAR BOOSTER
PAGES G13–G14
For more …

...ractice distinguishing between factual and unreal conditions.
...eck the statements that describe **unreal** conditions.
☐ 1. If they see something first-rate, they buy it.
☐ 2. If we take the bus to TechnoMart, we save a lot of time.
☐ 3. If you walked to the theater, you would get there late.
☐ 4. They won't get any phone calls if they don't have their cell phones.
☐ 5. If she were a photographer, she would sell her old camera and buy a new one.

8

**D** Complete each present factual conditional sentence.
1. Water _____ if you _____ its temperature to 100 degrees.
   *boil*        *raise*
2. If I _____ something that's really cutting edge, I _____ it.
   *see*                                                    *want*
3. She _____ her own beans if she _____ really great coffee.
   *grind*                              *want*
4. He always _____ state-of-the-art equipment if it _____ available.
   *use*                                              *be*

**E** Choose the correct form to complete each future factual conditional sentence.
1. If they _____ to get there fast, they _____ the express train.
   *want / will want*                        *take / will take*
2. If he _____ the product, the mosquitoes _____.
   *buys / will buy*                          *don't bite / won't bite*
3. If they _____ her tomorrow, they _____ her their new camera phone.
   *see / will see*                          *show / will show*
4. _____ the camera phone if they _____ it on sale?
   *Are you going to get / Do you get*        *offer / will offer*

**F** **PAIR WORK.** Take turns completing each present unreal conditional in your **own** way.
1. If I were an inventor, I …
2. If I could go anywhere in the world, …
3. If I needed a car, …

**CONVERSATION PAIR WORK**

Bring in advertisements for products from a newspaper, or use these ads. Use the vocabulary on page 88 to describe the products. Discuss whether or not to buy them.

**Start like this:**

**A:** I need a new _____. Do you think I should get the _____? …

**B:** _____ …

**Digicon B1X**
• cutting-edge technology
• 5.44 megapixel
US $3899

**Save $50**
US $379
**17" LCD Monitor**
Teknicon

**Micro Scanner**
• state-of-the-art
US $199

**Strawberry Palmtop** SPECIAL BUY
• handheld
• Internet capable
• secure digital
• media card slot
US $99
super special

**Digi-Phone**
• 2-line digital phone system
US $79

89

CONTROLLED PRACTICE

---

**GRAMMAR.** Grammar is presented with clear explanations and examples, integrating form, meaning, and use. Use of color ensures that students focus on the target grammar.

**GRAMMAR BOOSTER.** For those who want more, a Grammar Booster in the back of the Student's Book gives additional explanations, examples, grammar points, timely reviews, as well as more practice.

**CONTROLLED COMMUNICATION PRACTICE.** Students personalize the Conversation Model, using the new vocabulary and grammar, to confirm their progress at the end of the lesson.

**COMMUNICATION SUPPORT.** Realistic visual prompts provide support and ensure success.

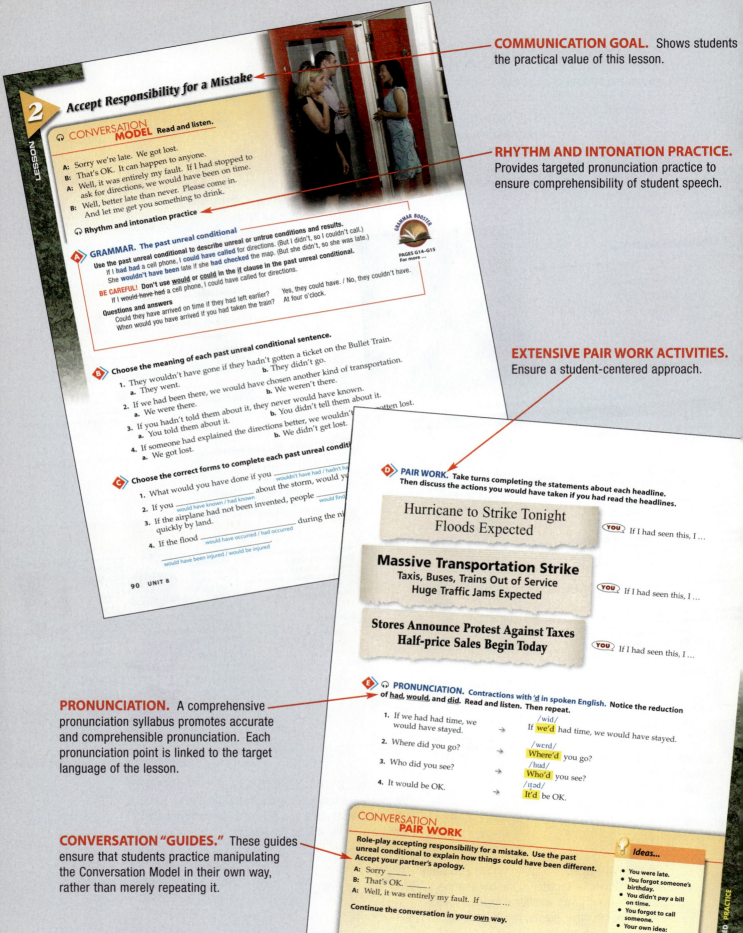

LESSON **2**

## Accept Responsibility for a Mistake

### CONVERSATION MODEL  Read and listen.

A: Sorry we're late. We got lost.
B: That's OK. It can happen to anyone.
A: Well, it was entirely my fault. If I had stopped to ask for directions, we would have been on time.
B: Well, better late than never. Please come in. And let me get you something to drink.

🎧 Rhythm and intonation practice

**A** **GRAMMAR. The past unreal conditional**

Use the past unreal conditional to describe unreal or untrue conditions and results.
If I **had had** a cell phone, I **could have called** for directions. (But I didn't, so I couldn't call.)
She **wouldn't have been** late if she **had checked** the map. (But she didn't, so she was late.)

**BE CAREFUL!** Don't use <u>would</u> or <u>could</u> in the <u>if</u> clause in the past unreal conditional.
If I ~~would have had~~ a cell phone, I could have called for directions.

GRAMMAR BOOSTER
PAGES G14–G15
For more …

**Questions and answers**
Could they have arrived on time if they had left earlier?    Yes, they could have. / No, they couldn't have.
When would you have arrived if you had taken the train?    At four o'clock.

**B** Choose the meaning of each past unreal conditional sentence.

1. They wouldn't have gone if they hadn't gotten a ticket on the Bullet Train.
   a. They went.               b. They didn't go.
2. If we had been there, we would have chosen another kind of transportation.
   a. We were there.          b. We weren't there.
3. If you hadn't told them about it, they never would have known.
   a. You told them about it.   b. You didn't tell them about it.
4. If someone had explained the directions better, we wouldn't ~~have~~ gotten lost.
   a. We got lost.             b. We didn't get lost.

**C** Choose the correct forms to complete each past unreal condit...

1. What would you have done if you _wouldn't have had / hadn't ha..._
2. If you _would have known / had known_ about the storm, would yo...
3. If the airplane had not been invented, people _would find..._ quickly by land.
4. If the flood _would have occurred / had occurred_ during the ni...
   _would have been injured / would be injured_

90  UNIT 8

---

**D** **PAIR WORK.** Take turns completing the statements about each headline.
Then discuss the actions you would have taken if you had read the headlines.

Hurricane to Strike Tonight
Floods Expected

(YOU) If I had seen this, I …

**Massive Transportation Strike**
Taxis, Buses, Trains Out of Service
Huge Traffic Jams Expected

(YOU) If I had seen this, I …

**Stores Announce Protest Against Taxes**
Half-price Sales Begin Today

(YOU) If I had seen this, I …

**E** 🎧 **PRONUNCIATION.** Contractions with '<u>d</u> in spoken English. Notice the reduction of <u>had</u>, <u>would</u>, and <u>did</u>. Read and listen. Then repeat.

1. If we had had time, we would have stayed.    →    /wid/  If **we'd** had time, we would have stayed.
2. Where did you go?    →    /wɛrd/  **Where'd** you go?
3. Who did you see?    →    /hud/  **Who'd** you see?
4. It would be OK.    →    /ɪtəd/  **It'd** be OK.

### CONVERSATION PAIR WORK

Role-play accepting responsibility for a mistake. Use the past unreal conditional to explain how things could have been different. Accept your partner's apology.

A: Sorry _____ .
B: That's OK. _____ .
A: Well, it was entirely my fault. If _____ …

**Continue the conversation in your <u>own</u> way.**

💡 Ideas…
• You were late.
• You forgot someone's birthday.
• You didn't pay a bill on time.
• You forgot to call someone.
• Your own idea:

CONTROLLED PRACTICE

**VOCABULARY.** Clear defining illustrations take the guesswork out of the meaning of new words and provide a permanent reference.

**FREE COMMUNICATION PRACTICE.** Offering students an opportunity to remember and use language taught in this AND previous lessons, *Top Notch* Interactions provide support for successful discussion.

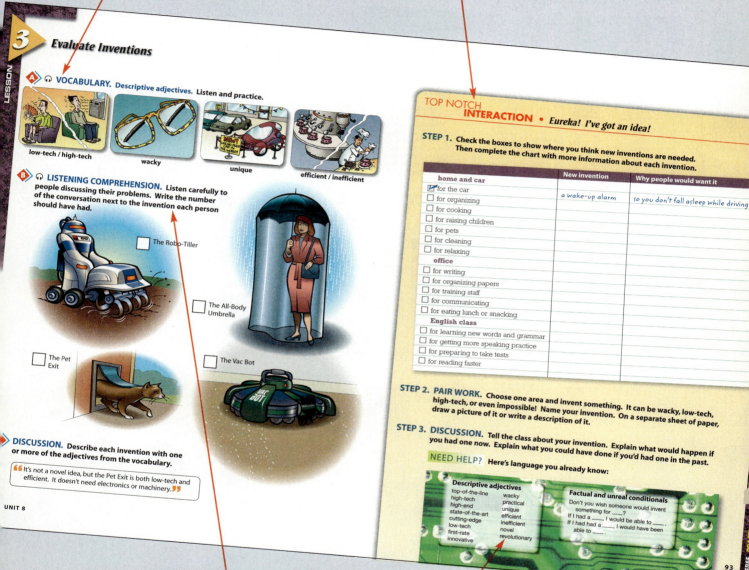

**LESSON 3**

**Evaluate Inventions**

**A** 🎧 **VOCABULARY.** Descriptive adjectives. Listen and practice.

low-tech / high-tech
wacky
unique
efficient / inefficient

**B** 🎧 **LISTENING COMPREHENSION.** Listen carefully to people discussing their problems. Write the number of the conversation next to the invention each person should have had.

The Robo-Tiller

The All-Body Umbrella

The Pet Exit

The Vac Bot

**DISCUSSION.** Describe each invention with one or more of the adjectives from the vocabulary.

"It's not a novel idea, but the Pet Exit is both low-tech and efficient. It doesn't need electronics or machinery."

UNIT 8

**TOP NOTCH**
**INTERACTION** • *Eureka! I've got an idea!*

**STEP 1.** Check the boxes to show where you think new inventions are needed. Then complete the chart with more information about each invention.

| home and car | New invention | Why people would want it |
|---|---|---|
| ☑ for the car | | |
| ☐ for organizing | a wake-up alarm | so you don't fall asleep while driving |
| ☐ for cooking | | |
| ☐ for raising children | | |
| ☐ for pets | | |
| ☐ for cleaning | | |
| ☐ for relaxing | | |
| **office** | | |
| ☐ for writing | | |
| ☐ for organizing papers | | |
| ☐ for training staff | | |
| ☐ for communicating | | |
| ☐ for eating lunch or snacking | | |
| **English class** | | |
| ☐ for learning new words and grammar | | |
| ☐ for getting more speaking practice | | |
| ☐ for preparing to take tests | | |
| ☐ for reading faster | | |

**STEP 2. PAIR WORK.** Choose one area and invent something. It can be wacky, low-tech, high-tech, or even impossible! Name your invention. On a separate sheet of paper, draw a picture of it or write a description of it.

**STEP 3. DISCUSSION.** Tell the class about your invention. Explain what would happen if you had one now. Explain what you could have done if you'd had one in the past.

**NEED HELP?** Here's language you already know:

**Descriptive adjectives**
top-of-the-line          wacky
high-tech                practical
high-end                 unique
state-of-the-art         efficient
cutting-edge             inefficient
low-tech                 novel
first-rate               revolutionary
innovative

**Factual and unreal conditionals**
Don't you wish someone would invent something for ____?
If I had a ____, I would be able to ____.
If I had had a ____, I would have been able to ____.

93

**LISTENING COMPREHENSION.** Listening tasks go beyond auditory discrimination to include critical thinking skills.

**NEED HELP?** Provides reminders to students of the language they have previously learned— in this unit and earlier units—that can be used in free communication.

## Discuss the Impact of Key Inventions in History

**A** **READING WARM-UP.** In what ways did people communicate words and ideas to each other before the invention of the telegraph, the telephone, the radio, and the computer?

**B** 🎧 **READING.** Read about the invention of printing. How do you think this invention changed the world?

# The Printing Press

Until the 6th or 7th century, all books had to be written by hand.

**ladle for pouring hot metal**

If you asked a large number of people what the most important invention has been, many would say the printing press. Others might say the wheel. But even though it's debatable whether the appearance of the printing press affected the course of history more than the wheel, the printing press ranks within the top two or three inventions in history.

Long before the telephone, the television, the radio, and the computer, the written word was the only way to communicate ideas to people too far away to talk with. Until the sixth or seventh century, all books had to be written

by hand. Creating a book was difficult, and in comparison with today, very few books existed. Therefore, very few people read books.

In the sixth and seventh centuries, the Japanese and Chinese invented a way to print pages by carving characters and pictures on wooden, ivory, or clay blocks. They would put ink on the blocks and then press paper onto the ink, printing a page from the block. This process is called letterpress printing. The invention of letterpress printing was a great advance in communication because each block could be inked many times and many copies of each page could be made. Many books could now be made. Therefore, many people

could read the same book.

Later, in the 11th century, another great advance occurred. The Chinese invented "movable" type. Each character was made as a separate block which could be used many times in many texts. This meant that pages could be created by putting together individual characters rather than having to have whole pages carved. Movable type was much more efficient than the earlier Japanese and Chinese print blocks because books could be created much more quickly by people with less skill.

In Europe, movable type was used for the first time in the 15th century. And there, Johannes Gutenberg invented typecasting, a way to make movable type much more quickly, by melting metal and pouring it into the forms of the letters. This greatly increased the speed of printing, and eventually made books available to many more people.

**carved print blocks**

**SOURCE:** Eyewitness Books: *Invention*. By Lionel Bender, Alfred A. Knopf, New York. ©

94 UNIT 8

**C** ▶ **DISCUSSION.**

1. How would life have been different if printing hadn't been invented?
2. In what ways do we communicate "in writing" today?
3. What makes an invention important? What do you think are the top two or three inventions in history?

**TOP NOTCH**
**INTERACTION • It's the greatest invention since the whee**

**STEP 1. PAIR WORK.** On your notepads, write your own ideas about how life chang result of each of these inventions. Then rank the four inventions in order of i

**2000 B.C.:** The plow loosens and turns the soil so crops can be planted efficiently.

**1802:** The steam locomotive permits transportation of products over long distances by train.

**1914:** The modern zipper permits the opening and closing of clothes without buttons and buttonholes.

**1920s:** The electric refrigerator keeps foo fresh.

| | Life before | Life after |
|---|---|---|
| the plow: | | |
| the train: | | |
| the zipper: | | |
| the refrigerator: | | |

**STEP 2. GROUP WORK.** Choose one of the inventions above or another invention. Present a report to your classmates about the impact the invention had in history.

❝ After the plow was invented, farmers could plant large areas in a short time. Then they could plant enough food to sell to other people. ❞

95

---

**CHECKPOINT.** Integrated-skills checkpoints permit students to consolidate, review, and confirm what they've learned.

**UNIT WRAP-UP.** A full-page illustration deliberately elicits and reviews all language from this unit, demonstrating to all students their mastery of new language.

# CKPOINT

**STENING COMPREHENSION.** Listen to the people
g about new products. Match the name of the
ct and the adjective that best describes it.

| Products | Adjectives |
|---|---|
| _ 1. The Ultraphone | a. cutting-edge |
| _ 2. Dinner-from-a-distance | b. efficient |
| _ 3. Kinder-TV | c. unique |
| _ 4. Ten Years Off | d. top-of-the-line |

**ck the statement that is true for each situation.**

We wouldn't have gotten lost if we had called in advance for directions.
- ☐ We called and we got lost.
- ☐ We didn't call and we got lost.
- ☐ We called and we didn't get lost.
- ☐ We didn't call and we didn't get lost.

. If the salesman were here, he would explain how the Omni works.
- ☐ The salesman is here, so he can explain how the Omni works.
- ☐ The salesman is here, so he can't explain how the Omni works.
- ☐ The salesman isn't here, but he can explain how the Omni works.
- ☐ The salesman isn't here, so he can't explain how the Omni works.

3. If Laura had bought the Ultraphone, she would have already sent those e-mails.
- ☐ Laura bought the Ultraphone and she has already sent those e-mails.
- ☐ Laura didn't buy the Ultraphone and she hasn't sent those e-mails yet.
- ☐ Laura bought the Ultraphone and she hasn't sent those e-mails yet.
- ☐ Laura didn't buy the Ultraphone and she has already sent those e-mails.

**Complete each conditional sentence.**

1. If I had a very fast car, _____.
2. Most people would look better if _____.
3. Will you buy a new car next year if _____?
4. If I had been born before there were cars, _____

**WRITING.** Choose one of the following inventions. Write
about how it changed life and what would have happened
if it had not been invented.

- the telephone
- the washing machine
- the microwave oven
- the computer

🎵 *TOP NOTCH* SONG
"Reinvent the Wheel"
Lyrics on last book page.

*TOP NOTCH* PROJECT
Choose an invention
appearing during your own
lifetime that has changed
your life. Make a presentation
to the class about the
invention.

*TOP NOTCH* WEBSITE
For Unit 8 online activities,
visit the *Top Notch*
Companion Website at
www.longman.com/topnotch.

**EXTRA *TOP NOTCH* FEATURES.**
Three exciting features add value to
*Top Notch* by extending language
practice and use.

**UNIT WRAP-UP**

- **Vocabulary.** Talk about the items in the store, using adjectives to describe them.
- **Grammar.** Complete the statements, using the factual and unreal conditional. Then make more statements.
  *If she buys the…*
  *If they bought the…*
  *If Dan hadn't bought the…*
- **Social Language.** Create conversations for the people.

✓ **Now I can …**
- ☐ describe an innovation.
- ☐ accept responsibility for a mistake.
- ☐ evaluate inventions.
- ☐ discuss the impact of key inventions in history.

97

**SELF-ASSESSMENT.** Students confirm mastery of the unit's communication goals.

# Other *Top Notch* Components

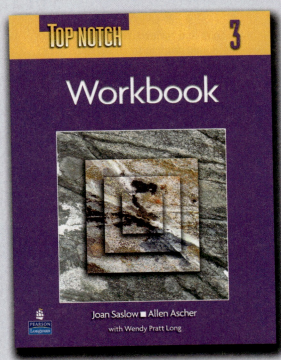

**WORKBOOK**

An illustrated workbook contains exercises that provide additional practice and reinforcement of language concepts and skills from the *Top Notch* Student's Book and its Grammar Booster.

**COMPLETE ASSESSMENT PACKAGE WITH EXAM***VIEW*® **SOFTWARE**

Ten easy-to-administer and easy-to-score unit achievement tests assess listening, vocabulary, grammar, social language, reading, and writing. Two review tests – one mid-book and one end-of-book – provide additional cumulative assessment. Two speaking tests assess progress in speaking.

In addition to the photocopiable achievement tests, Exam*View*® software enables teachers to customize tests that best meet their own needs.

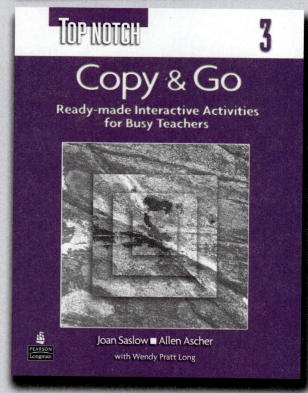

**COPY & GO: READY-MADE INTERACTIVE ACTIVITIES FOR BUSY TEACHERS**

Motivating games, puzzles, and other practice activities in convenient photocopiable form support Student's Book content and provide a welcome change of pace.

## COMPANION WEBSITE

A companion website at www.longman.com/topnotch provides numerous additional resources for students and teachers. This no-cost, high-benefit feature includes opportunities for further practice of language and content from the *Top Notch* Student's Book.

## CLASS AUDIO PROGRAM

The audio program contains listening comprehension activities, rhythm and intonation practice, and targeted pronunciation activities that focus on accurate and comprehensible pronunciation.

To prepare students to communicate with a variety of speakers, regional and non-native accents are included. Each class audio program also includes five *Top Notch Pop* songs in standard and karaoke form.

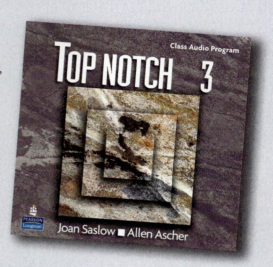

## TOP NOTCH TV

A hilarious TV-style situation comedy reintroduces language from each unit. Also includes authentic unrehearsed interviews and *Top Notch Pop* karaoke. Comes with Activity Worksheets and Teaching Notes.

# The *Top Notch* Teacher's Resource Disk

## A complete menu of free printable activities to personalize YOUR *Top Notch* classroom.

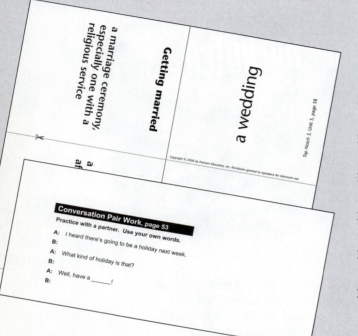

➤ **Vocabulary cards:** for games and other reinforcement activities

➤ **Pair work cards:** for an alternative approach to Conversation Pair Work

➤ **Grammar self-checks:** for reinforcement or for an inductive presentation

➤ **Cumulative vocabulary activities:** for additional vocabulary-building strategies

➤ **Learning strategies:** for conversation, listening, reading, and vocabulary building

➤ **Graphic organizers:** for reading and listening support

### a wedding

*Top Notch 3, Unit 5, page 58*

*Copyright © 2006 by Pearson Education, Inc. Permission granted to reproduce for classroom use.*

### Getting married

a marriage ceremony, especially one with a religious service

---

**Conversation Pair Work, page 53**
Practice with a partner. Use your own words.

A: I heard there's going to be a holiday next week.
B:
A: What kind of holiday is that?
B:
A: Well, have a _____ !
B:

---

NAME: _____ DATE: _____

### Grammar Self-check
(Unit 5, page 54)

**GRAMMAR. Adjective clauses with object relative pronouns**
Look at these sentences with adjective clauses.

> The person **who** comes for dinner should bring a gift.
> The person **who** (or **whom**) you invite should bring a gift.
> The book **that you bought** gives great information about holidays.
> The movie **you saw** is getting great reviews.
> The author **who wrote** that book did a great job.

**FIGURE IT OUT . . .**
**A. Subject or object? Fill in the blanks.**
1. In the first sentence, the relative pronoun *who* is the _____ subject / object of the clause.
2. In the second sentence, the relative pronoun *who* or *whom* is the _____ subject / object of the clause.

**B. Complete these grammar rules.**
1. When the relative pronoun is the object of the clause, it _____ may / may not be omitted.
2. When the relative pronoun is the subject of the clause, it _____ may / may not be omitted.

*ch 3*
*06 by Pearson Education. Permission granted to reproduce for classroom use.*

Unit 5

---

NAME: _____

### Cumulative Vocabulary Activ
(Unit 5)

**Association: ways to commemorate a holiday**

Write **at least** five words you associate with each way to
Use the words in the box first. Then add your own word
dictionary.

| colors | uniforms | temple | church | |
| dancing | party | religious | government | |
| shopping | crowds | hands | greetings | |

| Ways to commemorate a holiday | | |
|---|---|---|
| Set off fireworks | | |
| March in parades | | |
| Have picnics | | |
| Pray | | |
| Send cards | | |
| Give each other gifts | | |
| Wish each other well | | |
| Remember the dead | | |
| Wear costumes | | |

*Top Notch 3*
*Copyright © 2006 by Pearson Education. Permission granted for classroom use.*

Unit 5

---

NAME: _____ DATE: _____

### Learning Strategy
(Unit 5, page 55, Conversation)

**CONVERSATION STRATEGY: asking for help**

Asking for permission to ask a question is a polite way to ask for help or information.

**Ways to ask for help politely**
*with rising intonation*
- Do you mind if I ask you something?
- Could I ask you something?
- Would it be OK if I ask you something?

*with falling intonation*
- I wonder if I could ask you something.

**PRACTICE**
**A. Write three questions you could ask a classmate about rules at**
1. _____
2. _____
3. _____

**B. PAIR WORK.** Now role-play these conversations.
ask your question. Then ask your questions in Ex
A: _____
B: Sure. What is it?
A: (your question)

A: _____
B: Of course you could. What's up?
A: (your question)

A: _____
B: No problem.
A: (your question)

*Top Notch 3*
*Copyright © 2006 by Pearson Education. Permission granted to reproduce for classroom use.*

Unit 5

---

NAME: _____

| What happens? |
|---|
| 1. It lasts one day. |
| 2. It lasts three days |
| 3. It lasts one month |
| 4. People go shopp |
| 5. People clean the |
| 6. People offer gift the monks. |
| 7. People give to |
| 8. There are para |
| 9. People only e after sunset. |

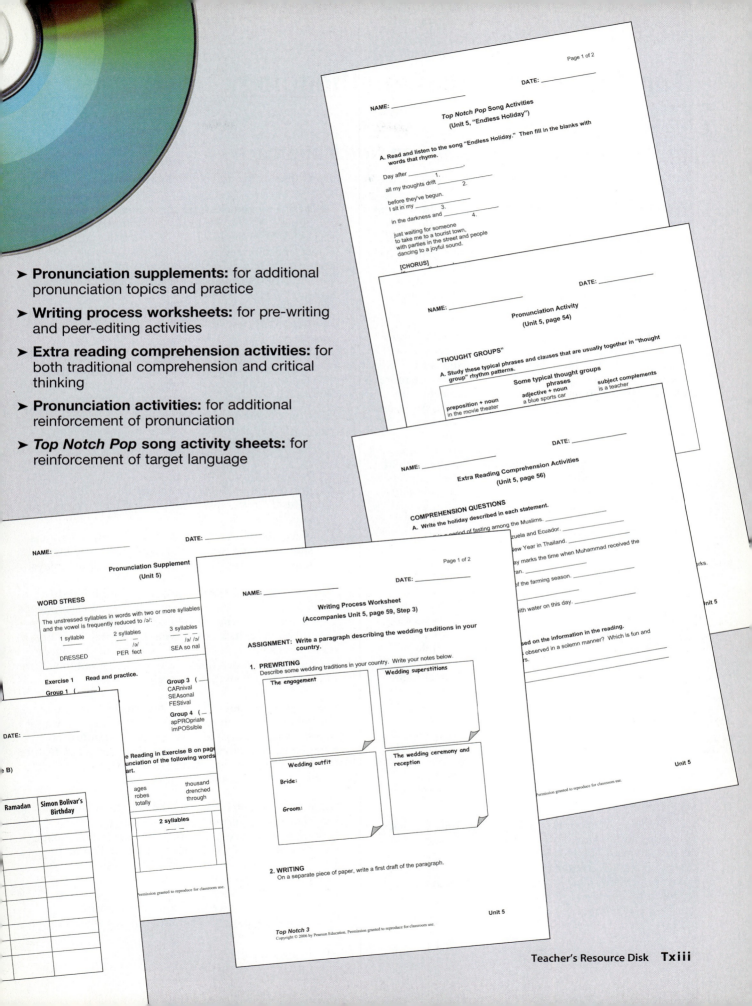

- ➤ **Pronunciation supplements:** for additional pronunciation topics and practice
- ➤ **Writing process worksheets:** for pre-writing and peer-editing activities
- ➤ **Extra reading comprehension activities:** for both traditional comprehension and critical thinking
- ➤ **Pronunciation activities:** for additional reinforcement of pronunciation
- ➤ *Top Notch Pop* **song activity sheets:** for reinforcement of target language

# *Top Notch:* A concise methodology

## The *Top Notch* approach

The following paragraphs describe the major features of the *Top Notch* approach.

**Explicit presentation of language.** So that students may use their textbook both to learn from in class and as a study tool, *Top Notch* provides explicit presentation of language. The heavily illustrated Student's Book depicts or defines all vocabulary taught for productive use; it provides clear grammar charts with explanations of form, meaning, and use; and it features numerous practical model conversations.

**English for today's world.** More than two out of every three speakers of English in today's world are non-native speakers. This fact has profound implications for English language instruction. Learners today are more likely than ever to use English to communicate with other non-native speakers in travel, business, study, and work. For that reason, in addition to presenting the traditional cultural-linguistic features of English and preparing students to communicate with native speakers of English, *Top Notch* deliberately helps students build cultural literacy. Numerous activities in the text prepare students to communicate with people from different cultures in formal and informal situations.

**Daily confirmation of progress.** Adult students are often highly motivated and anxious for results, and are unwilling to continue if they don't see progress. Moreover, they are often hesitant to reveal their lack of ability and are embarrassed to speak incorrectly. Materials and lessons need to provide observable results and safe opportunities for controlled and free practice. Students should leave each class session with clear knowledge of what they have achieved. Each daily lesson in *Top Notch* has a clearly identified communicative goal and culminates in an activity to confirm students' progress.

**Memorable conversation models.** *Top Notch* uses a selection of topics and short practical language models that represent the language adult students want and need to learn—for professional, social, and travel situations. Systematic guided practice helps to make these essential models memorable and transferable to students' own lives.

*Top Notch* has a practical social language syllabus that provides adult students with essential language for their real needs. In addition to classic level 3 topics, vocabulary, and grammar, *Top Notch 3* includes highly practical, communicative language, such as discussing types of medical treatments, expressing regrets about decisions, debating the pros and cons of issues, and so on.

**Deliberate movement from controlled to free practice.** If language is to be acquired, remembered, and accessible to students when they need it, ample practice is required. Because the language learner often lacks the opportunity to use English outside of the classroom, *Top Notch* offers opportunities for increasingly free and rigorous practice within the class.

**Learner-supportive instruction.** The following features provide support to students learning from *Top Notch*.

**Comprehensible directions.** The *Top Notch* Student's Book contains simple directions that students can readily understand and follow. Models and examples take any confusion out of what is expected.

**Conversation pair work guides.** Conversation pair work is supported with clear in-book speaking guides so students can practice with or without teacher observation.

**Notepadding.** Free-discussion activities are often preceded by notepad preparation so students have a clear and concrete stimulus to get them started and keep them going.

**Need Help?** A unique *Need Help?* feature reminds students of language they have previously learned that can be used in free discussions and role plays.

**Authentic, sourced reading texts.** To lend interest, seriousness, and authentic practice, the *Top Notch* Student's Book contains a variety of texts from authentic sources. Careful attention has been given to comprehensibility of these texts so that students are not frustrated. Source lines in the Student's Book show students that they have the ability to cope with real-world material.

**Real language.** Carefully exposing students to authentic, natural English, both receptively and productively, is a necessary component of building understanding and expression. All conversation models in *Top Notch* feature the language people really use, not "textbook English" written merely to exemplify grammar.

**Usage information backed by the Longman Corpus Network.** **CN** Informed by the Longman Corpus Network—Longman's unique computerized language database of over 328 million words of spoken and written English as well as learner errors—*Top Notch* provides concise and useful information about frequency, collocations, and typical native-speaker usage. Corpus Notes can be found at a glance on the Student's Book pages bound into this Teacher's Edition.

In addition, teachers are alerted to frequent learner errors so they can target their attention to troublesome vocabulary and structures.

***Top Notch Pop* songs.** Five songs especially composed and recorded for *Top Notch 3* provide focused language reinforcement as well as essential stress, intonation, and pronunciation practice, making language memorable and fun.

**Teacher's Resource Disk.** 🅢 Because teachers have differing ideas of what constitutes the best pedagogy, the Teacher's Resource Disk bound in the inside back cover of this book provides printable, ready-made classroom activities to extend or adapt each section of a *Top Notch* unit.

The following worksheets and cards can be printed from the Teacher's Resource Disk:

**Extra reading comprehension activities.** Each unit's reading selection appears on a worksheet with in-depth traditional comprehension and critical thinking questions.

**Writing process worksheets.** Brainstorming and peer-editing activities help students become better writers by offering them an opportunity to take initiative in generating ideas for writing and in correcting for accuracy and clarity.

**Learning strategies.** These activities teach and practice learning strategies students can apply over and over again, such as vocabulary building, skimming, summarizing, and clarification.

**Grammar self-checks.** Inductive grammar charts provide an alternative grammar presentation as well as cognitive activities to promote students' grammar awareness.

**Pronunciation activities and supplements.** Pair work activities provide extra practice of each unit's pronunciation point. Pronunciation supplements focus on additional pronunciation points that can be illustrated and practiced in the unit's conversation models.

**Vocabulary cards and cumulative vocabulary activities.** *Top Notch* vocabulary is further reinforced in two effective ways. Two-sided vocabulary flash cards come with teacher's notes that provide ideas for games, alternative presentations, substitution in pair work activities, and other ways to ensure vocabulary mastery. Cumulative vocabulary activities reinforce vocabulary meaning throughout the course through critical thinking and application of practical learning strategies.

**Pair work cards.** These cards reproduce each unit's guided conversation models. Partner A's part is on one card and Partner B's part is on another, with slots for controlled manipulation of vocabulary and social language. These cards get students "out of the book" and communicating.

**Graphic organizers.** Charts and visual representations enhance and extend activities in the *Top Notch* unit through classification and brainstorming activities.

***Top Notch Pop* song activities.** Using the lyrics to each of the *Top Notch Pop* songs, these activities provide practice of the target grammar and vocabulary embedded in the song.

**A Teacher's Edition as a management tool.** In the Lesson Planner beginning on page T2 of this Teacher's Edition, there are links to all components of *Top Notch 3*. Icons indicate places where extra and optional activities are available on the Teacher's Resource Disk, where *Top Notch* Workbook activities can be assigned, where an Achievement Test or a Speaking Test is available from the Complete Assessment Package, and when to use the *Top Notch TV* video. In addition, icons provide references to activities in *Copy & Go.* While the *Top Notch* Student's Book is a complete course without the need for additional components, those who have chosen to use one or more of the components will see them integrated at a glance in the Lesson Planner.

**A Student's Take-Home Super CD-ROM.** Located in the back of each *Top Notch* Student's Book, the Take-Home Super CD-ROM provides an opportunity for practice and self-study at students' own convenience. The disk contains a variety of exciting interactive activities for each unit: Speaking Practice, Interactive Workbook, Games and Puzzles, and *Top Notch Pop* Karaoke. The disk can also be played on an audio CD player to listen to the Conversation Models and hear and sing along with the five *Top Notch Pop* Songs.

**A "Pronunciator."** To remove any doubts about pronunciation of proper names in English, the *Top Notch* Companion Website includes a section in which proper names in *Top Notch* that are not heard on the Class Audio Program can be found transcribed in the International Phonetic Alphabet [IPA]. The transcription shows the way a native speaker of English is most likely to pronounce a word. When non-English names or places are included, the pronunciation given is that used in English, which may differ from the one used in the other language. For example, /mɛksɪkoʊ/ NOT /mɛhɪko/. To find the Pronunciator, go to the *Top Notch* Companion Website and click on "Pronunciator" in Teacher Resources.

# Methodology for the *Top Notch* course

**The following paragraphs describe suggestions for managing a *Top Notch* classroom.**

The goal of *Top Notch* is to prepare students to understand spoken and written English and to express themselves confidently, accurately, and fluently. Much practice is necessary to reach that goal. Because the typical student has limited opportunity to observe English and to practice it, *Top Notch* seeks to replicate as much as possible the authentic "voice" of English so that students can become successful in understanding, and to provide enough practice for students to truly acquire language.

Communicative teaching methodologies, especially at the lower levels of language instruction, often stop short of enabling students to bridge the gap between controlled and free practice. The student of today wants to be able to go beyond info-gaps and pair work activities to use English in real discussions about ideas with real people.

The following general methodology is recommended for *Top Notch*. Specific suggestions for teaching every exercise of the Student's Book are given in the Lesson Planner beginning on page T2. Note that the extent to which you use these recommendations is up to you. All suggestions may not be appropriate for all groups, and you should tailor the lesson to reflect your own background, personal approach, training, and the specific needs of your students.

**Pair work and collaborative activities.** On every page of *Top Notch*, opportunities for pair work, group work, and collaborative activities enable students to take a more active and creative role in learning and allow the maximum number of students to participate. These activities encourage students to use their own language resources, making the lesson more personalized and meaningful. They also ensure that students initiate as well as respond in English. Furthermore, in working together, students get to know each other faster and become more independent, relying less on the teacher for guidance and ultimately taking more responsibility for their own learning. We recommend the following approaches for pair and group work activities:

> **A student-centered approach.** Some students, particularly those accustomed to teacher-centered lessons, may not immediately see the benefits of working in pairs or groups. The first time you do pair and group work, point out to students that working together allows them more time to practice English and allows you to listen to more students individually.

> **Cooperative learning.** Encourage students to help and learn from each other. Whenever possible, try to elicit answers from other students before

answering a question yourself. If a student asks a question that was previously asked by another student, direct the question to the student who first asked the question. In restating in their own words information they have recently obtained, students internalize the language, increasing the likelihood that it will be retained.

**Flexible seating arrangement.** To ensure that students interact with a variety of partners, have students sit in a different location for each class. When dividing the class into pairs or groups, try to match students of different abilities. One method of forming groups is to have students count off according to the number of groups needed. (The 1s work together, the 2s work together, and so on.)

**Teacher monitoring.** During pair and group work activities, circulate around the room, keeping students on task and offering help as needed. When dividing the class into pairs, avoid playing a partner role yourself, as this will limit your ability to monitor and offer assistance to the class. If faced with an odd number of students, create a group of three students, with a third role added as a helper to encourage eye contact and to correct mistakes.

**Building student confidence.** Before asking students to speak in front of the class, build students' confidence by having them rehearse language in pairs, small groups, or chorally as a class. Students can also collaborate with a partner or group on writing exercises, either by completing the activity together or by comparing their answers.

**Time management.** To keep students on task, set time limits for each activity. End activities before most of the class is finished to avoid dead time. For students who finish early, prepare additional activities, either your own or ones from any of the *Top Notch* supplements. One idea, for example, would be to have students who have finished their Conversation Pair Work (see page Txxii) write the conversation that they created.

**Correction.** Most students of languages, particularly adult learners, like feedback and expect to be corrected when they make a mistake. However, recent research indicates that correcting errors in students' speech and writing is less effective in promoting correct language use than is commonly believed. Studies have shown that it is repeated exposure to correct usage, rather than constant correction, that results in the internalization of new language. In addition, excessive correction in a communicative course can embarrass and discourage students, making them reluctant to attempt the experimentation and practice essential to language acquisition. We recommend the following approaches for providing effective positive feedback and striking a balance between the need for correction and maintaining feelings of success:

**Accuracy.** For activities where accuracy is the focus, such as in the Conversation Pair Work, correct mistakes shortly after they occur. Immediate correction is important for controlled activities where students need guidance in using new language.

**Fluency.** For freer and more challenging activities where fluency is the focus, such as in the *Top Notch* Interactions, refrain from stopping the flow of student discussion with corrections. In these activities, accuracy is less important than the ability to communicate ideas and improvise with known language. Developing these improvisation skills is critical if students are to convert the English they have learned in the classroom into the English they need in their own lives. Interrupting students with corrections discourages this experimentation. Instead, take notes on common student mistakes and then review those errors as a class at the end of the activity.

**Self-correction.** Students are often able to correct their own mistakes. First, allow the student to finish the thought, then show by sound or gesture that there has been a mistake. Try to indicate where the mistake was and give the student an opportunity to self-correct. Some techniques for eliciting self-correction include counting off each word of the phrase on your fingers and pausing at the mistake, repeating the student sentence or pausing at the mistake, and prompting the student with a missing word. For example: S: *He has two child.* T: *He has two . . . ?* S: *He has two children.* A less intrusive method is to correct the student's mistake by reformulating what the student said without stopping the flow of conversation. For example: S: *He have a car.* T: *Oh, he has a car?* S: *Yes, he has a car.* Note that these techniques often prompt the student to self-correct.

**Selectivity.** Don't discourage or overwhelm students by correcting every mistake. Focus corrections on the skills that are being taught in that particular lesson or mistakes that prevent comprehension.

**Support.** Above all, avoid making students feel pressured. Give students enough time to think. Be careful not to stigmatize or embarrass students. Be aware that students may be sensitive to criticism in front of their peers and may prefer more private feedback. There is nothing more effective in promoting student practice than their belief that you are "on their side." To that end, it is suggested that you show approval for student experimentation, even if the language is inaccurate. Experimentation is an essential step in language mastery.

**Checking answers.** For exercises or homework requiring a written response, have students check their answers with a partner. This encourages students to correct their own mistakes and also helps students avoid the possible embarrassment of giving incorrect answers in front of the entire class. When the class has finished comparing answers, review the correct answers as a class, either by eliciting the answers from individual students or by having volunteers write their answers on the board. In classes with time constraints, write answers on the board and have the class self-correct.

**Repetition.** Repetition of the Conversation Models and the Vocabulary (see pages Txx and Txxi) helps students acquire comprehensible and accurate pronunciation, stress, and intonation. Repetition also helps to make language memorable, an important goal. On the Student's Take-Home Super CD-ROM and in the Class Audio Program, a pause following the speaker's utterance facilitates repetition and permits students to imitate the pronunciation and intonation of the native speaker on the audio. Teacher's notes provide specific suggestions for how to focus students' attention on rhythm, stress, and intonation for each Conversation Model. Here are some general options for using repetition to facilitate learning:

**Open or closed books.** For activities requiring students to listen and repeat, we recommend having students first listen while looking at the written form in their textbooks. This allows students to link the written form in the book to the sound they hear. In the next step, when students are asked to listen and repeat, have them listen and repeat with their books closed. This serves to reduce distractions and allows students to focus exclusively on listening and repeating rather than reading. It also reduces the confusing effect of English spelling on pronunciation.

**Practice drills.** Introduce short, fast-paced repetition drills to offer the class more pronunciation practice, reinforce word structures, and provide a fresh change of pace. Practice drills will also help students see how much they can personalize the language they are learning. Start by modeling a sentence from the Conversation Model and having the class repeat after you. For example: T: *Well, actually, I've been coughing.* Class: *Well, actually, I've been coughing.* Then prompt students to change the sentence. For example: T: *sneezing.* Students: *Well, actually, I've been sneezing.* Continue in this manner several times. Point to individual students and have them repeat. Modeling the new language before and after each student response helps students build auditory memory while providing them with a correct model for repetition.

**Pace.** Keeping the pace of repetition drills lively gives the greatest number of students a chance to speak and maximizes exposure to the language. If a student cannot respond or makes a mistake, move on quickly to another student and then return to the student who made the mistake. Maintaining the pace gives weaker students the time that they need to internalize and ultimately acquire new language.

**Realia—bringing the outside in.** Research has demonstrated that language is easier to comprehend and retain if presented in conjunction with sensory input such as pictures, sounds, props, and authentic documents. In addition, bringing real material into the classroom serves to motivate students and helps them understand the relevance of their language study to their own lives.

Projects in most units direct students to collect authentic documents; do Internet or library research; or bring in books, magazines, or other printed material. These materials provide real-world content for students to communicate about in English, whether or not the original material is in English. If English materials are available, they build awareness of authentic English in the world outside the classroom.

The Topic Preview on the first page of the unit and many of the readings come from authentic sources or are near-authentic documents created by integrating two or more authentic documents. Teaching notes in the Lesson Planner include suggestions for maximizing the value of this material.

**Elicitation.** Asking questions keeps the class active and involved and helps you to identify what students understand and what they do not. An effective method for eliciting language from the class is to first provide a model that students understand and then have them create language using that model. For instance, before eliciting a list of occupations from the class, provide examples by writing on the board several occupations

that students have learned. Some additional elicitation techniques to consider include the following:

**Warm-up.** Direct questions to the entire class before eliciting answers from individual students. This technique reduces the pressure on individual students to produce a response before they are ready and provides the class with a model of a correct response.

**One-word answers.** It is not always necessary for students to answer in full sentences. Often a one-word answer is sufficient to demonstrate understanding of the question and to respond appropriately. Using one-word answers is particularly valuable for beginning students because it allows them to communicate even if they have acquired only a little productive English. Moreover, it allows students to speak "real" language from the start, as one-word responses are often more authentic in informal contexts than full-sentence responses.

**Teaching multi-level classes.** To accommodate diverse levels within the same classroom, we recommend the following approaches:

**Modeling.** Use more advanced students to model activities. Advanced students, with their quicker comprehension time, are more likely to respond quickly and correctly. Modeling will allow weaker students, who need longer exposure time to new language, to use the stronger students' responses as a model and respond successfully.

**Grouping.** In pair and group work activities, vary the approach to grouping students to keep the activities fresh. Partnering more advanced students with weaker students encourages the class to help and learn from each other. Partnering students with similar ability levels also has advantages, as this allows pairs to speak at their own pace and level of production.

# Methodology for a *Top Notch* Unit

A *Top Notch* unit is made up of six two-page lessons:

▶ **Preview:** Introduction
▶ **Lesson 1:** Controlled practice
▶ **Lesson 2:** Controlled practice
▶ **Lesson 3:** Free practice
▶ **Lesson 4:** Free practice
▶ **Checkpoint:** Review

The icon  in this section indicates that extension activities can be printed from the Teacher's Resource Disk in the back of this Teacher's Edition.

## ▶ Preview

It is suggested that you open your *Top Notch* textbook to any unit in order to see each section described below.

The purpose of the Preview is to provide an introduction to the topic and the social language of the unit. It's important to understand that the Preview includes language at "+1" level. The reason for this is to expose students to the authentic language they will encounter in the world outside the classroom and to familiarize them with language they will be dealing with in the unit. Great care has been taken to ensure that +1 language is comprehensible. Embedded illustrations and contextual photographs were especially created to aid comprehension and motivate students.

When teaching *Top Notch* to a group for the first time, make students aware that they will not be expected to "learn" or "use" all the language in the Preview. The reason for including it is to give students a motivating glimpse of real language at a comprehensible level, to build their expectations of the topic and language that follows in the unit, to access some prior knowledge, and to build the strategy of determining meaning from context. Exercises and discussion questions in this Preview are written at the productive level of the student.

**TOPIC PREVIEW.** Begin each unit by asking a few questions about the content of the advertisement, menu, website, etc. that is featured in the Topic Preview. The purpose of Exercise A is to focus attention on the realia that follows. If necessary, model some answers to the questions in Exercise A yourself. Be sure to answer using language your students already know.

One of the purposes of including a piece of realia with +1 language is to teach students to find meaning in texts that contain some unknown language. Encourage students to use the illustrations and context to determine the meaning of unfamiliar words and phrases—an important learning strategy for understanding material above one's productive level. Help students build their ability to use illustrations and context by asking

questions that prompt students to do so. For example, if students don't know the words *non-fiction* and *fiction* on the first page of Unit 7, have them study the kinds of books listed under non-fiction and compare them to the titles listed under fiction. Ask *Which types of books are about real people and real events?* (non-fiction) *How can you describe fiction?* (books and stories about people or things that are imaginary)

Additional exercises on the left-hand page of the Preview get students to start talking about the unit topic. These discussion activities are designed so that students can use language they already know or that is readily available on the page. When grouping isn't specified, students can discuss in pairs or small groups. After students have discussed, review by asking a few students to share their responses with the whole class.

**SOUND BITES.** The Sound Bites on the right-hand page of the Preview are not a conversation for student practice, but rather for student observation. These examples of natural conversation will promote comprehension of authentic language and will begin to familiarize students with language they will learn later. An attempt has been made to include highly natural idiomatic language, language ordinarily not included in textbooks. Because the language is very appealing, many students will pick it up and make it their own. But that should not be your expectation or requirement.

Before students read and listen to the conversation, ask questions about the photo(s), if possible. For variety and to provide listening practice, you may sometimes want to have students listen with books closed. After students listen to the conversation, ask questions to check comprehension. Use the questions that are provided in each unit or your own questions. (Additional questions are included in the Lesson Plans in this book.) If students have listened with books closed, ask the comprehension questions, allow students to listen again, and then repeat the questions. Comprehension questions can be asked in open class, written on the board for students to answer with a partner, or read out loud for students to write answers to. If appropriate, ask additional questions that relate the content of the conversation to students' own lives.

Important new language in the Sound Bites is highlighted in the exercise(s) that follow. The meaning of almost all new language can be determined from the context of the conversation, but where doubts might occur, notes in the Lesson Plans offer suggestions for conveying meaning. Have students underline in the conversation the word, phrase, or sentence that is asked about in the exercise. Encourage students to reread the lines before and after the underlined portion of the conversation. You can also ask questions about the context that lead students to figure out the meaning of the new language.

**WHAT ABOUT YOU?** Each two-page Preview culminates in *What about you?* activities that prompt students to relate content from the Preview to their own lives, preferences, and opinions. Have students complete the What about you? exercise independently. Then talk about their responses. If a Pair Work or other speaking activity follows, your own responses can serve as a model. If the Pair Work activity asks partners to compare, ask a couple of students about their responses before pairs discuss. An option for this section is to have students use the third person to tell the class something about their classmate.

**UNIT GOALS.** Finally, note that each Preview lists in a box four communicative goals for the unit. These are the goals for the four lessons that follow.

 *Lessons 1 and 2*

Lessons 1 and 2 offer new language and controlled practice. Each lesson is titled with its communication goal, such as "Discuss a new product," so students see what they will learn to do in the lesson.

**CONVERSATION MODEL.** To build awareness and facilitate comprehension, begin by asking questions about the photo, if possible. Many questions are provided in the Lesson Plans, but it's not necessary to stop there. When you ask questions, however, be mindful of what students are capable of answering. Don't elicit language or information that students would not know prior to reading the conversation. Another option is for students to say as much as they can about the photo to a partner. Note that to preview the target grammar of the lesson, one or more examples of that grammar are embedded in the Conversation Model.

Play the recording of the Conversation Model or read it aloud yourself while students read and listen with books open. Then check students' understanding of the conversation by asking comprehension questions. The questions provided in the Lesson Plans help students focus on the essential information in the conversation and determine the meaning of any new language from context. The questions also prepare students to understand any grammar presentation that follows.

An alternative presentation technique, especially in stronger groups, is to have students listen to the conversation with books closed first. When electing this option, have students look at the picture first to build awareness of the social situation of the conversation.

**RHYTHM AND INTONATION PRACTICE.** Following the Conversation Model is a direction line for "Rhythm and intonation practice." This second recording of the model directs students to listen and repeat in the pauses. The pause following each line of the model is an opportunity for students to listen and focus on imitating the pronunciation, intonation, rhythm, and stress of the native speaker in the model. The Lesson Plans suggest specific rhythm, stress, and intonation points to pay attention to.

Some instructors like to have students look at the text as they repeat. Many prefer to have students do the rhythm and intonation practice with books closed, to avoid the interference of English spelling. We encourage experimentation to see which is more effective. With books closed, students listen and repeat after each line. Encourage students to imitate the rhythm, stress, and intonation of the conversation as closely as possible. Correct where necessary, helping students to pronounce the language clearly. Encourage students to continue practicing the rhythm and intonation using the Student's Take-Home Super CD-ROM included in the back of their textbook.

**Stress patterns.** To help teachers focus on the stress patterns of the Conversation Models, the stress patterns have been transcribed with a "Morse code-like" feature in the Lesson Plans.

**GRAMMAR.** Each new grammar structure is previewed in the Conversation Model so students read, hear, and understand the structure in context before they are required to manipulate it. Have students read the information in the Grammar box independently. Then ask them to look again at the Conversation Model and find and underline any examples of the new structure.

In the Grammar box, the new structure is presented through examples and clear, concise, easy-to-understand rules. The Lesson Plans offer specific suggestions for presenting the grammar from the box and for reinforcing the grammar taught in each unit. Students internalize grammatical structures when they have the opportunity to use them in a meaningful and relevant context. Suggestions prompt students to begin using the new structure in the context of their own lives to express opinions, preferences, and other ideas.

You can also use an inductive approach by printing out the Grammar Self-Checks (see below) or by writing the example sentences from the grammar chart on the board for discussion.

**THE GRAMMAR BOOSTER.** Following most Grammar boxes is an icon referring students to the Grammar Booster. In some cases, the grammar is expanded and presented more fully. In others, additional and related grammar points are included. Teachers and programs differ in their interest in grammar, so the Grammar Booster should be considered an option for teachers who want to go beyond what is normally included in a textbook for this level. In some cases, you may wish to direct stronger students who can do more to the Grammar Booster while not using it for the whole class. In addition to the presentations, the Grammar Booster contains confirming exercises.

Even if you elect not to use the Grammar Booster, students will still appreciate having additional material for permanent reference in their textbook.

Controlled exercises follow each grammar presentation in the Student's Book. The exercises provide written and/or oral practice with the structure(s) just taught and offer additional examples of its use in context. If necessary, model how to do the first item in each task. Have students complete the exercises independently, in pairs, or in small groups. Review answers in open class, or have students check answers with a partner. The Teacher's Edition contains all answers printed right on the Student's Book page facing the Lesson Plan.

**Grammar Self-Checks.** * If you prefer an inductive presentation of the grammar point, print out a Grammar Self-Check from the Teacher's Resource Disk. The Grammar Self-Checks are an inductive presentation and awareness activity for use in class. Grammar Self-Checks are also designed to check how well students understand the grammar, and can be used as a follow-up activity after the grammar charts have been presented.

**VOCABULARY.** Vocabulary is explicitly presented through pictures or definitions. The vocabulary presentations in the Student's Book serve to convey meaning of each new vocabulary item and to provide reference for self-study, especially valuable as students prepare for tests. Vocabulary in *Top Notch* is presented at word, phrase, and sentence level—including expressions, idioms, and collocations.

Students will use the vocabulary presented to manipulate the Conversation Pair Work at the end of the lesson. Begin by focusing students' attention on the illustrations or definitions. An option is to have students cover the words with a sheet of paper and look only at the pictures. Pairs can see which words and phrases they already know. Printable Vocabulary Cards are also available for this purpose on the Teacher's Resource Disk in the back of the Teacher's Edition (see below).

Play the audio program. If you don't have the audio program, read the words aloud as a model. Students listen and repeat. Note that singular count nouns are preceded by the indefinite article a/an. Students should use the article when they repeat. Depending on your students' language background, the concept of count and non-count nouns may provide a great challenge. Using the indefinite article to contrast singular count nouns with non-count nouns will help students to begin internalizing this difficult concept.

If necessary, clarify the meaning of any words or phrases students have difficulty understanding. Convey the meaning physically—through gestures, mime, or reference to people or objects in the room—or give examples or a simple definition. Specific ideas on how to do this are provided in the Lesson Plans.

When possible, personalize the vocabulary. Use the vocabulary to talk about or ask questions about content familiar to your students—for example, *Use the geographic adjectives and nouns to describe a spectacular place you've visited or even seen in a photo.* (Unit 10, page 116) In open class, or with pairs and small groups, have students talk about their likes/dislikes, preferences, plans, relationships, belongings, habits, etc., in relation to the vocabulary.

**Vocabulary cards.** For further practice with the vocabulary, print out the Vocabulary Cards from the Teacher's Resource Disk. These cards can be used for presentations and a variety of games and activities. An icon alerts you that cards are available.

**Cumulative vocabulary activities.** At the end of each unit, there is an icon for the Cumulative Vocabulary Activities. These activities are designed to provide both cumulative and cognitive practice of vocabulary learned in *Top Notch*. You can print out these Cumulative Vocabulary Activities from the Teacher's Resource Disk after completing the relevant Student Book units.

**Learning strategies for vocabulary building.** To enable students to learn strategies that can help them learn English more effectively, print out a Learning Strategies worksheets from the Teacher's Resource Disk. These worksheets include practical strategies students can apply throughout the course. For vocabulary learning, vocabulary building strategies such as word associations, classification, and marking stress are included.

---

*Throughout the Lesson Plans, each time you see this icon there is a printable extension activity from the Teacher's Resource Disk.

**PRONUNCIATION.** In addition to the rhythm and intonation practice, each unit provides practice with a specific pronunciation point. Play the audio program or read the examples to the class. Students first read and listen, then listen again and repeat. After students repeat, they can practice reading the examples to a partner. Pronunciation activities are generally related to each unit's content. Use the unit's content to provide additional examples. The Lesson Plans identify words or sentences within the unit—for example, in a Grammar box or another exercise—that students can practice reading to a partner with the correct intonation, pronunciation, or stress. An option is to have students exaggerate correct intonation, pronunciation, or stress when they practice. Remind students to also practice the pronunciation skill when they do the Conversation Pair Work activity at the end of the lesson.

**Pronunciation activities and supplements.** Extra interactive pronunciation activities provide more practice of the unit pronunciation point. In addition, each unit has a supplemental pronunciation activity that extends students' understanding of English pronunciation through further presentation and practice. You can print out both of these extra activities from the Teacher's Resource Disk whenever you see the icon.

**LISTENING COMPREHENSION.** Lessons 1 and 2 often contain exercises labeled Listening Comprehension. These short exercises serve to practice comprehension and recollection of the vocabulary or the grammar. Some exercises provide practice in simple auditory discrimination, but in most cases listening tasks require very careful listening for sense and critical thinking. The unit's major presentation of Listening Comprehension is included in Lessons 3 and 4 and is more fully described there (see below).

**Learning strategies for listening comprehension.** To help students to learn listening strategies, such as summarizing or taking notes, print out a Learning Strategies worksheet from the Teacher's Resource Disk.

**CONVERSATION PAIR WORK.** The Conversation Pair Work activity at the end of each lesson is the culminating activity. In this activity, students demonstrate progress and mastery of the lesson's communication goal. Most activities are facilitated by a "guide"—a version of the Conversation Model with blank slots for students to personalize as they like, using names, different vocabulary, or other appropriate social language they have learned. Illustrations and other cues are often provided to help students think of how to change the Conversation Model. This controlled practice is an essential first step, and it must be mastered before

students can be successful at applying the models to free conversation or discussion.

The most important way to maximize the value of this practice is to encourage experimentation, showing approval when students use a variety of possible slot fillers. <u>Be sure students don't think the point of the practice is to test their memory of the original Conversation Model.</u> It is exactly the opposite. As they practice, students should insert new language in the slots. The slots have been carefully chosen to offer a number of possibilities, based on what the students have learned. They should be largely foolproof.

Some slots have been included specifically because students have already learned a number of ways to express a particular thought. For instance, following "Thank you," a slot is provided because students can respond in a number of previously learned ways, such as "You're welcome," "No problem!" and "Sure!" Each slot has been tested to be sure students have enough language "in their pockets" to provide one or more responses. Having different pairs of students perform their Conversation Pair Work in front of the class reminds all students of how much social language they have learned.

Begin by reading the instructions out loud. Then model the conversation with a more advanced student to demonstrate that students should change the Conversation Model by filling in new language from the lesson or from other sources. If helpful, point out the language available on the two-page lesson for students to use. The Lesson Plans provide examples of conversations using language your students can produce. However, the conversation each pair of students creates will vary.

Students practice the Conversation Pair Work activity with a partner. The importance of this activity cannot be overstated, for it is in producing their own language in this controlled activity that students take their first steps toward truly free language. Encourage students to find a new partner for each Conversation Pair Work activity. As students practice, circulate and offer help as needed. Remind students to make eye contact during conversations, to encourage natural pronunciation and tone. An option is to have students practice the conversation a few times with different partners. Also, you can ask a couple of pairs to role-play their conversation for the class or have pairs role-play their conversations for each other.

**Pair work cards.** If you wish to get your students "out of the book" for conversation practice, print out Pair Work Cards from the Teacher's Resource Disk. These cards provide the Conversation Model guide split into two with Partner A's part on one card and Partner B's part on the other. Teaching suggestions are provided on the Teacher's Resource Disk. For example, one activity suggests students work in threes, with Partner C flashing Vocabulary Cards as cues for Partners A and B.

**Learning strategies for speaking.** 💿 If you want students to learn conversation strategies such as making small talk, politely responding to difficult questions, and keeping a conversation going, print out a Learning Strategies worksheet from the Teacher's Resource Disk.

## ▶ Lessons 3 and 4

Lessons 3 and 4 begin with a communication goal, such as "Discuss your reading habits," and culminate in a *Top Notch* Interaction in which students achieve that communication goal.

Lessons 3 and 4 open with either a reading or a listening. These exercises provide key input that leads students to free communication. Vocabulary is usually included and ranges from one-word items to phrases to collocations and idioms. Vocabulary meaning is clearly conveyed through illustrations, definitions, and/or contextual sentences. The vocabulary is usually used in the reading or listening and then practiced in the exercises and activities that follow.

**READING WARM-UP.** This exercise consists of a question or a series of questions that prompt students to start thinking about the topic of the reading. Before students read, they relate the content of the reading to their own lives. This process generates interest and aids understanding.

**READING.** All readings are based on authentic sources. When appropriate, the sources are identified. To avoid frustrating students at this level, we have had to simplify some of the language from the original sources, but we have taken great care to maintain the authentic character of the material. Students should be encouraged to understand the reading without looking up every new word in the dictionary. Reading in a foreign language always presents the challenge of *some* unknown language. Students need to learn that they can comprehend main ideas, can get specific information and infer information even without knowing every word. Comprehension activities always follow the reading, sometimes in the form of straight factual questions or true/false activities or clozes that demonstrate understanding of information or of vocabulary from context.

Note that all readings are recorded in the Class Audio Program. Listening to them gives excellent ear training for the rhythm, stress, and intonation of extended (as opposed to conversational) speech. It also helps students learn collocations—words that "go together" as phrases. It is recommended that students be given an opportunity to read and listen to each reading. You may choose to play the recording after students have already read the text or while they are reading. In some cases, you may choose to play the recording as a listening activity with closed books.

Read the Reading Warm-up question(s) out loud. Model the activity by answering the questions yourself. Students can answer the questions with a partner or in small groups. To review, ask a few students to share their responses with the class. Specific suggestions can be found in the Lesson Plans.

Before students read, have them look at any photos or illustrations. If appropriate, ask questions about these visuals. Give students a few minutes to look at the selection independently. Encourage them to look at the title and any headings to help give them an idea of what the reading is about. The instructions before most readings also ask a question to help focus students' attention as they read. Ask students to try to answer the question as they read. Then, if you choose, play the audio program and have students read along.

The readings contain language that students have not yet learned but that they should be able to comprehend through context and similarity to language they know. However, it is not necessary for students to know what every word means in order to understand the selection. Encourage students to guess at the meaning of new words as much as possible, or to comprehend as much as they can without understanding every word. After students read, ask questions or use activities that lead them to figure out the meaning of new language and that help them to identify the essential information from the reading. Such questions and activities are provided in the Lesson Plans.

Many of the exercises that follow the reading also prompt students to use context to figure out the meaning of new language or to identify the most important information from the reading. Read the directions for each exercise out loud, or ask for a volunteer to read them. Have students read the exercise items and then reread the selection independently. As students read, they can underline words or information in the reading that will help them to complete the exercise. Allow students a set period of time to refer to the reading as necessary to complete the exercise individually, in pairs, or in small groups. Have students check their work with a partner, have pairs or groups check their work with another pair or group, or review answers as a class. For a challenge, have students practice reading the selection out loud in small groups.

**Extra reading comprehension activities.** 💿 If you want more extensive comprehension questions than the ones that appear in the Student's Book, you can print them out from the Teacher's Resource Disk. The Extra

Reading Comprehension Activities contain both traditional comprehension and critical thinking questions.

**Learning strategies for reading.** 🖿 If you want students to learn reading strategies of predicting, summarizing main ideas, and vocabulary building, as well as others, you can print out a Learning Strategies worksheet from the Teacher's Resource Disk. Many students need encouragement to approach readings in this way.

**LISTENING COMPREHENSION.** Listening Comprehension activities in Lessons 3 and 4 provide the core listening practice of the unit, containing language at students' productive level as well as at the more challenging +1 level. Receptive-level language is comprehensible to students through context, intonation, and similarity to language they already know.

Point out to students that a major cause of lack of comprehension is the natural panic that occurs when learners hear unknown words. Explain that it is not necessary to understand every word to understand the selection. To maximize the effectiveness of these activities, avoid providing students with explanations of new language beyond any vocabulary that was taught prior to the Listening. If a student specifically asks about a new word, give the meaning, but do not spend a lot of time on it. Exposure to receptive-level language promotes students' language development and prepares students to communicate in the world outside the classroom.

In general, it is suggested that students listen to the selection the first time with books closed. (In some cases, the Lesson Plans provide an alternative approach.) In this way, students can focus on the "big picture" without the distraction of completing the exercise. Read out loud the portion of the directions that provides information about the speakers, setting, or situation. Alternatively, you might prefer to ask (after the first listening) *Who's talking? Where are the people? What are the people doing?* If students are not forthcoming with answers to those questions, you can restate the question, providing two answers from which to choose. The value of this practice is to convince students that they have, in fact, understood a good deal, even if they have not understood everything. This is an essential listening skill for foreign language learners.

Before students listen again and complete the exercise, have them look at the exercise to focus their attention on the specific listening task, such as listening for locations or opinions. Play the audio as many times as necessary for students to complete the activity. Do not approach these exercises as "tests." Repeated exposure to each listening sample has substantial instructional value. Increasing students' exposure to challenging language enhances their comprehension and confidence.

Review answers in open class, or have students check answers with a partner.

Note that the Listening Comprehension exercises are not on the Student's Take-Home Super CD-ROM. If you do not have the Class Audio Program, read the audioscript in the Lesson Plans out loud to your students.

**Accented speakers.** In order to accustom students to listening to English in the real world, the *Top Notch* audio program includes a number of non-native speakers of English as well as native speakers with regional variations of both American and British English. The Lesson Plans provide the language background of each accented speaker, information which may be interesting or informative to your class.

Note that accented speakers in *Top Notch* are heard only in receptive listening texts, not in productive models that students repeat.

***TOP NOTCH* INTERACTION.** Both Lessons 3 and 4 culminate in an activity labeled *Top Notch* Interaction. The goal of this activity is to engage students in free and open-ended discussions, role plays, debates, presentations, and writing.

Free discussion is the goal of all language learners. But foreign language students often have difficulty with free communication because the combination of gathering their thoughts and remembering the language they know is too challenging and often leads to silent panic. Students need to move beyond the controlled safety of models and info-gaps to more extensive self-expression. However, the nature of the foreign language setting makes success at free discussion elusive. The *Top Notch* Interactions are deliberately constructed to provide prepared opportunities for students to experiment and succeed, because each task elicits language that is known.

A series of steps prepares students so they will be successful. Notepad activities prompt students to make notes that organize their ideas and provide speaking or writing points for the discussions, presentations, or writing activities that follow. Students often compare notes with classmates for additional input. They also fill out surveys, answer questions, and look at a variety of visual stimuli such as menus, headlines, and bills. When it is time to actually discuss a topic, they already have the language and the ideas laid out in front of them.

An important feature of many *Top Notch* Interactions is *Need Help?* The *Need Help?* feature lists language that students have "in their pockets"—language learned in the current and previous units that students can use in the *Top Notch* Interactions. Massive opportunities for recycling language occur throughout *Top Notch*.

**WRITING.** Many *Top Notch* Interactions contain a writing activity. The Student's Book often contains an example to get students started, and there are suggestions in the Lesson Plans as well.

**Writing process worksheets.** 💿 For activities that emphasize the process of writing, print out Writing Process Worksheets. These worksheets provide brainstorming and peer-editing activities related to specific writing tasks. Through these activities, which provide an opportunity to take initiative in correcting their own work, students become better writers. An icon alerts you that a worksheet is available.

## ▶ *Checkpoint*

The Checkpoint reviews the essential content of the unit and offers students the opportunity to check their progress. It also allows you to identify any areas of particular difficulty that may require additional practice. The Checkpoint page begins with a listening comprehension exercise and generally ends with a writing task. The Lesson Plans suggest ways to start students writing and often offer outlines to help organize students' ideas. The Checkpoint page also includes exercises that review vocabulary, grammar, and social language from the unit.

Have students work individually to complete the Checkpoint exercises. Circulate to offer help as needed. Review the correct answers as a class. Note any areas of difficulty and provide additional instruction and practice as necessary.

**Top Notch Project.** Every *Top Notch* unit contains a project idea that is related to the unit's content. Projects allow students to use the language they have learned along with information from outside the classroom to complete real-life tasks such as researching travel destinations or researching a topic and then making a presentation. The Lesson Plans give detailed instructions on how to prepare students to complete the project. Provide students with the opportunity to present their completed projects to the class.

**Top Notch Companion Website.** The website contains resources for teachers and online activities for students to accompany each unit. These activities are appropriate for use at the end of each unit.

**Top Notch Pop Songs.** 💿 Five *Top Notch Pop* songs recycle language and make it both memorable and motivating. The *Top Notch Pop* songs are available in both traditional and karaoke versions on the Class Audio Program and in the traditional version only, on the Student's Take-Home Super CD-ROM. The *Top Notch TV* video contains the karaoke in classic visual form. Lyrics for the songs appear on the last page of the Student's Book. Activities to accompany each song can be printed out from the Teacher's Resource Disk. An

icon alerts you that a *Top Notch Pop* song activity is available.

**UNIT WRAP-UP.** A special feature of the *Top Notch* series is the full-page illustration at the end of each unit. Open-ended activities are designed to elicit from students language they know—vocabulary, social language, and grammar. The picture provides a clear visual context for practice and helps bridge the gap between language practice and authentic language use.

The bulleted vocabulary, grammar, social language, and writing activities on the Student's Book page prompt students to find and name items in the picture, ask and answer questions about the picture, create conversations between people in the picture, tell stories about people or situations in the picture, and more.

Specific suggestions for getting much more out of each illustration are given in the Lesson Plans. Depending on the focus of the Unit Wrap-Up, the Lesson Plans also provide lists of vocabulary items that can be found in the picture; examples of questions or sentences your students can produce to practice the unit's grammar; conversations for the people who are interacting in the picture; and stories your students can tell, using the language they know.

Have students work in pairs or small groups. Circulate and offer help as needed. To encourage the risk-taking and improvisation that are the major goals of these activities, avoid interrupting students with corrections. Instead, take notes on common student mistakes and review them as a class at the end of the activity. Encourage students to say as much as they can and to extend the suggested tasks as much as possible.

An optional oral assessment activity based on the full-page picture is provided in the Lesson Plans. These individual oral progress checks were designed to take no more than five minutes per student in order to make it possible to check class progress quickly. Note that the Complete Assessment Package provides complete Speaking Tests after Unit 5 and Unit 10.

Some options for the Unit Wrap-Up are the following:

➤ Allow students to look at the picture for one minute. Then have students close their books and write down all the vocabulary items they can remember from the picture. See who remembers the most items.

➤ In pairs, students write three true statements and three false statements about the picture. Regroup students into groups of four. One pair reads their statements, in random order, to the other pair, who replies *true* or *false*.

➤ One group (or pair) begins by saying a sentence about the picture, and the next group follows by saying another sentence. Groups that can no longer say anything are eliminated until only one group remains.

➤ Give students one minute to study the picture and remember all they can about it. Then have students close their books and form small groups. Ask questions about the picture and keep a record of the correct answers. After each question, allow the groups time to discuss and write down an answer. Review as a class, and see which group has the most correct answers.

➤ Working in pairs, students write one line of conversation for each person in the picture. Then each pair of students joins another pair. Pairs take turns reading their lines and guessing who in the picture is speaking.

➤ Have volunteers act out one of their conversations in front of the class. Students listen and guess which people in the picture are being portrayed.

➤ Have two volunteers act out their conversation in front of the class. The class listens and tries to remember exactly what was said. Working in pairs, students try to re-create the exact conversation they heard.

➤ In pairs, students write their conversation in dialogue form. Each pair then writes each line of its conversation on a separate slip of paper, mixes up the order of the slips, and gives them to another pair. The other pair must then put the conversation back in the correct order.

➤ Choose one of the example conversations from the Lesson Plans. Write all the lines from the conversation on the board in random order. Students try to re-create the conversation by putting the lines in order.

➤ Have students choose one person in the picture and write his or her biography. The details of the person's life should be based on what's in the picture, but students will have to make up much of the information. Have volunteers read their biographies to a group or to the class and have students guess who in the picture is being described.

**NOW I CAN ...** The last item on the page is a box that reiterates the four lesson goals from the unit. Note that all the goals are stated on the first page of the unit, and then stated one by one at the beginning of each of the four numbered lessons. Students can check the goals off at the end of the unit, demonstrating to themselves how much they've learned. Alternatively, they can check each one off at the end of each lesson.

**We sincerely hope you enjoy *Top Notch* and that you and your students find it an effective course.**

# TOP NOTCH

## English for Today's World

## 3

Joan Saslow ■ Allen Ascher

With *Top Notch Pop Songs and Karaoke*
by Rob Morsberger

PEARSON
Longman

# Scope and Sequence OF CONTENT AND SKILLS

GRAMMAR BOOSTER

| UNIT | Vocabulary* | Conversation Strategies | Grammar | |
|---|---|---|---|---|
| **1** **Cultural Literacy** Page 2 *Top Notch* Song: "It's a Great Day for Love" | • Terms for describing manners, etiquette, and culture | • Use <u>By the way</u> to introduce or change a topic • Use expressions such as <u>Do you mind if</u> and <u>Would it be rude to</u> to avoid offending some • Use <u>Actually</u> to politely correct someone • Begin a statement with <u>You know,...</u> to casually shift the focus of a conversation | • Tag questions: form and social use • The past perfect: form and use | • Tag questions: more practice • Verb tense review: simple present, present continuous, present perfect and present perfect continuous, simple past and past continuous, <u>used to</u>, past perfect |
| **2** **Health Matters** Page 14 | • Dental emergencies • Symptoms • Medical procedures • Types of treatments and practitioners • Medications | • Begin answers with <u>Well</u> to announce a willingness to act • Say <u>That's right</u> to confirm • Use <u>Really?</u> to indicate interest | • <u>May</u>, <u>might</u>, <u>must</u>, and <u>be able to</u>: possibility, conclusions, ability | • <u>May</u>, <u>might</u>, and <u>must</u>: degrees of certainty |
| **3** **Getting Things Done** Page 26 *Top Notch* Song: "I'll Get Back to You" | • Business and non-business services • Adjectives to describe services • Social events • Steps for planning a social event | • Repeat part of a question to clarify before answering • Begin a sentence with <u>I'm sorry but</u> to politely insist • Use <u>Sure</u> to affirm confidently | • The passive causative • Causatives <u>get</u>, <u>have</u>, and <u>make</u> | • The passive causative: the <u>by</u> phrase • Causatives <u>get</u>, <u>have</u>, and <u>make</u>: more practi • <u>Let</u> followed by an object and base form • Causative <u>have</u> and past perfect auxiliary <u>have</u> |
| **4** **Life Choices** Page 38 | • Fields for work or study • Reasons for changing your mind • Skills and abilities | • Say <u>Not bad</u> to respond casually to a question about well-being • Use <u>No kidding</u> to convey pleasant surprise • Say <u>Could be</u> to imply that you don't completely agree | • Future in the past: <u>was</u> / <u>were going to</u> and <u>would</u> • Perfect modals: meaning and form | • Review: future with <u>w</u> and <u>be going to</u> • Review: future meanin with present continuou simple present, and modals • Regrets about the past: <u>wish</u> + the past perfec <u>should have</u> and <u>ought to have</u> |
| **5** **Holidays and Traditions** Page 50 *Top Notch* Song: "Endless Holiday" | • Types of holidays • Ways to commemorate a holiday • Wedding terminology | • Use the expression <u>Same to you</u> to acknowledge well-wishes • Preface a question with <u>Do you mind if I ask</u> to make it less abrupt | • Adjective clauses with subject relative pronouns • Adjective clauses with object relative pronouns | • Adjective clauses: mor practice • Reciprocal pronouns: <u>each other</u> and <u>one another</u> • Reflexive pronouns • <u>By</u> + reflexive pronoun • Adjective clauses: <u>who</u> and <u>whom</u> for formal English |

iv      *In *Top Notch*, the term *vocabulary* refers to individual words, phrases, and expressions.

| Speaking | Pronunciation | Listening | Reading | Writing |
|---|---|---|---|---|
| • Make small talk with a stranger<br>• Ask how someone prefers to be addressed<br>• Get to know someone<br>• Describe rules of etiquette<br>• Discuss cultural changes | • Rising and falling intonation for tag questions | • Radio call-in show on etiquette<br>Task: identify the topics discussed<br>• People introducing themselves<br>Task: determine how people prefer to be addressed | • Flyer for an international language school<br>• Newspaper article about recent changes in Japanese culture<br>• Survey about cultural changes | • Advise visitors about culture and etiquette in your country<br>• Express your opinion on the importance of etiquette |
| • Make an appointment<br>• Describe dental problems and medical symptoms<br>• Show concern and empathy<br>• Explain preferences in medical treatments<br>• Talk about medications | • Intonation of lists | • Descriptions of dental emergencies<br>Task: identify problems<br>• Describing symptoms<br>Task: check the symptoms described<br>• Conversations between doctors and patients<br>Task: complete patient information forms | • Health advice for international travelers<br>• Overview of conventional and nontraditional health treatments | • Create a checklist for an international trip<br>• Write about the kinds of health care you use<br>• Complete patient information form |
| • Request express service<br>• Ask for and recommend a service provider<br>• Describe quality of service<br>• Plan a social event | • Emphatic stress to express enthusiasm | • Recommendations for service providers<br>Task: identify the service required<br>• Planning a social event<br>Task: order the steps and note who will do each step<br>• Requesting express service<br>Task: describe customer needs | • Service provider's website<br>• Tourist guide entry on buying custom-made clothing in Hong Kong | • Create an ad for a local service provider<br>• Identify hard-to-find services<br>• Write a story of a man's day, based on a complex illustration |
| • Greet someone you haven't seen for a while<br>• Explain a change in life and work choices<br>• Express regrets about life decisions<br>• Discuss skills, abilities, and qualifications | • Reduction of <u>have</u> in perfect modals | • Conversations about changes in life plans<br>Task: listen for the reasons the people changed their minds<br>• Interviews at a job fair<br>Task: match interviewees and qualifications<br>• Conversations about regrets<br>Task: infer whether there were regrets | • Work preference inventory<br>• Skills inventory<br>• Magazine article on the lifework of Mahatma Gandhi and Albert Schweitzer | • Recount the work and life decisions you have made and explain any regrets<br>• Report on the life of a great humanitarian |
| • Ask about and describe holiday traditions<br>• Ask for and give advice about customs<br>• Describe holidays, celebrations, and wedding traditions | • Rhythm: "thought groups" | • Descriptions of holidays<br>Task: identify the type of holiday and celebration<br>• Lecture on traditional Indian wedding customs<br>Task: correct the false statements<br>• Conversations about weddings<br>Task: determine each topic | • Magazine article describing three holiday traditions from around the world | • Describe in detail a holiday tradition in your country |

# Scope and Sequence OF CONTENT AND SKILLS

GRAMMAR BOOSTER

| UNIT | Vocabulary | Conversation Strategies | Grammar | |
|---|---|---|---|---|
| **6** **Disasters and Emergencies** Page 62 *Top Notch* Song: "Lucky to Be Alive" | • News sources • Severe weather events and other disasters • Emergency preparations and supplies • Terminology for discussing disasters | • Say <u>Will do</u> to accede to a request • Use <u>What a shame</u> to demonstrate empathy • Use <u>It says...</u> to indicate that information comes from a known source • Use <u>Thank goodness</u> to express relief | • Indirect speech: imperatives • Indirect speech: <u>say</u> and <u>tell</u>; tense changes | • Punctuation rules for direct speech • Indirect speech: optional tense changes |
| **7** **Books and Magazines** Page 74 | • Types of books • Ways to describe reading material • Some ways to enjoy reading | • Preface a request with <u>Do you mind if</u> to be more polite • Use <u>Not at all</u> to indicate that one doesn't mind • Say <u>What (adjective + noun)!</u> to express a compliment | • Noun clauses: embedded questions • Noun clauses as direct objects | • Embedded questions: usage and punctuation • Embedded questions with infinitives • Noun clauses with <u>that</u>: after mental activity verbs • Noun clauses with <u>that</u>: after other expressions |
| **8** **Inventions and Technology** Page 86 *Top Notch* Song: "Reinvent the Wheel" | • Mechanical inventions in history • Ways to describe innovative products | • Use <u>That depends</u> to indicate one needs more information • Say <u>It can happen to anyone</u> to show empathy when responding to an apology | • Conditional sentences: review • The unreal conditional | • <u>Unless</u> in conditional sentences • Clauses after <u>wish</u> • The unreal conditional: variety of forms |
| **9** **Controversial Issues** Page 98 | • Political terms and types of governments • Political and social beliefs • Controversial issues • Ways to disagree politely | • Use the expression <u>That's a good question</u> to imply that you are not sure of the answer or you want to avoid answering • Say <u>We'll have to agree to disagree</u> to politely end a disagreement with no hard feelings | • Non-count nouns for abstract ideas • Verbs followed by objects and infinitives | • Count and non-count nouns • Gerunds and infinitives: form • Review: gerunds and infinitives after certain verbs |
| **10** **Enjoying the World** Page 110 | • Geographical features • Ways to describe possible risks • Dangerous animals and insects • Positive and negative descriptions • Ways to describe the natural world | • Provide a reason to support and strengthen a warning • Use <u>Be sure to</u> to make an enthusiastic suggestion | • Infinitives with <u>too</u> + adjective • Prepositions of place to describe locations | • Infinitives with <u>too</u> + adjective: more practice • Infinitives with <u>enough</u> • Prepositions usage • Proper nouns: capitalization • Proper nouns: use of <u>the</u> |

| Speaking | Pronunciation | Listening | Reading | Writing |
| --- | --- | --- | --- | --- |
| • Convey a message for a third person<br>• Offer an excuse<br>• Report what you heard on the news<br>• Respond to good and bad news<br>• Discuss plans for an emergency<br>• Describe natural disasters | • Direct and indirect speech: rhythm | • Weather reports<br>Task: identify the weather event<br>• Emergency radio broadcast<br>Task: correct incorrect statements and report facts, using indirect speech<br>• News report on natural disasters<br>Task: identify the types of disasters | • Historic news headlines<br>• Magazine article describing variables that affect an earthquake's severity | • Write about a historic disaster<br>• Provide instructions on preparing for a disaster<br>• Explain the factors that contribute to the severity of an earthquake |
| • Recommend a book<br>• Give and accept a compliment<br>• Explain where you learned something<br>• Evaluate types of reading materials<br>• Describe your reading habits | • Sentence stress in short answers with <u>think</u>, <u>hope</u>, <u>guess</u>, or <u>believe</u> | • Descriptions of reading habits<br>Task: choose each speaker's preferences<br>• Conversations about books<br>Task: identify the type of book and infer if the speaker likes it | • Online bookstore website<br>• Magazine article about the popularity of, and attitudes about, comic books | • Write about your reading habits<br>• Review a book or other material you've read |
| • Discuss whether to purchase a product<br>• Accept responsibility for a mistake<br>• Reassure someone<br>• Describe a new invention<br>• Compare important inventions | • Contractions with '<u>d</u> (would) | • People describing problems<br>Task: select a useful invention for each person<br>• Discussions of new products<br>Task: determine which adjective best describes each product | • Magazine article describing the importance of the invention of the printing press | • Write about an invention that you think had a great impact |
| • Ask for and give advice about acceptable conversation topics<br>• State your opinion<br>• Express agreement or disagree politely<br>• Suggest solutions to global problems<br>• Debate pros and cons | • Stress to emphasize meaning | • Conversations about politics and social beliefs<br>Task: determine each person's political orientation<br>• Opinions about controversial ideas<br>Task: infer the speaker's opinion<br>• People arguing their views<br>Task: summarize arguments<br>• Radio news program<br>Task: identify the problems | • Authentic dictionary entries<br>• Magazine article defining global problems | • Describe a local or world problem and offer possible solutions<br>• Write the pros and cons of a controversial issue |
| • Warn about risks or dangers<br>• Ask and explain where a place is located<br>• Describe a natural setting<br>• Recommend a place for its beauty<br>• Debate a plan for economic development | • Voiced and voiceless <u>th</u> | • People discussing risks<br>Task: infer if the place is safe<br>• Description of a trip<br>Task: identify natural features<br>• Conversations about tourist destinations<br>Task: infer if the speaker recommends going | • Authentic maps<br>• Magazine article describing the pros and cons of eco-tourism | • Describe a spectacular natural setting<br>• Plan an eco-friendly development<br>• Create a tourism advertisement |

# Acknowledgments

## *Top Notch* International Advisory Board

The authors gratefully acknowledge the substantive and formative contributions of the members of the International Advisory Board.

**CHERYL BELL**, Middlesex County College, Middlesex, New Jersey, USA • **ELMA CABAHUG**, City College of San Francisco, San Francisco, California, USA • **JO CARAGATA**, Mukogawa Women's University, Hyogo, Japan • **ANN CARTIER**, Palo Alto Adult School, Palo Alto, California, USA • **TERRENCE FELLNER**, Himeji Dokkyo University, Hyogo, Japan • **JOHN FUJIMORI**, Meiji Gakuin High School, Tokyo, Japan • **ARETA ULHANA GALAT**, Escola Superior de Estudos Empresariais e Informática, Curitiba, Brazil • **DOREEN M. GAYLORD**, Kanazawa Technical College, Ishikawa, Japan • **EMILY GEHRMAN**, Newton International College, Garden Grove, California, USA • **ANN-MARIE HADZIMA**, National Taiwan University, Taipei, Taiwan • **KAREN KYONG-AI PARK**, Seoul National University, Seoul, Korea • **ANA PATRICIA MARTÍNEZ VITE DIP. R.S.A.**, Universidad del Valle de México, Mexico City, Mexico • **MICHELLE ANN MERRITT**, Proulex/ Universidad de Guadalajara, Guadalajara, Mexico • **ADRIANNE P. OCHOA**, Georgia State University, Atlanta, Georgia, USA • **LOUIS PARDILLO**, Korea Herald English Institute, Seoul, Korea • **THELMA PERES**, Casa Thomas Jefferson, Brasilia, Brazil • **DIANNE RUGGIERO**, Broward Community College, Davie, Florida, USA • **KEN SCHMIDT**, Tohoku Fukushi University, Sendai, Japan • **ALISA A. TAKEUCHI**, Garden Grove Adult Education, Garden Grove, California, USA • **JOSEPHINE TAYLOR**, Centro Colombo Americano, Bogotá, Colombia • **PATRICIA VECIÑO**, Instituto Cultural Argentino Norteamericano, Buenos Aires, Argentina • **FRANCES WESTBROOK**, AUA Language Center, Bangkok, Thailand

## Reviewers and Piloters

Many thanks also to the reviewers and piloters all over the world who reviewed *Top Notch* in its final form.

**G. Julian Abaqueta**, Huachiew Chalermprakiet University, Samutprakarn, Thailand • **David Aline**, Kanagawa University, Kanagawa, Japan • **Marcia Alves**, Centro Cultural Brasil Estados Unidos, Franca, Brazil • **Yousef Al-Yacoub**, Qatar Petroleum, Doha, Qatar • **Maristela Barbosa Silveira e Silva**, Instituto Cultural Brasil-Estados Unidos, Manaus, Brazil • **Beth Bartlett**, Centro Colombo Americano, Cali, Colombia • **Carla Battigelli**, University of Zulia, Maracaibo, Venezuela • **Claudia Bautista**, C.B.C., Caracas, Venezuela • **Rob Bell**, Shumei Yachiyo High School, Chiba, Japan • **Dr. Maher Ben Moussa**, Sharjah University, Sharjah, United Arab Emirates • **Elaine Cantor**, Englewood Senior High School, Jacksonville, Florida, USA • **María Aparecida Capellari**, SENAC, São Paulo, Brazil • **Eunice Carrillo Ramos**, Colegio Durango, Naucalpan, Mexico • **Janette Carvalhinho de Oliveira**, Centro de Linguas (UFES), Vitória, Brazil • **María Amelia Carvalho Fonseca**, Centro Cultural Brasil-Estados Unidos, Belém, Brazil • **Audy Castañeda**, Instituto Pedagógico de Caracas, Caracas, Venezuela • **Ching-Fen Chang**, National Chiao Tung University, Hsinchu, Taiwan • **Ying-Yu Chen**, Chinese Culture University, Taipei, Taiwan • **Joyce Chin**, The Language Training and Testing Center, Taipei, Taiwan • **Eun Cho**, Pagoda Language School, Seoul, Korea • **Hyungzung Cho**, MBC Language Institute, Seoul, Korea • **Dong Sua Choi**, MBC Language Institute, Seoul, Korea • **Jeong Mi Choi**, Freelancer, Seoul, Korea • **Peter Chun**, Pagoda Language School, Seoul, Korea • **Eduardo Corbo**, Legacy ELT, Salto, Uruguay • **Marie Cosgrove**, Surugadai University, Saitama, Japan • **María Antonieta Covarrubias Souza**, Centro Escolar Akela, Mexico City, Mexico • **Katy Cox**, Casa Thomas Jefferson, Brasilia, Brazil • **Michael Donovan**, Gakushuin University, Tokyo, Japan • **Stewart Dorward**, Shumei Eiko High School, Saitama, Japan • **Ney Eric Espina**, Centro Venezolano Americano del Zulia, Maracaibo, Venezuela • **Edith Espino**, Centro Especializado de Lenguas - Universidad Tecnológica de Panamá, El Dorado, Panama • **Allen P. Fermon**, Instituto Brasil-Estados Unidos, Ceará, Brazil • **Simão Ferreira Banha**, Phil Young's English School, Curitiba, Brazil • **María Elena Flores Lara**, Colegio Mercedes, Mexico City, Mexico • **Valesca Fróis Nassif**, Associação Cultural Brasil-Estados Unidos, Salvador, Brazil • **José Fuentes**, Empire Language Consulting, Caracas, Venezuela • **José Luis Guerrero**, Colegio Cristóbal Colón, Mexico City, Mexico • **Claudia Patricia Gutiérrez**, Centro Colombo Americano, Cali, Colombia • **Valerie Hansford**, Asia University, Tokyo, Japan • **Gene Hardstark**, Dotkyo University, Saitama, Japan • **Maiko Hata**, Kansai University, Osaka, Japan • **Susan Elizabeth Haydock Miranda de Araujo**, Centro Cultural Brasil Estados Unidos, Belém, Brazil • **Gabriela Herrera**, Fundametal, Valencia, Venezuela • **Sandy Ho**, GEOS International, New York, New York, USA • **Yuri Hosoda**, Showa Women's University, Tokyo, Japan • **Hsiao-I Hou**, Shu-Te University, Kaohsiung County, Taiwan • **Kuei-ping Hsu**, National Tsing Hua University, Hsinchu, Taiwan • **Chia-yu Huang**, National Tsing Hua University, Hsinchu, Taiwan • **Caroline C. Hwang**, National Taipei University of Science and Technology, Taipei, Taiwan • **Diana Jones**, Angloamericano, Mexico City, Mexico • **Eunjeong Kim**, Freelancer, Seoul, Korea • **Julian Charles King**, Qatar Petroleum, Doha, Qatar • **Bruce Lee**, CIE: Foreign Language Institute, Seoul, Korea • **Myunghee Lee**, MBC Language Institute, Seoul, Korea • **Naidnapa Leoprasertkul**, Language Development Center, Mahasarakham University, Mahasarakham, Thailand • **Eleanor S. Leu**, Souchow University, Taipei, Taiwan • **Eliza Liu**, Chinese Culture University, Taipei, Taiwan • **Carlos Lizárraga**, Angloamericano, Mexico City, Mexico • **Philippe Loussarevian**, Keio University Shonan Fujisawa High School, Kanagawa, Japan • **Jonathan Lynch**, Azabu University, Tokyo, Japan • **Thomas Mach**, Konan University, Hyogo, Japan • **Lilian Mandel Civatti**, Associação Cultural Brasil-Estados Unidos, Salvador, Brazil • **Hakan Mansuroglu**, Zoni Language Center, West New York, New Jersey, USA • **Martha McGaughey**, Language Training Institute, Englewood Cliffs, New Jersey, USA • **David Mendoza Plascencia**, Instituto Internacional de Idiomas, Naucalpan, Mexico • **Theresa Mezo**, Interamerican University, Río Piedras, Puerto Rico • **Luz Adriana Montenegro Silva**, Colegio CAFAM, Bogotá, Colombia • **Magali de Moraes Menti**, Instituto Lingua, Porto Alegre, Brazil • **Massoud Moslehpour**, The Overseas Chinese Institute of Technology, Taichung, Taiwan • **Jennifer Nam**, IKE, Seoul, Korea • **Marcos Norelle F. Victor**, Instituto Brasil-Estados Unidos, Ceará, Brazil • **Luz María Olvera**, Instituto Juventud del Estado de México, Naucalpan, Mexico • **Roxana Orrego Ramírez**, Universidad Diego Portales, Santiago, Chile • **Ming-Jong Pan**, National Central University, Jhongli City, Taiwan • **Sandy Park**, Topia Language School, Seoul, Korea • **Patrícia Elizabeth Peres Martins**, Instituto Brasil-Estados Unidos, Rio de Janeiro, Brazil • **Rodrigo Peza**, Passport Language Centers, Bogotá, Colombia • **William Porter**, Osaka Institute of Technology, Osaka, Japan • **Caleb Prichard**, Kwansei Gakuin University, Hyogo, Japan • **Mirna Quintero**, Instituto Pedagógico de Caracas, Caracas, Venezuela • **Roberto Rabbini**, Seigakuin University, Saitama, Japan • **Terri Rapoport**, Berkeley College, White Plains, New York, USA • **Yvette Rieser**, Centro Electrónico de Idiomas, Maracaibo, Venezuela • **Orlando Rodríguez**, New English Teaching School, Paysandu, Uruguay • **Mayra Rosario**, Pontificia Universidad Católica Madre y Maestra, Santiago, Dominican Republic • **Peter Scout**, Sakura no Seibo Junior College, Fukushima, Japan • **Jungyeon Shim**, EG School, Seoul, Korea • **Keum Ok Song**, MBC Language Institute, Seoul, Korea • **Assistant Professor Dr. Reongrudee Soonthornmanee**, Chulalongkorn University Language Institute, Bangkok, Thailand • **Claudia Stanisclause**, The Language College, Maracay, Venezuela • **Tom Suh**, The Princeton Review, Seoul, Korea • **Phiphawin Suphawat**, KhonKaen University, KhonKaen, Thailand • **Craig Sweet**, Poole Gakuin Junior and Senior High Schools, Osaka, Japan • **Yi-nien Josephine Twu**, National Tsing Hua University, Hsinchu, Taiwan • **Maria Christina Uchôa Close**, Instituto Cultural Brasil-Estados Unidos, São José dos Campos, Brazil • **Luz Vanegas Lopera**, Lexicom The Place For Learning English, Medellín, Colombia • **Julieta Vasconcelos García**, Centro Escolar del Lago, A.C., Mexico City, Mexico • **Carol Vaughan**, Kanto Kokusai High School, Tokyo, Japan • **Patricia Celia Veciño**, Instituto Cultural Argentino Norteamericano, Buenos Aires, Argentina • **Isabela Villas Boas**, Casa Thomas Jefferson, Brasilia, Brazil • **Iole Vitti**, Peanuts English School, Poços de Caldas, Brazil • **Gabi Witthaus**, Qatar Petroleum, Doha, Qatar • **Yi-Ling Wu**, Shih Chien University, Taipei, Taiwan • **Chad Wynne**, Osaka Keizai University, Osaka, Japan • **Belkis Yanes**, Freelance Instructor, Caracas, Venezuela • **I-Chieh Yang**, Chung-kuo Institute of Technology, Taipei, Taiwan • **Emil Ysona**, Instituto Cultural Dominico-Americano, Santo Domingo, Dominican Republic • **Chi-fang Yu**, Soo Chow University, Taipei, Taiwan, • **Shigeki Yusa**, Sendai Shirayuri Women's College, Sendai, Japan

# To the Teacher

## What is *Top Notch*?

- *Top Notch* is a six-level communicative English course for adults and young adults, with two beginning entry levels.
- *Top Notch* prepares students to interact successfully and confidently with both native and non-native speakers of English.
- *Top Notch* demonstrably brings students to a "Top Notch" level of communicative competence.

## Key Elements of the *Top Notch* Instructional Design

### Concise two-page lessons

Each easy-to-teach two-page lesson is designed for one class session and begins with a clearly stated communication goal and ends with controlled or free communication practice. Each lesson provides vocabulary, grammar, and social language contextualized in all four skills, keeping the pace of a class session lively and varied.

### Daily confirmation of progress

Adult and young adult students need to observe and confirm their own progress. In *Top Notch*, students conclude each class session with a controlled or free practice activity that demonstrates their ability to use new vocabulary, grammar, and social language. This motivates and keeps students eager to continue their study of English and builds their pride in being able to speak accurately, fluently, and authentically.

### Real language

Carefully exposing students to authentic, natural English, both receptively and productively, is a necessary component of building understanding and expression. All conversation models feature the language people really use; nowhere to be found is "textbook English" written merely to exemplify grammar.

### Practical content

In addition to classic topical vocabulary, grammar, and conversation, *Top Notch* includes systematic practice of highly practical language, such as: how to describe symptoms at a doctor's office, and how to ask for express service at a service provider such as a dry cleaner or copy center. In addition

to these practical applications, *Top Notch* continues development of its discussion syllabus with popular discussion topics ranging from explaining the holiday customs of one's country to polite discussions of government and politics—usable language today's students want and need.

### Memorable model conversations

Effective language instruction must make language memorable. The full range of social and functional communicative needs is presented through practical model conversations that are intensively practiced and manipulated, first within a guided model and then in freer and more personalized formats.

### High-impact vocabulary syllabus

In order to ensure students' solid acquisition of vocabulary essential for communication, *Top Notch* contains explicit presentation, practice, and systematic extended recycling of words, collocations, and expressions appropriate at each level of study. The extensive captioned illustrations, photos, definitions, examples, and contextualized sentences remove doubts about meaning and provide a permanent in-book reference for student test preparation. An added benefit is that teachers don't have to search for pictures to bring to class and don't have to resort to translating vocabulary into the students' native language.

### Learner-supportive grammar

Grammar is approached explicitly and cognitively, through form, meaning, and use—both within the Student's Book units and in a bound-in Grammar Booster. Charts provide examples and paradigms enhanced by simple usage notes at students' level of comprehension. This takes the guesswork out of meaning, makes lesson preparation easier for teachers, and provides students with comprehensible charts for permanent reference and test preparation. All presentations of grammar are followed by exercises to ensure adequate practice.

### English as an international language

*Top Notch* prepares students for interaction with both native and non-native speakers of English, both linguistically and culturally. English is treated as an international language, rather than the language of a particular country or region. In addition, *Top Notch* helps students develop a cultural fluency by creating an awareness of the varied rules across cultures for: politeness, greetings and introductions, appropriateness of dress in different settings, conversation do's and taboos, table manners, and other similar issues.

## Two beginning-level texts

Beginning students can be placed either in *Top Notch 1* or *Top Notch Fundamentals*, depending on ability and background. Even absolute beginners can start with confidence in *Top Notch Fundamentals*. False beginners can begin with *Top Notch 1*. The *Top Notch Placement Test* clarifies the best placement within the series.

## Estimated teaching time

Each level of *Top Notch* is designed for 60 to 90 instructional hours and contains a full range of supplementary components and enrichment devices to tailor the course to individual needs.

# Components of *Top Notch 3*

## Student's Book with Take-Home Super CD-ROM

The Super CD-ROM includes a variety of exciting interactive activities: Speaking Practice, Interactive Workbook, Games and Puzzles, and *Top Notch Pop* Karaoke. The disk can also be played on an audio CD player to listen to the Conversation Models and the *Top Notch Pop* songs.

## Teacher's Edition and Lesson Planner

Complete yet concise lesson plans are provided for each class. Corpus notes provide essential information from the *Longman Spoken American Corpus* and the *Longman Learner's Corpus*. In addition, a free *Teacher's Resource Disk* offers the following printable extension activities to personalize your teaching style:

- Grammar self-checks
- *Top Notch Pop* song activities
- Writing process worksheets
- Learning strategies
- Pronunciation activities and supplements
- Extra reading comprehension activities
- Vocabulary cards and cumulative vocabulary activities
- Graphic organizers
- Pair work cards

## Copy & Go: Ready-made Interactive Activities for Busy Teachers

Interactive games, puzzles, and other practice activities in convenient photocopiable form support the Student's Book content and provide a welcome change of pace.

## Complete Classroom Audio Program

The audio program contains listening comprehension activities, rhythm and intonation practice, and targeted pronunciation activities that focus on accurate and comprehensible pronunciation.

Because *Top Notch* prepares students for international communication, a variety of native *and* non-native speakers are included to ready students for the world outside the classroom. The audio program also includes the five *Top Notch Pop* songs in standard and karaoke form.

## Workbook

A tightly linked illustrated Workbook contains exercises that provide additional practice and reinforcement of language concepts and skills from *Top Notch* and its Grammar Booster.

## Complete Assessment Package with *ExamView®* Software

Ten easy-to-administer and easy-to-score unit achievement tests assess listening, vocabulary, grammar, social language, reading, and writing. Two review tests, one mid-book and one end-of-book, provide additional cumulative assessment. Two speaking tests assess progress in speaking. In addition to the photocopiable achievement tests, *ExamView®* software enables teachers to tailor-make tests to best meet their needs by combining items in any way they wish.

## Top Notch TV

A lively and entertaining video offers a TV-style situation comedy that reintroduces language from each *Top Notch* unit, plus authentic unrehearsed interviews with English speakers from around the world and authentic karaoke. Packaged with the video are activity worksheets and a booklet with teaching suggestions and complete video scripts.

## Companion Website

A Companion Website at www.longman.com/topnotch provides numerous additional resources for students and teachers. This no-cost, high-benefit feature includes opportunities for further practice of language and content from the *Top Notch* Student's Book.

# *Welcome to Top Notch!*

# About the Authors

## Joan Saslow

Joan Saslow has taught English as a Foreign Language and English as a Second Language to adults and young adults in both South America and the United States. She taught English and French at the Binational Centers of Valparaíso and Viña del Mar, Chile, and the Catholic University of Valparaíso. In the United States, Ms. Saslow taught English as a Foreign Language to Japanese university students at Marymount College and to international students in Westchester Community College's intensive English program as well as workplace English at the General Motors auto assembly plant in Tarrytown, NY.

Ms. Saslow is the series director of Longman's popular five-level adult series *True Colors: An EFL Course for Real Communication* and of *True Voices*, a five-level video course. She is author of *Ready to Go: Language, Lifeskills, and Civics*, a four-level adult ESL series; *Workplace Plus*, a vocational English series; and of *Literacy Plus*, a two-level series that teaches literacy, English, and culture to adult pre-literate students. She is also author of *English in Context: Reading Comprehension for Science and Technology*, a three-level series for English for special purposes. In addition, Ms. Saslow has been an author, an editor of language teaching materials, a teacher-trainer, and a frequent speaker at gatherings of EFL and ESL teachers for over thirty years.

## Allen Ascher

Allen Ascher has been a teacher and teacher-trainer in both China and the United States, as well as an administrator and a publisher. Mr. Ascher specialized in teaching listening and speaking to students at the Beijing Second Foreign Language Institute, to hotel workers at a major international hotel in China, and to Japanese students from Chubu University studying English at Ohio University. In New York, Mr. Ascher taught students of all language backgrounds and abilities at the City University of New York, and he trained teachers in the TESOL Certificate Program at the New School. He was also the academic director of the International English Language Institute at Hunter College.

Mr. Ascher has provided lively workshops for EFL teachers throughout Asia, Latin America, Europe, and the Middle East. He is author of the popular *Think about Editing: A Grammar Editing Guide for ESL Writers*. As a publisher, Mr. Ascher played a key role in the creation of some of the most widely used materials for adults, including: *True Colors, NorthStar, Focus on Grammar, Global Links*, and *Ready to Go*. Mr. Ascher has an M.A. in Applied Linguistics from Ohio University.

# UNIT 1

## Cultural Literacy

### UNIT GOALS

1 Meet someone and make small talk
2 Get to know someone
3 Be culturally literate
4 Discuss how culture changes over tir

**A** ▷ **TOPIC PREVIEW.** Look at the flyer for an international language school. Choose a place to study English.

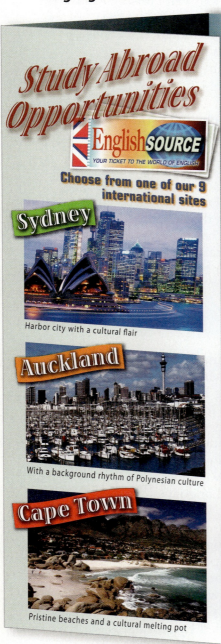

*Study Abroad Opportunities*

**EnglishSOURCE**
YOUR TICKET TO THE WORLD OF ENGLISH

**Choose from one of our 9 international sites**

**Sydney**

Harbor city with a cultural flair

**Auckland**

With a background rhythm of Polynesian culture

**Cape Town**

Pristine beaches and a cultural melting pot

**Shop and compare. EnglishSOURCE offers:**

- an international student body—over 35 countries represented!
- courses tailored to your available time—from one week to one year
- native teachers with university degrees
- arranged homestays near classes
- guaranteed achievement—or your money back!

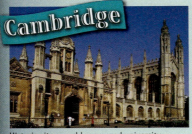

**Cambridge**

Historic city—world-renowned university—community of scholars

**Edinburgh**

Magnificent—from the medieval to the modern

**New York**

Capital of the world

**London**

The birthplace of English—home of the Crown

**San Francisco**

Human-size city—a delight for the eyes—near ocean and mountain peaks

**Toronto**

Canada's largest city—never run out of things to do, see, or buy

**B** ▷ **PAIR WORK.** Which site did you choose? Why? Answers will vary.

☐ because of the location
☐ because of the type of English spoken there
☐ because I have friends or relatives there
☐ other reason(s): _____

# Cultural Literacy

## How to plan a *Top Notch* lesson

Suggested teaching times for the activities in each two-page lesson add up to a total teaching time of 45–60 minutes. To plan a class of approximately 45 minutes, use the shorter estimated teaching times when a range is shown. To plan a class of 60 or more minutes, use the longer estimated teaching times when a range is shown. Your actual teaching time will vary from the times suggested, according to your needs, your schedule, and the needs of your class.

Activities labeled "Option" or "Challenge" are additional to the 45–60 minutes, and the estimated teaching time for each is noted with the activity. Similarly, any time you spend in class on the Grammar Booster is additional to the 45–60 minutes.

In addition to the notes, options, and challenges, you will see icons indicating other optional extensions to the material on the Student's Book page. These of course will also increase the time allotted to the lesson:

An extension activity from the Teacher's Resource Disk in the back of this Teacher's Edition

An episode from the *Top Notch TV* Video

A test from the Complete Assessment Package

At the end of each lesson is an item labeled "Extras." These are additional optional activities that can be assigned as homework or class work. The activities include exercises from the Grammar Booster, exercises from the Workbook, interactive activities from Copy & Go, and Pronunciation Supplements from the Teacher's Resource Disk.

Regarding the *Top Notch* Projects, please see the Introduction to this Teacher's Edition. It is impossible to estimate the amount of class time individual projects will take as many teachers prefer to spread projects out over a number of lessons or assign them for homework.

The *Top Notch* authors strongly encourage you to view these teacher's notes and accompanying options, challenges, and extensions as a menu of possibilities in creating the best lesson plan for you. You may wish to construct your lesson entirely with the options, challenges, and extensions, or, to extend the lesson by doing all possible activities. The times are provided to help you do that.

## A TOPIC PREVIEW

| Suggested teaching time: | 15 minutes |
|---|---|
| Your actual teaching time: | _____ |

- To begin, tell students that the flyer is for an international language school. Practice the reading strategy of scanning by asking students to read the text (quickly) to answer these questions: *What is the name of the school?* (English Source) *From how many countries do students come?* (more than 35) *In how many cities does this school offer courses?* (9)

- Ask students to name the countries the cities are in. (Sydney—Australia; Auckland—New Zealand; Cape Town—South Africa; Cambridge—England; Edinburgh—Scotland; New York—USA; London—England; San Francisco—USA; Toronto—Canada) If there is a world map in the classroom, ask a volunteer to point out the cities and countries.

- If you know that students in your class have done some international travel, ask if anyone has ever been to any of the cities in the pictures or knows interesting information about them. You may want to ask what they liked about the city.

- Tell students they can choose more than one site if they are interested in going to more than one place.

**Option:** To provide more practice with scanning, write the following questions on the board and ask students to read the flyer again for the answers. (1. Cambridge 2. Cape Town 3. London 4. Toronto 5. New York 6. San Francisco) [+5 minutes]

*1. Which city is the home of an old and famous university?*

*2. Which city has people from different cultures and backgrounds?*

*3. In which city was English born?*

*4. Which busy city is the largest in its country?*

*5. Which city is probably one of the most important in the world?*

*6. Which city is near both the mountains and the sea?*

## B PAIR WORK

| Suggested teaching time: | 5–10 minutes |
|---|---|
| Your actual teaching time: | _____ |

- Before students talk with their partners, encourage them to add any reason(s) the list does not include.

- To finish, students take turns saying why they chose a particular city. Encourage students to ask follow-up questions. Example: Student A: *I chose Edinburgh because I have relatives there.* Student B: *Really? Are they close relatives?* Student A: *Yes, my grandparents!*

- Take a poll of the class to find which site was the most popular.

**Option:** Ask if any students have ever taken an English course abroad. Encourage them to briefly talk about their experience by asking *Where? When? Did the course/trip help you improve your English?* [+5 minutes]

## C 🎧 SOUND BITES
(CD1, Track 2)

| Suggested teaching time: | 10–15 minutes |
|---|---|
| Your actual teaching time: | _____ |

- Pre-listening: To practice the strategy of prediction, ask students to cover the conversations and look at the pictures. Ask students to predict answers to these questions and write their information on the board. *Have the people known each other long? What are the people in the photos doing?* (Students may say: clapping, greeting each other, praying.)

- Ask students to answer the same questions after they read and listen. Then compare the answers with the students' predictions. (They are greeting each other. No, this is the first time they are meeting.)

- Have students read and listen again. To check comprehension, ask *Does Surat introduce himself first?* (No, Teresa introduces herself first.) *What does Teresa want to know?* (if Thais use their first names to address each other) *When does Surat say it's OK to use first names?* (at company meetings held in English)

- Direct attention to the information with the asterisk (*). (See also the culture note below.) Tell students that the *wai* is the name of the gesture Thais use to greet each other. Point out that men and women say the greeting a bit differently.

- Ask students to describe common formal and informal greetings in their country. Ask them to describe greetings they are familiar with from other countries. Examples: *In English-speaking countries people often shake hands in formal and informal situations. In Japan, people usually bow to each other in formal situations. In Spain and France, people usually kiss each other on both cheeks in informal situations.*

**Language note:** *M-hmm* is an informal way of saying *yes*.

**Culture note:** In Thailand, people greet each other with the *wai* (putting their hands together as in the photo), nodding slightly, and saying *Sawatdee-Khrab*, which means *Greetings*. A woman says *Sawatdee-Kaa* and a man says *Sawatdee-Khrab*. The *wai* hand position is also used when making an apology and when expressing thanks.

## D DISCUSSION

| Suggested teaching time: | 10 minutes |
|---|---|
| Your actual teaching time: | _____ |

- Group work. Form groups of three. Encourage students to share their opinions about each question. Point out that there are not correct answers to questions 1 and 3. Encourage students to give reasons for their answers.

- If you think students need help with question 2, tell students to think about the following: *What should you do when you're in a foreign country—follow the local customs or do things the way you do them in your own country?*

- Walk around the room and provide help as needed.

- To review, have volunteers from different groups answer one of the questions. (1. Possible answers: They are probably in Thailand. They might be business people or language teachers. 2. They are suggesting that when you are in a new place, you should follow the local customs. 3. Answers will vary.)

## WHAT ABOUT **YOU?**

| Suggested teaching time: | 5–10 minutes |
|---|---|
| Your actual teaching time: | _____ |

- Point out that students can identify different situations where they may want to be addressed differently; for example, on business trips, on school trips, on vacations.

- Pair work. Students take turns talking about how they would like to be addressed and give reasons for their choice.

- Ask various students to tell the class which item(s) they chose.

**Option:** Ask students about the different ways they are addressed daily. Examples: *Who calls you by your first name? Who uses your nickname? Who uses a title when they speak to you?* **[+5 minutes]**

**Language note:** A *nickname* is a shorter version of your name. It can also be a silly name or an endearing name usually used by your friends or family.

**Culture note:** In English-speaking countries, the order for names is first name (also known as your *given name*), middle name, and then last name (also known as your *surname* or *family name*). In the U.S., people usually call each other by their first names. In business situations, someone will often introduce a colleague with their full name and title, but after that use the person's first name.

## EXTRAS (optional)
**Workbook: Exercises 1–5**

🎧 **SOUND BITES.** Read along silently as you listen to a conversation at a business meeting in Thailand.

**TERESA:** Allow me to introduce myself. I'm Teresa Segovia, from Santiago, Chile. *Sawatdee-Kaa*.
**SURAT:** Where did you learn the *wai*?*
**TERESA:** Actually, a Thai friend in Chile taught me.

**SURAT:** *Sawatdee-Khrab*. Nice to meet you, Ms. Segovia. I'm Surat Leekpai.
**TERESA:** Nice to meet you, too. But please call me Terri.
**SURAT:** And please call me Surat. It's easier to say than Leekpai!

**TERESA:** Do you mind my asking you the custom here? Are most people on a first-name basis? **CN1**
**SURAT:** At company meetings in English, absolutely. In general, though, it's probably best to watch what others do. You know what they say: "When in Rome…" **CN2**
**TERESA:** M-hmm… "do as the Romans do!"

*Thais greet each other with a gesture called the "wai" and by saying "Sawatdee-Kaa" (women) / "Sawatdee-Khrab (men)."

**CN1 Corpus Notes:**
Two people can *be on a first-name basis* or a person can be *on a first-name basis with (someone).* Each has about the same level of frequency in American English.

**CN2 Corpus Notes:**
*You know what they say* is almost always used to introduce a common expression, proverb, or piece of information that the listener probably already knows.

D **DISCUSSION.**

1. Why do you think Teresa greets Surat with the *wai*?
2. Why do Surat and Teresa say, "When in Rome, do as the Romans do!"?
3. When do you think people should use first names with each other? When do you think they should use titles and last names?

## WHAT ABOUT **YOU?**

**If you take a trip to another country, how would you like to be addressed?** Answers will vary.

- ☐ 1. I'd like to be called by my title and my family name.
- ☐ 2. I'd like to be called by my first name.
- ☐ 3. I'd like to be called by my nickname.
- ☐ 4. I'd prefer to follow the local customs.

# **1** *Meet Someone and Make Small Talk*

## 🎧 CONVERSATION MODEL **Read and listen.**

**A:** Good morning. Beautiful day, isn't it?
**B:** It really is. By the way, I'm Kazuko Toshinaga.
**A:** I'm Jane Quitt. Nice to meet you.
**B:** Nice to meet you, too.
**A:** Do you mind if I call you Kazuko?
**B:** Absolutely not. Please do.
**A:** And please call me Jane.

🎧 **Rhythm and intonation practice**

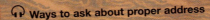

🎧 **Ways to ask about proper address**

Do you mind if I call you [Kazuko]?
Would it be rude to call you [Kazuko]?
What would you like to be called?
How do you prefer to be addressed?
Do you use Ms. or Mrs.?

---

### Ⓐ GRAMMAR. **Tag questions: form and social use**

Use tag questions to confirm information you already think is true or to encourage someone to make small talk.

| statement | tag question | answer |
|---|---|---|
| You're Kazuko, | **aren't you**? | Yes, I am. / No, I'm not. **CN** |
| You speak Thai, | **don't you**? | Yes, I do. / No, I don't. |
| They'll be here later, | **won't they**? | Yes, they will. / No, they won't. |
| They didn't know, | **did they**? | Yes, they did. / No, they didn't. |
| It's a beautiful day, | **isn't it**? | Yes, it is. / No, it isn't. |

When the statement is affirmative, the tag question is negative. When the statement is negative, the tag question is affirmative.
He**'s** late, **isn't** he?    He **isn't** late, **is** he?

**BE CAREFUL!** Use pronouns, not names or nouns, in tag questions.
Machu Picchu was built by the Incas, wasn't it? (NOT ~~wasn't Machu Picchu?~~)

Use <u>aren't</u> for negative tag questions after <u>I am</u>.
I'm on time, **aren't** I?  BUT I'm not late, am I?

GRAMMAR BOOSTER

**PAGE G1**
**For more …**

---

### Ⓑ 🎧 PRONUNCIATION. **Intonation of tag questions. Read and listen. Then listen again and repeat.**

**Use rising intonation when you're not sure if the listener will agree, and you expect an answer.**

People use first names here, don't they?

That movie was great, wasn't it?

**CN** Corpus Notes:
Many learners get confused when forming tag questions with sentences with *your*. For example: *Your favorite sport is baseball, aren't you?* rather than *Your favorite sport is baseball, isn't it?*

**Use falling intonation when you think the listener will agree.**

It's a beautiful day for a walk, isn't it?

You're studying in Chicago next year, aren't you?

# LESSON
# 1 *Meet Someone and Make Small Talk*

**A:** ˙ ˙ — ˙˙ — ˙ — ˙˙
Do you mind if I call you Kazuko?

**B:** —˙ — ˙ — ˙ — ˙
Absolutely not. Please do.

**A:** ˙ — ˙ ˙ — ˙ —
And please call me Jane.

## 🎧 CONVERSATION **MODEL**
**(CD1, Tracks 3,5)**

| Suggested teaching time: | 5–10 minutes |
|---|---|
| Your actual teaching time: | _____ |

- After students read and listen, ask *What are the women's first names?* (Kazuko and Jane) *What gesture are they using to greet each other?* (shaking hands)
- Have students listen, study, then repeat the questions about addressing someone in the small box.
- You may want to write ways to respond to the questions on the board. Examples: 1. and 2. *Absolutely not. Not at all. No, that's fine.* 3. *Please call me [Name]. You can call me [Name].* 4. *Most people call me [Name]. [Name] is fine with me.* 5. *I use [Title].*
- Pair work. Take turns asking and answering the questions.
- To introduce the topic of small talk, ask *How does Jane start the conversation?* (She says "Good morning" and talks about the weather.)
- Write a list of topics on the board: *weather, family, school, religion, age, occupation, politics, relationships.*
- Ask students to say which topics are considered appropriate for small talk in their culture.

**Culture note:** Appropriate topics for small talk vary in different countries. In many English-speaking countries, appropriate topics are the weather, the food you are eating, sports, popular movies, music.

## 🎧 Rhythm and intonation practice
**(CD1, Track 4)**

| Suggested teaching time: | 5 minutes |
|---|---|
| Your actual teaching time: | _____ |

- Have students repeat each line chorally.
- Make sure students:
  ○ pause after *day* and use rising intonation for *isn't it?*
  ○ pause after *way* in *By the way, I'm Kazuko Toshinaga.*
  ○ link the *t* and *y* in *meet you* to form *ch.*
  ○ use rising intonation for *Do you mind if I call you Kazuko?*
  ○ use the following stress pattern:

**STRESS PATTERN\***

**A:** ˙ — ˙ ˙ — ˙ ˙ — ˙˙
Good morning. Beautiful day, isn't it?

**B:** ˙ —˙ — ˙ — ˙ ˙˙ — ˙˙ — ˙
It really is. By the way, I'm Kazuko Toshinaga.

**A:** — — — ˙ — ˙ —˙ ˙
I'm Jane Quitt. Nice to meet you.

**B:** — ˙ — ˙ — ˙
Nice to meet you, too.

## A GRAMMAR

| Suggested teaching time: | 15 minutes |
|---|---|
| Your actual teaching time: | _____ |

- Direct attention to the box and have students read the first explanation and study the examples.
- Tell students that a tag question comes after a statement. Point out the tag questions in blue.
- Point out that the auxiliary or verb in the tag question matches the verb in the statement. Have students look at examples 1 and 5. If the verb *be* is used in the statement, then *be* is needed in the tag question.
- In examples 2 and 4 point out that the verbs in the statements are the present and past tense. Tell students that these tag question need the auxiliaries *do* and *did* because it is <u>not</u> the verb *be*.
- Point out example 3. The future *will* is used in the statement and *will* is needed in the tag question.
- Direct attention to the short answers (the third column).
- It's important for students to understand that the listener is supposed to agree or disagree with the information in the statement, not with the tag question.
- To check comprehension, ask students a variety of questions that are true and false for your group. Examples: *You're [student's correct name], aren't you?* (Yes, I am.) *You're [student's incorrect name], aren't you?* (No, I'm not.) *This class starts at [incorrect time], doesn't it?* (No, it doesn't.)
- Direct attention to the second explanation and have students study the examples.
- Ask students to read the last two explanations.
- To check comprehension, ask students to identify mistakes with *am / are* and pronouns. Examples: *I'm not going to pass this class, aren't I?* (am I) *Jane went shopping yesterday, didn't Jane?* (didn't she)

**Language note:** In British English, it is possible to use an affirmative tag question after an affirmative statement to confirm information.

 **Grammar Self-Checks**

## B  🎧 PRONUNCIATION
**(CD1, Track 6)**

| Suggested teaching time: | 5 minutes |
|---|---|
| Your actual teaching time: | _____ |

- First listening: Have students listen.
- Second listening: Have students listen and repeat.

 **Pronunciation Activities**

---

\* The dots [˙] and dashes [—] indicate the stress used in the recording. While there may be other correct ways to stress each of these utterances, what you see here is a representation of the stress you'll hear on the audio.

### C Complete each statement . . .

| Suggested teaching time: | 5 minutes |
|---|---|
| Your actual teaching time: | _____ |

- Do the first item with the class. Clarify that the correct answer is *isn't he* by pointing out that the statement uses "is" in the affirmative form, so the tag question requires "is" in the negative form. Also, the pronoun *he* is needed, not the person's name (Robert) which should not be repeated.

- Encourage students to underline the verb in each statement before writing the tag questions.

- Have students compare answers with a partner. Then review as a class.

### D PAIR WORK

| Suggested teaching time: | 5–10 minutes |
|---|---|
| Your actual teaching time: | _____ |

- Review the writing model with the class. Then read the model tag question out loud.

- Ask students to provide other possible tag questions about the facts on the notepad. Examples: *You grew up here, didn't you? You started studying English long ago, didn't you?*

- Tell students to write at least five or six facts about themselves and their families. Point out that they should include present and past information.

- Point out / remind students they will ask tag questions to confirm their partner's information (not their own).

- Encourage students to use falling information in their tag questions because they are confirming information.

- Walk around the room and provide help as needed.

> **Language note:** If the speaker asks a tag question you agree with, for example, *It's a great concert, isn't it?* you can say *Yes, it (really) is. / Yes. / It sure is. / I agree.* If you don't agree, it is polite to give your opinion or a reason why. For example, *Well, I think the music is too loud. / No, it really isn't. I don't like this kind of music.*

## CONVERSATION **PAIR WORK**

| Suggested teaching time: | 5–10 minutes |
|---|---|
| Your actual teaching time: | _____ |

- To get students ready for the activity, have students read the conversation model on page 4 again. You may also want to have students listen to the model.

- Write on the board:
  1. it / nice day
  2. it / getting warmer / colder
  3. you / student here
  4. you / live around here

- To practice making questions for making small talk, ask students to make tag questions with the information on the board. Examples: *It's a nice day, isn't it? It's getting warmer, isn't it? You're a student here, aren't you? You don't live around here, do you?*

- Remind students that intonation they use "sends a message." See page 4, Exercise B.

- Choose a more confident student and role-play a conversation. Encourage students to ask follow-up questions.

- Ask students to walk around and meet at least five classmates.

- Walk around the room and provide help as needed. Encourage students to use the correct rhythm and intonation.

 **Pair Work Cards**

 **Learning Strategies**

## EXTRAS (optional)

**Grammar Booster**
**Workbook: Exercises 6–11**
**Copy & Go: Activity 1**

 **Pronunciation Supplements**

**C** Complete each statement with a tag question.

1. Robert Reston is the director of the English program, __isn't he__?

2. There weren't any openings at the San Francisco location, __were there__?

3. They're all going to enroll in the Chicago course, __aren't they__?

4. I'm not too late to sign up, __am I__?

5. She prefers to be addressed by her title and last name, __doesn't she__?

6. The letters of acceptance will be mailed in March, __won't they__?

7. Australia has been a terrific place to learn English, __hasn't it__?

8. It was a great day, __wasn't it__?

**D** **PAIR WORK.** Write a few facts about yourself. Give the paper to your partner to read for a minute. Then take back the paper and confirm the information with tag questions.

> **"** Your parents are from Italy, aren't they? **"**

> I grew up here, but my parents are from Italy. I started studying English when I was in primary school.

## CONVERSATION
### PAIR WORK

**Meet your classmates. Ask them how they'd like to be addressed. Use tag questions to make small talk about the weather and other subjects.** Answers will vary.

# Get to Know Someone

## 🎧 CONVERSATION MODEL Read and listen.

**A:** Hi. I'm Sylvia Contreras.

**B:** Conrad Schmitt. Nice to meet you, Sylvia. You know, you look familiar. You were in this class last term, weren't you?

**A:** No, actually, I wasn't. I hadn't arrived here yet when the class began.

🎧 **Rhythm and intonation practice**

**A** **GRAMMAR.** **The past perfect: form and use** ───────

Form the past perfect with <u>had</u> and a past participle of the main verb.

                past participle
By 2001, she **had** already **met** her husband.

**Use the past perfect to describe something that happened before a specific time in the past.**
By April, he **had started** his new job.
At 3:00, we **hadn't** yet **heard** the news.

**Use the past perfect with the simple past tense to show which of two past events occurred first.**
I **had** already **seen** the movie when it **came** out on DVD. (First I saw it. Then it came out on DVD.)

**Note that in informal speech we often use the simple past tense instead of the past perfect. The words <u>before</u> and <u>after</u> can help clarify the order of the events in informal speech.**
By April, he started his new job.
Before I graduated, I learned to speak Greek.
I became a good driver after I got my own car.

**GRAMMAR BOOSTER**

**PAGES G1–G3**
For more …

**B** **Choose the correct meaning for each statement.**

1. "When they decided to open a language school in Scotland, I had already decided to study in San Francisco."
   - ☐ First they decided to open the language school in Scotland. Then I decided to study in San Francisco.
   - ☑ First I decided to study in San Francisco. Then they opened a language school in Scotland.

2. "By the time she was twenty, she had studied at two language schools."
   - ☐ She turned twenty before she studied at two language schools.
   - ☑ First she studied at two language schools. Then she turned twenty.

3. "We had already applied for the study abroad program when they canceled it."
   - ☑ First we applied for the program. Then they canceled it.
   - ☐ First they canceled the program. Then we applied for it.

# 2 ►Get to Know Someone

## 🎧 CONVERSATION MODEL
**(CD1, Track 7)**

| Suggested teaching time: | 5–10 minutes |
|---|---|
| Your actual teaching time: | _____ |

- After students read and listen, ask *Why does Conrad think Sylvia was in the same class the previous term?* (He feels like he knows her already.) *Why wasn't she in that class last term?* (because she arrived after the class began)

## 🎧 Rhythm and intonation practice
**(CD1, Track 8)**

| Suggested teaching time: | 5 minutes |
|---|---|
| Your actual teaching time: | _____ |

- Have students repeat each line chorally.
- Make sure students:
  - pause after *actually.*
  - stress <u>Nice</u>, <u>meet</u>, and <u>Syl</u>via in *Nice to meet you, Sylvia.*
  - use rising intonation for *weren't you* in *You were in this class last term, weren't you?*
  - use the following stress pattern:

┌─ **STRESS PATTERN** ──────────────
— — — ·· · — ·
**A:** Hi. I'm Sylvia Contreras.

— · — · — · —·· · ·
**B:** Conrad Schmitt. Nice to meet you, Sylvia. You know,

— · · — · · · · · —
you look familiar. You were in this class last term,

— · ·
weren't you?

— — · ·· · — · — · · — · · ·
**A:** No, actually, I wasn't. I hadn't arrived here yet when

· — · ·
the class began.
└────────────────────────────────

## 🅐 GRAMMAR

| Suggested teaching time: | 15–20 minutes |
|---|---|
| Your actual teaching time: | _____ |

- Direct attention to the first explanation and example.
- Point out that the past perfect is formed with *had* + a past participle.
- Tell students that *already* is not necessary, but adds emphasis to show something finished.
- Point out that *already* is placed between *had* and the past participle. Give more examples: *By 1995, I had already started my first job as a teacher. At 5:00, I had already finished cooking dinner.*
- Review how past participles are formed: *What verb is* met *the past participle of?* (meet) *Is* meet *a regular or an irregular verb?* (irregular) *What do regular past participles end in?* (-ed) *Example:* marry / married

**Option:** To provide practice with past participles, ask students to say the past participle of various verbs. Examples: *choose* (chosen), *live* (lived), *introduce* (introduced), *call* (called). **[+5 minutes]**

- Have students read and study the second explanation.
- To make sure students understand the order of when each event happened, ask *What specific past time is mentioned in the first example?* (April) *What happened before April?* (He started his new job.)
- Point out that the specific time in the past is often a phrase starting with *By [point in time]* . . . Examples: *By Saturday, By yesterday afternoon, By lunch time*
- To check comprehension, ask students the following question: *What had you already done by ([eight]) o'clock this morning?* (Possible answers: I had eaten breakfast. I had taken the dog for a walk. I had taken a shower.) Say a different time each time you ask a new student.
- Point out that *yet* in negative statements adds emphasis about something not completed. Point out in the example that *yet* can be placed between *hadn't* and the past participle. Also point out the placement of *yet* in the conversation model: *I hadn't arrived here yet when class began.*
- Have students read the third explanation (the use of the past perfect with the simple past) and study the example.
- To convey the time relationship between the two past events, draw a timeline on the board and write the information.

*1. I saw the movie.       The movie came out on DVD.*

- Review the timing of the two events by saying *First I saw the movie. Then it came out on DVD. I had already seen the movie when it came out on DVD.*
- Ask students to make a timeline and write three sentences about their own lives using the simple past and the past perfect with *when, already,* or *yet.*
- Pair work. Have students share their sentences.
- Have students read the last two explanations (using the simple past in informal speech) and study the examples.
- To check comprehension, ask *When can the simple past be used instead of the past perfect?* (in informal speech)
- Ask students to rewrite the example in the book with the past perfect instead of the past tense. (By April, he had started his new job.)

 **Grammar Self-Checks**

## 🅑 Choose the correct . . .

| Suggested teaching time: | 5 minutes |
|---|---|
| Your actual teaching time: | _____ |

- Ask students to do the first item and review the correct answer with the class. Ask *What happened first—they decided to open a school in Scotland or the person decided to study in San Francisco?* (The person decided to study in San Francisco.)

**T6**

 **Lynn Todd . . .**

Suggested teaching time: 5–10 minutes
Your actual teaching time: _____

- Review the example first.
- Remind students that they will need to use the past perfect tense because it is almost the end of the day and they are describing what happened before a specific time in the past.
- Encourage students to pay attention to the verbs used in the to-do list as they will need them to write the answers. Ask students which verbs are needed for *Exam!* and *Lunch with Lainie.* (take an exam, have lunch with someone)
- Have students check answers with a partner and review as a class.

**Challenge:** Write on the board:

> 1. *You had invited friends to dinner at your house at 6:00 P.M. They arrived at 5:00.*
> 2. *You had called for a car service to pick you up at 9:00 A.M. to take you to the airport. The car arrived at 8:00 A.M.*

Pair work. Students take turns telling a short story of what happened in each situation. Encourage students to talk about what they had or hadn't done up to the earlier point of time in each situation. Remind students they will use present perfect and the simple past. Example: *When the doorbell rang, I had already set the table but I hadn't finished cooking yet. I had taken a shower already, so I was lucky!* **[+10 minutes]**

## CONVERSATION **PAIR WORK**

Suggested teaching time: 10 minutes
Your actual teaching time: _____

- To get students ready for the activity, have students read the conversation model on page 6 again. You may also want to have students listen to the model.
- If necessary, review how to form tag questions on page 6, Exercise A.
- Choose a more confident student and role-play a conversation. Encourage students to continue their conversations by asking follow-up questions.
- Walk around the room and provide help as needed. Make sure students switch roles.
- Encourage students to use the correct rhythm and intonation.

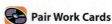 **Pair Work Cards**

## EXTRAS (optional)

**Grammar Booster**
**Workbook: Exercises 12–16**
**Copy & Go: Activity 2**

**4.** "I had received my acceptance letter when they closed the school."

☑ First I received my acceptance letter. Then they closed the school.

☐ First they closed the school. Then I received my acceptance letter.

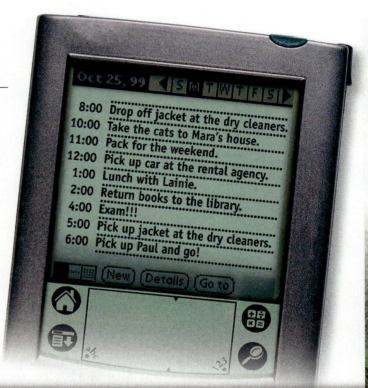

**C** Lynn Todd is taking a weekend trip. It's almost 6:00 P.M. Read her "to-do" list and complete the statements, using <u>already</u> or <u>not yet</u>.

1. At 8:30 Lynn _had already dropped off_ her jacket, but she _hadn't yet taken_ the cats to Mara's house.

2. By 11:00 she _had already taken_ the cats to Mara's house, but she _hadn't yet packed_ for the weekend.

3. At 12:45 she _had not yet had / eaten_ lunch with Lainie, but she _had already picked up_ the car.

4. By 2:10 she _had already returned_ the books to the library, but she _had not yet taken_ her exam.

5. At 5:15 she _had not yet picked up_ Paul, but she _had already picked up_ her jacket at the dry cleaners.

Oct 25, 99 〈 S M T W T F S 〉

8:00 Drop off jacket at the dry cleaners.
10:00 Take the cats to Mara's house.
11:00 Pack for the weekend.
12:00 Pick up car at the rental agency.
1:00 Lunch with Lainie.
2:00 Return books to the library.
4:00 Exam!!!
5:00 Pick up jacket at the dry cleaners.
6:00 Pick up Paul and go!

(New) (Details) (Go to)

abc

---

## CONVERSATION
### PAIR WORK

**Role-play getting to know someone, using one of the imaginary situations. Use the guide, or create a new conversation.**
Answers will vary.

**A:** _____ , I'm _____ .

**B:** _____ . Nice to meet you, _____ . You know, you look familiar. _____ ?

**A:** _____ …

**Continue the conversation in your <u>own</u> way.**

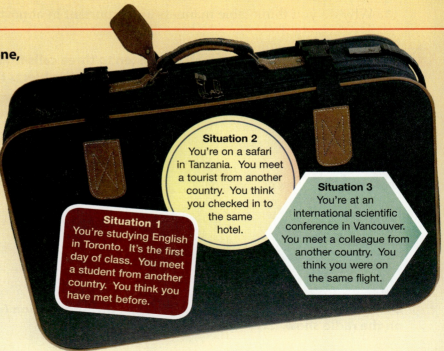

**Situation 2**
You're on a safari in Tanzania. You meet a tourist from another country. You think you checked in to the same hotel.

**Situation 3**
You're at an international scientific conference in Vancouver. You meet a colleague from another country. You think you were on the same flight.

**Situation 1**
You're studying English in Toronto. It's the first day of class. You meet a student from another country. You think you have met before.

CONTROLLED PRACTICE

# 3 Be Culturally Literate

## A ⌒ VOCABULARY. Manners and etiquette. Listen and practice.

**etiquette**   the "rules" of polite behavior

When traveling, it's important to be aware of the etiquette of the culture you will be visiting.

**cultural literacy**   knowing about and respecting the culture of others and following their rules of etiquette when interacting with them

In today's world, cultural literacy is essential to success and good relations with others.

**table manners**   rules for polite behavior when eating with other people

Table manners differ from culture to culture.

**punctuality**   the social "rules" about being on time

Punctuality is considered more important in some cultures than in others.

**impolite**   not polite, rude **CN**

All cultures have rules for polite and impolite behavior.

**offensive**   extremely rude or impolite **CN**

In some cultures, it's offensive to take pictures of people without their permission.

**customary**   usual or traditional in a particular culture

In many cultures, handshakes are customary when meeting someone for the first time.

**taboo**   not allowed because of very strong cultural or religious rules against behavior or topics that are considered very offensive

It's taboo to eat pork in some religions.

**CN** Corpus Notes:
It is much more common to say *impolite to [do something]* than *impolite to [someone]*. However, it is more common to say *offensive to [someone]* than *offensive to [do something]*.

## B DISCUSSION.

1. What are some good ways to teach children etiquette? Give specific examples, using words from the vocabulary.

2. Do you know any differences between your culture and others?

3. Why do you think table manners are important in almost all cultures?

## C ⌒ LISTENING COMPREHENSION. Listen to three calls from a radio show. Then look at the chart and listen again to each call. Check the subjects that were discussed.

| What subjects were discussed? | 1. Arturo and Jettrin | 2. Hiroko and Nadia | 3. Javier and Sujeet |
|---|---|---|---|
| table manners | ☐ | ☐ | ☑ |
| greetings | ☑ | ☐ | ☐ |
| dress and clothing | ☐ | ☑ | ☐ |
| male and female behavior | ☐ | ☑ | ☐ |
| taboos | ☑ | ☐ | ☑ |
| offensive behavior | ☐ | ☑ | ☑ |
| punctuality | ☐ | ☐ | ☐ |
| language | ☐ | ☑ | ☐ |

## D DISCUSSION. In small groups, summarize the information from each of the calls on the radio show. Listen again if necessary.

# LESSON

# 3 ▶ Be Culturally Literate

## A 🎧 VOCABULARY
**(CD1, Track 9)**

| Suggested teaching time: | 5 minutes |
|---|---|
| Your actual teaching time: | _____ |

- Ask students to identify the pictures of the three items. (a fork, chopsticks, a plate)

- Have students listen to the words and study the definitions. Then have students listen and repeat.

- To check comprehension, ask the following questions and encourage students to give examples. *What are some basic rules of etiquette in this country? Is punctuality considered important here? What are one or two behaviors that are considered offensive in this country? Are handshakes customary here?*

**Option:** Write on the board: *cultural literacy, table manners, punctuality.* Ask students to match the word with the following definitions they hear: *behaving politely when eating* (table manners); *being familiar with the etiquette of other cultures* (cultural literacy); *being on time to appointments, meetings, events* (punctuality). Then add to the board: *impolite, offensive, customary, taboo.* Tell students you are going to give examples and they should say which word matches each one: *Doing something that is not allowed (forbidden) in a certain culture* (taboo); *not saying please or thank you* (impolite); *saying rude or insulting things to a person* (offensive); *saying hello to people you meet every day* (customary).
**[+10 minutes]**

 **Vocabulary Cards**

 **Learning Strategies**

## B DISCUSSION

| Suggested teaching time: | 5–10 minutes |
|---|---|
| Your actual teaching time: | _____ |

- Form small groups. Encourage students to take notes as they discuss each question and to use as many of the vocabulary words as they can.

- If students need help generating ideas, offer the following ideas: 1. Demonstrate good manners. Remind children to say *please* and *thank you.* Praise/compliment them when they use good manners. 2. Think about movies or shows you have seen about other cultures. 3. Good table manners make the meal more pleasant for everyone. They help make a good impression, for example, in business situations.

- Ask various groups to answer one of the questions. Encourage follow-up questions.

## C 🎧 LISTENING COMPREHENSION
**(CD1, Track 10)**

| Suggested teaching time: | 15–20 minutes |
|---|---|
| Your actual teaching time: | _____ |

- Note: The three conversations in this exercise are substantially longer than other audio material in *Top Notch 3.* These notes encourage you to treat each listening as a separate activity to make the task more manageable for your students.

- Before listening, have students study the chart. Review any words in column 1 that students are not sure about.

- Tell students they are going to listen to and take notes for the conversations separately.

- To make sure students understand the format and purpose of the radio show, first have students listen to the radio announcer introducing the show and the guests. Ask students to listen for the answers to these questions: *How many guests are there in the studio?* (three) *What were they invited for?* (to answer questions about etiquette in their cultures) *Where are they from?* (Thailand, Dubai, and Nepal) If there is a map in the room, point out the countries.

- Then have students listen to Conversation 1 and check boxes in the first column of the chart. Ask them to compare answers with a partner. You may want students to listen again.

- Review the answers with the class. You may want students to listen again to reconfirm answers.

- Then have students listen to Conversations 2 and 3 following the same procedure.

- Note: You may want to tell students there is one distractor—one item on the list of subjects is not talked about in any conversation. (punctuality)

**Option:** To provide more listening practice, write the following questions (without the answers) on the board and have students listen for the answers:

> 1. *Where is Jettrin from? What two taboos does he talk about?*
> 2. *Where is Nadia from? Can people take any photos they want to?*
> 3. *Where is Sujeet from? What are some taboos and behaviors to know about when in Nepal?*

(1. Thailand. Not touching people's heads and not to show the bottom of their feet. 2. The United Arab Emirates. No, they should not take pictures of Muslim women, and they need to ask a man for permission to take his picture. 3. Nepal. People eat with their right hand, visitors can use a fork, and people from Nepal don't eat beef. Take off shoes and ask if visitors are allowed to enter.) **[+15 minutes]**

 **Learning Strategies**

**AUDIOSCRIPT for Exercise C is on pages T9 and T11.**

## D DISCUSSION

| Suggested teaching time: | 5 minutes |
|---|---|
| Your actual teaching time: | _____ |

- Group work. Form groups of three.

- Tell students to use the boxes they checked on page 8 and their notes from the listening.

- Ask various groups to choose one call and to summarize it. Encourage students to be brief and clear. Ask the class to add any relevant information.

# TOP NOTCH **INTERACTION**

| Suggested teaching time: | 15–20 minutes |
|---|---|
| Your actual teaching time: | _____ |

## STEP 1. PAIR WORK.

- Encourage students to keep their notes for each item brief.
- You may want to give students a copy of the graphic organizer so they can write their notes and add notes in Step 2.

| | |
|---|---|
| Greet someone: first time | |
| Greet someone: men vs. women | |
| Address someone formally: when and how? | |
| Address someone informally: when and how? | |
| Table manners: do's and don'ts | |
| Taboo food and beverages | |
| Taboo topics of conversation | |
| Being punctual: customs | |
| Customary gifts when visiting someone's home | |
| Taboo gifts | |
| Dressing modestly: where and when? | |
| Other helpful information | |

 **Graphic Organizers**

## STEP 2. DISCUSSION.

- Organize students' answers on the board according to each question. Identify the items students did not agree on with a check mark or other symbol.

## STEP 3. WRITING.

- Before students write, have them review their notes and the information on the board.
- Tell students to group information that is similar or about the same topic together. For example, conversation topics, punctuality, and gifts can be grouped into one paragraph about what people should do when visiting someone's home.
- Ask students to include one or two simple introductory sentences to identify the topic of their article. Examples: *The following information can be helpful for visitors arriving for the first time in [country].* OR *Every country has its own ideas about proper etiquette. Here are some tips when you visit [country].*
- Encourage students to include one or two sentences at the end to summarize their article. Examples: *Knowing the customs and taboos when visiting a new place can help make your experience a success.* OR *Hopefully this information will help increase your cultural literacy before your next trip to Peru!*
- Walk around the room as students write and provide help as needed.

 **Writing Process Worksheets**

**AUDIOSCRIPT**

**AUDIOSCRIPT for Exercise C, page T8**

CALL 1 Arturo and Jettrin [F1 = British, M1 = Thai, F2 = Arabic, M2 = Indian, M3 = Spanish]

**F1:** Good morning, world. This is Millicent McKay in Brussels with today's worldwide Cultural Literacy Update. If you're new to the program, here's the format: In the studio three people take your phone calls and answer your questions about etiquette in their countries. Today's guests are Jettrin from Thailand, Nadia from Dubai in the United Arab Emirates, and Sujeet from Nepal. We're all first-name here, so let me welcome Jettrin, Nadia, and Sujeet.

**M1:** Sawatdee Khrab, Millicent. Good morning! I'm Jettrin from Thailand.

**F2:** Hello. It's nice to be with you. I'm Nadia from Dubai.

**M2:** And good morning, Millicent, Jettrin, and Nadia. Sujeet here from Nepal.

**F1:** OK. Let's get started. I see our first caller is on the line. Hello, Arturo from Montevideo. You're on the air.

**M3:** Good morning—actually, good evening. It's 10:30 at night here in Montevideo. Here's my question: I'm traveling on business to Thailand next month, and I'll be working with Thai business managers from my company. What should I know?

**M1:** Hello, Arturo. Jettrin here. Just a couple of things: First a taboo: Don't touch anyone's head, not even a child's.

**M3:** Hmm? Well, I don't ordinarily touch people's heads, but if you don't mind my asking, what's wrong with touching someone's head?

**M1:** Well, we believe the head is where the person's soul lives. So it's very disrespectful and offensive to touch a person's head.

**M3:** Any other tips?

**M1:** Well, when you are seated, be sure not to cross your legs in such a way that others can see the bottom of your foot.

**M3:** Actually, I knew that. But don't worry. It's good to be reminded. I do have one more specific question before I hang up.

**M1:** Sure. What's that?

**M3:** In Uruguay it's customary to shake hands, and I know Thai people greet each other with the wai. Will it seem impolite for a foreigner to do the wai?—and what happens if I don't do it right? Will that be offensive?

**M1:** Absolutely not! Just put the palms of your hands together on your chest and bow slightly. Say "Sawatdee–khrab." For the women listening, you say "Sawatdee–kaa." You will warm our hearts with that. Don't worry if you don't do it exactly the way Thais do it. And don't worry about the pronunciation. Have a wonderful trip to Thailand. Try to do some sightseeing. And taste our wonderful food!

**M3:** Thanks so much.

**F1:** Thank YOU, Jettrin and Arturo for a good lesson in cultural literacy. Let's take a break and then another call.

CALL 2 Hiroko and Nadia [F3 = Japanese]

**F1:** Welcome back, listeners. This is Millicent McKay with a worldwide town meeting, answering all your questions about do's and taboos around the world. Let's say hello to Hiroko from Osaka, Japan. Hiroko, you're on the air.

**AUDIOSCRIPT continues on page T11.**

## EXTRAS (optional)

Workbook: Exercises 17–19
Copy & Go: Activity 3

## **INTERACTION** • *Know before you go!*

**STEP 1. PAIR WORK.**
**On the notepad, make notes about what visitors to your country should know.**
Answers will vary.

**STEP 2. DISCUSSION.**
**Combine everyone's notes on the board. Does everyone agree?**

**STEP 3. WRITING.**
**Write an article to help a visitor be culturally literate about your country. Use important information from your notepad and the board.**

How do people greet each other when they meet for the first time?

Are greetings customs different for men and women? How?

When and how do you address people formally?

When and how do you address people informally?

What are some do's and don'ts for table manners?

Are certain foods or beverages taboo?

What are some taboo conversation topics?

What are the customs about punctuality?

What is a customary gift if you are visiting someone's home?

Are there any gift taboos (kinds of flowers, etc.)?

Are there some situations or places where you should dress modestly?

What else should a visitor know?

# 4 ▶ Discuss How Culture Changes over Time

 **READING WARM-UP.** Can you think of an example of how etiquette and culture change over time?

 🎧 **READING.** Read the article. Is Japanese culture more or less formal than it was in the past?

## Japanese Workers Get Word from on High: Drop Formality

### By NORIMITSU ONISHI

HIROSHIMA, Japan, Oct. 30, 2003 — The change in policy came directly from the Tokyo headquarters of Elpida Memory, a semiconductor maker.

Elpida's 1,366 workers were told to stop addressing each other by their titles and simply to add the suffix -san to their names. Many Japanese have dropped the use of titles to create a more open — and, they hope, competitive — culture. This change mirrors other changes in Japanese society, experts say. Equality-minded parents no longer emphasize honorific language to their children, and most schools no longer expect children to use honorific language to their teachers. What is clear is that the use of honorific language, called keigo, to elevate a person or humble one-self, has especially fallen out of use among young Japanese.

Naomi Sugi, a secretary at the Elpida factory, has hesitantly begun addressing her boss as "Mr. Yamamoto" instead of "President Yamamoto."

Japanese, perhaps more than any other language, has long taken account of social standing. In Japanese, there are many ways to say I or you, calibrated by age, circumstance, gender, social position and other factors. Verb endings, adjectives and entire words also shift according to the situation.

These days, companies hope the use of -san — less cumbersome than the longer titles traditionally used — will allow workers to exchange ideas more freely and make decisions more quickly. In 2001, 59 percent of companies with more than 3,000 employees had adopted such a policy, compared with 34 percent in 1995, according to the Institute of Labor Administration of Japan.

"It's easier to talk now," said Kazuyoshi Iizuka, a 32-year-old employee at the Tokyo headquarters of Elpida. The factory's president, Takehiko Kubota, 59, who describes himself as "old-fashioned," sent an e-mail message on Sept. 5 explaining the policy to his staff.

 **Answer the following questions, according to the information in the article.**

1. What are some recent changes in the social use of the Japanese language? Many have dropped the use of titles and instead have added the suffix –san to their names. Also, parents no longer emphasize honorific language to their children.

2. How has Japanese business culture changed? It has become less formal.

 **DISCUSSION.** What do you think could be some positive and negative results of the changes described in the article?

LESSON

# 4 Discuss How Culture Changes over Time

## A READING WARM-UP

| Suggested teaching time: | 5 minutes |
|---|---|
| Your actual teaching time: | _____ |

- Ask questions to prompt students. Examples: *Think about fashion. Could women always wear pants? Think about families. Could children always speak when sitting at a table with adults? Think about the workplace. Could people always address their employers or bosses by their first names?*

- Ask various students for their answers.

## B 🎧 READING
(CD1, Track 11)

| Suggested teaching time: | 10–15 minutes |
|---|---|
| Your actual teaching time: | _____ |

- To practice the strategy of predicting, have students look at the photo and the headline and ask questions. Examples: *What country is this article about?* (Japan) *What kind of changes do you think the article talks about?* (business culture changes / culture changes in the workplace)

- Ask students to give examples from the article to support their answer to the question in the direction line. (Less formal. Paragraph 2: Workers were told to stop using titles when speaking to colleagues. Paragraph 2: Many parents and teachers are not requiring students to use honorific language.)

**Option:** Use this option if you want to use the reading as a listening activity. Books closed. Write the following questions on the board.

1. *Are the Japanese becoming more or less formal?*
2. *What affects the type of language or words you choose in Japanese?*
3. *Who started the change at the factory in the article?*

Have students listen and write their answers. Then have students read the text to confirm their answers. Review the answers as a class. (1. less formal 2. How and what you say in Japanese is affected by who you are talking to: an older person, a boss, a teacher, a child, etc. 3. the administration / headquarters)
[+10 minutes]

 **Learning Strategies**

## C Answer the following questions . . .

| Suggested teaching time: | 5 minutes |
|---|---|
| Your actual teaching time: | _____ |

- Tell students to scan the article to find the answers to the questions. Encourage students to take notes or to underline important information.

- Have students compare answers with a partner. Then review as a class.

**Option:** To provide more practice scanning a text for specific information, ask these questions one at a time and ask the class to (quickly) read the article to find the answer. Students should call out the answer as soon as they find it: *How many workers work at Elpida Memory?* (1,366) *What's the Japanese name for honorific language?* (keigo) *What percentage of companies adopted the use of -san in 2001?* (59%) *When did Elpida's president communicate the new policy to his staff?* (on Sept. 5) *Who is Kazuyoshi Iizuka?* (an employee of Elpida) *Who is Takehiko Kubota?* (the factory's president) [+5 minutes]

 **Extra Reading Comprehension Activities**

## D DISCUSSION

| Suggested teaching time: | 5–10 minutes |
|---|---|
| Your actual teaching time: | _____ |

- Write two columns on the board with one example under each.

| <u>Positive results</u> | <u>Negative results</u> |
|---|---|
| 1. People will work in a friendlier environment. | 1. Workers will start demanding other changes. |

- Group work. Form groups of three. Encourage students to write notes during their discussion using two columns and examples.

- Ask various groups to say one result from their discussion. You may want to add students' ideas to the columns on the board.

**Challenge:** Group work. Form groups of four. To provide more practice, write the following questions on the board and ask students to discuss them. Encourage students to use information from the reading as well as their own experiences and opinions. Then ask different groups to share one of their answers with the class.
[+10 minutes]

1. *Why did the New York Times think their readers would be interested in the information in this article?*
2. *Why do you think most people enjoy reading and learning about the customs of other people and places?*

# TOP NOTCH **INTERACTION**

| | |
|---|---|
| Suggested teaching time: | 20–25 minutes |
| Your actual teaching time: | _____ |

## STEP 1. Have cultural . . .

• Before students complete the survey, direct attention to the title of the activity "Is change for the better?" Point out the title refers to changes happening to culture.

• Direct attention to *Are you a dinosaur . . .* on the right and have students read it.

• To check comprehension ask *Why do you think the dinosaur is used to describe someone who doesn't like change?* (because it's a prehistoric animal that never changed / didn't evolve into another animal) *Why is the chameleon used to describe someone who adapts to change?* (because this animal can change its color to match the colors around it / to survive.).

• Tell students to fill in the survey, count the number of *yes* answers, and then find the information that describes how they feel about change.

**Option:** Group work. Form small groups. Have students compare which description—dinosaur or chameleon—their scores earned. Do they feel the description is true? Not true? **[+5 minutes]**

**Language note:** The expression *If it isn't broken, don't fix it!* means if something is working OK, then don't change anything. Often the slang version is used: *If it ain't broke, don't fix it!* The expression *Easy does it!* is usually used to tell someone to slow down and / or be careful. The expression *Out with the old, in with the new!* means someone looks forward to and can make changes easily.

## STEP 2. PAIR WORK.

• Review the model with the class.

• Remind students they should give examples to support why they think each of the cultural items has changed a little or a lot. Example: *I think table manners have changed a lot. Young people don't seem to have any!*

## STEP 3. DISCUSSION.

• Group work. Have pairs combine to form groups of four.

• Point out the NEED HELP? section and review the expressions. You may want to have students repeat.

• Encourage students to give examples and to ask each other follow-up questions.

• Walk around the room and provide help as needed.

**Option:** Ask various groups to say if they agreed or not and to explain why. **[+5 minutes]**

**AUDIOSCRIPT**

**AUDIOSCRIPT continued from page T9.**

**F3:** Thank you, Millicent. My husband and I are going to Dubai. He's a banker and has business there, but I'm going with him as a tourist. I'm very interested in all kinds of culture, and I understand Dubai is very different from Japan. I have three questions.

**F2:** Hello, Hiroko. Nadia on the line.

**F3:** Thanks, Nadia. If I'm alone, can I walk on the street or drive a car? When we went to Saudi Arabia, women were not permitted to go out alone or drive.

**F2:** Absolutely. As a woman traveler, you will have no difficulty getting around, even if you are alone. You can drive, and as long as you dress modestly, you can wear whatever you like.

**F3:** Second question: I don't speak any Arabic.

**F2:** Again, no problem. As you know, Arabic is the official language of Dubai, but English is commonly used in tourism and commerce.

**F3:** You speak very good English, Nadia. Where did you learn it?

**F2:** I actually am an English teacher. I learned my English in the United States, at the University of Wisconsin.

**F3:** And my last question: I'm an amateur photographer. Will I be able to take pictures in Dubai?

**F2:** Well, yes, but you should know that it is considered offensive to take pictures of Muslim women here.

**F3:** Oh. I'm glad I asked. What about pictures of men?

**F2:** Well, yes, just be sure to ask permission.

**F3:** I don't know how to thank you. I'm really looking forward to the trip!

**F1:** We'll be right back with our final call.

CALL 3 Javier and Sujeet [M4 = Mexican]

**F1:** I think we have time for one more caller. Javier from Mexico City! Welcome to the show. How can we help you?

**M4:** [Mexican accent] I'm going to Nepal next month on an international trek. I will be staying with a Nepalese family for a weekend, and I want to be sure I don't offend anyone. Mexico is very different from Nepal.

**F1:** Well, . . . let's ask Sujeet to comment.

**M2:** Hi, Javier. Let's talk about table manners. First of all, Nepalese don't usually use spoons, forks, or knives.

**M4:** No? So how do the people eat? How will I eat?

**M2:** Well, your hosts will eat with their right hand, never the left hand. But I'm sure they'll provide you with spoons and forks. If they are welcoming foreigners into their home, they'll want you to be comfortable. But remember one important taboo: Beef is strictly forbidden as a food in both Hindu and Buddhist homes. Our typical food, however, is wonderful and very flavorful and healthy.

**M4:** That's great, because I'm Mexican, and we have great food in Mexico, too. I love good food when I travel. Sujeet, I'm very interested in culture but I don't know much about Hinduism and Buddhism. What can you tell me?

**M2:** Well, if you visit a Hindu temple or a Buddhist shrine, you must remove your shoes. Or, if you prefer, you can wear open sandals. Check first; in some Hindu temples, non-Hindus can't enter. And, very important, don't take leather things near the temple. And if you want to take a picture, be sure to ask before using your camera.

**M4:** Thanks so much. I feel very prepared now.

**M2:** My pleasure.

**F1:** Well that's all we have time for today. Until next time, this is Millicent McKay in Brussels, reminding you that in today's world cultural literacy is an essential survival skill.

## EXTRAS (optional)

**Workbook:** Exercises 20–22
**Copy & Go:** Activity 4

## INTERACTION • *Is change for the better?*

**STEP 1.** Have cultural features changed a little or a lot in the last fifty years? Complete the survey. Answers will vary.

# Culture Survey

| | have changed a little | have changed a lot | Is the change for the better? (YES or NO) | |
|---|---|---|---|---|
| 1. Table manners | ☐ | ☐ | ☐ | ☐ |
| 2. Musical tastes | ☐ | ☐ | ☐ | ☐ |
| 3. Dating customs | ☐ | ☐ | ☐ | ☐ |
| 4. Clothing customs | ☐ | ☐ | ☐ | ☐ |
| 5. Rules about formal behavior | ☐ | ☐ | ☐ | ☐ |
| 6. Rules about punctuality | ☐ | ☐ | ☐ | ☐ |
| 7. Forms of address | ☐ | ☐ | ☐ | ☐ |
| 8. Male / female roles in the workplace | ☐ | ☐ | ☐ | ☐ |
| 9. Male / female roles in the home | ☐ | ☐ | ☐ | ☐ |

Total YES answers: _____

## Are you a dinosaur or a chameleon?

How many times did you check YES in the third column?

**0–3 = Definitely a dinosaur.** You prefer to stick with tradition. Your motto: "If it isn't broken, don't fix it!"

**4–6 = A little of both.** You're willing to adapt to change, but not too fast. Your motto: "Easy does it!"

**7–9 = Definitely a chameleon.** You adapt to change easily. Your motto: "Out with the old, in with the new!"

**STEP 2. PAIR WORK.** Compare and discuss your answers and give specific examples of changes for each answer.

> **❝** I think clothing customs have become less modest. My mother had to wear a uniform to school. But by the time I started school, girls had stopped wearing them. Now girls can go to school in jeans and even shorts! **❞**

**STEP 3. DISCUSSION.**

• What are the advantages and disadvantages of the changes in your culture? Does everyone think change is good?

• Do older and younger people disagree about culture change? Do men and women disagree?

NEED HELP? Here's language you already know:

**Formality and informality**
be on a first-name basis
prefer to be addressed by
their first [last] names /
titles and family
names

**Agree about facts**
[People don't use titles
as much], do they?
[Clothing customs used
to be more modest],
didn't they?

**Agree in general**
I agree. I think
you're right.

**Disagree in general**
I disagree.
Actually, I don't agree,
because ——.
Really? I think ——.

# UNIT 1
# CHECKPOINT

**A** 🎧 **LISTENING COMPREHENSION.** **Listen to the conversations of people introducing themselves. Check the statement in each pair that's true.**

1. ☐ She'd like to be addressed by her title and family name.
   ☑ She'd like to be addressed by her first name.

2. ☐ She'd prefer to be called by her first name.
   ☑ She'd prefer to be called by her title and last name.

3. ☑ It's customary to call people by their first name there.
   ☐ It's not customary to call people by their first name there.

4. ☑ He's comfortable with the policy about names.
   ☐ He's not comfortable with the policy about names.

5. ☐ She prefers to use the title Mrs.
   ☑ She prefers to use the title Dr.

**B** **Complete each statement with a tag question.**

1. You're not from around here, __are you__?

2. You were in this class last year, __weren't you__?

3. They haven't been here since yesterday, __have they__?

4. It's impolite to ask people their age, __isn't it__?

5. These chrysanthemums are an OK gift here, __aren't they__?

6. I met you on the tour in Nepal, __didn't I__?

7. We'll have a chance to discuss this tomorrow, __won't we__?

8. By 10:00 he had already picked up her passport, __hadn't he__?

**C** **Complete each statement.**

1. Behaving impolitely when eating with others is an example of bad __table manners__.

2. Each country has customs and traditions about how to behave in social situations. The rules are sometimes called __etiquette__.

3. Each culture has its own sense of __punctuality__. It's important to understand people's ideas about lateness.

**D** **WRITING. Is etiquette important? On a separate sheet of paper, explain your opinion. Include some or all of the words in the box.**

| | | |
|---|---|---|
| impolite | polite | taboo |
| table manners | formal | informal |

*TOP NOTCH* **SONG**
"It's a Great Day for Love"
Lyrics on last book page.

*TOP NOTCH* **PROJECT**
Make a cultural literacy guidebook. Find cultural information about countries you'd like to visit on the Internet.

*TOP NOTCH* **WEBSITE**
For Unit 1 online activities, visit the *Top Notch* Companion Website at www.longman.com/topnotch.

A chrysanthemum. Chrysanthemums are an inappropriate social gift in some countries.

# UNIT 1 CHECKPOINT

 **⌒ LISTENING COMPREHENSION**
(CD1, Track 12)

| Suggested teaching time: | 5–10 minutes |
| --- | --- |
| Your actual teaching time: | _____ |

• Before listening, have students read the statements.

• Have students compare answers with a partner. Then review as a class.

**Option:** Have students listen to the recording and write the information that supports each answer. (1. Please call me Ana. 2. Mrs. Denman would be fine. 3. The policy is generally first name. 4. Not at all. "Robert's" fine with me. 5. I use "doctor.") **[+5 minutes]**

**AUDIOSCRIPT**

CONVERSATION 1 [F = Spanish]
F: Good morning. I'm Dr. Ana Montoya.
M: Good morning, Dr. Montoya.
F: Please call me Ana.

CONVERSATION 2 [F = British]
M: Hi. I'm Larry Lockhart.
F: Hi. I'm Winnie Denman. Nice to meet you.
M: Nice to meet you, too. By the way, how would you prefer to be addressed?
F: Mrs. Denman would be fine.

CONVERSATION 3 [F1 = Brazilian]
F1: Excuse me. I'm Sofia Peres. I'm looking for Martin Page.
F2: Certainly, Ms. Peres. I'm Ramona Wright. Martin's right over there. Come. I'll introduce you.
F1: Thanks. And would it be rude if I called him Martin?
F2: No, that's fine. And while you're at it, feel free to call me Ramona.
F1: And please call me Sofia.

CONVERSATION 4
M: Hi. I'm Robert Morse, the new English instructor.
F: Oh, hello, Dr. Morse. I'm Laura Lane, the department secretary. I'll take you to your class. By the way, how would you like to be introduced to the class?
M: Well, what's the custom here?
F: We're pretty informal. The policy is generally first name. We think it makes for a more conversational English class. Do you mind?
M: Not at all. "Robert's" fine with me!

CONVERSATION 5 [F1 = Japanese]
F1: Hello. I'm Mayumi Sato. I'm pre-registered for the conference.
F2: Certainly. Let me make up your name badge. Do you prefer Ms. or Mrs.?
F1: Actually, neither. I use "doctor."
F2: Of course, Dr. Sato. Here you go.
F1: Thanks!

 **Complete each statement . . .**

| Suggested teaching time: | 5 minutes |
| --- | --- |
| Your actual teaching time: | _____ |

• Before students complete the statements, review tag questions on page 4.

• Have students compare answers with a partner. Then review as a class.

**Option:** To provide more practice, write something true and false about yourself on the board: *I live in a house / an apartment. I'm going to [the mall] / [the beach] this weekend.* Ask students to make tag questions to check which information is true. Remind students that falling intonation means the speaker is confirming information he or she knows and rising intonation means the speaker doesn't know and wants the correct information. Examples: Student A: *You live in a house, don't you?* [falling intonation] Teacher: *Actually, I don't. I live in an apartment.* Student A: *Oh!* Student B: *You're going to the beach this weekend, aren't you?* [rising intonation] Teacher: *Why yes, I am.*

Pair work. Ask students to write about themselves including true and false information. Then take turns asking tag questions and using the correct intonation. **[+5 minutes]**

 **Complete each statement.**

| Suggested teaching time: | 5 minutes |
| --- | --- |
| Your actual teaching time: | _____ |

• Have students compare answers with a partner. Then review as a class.

**Option:** To provide more practice, call out key phrases and ask students to say the matching words from page 8, Exercise A. Say *Arriving on time* (punctuality) *Insulting someone* (offensive) *Chewing with your mouth open* (bad table manners) *Rules of polite behavior* (etiquette) *Not saying "Thank you"* (impolite) *Eating beef in India* (taboo) *Saying "Good morning"* (customary). **[+5 minutes]**

 **WRITING**

| Suggested teaching time: | 10–15 minutes |
| --- | --- |
| Your actual teaching time: | _____ |

• Before students write, brainstorm ideas why etiquette is important and write them on the board. Examples: *Knowing the rules of etiquette makes you feel more comfortable. Etiquette rules help you know what is customary, impolite, or taboo in different situations.*

• Walk around the room and provide help as needed.

 **Writing Process Worksheets**

 ***Top Notch Pop* Song Activities**
(CD1, Track 13)

***TOP NOTCH* PROJECT**

**Idea:** Brainstorm with the class topics that could be included in a cultural literacy guidebook. Examples: *table manners, taboos, offensive behavior, dress / clothing, greeting, gifts, punctuality,* etc. Form small groups. Encourage students to assign tasks, for example, who will do research on the Internet, who will collect the information in one document, who will edit and review the final information.

# UNIT WRAP-UP

Suggested teaching time: 20–25 minutes
Your actual teaching time: _____

## Grammar

- If your class is not familiar with the location in the picture, point out that these are the ancient ruins of Machu Picchu in Peru. Also see Culture note below.

- Pair work. Students take turns making statements with questions tags about the picture. Encourage students to use the correct rhythm and intonation.

**Your students can say . . .**

It's a nice place, isn't it? The view is beautiful, isn't it? This was an Incan city, wasn't it? It's a very old city, isn't it? This is only part of the city, isn't it? These rooms were parts of houses, weren't they? Lots of tourists visit this city, don't they?

**Challenge: Around the world.** Pair work. Have students talk about interesting places they have visited or they know about. Students should keep the conversation going by asking tag questions. Student A: *I was in Egypt last year.* Student B: *Really? The pyramids are impressive, aren't they?* Student A: *They really are. I visited the largest one.* Student B: *It's very scary to be inside one, isn't it?* [+5 minutes]

**Culture note:** Machu Picchu, the remains of an ancient city of the Inca Empire, is situated in the Andes mountains in Peru. It is believed to have been built in the mid-1400s. The ruins are located about 600 meters (1,950 feet) above the Urubamba River and cover about 13 square kilometers (5 square miles). The site was rediscovered by archeologists in 1911 and has become a popular tourist destination.

## Social Language

- Role-play the model in the book with a student.

- Before students create the conversations, they may want to decide on a name for each person in the picture.

**Your students can say . . .**

**A:** Beautiful place, isn't it? **B:** Yes. It's great. By the way, I'm [first name] [last name]. **A:** I'm [first name] [last name]. Nice to meet you. **B:** Nice to meet you, too. **A:** How do you prefer to be addressed?/What would you like to be called? **B:** [First name] is fine with me. /[First name] would be fine. **B:** OK. And please call me [first name].

**A:** Hi, I'm [first name] [last name]. **B:** [First name] [last name]. Nice to meet you, [first name]. By the way, this is [first name] [last name]. **A:** Nice to meet you, [first name]. You know, you look familiar. Weren't you [on the Lima tour] on [Monday]? **B:** No, actually, we weren't. We hadn't yet arrived in [Peru] by then. **A:** This place is fantastic, isn't it? **B:** It really is.

## Writing

- Brainstorm ideas students can write about and write them on the board. Examples: *where the people are from, why they are enjoying the Machu Picchu tour, why they enjoy meeting people from other cultures, what other places they might be interested in visiting,* etc.

- As students write, walk around the room and provide help as needed.

**Option: What's your story?** Pair work. Students exchange papers or take turns reading their paragraph(s) out loud. Encourage students to give each other feedback on vocabulary and verb tenses. [+10 minutes]

**Individual oral progress check (optional)**

- Use the illustration on page 13. Encourage the student to use material (vocabulary, grammar, rhythm and intonation) practiced in this unit.

- Evaluate the student on correctness and intelligibility.

- Tell the student to ask you four questions about the picture using tag questions. Encourage the student to practice using rising and falling intonation. Examples: **S:** *This is Machu Picchu, isn't it?* **T:** *Yes, it is.* **S:** *These are ruins of an Inca city, aren't they?* **T:** *Yes, they are.* **S:** *They aren't located in a city, are they?* **T:** *No, they aren't. They're on a mountain.* **S:** *A lot of tourists visit Machu Picchu, don't they?* **T:** *Yes, they do. It's a very famous place!*

- Point to one of the pictures of people talking and tell the student that together you are going to role-play a conversation. Tell the student you will start with small talk and then the student should introduce him / herself. Example: **T:** *Hi. Nice place, isn't it?* **S:** *Yes, it is. I'm [first name] [last name].* **T:** *Nice to meet you. I'm [first name] [last name].* **S:** *You can call me [Name].* **T:** *OK.* **S:** *What would you like to be called?* **T:** *[Name] is fine.* **S:** *This is my first time here. It's wonderful . . .*

 **Cumulative Vocabulary Activities**

 You may wish to use the video and activity worksheets for Unit 1 at this point.

 **Complete Assessment Package Unit 1 Achievement Test**

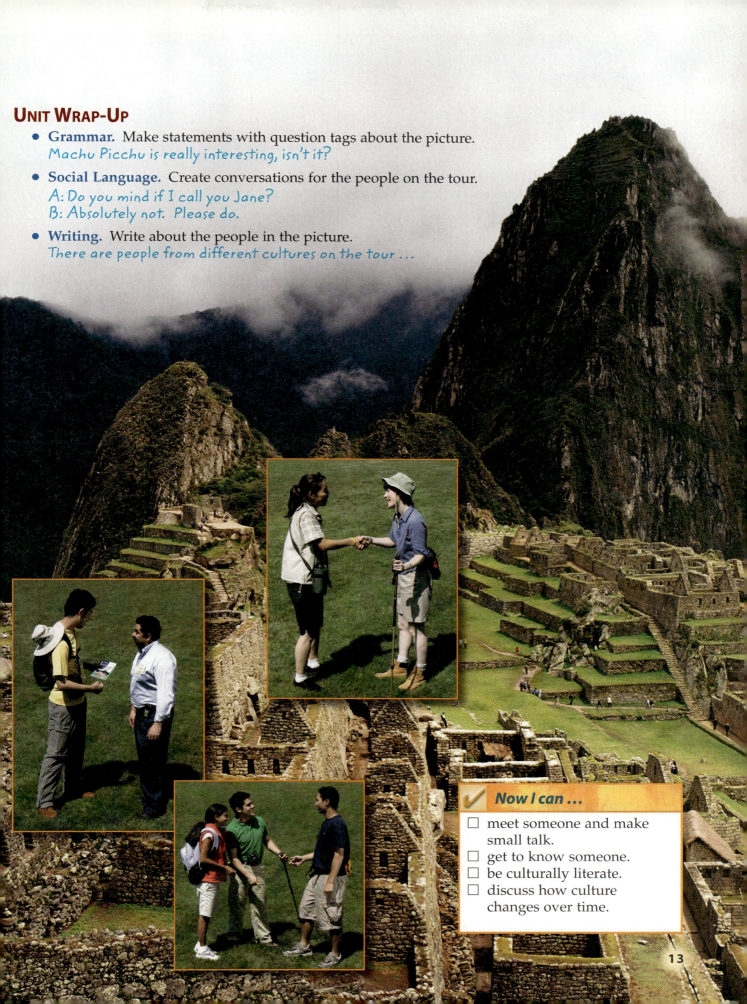

## UNIT WRAP-UP

- **Grammar.** Make statements with question tags about the picture.
  *Machu Picchu is really interesting, isn't it?*

- **Social Language.** Create conversations for the people on the tour.
  *A: Do you mind if I call you Jane?*
  *B: Absolutely not. Please do.*

- **Writing.** Write about the people in the picture.
  *There are people from different cultures on the tour ...*

✓ **Now I can ...**

- ☐ meet someone and make small talk.
- ☐ get to know someone.
- ☐ be culturally literate.
- ☐ discuss how culture changes over time.

## Health Matters

**UNIT GOALS**

1 Make an appointment to see a denti
2 Describe symptoms at a doctor's offi
3 Discuss types of medical treatments
4 Talk about medications

 **TOPIC PREVIEW.** Read the health checklist for international travelers. Which tips do you think are the most important?

# Before you go...

### A checklist for international travelers

**✔ Vaccinations**

You may be required to get vaccinated before you are allowed to enter certain countries. Check the immunization requirements of the country you are visiting. The farther "off the beaten path" you travel, the more important it is to be protected from illness and disease.

**✔ Eyewear**

If you wear glasses or contact lenses, get a copy of your prescription before you go. Carry it with you in case you break or lose your eyewear. Or be sure to carry an extra pair with you.

**✔ Dental care**

There's nothing more frightening than having a toothache when you're far from home. Have a dental check-up before you leave on a long trip to avoid any problems.

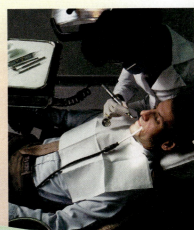

**✔ Medications**

Talk to your doctor before your trip. Your doctor may be able to write a prescription for extra medication or give you tips for staying healthy while traveling. Buy and pack a supply of all medications you take regularly. Carry your medications in your carry-on bags. If you lose your luggage, you will still have them.

**SOURCE:** www.atevo.com

 **PAIR WORK.** In addition to medical items, what else should go on a checklist for an international trip? Write a list with your partner.
Answers will vary.

### CHECKLIST

☑ _____

☑ _____

☑ _____

☑ _____

# UNIT 2

# Health Matters

 **TOPIC PREVIEW**

| Suggested teaching time: | 15 minutes |
|---|---|
| Your actual teaching time: | _____ |

- Tell students they're going to read about things a traveler should remember to do before taking a trip.

- Write on the board:

  *A checklist for _____*

- Ask students for situations when they might make a checklist and write the list on the board. Examples: *traveling, shopping, moving, cooking something, office supplies, a party, a wedding, school*, etc.

- After students read, check comprehension by asking *What should travelers do to be protected from local illnesses and diseases?* (get vaccinated, get extra medication) *What should they do to stay healthy on their trip?* (pack regular medications) *What should they do if they wear glasses or contact lenses?* (pack an extra pair, bring a copy of their prescription) *What should they do to take care of their teeth?* (have a dental check-up before leaving).

- Pair work. Have students discuss which tips are more important and put them in order starting with the most important. Encourage them to include reasons for their choices.

- Ask pairs to write their final lists on the board and have the class compare them. Did any groups have the same order?

**Option:** Point out the first sentence under Dental Care *There's nothing more frightening than having a toothache. . . .* Ask students to say other emergencies or events that would be frightening when on an international trip. Examples: *breaking [a leg], needing an operation, losing a passport, having your rented car break down on a back road*, etc. **[+5 minutes]**

**Option:** Pair work. Students take turns saying the things from the checklist they do or don't / didn't do before traveling and the things they've learned they should do. Examples: Student A: *I always pack my medications, but I never pack them in my carry-on bag. I will next time. That way, if I lose my luggage, I'll still have them.* Student B: *On one trip, I didn't pack my glasses and I didn't know my prescription information. Never again!* **[+5 minutes]**

**Language note:** To practice the reading skill of understanding vocabulary from context, encourage students to use information in this text (and in future reading texts) to help them figure out the meaning of words they don't know. Students may need help with the following words: *get vaccinated* (to give someone a substance containing the weak form of the virus causing a disease in order to protect him / her from that disease); *immunization requirements* (vaccinations that are usually needed for travel, school, etc.); *off the beaten path* (places not visited by most people); *prescription* (a piece of paper / information from a doctor requesting medicine a patient needs).

**B** **PAIR WORK**

| Suggested teaching time: | 5–10 minutes |
|---|---|
| Your actual teaching time: | _____ |

- Tell students they can include more health-related items and / or other types of ideas. Examples: *find out about the local weather so you can pack the right clothes, buy a small first-aid kit, find out what to do when you have jet lag, take prescription medicines in original bottles for airport security, make extra copies of your passports and travel documents*, etc.

- Walk around the room and provide help as needed.

- Ask various pairs to say two items on their list. You may want to create a list on the board.

**Challenge:** Brainstorm with the class and write on the board a list of topics related to planning and taking an international trip. Examples: *booking a hotel, making airline reservations, collecting / preparing necessary travel documents, packing your suitcase(s), finding out about local customs and etiquette, finding out about the local currency,* etc. Pair work. Ask each pair to choose one topic and write a checklist of two or three items. Have pairs combine with another pair to share their lists. (Students may say: Booking a hotel: Book your rooms in advance and ask for a confirmation number, ask if any meals are included, reconfirm your reservation a week before you leave. Travel documents: Make sure you have a valid passport. Find out if you need a visa. Get an international driving license.) **[+15 minutes]**

## C  SOUND BITES

(CD1, Track 15)

| | |
|---|---|
| Suggested teaching time: | 10 minutes |
| Your actual teaching time: | _____ |

- Pre-listening: Have students cover the conversations and look at the pictures. Ask them to make predictions for the following questions: *Where are the men? Who do you think they are? What do you think they are talking about?* (Possible answers: at the front desk in a hotel; a hotel guest and a hotel clerk; the guest is asking for something / maybe he has a problem) *Who is the woman on the right and where are they?* (Possible answers: a doctor or dentist; in a [doctor's] office, in a hospital)

- After reading and listening, ask students the same questions.

- Write on the board:
    1. *What does the guest ask the clerk to recommend?*
    2. *Why was the guest able to make an appointment?*

- To check comprehension, ask students to read and listen again and then answer the questions. (1. a dentist; one who speaks English 2. another patient cancelled / didn't come)

> **Language note:** The omission or reduction of sounds (elision) is common in rapid, spoken English. Point out that the full form of *Thought I'd better* is *I thought I'd better.*

> **Culture note:** The dolls on the front desk in the first picture are *Matryoshka*, a typical Russian souvenir. They are nesting dolls and usually have seven different-sized dolls that fit one into the other. Larger collections can consist of over fifty dolls! They are made of hand-painted wood and are finished in lacquer.

## D  Check the statements . . .

| | |
|---|---|
| Suggested teaching time: | 5 minutes |
| Your actual teaching time: | _____ |

- Encourage students to identify things in the pictures or underline information in the conversations above that support their answers.

- Have students compare answers with a partner. Then review as a class.

## E IN OTHER WORDS

| | |
|---|---|
| Suggested teaching time: | 5–10 minutes |
| Your actual teaching time: | _____ |

- Encourage students to identify who says the phrases and to use the context of the conversation to help work out their meaning.

- Have students compare answers with a partner. Then review as a class.

- Other possible answers include: 1. Someone told me, Is it me . . . ? 2. seeing me 3. is so painful 4. let me check (your tooth).

## WHAT ABOUT **YOU?**

| | |
|---|---|
| Suggested teaching time: | 5–10 minutes |
| Your actual teaching time: | _____ |

- Write on the board:
    *What was the problem?*
    *Where were you?*
    *How did it happen?*
    *What happened in the end?*

- Ask students to use the outline on the board to organize some notes about an emergency. Students can also write about someone they know.

- Encourage students to use a dictionary if necessary.

- Role-play the model with a student. Ask the student to say the model in the speech bubble and then you ask a follow-up question. Examples: *Did you stay in the hospital?* OR *What did the doctor do?*

- Form small groups. Ask students to use their notes as a guide to talk about their experiences. Encourage students who are listening to ask follow-up questions.

- Walk around the room and provide help as needed.

- Ask some volunteers to give a brief summary of their emergency experience in front of the class.

## EXTRAS (optional)

**Workbook: Exercises 1–3**

**C** 🎧 **SOUND BITES.** Read along silently as you listen to two short conversations in Russia.

**GUEST:** I need to see a dentist as soon as possible. I think it's an emergency. I was wondering if you might be able to recommend someone who speaks English. **CN1**

**CLERK:** Actually, there's one not far from here. Would you like me to make an appointment for you?

**CN1 Corpus Notes:**
*Could you recommend. . .* is much more common than *I was wondering if you might be able to recommend. . . .* However, the latter is considered much more polite in register.

**DENTIST:** So I hear you're from overseas. **CN2**

**PATIENT:** Yes. From Venezuela. Thanks for fitting me in. This tooth is killing me.

**DENTIST:** Luckily, I had a cancellation. Glad to be of help.

**PATIENT:** I really appreciate it. Thought I'd better see someone right away.

**DENTIST:** Well, let's have a look.

**D** Check the statements that you are sure are true. Explain your answers.

☑ **1.** The hotel guest is having a dental emergency.

☐ **2.** The hotel guest is on vacation.

☑ **3.** The hotel clerk offers to call the dentist.

☑ **4.** It was easy to get an appointment with the dentist.

**CN2 Corpus Notes:** In the expression *I hear [noun clause]. . .,* that is almost always not used. For example, *I hear ~~that~~ you're from overseas.*

**E** **IN OTHER WORDS.** Explain the meaning of each underlined phrase. Answers may vary. Possible answers include:

**1.** "So I hear you're from overseas." I understand

**2.** "Thanks for fitting me in." giving me an appointment so quickly

**3.** "This tooth is killing me." hurts very badly

**4.** "Well, let's have a look." I'll examine you now

## WHAT ABOUT **YOU?**

Have you ever had a medical or dental emergency? Where were you? What happened? What did you do?

❝ Last year, I went skiing and I broke my arm. I had to go to the emergency room at the hospital. ❞

# 1 Make an Appointment to See a Dentist

🎧 **CONVERSATION MODEL** Read and listen.

**A:** Hello. I wonder if I might be able to see the dentist today. I'm here on business, and I have a toothache. `CN1`

**B:** Oh, that must hurt. Are you in a lot of pain? `CN2`

**A:** Yes, actually, I am.

**B:** Well, let me check. Could you be here by 3:00?

**A:** Yes. That would be fine. I really appreciate it.

🎧 **Rhythm and intonation practice**

**A** 🎧 **VOCABULARY.** Dental emergencies. Listen and practice.

**I have a toothache.**

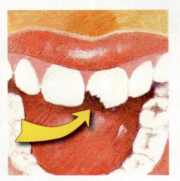
**I broke a tooth.**

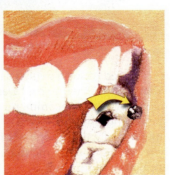
**I lost a filling.**

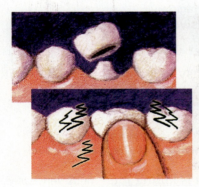
**My crown is loose.**

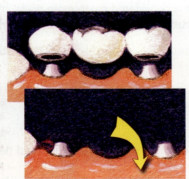
**My bridge came out.**

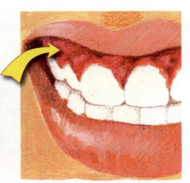
**My gums are swollen.**

**B** 🎧 **LISTENING COMPREHENSION.** Listen to the conversations. Complete each statement to describe the dental problem.

1. The man lost ___a tooth___ .

2. The woman's ___bridge___ is loose.

3. The man's ___filling___ came out.

4. The woman just broke ___a crown___.

`CN1` **Corpus Notes:**
A common learner error is to say or write, *I'm here for business* instead of *on business*. Make sure students do not make this error.

`CN2` **Corpus Notes:**
When asking about pain in a specific body part, it is more common to ask *Does your ___ hurt?* than *Do you have pain in your ___?* However, it is not common to ask *Do you hurt?*

## LESSON 1

# Make an Appointment to See a Dentist

## 🎧 CONVERSATION MODEL
### (CD1, Track 16)

| Suggested teaching time: | 5 minutes |
|---|---|
| Your actual teaching time: | _____ |

• After students read and listen, check comprehension by asking *What kind of problem does the woman have?* (She has a toothache. She's in pain.) *How is the assistant able to help her?* (He gives her an appointment for three o'clock [today].)

## 🎧 Rhythm and intonation practice
### (CD1, Track 17)

| Suggested teaching time: | 5 minutes |
|---|---|
| Your actual teaching time: | _____ |

• Have students repeat each line chorally.
• Make sure students:
  ○ pause after *business.*
  ○ stress <u>that</u> and <u>hurt</u> in *Oh, that must hurt.*
  ○ use rising intonation for *Are you in a lot of pain?*
  ○ use rising intonation for *Could you be here by 3:00?*
  ○ use the following stress pattern:

┌─STRESS PATTERN─────────────────────┐
|  —  •  •  •  •  •  •  —  •  •  •  •  •  —  |
| **A:** Hello. I wonder if I might be able to see the dentist |
|  •  •  •  •  •  —  •  •  •  •  •  •  —  |
| today. I'm here on business, and I have a toothache. |
|  —  —  •  •  —  •  •  —  •  •  •  —  |
| **B:** Oh, that must hurt. Are you in a lot of pain? |
|  •  —  •  —  •  •  |
| **A:** Yes, actually, I am. |
|  •  —  •  —  •  —  •  •  •  •  •  —  |
| **B:** Well, let me check. Could you be here by three o'clock? |
|  —  •  —  •  •  •  —  •  •  •  —  •  •  •  |
| **A:** Yes. That would be fine. I really appreciate it. |
└────────────────────────────────────┘

## 🅐 🎧 VOCABULARY
### (CD1, Track 18)

| Suggested teaching time: | 5 minutes |
|---|---|
| Your actual teaching time: | _____ |

• Have students listen and study the statements.
• Then have students listen and repeat chorally.

**Language note:** Point out that the words in the vocabulary section have other possible collocations (combinations). Examples: *I broke a tooth / a crown / a bridge. I lost a filling / a tooth / a crown. My tooth / My bridge / My crown is loose. My filling / My crown / My tooth / My bridge came out.* You may want to write some examples on the board.

 **Vocabulary Cards**

## 🅑 🎧 LISTENING COMPREHENSION
### (CD1, Track 19)

| Suggested teaching time: | 5–10 minutes |
|---|---|
| Your actual teaching time: | _____ |

• Before listening, have students read the sentences.
• Pause after each conversation to allow students time to complete the statements.
• Review answers as a class.

**Option:** Group work. Form groups of four. Students take turns telling each other if they have ever had any of the dental problems in Exercise A. Encourage students to ask follow-up questions to find out what happened. Example: Student A: *I once had a terrible toothache.* Student B: *Really? Did you go to the dentist?* Student A: *Yes. He said I had lost a filling.* Student B: *That probably hurt!* **[+5 minutes]**

**Option:** Draw the following chart on the board (without the answers). To provide more listening practice, ask students to listen again and complete the chart. Review the answers with the class. You may want students to listen again to confirm the correct answers **[+10 minutes]**

| Question / Conversation | 1 | 2 | 3 | 4 |
|---|---|---|---|---|
| 1. What was the patient doing when the accident happened? | skiing | about to go sightseeing | having dinner | we don't know |
| 2. Does the patient say he / she is in pain? | yes | no | yes | no |

🔵 **Graphic Organizers**

**AUDIOSCRIPT**

CONVERSATION 1 [M = U.S. Regional, Southern]
**F:** Hello, Mr. Lee. What brings you in today?
**M:** Well, I was skiing at Mount Gladding and I had a bit of an accident.
**F:** Oh really . . .
**M:** Yeah. I fell down pretty hard and I guess I hit a tree. My mouth hurt pretty bad, and when I got up I realized that I had lost a tooth.
**F:** Oh, no! I hope you're not in a lot of pain.
**M:** It isn't too bad. I just can't believe it happened. I feel so stupid.
**F:** Hey, it happens all the time. Why don't you sit back and let me take a look.

CONVERSATION 2 [F = Columbian]
**M:** So tell me, Mrs. Ochoa, what happened?
**F:** Well we were about to go sightseeing, and suddenly I felt something.
**M:** What was it?
**F:** Well that's what my husband said. "What is it?" he says. So I say, "I can't believe it. My bridge is loose!"
**M:** Oh, I see.
**F:** So he says, "Maybe you'd better see a dentist." And I'm thinking, Where am I going to find a dentist here? Luckily we asked at the hotel and they gave me a referral.
**M:** Well, I'm glad I could help.

**AUDIOSCRIPT continues on page T20.**

T16

##  GRAMMAR

| Suggested teaching time: | 10–15 minutes |
| Your actual teaching time: | _____ |

- Tips for organizing information on the board: Use one side of the board to write the grammar examples offered in these notes. This creates a list of helpful information that students can refer to as they practice.

- Direct attention to the box and have students read the first explanation and study the examples.

- Write on the board: *1. Kevin may / might come tomorrow. Maybe Kevin will come tomorrow.*

- Tell students that both sentences mean we're not sure if Kevin will come tomorrow.

- Point out that the negatives are *may not* and *might not.* Write <u>not</u> between *might* and *come* on the board. *Kevin may / might not come tomorrow.*

**Option:** Write on the board: *A: Saturday morning, go shopping B: Sunday afternoon, go to the movies*

Pair work. To check comprehension, ask students to write sentences using *may* and *might* and the information on the board. Encourage students to also make negative sentences and to add information about who else is going, why they are going, etc. To review ask various pairs to say one sentence about each day. Make necessary corrections. **[+10 minutes]**

- Have students read the second explanation and study the examples.

- Write on the board: *2. Sarah didn't come to work. She <u>must</u> be ill. 3. Sarah came to work. She must not be ill.*

- To help clarify, say *Use* must *when you are not 100% certain, but you are almost sure that something is true.* Point out that the negative is <u>must not</u>.

**Option:** To check comprehension, ask students to use *must* or *must not* to make conclusions about various situations you say. Examples: *I didn't have [breakfast].* (You must be hungry.) *I had a huge [lunch]!* (You must not be hungry!) *I worked very late yesterday.* (You must be tired. / You must be busy at work.) *I just broke a tooth.* (That must hurt. / You must be in pain.) **[+5 minutes]**

- Have students read the third explanation and study the example.

- Point out that *be able to* and *can* have the same meaning. Point out that *can* is not used with *will.*

- Have students read the Note and study the examples.

- Point out that *may, might,* and *must* come before *be able to* and *have to.* Also point out that *be able to* and *have to* are followed by a base verb.

- Write on the board: *4. Brad might <u>be able to</u> be at the office by 8:00. 5. Sue might <u>have to</u> be at the office by 8:00.*

- To clarify the difference between *be able to* and *have to,* say *Be able to expresses ability. Number 4 tells us that it's possible Brad can arrive at the office by 8:00, but no one is demanding it.* Have to *shows something that is necessary. Number 5 tells us Sue's boss wants her to be at the office by 8:00.*

**Option:** To check comprehension, ask various students to say what they will be able to do later today, tomorrow, etc. Examples: *I'll be able to leave work early today. We'll be able to get tickets for the concert tomorrow tonight.* **[+5 minutes]**

**Language note:** The contraction for *will not be able to* is *won't be able to.* *May not* cannot be contracted. The contraction of *must not—mustn't—*is only used for prohibition, not for making a conclusion.

 Grammar Self-Checks

##  PAIR WORK

| Suggested teaching time: | 5 minutes |
| Your actual teaching time: | _____ |

- If students need support, brainstorm situations in which your students might want to or have to use English. Examples: *reading, watching movies, doing grammar exercises, writing e-mails, listening to music, traveling, visiting the* Top Notch *website!*

- Encourage students to ask each other follow-up questions during the discussion. Example: Student A: *I might be able to practice English at work this week.* Student B: *Great! How?* Student A: *Well, I might have to write a report in English for my boss.*

- To review, ask various pairs to say one of their answers. Make sure they use *may* and / or *might.*

## 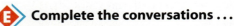 Complete the conversations . . .

| Suggested teaching time: | 5 minutes |
| Your actual teaching time: | _____ |

- Have students compare answers with a partner. Then review with the class.

## CONVERSATION **PAIR WORK**

| Suggested teaching time: | 5–10 minutes |
| Your actual teaching time: | _____ |

- To get ready for the activity, have students read and listen to the conversation model on page 16 again.

- To review the necessary vocabulary, ask students to say different dental emergencies and write them on the board. If necessary, review page 16.

- Review questions a dentist's assistant might ask. Examples: *What's the problem? Are you in a lot of pain? Have you been here before? Could you be here by [3:00]?*

- Role-play a conversation.

- Make sure students change roles at least one time. Encourage students to ask follow-up questions.

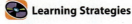 Pair Work Cards

🔲 Learning Strategies

## EXTRAS (optional)

Grammar Booster
Workbook: Exercises 4–9
Copy & Go: Activity 5

**C** **GRAMMAR.** May, might, must, and be able to

**May or might for possibility**  **CN**

Use **may** or **might** and the base form to express possibility. They have the same meaning.
> The dentist **may** (or **might**) **have** some time to see you.
> Barbara **might** (or **may**) **not need** a new filling.

**Must for conclusions**

Use **must** and the base form of a verb when something is almost certainly true.
> John just broke a tooth. That **must hurt**.
> The dentist told me to come next week. It **must not be** an emergency.

**CN** **Corpus Notes:**
*Might* is used much more frequently than *may* in spoken English to express possibility. *May* is typically used in more formal English.

**Be able to for ability or possibility**

**Be able to** has the same meaning as **can**.
> She**'ll be able to see** you tomorrow. = She **can see** you tomorrow.

Note: You can use **be able to** or **have to** with **may**, **might**, or **must**.

| | | | |
|---|---|---|---|
| Dr. Sharp | **may** | **be able to** | **help** you. |
| I | **might not** | **be able to** | **get** there till 6:00. |
| You | **might** | **have to** | **get** a new crown. |
| She | **must not** | **have to** | **go** to work today. |

GRAMMAR BOOSTER

**PAGE G3**
**For more …**

 **D** **PAIR WORK.** Discuss the questions. Use **may** or **might**.
Answers will vary.
1. When will you practice English outside class this week?
2. When will you need to use English in your life?

 **E** Complete the conversations by drawing conclusions with **must** or **must not**.

1. **A:** You look terrible! Your tooth ___must___ really hurt.
   **B:** It does.

2. **A:** Did you call the dentist?
   **B:** Yes, but no one is answering. The dentist ___must not___ be in today.

3. **A:** Bill had a bad toothache this morning.
   **B:** No kidding. Then he ___must not___ be able to come to the meeting today.

4. **A:** Where's Alice?
   **B:** Well, I heard she lost a filling, so she ___must___ be at the dentist.

## CONVERSATION PAIR WORK

**Role-play making an appointment to see a dentist. Start like this:**
Answers will vary.

**A:** Hello. I wonder if I might be able to see the dentist today. _____ .

**B:** _____ …

CONTROLLED PRACTICE

## Describe Symptoms at a Doctor's Office

LESSON 2

🎧 **CONVERSATION MODEL** Read and listen.

**A:** You must be Mr. Brown. You're here for a blood test, aren't you?
**B:** That's right.
**A:** And is anything bothering you today?
**B:** Well, actually, I've been coughing.
**A:** Really? Well, why don't you have a seat? I'll see if the doctor can see you. **CN**

🎧 **Rhythm and intonation practice**

**CN** **Corpus Notes:** You can also say *take a seat* when asking someone to sit down but *have a seat* is used much more frequently in spoken English.

**A** 🎧 **VOCABULARY. Symptoms. Listen and practice.**

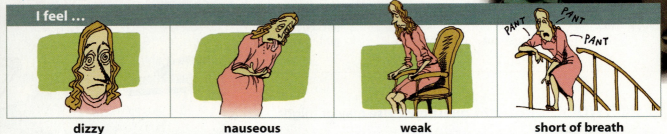

I feel ...
dizzy    nauseous    weak    short of breath

I've been ...
vomiting    coughing    sneezing    wheezing

I have pain in my ...
chest    hip    ribs    abdomen

**B** 🎧 **PRONUNCIATION. Intonation of lists. Listen. Then listen again and repeat.**

1. I feel **weak** and **dizzy**.

2. I've been **sneezing, coughing,** and **wheezing**.

3. I have pain in **my neck, my shoulders, my back,** and **my hip**.

# LESSON 2

## Describe Symptoms at a Doctor's Office

### 🎧 CONVERSATION **MODEL**
(CD1, Track 20)

| | |
|---|---|
| Suggested teaching time: | 5–10 minutes |
| Your actual teaching time: | —————— |

- To practice the strategy of identifying context before listening, ask students to look at the picture and say who they think the people are. (Students may say: the woman—doctor, doctor's assistant, nurse, nurse practitioner; the man—a patient, another doctor)

- To check comprehension after students read and listen, ask *Who is Mr. Brown?* (a patient) *Why does he have an appointment today?* (to have a blood test) *What does he say about his health?* (He's been coughing.)

### 🎧 Rhythm and intonation practice
(CD1, Track 21)

| | |
|---|---|
| Suggested teaching time: | 5 minutes |
| Your actual teaching time: | —————— |

- Have students repeat each line chorally.
- Make sure students:
  ○ use falling intonation for the confirmation tag question *aren't you?*
  ○ use rising intonation for *Is anything bothering you today?*
  ○ pause before and after *actually.*
  ○ use falling intonation for *Why don't you have a seat?*
  ○ use the following stress pattern:

---STRESS PATTERN---

**A:** You must be Mister Brown. You're here for a blood

test, aren't you?

**B:** That's right.

**A:** And is anything bothering you today?

**B:** Well, actually, I've been coughing.

**A:** Really? Well, why don't you have a seat? I'll see if the

doctor can see you.

---

### A 🎧 VOCABULARY
(CD1, Track 22)

| | |
|---|---|
| Suggested teaching time: | 10–15 minutes |
| Your actual teaching time: | —————— |

- Have students listen and study the words. Then have students listen and repeat chorally.

- Point out that the second group of symptoms need *I've been +___ ing.* You may also want to tell students that *I've been ____ ing* usually includes *a lot, all, for [two] hours, for the last few days,* etc. to give information about how long they've had the symptom.

- Write on the board:
  *Situation 1: You've eaten too much [chocolate].*
  *Situation 2: You have a very bad cold.*
  *Situation 3: You've been exercising too much!*

- Pair work. Ask students to take turns using the vocabulary in Exercise A to make sentences about each situation.

- Point out that they should use *I feel* with words from group 1, *I've been* with group 2, and *I have pain in my* for group 3. (Students may say: 1. I've been vomiting; I have pain in my abdomen. 2. I've been coughing a lot. I feel weak. 3. I have pain in my chest. I have pain in my hip.)

- Ask various students to say one of their sentences. Make necessary corrections.

**Option:** To provide more practice, ask students to say when or why they might have the symptoms in Exercise A. Examples: *I feel dizzy when I look down from a tall building. I feel nauseous when I travel by plane. I have a bad cold, so I've been coughing a lot. I fell off my bicycle, and now I have a pain in my hip.* [**+5 minutes**]

> **Language note:** You may want to point out that *I have pain in my [chest]* and *I have a pain in my [chest]* are both correct. An informal way to say *vomit* is *throw up.*

 **Vocabulary Cards**

 **Learning Strategies**

### B 🎧 PRONUNCIATION
(CD1, Track 23)

| | |
|---|---|
| Suggested teaching time: | 5 minutes |
| Your actual teaching time: | —————— |

- First listening: Have students listen and study the examples.

- Second listening: Have students listen and repeat chorally.

**Option:** Pair work. Students make a list of symptoms they have. Tell students they can be dramatic and encourage them to combine vocabulary. Example: *I feel weak and nauseous, and I've been coughing, sneezing, and vomiting.* Walk around and encourage students to use the correct intonation for their lists. [**+5 minutes**]

 **Pronunciation Activities**

**T18**

## C  LISTENING COMPREHENSION
(CD1, Track 24)

| Suggested teaching time: | 10 minutes |
| Your actual teaching time: | _____ |

- Before listening, have students study the chart.
- Point out that the first three column heads in the chart use the noun forms of the symptoms. Say the noun forms and ask students to give you the adjective forms. (dizzy, nauseous, weak)
- You may want to pause after each conversation to allow students time check the columns and write about the pain.
- Have students compare answers with a partner. Then have them listen again to confirm their answers.
- Review the answers with the class.

**AUDIOSCRIPT**

CONVERSATION 1
**M:** What seems to be the problem today, Mrs. Gilles?
**F:** Well, I've been feeling pretty dizzy for the last few days. I have to lie down all the time. I feel really weak and I have so little energy—I can't even make myself lunch or dinner.
**M:** I'm sorry to hear that.
**F:** And I can hardly walk up stairs. I'm so short of breath whenever I try.
**M:** Any pain?
**F:** Funny you should ask. I have pain in my shoulder, too.

CONVERSATION 2 [F = Chinese]
**F:** Is there anything bothering you today, Mr. Baker?
**M:** Well, when I woke up this morning I felt terrible. I had this pain in the back of my neck, and I thought I'd better get in to see the doctor right away.
**F:** Have you been coughing?
**M:** A lot, actually. I've had a bad cold for over a week now.
**F:** That might explain the pain you've been feeling in your neck. I'm going to give you something for that cold.

CONVERSATION 3 [M = Australian]
**M:** The doctor will be right with you, Ms. Rice. Have you not been feeling well?
**F:** Not great, actually. And I've been sneezing like crazy.
**M:** Oh, that's too bad.
**F:** Anyway, today my back is killing me. So I thought, that's it, I'd better come in.
**M:** Come. I'll take you in to see the doctor.

CONVERSATION 4
**F:** You're here to see Dr. Fox?
**M:** Yes, I am. I've been really sick.
**F:** Oh, I'm sorry to hear that. Have you been nauseous?
**M:** Oh yeah.
**F:** Any vomiting?
**M:** Yes. I'm afraid I've been throwing up everything I eat.
**F:** Any dizziness?
**M:** Not really. Just nauseousness.
**F:** Well, Dr. Fox will be with you in a moment.

CONVERSATION 5
**M:** You're Ms. Pearlman?
**F:** Yes, I am.
**M:** The doctor will be with you soon. Can I ask you a few questions?

**F:** OK.
**M:** What brings you in today?
**F:** Well, I've been wheezing a lot since yesterday. I don't know what's wrong. It's really annoying.
**M:** Are you allergic to anything?
**F:** Not that I can think of.
**M:** Any other symptoms?
**F:** Not really.

CONVERSATION 6 [M = Egyptian]
**F:** Mr. Rashid?
**M:** That's me.
**F:** Hello, Mr. Rashid. The doctor will see you in just a moment. Are you in a lot of pain?
**M:** Well, my hip has been bothering me a lot for the past two days. It hurts all the time.
**F:** Hmm. Did you fall or have an accident?
**M:** Not that I can remember.
**F:** Any pain anywhere else? In your knees? Your elbows?
**M:** No.

## D  VOCABULARY
(CD1, Track 25)

| Suggested teaching time: | 5 minutes |
| Your actual teaching time: | _____ |

- Have students listen and study the words. Then have students listen and repeat chorally.
- If you feel it is appropriate, ask various students questions about their own lives. Examples: *Have you ever had an X-ray? When did you last get an injection?*

 **Vocabulary Cards**

## CONVERSATION **PAIR WORK**

| Suggested teaching time: | 5–10 minutes |
| Your actual teaching time: | _____ |

- To get students ready for the activity, have students read the conversation model on page 17 again. You may also want to have students listen to the model.
- If necessary, review the vocabulary for symptoms by having students take turns pantomiming (acting out) problems and guessing symptoms.
- Choose a more confident student and role-play a conversation. Encourage students to ask follow-up questions.
- Walk around the room and provide help as needed. Encourage students to use the correct rhythm and intonation.
- Make sure each student plays both roles.

 **Pair Work Cards**

## EXTRAS (optional)

**Grammar Booster**
**Workbook: Exercises 10–14**
**Copy & Go: Activity 6**

**Pronunciation Supplements**

🎧 **LISTENING COMPREHENSION.** Listen to the conversations. Check the symptoms each patient describes. If the patient has any pain, where is it? Listen again to check your work.

|  | dizziness | nausea | weakness | vomiting | coughing | sneezing | wheezing | pain | if pain, where? |
|---|---|---|---|---|---|---|---|---|---|
| 1. | ☑ | ☐ | ☑ | ☐ | ☐ | ☐ | ☐ | ☑ | shoulder |
| 2. | ☐ | ☐ | ☐ | ☐ | ☑ | ☐ | ☐ | ☑ | back of neck |
| 3. | ☐ | ☐ | ☐ | ☐ | ☐ | ☑ | ☐ | ☑ | back |
| 4. | ☐ | ☑ | ☐ | ☑ | ☐ | ☐ | ☐ | ☐ | |
| 5. | ☐ | ☐ | ☐ | ☐ | ☐ | ☐ | ☑ | ☐ | |
| 6. | ☐ | ☐ | ☐ | ☐ | ☐ | ☐ | ☐ | ☑ | hip |

**D** 🎧 **VOCABULARY.** Medical procedures. Listen and practice.

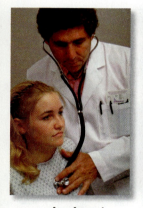
a checkup /
an examination

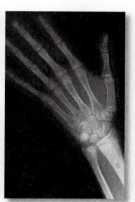
an X-ray

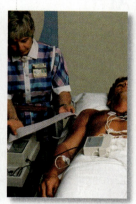
an EKG

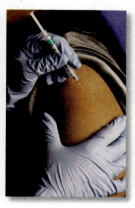
a shot /
an injection

a blood test

## CONVERSATION PAIR WORK

Role-play a visit to the doctor's office. Before you begin, choose a time and medical procedure and write it in the appointment book. Use the guide, or create a new conversation. Answers will vary.

**A:** You must be _____ . You're here for _____ , aren't you?

**B:** _____ .

**A:** And is anything bothering you today?

**B:** Well, actually, _____ .

**A:** _____ .

### APPOINTMENTS

|  | patient's name | medical procedure |
|---|---|---|
| 8:00 | | |
| 9:00 | | |
| 10:00 | | |
| 11:00 | | |
| **12:00** | | |
| 1:00 | | |
| 2:00 | | |
| 3:00 | | |
| 4:00 | | |
| 5:00 | | |
| 6:00 | | |
| 7:00 | | |

# 3 ▶ Discuss Types of Medical Treatments

 **A** ▶ **READING WARM-UP.** What do you do when you get sick or you're in pain?

**B** ▶ 🎧 **READING.** Read the article. Which health treatments have you tried?

## CONVENTIONAL MEDICINE

The beginnings of conventional medicine can be traced back to the fifth century B.C. in ancient Greece. It is based on the scientific study of the human body and illness. In the last century, there has been great progress in what doctors have been able to do with modern surgery and new medications. These scientific advances have made conventional medicine the method many people choose first when they need medical help.

**Surgical techniques have greatly improved over the last century.**

## HOMEOPATHY

Homeopathy was founded in the late eighteenth century in Germany. It is a low-cost system of natural medicine used by hundreds of millions of people worldwide, particularly in India, France, Germany, and the United Kingdom. Homeopathic remedies always come from plants and other natural sources, and they are designed to try to get the body to heal itself. The remedies are usually taken under the tongue.

**Homeopathic remedies are popular in many countries.**

## HERBAL THERAPY

Herbal medicine, often taken as teas or pills, has been practiced for thousands of years in almost all cultures around the world. In fact, many conventional medicines were discovered by scientists studying traditional uses of herbs for medicinal purposes. The World Health Organization claims that 80% of the world's population uses some form of herbal therapy for their regular health care.

**Herbs are used to treat many ailments.**

## ACUPUNCTURE

Acupuncture originated in China over five thousand years ago. Today, it is used worldwide for a variety of problems. Acupuncture needles are inserted at certain points on the body to relieve pain and /or restore health. Many believe acupuncture may be effective in helping people stop smoking as well.

**An acupuncturist inserts needles at certain points on the body.**

## CHIROPRACTIC

Chiropractic was introduced in the U.S. in 1895 and is now used by 15 million people worldwide for the treatment of pain, backache, injuries and some illnesses. Chiropractic uses no medications, but it is sometimes practiced along with herbal or homeopathic therapies.

**A chiropractor adjusts a patient's spine.**

## SPIRITUAL HEALING

Also known as faith healing, or mind and body connection, various forms of spiritual healing exist around the world. This is a form of healing that uses the mind or religious faith to treat illness. A number of conventional doctors even say that when they have not been able to help a patient, spiritual healing just may work.

**Many believe meditation or prayer may help heal disease.**

**SOURCES:** www.alternativemedicine.com and www.holisticmed.com

# LESSON 3

## Discuss Types of Medical Treatments

**AUDIOSCRIPT continued from Exercise B, page T16.**

CONVERSATION 3 [F = Indian, M = Arabic]
**F:** Hello, Mr. Aboud. I'm Dr. Patel.
**M:** Hi. Thanks for fitting me in. Did they tell you I'm from out of town?
**F:** Yes. Where from?
**M:** Lebanon . . . Beirut.
**F:** And you had a dental emergency? Too bad. OK, Mr. Aboud. Tell me what happened.
**M:** I'm afraid one of my fillings came out.
**F:** How do you think THAT happened?
**M:** Well, I went out to dinner last night at a pretty nice restaurant. But about halfway through the meal I felt something funny.
**F:** Your filling, huh? Does it hurt?
**M:** A little bit. Whenever I drink something cold.
**F:** Well, I can take care of that. But you should see your dentist when you get back home, OK?

CONVERSATION 4 [F = Brazilian]
**M:** Are you the three o'clock appointment?
**F:** That's right. Stella Texeira.
**M:** The dentist will see you in just a minute. What brings you into the office today?
**F:** Well, I think I broke something.
**M:** Not a tooth!
**F:** No I don't think so. I think it was this crown, right here.
**M:** Oh, that's too bad. Didn't you say you were from out of town?
**F:** Yes. I'm from Brazil.
**M:** Really! Well don't worry. I'm sure the dentist can help you.

### A ▷ READING WARM-UP

| Suggested teaching time: | 5–10 minutes |
| Your actual teaching time: | _____ |

• Group work. Form small groups. Students take turns saying what they do when they get sick or when they are in pain. Examples: Student A: *When I get sick, I go to bed.* Student B: *When I'm in pain, I usually take some medication.* Student C: *When I feel nauseous, I drink some tea.*

• Encourage students to offer information about more than one situation.

• Ask various students to share one of their situations with the class.

### B ▷ 🎧 READING

**(CD1, Track 26)**

| Suggested teaching time: | 10–15 minutes |
| Your actual teaching time: | _____ |

• To draw on students' schema (prior knowledge), have students look at the pictures and subheadings and make simple statements about what they already know about each medical treatment. Examples: *I drink [chamomile] tea when my stomach hurts. Acupuncture uses needles.*

• Pair work. Students take turns telling each other which treatments they have tried.

**Option:** Use this option if you want to do a listening activity. Books closed. Write the following chart (without the answers) on the board. Have students listen and complete the chart. Then have students read the text to confirm their answers. **[+15 minutes]**

| Treatments | What does it use / what is done? | Where did it start? |
|---|---|---|
| Conventional medicine | medications, surgery | Greece |
| Homeopathy | plants and other natural sources | Germany |
| Herbal therapy | herbs (teas and pills) | around the world |
| Acupuncture | needles | China |
| Chiropractic | adjusts the back | U.S. |
| Spiritual healing | the mind; religious faith | all over the world |

 **Graphic Organizers**

 **Extra Reading Comprehension Activities**

 **Learning Strategies**

**Language note:** *Chiropractic treatment* includes pressing on and moving the bones in the back.

 **DISCUSSION**

| Suggested teaching time: | 10 minutes |
| Your actual teaching time: | _____ |

- Group work. Form groups of three or four. Encourage students to take notes as they talk that help summarize their discussion.
- Ask students to use the vocabulary from previous lessons, such as symptoms (page 18), medical procedures (page 19), and the information in the reading to talk about why certain treatments may be more popular.
- To finish the activity, have various groups choose one treatment and summarize why they think it is popular and the reason(s) why.
- Encourage the class to ask follow-up questions. Examples: Student A: *Conventional medicine is popular because people feel safe with doctors.* Student E: *But we hear about so many doctors who are not even friendly to their patients.* Student B: *I think many people just want someone who is trained in modern methods and has experience. Maybe it's not important to them that the doctor is nice.*

 **WHAT DO YOU THINK?**

| Suggested teaching time: | 5 minutes |
| Your actual teaching time: | _____ |

- Have students compare their answer choices with a partner. Encourage them to explain why they chose a particular answer.
- Ask various students to tell the class one of their suggestions. Encourage the class to ask follow-up questions.

**Option:** Pair work. Students take turns saying if they agree or disagree with the opinions of the people in the pictures and explaining why. **[+5 minutes]**

## TOP NOTCH **INTERACTION**

| Suggested teaching time: | 15–20 minutes |
| Your actual teaching time: | _____ |

### STEP 1. PAIR WORK.

- Have students listen to and read the list of practitioners. Then have them listen and repeat chorally.
- Clarify the task: First students fill in the first column with their own information. Then they discuss their answers and take notes about their partner.
- Encourage students to explain their choices.

### STEP 2. DISCUSSION.

- You may want to do this activity in small groups.
- Role-play the models for the class.
- Before students begin their discussions, brainstorm different ways to say if a treatment works or not. Examples: *It works for me. It helped me with my [backache]. It helped my body to heal itself. It relieved my pain. I felt a lot better.*
- Walk around the room and provide help as needed.
- Take a poll to find out which type of treatment is the most popular in the class.

### STEP 3. WRITING.

- Encourage students to use the grammar and vocabulary from this unit.
- Students should also include ideas and information they discussed in Steps 1 and 2.

 **Writing Process Worksheets**

### EXTRAS (optional)

Workbook: **Exercises 15–20**
Copy & Go: **Activity 7**

**C** **DISCUSSION.** Which of the treatments in the reading are available in your country? Which ones are the most popular? Why?

**D** **WHAT DO YOU THINK?** Match each patient to a treatment. Explain your answers. In some cases, more than one therapy might be appropriate.

Answers may vary. Possible answers include:

1. ❝I want to avoid taking any strong medications or having surgery.❞

   This patient might prefer <u>chiropractic, acupuncture</u>.

2. ❝I believe you have to heal yourself. You can't just expect doctors to do everything for you.❞

   This patient might prefer <u>homeopathy, spiritual healing</u>.

3. ❝I wouldn't use a health care method that isn't strongly supported by scientific research.❞

   This patient might prefer <u>conventional medicine, chiropractic</u>.

## TOP NOTCH
### INTERACTION • *What works for you?*

**STEP 1. PAIR WORK.** Discuss the medical treatments and practitioners you would choose for each ailment. Take notes on your notepad.

**Practitioners**
a conventional doctor
a homeopathic doctor
an acupuncturist
an herbal therapist
a chiropractor
a spiritual healer

|  | You | Your partner |
|---|---|---|
| a cold | *Answers will vary.* |  |
| a headache |  |  |
| nausea |  |  |
| back pain |  |  |
| a high fever |  |  |
| a broken finger |  |  |

**STEP 2. DISCUSSION.** Compare the kinds of health care you and your classmates use. Explain why you use them.

❝I've tried acupuncture a number of times. It really helped with my back pain.❞

❝I would never try herbal medicine. I don't think it works.❞

❝I see a homeopathic doctor regularly, but my husband doesn't believe in that.❞

**STEP 3. WRITING.** On a separate sheet of paper, write about the health care you use.

**FREE PRACTICE**

## 4 ▶ Talk about Medications

### A ▶ 🎧 VOCABULARY. Medications.
Listen and practice.

🎧 **Medicine label information**
**Dosage:** Take 1 tablet by mouth every day.
**Warnings:** Do not take this medication if you are pregnant or nursing a baby.
**Side effects:** May cause dizziness or nausea.

**a painkiller**

**cold tablets**

**a nasal spray / a decongestant**

**eye drops**

**an antihistamine**

**cough medicine**

**an antibiotic**

**an antacid**

**an ointment**

**vitamins**

### B ▶ 🎧 LISTENING COMPREHENSION.
Listen to each patient talk with a doctor. Use the vocabulary to fill out the chart for each patient.

NAME: _Valerie Ramazan_

| | NO | YES | |
|---|---|---|---|
| Is the patient currently taking any medication? | ☐ | ☑ | If so, which type? _painkillers_ |
| Are there any possible side effects? | ☐ | ☑ | If so, what are they? _nausea, vomiting_ |
| Did the doctor give the patient a prescription? | ☐ | ☑ | |

NAME: _Lucy Fernandez_

| | NO | YES | |
|---|---|---|---|
| Is the patient currently taking any medication? | ☐ | ☑ | If so, which type? _antacid, painkiller_ |
| Are there any possible side effects? | ☐ | ☑ | If so, what are they? _tiredness_ |
| Did the doctor give the patient a prescription? | ☐ | ☑ | |

NAME: **Mark Goh**

| | NO | YES | |
|---|---|---|---|
| Is the patient currently taking any medication? | ☐ | ☑ | If so, which type? _eye drops_ |
| Are there any possible side effects? | ☑ | ☐ | If so, what are they? ___ |
| Did the doctor give the patient a prescription? | ☐ | ☑ | |

## LESSON

# 4 ▶ *Talk about Medications*

 **A** 🎧 **VOCABULARY**
**(CD1, Tracks 27, 28)**

| Suggested teaching time: | 10–15 minutes |
|---|---|
| Your actual teaching time: | _____ |

- Have students listen and read the label of the prescription container. Then listen and repeat.

- Write on the board:

  *1. dosage*    *a. things you shouldn't do*
  *2. warnings*    *b. symptoms a medication can cause*
  *3. side effects*    *c. how much medicine and when to take it*

- To check comprehension, ask students to match the words with the definitions. (1-c, 2-a, 3-b)

- Have students listen and study the medications. Then have students listen and repeat chorally.

- To provide practice, have students work in small groups and make statements or suggestions about what kind of ailment or symptoms the medications could be used for. Students can review vocabulary for symptoms on page 18. Examples: *Take a painkiller for a headache or for pains in your body. I'm allergic to dust so I often take an antihistamine.*

- Point out the verb + noun combinations students will need: *use* a nasal spray, a decongestant, an antihistamine, an ointment; *get* a prescription; *take* [all others]. You may want to write them on the board.

**Culture note:** In most English-speaking countries, a doctor writes a prescription and it's filled at a pharmacy. Labels on prescription medicines include the patient's name, doctor's name, name of the drug, dosage, any warnings or side effects, how many times this prescription can be refilled, and an expiration date. Medicines that don't need a prescription are *over-the-counter medicines* or *OTCs*.

 🔵 **Vocabulary Cards**

 🔵 **Learning Strategies**

**B** 🎧 **LISTENING COMPREHENSION**
**(CD1, Track 29)**

| Suggested teaching time: | 15–20 minutes |
|---|---|
| Your actual teaching time: | _____ |

- Before listening, have students look at the charts to check which information they should listen for.

- Pause after each conversation so students can write.

- Have students compare answers with a partner and review as a class.

**◀ AUDIOSCRIPT ▶**

CONVERSATION 1 [M = Korean, F = Turkish]
**M:** Ms. Ramazan? I'm Dr. Kim. I understand you're a long way from home.

---

**F:** That's right. I'm here on business. From Turkey.
**M:** But you're not feeling well?
**F:** It's my back. It's really been killing me for several days now.
**M:** Are you taking anything?
**F:** Just some painkillers. But they're really not helping.
**M:** Let me give you a prescription for Percotrol. It's a very effective painkiller. I think you might find it very helpful.
**F:** Does it have any side effects?
**M:** Very rarely. In some people it causes nausea or vomiting. But I really don't think you'll have to worry. Call me if you feel at all nauseous, OK?
**F:** Thanks.
**M:** The dosage is one tablet in the morning, one in the evening, during meals. You'll see a full set of instructions when you pick up your prescription downstairs.
**F:** Thank you, Dr. Kim.

CONVERSATION 2 [M = Japanese, F = Mexican]
**M:** Lucy Fernandez? I'm Dr. Hirano.
**F:** Thanks so much for fitting me in.
**M:** My pleasure. Where are you from?
**F:** Mexico. I'm here on business.
**M:** You're a long way from home! What can I do for you today?
**F:** Well, I've got a splitting headache, and I've been kind of nauseous since Monday.
**M:** You must feel terrible. Are you currently taking any medication?
**F:** I've been taking an antacid and a painkiller.
**M:** Are you allergic to any medications?
**F:** I think I might be allergic to penicillin. But I'm not sure.
**M:** Well, that's OK. Keep taking the painkiller for that headache. But you can stop taking the antacid. I'm going to give you a prescription for your nausea. Take it twice a day.
**F:** Will there be any side effects?
**M:** It might make you a little tired during the day. But chances are you'll be fine. Call me if you don't feel better.

CONVERSATION 3 [M = Chinese]
**M:** Dr. Benson? Hi, I'm Mark Goh.
**F:** Hello, Mr. Goh. I hear you're not from around here.
**M:** Right. I'm visiting from Hong Kong for a few weeks.
**F:** You've come a long way to see a doctor! Well, what can I do for you today?
**M:** My eyes have been really red for about a week now.
**F:** Have you been using any medication?
**M:** Well I got some eye drops at the drugstore, but they aren't helping.
**F:** For your condition, I think you might want something stronger. I'm going to give you a prescription for an eye ointment. Use it twice a day, and wash your eyes several times a day.
**M:** OK.
**F:** It's a strong medication, but there aren't any side effects you need to worry about. If you keep your eyes clean, the ointment should do the trick.
**M:** Thanks.
**F:** Will you still be here next week? I'd like you to come back to see me.
**M:** Yes, I'll still be here.
**F:** Good. You can make an appointment at the front desk on your way out.
**M:** Thanks, Doctor.

**T22**

# TOP NOTCH **INTERACTION**

Suggested teaching time: 20–25 minutes
Your actual teaching time: _____

## STEP 1. Imagine you are . . .

- Point out that students can complete the form with either true or imaginary information.
- Walk around the room and provide help as needed.

## STEP 2. ROLE PLAY.

- Have students read the list of roles in the small box and the descriptions of the four situations.
- Point out the NEED HELP? section and review the expressions. You may want students to repeat chorally.
- You may want to review the following questions in the NEED HELP? section to make sure students are familiar with the vocabulary and meaning: *Is it urgent?* (Is it an emergency?) *Are there any side effects?* (Will it make you feel anything unusual?)
- Encourage students to use as many of the expressions in the box as they can. You may want to ask them to check off the ones they use.
- Choose one or two students and role-play two different situations.
- Walk around the room and provide help as needed.
- Ask pairs of students to role-play one of their situations in front of the class.

## EXTRAS (optional)

**Workbook: Exercises 21–23**
**Copy & Go: Activity 8**

# INTERACTION • *Are you currently taking any medication?*

**STEP 1.** **Imagine you are visiting the doctor. Complete the patient information form.**
Answers will vary.

## Patient Information Form

NAME: _____

1. What are your symptoms?
☐ dizziness    ☐ weakness    ☐ shortness of breath
☐ coughing    ☐ sneezing    ☐ wheezing
☐ nausea    ☐ vomiting    ☐ pain (where?_____)
☐ other:_____

2. How long have you had these symptoms?_____

3. Are you currently taking any medications?
   If so, what?_____

4. Are you allergic to any medications?
   If so, which?_____

**STEP 2.** **ROLE PLAY. Take turns playing different roles. Use your patient information form. Include the following scenes:** Answers will vary.

**Roles**
a patient
a colleague / classmate
a doctor
a receptionist

1. The colleague or classmate recommends a doctor.
2. The patient calls the receptionist to make an appointment.
3. The receptionist greets the patient at the office.
4. The doctor asks about the problem and suggests a treatment.

NEED HELP? **Here's language you already know:**

**Finding a doctor**

Could you recommend ____?
I'd like to make an appointment to see ____.
I think it's an emergency.
I really appreciate it.

**At the doctor's office**

Is it an emergency?
Why don't you have a seat?
You must be ____.
I'll see if the doctor can see you.
The doctor will be right with you.

**The doctor**

Luckily, I had a cancellation.
Glad I'm able to help you out.
It's a good idea to ____.
You should ____.
You may have to ____.
Let's have a look.
That must hurt.

**The patient**

Thanks for fitting me in.
My ____ is killing me.
I feel [dizzy].
I've been [coughing].
I have pain in my [ankle].
I thought I'd better see someone right away.
Are there any side effects?

**A** 🎧 **LISTENING COMPREHENSION.** **Listen to the conversations.**
**Complete the statements.**

1. The patient lost a __filling__ .

2. The doctor wrote a prescription for an __Clear Aid__ .

3. The doctor wants the patient to get an __X-ray__ .

4. The patient wants to see an __acupuncturist__

Answers may vary. Possible answers include:

**B** **Suggest a medication for each of the people.**

    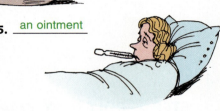

5. __an ointment__

1. __a painkiller__   2. __an antihistamine__   3. __an antacid__   4. __eye drops__   6. __cold tablets__

**C**  **Complete each conversation with a statement using must.** Answers will vary. Possible answers include:

1. **A:** I feel weak and dizzy, and I've been vomiting all morning.
   **B:** You __must feel terrible__ .

2. **A:** My brother stayed up all night dancing. He got home at 7:00 A.M.
   **B:** He __must be very tired__ .

3. **A:** I tried to make an appointment with a dentist, but they can't fit me in this week.
   **B:** They __must be busy__ .

4. **A:** My daughter is getting married next week.
   **B:** You __must be excited__ .

**D** **Rewrite each statement, using may (or might) and be able to.** Answers may vary. Possible answers include:

1. Maybe the doctor can see you tomorrow.
   __The doctor might be able to see you tomorrow.__

2. Maybe an acupuncturist can help you.
   __An acupuncturist may be able to help you.__

3. Maybe the hotel can recommend a good dentist.
   __The hotel might be able to recommend a good dentist.__

4. Maybe she can't come to the office before 6:00.
   __She may not be able to come to the office before 6:00.__

5. Maybe you can buy an antihistamine in the gift shop.
   __You might be able to buy an antihistamine in the gift shop.__

 *TOP NOTCH* **PROJECT**
Use a bilingual dictionary to make a list of more medical and dental vocabulary.

 *TOP NOTCH* **WEBSITE**
For Unit 2 online activities, visit the *Top Notch* Companion Website at www.longman.com/topnotch.

# UNIT 2 CHECKPOINT

## A  LISTENING COMPREHENSION
**(CD1, Track 30)**

| Suggested teaching time: | 10 minutes |
|---|---|
| Your actual teaching time: | _____ |

- Have students compare answers with a partner. Then review as a class.

**Option:** To provide more practice, tell students that the cause or reason for the problem is given for three of the patients. Have them listen to the conversations again and write the cause or reason. (1. eating candy / something hard  2. allergies  3. skiing fast and falling down.  4. not known)  **[+5 minutes]**

### AUDIOSCRIPT

**CONVERSATION 1**
**M:** So what's bothering you today?
**F:** Well, I've had some pain in my tooth. Here on the right side.
**M:** Let's have a look. Hmm . . . Looks like you lost a filling.
**F:** Really? My regular dentist just put that in a month ago!
**M:** Have you eaten anything hard, or chewy or crunchy lately?
**F:** Uh-oh. I think that's it. It was probably that candy I ate two days ago.
**M:** Well, how about we take care of that right now, OK?
**F:** Thanks.

**CONVERSATION 2**
**F:** Thanks for fitting me in. I've been sneezing like crazy all day. I thought I'd better come in and get something.
**M:** Allergies?
**F:** Mm-hmm. I get them every spring at this time. I don't know if it's the trees or the flowers or what. But my eyes get red. I sneeze.
**M:** Well, I can give you a prescription to take care of that. ClearAid is a very good antihistamine.
**F:** Thanks. I'd really appreciate that.

**CONVERSATION 3**
**F:** You must be in a lot of pain.
**M:** I am. My leg really hurts a lot.
**F:** You said you were skiing?
**M:** Yes. I guess I went a little too fast.
**F:** Well don't worry about that now. Let's get you into radiology and then we'll know if you've broken anything or not. Have you ever been X-rayed before?
**M:** Just for my teeth.

**CONVERSATION 4**
**M:** You look like you're in a lot of pain.
**F:** Yes. My back's been killing me for several days now. I've been taking painkillers several times a day.
**M:** And that hasn't helped?
**F:** Not really. I still can't sit. I can't stand. All I can do is lie down.
**M:** Well, I could write you a prescription for a stronger medication if you like. That might help.
**F:** I don't know. Everyone says acupuncture is good for pain. Do you think I should try that?
**M:** Sometimes it helps. I could give you a referral if you like.
**F:** I'd like that. I need to try something else.

## B  Suggest a medication . . .

| Suggested teaching time: | 5–10 minutes |
|---|---|
| Your actual teaching time: | _____ |

- Encourage students to look at which part of the body has the problem.
- To review, ask students to use complete sentences to say what the problem is and which medication the person should take. Examples: *She has a headache. She needs a painkiller. He has allergies. He needs an antihistamine.*
- To provide more practice, write the following ailments and medications in two columns on the board. Ask students to match them. Have students compare answers with a partner and review as a class. (1. b 2. d or a  3. a or d  4. f 5. e 6. c)

| | |
|---|---|
| 1. burns | a. antihistamine |
| 2. a stuffy nose | b. ointment |
| 3. an allergy | c. cold tablets |
| 4. a burning feeling in your stomach | d. nasal spray / decongestant |
| 5. a headache | e. painkiller |
| 6. a cold | f. antacid |

## C  Complete each conversation . . .

| Suggested teaching time: | 5 minutes |
|---|---|
| Your actual teaching time: | _____ |

- Review the example first.
- Review answers by having two students read the sentences for A and B. Make necessary corrections.

**Option:** Pair work. Students take turns role-playing the corrected conversations. **[+5 minutes]**

## D  Rewrite each statement . . .

| Suggested teaching time: | 5–10 minutes |
|---|---|
| Your actual teaching time: | _____ |

- Review the example first.
- Have students compare answers with a partner. Then review as a class.

🔘 *Top Notch Pop* Song Activities

### *TOP NOTCH* PROJECT

**Idea:** Pair work. Ask students to write a list of ten items of medical or dental vocabulary they would like to know in English. Have pairs join other pairs and share the new words.

**Idea:** Form small groups. Have students find and read a short medical article in English on the Internet or in a magazine and make a list of dental or medical vocabulary. Encourage them to work out their meaning from context or look them up in a dictionary.

# UNIT WRAP-UP

Suggested teaching time: 20–25 minutes
Your actual teaching time: _____

## Vocabulary

• Ask *Where are these people?* (2nd floor: at a dentist's office; 1st floor: at a medical office / at a doctor's office / at a clinic)

• Pair work. Encourage students to take notes and to write the vocabulary in three groups: treatments, procedures, ailments. Remind students to talk about anything having to do with a dental or medical situation.

┌─ **Your students can say . . .** ─────────────
a check-up, an examination, an X-ray, an EKG, a shot / an injection, a blood test, conventional medicine, homeopathy, herbal therapy, acupuncture, chiropractic, spiritual healing He has a toothache / a backache / pain in his arm. The dentist is looking at an X-ray. The patient needs an injection. He is having a check-up. She feels dizzy / nauseous / weak / short of breath. He has been vomiting / coughing / sneezing / wheezing. She has pain in her chest / hip / ribs / abdomen.
└──────────────────────────────────────────────

## Grammar

• Review the example first.

• You may want to have students label each person with a number and use that number to identify which people or situation they are describing.

• Have students compare answers with a partner.

• Ask various students to say one or two of their sentences.

┌─ **Your students can say . . .** ─────────────
He might need an appointment with the dentist. He might have to get a new crown. He may have to get a new filling. She must be in pain. She might be going on a trip. He must need to see a doctor. He might have a cold. She must have an infection. He must need an injection. He must feel nauseous. She might need a blood test.
└──────────────────────────────────────────────

## Social Language

• Role-play the model first.

• Pair work. Ask students to write as many conversations as they can.

• Ask various pairs to role-play one of their conversations. Make necessary corrections.

┌─ **Your students can say . . .** ─────────────
**A:** You're here to see Dr. [Jones]? **B:** Yes, that's right. I feel [dizzy and weak]. **A:** Oh, I'm sorry to hear that. I'm sure the doctor can help you.

**A:** I wonder if I might be able to get an appointment today. I'm here on [business], but I've been [vomiting a lot]. **B:** Are you in pain? **A:** Yes, actually, I am. My stomach really hurts. **B:** Well, don't worry. I'm sure Dr. [Jones] can help you.
└──────────────────────────────────────────────

┌────────────────────────────────────────────────
**A:** I'd like to make an appointment to see Dr. [Jones]. **B:** Well, let me check. Could you be here by [three o'clock]? **A:** Yes, that would be fine. Thanks for fitting me in.

**A:** Hello, [Miss Black]. Tell me what happened. **B:** Well, I was [washing the car] when I felt [dizzy]. And then I had pain in my [chest]. **A:** I understand. Are you in a lot of pain now? **B:** It isn't too bad.

**A:** Hello, [patient's name] What brings you in today? **B:** I've been [coughing]. **A:** Oh, that's too bad. Any other symptoms? **B:** Yes, I feel [weak]. **A:** Well, I'm going to give you a prescription for some [cough medicine]. **B:** Does it have any side effects? **A:** It might [make you tired] so take it at night.
└────────────────────────────────────────────────

## Writing

• Encourage students to include deductions about what is happening. Remind students to use *may* and *might* for possibility and *must* for necessity.

• As students write, walk around the room and provide help as needed.

**Option: Which one?** In small groups or in front of the class, have volunteers pick one scene in the picture and read their description out loud. The class guesses which situation is being described. **[+5 minutes]**

┌─ **Individual oral progress check (optional)** ─
• Use the illustration on page 25. Encourage the student to use material (vocabulary, grammar, rhythm and intonation) practiced in this unit.

• Evaluate the student on correctness and intelligibility.

• Tell the student you are going to ask questions about various people in the waiting area and he / she should make a statement of deduction using *may, might* or *must.* Examples: T: *Why does the man on the telephone need an appointment?* S: *He might be on a business trip and he feels weak and nauseous.* T: (pointing) *Why do you think this man is at the medical office?* S: *He may need a vaccination for an overseas trip.* T: (pointing) *Who do you think this woman wants to see?* S: *She must need to see a chiropractor for her back problem.*

• Tell the student you are going to role-play a conversation between a patient and a receptionist (on the telephone or in person). The student should play the patient. Example: T: *Hello. Dr. Brown's office.* S: *Hi. I'd like to make an appointment for a check-up.* T: *OK. Can you come in next Tuesday at 10:00?* S: *Yes, I can. I'd like a blood test and a complete examination.*
└────────────────────────────────────────────────

 **Cumulative Vocabulary Activities**

 You may wish to use the video and activity worksheets for Unit 2 at this point.

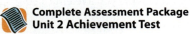 **Complete Assessment Package Unit 2 Achievement Test**

# UNIT WRAP-UP

- **Vocabulary.** Name all the treatments, procedures, and ailments you can see in the picture.
  *backache, X—ray, …*

- **Grammar.** Make statements with <u>may</u> or <u>might</u> and <u>must</u>.
  *She must have a backache.*

- **Social Language.** Create conversations for the people.
  *A: I wonder if I might be able to see the dentist today.*
  *B: Is it an emergency?*

- **Writing.** Write about what is happening in the picture.
  *The medical office is very busy today. There are a lot of…*

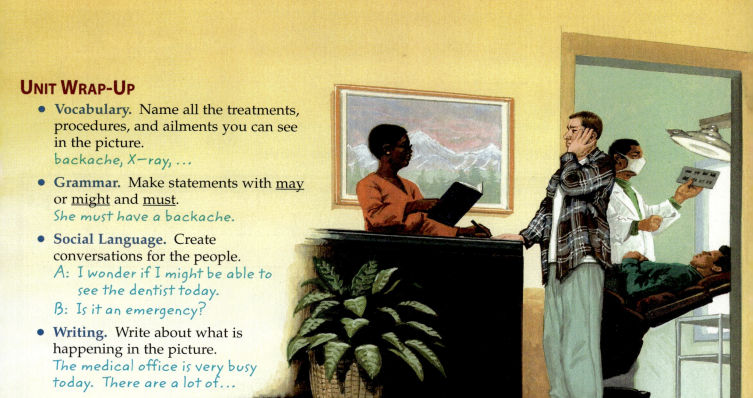

### ✔ Now I can …

- ☐ make an appointment to see a doctor or dentist.
- ☐ describe symptoms at a doctor's office.
- ☐ discuss types of medical treatments.
- ☐ talk about medications.

# UNIT

# Getting Things Done

**UNIT GOALS**

1 Request express service
2 Ask for a recommendation
3 Evaluate the quality of service
4 Plan a social event

**A** **TOPIC PREVIEW.** Look at the business services website.

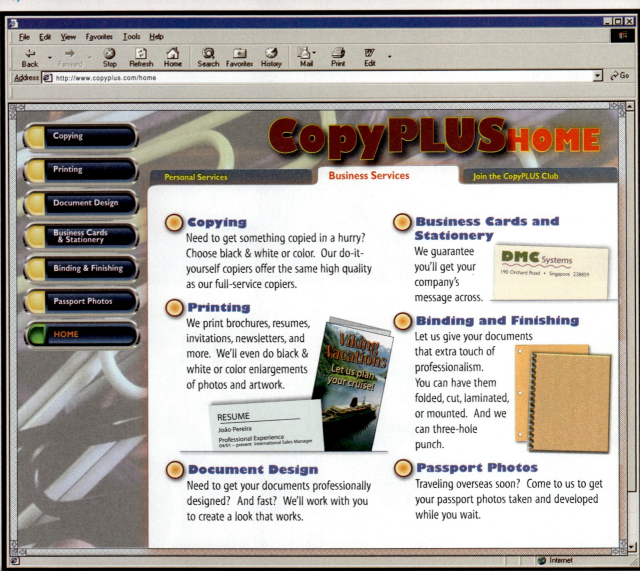

File  Edit  View  Favorites  Tools  Help

Back  Forward  Stop  Refresh  Home  Search  Favorites  History  Mail  Print  Edit

Address  http://www.copyplus.com/home

## CopyPLUS HOME

Personal Services    Business Services    Join the *CopyPLUS* Club

- Copying
- Printing
- Document Design
- Business Cards & Stationery
- Binding & Finishing
- Passport Photos
- HOME

**Copying**
Need to get something copied in a hurry? Choose black & white or color. Our do-it-yourself copiers offer the same high quality as our full-service copiers.

**Printing**
We print brochures, resumes, invitations, newsletters, and more. We'll even do black & white or color enlargements of photos and artwork.

RESUME
João Pereira
Professional Experience
04/01 – present  International Sales Manager

*Viking Vacations*
Let us plan your cruise!

**Document Design**
Need to get your documents professionally designed? And fast? We'll work with you to create a look that works.

**Business Cards and Stationery**
We guarantee you'll get your company's message across.

DMC Systems
190 Orchard Road • Singapore 238859

**Binding and Finishing**
Let us give your documents that extra touch of professionalism. You can have them folded, cut, laminated, or mounted. And we can three-hole punch.

**Passport Photos**
Traveling overseas soon? Come to us to get your passport photos taken and developed while you wait.

Internet

**B** **DISCUSSION.** When might you need each of these services? Give examples.

> If I started my own business, I might want to print some brochures.

> If I travel overseas, I'll need a passport.

# Getting Things Done

 **TOPIC PREVIEW**

| Suggested teaching time: | 10–15 minutes |
| Your actual teaching time: | _____ |

- Pre-reading: Books closed. Have students imagine they own a business. Ask them to brainstorm different business services they might need during a business day. Examples: *sending packages; making (photo) copies, making travel arrangements, buying office supplies, etc.* You may want to write them on the board.

- To practice the reading strategy of scanning, ask students to look at headings and subheadings of the text and find the name of the company (CopyPLUS) and the different kinds of services they offer. (copying, printing, document design, business cards and stationery, binding and finishing, passport photos)

- If students did not say the business services identified in the reading during brainstorming, add them to the list.

- Then have students read the text. Encourage them to work out the meaning of unknown words and phrases as they read. The pictures can also help.

- Write on the board:
  *Projects*:
  1. *Design a newsletter*
  2. *Translate a business document*
  3. *Make color copies*
  4. *Print a resume*
  5. *Repair a copier*
  6. *Cut party invitations*
  7. *Fold holiday cards*
  8. *Take a family photo*

- Pair work. To check comprehension, ask students to scan the text to answer the question: *Can CopyPLUS do these projects?* (1. yes  2. no  3. yes  4. yes  5. no  6. yes  7. yes  8. no)

- Review as a class. Encourage students to support their answers with information from the text.

**Language note:** The omission of words or a phrase (ellipsis) that are not necessary for understanding the message is common in rapid, spoken English. It is also common in written texts, such as advertisements, personal letters, and e-mails. Point out the full forms of the folowing: *Need to get . . . = Do you need to get . . .* and *Traveling overseas soon? = Are you traveling overseas soon?*

**Language note:** Students may need help with the following words: *enlargement* (something printed or copied again in a larger size); *stationery* (special paper for writing, usually with matching envelopes); *binding* (fastening pieces of paper together and usually putting on a cover); *laminated* (covered with a layer of thin plastic); *mounted* (fastening a picture or photograph to a larger piece of paper).

 **DISCUSSION**

| Suggested teaching time: | 10 minutes |
| Your actual teaching time: | _____ |

- Review the models first.

- Group work. Form groups of three. Encourage students to give examples for each service.

- Tell students they can also discuss services they might already use.

- To finish the activity, ask various students to say one service they might need and for what. Example: Student A: *I often get documents copied.* Student B: *Don't you have a copier in the office?* Student A: *Yes. But it doesn't make color copies.*

## SOUND BITES
(CD2, Track 2)

| Suggested teaching time: | 5–10 minutes |
|---|---|
| Your actual teaching time: | _____ |

• To check comprehension, ask students to summarize Sue and Kim's conversation. (Possible answers: Both Kim and Sue are in a hurry. Kim needs color copies a.s.a.p. / right away. She also needs to make sure the copies arrive in Singapore early Monday morning. Sue needs to have the tailor put / sew new buttons on a jacket.)

• Point out that *a.s.a.p.* is said with the four letters A-S-A-P.

## D IN OTHER WORDS

| Suggested teaching time: | 10 minutes |
|---|---|
| Your actual teaching time: | _____ |

• Encourage students to identify who says the phrases and to use the context of the conversation to help work out their meaning.

• Have students compare answers with a partner and review as a class. Make necessary corrections.

• Other possible answers are: 1. very busy 2. do this job fast 3. right away 4. see you later.

## WHAT ABOUT **YOU?**

| Suggested teaching time: | 10–15 minutes |
|---|---|
| Your actual teaching time: | _____ |

• Have students look at the pictures and review the types of services.

• You may want to brainstorm other services students know and write them on the board. Examples: *installing home appliances, painting, gardening, translation services, computer services, food delivery*

• Provide an example for the class. Encourage students to ask each other follow-up questions. Examples: Student A: *I use ArriveQuick, a courier service.* Student B: *Why?* Student A: *I often send gifts to my sister, who lives in Italy.* Student C: *I used a copying service last year.* Student D: *Was it expensive?* Student C: *Yes, but it was so efficient. It saved us a lot of time.*

• Walk around the room and provide help as needed.

**Option:** Ask various students to report to the class about one of the services their partners used.
[+10 minutes]

## EXTRAS (optional)

**Workbook: Exercises 1–3**

## C 🎧 SOUND BITES. Read along silently as you listen to a natural conversation.

**SUE:** You look like you're in a hurry!
**KIM:** I am. I've got to get 50 color copies made a.s.a.p.* I hope they can do a rush job. **CN1**
**SUE:** They must get requests like that all the time.
**KIM:** I sure hope so. But that's not all.
**SUE:** What else?

*a.s.a.p. = as soon as possible

**CN1 Corpus Notes:**
The acronym *a.s.a.p.* is used frequently in spoken English and informal writing, such as in e-mails.

**KIM:** Then I've got to get it all air expressed so it arrives in Singapore first thing Monday morning. **CN2**
**SUE:** I won't keep you then. Actually, I'm in a bit of a hurry myself. I need to have the tailor put new buttons on this jacket.
**KIM:** OK. I'll call you tonight.
**SUE:** Great!

**CN2 Corpus Notes:**
The use of *first thing* as an adverb is especially common in spoken and informal English.

## D IN OTHER WORDS. Read the conversation again and restate the following underlined words and phrases in your own way.

Answers will vary. Possible answers include:

1. You look like you're <u>in a hurry</u>. really busy
2. I hope they can <u>do a rush job</u>. get the job done quickly
3. <u>first thing</u> Monday morning before anything else
4. I <u>won't keep you</u> then. will let you go

## WHAT ABOUT YOU?

**PAIR WORK.** Which business and non-business services have you used in the last year? Who was the service provider? Which other services have you used? Answers will vary.

 ☐ copying
 ☐ printing
 ☐ housecleaning
 ☐ car repair
 ☐ tailoring
 ☐ courier service

# 1 Request Express Service

## CONVERSATION MODEL Read and listen.

**A:** Do you think I could get this dry-cleaned by Thursday?

**B:** Thursday? That might be difficult.

**A:** I'm sorry, but it's pretty urgent. I need it for a friend's wedding this weekend.

**B:** Well, in that case, I'll see what I can do. But it won't be ready until after four o'clock. **CN**

**A:** I really appreciate it. Thanks.

**Rhythm and intonation practice**

**CN Corpus Notes:**
*I'll see what I can do* has the same meaning as *I'll try* but *I'll see what I can* do is typically used in conversation.

## A VOCABULARY. Services. Listen and practice.

**dry-clean a suit**

**develop / process film**

**repair shoes**

**frame a picture**

**deliver a package**

**lengthen / shorten a skirt**

**enlarge photos**

**print a sign**

**copy a report**

## LESSON

# 1 Request Express Service

## 🎧 CONVERSATION MODEL
### (CD2, Track 3)

| Suggested teaching time: | 5 minutes |
|---|---|
| Your actual teaching time: | _____ |

• After students read and listen, ask *Why does the woman need her jacket cleaned so quickly?* (She needs it for a friend's wedding on the weekend.) *When will the jacket be ready?* (by Thursday, but after four o'clock)

• If necessary, explain that *dry-clean* means to clean cloth / fabric with chemical solvents using little or no water.

## 🎧 Rhythm and intonation practice
### (CD2, Track 4)

| Suggested teaching time: | 5 minutes |
|---|---|
| Your actual teaching time: | _____ |

• Have students repeat each line chorally.
• Make sure students:
  ○ use rising intonation for *Do you think I could get this dry-cleaned by Thursday?*
  ○ use rising intonation for *Thursday?*
  ○ pause after *I'm sorry.*
  ○ stress <u>need</u>, <u>wedding</u> and <u>week</u>end in *I need it for a friend's wedding this weekend.*
  ○ pause before and after *in that case.*
  ○ stress <u>real</u>ly and ap<u>pre</u>ciate in *I really appreciate it.*
  ○ use the following stress pattern:

### STRESS PATTERN

**A:** Do you think I could get this dry-cleaned by Thursday?

**B:** Thursday? That might be difficult.

**A:** I'm sorry, but it's pretty urgent. I need it for a friend's wedding this weekend.

**B:** Well, in that case, I'll see what I can do. But it won't be ready until after four o'clock.

**A:** I really appreciate it. Thanks.

## 🔺A 🎧 VOCABULARY
### (CD2, Track 5)

| Suggested teaching time: | 5–10 minutes |
|---|---|
| Your actual teaching time: | _____ |

• Have students listen and study the phrases. Then have students listen and repeat chorally.

• Pair work. To provide practice, ask students to take turns describing the pictures without using the vocabulary or saying which service it is and then guessing which one it is. Point out that the student describing can talk about people, objects, use any tense, etc., but the person guessing only needs to say <u>the service</u>. Example: Student A: *This person works with clothes. She cleans them but she doesn't wash them in water.* Student B: *Dry clean!* Student B: *This person makes a lot of the same thing. For example, if I have one but I want fifty, this person does this.* Student A: *Copy!* (or *Make copies*)

**Option:** Pair work. Student A closes the book. Student B says a verb from the exercise. Then Student A says the verb plus a noun to make the verb phrase. Example: Student A: *frame* Student B: *frame a picture* Student B: *process* Student A: *process film* **[+5 minutes]**

**Option:** Pair work. To provide more practice, ask students to brainstorm other nouns that can be used with the verbs (except for *process / develop film*). Examples: *dry-clean—a jacket, a raincoat, a blouse; repair—a car, a copier; frame—a painting, a photo; deliver—a letter, a box; lengthen / shorten—pants, a dress; enlarge—artwork, a picture; print—a document, a card* **[+5 minutes]**

> **Language note:** Other ways to say *get a document copied* are *get it duplicated* or *get it xeroxed* /zɪrɑkst/. To *xerox something* comes from the trademark *Xerox,* which is the name of a company that makes copy machines.

 **Vocabulary Cards**

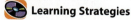 **Learning Strategies**

##  GRAMMAR

| Suggested teaching time: | 10–15 minutes |
|---|---|
| Your actual teaching time: | _____ |

- Direct attention to the Grammar box and have students read the first explanation and study the examples.

- Write on the board:
  1. I <u>got</u> my shoes <u>repaired</u>.
  2. I <u>had</u> my shoes <u>repaired</u>.

- Point out that the passive causative is formed with *got* or *had* + object (*shoes*) + past participle (*repaired*).

- Write on the board:
  3. Kim cleaned the carpet.
  4. Kim had the carpet cleaned.

- To check comprehension of the usage of the passive causative, ask students to identify the difference between the two sentences. (1. Kim cleaned the carpet herself. 2. Someone else cleaned Kim's carpet.)

- Direct attention to the different forms of *get* and *have* in the Grammar box. Point out that the passive causative can be used in all tenses.

- Write on the board:

| I | had | my car repaired. |
|---|---|---|
| | am getting | |
| | will have | |

- Point out that the past participle (*repaired*) remains the same with the different tenses and modals.

- Have students read the last explanation and study the examples.

- Write on the board:
  5. Sue needs to get this report copied.
  6. She needs to get this report copied by Frank.

- Point out that in the first example what is important to know is that Sue needs copies. In the second example *by Frank* is included because <u>who's</u> doing the copying is important for the reader / listener.

**Option:** To provide more practice, draw the following chart on the board. First ask students to add two more activities. Then have them identify which activities they do themselves and which they use services for. Group work. Combine pairs. Students take turns sharing information about themselves and their partner. Example: Student A: *I always clean my house on Fridays. Gina doesn't have time to clean, so she has it cleaned once a week—usually on Mondays.* **[+15 minutes]**

| Activity | Me | My partner |
|---|---|---|
| Clean the house / apartment | | |
| Paint the house / apartment | | |
| Get a haircut | | |
| Wash the car | | |
| Wash clothes | | |
| Other: | | |
| Other: | | |

 **Grammar Self-Checks**

##  🎧 LISTENING COMPREHENSION
(CD2, Track 6)

| Suggested teaching time: | 5 minutes |
|---|---|
| Your actual teaching time: | _____ |

- Pause after each conversation to allow students time to complete the statements.

- To review the answers with the class, have students say the complete sentences.

**AUDIOSCRIPT for Exercise C is on page T31.**

##  Use the cues . . .

| Suggested teaching time: | 5 minutes |
|---|---|
| Your actual teaching time: | _____ |

- Do the first item with the class.

- Review answers by having students read their questions out loud. Make necessary corrections.

## 🅴 PAIR WORK

| Suggested teaching time: | 5 minutes |
|---|---|
| Your actual teaching time: | _____ |

- Role-play the example with a student.

- Walk around the room and provide help as needed. Make sure students are using the passive causative and encourage students to ask each other follow-up questions.

- Ask various pairs to role-play a conversation about a service.

## CONVERSATION **PAIR WORK**

| Suggested teaching time: | 5–10 minutes |
|---|---|
| Your actual teaching time: | _____ |

- To get students ready for the activity, have students read the conversation model on page 28 again. You may want to also have students listen to the model.

- Point out that in the conversation Sue doesn't say *this jacket* but just *this*. Explain that *this, that, these,* and *those* are often used without the noun when the speaker is either holding or pointing to something and it is clear what is being referred to.

- To review the passive causative and services, have students look at Exercise A page 28. Students should take turn saying sentences about different items that match each service. Example: *You can get a jacket or a tie dry-cleaned.* Note: There aren't other possibilities for *developing / processing a film.*

- Review the ideas on the orange tag on the hanger.

- Choose a more confident student and role-play a conversation.

- Walk around the room and provide help as needed.

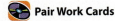 **Pair Work Cards**

## EXTRAS (optional)

**Grammar Booster**
**Workbook: Exercises 4–9**
**Copy & Go: Activity 9**

**B** **GRAMMAR.** **The passive causative** **CN**

Use <u>get</u> or <u>have</u> with an object and the past participle to talk about arranging services.
<u>Get</u> and <u>have</u> have the same meaning in the passive causative.

|  | <u>get</u> / <u>have</u> | object | past participle |  |
|---|---|---|---|---|
| They | **got** | their vacation photos | **enlarged**. |  |
| I need to | **get** | this report | **copied**. |  |
| We | **'re having** | the office | **cleaned** | tomorrow. |
| She can | **have** | her film | **developed** | in an hour. |

A <u>by</u> phrase is used when the speaker thinks that information is important.
We're having the office cleaned **by Royal Cleaning Services**.
They got the copier repaired yesterday. (no <u>by</u> phrase; not necessary to know by whom)

GRAMMAR BOOSTER

PAGE G4
For more …

**C** 🎧 **LISTENING COMPREHENSION.** **Listen to the conversations.**
**Complete each statement with the item and a service.**

1. He wants to get his ___shirts___ ___done___ .
2. She needs to get her ___pants___ ___lengthened___ .
3. He needs to have his ___camera___ ___repaired___ .
4. She wants to have a ___painting___ ___framed___ .

**D** **Use the cues to write questions with the passive causative.**

1. Would it be possible to / these pictures / frame / by next week? ___Would it be possible to get these pictures framed by next week?___

2. Could I / these shoes / repair / here? ___Could I have these shoes repaired here?___

3. Can I / this shirt / dry-clean / by tomorrow? ___Can I get this shirt dry-cleaned by tomorrow?___

4. Where can I / these gloves / gift wrap? ___Where can I have these gloves gift wrapped?___

5. Is it possible to / these photos / enlarge / before 5:00? ___Is it possible to get these photos enlarged before 5:00?___

**E** **PAIR WORK.** **Where do you go for these services? Use the passive causative.**

dry-clean clothes      cut hair      process film      make photocopies

repair shoes

❝ Where do you get your clothes dry-cleaned? ❞

❝ I usually get them dry-cleaned at … ❞

# CONVERSATION
## PAIR WORK

**Role-play asking for express service.** Answers will vary.

**A:** Do you think I could _____ by _____?

**B:** _____? That might be difficult.

**A:** _____ …

**Continue the conversation in your <u>own</u> way.**

Ideas for why you might be in a rush:
for a wedding
for a business trip
for a vacation
for a new job

CONTROLLED PRACTICE

29

# 2 ▶ *Ask for a Recommendation*

 **CONVERSATION MODEL** **Read and listen.**

**A:** I have to get this to Chicago a.s.a.p. Can you recommend a courier service?

**B:** Why don't you have Aero Flash take care of it?

**A:** Have you used them before?

**B:** Sure. They're really reliable. And they can deliver a package anywhere in the world in two business days.

 **Rhythm and intonation practice**

**A** ▶ **GRAMMAR.** **Causatives get, have, and make** **CN**

Use the causative to show that one person causes another person to do something.
With **get**, use an object and an infinitive. With **have**, use an object and a base form of a verb.

|  |  | object | infinitive |  |
|---|---|---|---|---|
| I | **got** | my brother | **to help** | me finish the job. |

|  |  | object | base form |  |
|---|---|---|---|---|
| She | **had** | her assistant | **plan** | the meeting. |

To suggest an obligation, use **make** with an object and a base form.
I **made** my brother **help** me finish the job.

**CN** **Corpus Notes:**
Using an infinitive after *make* and an object, instead of a base form, is a common learner error. Example: *He made them to finish the job early.* Make sure students are aware of this.

GRAMMAR BOOSTER

**PAGES G4–G5**
**For more …**

**B** ▶ **Correct the error in each sentence.**

1. Why don't you have your assistant t~~o~~ call them?
2. Why didn't you get your sister ^to^ help you?
3. I'll never be able to get the dry cleaner ^to^ do this by tomorrow!
4. You should have the hotel t~~o~~ give you your money back.
5. Why don't you make your brother t~~o~~ wash the dishes?
6. I'm sure we can get the store ^to^ process the film in an hour.

**C** ▶  **VOCABULARY.** **Adjectives to describe services.** **Listen and practice.**

**reliable** can be trusted to keep a promise
**reasonable** doesn't charge too much money
**fast** does the job in a short time
**honest** does not lie or cheat
**efficient** doesn't waste time
**helpful** is willing to help
**professional** does a very good job

## LESSON

# 2 ▶ *Ask for a Recommendation*

## 🎧 CONVERSATION **MODEL**
**(CD2, Track 7)**

| Suggested teaching time: | 5–10 minutes |
|---|---|
| Your actual teaching time: | _____ |

- After students read and listen, ask *Where does the package need to go?* (Chicago) *Why does the woman recommend Aero Flash?* (She has used them before, and they are reliable and fast.)
- Point out that *business days* refer to the weekdays.

## 🎧 Rhythm and intonation practice
**(CD2, Track 8)**

| Suggested teaching time: | 5 minutes |
|---|---|
| Your actual teaching time: | _____ |

- Have students repeat each line chorally.
- Make sure students:
  - use rising intonation for *Can you recommend a courier service?*
  - use falling intonation for *Why don't you have Aero . . .*
  - stress new information in a sentence, like <u>Aero Flash</u>.
  - use rising intonation for *Have you used them before?*
  - use the following stress pattern:

**┌─ STRESS PATTERN ─────────────────────**

**A:** I have to get this to Chicago a.s.a.p. Can you

recommend a courier service?

**B:** Why don't you have Aero Flash take care of it?

**A:** Have you used them before?

**B:** Sure. They're really reliable. And they can deliver a

package anywhere in the world in two business days.

**└──────────────────────────────────────**

## Ⓐ GRAMMAR

| Suggested teaching time: | 10–15 minutes |
|---|---|
| Your actual teaching time: | _____ |

- Direct attention to the box and have students read the first explanation and examples.
- Write on the board:

1. I ___ <u>got</u> ___ my sister ___ <u>to help</u> me.
2. ___ <u>had</u> ___ ___ <u>help</u>.

- Point out the two ways to form the causative:
  1. *got* + person / people + infinitive or
  2. *have* + person / people + base form.

- Write on the board:
  3. *I asked my sister to mail the letters.*
  4. *My father asked us to wash his car.*
- Pair work. To check comprehension, ask students to rewrite the sentences will *get* and *have*.
- Review as a class. (3. I had my sister mail the letters. I got my sister to mail the letters. 4. My father had us wash his car. My father got us to wash his car.)
- Have students read the second explanation and study the example.
- Write on the board: 5. *Sally <u>made</u> her son <u>clean</u> his room.*
- Point out that the causative for obligation includes *make* + person / people + the base form. This form means the person or people doing the action <u>don't</u> or <u>didn't</u> have a choice.

> **Language note:** *Get* implies you persuaded the person to do something. *Have* implies you asked the person to do something.

 **Grammar Self-Checks**

## Ⓑ ▶ Correct the error . . .

| Suggested teaching time: | 5 minutes |
|---|---|
| Your actual teaching time: | _____ |

- Review the example first. Remind students that the causative *have* needs the base form, not the infinitive.
- Have students compare answers with a partner.

## Ⓒ ▶ 🎧 VOCABULARY
**(CD2, Track 9)**

| Suggested teaching time: | 5 minutes |
|---|---|
| Your actual teaching time: | _____ |

- Have students listen and study, then repeat.
- Write on the board: *reliable   reasonable   fast   honest*
- Have students number a paper from one (1) to four (4). Have students say which words describe the services they will hear about.
- Say 1. *They can deliver packages in one day.* (fast) You may want to stop after each sentence and go over the answer. 2. *It's true. When they say you can pick it up by four, it's really ready!* (reliable) 3. *If it's not broken, they'll let you know. They don't just fix things and charge you.* (honest) 4. *I know it's a big job, but their prices are actually very good.* (reasonable)
- Tell students to add five (5) to seven (7) on their lists. Then add to the board: *efficient. helpful. professional.*
- Say 5. *They always answer your questions and make you feel comfortable.* (helpful) 6. *They do it fast and well.* (efficient) 7. *They are responsible and they do a good job.* (professional)

 **Vocabulary Cards**

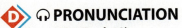 **⌒ PRONUNCIATION**

(CD2, Track 10)

| Suggested teaching time: | 5 minutes |
|---|---|
| Your actual teaching time: | _____ |

• First listening: Have students listen and study the examples.

• Second listening: Have students listen and repeat chorally.

**Option:** Pair work. Students take turns asking and answering questions about services using emphatic stress in their answers. Example: Student A: *Why do you have your clothes dry-cleaned at Brenda's?* Student B: *Because they're incredibly fast.* **[+5 minutes]**

 **Pronunciation Activities**

 **Circle the best adjective . . .**

| Suggested teaching time: | 5 minutes |
|---|---|
| Your actual teaching time: | _____ |

• Review the first item with the class. Make sure students understand the correct adjective is *helpful* because they delivered the product right to their office.

• Encourage students to underline the information that supports their choice of adjective.

• Have students compare answers with a partner. Then review as a class.

**Option:** Pair work. Have students take turns reading each situation out loud using emphatic stress. **[+5 minutes]**

## CONVERSATION **PAIR WORK**

| Suggested teaching time: | 5–10 minutes |
|---|---|
| Your actual teaching time: | _____ |

• To get students ready for the activity, have students read the conversation model on page 30 again. You may also want to have students listen to the model.

• Review the ideas on the right. Make sure students understand they are different situations they can role-play.

• To review adjectives, ask students to choose two adjectives that describe each service provider in the advertisements and to make sentences. Example: *Speedy Copy Services is fast. I think they must also be reliable.*

• Choose a more confident student and role-play a conversation.

• Walk around the room and provide help as needed. Encourage students to use the correct rhythm and intonation.

**Challenge:** Ask various students to report their partner's recommendations to the class. Encourage students to use adjectives to explain why their partner recommended a particular business. **[+10 minutes]**

 **Pair Work Cards**

## EXTRAS (optional)

**Grammar Booster**
**Workbook:** Exercises 10–15
**Copy & Go:** Activity 10

 **Pronunciation Supplements**

**AUDIOSCRIPT**

**AUDIOSCRIPT for Exercise C, page T29**

CONVERSATION 1
**M1:** Can you recommend a good dry-cleaner? I want to get my shirts done and I don't like the place I'm using now.
**M2:** Sure. Try Downtown Cleaners.

CONVERSATION 2
**F1:** I'm looking for a good tailor. My new pants are too short.
**F2:** You should take them to mine. I'm sure you can get them lengthened there.

CONVERSATION 3
**M:** I wonder if you could help me with something. My camera isn't working right. Do you know a good place for repairs?
**F:** You can try Hoyt Camera. People say they're very good.

CONVERSATION 4 [F = French]
**M:** That's a terrific painting. Where'd you get it?
**F:** Oh, we bought that on our trip to New Zealand.
**M:** Really! You should get it framed.
**F:** I'd like to. Got any suggestions where to get that done?
**M:** I'll ask around.

**D** 🎧 **PRONUNCIATION.** **Emphatic stress to express enthusiasm.** **Listen and repeat.**

1. They're **REALly** reliable.
2. They're **inCREDibly** fast.

3. He's **exTREMEly** helpful.
4. She's **SO** professional.

**E** **Circle the best adjective for each situation.**

1. "Link Copy Service was so (reasonable /(helpful)/ honest). They delivered the job to my office before I had to leave for the airport."

2. "I find Portello's to be extremely (professional / fast /(reasonable)). I've shopped around and I can't find another service with such low prices."

3. "If you're looking for a good housecleaning service, I'd recommend Citywide Services. They're incredibly (efficient)/ reliable / honest). They have two people working together to complete the job in no time at all."

4. "What I like about Dom's Auto Service is that they're so (fast / reasonable / (honest)). There are so many other places that you can't trust. But at Dom's they always tell you the truth."

# CONVERSATION
## PAIR WORK

**Role-play asking for a recommendation. Use the guide and the ads, or create your own conversation.** Answers will vary.

**A:** I have to _____ a.s.a.p. Can you recommend a _____?
**B:** Why don't you have _____ take care of it?
**A:** Have you used them before?
**B:** _____ …

**Continue the conversation in your own way.**

**Ideas:**
You need someone to make 200 color copies of a report.

You need someone to send a package to Moscow.

You need someone to dry–clean your suit / dress / jacket before an important meeting.

You need someone to service your car before a long trip.

a copy service

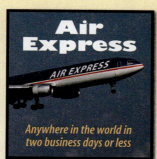
a courier service

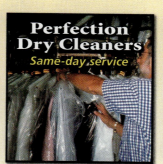
a dry cleaner

an auto repair shop

# 3 ▸ *Evaluate the Quality of Service*

**A** ▸ **READING WARM-UP.** Have you ever bought handmade clothing or other handmade things? Do you prefer handmade or factory-made?

**B** ▸ 🎧 **READING.** Read the tourist information for visitors to Hong Kong. Are there services like these in your city or town?

---

**PLACES TO SHOP**

## HONG KONG TAILORS

The famous Hong Kong 24-hour suit is a thing of the past, but you can still have clothes custom-made in a few days. Today, prices are no longer as low as they once were, but they're often about what you'd pay for a ready-made garment back home; the difference, of course, is that a tailor-made garment should fit you perfectly. The workmanship and quality of the better established shops rival even those of London's Savile Row—at less than half the price. A top-quality men's suit will run about HK$7,000 (US$910) or more, including fabric, while a silk shirt can cost HK$600 (US$78).

Tailors in Hong Kong will make almost any garment you want—suits, evening gowns, wedding dresses, leather jackets, even monogrammed shirts. Many tailors offer a wide range of cloth from which to choose, from cotton and linen to very fine wools, cashmere, and silk. Hong Kong tailors are excellent at copying fashions. Bring a picture or drawing of what you want.

You should allow three to five days to have a garment custom-made, with at least two or three fittings. If you aren't satisfied during the fittings,

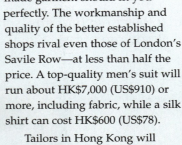

You can choose from a variety of fabrics.

linen
cotton
wool
cashmere
silk

At your first fitting, the tailor will take your measurements. At your next fitting, the tailor will make alterations until you're satisfied.

speak up. Alterations should be included in the original price. If, in the end, you still don't like the finished product, you don't have to accept it. However, you will forfeit the deposit you are required to pay before the tailor begins working, usually about 50% of the total cost.

With more than 2,500 tailoring establishments in Hong Kong, it shouldn't be any problem finding one. Some of the most famous are located in hotel shopping arcades and shopping complexes, but the more upscale the location, the higher the prices.

You can get anything made—from an evening gown to a monogrammed shirt.

Once you've had something custom-made and your tailor has your measurements, you will more than likely be able to order additional clothing later, even after you've returned home!

Be specific about the details you want, such as the lining or the buttons.

**SOURCE:** *Frommer's Hong Kong*, 7th edition

# 3 ► Evaluate the Quality of Service

## A ► READING WARM-UP

| Suggested teaching time: | 5 minutes |
|---|---|
| Your actual teaching time: | _____ |

- Write in two columns on the board:
  handmade    factory-made

- Ask students to say different handmade clothes and factory-made things they have bought and make a list on the board. Encourage students to describe what made them decide to buy an item.

- As students say what they might prefer or like about each form of production, write the reasons under each heading on the board.

> **Language notes:** If necessary, clarify the meaning of *handmade* (made by hand, not by a machine) and *factory-made* (made by a machine in a factory).

## B ► 🎧 READING
### (CD2, Track 11)

| Suggested teaching time: | 10–15 minutes |
|---|---|
| Your actual teaching time: | _____ |

- To practice the reading strategy of scanning have students look at the headline and the photos. Then have them quickly read the text and answer these questions: Examples: *What is the article about?* (Hong Kong tailors, clothes you can have made in Hong Kong) *What can the tailors make?* (suits, gowns, wedding dresses, jackets, monogrammed shirts) *How long does it take for a tailor to finish your garment?* (three to five days) *How many tailor businesses are there in Hong Kong?* (more than 2,500)

- If you need to clarify the meaning of the fabrics, give examples of clothes that are typically made of them. Examples: *Many T-shirts are made of cotton. Jackets and dresses are often made of linen. Warm sweaters are often made of wool or cashmere. Some ties are made of silk.* You can also point to clothes made of the different fabrics if they are available in the classroom.

**Option:** Ask students to imagine they won a prize: a garment of their choice custom-made by a Hong Kong tailor. Pair work. Students take turns saying what garment they would like to have custom-made and when they would wear it. Examples: *I'd like a monogrammed shirt, and I'd wear it at important business meetings. I'd like an evening gown for my sister's wedding.* Ask various students to report to the class about the garments their partners would have custom-made.
[+5 minutes]

**Option:** Use this option if you want to do a listening activity. Books closed. Write the following sentences on the board. Have students listen and put them in the correct order. Then have students read the text to confirm their answers. (a. 5 b. 1 c. 4 d. 2 e. 3)
[+10 minutes]

   a. *Now you can order clothes without having to travel to Hong Kong.*
   b. *Tell the tailor the type of garment you want.*
   c. *Pick up the garment and pay the remaining 50 percent of the price.*
   d. *Pay a deposit of about 50 percent of the total cost.*
   e. *Attend two or three fittings to try on the garment.*

 **Extra Reading Comprehension Activities**

 **Learning Strategies**

 **PAIR WORK**

| Suggested teaching time: | 10 minutes |
|---|---|
| Your actual teaching time: | _____ |

- Ask students to underline any information in the text that supports their answers.
- Have students compare answers with a partner and then review as a class.

 **Extra Reading Comprehension Activities**

 **DISCUSSION**

| Suggested teaching time: | 5–10 minutes |
|---|---|
| Your actual teaching time: | _____ |

- Group work. Form groups of three or four. Encourage students to support their views with examples from the reading text on page 32.
- Ask various students to say whether the Hong Kong tailoring services sound like a good deal to them or not and why.

**Challenge:** Pair work. Ask students to scan the text for at least four advantages in having a garment custom-made in Hong Kong. Have pairs compare answers with another pair. To review, ask students for their answers and write a list on the board. The following are advantages mentioned in the text: **[+10 minutes]**

1. You can have the garment custom-made in only three to five days.
2. The garment will cost as much as a ready-made garment at home.
3. The garment will cost less than half the price it costs in London.
4. The garment will fit you perfectly.
5. You can easily find a tailoring establishment because there are over 2,500.
6. You can find a tailor that suits your price needs.
7. Hong Kong tailors will make almost any kind of garment you want.
8. Hong Kong tailors offer a variety of fabrics to choose from.
9. You don't have to accept the garment if you're not fully satisfied.
10. You can order another garment when you're back home.

## TOP NOTCH **INTERACTION**

| Suggested teaching time: | 15–20 minutes |
|---|---|
| Your actual teaching time: | _____ |

### STEP 1. What services . . . ?

- If necessary, point out that *speed* refers to how fast, *reliability* means you can depend on something, and *workmanship* refers to the quality of someone's work.
- Encourage students who don't remember the name of a business to think of another way to identify it. Examples: *the one on the corner, the one at the mall, the one opposite my office*
- Have students talk to their partners about the reasons why they choose the services they use. Example: *I use RushEx to have my packages delivered because they are cheap. You use FastTrack to have packages delivered because they're fast.*

### STEP 2. DISCUSSION.

- Write on the board:
  *Speed*:
  *Reliability*:
  *Price*:
  *Workmanship*:
- Review adjectives to describe services on page 30. Then have students say which of these adjectives can be used in the categories on the board. Add their answers to the board. (Possible answers: speed: fast, efficient; reliability: reliable, honest, professional; price: reasonable, honest; workmanship: reliable, professional)
- Group work. Form groups of four. Ask students to explain why they recommend a particular local business, using their chart as a guide. Encourage students to use as many adjectives as they can.
- Walk around the room and provide help as needed. Make sure students use the causatives *have, get,* and *make* correctly. Make necessary corrections.

### STEP 3. WRITING.

- Have students look at the advertisements on page 31. Point out how advertisements include the name of the business and some brief information about the quality of the service or the workmanship.
- Remind students to use the vocabulary in this and previous units.
- Walk around the room as students write and provide help as needed.

**Option:** Ask various students to come to the front and write their advertisements on the board. Ask the class questions about the advertisements such as *What's this advertisement for? What's the name of the business? Do they offer a good service? Why?* **[+10 minutes]**

 **Writing Process Worksheets**

### EXTRAS (optional)

Workbook: Exercises 16–19
Copy & Go: Activity 11

**C** **PAIR WORK.** **Check the statements that are true, according to the article. Find the information to support your answers in the reading.**

☑ 1. You used to be able to get a suit made in 24 hours in Hong Kong.

*The famous Hong Kong 24-hour suit is a thing of the past . . .*

☑ 2. If you buy a ready-made garment at a store at home, it will cost about the same as a custom-made garment in Hong Kong.

*. . . but they're often about what you'd pay for a ready-made garment back home . . .*

☐ 3. If you get a garment made on Savile Row, you will pay about 50 percent less than you would pay for the same garment made in Hong Kong.

*The workmanship and quality of the better established shops rival even those of London's Savile Row—at less than half the price.*

☐ 4. If you don't like the garment you ordered, you can get all your money back.

☐ 5. If you want to pay a low price for a custom-made garment, go to an upscale hotel shopping arcade. *. . . the more upscale the location, the higher the prices.*

*However, you will forfeit the deposit you are required to pay . . . about 50% of the total cost.*

**D** **DISCUSSION.** **Do you think the Hong Kong tailoring services described in the tour guide sound like "a good deal"? What's more important to you—price or quality?**

---

# TOP NOTCH
## INTERACTION • *They're the best!*

**STEP 1.** **What services do you use? Complete the chart. Write the name of the business, and check the reasons why you use that service. Then compare your chart with your partner's.** *Answers will vary.*

| | name of business | speed | reliability | price | workmanship | location |
|---|---|---|---|---|---|---|
| dry cleaning | | ☐ | ☐ | ☐ | ☐ | ☐ |
| photo processing | | ☐ | ☐ | ☐ | ☐ | ☐ |
| auto repair | | ☐ | ☐ | ☐ | ☐ | ☐ |
| bicycle repair | | ☐ | ☐ | ☐ | ☐ | ☐ |
| tailoring | | ☐ | ☐ | ☐ | ☐ | ☐ |
| express delivery | | ☐ | ☐ | ☐ | ☐ | ☐ |
| shoe repair | | ☐ | ☐ | ☐ | ☐ | ☐ |
| hair stylist | | ☐ | ☐ | ☐ | ☐ | ☐ |
| other: | | ☐ | ☐ | ☐ | ☐ | ☐ |

**STEP 2.** **DISCUSSION.** **Recommend local businesses to your classmates. Explain why you use them.**

> **❝**I always get my clothes dry-cleaned at Royal Dry Cleaners on 45th Road. They're really fast, and the prices are quite reasonable.**❞**

**STEP 3.** **WRITING.** **Write an advertisement for a local service that you use and like. Describe the quality of the service and the workmanship.**

# Plan a Social Event

**A** 🎧 **VOCABULARY.** Steps for planning a social event. Listen and practice.

**make a guest list**

**pick a date, time, and place**

**make a budget**

**assign responsibilities**

**send out invitations**

**call a caterer**

**hire a DJ**

**decorate the room**

**B** 🎧 **LISTENING COMPREHENSION.** Listen to the conversation. Number the steps in order. Then listen again and check who will do each step.

| | | She'll do it herself. | She'll get help. |
|---|---|:---:|:---:|
| _1_ | make a guest list | ☑ | ☐ |
| _3_ | pick a date and time | ☑ | ☐ |
| _4_ | pick a place | ☑ | ☐ |
| _2_ | make a budget | ☑ | ☐ |
| _9_ | assign responsibilities | ☑ | ☐ |
| _8_ | send out invitations | ☐ | ☑ |
| _5_ | call a caterer | ☑ | ☐ |
| _6_ | hire a DJ | ☑ | ☐ |
| _7_ | decorate the room | ☐ | ☑ |

# LESSON

# 4 *Plan a Social Event*

## A 🎧 VOCABULARY
**(CD2, Track 12)**

| Suggested teaching time: | 10–15 minutes |
|---|---|
| Your actual teaching time: | _____ |

- Have students listen and study the phrases.
- Then have students listen and repeat chorally.
- To provide more practice, write the following words and the chart (without answers) on the board. Books closed. Then ask students to fill in the words to match the correct verb.

| | | | |
|---|---|---|---|
| a caterer | a date | a budget | responsibilities |
| a guest list | invitations | a task | the walls |
| a DJ | the room | a time | holiday cards |

| make | call or hire | pick | assign | decorate | send out |
|---|---|---|---|---|---|
| a budget | a DJ | a date | responsibilities | the room | invitations |
| a guest list | a caterer | a time | a task | the walls | holiday cards |

 **Graphic Organizers**

**Language note:** If necessary, clarify the meaning of *DJ* (*disc jockey:* someone who plays records, tapes, and CDs to provide music at a party), *caterer* (a person or a company that is paid to provide and serve food and drinks at an event), and *budget* (a plan of how much you'll spend and how you will spend it).

 **Vocabulary Cards**

## B 🎧 LISTENING COMPREHENSION
**(CD2, Track 13)**

| Suggested teaching time: | 15–20 minutes |
|---|---|
| Your actual teaching time: | _____ |

- Before listening, tell students they are going to listen to a woman talk about plans for a party. Clarify that they will listen two times and write the numbers to order the steps. Then they will listen again to identify who will do each step.
- First listening: Students should listen for when the speaker will do things. Let them know the speaker sometimes backtracks during the conversation. Have students compare answers.
- Second listening: Listen to confirm answers.
- Review the order of the steps as a class.
- Third listening: Have students listen and identify which tasks the speaker will do and which tasks others will do.
- Review answers as a class. You may want to have students listen again to confirm the correct answers.

 **Learning Strategies**

## AUDIOSCRIPT

**F:** Ugh. My boss is making me plan the holiday party this year.

**M:** What's wrong with that? Sounds like fun.

**F:** It's a LOT of work. This is a pretty big event, you know. Over a hundred people! I don't even know where to begin.

**M:** Well, what needs to be done first?

**F:** Oh, I guess I could start by choosing the date and time.

**M:** Well, why don't you talk to your colleagues and get a sense of what they'd like to do?

**F:** Not a bad idea.

**M:** Then what?

**F:** Then I guess it's the location. I hated the place where they held the party last year. It was way too close to the office.

**M:** What was wrong with that?

**F:** Who wants to party near the office? I want to try something different—in a fun part of town. You know?

**M:** Oh, I get it. How about down around the city market? A lot of people have events around there.

**F:** Great idea! I'll make some phone calls tomorrow. And maybe I can get some of my colleagues to give me some more ideas.

**M:** Makes sense. So then what?

**F:** Well, with so many people coming, I guess the guest list would be the next thing to think about.

**M:** Come to think of it, you should probably make the guest list BEFORE you choose a place. You've got to know how many people you're going to have first.

**F:** Good point. I'll do that tomorrow before I make any phone calls.

**M:** What about food? You must get a big event like this catered, right?

**F:** Oh, definitely. This is a pretty formal event.

**M:** Well, that would be the next step. Once you know how many people are coming and where it's going to be. Who knows, you might want to have it right in a restaurant.

**F:** Right ... Hey, wait a minute! We missed something important. I've got to make a budget first.

**M:** Like right after you've made your guest list, right?

**F:** Right. Because I'll know then how much I can spend per person. See what I mean? There's a lot to do!

**M:** So far so good. What's next?

**F:** Well, we've got to have music. So I'll need to find a DJ.

**M:** You know, one of the guys at work—his wife does that. Want me to get her number for you?

**F:** That would be great. Thanks. Oh, and decorations! They usually do a great job decorating the room for these parties. I'm sure I can get someone to take care of that. I'd better include it on my list so I don't forget.

**M:** Well ... that sounds pretty much like everything, no?

**F:** I think so ... Ah—invitations. They're going to want me to send out some nice invitations to get everyone in the mood.

**M:** OK, that should be everything. So—why don't you get some help from your colleagues. Surely you're not expected to do it all, right?

**F:** No, you're right. When I'm done I'll make a list and assign responsibilities. There are at least five people in the office who have already said they'd help. I'm sure I can get them to do the invitations and decorations. And I can take care of the rest.

**M:** Not too bad.

**F:** Thanks. That really helped.

**T34**

# TOP NOTCH **INTERACTION**

Suggested teaching time:  20–25 minutes
Your actual teaching time:  _____

## STEP 1. Take the survey . . .

- Clarify that there are four tasks for Step 1:  Fill out the survey, add up the checks in each column to find the description that matches, check the descriptions under the survey to find out which one describes you, and then talk to a partner.

- Take a poll to see which students matched the different descriptions.

- Ask various students if they agree with the result of their survey.

**Language note:** If necessary, clarify the meaning of *wild* (exciting and fun) and *the best of both worlds* (enjoying the advantages of two different things at the same time).

## STEP 2. GROUP WORK.

- Have students look at the pictures in the ideas box.  If necessary, clarify the meaning of a *TGIF party* (a party where people celebrate that the work week is finished because it's Friday), *a talent show* (a party in which people show how well they sing, dance, tell jokes, etc.), and a *karaoke* /kɑeriouki/ *party* (a party where people sing to recorded music for fun).

- Brainstorm and write on the board other social events the class might like to attend.  Examples: *going bowling, having dinner, having a picnic, going dancing, going to a concert,* etc.

- Review phrases for making suggestions during the discussion.  Examples: *Why don't we . . . ?  How about . . . ?  Maybe we could . . . I think we should . . .*

- Form groups of three or four.  Encourage each group to choose one social event to plan.

- Ask various groups to summarize for the class the event they planned.

**Culture note:**  In the U.S. and Canada people say T-G-I-F (Thank Goodness It's Friday) to show they are happy the work or school week is finished and the weekend is coming.  Karaoke /kɑeriouki/, which originated in Japan, is an event where people sing famous pop songs along with the original music.

## EXTRAS (optional)

**Workbook:  Exercises 20–23**
**Copy & Go:  Activity 12**

**STEP 1.** **Take the survey. Compare your answers with a partner's.** Answers will vary.

# What kind of
# personality
# do you have?

### Check which activities you would rather do. Choose from column A or column B.

| Column A | | Column B |
|---|---|---|
| ○ spend money | **or** | ○ plan a budget |
| ○ assign responsibility | **or** | ○ take responsibility |
| ○ design invitations | **or** | ○ send invitations |
| ○ play your own music | **or** | ○ hire a DJ |
| ○ decorate a room | **or** | ○ make a guest list |
| ○ bring your own food | **or** | ○ call a caterer |
| ○ dance | **or** | ○ watch other people dance |
| ○ sing | **or** | ○ listen to other people sing |
| ○ hire someone to clean | **or** | ○ clean up after a party |

### If you chose:

**five or more from column A,**
   you're the wild and creative type! You'd be a lot of fun at a party!

**five or more from column B,**
   you're a born leader! You could plan a great party!

**about the same from each column,**
   you're the best of both worlds!

**Some ideas:**

An end-of-year party? A birthday party? A TGIF* party?
*Thank Goodness It's Friday!

A talent show? A karaoke party?

An English practice day?

**STEP 2.** **GROUP WORK.** **Plan a social event for your class. Choose a type of event and discuss the steps you would need to take. Write the actions in your notepad.**

| Type of event: | |
|---|---|
| Steps: | |
| | |
| | |
| | |
| | |
| | |

**A** 🎧 **LISTENING COMPREHENSION.** **Listen to each conversation.**
**Write a sentence to describe what the customer needs and when.**

1. _She needs to get her dress dry-cleaned by Friday._
2. _He needs to get his pants shortened by Wednesday._
3. _He needs his film processed by 4:00._
4. _She needs to get a sign printed by Wednesday._

**B** **Complete each statement or question with a noun. Use your own words.** Answers may vary.
Possible answers include:

1. Can I get my _____suit_____ dry-cleaned here?
2. I'd like to have these _____pants_____ lengthened.
3. Where can I get these _____skirts_____ shortened?
4. Can you tell me where I can get some _____reports_____ copied?
5. Where did she get her _____pictures_____ framed?
6. How much did he pay to have his _____shoes_____ repaired?
7. I need to get some _____signs_____ printed.
8. I'm in a hurry to have my _____film_____ processed.

**C** **Complete each causative statement in your own way.**
**Begin with the base form of a verb or an infinitive.** Answers may vary. Possible answers include:

1. I got the teacher _to help me with my writing_ .
2. At the end of the meal, I had the waiter _bring the bill_ .
3. Before my last vacation, I got the travel agent _to reserve a car for me_ .
4. When I was young, my mother always made me _clean my room_ .
5. When you arrive, you should get the hotel _to make an appointment for you_
6. Don't forget to have the gas station attendant _wash the windshield_ .
7. If you come for dinner, I promise I won't make you _wash the dishes_ .
8. Sad movies always make me _feel sad_ .
9. Maybe you can get your friend _to come with us_ .
10. You should have Air Express Courier Service _deliver it_ .

**D** **WRITING.** **What kinds of services are difficult to find?**
**Write about the services you would like to have in your**
**neighborhood.**

🎵 **TOP NOTCH SONG**
"I'll Get Back to You"
Lyrics on last book page.

▶ **TOP NOTCH PROJECT**
Have a real social event for
the class. Invite other classes
to join you.

▶ **TOP NOTCH WEBSITE**
For Unit 3 online activities,
visit the *Top Notch*
Companion Website at
www.longman.com/topnotch.

# UNIT 3 CHECKPOINT

 **A** 🎧 **LISTENING COMPREHENSION**
(CD2, Track 14)

| | |
|---|---|
| Suggested teaching time: | 10–15 minutes |
| Your actual teaching time: | _____ |

- Review the example first by listening to the first conversation.
- Pause after each conversation to allow students time to write.
- Review as a class by having students read the sentences out loud. Make any necessary corrections.

**AUDIOSCRIPT**

CONVERSATION 1
**F:** I'd like to get this dress dry-cleaned.
**M:** OK. It'll be ready on Monday.
**F:** I'm in a bit of a rush. Any chance I could get it done by Friday?
**M:** I'll see what we can do.

CONVERSATION 2
**M1:** I need to get these pants shortened. Can I get them back Wednesday?
**M2:** I don't know. We're pretty busy this week.
**M1:** I'd really appreciate it.
**M2:** We'll try. But it might not be ready till Thursday. OK?

CONVERSATION 3
**M:** Can you do a rush on processing this film?
**F:** That depends. When do you need it by?
**M:** How about 4:00?
**F:** Oh, that should be no problem. With our one-hour service, you'll have it by three.
**M:** Terrific!

CONVERSATION 4
**F:** I'd like to get a sign printed. Does it take long to do?
**M:** Just one sign? Not too long. You can have it by Thursday.
**F:** Gee. I'd appreciate it if you could get it done a little sooner. I'm on a bit of a tight schedule.
**M:** How about Wednesday? Is that OK?
**F:** That would be perfect. Thanks.

**B** **Complete each . . .**

| | |
|---|---|
| Suggested teaching time: | 5 minutes |
| Your actual teaching time: | _____ |

- Encourage students to look at the verbs used to help them decide how to complete each item.
- Have students compare answers with a partner.
- Ask various students for their information and make a list of possible answers on the board.

**Option:** To provide further practice, have volunteers reply to your statements with a passive causative question. *Why don't you ___?* Remind students to use the vocabulary from the unit and *get* or *have.* Examples: *My pants are too long.* (Why don't you have them shortened?) *The copier is broken.* (Why don't you have it repaired?) *I've bought a beautiful painting.* (Why don't you have it framed?) *My white jacket is stained with blue ink.* (Why don't you have it dry-cleaned?) *I need 50 copies of this test a.s.a.p.* (Why don't you have it copied at Quick Copy Service?) *I need a new sign for the door of this room.* (Why don't you have it printed?) **[+5 minutes]**

**C** **Complete each causative . . .**

| | |
|---|---|
| Suggested teaching time: | 5 minutes |
| Your actual teaching time: | _____ |

- Write on the board:

| I | got had made | my brother _____ |
|---|---|---|

- To review, have volunteers create sentences. Examples: *I got my brother to drive me to school. I had my brother buy my concert ticket.* Point out the corresponding structure: *get* + person + infinitive; *have* + person + base form.
- Review the function of the causative *make:* someone is obligated to do something.
- After students complete the statements, have them compare answers with a partner. Then review as a class.

**D** **WRITING**

| | |
|---|---|
| Suggested teaching time: | 10–15 minutes |
| Your actual teaching time: | _____ |

- Before students write, brainstorm services that are difficult to find in the area of the school or where students live and write them on the board.
- Encourage students to use the adjectives to describe the quality of the services they would like the businesses to have.
- Walk around the room and provide help as needed.

 **Writing Process Worksheets**

 *Top Notch Pop* **Song Activities** (CD2, Track 15)

***TOP NOTCH* PROJECT**

**Idea:** As a class, make a list of the guests who will be invited. Form four groups and assign each group one of the following to think about and plan: food and drinks, music, invitations, decorations. Encourage each group to take notes as it plans. Finally, have each group report its ideas and suggestions to the class. Once the class has agreed on the details, pick a date, send out the invitations, and have fun!

**T36**

# UNIT WRAP-UP

| Suggested teaching time: | 15–20 minutes |
|---|---|
| Your actual teaching time: | _____ |

## Social Language

• Have students look at the picture. Review what kinds of problems the man in the pictures is having today. You may want to give the man a name. (He needs to get a package to L.A. right away, the copier doesn't work, his pants are too long, he got in a car accident / he hit something with his car).

┌─ **Your students can say . . .** ─┐

**A:** I have to get this to Los Angeles / L.A. a.s.a.p. Can you recommend a courier service? **B:** Why don't you have [AirTran] take care of it? **A:** Have you used them before? **B:** Yes. They are really [reliable].

**A:** I'm looking for a good courier service. I need to get this package delivered to Los Angeles. **B:** You can try [FlyBy]. They're extremely [efficient].

**A:** The copier isn't working right. Do you know a good service? **B:** Yes. You can have [QuickFix] repair it. They are really [reasonable].

**A:** Do you think I could get these pants shortened by [Thursday]? **B:** [Thursday]? That might be difficult. **A:** I'm sorry but I need them for a/an [business dinner] on [Friday night]. **B:** Well, in that case, I'll see what I can do. **A:** I really appreciate it. Thanks.

**A:** I need to get my car repaired. Can you do it this week? **B:** I don't know. I'm very busy this week. **A:** Can you get it done next week? **B:** Yes. Next week would be fine.

**A:** I need my car repaired. **B:** What happened? **A:** Well, I hit the wall in the garage. **B:** Oh, no! What do you need to have done? **A:** I need to get a new headlight.

**Challenge: Service anyone?** Group work. Form groups of four. Ask students to make a list of all the services they used or requested this week. Ask each group to check and correct the statements in their group. Walk around the room and provide help as needed. **[+10 minutes]**

## Grammar

• Pair work. Ask students to write as many sentences as they can.

• Ask students to exchange papers with another pair and read each other's lists.

┌─ **Your students can say . . .** ─┐

He has to get a package delivered. He needs to have the package in L.A. by tonight! He needs to get the copier repaired. He needs to have some documents copied. He wants to have his pants shortened. He needs to get his car repaired. He needs to make an appointment for the car.

## Writing

• Draw a chart on the board:

| Where? | What happened? | What does he need or want? |
|---|---|---|
| In the office | | |
| After work | | |
| At home | | |

 **Graphic Organizers**

• Before students write, ask them to make notes in the chart. Point out that the chart can help them organize their ideas.

• Tell students to use specific sentence beginnings such as *In the office, After work,* and *At home* in their paragraphs.

• Remind students to use the vocabulary and grammar from this and previous units.

• As students write, walk around the room and provide help as needed.

┌─ **Individual oral progress check (optional)** ─┐

• Use the illustration on page 37. Encourage the student to use material (vocabulary, grammar, rhythm and intonation) practiced in this unit.

• Evaluate the student on correctness and intelligibility.

• Tell the student to answer questions using the passive causative. Examples: *Why is the man holding a package?* (He has to get it delivered) *What does the man's colleague say about the copy machine?* (You need to call someone and have it repaired.) *What is he telling the woman who is wearing glasses?* (He wants to have his pants shortened.) *Why is he phoning Bart's Auto Repair?* (He has to have his car repaired a.s.a.p.)

• Point to the top right-hand picture (the man holding the package) and tell the student that together you are going to role-play a conversation. The situation is that the man needs a recommendation for a good courier service. Remind the student to use the causative passive with *get, have,* and *make* when possible. Tell the student that you are the woman and you will start. Example: T: *Hi, [Joe]. What's going on?* S: *Hi, [Sue]. I need to get this package to L.A. tonight! Can you recommend a reliable courier service?* T: *Yes. It's called AlreadyThere.* S: *Are they fast? I made my boss give me this project, so it's really important!* S: *Well, I had to have a package delivered to Japan overnight last week and they were fast and reasonable.* T: *OK, thanks.*

 **Cumulative Vocabulary Activities**

 You may wish to use the video and activity worksheets for Unit 3 at this point.

**Complete Assessment Package**
**Unit 3 Achievement Test**

## UNIT WRAP-UP

- **Social Language.** Create conversations for the people.
  *I've got to get this to Los Angeles a.s.a.p.*

- **Grammar.** Use the passive causative to describe the services the man wants or needs.

- **Writing.** Tell the story of the man's day.

**Now I can ...**

- ☐ request express service.
- ☐ ask for a recommendation.
- ☐ evaluate the quality of service.
- ☐ plan a social event.

37

# UNIT 4

## Life Choices

**UNIT GOALS**

1. Explain a change in life and work ch[...]
2. Express regrets about decisions
3. Discuss skills, abilities, and qualificati[...]
4. Discuss work and life decisions

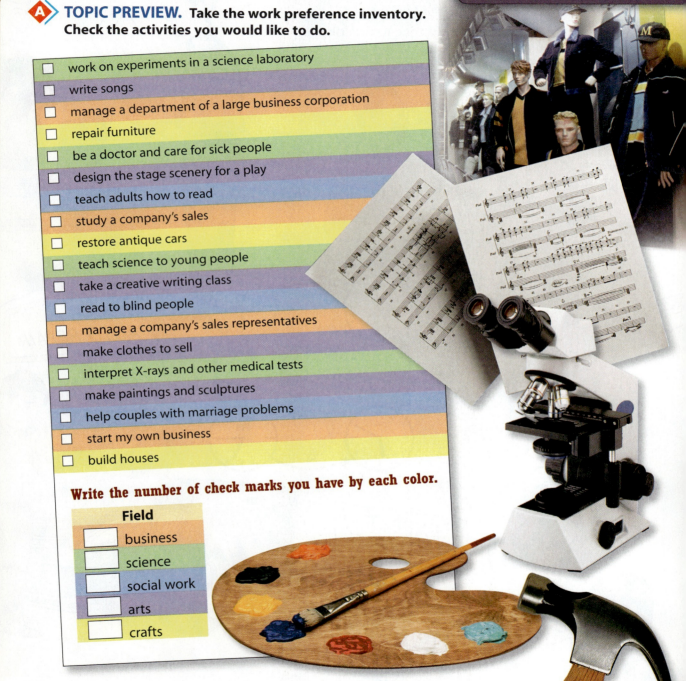

**A** ▷ **TOPIC PREVIEW.** Take the work preference inventory. Check the activities you would like to do.

- ☐ work on experiments in a science laboratory
- ☐ write songs
- ☐ manage a department of a large business corporation
- ☐ repair furniture
- ☐ be a doctor and care for sick people
- ☐ design the stage scenery for a play
- ☐ teach adults how to read
- ☐ study a company's sales
- ☐ restore antique cars
- ☐ teach science to young people
- ☐ take a creative writing class
- ☐ read to blind people
- ☐ manage a company's sales representatives
- ☐ make clothes to sell
- ☐ interpret X-rays and other medical tests
- ☐ make paintings and sculptures
- ☐ help couples with marriage problems
- ☐ start my own business
- ☐ build houses

**Write the number of check marks you have by each color.**

| | Field |
|---|---|
| ☐ | business |
| ☐ | science |
| ☐ | social work |
| ☐ | arts |
| ☐ | crafts |

**B** ▷ **DISCUSSION.** Which field did you have the most check marks for? What are some jobs in that field? Do you have a job in that field now? Would you like to? Is that job the same job you wanted when you were younger?

# Life Choices

## A TOPIC PREVIEW

| Suggested teaching time: | 5–10 minutes |
|---|---|
| Your actual teaching time: | _____ |

- Before students start the activity, have them look at the pictures. Ask *What jobs or occupations could be represented by the pictures?* Encourage students to say the jobs or occupations, not the objects that represent them. Examples: *fashion designer or model, musician or composer, scientist or doctor, painter or artist, carpenter or builder.*

- Ask students to review the activities listed and tell them that a *work preference inventory* is a list of tasks or activities to measure or show someone's occupational interests.

- You may want to ask if anyone has ever taken this type of inventory before.

- Have students check the activities they are interested in, count up check marks according to color, and write the totals at the bottom (according to color).

**Language note:** A *craft* is a job or occupation that requires skills to make or fix things, such as furniture, jewelry, objects out of glass, etc.

**Culture note:** Career inventories can help people have a better understanding of what their job / career options are. These inventories and assessments are designed to measure someone's interests or skills, indicate personality preferences, and identify work-related and life values. In most English-speaking countries, these tools are used by career guidance companies and even schools with the goal of helping people make successful career choices.

- ○ Science: scientist, researcher, doctor, technician, biologist
- ○ Social work: social worker, therapist, marriage counselor
- ○ Arts: songwriter, musician, painter, sculptor, fashion designer, graphic designer
- ○ Crafts: woodworker, builder, carpenter, architect, jewelry designer

- Ask students about what they do now. Examples: *Does their present job match the results of their inventory? Are they doing now what they had thought about as a child?*

- Note: If many of your students have not yet entered the workforce, ask them to talk about what kind of job or career they are thinking about in the future. Encourage them to give reasons for their choices and to ask each other follow-up questions. Example: Student A: *I really want to be a doctor.* Student B: *A doctor? Why?* Student A: *I like learning about the body and how it works.* Student C: *But are you interested in working with people?* Student A: *Yes. I especially want to work with children.*

- For a class not yet in the workforce, take a poll to see which fields the students are most interested in.

**Option:** Group work. Form small groups. Ask students to take turns talking about the jobs and occupations of family members and friends. Are most of them happy in their jobs? Are they doing what they had thought about or dreamed about when they were young? **[+10 minutes]**

## B DISCUSSION

| Suggested teaching time: | 10 minutes |
|---|---|
| Your actual teaching time: | _____ |

- Group work. Form groups of two or three.

- Work with the class to identify different jobs in the fields. Write the different fields in columns on the board.

  Business   Science   Social work   Arts   Crafts

- Then ask the groups to make lists of jobs or occupations in each field. Students can also use items from the list of activities above.

- Students may say:

- ○ Business: manager, sales analyst, accountant, sales director, stockbroker

##  SOUND BITES

(CD2, Track 17)

| | |
|---|---|
| Suggested teaching time: | 10 minutes |
| Your actual teaching time: | _____ |

- Note: Ann has a Jamaican accent.
- Write the following questions on the board:
  1. *What is the relationship between the women? Give your reasons.*
  2. *What is the woman in pink daydreaming (thinking) about?*
- Pair work. Before reading and listening, ask students to look at the pictures and predict the answers to these questions. Ask various students for their ideas and write them on the board. (Students may say: 1. mother / daughter, boss / employee, co-workers, teacher / student 2. an important decision, her job, a problem)
- After reading and listening, ask students for answers to the questions on the board based on the conversation. (1. boss / employee or co-workers 2. changing her career / job)
- Point out the ellipsis (omission of words or phrases) *Think so?* The full form is *Do you think so?*

> **Language note:** Students may need help with the following words: *daydream* (to think about something nice, for example, something you would like to happen, especially when this makes you forget what you should be doing); *a shortage* (a situation in which there is not enough of something).

##  Check the statements . . .

| | |
|---|---|
| Suggested teaching time: | 5 minutes |
| Your actual teaching time: | _____ |

- Encourage students to underline the information in the conversation that supports their answers. (1. Since when have you been interested in . . . 2. . . . instead of doing these useless reports 3. I wish I'd gone to medical school . . . 4. Maybe it's not too late.)
- Have students compare answers with a partner. Then review as a class.

## IN OTHER WORDS

| | |
|---|---|
| Suggested teaching time: | 5–10 minutes |
| Your actual teaching time: | _____ |

- Encourage students to identify who says each statement and to use the context of the conversation to help work out the meaning.
- Have students compare answers with a partner. Then review as a class.

## WHAT ABOUT **YOU?**

| | |
|---|---|
| Suggested teaching time: | 10–15 minutes |
| Your actual teaching time: | _____ |

- If you think your students will feel more comfortable with less personal topics, you may want to use the following topics instead. Write on the board:
  *a car you bought / didn't buy*
  *a trip you took / didn't take*
  *an invitation you accepted / didn't accept*
  *an investment you made / didn't make*
  *other:*
- Encourage students to make notes about any regrets and the decisions they wish they could change before they speak.
- Group work. Form groups of three or four. Remind students to ask each other follow-up questions to find out why their partners regret a decision and what they wish they could change now.
- Walk around the room and provide help as needed.
- Ask various students to briefly tell the class about one decision they wish they could change.

**Challenge: Writing task.** Ask students to write a paragraph explaining a decision they regret and the change they would like to make. **[+ 15 minutes]**

## EXTRAS (optional)

**Workbook:** Exercises 1–5

**C** 🎧 **SOUND BITES.** Read along silently as you listen to a natural conversation.

**ANN:** Ruth! This report's due tomorrow. What are you dreaming about?

**RUTH:** You know, I wish I'd gone to medical school instead of business school.

**ANN:** What? Since when have you been interested in medicine? **CN1**

**RUTH:** Well, when I read about doctor shortages and terrible diseases, I think about how I could have made a difference in this world, an important difference… instead of doing these useless reports!

**ANN:** Well, you're young. Maybe it's not too late.

**RUTH:** Think so?

**ANN:** Sure. But do you think maybe you could get your head out of the clouds and get back on task now? **CN2**

**RUTH:** Sorry about that. You can count on me.

**CN1** Corpus Notes:
*Interested* is immediately followed by *in* more than any other word in both spoken and written English.

**D** **Check the statements that are true.**

☑ 1. Ann is surprised to hear about Ruth's interest in medicine.
☐ 2. Ruth thinks business is more useful than medicine.
☑ 3. Ruth would like to be a doctor.
☑ 4. Ann suggests that it's possible for Ruth to change careers.

**CN2** Corpus Notes:
In spoken English, common collocations with *task* are *get (back) on task, stay on task,* or *be on task. On track* has the same meaning and is slightly more common.

**E** **IN OTHER WORDS.** With a partner, restate each of the following statements in another way.
Answers may vary. Possible answers include:

1. "I could have made a difference in this world…" I could have done something more important than this.

2. "Maybe it's not too late." You can still do it.

3. "…could [you] get your head out of the clouds and get back on task now?" Can you stop thinking about that now, and get your work done?

4. "You can count on me." You can trust me to get it done.

---

**WHAT ABOUT YOU?**

**What regrets do you have in your life? What decisions do you wish you could change?**

☐ a job choice          ☐ your studies          ☐ a friendship that ended
☐ a job change          ☐ your marriage / divorce          ☐ other: _____

# 1 Explain a Change in Life and Work Choices

## 🎧 CONVERSATION MODEL  Read and listen.

**A:** Hey, Art! Long time no see. **CN1**

**B:** Ben! How have you been?

**A:** Not bad, thanks. So what are you doing these days?

**B:** Well, I'm in dental school.

**A:** No kidding! I thought you had other plans.

**B:** That's right. I was going to be an artist, but I changed my mind.

**A:** How come?

**B:** Well, it's hard to make a living as a painter! **CN2**

**CN1 Corpus Notes:** Students should be aware that *Long time no see* is a fixed phrase that stands alone. Learners commonly make errors with this expression like *It's been a long time no see* or *Long time no see for six years.*

## 🎧 Rhythm and intonation practice

**CN2 Corpus Notes:** A person can *make a living as a [doctor/cook etc.]* or *make a living by [teaching/selling cars etc.].* Use of *as* and a job title is the most frequent.

**A** **GRAMMAR. Future in the past: <u>was</u> / <u>were going to</u> and <u>would</u>**

Use <u>was</u> / <u>were going to</u> + the base form of a verb to express future plans someone had in the past.
  I **was going to get** married, but I changed my mind.
  I believed I **was going to have** a lot of children, but I was wrong.

  **Weren't** you **going to study** law?       Yes, I was. / No, I wasn't.
  Who **was going to teach** this class?       My sister was.
  Where **were they going to study**?       In Prague.

<u>Would</u> + the base form of the verb can also express future in the past, but only after statements of knowledge or belief.
  She thought she **would be** a doctor, but she changed her mind.
  We always believed they **would get** married, but they never did.

GRAMMAR BOOSTER
**PAGES G5–G7**
For more …

**B** Read each person's New Year's resolution from January 2000, the turn of the century. Write what each person was going to do.

Ivan Potok

Marie Duclos

Sylvia Strook

Robert Park

"I'm going to stop smoking."
*Ivan was going to stop smoking.*

"I'm going to apply to law school."
*Marie was going to apply to law school.*

"I'm going to find a husband."
*Sylvia was going to find a husband.*

"I'm going to marry Sylvia Strook."
*Robert was going to marry Sylvia.*

# LESSON 1

# Explain a Change in Life and Work Choices

## 🎧 CONVERSATION **MODEL**

**(CD2, Track 18)**

| | |
|---|---|
| Suggested teaching time: | 5 minutes |
| Your actual teaching time: | _____ |

- After students read and listen, ask *What school is Art in?* (dental school) *Why is his friend Ben surprised?* (Ben thought Art wanted to do something else.) *Why did Art change his mind?* (He wanted to make more money. / He wouldn't earn much money as a painter.)
- Point out that *Not bad* in this context means *I'm OK* or *I'm all right.*

## 🎧 Rhythm and intonation practice

**(CD2, Track 19)**

| | |
|---|---|
| Suggested teaching time: | 5 minutes |
| Your actual teaching time: | _____ |

- Have students repeat each line chorally.
- Make sure students:
  - use falling intonation for *How have you been?* and *So what are you doing these days?*
  - pause after *Well* and after *but.*
  - use falling intonation for *but I changed my mind* and *How come?*
  - use the following stress pattern:

### STRESS PATTERN

**A:** Hey, Art! Long time no see.

**B:** Ben! How have you been?

**A:** Not bad, thanks. So what are you doing these days?

**B:** Well, I'm in dental school.

**A:** No kidding! I thought you had other plans.

**B:** That's right. I was going to be an artist, but I changed my mind.

**A:** How come?

**B:** Well, it's hard to make a living as a painter!

## 🔺Ⓐ GRAMMAR

| | |
|---|---|
| Suggested teaching time: | 5–10 minutes |
| Your actual teaching time: | _____ |

- Direct attention to the box and have students read the first explanation and study the examples.

---

- To check comprehension, ask students questions. *What plans did this person have?* (to get married) *Did she get married?* (No.) *Why not?* (She changed her mind.)
- To help clarify, say *Use the future in the past to talk about things you planned to do. Maybe you did or didn't do them.*
- Point out the words in blue and review how to form the future in the past: *was / were going to* + base form of the verb.
- Group work. Form groups of three. Have students say one thing they wanted to do but didn't. They should give the reason why they didn't. Tell students to write notes about what their partners say to use in the next activity. Examples: *I was going to buy a new car, but I didn't have enough money. We were going to go on vacation, but my sister broke her leg.*
- Then have students in the same groups ask each other detail questions using the future in the past. Examples: Student A: *When were you going to buy a car?* B: *At the end of summer.* Student C: *Where were you going to go on vacation?* Student A: *To Hawaii!*
- Have students read the last explanation and study the examples.
- Review the four verbs of knowledge and belief: *think, believe, know, be sure.*
- Write on the board:
  1. *She thought he was going to the party.*
  2. *They knew they were going to be late.*
- To check comprehension, ask students to rewrite these sentences using *would* + base form to express future in the past. (1. She thought he would go . . . 2. They knew they would be . . .)

 **Grammar Self-Checks**

## 🔶Ⓑ Read each person's . . .

| | |
|---|---|
| Suggested teaching time: | 5 minutes |
| Your actual teaching time: | _____ |

- Review the example first.
- Review answers as a class.

**Option:** Write resolutions for each person using verbs of belief + *would* + base form. (Ivan was sure he would stop . . . Marie thought she would apply . . . Sylvia believed she would find . . . Robert knew he would marry . . .) **[+5 minutes]**

> **Culture note:** A popular tradition around the world is making New Year's resolutions. A *resolution* is a promise to do something. Typical resolutions often include everyday practical ideas, such as quitting smoking, losing weight, studying harder, etc.

**T40**

## C 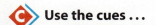 Use the cues . . .

| Suggested teaching time: | 5 minutes |
|---|---|
| Your actual teaching time: | _____ |

• Do the first item with the class.

• Have students compare answers with a partner. Then review as a class.

## D DISCUSSION

| Suggested teaching time: | 5 minutes |
|---|---|
| Your actual teaching time: | _____ |

• Form small groups. Role-play the model with a student.

• Ask students from different groups to say whether they had similar or different beliefs and expectations. Examples: *[Name] and I both thought we would buy new cars this year and we did. [Name] was going to be a teacher, but I was going to be an architect.*

• Note: If you have younger students, encourage them to think about any type of plan or belief they had in the past. Examples: *I believed I would be a famous singer. I was going to fly a plane around the world!*

## E 🎧 VOCABULARY
**(CD2, Track 20)**

| Suggested teaching time: | 5 minutes |
|---|---|
| Your actual teaching time: | _____ |

• Have students listen and study the sentences.

• Then have students listen and repeat chorally.

**Option:** To provide more practice, say the following sentences and ask students to identify which vocabulary phrase matches each one: 1. *I studied really hard but I failed the exam.* (I didn't pass.) 2. *I have to work two jobs now to earn enough money.* (It's hard to make a living.) 3. *I was going to travel around the world, but my family thinks I'm crazy, so I'm not going.* (My family talked me out of it.) 4. *I used to drink only coffee; now I drink tea.* (My taste(s) changed.) 5. *I was going to go out to dinner after class, but I think I'll just go home.* (I just changed my mind.) **[+5 minutes]**

## F 🎧 LISTENING COMPREHENSION
**(CD2, Track 21)**

| Suggested teaching time: | 5–10 minutes |
|---|---|
| Your actual teaching time: | _____ |

• Pause after the first conversation and review the example. Then pause after each conversation to allow students time to write the reasons.

• Have students compare answers with a partner. Then review as a class.

**Option:** Have students listen and write the original plans people had using *was going to* or *would* for future in the past. (1. She was going to be a sculptor. 2. He thought he would marry a Spanish dancer. 3. She thought she would be a lawyer. 4. She was going to marry a Swede.) **[+5 minutes]**

---

### AUDIOSCRIPT

**CONVERSATION 1**
**M:** So what did you want to be when you grew up?
**F:** Me? I actually wanted to be a sculptor. And I was one for about five years.
**M:** Really!? So how come you're an architect now?
**F:** Do you know how hard it is to make a living being a sculptor?
**M:** I can imagine.

**CONVERSATION 2**
**F:** Weren't you going to marry that beautiful Spanish dancer—what was her name—Pilar?
**M:** You remember?! You're amazing!
**F:** Who could forget Pilar?
**M:** Hmmm. Well, she was something else!
**F:** What made you change your mind?
**M:** I never really changed my mind. My parents talked me out of it.

**CONVERSATION 3** [M = Russian]
**M:** I always thought you would be a lawyer.
**F:** What do you mean?
**M:** Well, you love to argue, and you love to win.
**F:** To tell you the truth, I really thought I would be a lawyer too, but I didn't pass the entrance exam. I took it twice.
**M:** You're kidding!
**F:** Well, there's more to law than arguing and winning.

**CONVERSATION 4**
**F1:** I remember that gorgeous Swede you were going to marry.
**F2:** Oh, yes. Sven Svenson. He was some hunk.
**F1:** Whatever happened?
**F2:** I guess my tastes changed. I married Luigi instead.

---

## CONVERSATION **PAIR WORK**

| Suggested teaching time: | 5–10 minutes |
|---|---|
| Your actual teaching time: | _____ |

• To get students ready for the activity, have students read the conversation model on page 40 again. You may also want to have students listen to the model.

• Review the topics list. Students may want to add ideas.

• Brainstorm ways to answer *How have you been?* Examples: *Not bad / Fine / Great, thanks.*

• Choose a more confident student and role-play a conversation.

• As students interact, walk around the room and provide help as needed. Encourage students to use the correct rhythm and intonation.

🔵 **Pair Work Cards**

🔵 **Learning Strategies**

## EXTRAS (optional)

**Grammar Booster**
**Workbook: Exercises 6–11**
**Copy & Go: Activity 13**

**C** Use the cues to make statements with <u>would</u>.

1. In 1990 Sam thought / be / a lawyer, but he decided against it.
   In 1990 Sam thought he would be a lawyer, but he decided against it.
2. When I was young, I believed / study Chinese, but I never did.
   When I was young, I believed I would study Chinese, but I never did.
3. Everyone was sure / Bill and Stella / get a divorce, but they didn't!
   Everyone was sure Bill and Stella would get a divorce, but they didn't!
4. We didn't know / we / have so many children, but now we have six!
   We didn't know we would have so many children, but now we have six!

**D** DISCUSSION. Compare the plans and beliefs you had about your own future when you were young.

❝When I was young, I thought I would be a teacher.❞

❝That's amazing! I thought I was going to be a teacher too, but I changed my mind.❞

**E** 🎧 VOCABULARY. Reasons for changing your mind. Listen and practice. **CN**

I wanted to be a rock star, but **my tastes changed**.

I was going to be an artist, but **it's hard to make a living as an artist**.

I thought I would be a lawyer, but **I didn't pass the exam**.

I wanted to be a firefighter, but **my family talked me out of it**.

I was going to marry George, but **I just changed my mind**.

**CN** Corpus Notes: The phrase *change your mind* collocates most frequently with *about.* You can change your mind about something (*[This] book . . . may change your mind about your choice*) or about doing something (*I changed my mind about marrying George*).

**F** 🎧 LISTENING COMPREHENSION. Listen to the conversations. Then listen again. Write the reason each person changed his or her mind.

| Reason | |
|---|---|
| **1.** *It was hard to make a living as a sculptor.* | **3.** She didn't pass the entrance exam. |
| **2.** His parents talked him out of it. | **4.** Her tastes changed. |

## CONVERSATION
### PAIR WORK

**Topics**
marriage
work
studies
children
your idea: _____

Role-play meeting someone you haven't seen for a while. Talk about changes in your life plans. Use the speech balloons and the topics for ideas. Answers will vary.

❝Long time no see!❞

❝So what are you doing these days?❞

❝I was going to _____, but I changed my mind.❞

❝How have you been?❞

❝How come?❞

❝Well,_____.❞

# *Express Regrets about Decisions*

## CONVERSATION MODEL  Read and listen.

**A:** I should have married Steven.
**B:** Why do you think that?
**A:** Well, I might have had children by now.
**B:** Could be. But you never know. You might not have been happy.
**A:** True.

 **Rhythm and intonation practice**

**A**  **GRAMMAR.** Perfect modals: meaning and form

Express regrets about past actions with <u>should have</u> and a past participle.
I **should have studied** medicine. (But unfortunately, I didn't.)
She **shouldn't have divorced** Sam. (But unfortunately, she did.)

Speculate about the past with <u>would have</u>, <u>could have</u>, <u>may have</u>, and <u>might have</u>, and a past participle.
I should have married her. We **would have been** happy.
He **could have made** a better career choice.
I **may have failed** the entrance exam. It was very hard.
He **may** (or **might**) not **have been** able to make a living as a painter.

Draw conclusions about the past with <u>must have</u> and a past participle.
He's not here. He **must have gone** home early. (Probably—but I don't know for sure.)
They didn't buy the house. The price **must not have been** acceptable. (Probably—but I don't know for sure.)

GRAMMAR BOOSTER
**PAGE G7**
**For more …**

**B**  **PAIR WORK.** Share your regrets. Answers will vary.

**Partner A:** Tell your partner what you regret about your life, your studies, your work, or your actions in the past. Use <u>should have</u> or <u>shouldn't have</u>.

**Partner B:** Ask why or why not.

"I should have studied architecture."

"Why?"

"I would have been a great architect!"

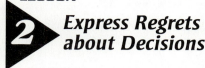

# LESSON 2

## Express Regrets about Decisions

### 🎧 CONVERSATION MODEL
**(CD2, Track 22)**

| | |
|---|---|
| Suggested teaching time: | 5 minutes |
| Your actual teaching time: | _____ |

- After students read and listen, ask *What does the first woman / speaker regret?* (that she didn't marry Steven) *Why?* (She wants kids. She thinks she would have kids now.)
- Point out that *Could be* means *That could be true.*

### 🎧 Rhythm and intonation practice
**(CD2, Track 23)**

| | |
|---|---|
| Suggested teaching time: | 5 minutes |
| Your actual teaching time: | _____ |

- Have students repeat each line chorally.
- Make sure students:
  - stress <u>Steven</u> in *I should have married Steven.*
  - use falling intonation for *Why do you think that?*
  - pause after *Well.*
  - stress <u>never</u> in *But you never know.*
  - stress the negative information <u>not</u> and <u>happy</u> in *You might not have been happy.*
  - use the following stress pattern:

---
**STRESS PATTERN**

**A:** I should have married Steven.

**B:** Why do you think that?

**A:** Well, I might have had children by now.

**B:** Could be. But you never know. You might not have

been happy.

**A:** True.

---

**Pair Work Cards**

### 🔺 A GRAMMAR

| | |
|---|---|
| Suggested teaching time: | 15 minutes |
| Your actual teaching time: | _____ |

- Tips for organizing information on the board: Use one side of the board specifically for the examples in these grammar notes. The list creates a useful reference for students while practicing.
- Direct attention to the box and have students read the first explanation and study the examples.

- Write on the board:
  > 1. I <u>should have brought</u> my raincoat.
- To help clarify meaning, say *I didn't bring a raincoat. Now I regret it.*
- Point out the form: *should + have + past participle.*
- Ask students to turn to a classmate and use *should have* to express a regret. Examples: *I should have studied more. I should have taken a taxi this morning.*
- Have students read the second explanation and study the examples.
- Write the following on the board:
  > 2. I should have studied for the exam. I <u>would have passed</u>.
  > 3. I should have taken the exam. I <u>could have passed</u>.
  > 4. The exam was difficult, but I <u>may / might have passed</u>.
- Ask students turn to a classmate and talk about how to clarify each situation. Tell students to say what *did* or *didn't happen* and then the phrase *Now I look back and think . . .*
- Give an example. Say *Number two. I didn't study for the exam. Now I look back and think I had a good chance of passing.*
- Review the meaning of each example. Examples: 2. see above 3. *I didn't take the exam. Now I look back and think I had a chance of passing.* 4. *I took the exam. Now I look back and think that maybe I passed. But I still don't know.*
- Point out that the negative is formed by adding *not* after the modal. Write on the board:
  > 5. I'm glad I didn't take the exam. I <u>wouldn't have passed</u>.
  > 6. The exam was easy, but I <u>may/might not have passed</u>.
- Have students read the last explanation and study the examples.
- Write on the board:
  > 7. Susan didn't call back. She must have forgotten.
  > 8. She must not have gotten your message.
- To help clarify, tell students that using *must* means you are saying why <u>you</u> think or believe something happened or why someone did something.
- Write on the board:
  > 9. [Name] was late for class today.
- To check comprehension, ask students to turn to a classmate and draw conclusions about why that person was early (or late) to class today. Examples: *He / she must have come by car and not bus. He / she must have missed the bus. He / she must have met a friend on his/her way. He / she must have overslept.*

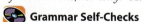
**Grammar Self-Checks**

### 🔺 B PAIR WORK

| | |
|---|---|
| Suggested teaching time: | 5–10 minutes |
| Your actual teaching time: | _____ |

- Review the task and role-play the model with a student. Encourage students to ask follow-up questions and give reasons.
- After students finish a conversation, ask them to change roles.

## C  PRONUNCIATION
(CD2, Track 24)

Suggested teaching time: 5 minutes
Your actual teaching time: _____

- First listening: Have students listen and study the examples.
- Second listening: Have students listen and repeat chorally.
- Pair work. Have students practice the reduction of *have* in perfect models by saying the example sentences in the Grammer box (page 42). Encourage students to give each other feedback.

**Language note:** The auxiliary *have* is reduced in spoken English because it is a *function word*. Function words—for example, auxiliaries *(have)*, articles *(a, an, the)*, prepositions *(on, in, at, for,* etc.), pronouns *(he, his, him,* etc.), conjunctions *(and, or, but,* etc.), and forms with *be (he's, they're,* etc.)—are often reduced because they do not provide the important information in a sentence. *Content words*—such as nouns, verbs, adjectives, and adverbs—are never reduced.

 **Pronunciation Activities**

## D PAIR WORK

Suggested teaching time: 5–10 minutes
Your actual teaching time: _____

- First review the example sentence and the model answers.
- Walk around the room and provide help as needed. Encourage students to use all of the grammar forms.
- To review, call on various pairs to say their speculation and conclusion about one item. Make necessary corrections.

## CONVERSATION **PAIR WORK**

Suggested teaching time: 5–10 minutes
Your actual teaching time: _____

- To get students ready for the activity, have students read the conversation model on page 42 again. You may also want to have students listen to the model.
- Review the ideas in the box. Ask students to add their own idea.
- Before students begin, ask them to write some notes about their regret(s). Have them include the reason(s) and what they think might have happened if things had been different.
- Choose a more confident student and role-play a conversation.
- As students interact, walk around the room and provide help as needed. Encourage students to use the correct rhythm and intonation.

**Challenge:** Group work. Combine pairs to form groups of four. Students take turns reporting their partners' regrets and adding their opinions. Example: Student A: *Brandon says he should have moved to the mountains. I think he might have had a boring life in the mountains.* Student B: *But I think I might have been happier there than here in the city.* Student C: *And you would have had a quieter life.* Student D: *I agree.*
**[+10 minutes]**

 **Pair Work Cards**

## EXTRAS (optional)

**Grammar Booster**
**Workbook: Exercises 12–17**
**Copy & Go: Activity 14**

 **Pronunciation Supplements**

🎧 **PRONUNCIATION. Reduction of __have__ in perfect modals. Listen to the reduction of __have__ in perfect modals. Then repeat.**

/ʃʊṭəv/
1. I should have married Marie.

/naṭəv/
3. We may not have seen it.

/maiṭəv/
2. They might have left.

/cʊṭəv/
4. She could have been on time.

**D** **PAIR WORK. Provide reasons for each of the following statements.**
**Partner A: Speculate with __may have__ / __may not have__ or __might have__ / __might not have__.**
**Partner B: Draw a conclusion with __must have__ or __must not have__.** Answers will vary.

Example: John is late for dinner.

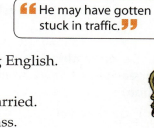

❝ He may have gotten stuck in traffic. ❞

❝ He must have forgotten. ❞

1. My brother stopped studying English.
2. Claire left her husband.
3. Glen is 40, and he just got married.
4. They canceled the English class.
5. All the students failed the exam.

## CONVERSATION PAIR WORK

**Express more regrets with your partner. Use the guide and the ideas from the box, or create a new conversation.** Answers will vary.

**A:** I should have _____ .
**B:** Why do you think that?
**A:** Well, I might have _____ .
**B:** Could be. But you never know.
    You might _____ …

**Continue the conversation in your __own__ way.**

💡 *Some ideas…*
● taken a job [at Microsoft]
● bought a [sports car]
● studied [medicine]
● married [Pat]
● your own idea:
  _____

**CONTROLLED PRACTICE**

# 3 ▷ Discuss Skills, Abilities, and Qualifications

**A** ▷ ⌒ **VOCABULARY. Skills and abilities. Listen and practice.**

**talents**  abilities in art, music, mathematics, etc. that you are born with
  She was born with talents in both mathematics and art.

**skills**  abilities that you learn, such as cooking, speaking a foreign language, or driving
  She has several publishing skills: writing, editing, and illustrating.

**experience**  time spent working at a job in the past
  Sally has a lot of experience in sales. She has worked at three companies.

**knowledge**  understanding of or familiarity with a subject, gained from experience or study
  Anna has extensive knowledge of the history of film. You can ask her which classics to see.

**B** ▷ ⌒ **LISTENING COMPREHENSION. Listen to nine people being interviewed at an international job fair. Stop after each interview and match each interviewee with his or her qualification.**

| Interviewee | Qualification |
|---|---|
| _h_ **1.** Sonia Espinoza | **a.** a good memory |
| _d_ **2.** Silvano Lucastro | **b.** artistic ability |
| _f_ **3.** Ivan Martinovic | **c.** mathematical ability |
| _i_ **4.** Agnes Lukins | **d.** logical thinking |
| _e_ **5.** Elena Burgess | **e.** compassion |
| _b_ **6.** Karen Trent | **f.** manual dexterity |
| _g_ **7.** Ed Snodgrass | **g.** common sense |
| _c_ **8.** Akiko Uzawa | **h.** athletic ability |
| _a_ **9.** Mia Kim | **i.** leadership skills |

**C** ▷ **PAIR WORK. With your partner, classify each qualification from exercise B. Do you agree on all the classifications? Discuss your opinions.** Answers will vary.

> ❝I think artistic ability is a talent. You're born with it.❞

> ❝I disagree. I think if you study art, you can develop artistic ability. I think it's a skill.❞

| A talent | A skill |
|---|---|
| artistic ability | |
| | |
| | |
| | |
| | |

**LESSON**

# 3 Discuss Skills, Abilities, and Qualifications

## A 🎧 VOCABULARY
**(CD2, Track 25)**

| Suggested teaching time: | 10 minutes |
|---|---|
| Your actual teaching time: | _____ |

- Have students listen and study the words and the definitions.
- Then have students listen and repeat chorally.
- Write the following sentences on the board. To check comprehension, ask students to fill in the blanks with the vocabulary words from Exercise A. (1. experience 2. skills 3. talent 4. knowledge)

  *1. He has done this kind of job before, so he has some ___.*
  *2. She types fast and knows at least three computer programs. She has the ___ we need for this position.*
  *3. She sings beautifully and plays the violin. She has a lot of ___.*
  *4. They studied 20th-century European politics. I'm sure they have a lot of background ___ on the history of World War II.*

 **Vocabulary Cards**

 **Learning Strategies**

## B 🎧 LISTENING COMPREHENSION
**(CD2, Track 26)**

| Suggested teaching time: | 15–20 minutes |
|---|---|
| Your actual teaching time: | _____ |

- Point out that a *qualification* is a skill, personal quality, or experience that makes you right for a particular job.
- You might want to clarify that people who have *manual dexterity* are good with their hands, people who have *compassion* for others understand other people's feelings, and people who have *leadership skills* can manage people or groups very well.
- Have students listen to the first interview and review the example. Ask students to listen again for the information that supports the correct answer. (She plays tennis, golf, and she's on a basketball team. She's won a few swimming contests, and she teaches swimming.)
- Ask students to make notes as they listen to the other interviews. They should listen for what the person does and what gives the person good qualifications.
- Review the answers as a class. Ask students to give the information that supports an answer.

**AUDIOSCRIPT**

CONVERSATION 1  [F = Spanish]
**M:** Good morning.
**F:** Hello. I'm Sonia Espinoza. I'm interested in the job as director of the sports program. The one on the cruise ship.
**M:** Do you have any experience with sports programs or any special athletic ability?

**F:** Yes. I play tennis, golf, and I'm on a basketball team. I've won a few swimming contests, and I've been teaching swimming at a club for five years. I actually thought I would be an Olympic swimmer, but I'm not good enough for that.

CONVERSATION 2  [M2 = Italian]
**M1:** Good morning. Please come in.
**M2:** Thank you. I'm Silvano Lucastro. I'm interested in working in an international company, but I'm not sure what jobs might be available.
**M1:** OK. Tell me something about yourself. What do you see as your strengths?
**M2:** Well, I'm very logical. I can figure things out when other people can't. Whenever there is a problem, people bring it to me to look for an answer. I write everything down in a list and then think about every solution. It's a good way to solve problems.

CONVERSATION 3  [M2 = Slavic]
**M1:** Hello. Please come in and have a seat.
**M2:** Thanks.
**M1:** Which job are you interested in?
**M2:** Well, I'm not sure. I don't have a family yet, and my English is pretty good. I'd love to work somewhere outside of the country for a while, but I don't have much work experience.
**M1:** That's OK. We have jobs for people at every level. Please tell me about your qualifications.
**M2:** Well, ever since I was a child, I've been great with my hands.
**M1:** Hmm. Manual dexterity … Can you tell me a little more?
**M2:** Sure. People always tell me that I'm good at fixing things. I love to fix things that are broken.
**M1:** That's great. I actually know of a nice position that might be just right for you … in the U.S., working for a Ukrainian piano company. Let me get your personal information. Please spell your name.
**M2:** It's Ivan Martinovic. That's M-A-R-T-I-N-O-V-I-C.

CONVERSATION 4
**M:** Good afternoon.
**F:** Hi! I'm Agnes Lukins, and I'm a people person.
**M:** A people person. Could you please explain what you mean, Ms. Lukins?
**F:** I just love working with people. And, actually, people like working with me … and for me. They say I'm a good boss.
**M:** So would you say you have strong leadership qualities?
**F:** I guess so. I manage people well and my last two jobs have been in management. I'd like to know if there's anything available abroad … maybe in Mexico? I can speak Spanish.
**M:** Let's have a look at the possibilities there.

**AUDIOSCRIPT continues on page T45.**

## C PAIR WORK

| Suggested teaching time: | 5–10 minutes |
|---|---|
| Your actual teaching time: | _____ |

- Review the difference between a talent and a skill by asking *Which is an ability you learn?* (skill) *What is an example of a talent?* (art, music)
- Role-play the model with a student.
- Point out that it's not necessary to agree with your partner. Encourage students to give reasons why they chose talent or skill for each qualification.

# TOP NOTCH **INTERACTION**

| Suggested teaching time: | 15–20 minutes |
|---|---|
| Your actual teaching time: | _____ |

## STEP 1. Take the skills ...

- To practice scanning, have students (quickly) read and ask *What's this inventory for?* (to prepare yourself for a job interview or an interview for a school) *What kind of information will you need to share?* (things you're interested in, your qualifications, your background experience)

- Encourage students to look back in the unit for help with vocabulary.

## STEP 2. On the notepad ...

- Review the example.

- Brainstorm other examples with the class.

- Walk around the room and provide help as needed.

## STEP 3. ROLE PLAY.

- Point out the NEED HELP? section and review the questions and answers.

- Encourage students to use their imagination, as well as the vocabulary and grammar from this unit.

- You may want to write the following chart on the board and have students take notes.

- Walk around the room and provide help as needed.

---

**Interview form**

Name: _____    Date: _____

Fields of interest:
- ☐ business    ☐ science    ☐ education
- ☐ art    ☐ manufacturing    ☐ social work
- ☐ other _____

Talents:

Skills:

Work experience:

Special knowledge:

---

🔵 **Graphic Organizers**

**Challenge.** Ask various students to report the results of their interview to the class. Students should give a brief overview of their partners' skills and qualifications. If their partners already have a job, ask them to explain why they think their partners have / don't have the right job for them. If their partners don't have a job, ask students to offer some career advice. **[+10 minutes]**

## EXTRAS (optional)

**Workbook: Exercises 18–21**
**Copy & Go: Activity 15**

---

**◉ AUDIOSCRIPT**

**AUDIOSCRIPT continued from Exercise B, page T44**

CONVERSATION 5 [F = Australian]
**M:** Come in. You're Elena Burgess, aren't you?
**F:** Yes, that's right. I see you have two jobs available for psychologists. I just finished my studies, and I'm not sure which job to apply for. This would be my first job.
**M:** Well, please tell me about yourself. What do you see as your strengths?
**F:** Strengths? Hmm ... Well, people say I have a lot of compassion.
**M:** You're compassionate? In what way?
**F:** I'm able to understand other people's feelings—to put myself in their shoes. I think I must have gotten that from my parents. Both my parents are psychologists, too.

CONVERSATION 6
**M:** Good afternoon. You must be Karen Trent.
**F:** Yes ... I'm looking for a job.
**M:** Certainly, Ms. Trent. What kind of experience do you have?
**F:** Well, I'm a painter. I painted the murals at the new Design Center reception area.
**M:** Really? Those are beautiful! I understand they won a prize. You do have a lot of talent.
**F:** Thanks! I actually have a teaching certificate in art, and I'd love to work with children. Is there anything available in Europe? I speak French and German as well as English, and I'd love a chance to practice!

CONVERSATION 7 [M2 = U.S. Southern, regional]
**M1:** Please come in and have a seat.
**M2:** Thank you. I'm Ed Snodgrass, and I'm a student. I'm looking for some kind of a summer job ... maybe in Thailand? Would that be possible?
**M1:** Asia. Well, let's see. Tell me something about your skills and abilities.
**M2:** Well, I'm pretty young, but people have always said I have a lot of common sense.
**M1:** Now that DOES sound good. What specifically do you mean?
**M2:** Well, I don't really have a lot of experience or skill, but I have a talent for just knowing what to do. Things seem pretty simple to me. I just seem to be able to figure out what to do when others can't.

CONVERSATION 8 [F = Japanese]
**M:** Please come in and have a seat.
**F:** Thank you very much. I'm Akiko Uzawa. I've been working as a computer programmer, but I'm interested in moving to information technology. I see there's a job available with a multinational.
**M:** Yes, that's right. This would be a change for you, Ms. Uzawa. What makes you feel you would be good at information technology?
**F:** Well, I went into programming because I was always good at math. I think with my background in mathematics I understand the needs and problems of people in IT.

CONVERSATION 9
**M:** Hello. Are you Mia Kim?
**F:** Yes, that's right. I'm currently working as a receptionist at a law firm, but I've just finished a course as a legal secretary and I'd like to apply for the opening in Paris.
**M:** Paris? Do you speak French?
**F:** Yes. I have a good knowledge of French. My parents both worked in France for a Korean company, and I went to a French-speaking school.
**M:** What do you see as your strengths?
**F:** Well, I have a great memory for details. Also for faces and facts. I hope you'll consider me for this job.

**STEP 1. Take the skills inventory.** Answers will vary.

## Careers, Jobs, Advanced Studies AND YOU

Whether you're looking for a job or interviewing for a school, interviewers expect you to answer questions about your interests, talents, skills, and experience. Take this inventory to prepare yourself for those questions.

**Interests**
**Check the fields that interest you:**
- ☐ business
- ☐ science
- ☐ education
- ☐ art
- ☐ manufacturing
- ☐ other _____

**Qualifications**
**Check the qualifications you believe you have:**
- ☐ manual dexterity
- ☐ logical thinking
- ☐ mathematical ability
- ☐ common sense
- ☐ athletic ability
- ☐ artistic ability
- ☐ compassion
- ☐ a good memory
- ☐ leadership skills
- ☐ other _____

**Experience**
**Briefly note information about your experience, skills, and any special knowledge you have.**

Experience: _____

Skills: _____

Special knowledge: _____

| Qualification | Example |
|---|---|
| mathematical ability | I love number puzzles. I'm great at them! |

**STEP 2. On the notepad, write specific examples of your qualifications.**

| Qualification | Example |
|---|---|
| | |
| | |
| | |
| | |

**STEP 3. ROLE PLAY.** Role-play an interview for a job, for career advice, or for entry into a school. Talk about interests, qualifications, skills, and experience.

NEED HELP? **Here's language you already know:**

**Interviewer**
Please tell me something about your [skills].
Do you have knowledge of [Arabic]?
What kind of [talents] do you have?
What [work] experience do you have?

**Interviewee**
I have experience in [teaching].
I don't have much experience.
I'm good at [math].
I have three years of [French].

FREE PRACTICE

45

# 4 Discuss Work and Life Decisions

 **READING WARM-UP.** Can you name some great humanitarians—people who have made or who are making an important difference in the world?

**B** 🎧 **READING.** Read about the lifework of two humanitarians. Why do you think these people are internationally known?

## PEOPLE WHO CHANGED THE WORLD

### Mahatma Gandhi

*"Non-violence is not a weapon of the weak. It is a weapon of the strongest and the bravest."* —Mahatma Gandhi

Mohandas Karamchand Gandhi believed that the way people behave is more important than what they accomplish. Gandhi studied law but became known for social action. He practiced non-violence to help India achieve independence from Britain.

In 1947, India was granted independence, but the country was broken into two states—India and Pakistan—and fighting between Hindus and Muslims began. But Gandhi believed in an India where Hindus and Muslims could live together in peace. On January 13, 1948, at the age of 78, Gandhi began a fast, not eating anything for days, with the purpose of stopping the war. After five days, the opposing leaders said they would stop the fighting and Gandhi broke his fast and started eating again.

Sadly, twelve days later Gandhi was assassinated by a Hindu fanatic who strongly opposed his vision of an India for both Hindus and Muslims. The Indian people called Gandhi "Mahatma," meaning "Great Soul."

**Mahatma Gandhi**
Indian Spiritual / Political Leader and Humanitarian 1869–1948

### Albert Schweitzer

*"Man must cease attributing his problems to his environment, and learn again to exercise his will—his personal responsibility."*
—Albert Schweitzer

Albert Schweitzer was born in Alsace, Germany, which is now a part of France. By the time he was 21, Schweitzer had decided on the course for his life. For nine years he would dedicate himself to the study of science, music, and religion. Then he would devote the rest of his life to serving humanity directly. Before he was 30, he was a respected writer, an organist, and an expert on the life and work of Johann Sebastian Bach.

In 1904, Schweitzer was inspired to help sick people in the world, so he studied medicine at the University of Strasbourg. He

**Albert Schweitzer**
German Philosopher, Physician, and Humanitarian 1875–1965

founded a hospital in French Equatorial Africa in 1913. Over the years, he built a large hospital that served thousands of Africans. In 1952, Schweitzer received the Nobel Prize for Peace. He used his $33,000 Nobel Prize to expand the hospital and to build a place to take care of people who had the terrible disease of leprosy.

Schweitzer based his personal philosophy on a love and respect for life and on a deep commitment to serve humanity through thought and action.

**SOURCE:** Adapted from www.lucidcafe.com

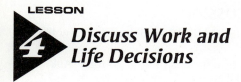

# LESSON 4
## Discuss Work and Life Decisions

 **A  READING WARM-UP**

| Suggested teaching time: | 5 minutes |
|---|---|
| Your actual teaching time: | _____ |

- Explain or elicit that a *humanitarian* is someone who works to help improve bad living conditions and/or prevent unfair treatment of people.

- If students need ideas, brainstorm other humanitarians. Examples: *Mother Teresa, Nelson Mandela, Bill and Melinda Gates.*

> **Culture note:** Some other well-known humanitarians: **Mother Teresa,** a Roman Catholic nun, was born in Macedonia in 1910. In 1948 she began to live among and care for the poor and the sick in India. In 1979 she won the Nobel Peace Prize for her humanitarian work. Mother Teresa died in 1997. **Nelson Mandela** was born in South Africa in 1918. In 1942 he set up a law firm to fight for the rights of black people. In 1963 he was arrested and imprisoned for leading a movement against discrimination. He spent 27 years in prison. Mandela was released in 1990 and won the Nobel Peace Prize in 1993. He went on to become the first black president of a multiracial South Africa in 1994. **Bill and Melinda Gates** have created a foundation with more than $27 billion to support philanthropic initiatives in the areas of global health and learning. They want to help make sure that advances in these critical areas will be available for all people.

**B  🎧 READING**
### (CD2, Track 27)

| Suggested teaching time: | 10–15 minutes |
|---|---|
| Your actual teaching time: | _____ |

- Have students scan the text for the names of the two people the article is about.

- To draw on students' prior knowledge, ask students what they already know about Gandhi and Schweitzer. Point out that they can make simple statements. Example: *Gandhi lived in India. Schweitzer was a doctor.*

- After students read the article, ask various students to give their opinions about why these men are famous.

**Option:** Use this option if you want to do a listening activity. Books closed. Draw a Venn diagram on the board. First ask students to listen and write the details about each man in his assigned circle. Then ask students to find any information that is common for both men and write those details in the middle area where the circles overlap. (Common for both: served humanity, brought change without violence)
**[+15 minutes]**

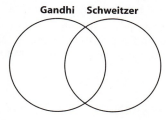

Gandhi    Schweitzer

 **Graphic Organizers**

**Option:** Write the following statements on the board.
1. *Gandhi developed a non-violent method to win the independence of India.*
2. *He stopped eating to fight for independence for his country.*
3. *Gandhi was killed by someone from his own country.*
4. *Schweitzer studied for many years before he started helping people.*
5. *He was born in Germany but helped the people in Africa.*
6. *He used his Nobel Prize to continue his studies.*

To practice the reading strategy of skimming (for information), ask students to read the article and check the statements that are true. Encourage students to underline information in the reading that supports their answers. Review as a class. (1. T  2. F  3. T  4. T  5. F)  **[+10 minutes]**

 **Extra Reading Comprehension Activities**

 **Learning Strategies**

## C  PAIR WORK

| Suggested teaching time: | 5 minutes |
|---|---|
| Your actual teaching time: | _____ |

- Encourage students to use the grammar items listed in the direction line. Examples: *Schweitzer and Gandhi must have been really nice people. They may have thought about helping people even when they were children. They could have had jobs that paid more.*

- To review, ask various students to say one or two of their ideas about Gandhi or Schweitzer. Make any necessary corrections to statements using *must / might / may / could have.*

## D DISCUSSION

| Suggested teaching time: | 5–10 minutes |
|---|---|
| Your actual teaching time: | _____ |

- Review Gandhi's and Schweitzer's humanitarian acts by asking students to read the text again (page 46) and underline the information they need for the discussion. (Gandhi: dedicated his life to non-violence, developed a method of directing social action and used it to help obtain independence for India, fasted to help stop the fighting; Schweitzer: studied medicine and dedicated his life to helping others, built a large hospital, used his prize money to expand the hospital)

- Remind students to include in their discussion other humanitarians and what they have done.

- To review, ask various students to share one or two of their thoughts about Gandhi, Schweitzer, or another humanitarian. Encourage the class to ask follow-up questions.

## TOP NOTCH **INTERACTION**

| Suggested teaching time: | 20–25 minutes |
|---|---|
| Your actual teaching time: | _____ |

## STEP 1. On your notepad . . .

- Review the example. Point out that students can write about plans they had in relation to work, studies, marriage, trips, place where they live, etc.

- Encourage students to write about at least two or three plans that changed. Tell students to make notes about having any regrets and if and how things would have been different.

- If your students are younger, you can encourage them to imagine they are older and to use ideas and plans they are thinking about now to do the activity.

- As students make their notes, walk around the room and provide help as needed.

## STEP 2. DISCUSSION.

- Point out the NEED HELP? section and review the expressions.

- Group work. Form groups of three or four. Ask students to make sure to express interest, offer encouragement, and ask follow-up questions during the discussion.

- As students talk, walk around the room and provide help as needed.

**Option:** Ask students from different groups to report about a past plan made by someone in their group that changed. **[+10 minutes]**

## STEP 3. WRITING.

- You may want to offer an alternative topic. For example, students can write about someone else: a famous person, a character in a book, someone they know, etc., whose plans changed.

- To help students organize the information into three paragraphs, write on the board:
    1: *your plan, why you changed/didn't change your mind, what happened*
    2: *why you have/don't have any regrets, what would have been different if you had made a different decision*
    3: *general comments about your life now*

- As students write, walk around the room and provide help as needed.

 Writing Process Worksheets

## EXTRAS (optional)

**Workbook:** Exercises 22–25
**Copy & Go:** Activity 16

**C** PAIR WORK. Use <u>must have</u>, <u>might have</u>, <u>may have</u>, and <u>could have</u> to discuss the following questions. Answers will vary.

1. Why do you think Schweitzer and Gandhi spent their lives helping other people?

2. Instead of being humanitarians, what might Gandhi and Schweitzer have been? What could they have done with their lives?

**D** DISCUSSION. In what ways are Mahatma Gandhi and Albert Schweitzer humanitarians? Do you admire how they chose to live their lives? Do you know any other humanitarians? What did they do?

## TOP NOTCH
### INTERACTION • *It's never too late!*

**STEP 1.** On your notepad, list some plans that changed in your life. Write if you have regrets about the change.

| Plans that changed | Any regrets? |
|---|---|
| I was going to be a teacher, but I changed my mind. | I have no regrets. |

| Plans that changed | Any regrets? |
|---|---|
| | |
| | |
| | |

**STEP 2. DISCUSSION.** Discuss the plans that changed in your life. What could you have been? What might you have done? Are you sorry about it or happy about it?

**NEED HELP?** Here's language you already know:

| Express regrets | Talk about past plans | Explain changes in plans | Express interest and offer encouragement |
|---|---|---|---|
| I could have ____ . | I was going to ____ , but ____ . | I changed my mind. | Maybe it's not too late. |
| I might have ____ . | I thought I would ____ , but ____ . | My family talked me out of it. | You're still young. |
| I should have ____ . | | It's hard to make a living as a (painter). | You never know. |
| I wish I had ____ . | | My tastes changed. | Maybe you would have hated it. |

**STEP 3. WRITING.** Gandhi and Schweitzer had plans for their lives, but their plans changed. On a separate sheet of paper, write about your life. What were you going to do or be? What did you think you would be? Did you change your mind? What happened? Do you have any regrets? Explain.

FREE PRACTICE

**A** 🎧 **LISTENING COMPREHENSION. Listen to the conversations. Complete the chart.**

| | Why did the person change his / her mind? | Any regrets? |
|---|---|---|
| **1.** | His parents convinced him it would be hard to have a family. | yes / (no) |
| **2.** | She lost interest and got another job offer. | (yes) / no |
| **3.** | She wasn't getting paid enough. | yes / (no) |
| **4.** | His English wasn't good enough. | (yes) / no |

**B** **Complete each statement of belief about the future, using <u>would</u>.** Answers may vary. Possible answers include:

1. When I was a child, I thought I <u>would be a doctor when I grew up</u>

2. My parents believed <u>I would be successful when I grew up</u>.

3. My teachers were sure <u>I would be a news reporter</u>.

4. When I finished school, I didn't know <u>I would later go to medical school</u>.

**C** **Explain the meaning of each of the following qualifications. Then write an occupation or course of study for a person with each qualification.** Answers may vary. Possible answers include:

| Qualification | Definition | Occupation or Study |
|---|---|---|
| **1.** athletic ability | able to play sports very well | professional tennis player |
| **2.** artistic ability | showing skill and imagination in an art | painter |
| **3.** mathematical ability | showing skill in the science of numbers | mathematician |
| **4.** logical thinking ability | able to think carefully, using formal methods | philosophy professor |
| **5.** a good memory | able to recall information easily | scientist |
| **6.** leadership skills | being good at leading a team, organization, or country | business management |

**D** **Write answers to the questions about your <u>own</u> skills and qualifications.** Answers will vary.

1. What talents do you have? _____

2. What work experience do you have? _____

3. What skills do you have? _____

4. What special knowledge do you have? _____

**E** **WRITING. On a separate sheet of paper, write a paragraph about Mahatma Gandhi, Albert Schweitzer, or another great humanitarian. Use <u>was going to</u>, <u>would</u>, <u>may</u> or <u>might have</u>, <u>must have</u>, and <u>should have</u> in your paragraph.**

*TOP NOTCH* **PROJECT**
Write advertisements for jobs. Include requirements for experience and skills.

*TOP NOTCH* **WEBSITE**
For Unit 4 online activities, visit the *Top Notch* Companion Website at www.longman.com/topnotch.

# UNIT 4 CHECKPOINT

## A 🎧 LISTENING COMPREHENSION
### (CD2, Track 28)

| | |
|---|---|
| Suggested teaching time: | 10 minutes |
| Your actual teaching time: | _____ |

- Review reasons for changing your mind (page 41).
- Encourage students to use vocabulary from this unit.
- Pause after each conversation to allow students time to write their answers.
- Have students compare answers with a partner. Then review as a class.

**Option:** Have students listen to the recording again and make notes about the plan that each person changed. (1. He was going to get married. 2. She was going to accept a teaching position in Peru. 3. She was going to be an art teacher. 4. He was going to be an interpreter at the United Nations.) **[+10 minutes]**

### AUDIOSCRIPT

CONVERSATION 1
**F:** What happened? Weren't you going to get married?
**M:** Yes, but my parents were against the marriage.
**F:** How come?
**M:** My fiancé had to travel all the time for her work, and my parents convinced me that it would be hard to have a family. In the end, I agreed with them.
**F:** No regrets?
**M:** None.

CONVERSATION 2
**F:** I wish I'd accepted the teaching position in Peru.
**M:** Why didn't you?
**F:** Well, I thought I wanted to live outside of this country, but then I lost interest. I got a good job offer here.
**M:** Are you sorry about it now?
**F:** I guess I am. I would have had a much more exciting life.

CONVERSATION 3
**M:** Didn't you use to teach painting?
**F:** Yes. I thought I would always teach art.
**M:** So how come you're a lawyer?
**F:** I have pretty expensive tastes. And I wasn't getting paid enough … And it turns out that I really like law.
**M:** So all's well that ends well!
**F:** You bet!

CONVERSATION 4 [M = French]
**F:** I thought you were going to be an interpreter at the United Nations?
**M:** Well, I was, but I tried twice, and my English wasn't good enough, so I couldn't. The exam is extremely hard.
**F:** That's too bad.
**M:** Yes, I wish I had studied more.

## B Complete each statement . . .

| | |
|---|---|
| Suggested teaching time: | 5 minutes |
| Your actual teaching time: | _____ |

- To review, ask various students to read their sentences out loud.

## C Explain the meaning . . .

| | |
|---|---|
| Suggested teaching time: | 5–10 minutes |
| Your actual teaching time: | _____ |

- Have students review the vocabulary and information about qualifications on page 44.
- Have students compare answers with a partner. Then review as a class.

## D Write answers . . .

| | |
|---|---|
| Suggested teaching time: | 5 minutes |
| Your actual teaching time: | _____ |

- Provide an example for item 1 by answering the question about yourself. Example: *I can sing well and I'm good at art.*
- To review, ask various students for their answers. Make necessary corrections.

## E WRITING

| | |
|---|---|
| Suggested teaching time: | 10–15 minutes |
| Your actual teaching time: | _____ |

- If necessary, have students review the grammar presented on pages 40 and 42.
- You may want to provide the students with the following examples about Mother Teresa:

    *Mother Teresa was going to live in a convent, but she changed her mind.*
    *If she had stayed in the convent, she might not have become famous.*
    *She must have felt deep compassion for the people in need around her.*

 **Writing Process Worksheets**

### *TOP NOTCH* PROJECT

**Idea:** Ask students to find advertisements for jobs on the Internet or in English newspapers to use as models. Group work. Form groups of four. Ask each group to write two advertisements. Hang the ads on the board, and have students walk around and read them. Then ask volunteers to say which job(s) they would apply for and why.

**Idea:** Ask students to research jobs on the Internet in their professions or in the field they would like to work in. Then have students write their "ideal advertisement." Point out that students are creating an ad that describes their dream job! Make sure they include qualifications necessary for this job.

# UNIT WRAP-UP

| Suggested teaching time: | 10–15 minutes |
| --- | --- |
| Your actual teaching time: | —————— |

## Narration

- Write the following information in three columns on the board:

  Michael    Carlota

  Mother and father's dream
    for their child
  Child's dream when he / she
    was young
  The actual choice and any
    regrets

- Ask students to study the pictures and the story and write notes to prepare their story.

- Pair work. Encourage students to use time expressions as they tell the story of Michael and Carlota. Examples: *When Michael was a baby . . . After graduating from medical school . . .*

- Encourage students to use the grammar from this unit to offer reasons Michael and Carlota changed their minds. Examples: *Michael's mother must have talked him out of being a pilot. Carlota might have thought it was hard to make a living as a photographer.*

**Option: Our version.** Group work. Combine pairs and ask students to take turns telling their stories. Walk around the room and provide help as needed.
**[+10 minutes]**

### Your students can say . . .

When Michael was born, his father thought he would be a pilot. His father must have been a pilot. Michael's mother thought he would be a doctor. She might have admired doctors. When Carlota was a baby, her mother thought she would be a photographer. Carlota's mother might have been a photographer. Carlota's father thought she would be a doctor. Carlota's father must have been a doctor.

When Michael was a schoolboy, he was going to be a pilot. When Carlota was a young girl, she believed she would be a photographer. Michael might have just changed his mind. His mother may have talked him out of being a pilot. His mother must have persuaded him to become a doctor. Carlota may have thought it was hard to make a living as a photographer. Her father must have talked her out of being a photographer.

Now Michael thinks he should have been a pilot, and Carlota thinks she should have been a photographer. Michael thinks he would have been happier if he had become a pilot. Carlota thinks life would have been much more exciting if she had been a photographer.

### Individual oral progress check (optional)

- Use the illustration on page 49. Encourage the student to use material (vocabulary, grammar, rhythm and intonation) practiced in this unit.

- Evaluate the student on correctness and intelligibility.

- Tell the student you are going to ask questions about Michael's dreams and his parent's plans for him. Ask him / her to give full answers. Ask *What did Michael's father think Michael would be?* (He thought he would / was going to be a pilot.) *What did his mother believe he would be?* (She believed he would / was going to be a doctor.) *What did Michael think he would be when he was a boy?* (He thought he would / was going to be a pilot.)

- Tell the student that together you are going to role-play an interview. You are the interviewer and the student is either Michael or Carlota. Ask the student to answer your questions based on the pictures on this page. The student can also add information if necessary. Encourage the student to use the grammar from this unit. Example:
T: *What did you believe you would be when you were a child?* S: *I thought I was going to be a photographer.* T: *What do you do now?* S: *I'm a doctor.* T: *Why did you change your mind?* S: *My mother believed I could have been a great photographer, but my father wanted me to be a doctor.* T: *How would your life have been different if you had changed your decision?* S: *I would have traveled all over the world. I could have had an exciting life.*

 **Cumulative Vocabulary Activities**

 You may wish to use the video and activity worksheets for Unit 4 at this point.

 **Complete Assessment Package Unit 4 Achievement Test**

# UNIT WRAP-UP

- **Narration.** Tell the life story of the Wileys. Talk about the expectations their parents had, their own expectations, and what happened.

|  | **Michael** | **Carlota** |
|---|---|---|

**1980** — Their parents' plans and dreams for them

**1990** — Their wishes and dreams for themselves

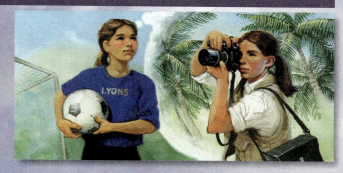

**Now** — Their actual choices and regrets

## Now I can ...

- ☐ explain a change in life and work choices.
- ☐ express regrets about decisions.
- ☐ discuss skills, abilities, and qualifications.
- ☐ discuss work and life decisions.

# UNIT 5

## Holidays and Traditions

### UNIT GOALS

1 Find out about a holiday
2 Ask about the customs of another culture
3 Describe a holiday or celebration
4 Explain wedding traditions

**A** **TOPIC PREVIEW.** Look at the pictures. Which traditions are you familiar with? Which ones would you like to know more about?

▲ A mariachi band in the State of Jalisco, Mexico, where mariachi was born

▲ A Korean couple dressed in the traditional hanbok

Egyptians buying traditional sweets for the feast of Eid ul-Fitr at the end of Ramadan, the most important observance in Islam ▼

▲ Thanksgiving in the United States, featuring turkey, the traditional Thanksgiving food

People in Rio de Janeiro, Brazil, enjoying Carnaval, Brazil's world-famous celebration ▼

▲ People in Hong Kong celebrating the Chinese New Year

**B** **DISCUSSION.** Why do people think it is important to keep traditions alive? Do you think it is important to learn about the customs and traditions of other religions and cultures?

# Holidays and Traditions

 **A** **TOPIC PREVIEW**

| Suggested teaching time: | 10–15 minutes |
|---|---|
| Your actual teaching time: | _____ |

- Write on the board:
  *What? When? Why?*

- Group work. Form groups of three. To use the strategy of schema building (activating students' prior knowledge), have students share what they may already know about the traditions in the pictures. This could be vocabulary, locations, activities, etc.

- Encourage students to ask questions about the traditions in the pictures they want to know more about. Examples: *I want to know more about mariachi because I'm very interested in music. I'd like to know if Korean couples wear hanbok when they get married.*

- Ask various students to say one tradition they would like to know more about and why.

**Culture note:** **Mariachi** is festive and romantic music. Modern mariachi bands play trumpets, violins, a small guitar *(vihuela)*, and a large guitar *(guitarrón)*. Mariachi music is played on holidays, to celebrate important events, as well as to entertain in restaurants and at parties. **Hanbok** is the name of traditional Korean clothing worn by men and women on traditional holidays or special occasions, such as weddings. Women usually wear a long dress or skirt, and men, wide pants, a shirt, and a short jacket. The **Chinese New Year** follows the lunar calendar and takes place between January and the middle of February. It is the most important Chinese holiday. People decorate their homes with red paper decorations and prepare traditional foods for families and friends. There are fireworks and parades with large dragons, which symbolize strength and happiness. **Thanksgiving,** a national holiday in the United States, is celebrated on the fourth Thursday in November. Families and friends get together and "give thanks" for all they have. Thanksgiving is also celebrated in Canada on the second Monday of October. **Carnaval** is a four-day celebration celebrated in many other countries; for example, Venezuela, Argentina, and Spain. But the most famous celebrations take place in Rio de Janeiro, Brazil. It is a four-day celebration in February or March. There are colorful parades, full of music and dancing people. **Eid ul-Fitr** comes at the end of Ramadan when Muslims celebrate the end of a period of fasting. It is traditional for people to decorate their homes, visit with friends and family, and serve sweets.

**B** **DISCUSSION**

| Suggested teaching time: | 10 minutes |
|---|---|
| Your actual teaching time: | _____ |

- Write on the board:
  *An old tradition in my country is ____.*

- Ask students to brainstorm and fill in the blank. Have them write some notes on a separate piece of paper about the importance of the tradition.

- Group work. Form small groups. Encourage students to share their opinions and ideas and to use their notes as they discuss the questions.

- Walk around the room and provide help as needed.

- Ask various students to say one of their reasons why we should keep traditions alive. Write a list on the board. Examples: *Traditions create a sense of identity. They remind or teach about important historical events. Traditions develop a sense of community. They reflect the values of a culture.*

- Then ask different students for their opinions about the importance of learning about other cultures' customs and traditions. Examples: *It can help us understand other cultures. Learning about others helps teach respect for different ways of thinking and doing things.*

**Challenge:** Student project. Students can work individually or in small groups. Ask students to choose one of the traditions in the pictures and do some research. Have them give a brief presentation to the class about the event. **[timing will vary]**

## C  SOUND BITES
(CD3, Track 2)

| Suggested teaching time: | 10 minutes |
|---|---|
| Your actual teaching time: | _____ |

- Note: Maya is from Malaysia and Min-Jin is from Korea.

- After reading and listening, ask students to (use their own words) summarize the description of the holiday. (Possible answer: *Chuseok, a Korean harvest festival, takes place in September or October. Everyone visits their family and relatives.*)

- Point out that *Oh yeah?* means *Really?*

- Draw the following diagram on the board. Ask students to write the name of a harvest festival (or other holiday) they know and then brainstorm and write the information that answers each question. Example: *The harvest festival of Thanksgiving is celebrated in the U.S. on the fourth Thursday in November. Families and friends get together for the day and share a wonderful meal. The traditional foods served on Thanksgiving—turkey, potatoes, and vegetables—are symbols of a successful harvest.* etc.

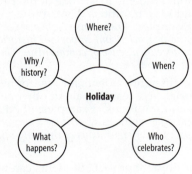

 **Graphic Organizers**

- Pairs or small groups. Have students share their diagrams and information with their partners. Encourage students to ask for clarification and to ask follow-up questions.

> **Culture note:** *Harvest* is the time when crops (vegetables, fruit, grains, etc.) are ripe and then picked or taken from the field. *Chuseok* (or *Chu Suk*) is one of the most important holidays in Korea. People get together with their families, share stories and memories, and celebrate by singing, dancing, playing games, and eating traditional food. Many Koreans travel to the towns where their ancestors are buried.

## D  IN OTHER WORDS

| Suggested teaching time: | 5 minutes |
|---|---|
| Your actual teaching time: | _____ |

- Encourage students to first identify who says the phrases and to use the context of the conversation to help work out their meanings.

- Other possible answers are: 1. That dress is beautiful. 2. It's in September. 3. We (go) see our relatives. 4. The train stations are full of people. 5. The traffic is very heavy.

- Have students compare answers with a partner. Then review as a class. Make necessary corrections.

## E On a separate . . .

| Suggested teaching time: | 5–10 minutes |
|---|---|
| Your actual teaching time: | _____ |

- Tell students they can use the words to describe one holiday or various holidays.

- You may want to give an example: *Thousands of people celebrate Carnaval in Rio de Janiero. The streets are mobbed and it's almost impossible to move!*

- To review, have various students read one or two of their sentences out loud in small groups or in front of the class. Encourage the class to listen for the target word or phrase and make necessary corrections.

## WHAT ABOUT YOU?

| Suggested teaching time: | 5–10 minutes |
|---|---|
| Your actual teaching time: | _____ |

- Group work. Form small groups. Students take turns sharing their information using complete sentences.

- Encourage students to ask each other follow-up questions. Example: Student A: *After a wedding ceremony, as the bride and groom are leaving, people throw rice at them.* Student B: *Why rice?* Student A: *It's supposed to bring good luck and lots of children!*

- Walk around the room and provide help as needed.

- Ask volunteers to share with the class any information they learned about that was new or unusual.

## EXTRAS (optional)
**Workbook: Exercises 1–3**

 **SOUND BITES.** Read along silently as you listen to a conversation during a coffee break at an international meeting.

**MAYA:** Wow! That dress Su-min is wearing is spectacular. What was the occasion?

**MIN-JIN:** Chuseok. The dress is called a hanbok.

**MAYA:** Did you say "Chuseok"? What's that—a holiday?

**MIN-JIN:** That's right. It's a Korean harvest celebration. It takes place in September or October each year. **CN1**

**CN1 Corpus Notes:** *In* follows *take place* more than any other word. The prepositions *at* and *on* are second and third most frequent.

**MAYA:** Oh yeah? What does everybody do?

**MIN-JIN:** We get together with our relatives. The airports and train stations are mobbed with passengers, **CN2** and the roads are impossible. It takes hours to get anywhere.

**MAYA:** Every country's got at least one holiday like that!

**CN2 Corpus Notes:** The verb *mob* is most frequently used in the passive voice.

**D** **IN OTHER WORDS.** **Say each statement in another way.** Answers may vary. Possible answers include:

1. That dress is spectacular.
   I really like that dress.
2. It takes place in September.
   It happens in September.
3. We get together with our relatives.
   We visit our relatives.

4. The train stations are mobbed with passengers. The train stations are very crowded.

5. The roads are impossible.
   The traffic is very bad.

**E** On a separate sheet of paper, write five sentences about holidays in your country. Use the following words or phrases: **spectacular**, **take place**, **get together with**, **mobbed with people**, and **impossible**.

## WHAT ABOUT YOU?

Complete the chart. Give examples and information about holiday traditions in your country.

| a clothing item: | When is it worn? |
|---|---|
| a type of music: | When is it played? |
| a food: | When is it eaten? |
| a dance: | When is it danced? |
| a special event: | What happens? |

# Find out about a Holiday

🎧 CONVERSATION **MODEL** **Read and listen.**

**A:** I heard there's going to be a holiday.

**B:** That's right. The Harvest Moon Festival.

**A:** What kind of holiday is that?

**B:** It's a seasonal holiday that takes place in autumn. People spend time with their families and eat moon cakes. **CN**

**A:** Well, have a great Harvest Moon Festival!

**B:** Thanks! Same to you!

🎧 **Rhythm and intonation practice**

🎧 **Types of holidays**
seasonal
historical
religious

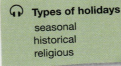
a moon cake

**A** 🎧 **VOCABULARY.**
**Ways to commemorate a holiday.** **Listen and practice.**

set off fireworks

march in parades

have picnics **CN**

pray

send cards

give each other gifts

wish each other well

remember the dead

wear costumes

**CN** Corpus Notes:
*With, in,* and *on* are the prepositions that most frequently follow *spend time.* It is also common to say *spend time (doing something).*

Another option is to use *go on a picnic,* but *have a picnic,* is used more frequently.

**B** 🎧 **LISTENING COMPREHENSION.** **Listen carefully to the descriptions of holidays.**
**Write the type of holiday and what people do to celebrate.**

|  | Type of holiday | What people do to celebrate |
|---|---|---|
| Mardi Gras (U.S.) | religious | wear costumes, have a parade |
| Bastille Day (France) | historical | dance in the streets, eat all kinds of food, military parades, fireworks |
| Tsagaan Sar (Mongolia) | seasonal | wear new clothes, clean every corner of their house, make traditional food, give gifts |

## LESSON 1
# Find out about a Holiday

### 🎧 CONVERSATION **MODEL**
(CD3, Tracks 3, 5)

| Suggested teaching time: | 5 minutes |
|---|---|
| Your actual teaching time: | _____ |

- After students read and listen, ask *What's special about next week?* (a holiday, the Harvest Moon Festival) *Why does the woman say it's seasonal?* (People celebrate this holiday each year in autumn.)
- Have students listen to the holidays and repeat.
- Review when or why they happen.

**Option:** Group work. Form small groups. Ask students to write down one or two examples they know for each type of holiday (in the box). Write student answers in three groups on the board. **[+ 5 minutes]**

> **Culture note:** In China, the Harvest Moon Festival celebrates the biggest, brightest full moon of the year. After the sun had set, farmers used to continue harvesting. During the festival, families get together to eat moon cakes—small round pastries with traditional fillings, like red bean paste, or more modern fillings like fruit and jam. In Korea, this festival is called *Chuseok* (or *Chu Suk*), and in Vietnam, *Trung Thu*.

### 🎧 Rhythm and intonation practice
(CD3, Track 4)

| Suggested teaching time: | 5 minutes |
|---|---|
| Your actual teaching time: | _____ |

- Have students repeat each line chorally.
- Make sure students:
  - use falling intonation for *What kind of holiday is that?*
  - stress new and important information such as <u>sea</u>sonal, <u>hol</u>iday, and <u>autumn</u> in *It's a seasonal holiday that takes place in autumn.*
  - use the following stress pattern:

**STRESS PATTERN**

```
      •  __   •    •    •  •   •  __ •  •
A:  I heard there's going to be a holiday.

    __   •    •    •    __   __ • •
B:  That's right. The Harvest Moon Festival.

      •  __   __  __ • •   __
A:  What kind of holiday is that?

    •  •  __  •  •     •  __   •    •  •   •  __
B:  It's a seasonal holiday that takes place in autumn.

    __   •   •   •    __   • •  •   __
    People spend time with their families and eat moon
      •
    cakes.

      •   •   __  •   __  •  •   __   •
A:  Well, have a great Harvest Moon Festival!

    __   •   •   __
B:  Thanks!  Same to you!
```

### 🅐 🎧 VOCABULARY
(CD3, Track 6)

| Suggested teaching time: | 5–10 minutes |
|---|---|
| Your actual teaching time: | _____ |

- Have students listen and study the vocabulary. Then have students listen and repeat chorally.
- Pair work. Ask students to write down one occasion or holiday for each vocabulary phrase. Provide an example: *We set off fireworks and march in parades on Independence Day.*
- To review, ask students to say their examples using complete sentences.

> **Culture note:** The people depicted for *pray* are praying in the Muslim tradition. The people depicted for *wish each other well* are dressed for New Year's Eve, the last night of the year. The people depicted for *wear costumes* are celebrating Halloween—a U.S. holiday for children. Many adults also enjoy dressing up for Halloween parties.

 Learning Strategies

### 🅑 🎧 LISTENING COMPREHENSION
(CD3, Track 7)

| Suggested teaching time: | 10 minutes |
|---|---|
| Your actual teaching time: | _____ |

- Have students study the chart. If there is a world map in the classroom, point out the countries.
- Pre-listening: Ask students to say the three types of holidays they should use in the first column. (seasonal, historical, religious)
- First listening: Stop the recording after each description to allow students time to write.
- Have students compare answers with a classmate.
- Second listening: To practice note-taking, make sure students understand that they should write words and phrases, not sentences.
- Review as a class. Encourage students to use their notes to make complete sentences as they give their answers. Example: *Mardi Gras is a religious holiday.*

**AUDIOSCRIPT**

LISTENING 1

**M:** There are Mardi Gras celebrations in many places in the world, but the Mardi Gras celebrations in New Orleans in the United States are world-famous. Mardi Gras means "fat Tuesday," and usually occurs in February. It began as a religious holiday in which people could really enjoy themselves before the more solemn Catholic celebration of Lent. Now it's considered to be "the biggest party in the world," and people travel from all over to enjoy the celebrations. On this day, people wear really wild costumes and dance in a huge parade to New Orleans' famous jazz music. Along the parade route, people in the parade throw purple, green and gold colored necklaces, candy, and other things to the people who are watching.

**AUDIOSCRIPT continues on page T55.**

##  GRAMMAR

| Suggested teaching time: | 5–10 minutes |
|---|---|
| Your actual teaching time: | _____ |

- Tips for organizing information on the board: Write all of the examples from these grammar notes on one side of the board. This creates a helpful reference list for students while doing the practice activities.

- Direct attention to the box and have students read the first explanation and study the examples.

- Write on the board:

  1. The Harvest Moon Festival is a (holiday) that takes place in autumn.
  2. A gift is (something) that you give as a present.

- To help clarify, point out that an adjective clause (underlined) gives information about a noun or a pronoun (circled).

- Write on the board:

  3. My sister is the girl __ is wearing a costume.
  4. Mariachi is a kind of music __ was born in Mexico.
  5. Anyone __ comes to the party should bring something to eat.

- To check comprehension, ask students to fill in the blanks with *who* or *that*. Review as a class. (3. who or that  4. that  5. who or that)

- Have students read the Be Careful! explanation and study the example.

- Write on the board:

  6. Carnaval is a holiday that it is celebrated in many countries.
  7. My brother is the boy who he is carrying the flag.

- To check comprehension, have students correct the sentences by crossing out the unnecessary word in each adjective clause. (6. it  7. he)

 **Grammar Self-Checks**

##  Underline the adjective clauses . . .

| Suggested teaching time: | 5 minutes |
|---|---|
| Your actual teaching time: | _____ |

- Review the example first. Encourage students to follow the steps outlined in the direction line.

- Have students compare answers with a partner. Then review as a class.

## E PAIR WORK

| Suggested teaching time: | 5 minutes |
|---|---|
| Your actual teaching time: | _____ |

- Review the models first.

- You may want to provide more models on the board:

  . . . is a celebration that . . .
  . . . is someone who . . .
  . . . are the people who . . .
  . . . is something that . . .
  . . . is the traditional food that . . .

- To review, first provide controlled feedback by asking various pairs for one of their sentences and making necessary corrections.

- Then combine pairs and have them exchange papers. Tell students to focus on adjective clauses and relative pronouns as they correct each other's sentences.

- Walk around the room and provide help as needed.

**Challenge:** Group work. Form groups of three. Students take turns describing a holiday using adjective clauses and having their partners guess. Students can choose a holiday in this unit or others they know. Example: Student A: *It's a holiday that takes place in December.* Student B: *Hannukah?* Student A: *No. It's a holiday that happens on the last day of December.* Student C: *New Year's Eve!* **[+10 minutes]**

## CONVERSATION **PAIR WORK**

| Suggested teaching time: | 5–10 minutes |
|---|---|
| Your actual teaching time: | _____ |

- To get students ready for the activity, have students read the conversation model on page 52 again. You may also want to have students listen to the model.

- Encourage students to describe the holiday by using adjective clauses to provide extra information. If necessary, students can refer to the grammar in Exercise C.

- Choose a more confident student and role-play a conversation. Encourage students to ask follow-up questions to continue the conversation.

- Walk around the room and provide help as needed. Encourage students to use the correct rhythm and intonation.

**Culture note:** Good wishes are appropriate for celebratory holidays. However, it would not be appropriate to say "Have a nice ___" for a serious holiday, for example, one that commemorates the dead.

 **Pair Work Cards**

## EXTRAS (optional)

**Grammar Booster**
**Workbook: Exercises 4–9**
**Copy & Go: Activity 17**

**GRAMMAR.** **Adjective clauses with subject relative pronouns**

Use an adjective clause to identify or give information about a noun or an indefinite pronoun such as <u>someone</u>, <u>something</u>, etc. Begin an adjective clause with the relative pronouns <u>who</u> or <u>that</u> for adjective clauses that describe people. Use <u>that</u> for adjective clauses that describe things.

A mariachi singer is someone **who** (or **that**) **sings traditional Mexican music**.
Carnaval is a great holiday for people **who** (or **that**) **like parades**.
Anyone **who** (or **that**) **doesn't wear a costume** can't go to the festival.
Halloween is a celebration **that takes place in October**.
The parade **that takes place on Bastille Day** is very exciting.

**BE CAREFUL!** Don't use a subject pronoun after the relative pronoun.
Don't say: Halloween is a celebration that ~~it~~ takes place in October.

**PAGES G7–G9**
**For more …**

**D** Underline the adjective clauses and circle the relative pronouns. Then draw an arrow from the relative pronoun to the noun or pronoun that it describes.

1. Ramadan is a religious tradition (that) is observed by Muslims all over the world.

2. Chuseok is a Korean holiday (that) celebrates the yearly harvest.

3. The gifts (that) people usually give to each other are not very expensive.

4. In the United States, a person (who) is invited for dinner often brings a gift to eat or drink.

5. The Day of the Dead in Mexico is a celebration (that) takes place in November.

6. The celebrations (that) take place in Brazil during Carnaval are a lot of fun.

**E** **PAIR WORK.** Create five sentences with adjective clauses to describe some holidays in your country. Use the models to begin. Answers will vary.

| … is a (religious) holiday that… | … is a great holiday for people who… |

## CONVERSATION
### PAIR WORK

**Role-play a conversation with a visitor to your country. Exchange information about holidays. Start like this, or create a new conversation.** Answers will vary.

**A:** I heard there's going to be a holiday next _____ .
**B:** That's right. _____ .
**A:** What kind of holiday is that?
**B:** _____ …

**Continue the conversation in your <u>own</u> way.**

**Ways to give good wishes on holidays**
Have a nice / good / great [Carnaval]!
Have a happy [New Year]!
Enjoy yourself on [Chuseok]!

**53**

**CONTROLLED PRACTICE**

# Ask about the Customs of Another Culture

## ⌒ CONVERSATION MODEL  Read and listen.

**A:** Do you mind if I ask you something?

**B:** Of course not. What's up?

**A:** I'm not sure of the customs here. When you're invited for dinner, should you bring the host a gift?

**B:** Yes. That's a good idea. But the gift that you bring should be small.

**A:** Would flowers be appropriate?

**B:** Absolutely perfect!

**A:** Thanks. It's a good thing I asked.

⌒ **Rhythm and intonation practice**

---

**A** ▸ **GRAMMAR.  Adjective clauses with object relative pronouns**

**In some adjective clauses, the relative pronoun is the subject of the clause.**
The person **who comes for dinner** should bring a gift.
[who = subject because he or she is the performer of the action]

**In other adjective clauses, the relative pronoun is the object of the clause.**
The person **who** [or **whom**] **you invite** should bring a gift.
[who (or whom) = object because he or she is the receiver of the action]

**When the relative pronoun is the object of the clause, it may be omitted.**
The book **that you bought** gives great information about holidays. OR
The book **you bought** gives great information about holidays.

**When the relative pronoun is the subject of the clause, it may NOT be omitted.**
The author **who wrote that book** did a great job.
NOT ~~The author wrote that book did a great job~~.

GRAMMAR BOOSTER
**PAGE G9**
**For more …**

---

**B** ▸ ⌒ **PRONUNCIATION.  "Thought groups."  Notice how rhythm indicates how thoughts are grouped.  Listen and repeat.**

1. The person who comes for dinner should bring flowers.
2. The man we invited to the party is from Senegal.
3. The song that you were listening to is fado music from Portugal.
4. The Cherry Blossom Festival is a holiday that is celebrated in Japan every spring.

maracas, traditional musical instruments of the Caribbean and Latin America

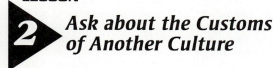

# LESSON 2

## Ask about the Customs of Another Culture

### 🎧 CONVERSATION MODEL
(CD3, Track 8)

| Suggested teaching time: | 5 minutes |
|---|---|
| Your actual teaching time: | _____ |

- After students read and listen, ask *What is a host?* (the person who invites you to an event) *What custom is the man asking about?* (what to do when you're invited to someone's home for dinner) *What is the woman's opinion about giving flowers?* (She thinks it's a very good idea.)

**Language note:** Many traditional definitions present *bring* and *take* as having somewhat different meanings. In spoken English, however, few native speakers differentiate between them.

### 🎧 Rhythm and intonation practice
(CD3, Track 9)

| Suggested teaching time: | 5 minutes |
|---|---|
| Your actual teaching time: | _____ |

- Have students repeat each line chorally.
- Make sure students:
  ○ use rising intonation for *Do you mind if I ask you something?*
  ○ use falling intonation at the end of *What's up?*
  ○ use rising intonation for *should you bring the host a gift?*
  ○ use rising intonation for *Would flowers be appropriate?*
  ○ use the following stress pattern:

---STRESS PATTERN---

**A:** Do you mind if I ask you something?

**B:** Of course not. What's up?

**A:** I'm not sure of the customs here. When you're invited for dinner, should you bring the host a gift?

**B:** Yes. That's a good idea. But the gift you bring should be small.

**A:** Would flowers be appropriate?

**B:** Absolutely perfect!

**A:** Thanks. It's a good thing I asked.

### 🔷 A GRAMMAR

| Suggested teaching time: | 10–15 minutes |
|---|---|
| Your actual teaching time: | _____ |

- Direct attention to the box and have students read the first explanation and study the example.
- Write on the board:
  *1. The friend who sent me flowers lives in Paris.*
- Ask students to identify the adjective clause (who sent me flowers). Underline the clause.
- To help clarify, say *"Who" is the subject of the clause. My friend is the performer (doer) of the action of sending me flowers.*
- Have students read the second explanation and study the example.
- Write on the board:
  *2. She is the woman who Peter invited to the party.*
- Ask students to identify the clause (who Peter invited to the party). Underline the clause.
- To help clarify, ask *Who is the performer of the action inviting?* (Peter). Then tell students *The woman is the receiver of the action so "Who" is the object, not the subject.*
- Have students read the third and fourth explanations and study the examples. Tell them to keep in mind subject vs. object of a clause as they read.
- To check comprehension, direct attention to *who* in sentence 2 on the board. Say *When "who" is the object of the clause, it can be omitted.* Then erase *who*.
- Direct attention to *who* in sentence 1 and ask *If "who" is the subject of the clause, can I omit it?* (no)

**Language note:** Both *who* and *whom* can be used in the object position but *who* is more common in everyday speech. Most native speakers use the subject relative pronoun *that* instead of *who*.

 **Grammar Self-Checks**

### 🔷 B 🎧 PRONUNCIATION
(CD3, Track 10)

| Suggested teaching time: | 10 minutes |
|---|---|
| Your actual teaching time: | _____ |

- First listening: Have students listen and study the examples. Point out that the adjective clauses form "natural" thought groups.
- Second listening: Have students listen and repeat.
- To provide more practice, have students practice saying the sentences in the Grammar box focusing on thought groups.

**Language note:** A *thought group* is a group of words said together in the rhythm of a sentence in order to help convey a meaning or message more clearly. The speaker often pauses between groups.

 **Pronunciation Activities**

## C  PAIR WORK

| Suggested teaching time: | 5–10 minutes |
|---|---|
| Your actual teaching time: | _____ |

- Review the example first. To make sure students understand the correct answer, ask *Why can the relative pronoun "that" be deleted?* (because it is the object of the clause)
- Remind students that relative pronouns that are subjects of clauses cannot be deleted.
- Encourage students to identify the adjective clauses first.
- Both items 2 and 5 could be *whom,* but *who* is increasingly used as the object pronoun.
- Review answers as a class.

**Option:** To provide more practice, write the following statements on the board. Ask students to identify and cross out relative pronouns that can be omitted. (sentences 1 and 5: relative pronouns can't be omitted; sentences 2, 3, 4: they can be omitted) **[+5 minutes]**

1. *Carnaval is a holiday that is very popular in Brazil.*
2. *Carnaval is a holiday that I have always enjoyed.*
3. *I gave her the flowers that I picked from my garden.*
4. *I can't find the gift that she gave me.*
5. *I saw some friends who were marching in a parade.*

**Culture note:** *La Tomatina* is a wild festival during which thousands of people throw tomatoes at each other for two hours!

## D  Correct the error . . .

| Suggested teaching time: | 5 minutes |
|---|---|
| Your actual teaching time: | _____ |

- Review the example first. Remind students that a clause can't have two subjects.
- Have students compare answers with a partner. Then review as a class.

## CONVERSATION **PAIR WORK**

| Suggested teaching time: | 5–10 minutes |
|---|---|
| Your actual teaching time: | _____ |

- To get students ready for the activity, have students read the conversation model on page 54 again. You may also want to have students listen to the model.
- Have students read the ideas in the box. Then ask students to write one question someone might ask for each situation.

- Ask students for their questions and make a list on the board. Examples: Someone invites you out for dinner: *Should I offer to pay the check? Should I invite the person out for dinner the next week?* Someone invites you to a party: *Should I bring the host a gift? Should I let the person know if I'm coming or not?* Someone gives you a gift: *Should I open it in front of the person? Should I put it away without opening it?* Someone makes a special effort to help you: *Should I offer to do a favor in return? Should I send a thank-you card?*
- Choose a more confident student and role-play a conversation.
- Walk around the room and provide help as needed. Encourage students to use the correct rhythm and intonation.

 **Pair Work Cards**

 **Learning Strategies**

## EXTRAS (optional)

**Grammar Booster**
**Workbook: Exercises 10–12**
**Copy & Go: Activity 18**

 **Pronunciation Supplements**

### AUDIOSCRIPT

**AUDIOSCRIPT continued from Exercise B, page T52.**

LISTENING 2
**F:** Celebrated on July 14th, Bastille Day is France's most important national holiday. It celebrates the attack on the hated Bastille prison, which marked the beginning of the French Revolution that led to modern France. It's a joyous holiday in which people celebrate being French. You can see people dancing in the streets together and eating all kinds of food. Usually in the morning there are military parades with French flags flying all over. And in the evening, fireworks are set off and families sit together to watch them.

LISTENING 3
**M:** Tsagaan Sar—or White Month—is a celebration of the lunar new year in Mongolia. It's held for three days in February or March. Before the first day of the celebration, families clean every corner of their house. During this time, people wear new clothes—usually traditional Mongolian clothing—and they make lots of traditional foods. They also give each other gifts, and especially enjoy giving gifts to their children. One of the ways Mongolians really enjoy themselves during this holiday is to watch wrestling matches and horse races. All these activities symbolize starting the new year clean, rich, and happy.

**PAIR WORK.** **Discuss whether the relative pronoun can be deleted. If it can be deleted, cross it out.**

1. The traditional Chinese dress ~~that~~ she has is called a cheongsam.

2. The man ~~who~~ you were talking with plays in a mariachi band.

3. Anzac Day is a holiday ~~that~~ people in Australia and New Zealand celebrate to remember the soldiers who died in wars.

4. People who visit other countries should find out about the local customs.

5. The young people ~~whom~~ you saw in the parade today were all wearing traditional costumes.

 **Correct the error in each sentence.**

1. Putting butter on a child's nose is a birthday tradition that ~~it~~ is celebrated on the Atlantic coast of Canada.

2. On the Day of the Dead, Mexicans remember family members who ~~they~~ have died.

3. The older couple we saw at the restaurant ~~they~~ were doing the tango.

4. La Tomatina is a festival that ~~it~~ is celebrated in Bunol, Spain.

5. The singer <u>who</u> performed at Casey Hall last night is well known all over Europe.

A bouquet of flowers is a popular gift in many countries.

## CONVERSATION PAIR WORK

**Role-play a conversation with a visitor to your country. Discuss customs. Use the guide and the ideas from the box, or create a new conversation.** Answers will vary.

**A:** Do you mind if I ask you something?

**B:** Of course not. What's up?

**A:** I'm not sure about the customs here. When _____?

**B:** _____ …

**Continue the conversation your <u>own</u> way.**

💡 **Some ideas…**

- someone invites you out for dinner
- someone invites you to a party
- someone gives you a gift
- someone makes a special effort to help you

**3** ▶ *Describe a Holiday or Celebration*

**A** ▶ **READING WARM-UP.** What are your favorite holiday traditions?

**B** ▶ 🎧 **READING.** Read about some holiday traditions and observances from around the world. Are any of them familiar to you?

# HOLIDAYS AROUND THE WORLD

## Thailand's Wet Water Festival

Songkran marks the start of the Buddhist New Year in Thailand. It is a wild and wonderful festival in which people of all ages have fun dousing each other with water for three solid days. If you decide to stay indoors, you'll miss out on a great time!

Songkran began nearly a thousand years ago to celebrate the beginning of the farming season. It is a time when Thai people routinely do a thorough cleaning of their homes. Additionally, people make offerings to local temples and provide food and new robes for monks.

During Songkran there is singing and dancing in the streets, and lots of water. Visitors should expect to become totally drenched—and love every minute of it! On every side street, you'll find children waiting to throw water at you. Bus riders also need to be careful. Some people have been known to hurl buckets of water through open windows!

People douse each other with water during Songkran.

## Ramadan, the Month of Fasting

"May you be well throughout the year," is the typical greeting during Ramadan, the ninth month of the Islamic calendar, a special month of the year for over one billion Muslims throughout the world. According to Islamic tradition, Ramadan marks the time when Muhammad received the word of God through the Koran. Throughout the month, Muslims fast—totally abstaining from food and drinks from the break of dawn until the setting of the sun. The usual practice is to have a pre-fast meal before dawn and a post-fast meal after sunset. It is also a time of increased worship and giving to the poor and the community. Ramadan ends with the festival of Eid ul-Fitr—three days of family celebrations—and eating!

## Simon Bolivar's Birthday

Simon Bolivar was born on July 24, 1783 in Caracas, Venezuela. He is known throughout Latin America as "The Liberator" because of his fight for independence from Spain. He led the armies that freed Venezuela, Bolivia, Colombia, Ecuador, Peru, and Panama. He is memorialized in many ways, but two countries celebrate his birthday every July 24th—Venezuela and Ecuador. On that day, schools and most general businesses are closed and there are military parades and government ceremonies. But the malls are open and people usually use the holiday to go shopping.

Worshippers pray during Ramadan.

Bolivar led the fight for independence from Spain.

**SOURCES:** www.muhajabah.com and www.colostate.edu

# 3 Describe a Holiday or Celebration

## A READING WARM-UP

| Suggested teaching time: | 5–10 minutes |
|---|---|
| Your actual teaching time: | _____ |

• Ask students to say some of their favorite traditions for special events or holidays and make a list on the board. Examples: *decorating for [holiday], going on a picnic for my birthday, preparing traditional food for [holiday], visiting my relatives on [holiday],* etc.

• You may want to ask students to say some holidays or traditions they know and like from other cultures and countries.

## B 🎧 READING

(CD3, Track 11)

| Suggested teaching time: | 10–15 minutes |
|---|---|
| Your actual teaching time: | _____ |

• To practice the reading strategy of scanning, ask students to read the article (quickly) and underline the name, reason, date, and location for each holiday.

• Ask students to give their answers in complete sentences. (Possible answers: Songkran begins the Buddhist new year in Thailand. / Ramadan celebrates when Mohammad got the word of God from the Koran. It takes place all over the world in the ninth month of the Islamic calendar. / Simon Bolivar's birthday is celebrated on July 24th in Venezuela, Bolivia, and Ecuador. OR Simon Bolivar is famous for fighting for independence for many countries in Latin American and his birthday, July 24, is celebrated in Venezuela, Bolivia, and Ecuador.)

**Option:** Use this option if you want to do a listening activity. Books closed. Draw the following chart (without the answers) on the board. Ask students to check the information that matches each holiday. Then have students read the text to check their answers.
**[+10 minutes]**

| What happens? | Wet Water Festival | Ramadan | Simon Bolivar's Birthday |
|---|---|---|---|
| 1. It lasts one day. | | | ✓ |
| 2. It lasts three days. | ✓ | | |
| 3. It lasts one month. | | ✓ | |
| 4. People go shopping. | | | ✓ |
| 5. People clean their homes. | ✓ | | |
| 6. People offer gifts to God and the monks. | ✓ | | |
| 7. People give to the poor. | | ✓ | |
| 8. There are parades and ceremonies. | | | ✓ |
| 9. People only eat before dawn and after sunset. | | ✓ | |

**Language note:** Students may need help with the following words: *douse* (to cover something in water); *robe* (a long loose piece of clothing, especially worn for official and religious ceremonies); *drenched* (completely wet); *hurl* (to throw something violently); *Koran* (the holy book of Islam); *abstain* (to not do something or to stop doing something); *liberator* (a person who frees a person or country from someone's control).

**Language note:** You may want to point out the prefixes *pre-* (before) and *post-* (after). *Pre-* and *post-* combine with nouns to form compound nouns. Examples: *pre-fast meal, post-fast meal, pre-dawn breakfast, post-sunset dinner.*

**Culture note:** The name of the place where different religions pray or worship varies. Muslims → mosque, Jews → synagogue, Buddhists → temple, Christians → church.

 **Extra Reading Comprehension Activities**

**Learning Strategies**

**Graphic Organizers**

## DISCUSSION

- Ask students to read the article again and underline information they could use to discuss the questions.

- Group work. Form groups of three or four. Encourage students to use their notes as they talk.

- Answers for question 1: Thailand's Wet Water Festival: *seasonal holiday*; Ramadan: *religious holiday*; Bolivar's birthday: *historical holiday*.

- For question 2, ask students to give supporting reasons for their choice of the most interesting holiday. Examples: Songkran: *It sounds like fun, and it's so different from serious holidays.* Ramadan: *It's important to remember others who don't have what we do.* Bolivar's birthday: *He is an important part of our history, and we need to show our respect.*

- For question 3, you may want to encourage students to compare only one holiday with one of the holidays in the article (two at a time).

- To help students organize their ideas for question 3, draw the following Venn diagram on the board and ask students to write their ideas in the circles. The details that the holidays have in common should be written in the middle / overlapping area of the circles. Then walk around the room and provide help as needed.

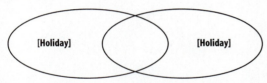

 **Graphic Organizers**

 **Extra Reading Comprehension Activities**

## TOP NOTCH **INTERACTION**

### STEP 1. PAIR WORK.

- Make sure students only write notes, not complete sentences, on the notepad.

- You may want to encourage students to point out what they like or dislike about the customs and traditions of a holiday.

**Option:** Take a poll to find out what three holidays your students chose to write notes about.   **[+5 minutes]**

### STEP 2. ROLE PLAY.

- Point out the NEED HELP? section and review the expressions.

- Have students switch roles and work with a new partner.

- Ask pairs of students to role play one of their conversations in front of the class.

### EXTRAS (optional)

Workbook: **Exercises 13, 14**
Copy & Go: **Activity 19**

 **DISCUSSION.**

1. How would you categorize each of the holidays in the article—religious, seasonal, or historic?

2. Which holiday or tradition do you find the most interesting? Why?

3. Do you know any holidays, observances, or traditions that are similar to these? What are they? How are they similar and different?

## TOP NOTCH
### INTERACTION • *Do you mind if I ask you something?*

**STEP 1. PAIR WORK.** Choose three holidays in your country. Discuss them and write some notes about them on your notepad. Answers will vary.

| A historic holiday | A religious holiday | A seasonal holiday |
|---|---|---|
| name of holiday: | name of holiday: | name of holiday: |
| typical foods: | typical foods: | typical foods: |
| typical clothing: | typical clothing: | typical clothing: |
| other traditions: | other traditions: | other traditions: |

**STEP 2. ROLE PLAY.** Take turns with a different partner. One of you is a visitor to your country. Ask about and explain your holidays and traditions. Use your notepad for ideas.
Answers will vary.

NEED HELP? **Here's language you already know:**

**Resident**
It's a great day for ——.
It's customary to ——.
It's offensive to ——.
—— is taboo.
It's impolite to ——.
It's probably best to ——.
That must be ——.
You can eat ——.
You can wear ——.

**Visitor**
Do you mind if I ask you ——?
I hear people ——.
Is it possible to ——?
What do people do?
I'm not sure of the customs here.
Would —— be appropriate?
It's a good thing I asked!
It's a ——, isn't it?

traditional Japanese origami

# 4 ▸ *Explain Wedding Traditions*

**A** ▸ 🎧 **VOCABULARY. Getting married. Listen and practice.**

**an engagement**   an agreement to marry someone

**get engaged**   agree to marry **CN**

**a ceremony**   a formal set of actions used at an important social or religious event such as a wedding

**a wedding**   a marriage ceremony, especially one with a religious service

**a reception**   a large formal party after a ceremony

**a honeymoon**   a vacation taken by two newlyweds

🎧 **The wedding couple**
**a bride**  a woman at the time she gets married
**a groom**  a man at the time he gets married
**newlyweds**  the bride and groom after the wedding

**CN** **Corpus Notes:**
A person gets engaged *to*, not *with*, another person. This is a common learner error; be sure students are aware of this.

**B** ▸ **Read about some wedding traditions in many English-speaking countries. Then use the vocabulary to describe a wedding tradition you are familiar with.**

The bride throws her bouquet after **the wedding ceremony**. The woman who catches the bouquet is believed to be the next to get married.

The newlyweds cut the cake together **at the wedding reception**.

The groom carries the bride "across the threshold," through the doorway into their new home. Soon after the wedding, they **go on their honeymoon**.

**C** ▸ 🎧 **LISTENING COMPREHENSION. Listen carefully to Part 1 of a lecture about a traditional wedding in India. Then read the statements and listen again. Check the statements that are true. Correct the statements that are false.**

**PART 1. Before the wedding**

☑ **1.** A traditional Hindu wedding celebration can last for more than five days.

☐ **2.** The wedding date is chosen based on the ~~date the bride prefers.~~ ⌄ bride and groom's birthdays, and other details, to bring good luck.

☐ **3.** Musicians visit the ~~bride~~'s home and play traditional music. *groom*

☑ **4.** The groom's relatives wash the groom with coconut or olive oil.

☐ **5.** An older person in the family offers the groom ~~food.~~ *money*

☑ **6.** The bride's relatives paint her face, arms, hands, and feet.

# LESSON 4 Explain Wedding Traditions

## A 🎧 VOCABULARY
**(CD3, Track 12)**

| Suggested teaching time: | 5 minutes |
|---|---|
| Your actual teaching time: | _____ |

- Have students listen and study the words and the definitions. Then have students listen and repeat chorally.
- Write on the board:
  - *a wedding reception*
  - *an engagement*
  - *a honeymoon*
  - *a wedding ceremony*
- Books closed. To check comprehension, ask students to put them in the order in which the events take place. (1. an engagement  2. a wedding ceremony 3. a wedding reception  4. a honeymoon)
- Review as a class.

 **Vocabulary Cards**

## B Read about ...

| Suggested teaching time: | 10 minutes |
|---|---|
| Your actual teaching time: | _____ |

- Group work. Form small groups.
- Write the following on the board:
  1. *Think about weddings you have attended. How were they different?*
  2. *Describe wedding traditions from when your grandparents or great-grandparents married.*
  3. *List some popular honeymoon trips. Compare them to places your parents' generation traveled to.*
- Group work. Have students discuss each item.

**Language note:** The *threshold* is the area of the floor at an entrance (door).

## C 🎧 LISTENING COMPREHENSION
**(CD3, Tracks 13,14)**

| Suggested teaching time: | 10–15 minutes |
|---|---|
| Your actual teaching time: | _____ |

- Part 1: Have students listen and read the statements. Then have students listen again to check the answers. Remind students to correct the false statements as they listen.
- Review the answers as a class. You may want students to listen to Part 1 again to confirm the correct answers and information.

## AUDIOSCRIPT

**PART 1**

**F:**  In India, Hindu wedding traditions vary from state to state. But most families are known to go out of their way to make a wedding a huge celebration which can last for as long as five days or more. It is common for wedding preparations to start a year before the actual date. After a couple gets engaged to be married, the date for the wedding is chosen very carefully based on the bride and groom's birthdays—and other details—to bring good luck.

Two days before the wedding, celebrations begin at the groom's home. This is called "Making the Groom." Musicians visit his home as early as four in the morning and play traditional music while the groom's relatives and neighbors come to see him. While there, they make decorations from mango leaves, which will later be used at the wedding ceremony. Next, someone washes the groom with coconut or olive oil. His face is painted with a black dot on each cheek and a spot between his eyes. Then an older person in the family offers the groom money as a gift.

The bride goes through a ceremony before the wedding called "Making the Bride." Her face, arms, hands, and feet are painted attractively by her relatives, leaving her skin a red color. This process takes many hours to do and requires a lot of patience.

**PART 2**

**F:**  The wedding ceremony is usually held in the evening. When the bride and groom arrive, there is a lot of noise and music. Members of the family wash their feet and sprinkle flowers and water on them. The couple sits in chairs under a special roof made of leaves and flowers. While the bride is seated behind a cloth so the groom can't see her, the guests eat and enjoy the wedding feast. Then when it's near the end of the feast, the cloth is removed and the music is played again. It is considered bad luck to sneeze at this moment. All the guests clap their hands while the music is playing. Then one by one the guests come to the couple and throw rice grains at their heads for prosperity. Everyone wishes the couple well. Then the couple gives each other rings made of flowers and handfuls of rice. The groom places a golden necklace over the bride's neck.

Finally, the groom places a second necklace around the bride's neck to signify the end of the wedding.

- Part 2: Have students listen and read the statements. Then have students listen again to check the answers. Remind students to correct the false statements as they listen.

- Review as class. You may want students to listen to Part 2 again to confirm correct answers and information.

 **Learning Strategies**

 **DISCUSSION**

| Suggested teaching time: | 5–10 minutes |
|---|---|
| Your actual teaching time: | —————— |

- Group work. Form groups of three or four.

- You may want to suggest that students go through the list of statements and compare each one to the wedding traditions they know.

- Ask various students to say which tradition from the listening was the most interesting. Encourage students to offer follow-up comments or to ask questions. Example: Student A: *I think it's interesting and fun that the wedding celebration lasts so long.* Student B: *Yes, especially for guests who have to travel far to get there.*

## TOP NOTCH **INTERACTION**

| Suggested teaching time: | 15–20 minutes |
|---|---|
| Your actual teaching time: | —————— |

### STEP 1. PAIR WORK.

- To review the sayings and proverbs, ask students to say what they mean. Encourage students to use the vocabulary from Exercise A. (Possible answers: Italian saying: It's easier to find a wife for a son than to find a husband for a daughter. Irish saying: Getting married is easy, it's living together that's difficult. South African proverb: If you don't have children when you are married, you are not really husband and wife. Polish saying: Women cry before the wedding because they are happy and emotional; men cry after because they regret their decision to marry. British saying: The newlyweds will have a happy marriage if the bride wears the things described in the saying.)

- Ask various students if they like the sayings or not and ask them to briefly explain why.

- Then ask students to say proverbs or sayings they know about weddings and marriage. You may want to write them on the board.

**Language note:** You may want to point out the difference between the words *wedding* (a ceremony at which two people become married) and *marriage* (the relationship between two people who are married). Examples: *That silver tray was a wedding present. They had a long and happy marriage.*

**Culture note:** The proverb from the U.K. expresses superstitions associated with weddings. If the bride wears something old, her old friends will remain close during the marriage. If she wears something new, the newlyweds will have a prosperous future. If someone from the bride's family lends her something to wear—which she will then have to give back—the couple will have a happy marriage. If the bride wears something blue, the couple will be faithful to each other.

### STEP 2. GROUP WORK.

- Encourage students to make notes and not to write complete sentences.

- Walk around the room to help with any words they might need.

### STEP 3. WRITING.

- To help students organize their thoughts and information before writing, you may want to write the following outline on the board:
    1. briefly introduce topic (wedding tradition)
    2. describe what happens / traditions before the wedding
    3. describe traditions during the wedding ceremony
    4. describe traditions at and after the reception
    5. write a short personal comment to conclude

- Walk around the room as students write and provide help as needed.

 **Writing Process Worksheets**

## EXTRAS (optional)

**Workbook: Exercises 15–18**
**Copy & Go: Activity 20**

**Now listen carefully to Part 2 of the lecture. Then read the statements and listen again. Check the statements that are true. Correct the statements that are false.**

**PART 2.** **On the day of the wedding**

    ☐  **7.** Relatives wash the bride's and groom's ~~hands~~. *feet*

    ☑  **8.** The bride is seated behind a cloth so the groom cannot see her.

    ☑  **9.** Relatives throw rice grains at the bride and groom.

    ☑  **10.** The couple gives each other rings made of flowers and some rice.

    ☐  **11.** The groom places a ~~flower~~ necklace over the bride's neck. *golden*

**D** **DISCUSSION.** **Are any of the traditions described in the listening similar to those in your country? Which traditions sounded the most interesting to you? Why?**

---

## TOP NOTCH
### INTERACTION • *Something old and something new*

**STEP 1. PAIR WORK.** **Read the sayings and proverbs about weddings and marriage. Explain what you think each one means. Do you find any of them offensive? What sayings or proverbs about weddings do you know in your own language?** Answers will vary.

Marry off your son when you wish. Marry off your daughter when you can.
**Italy**

Marriages are all happy. It's having breakfast together that causes all the trouble.
**Ireland**

Marriage is just friendship if there are no children.
**South Africa**

The woman cries before the wedding and the man after.
**Poland**

A bride should wear something old and something new, something borrowed, and something blue.
**the U.K.**

**STEP 2. GROUP WORK.** **On your notepad, make a list of traditions for weddings in your country. Compare your lists with those of other groups.**

before a wedding:

at a wedding ceremony:

**STEP 3. WRITING.** **Write a paragraph describing the wedding traditions in your country.**

after a wedding:

# UNIT 5
# CHECKPOINT

**A** 🎧 **LISTENING COMPREHENSION.** Listen to each conversation and check the occasion or people they are talking about.

1. ☐ the engagement   ☐ the reception   ☑ the honeymoon
2. ☑ the engagement   ☐ the reception   ☐ the honeymoon
3. ☑ the bride         ☐ the groom       ☐ the relatives
4. ☐ the bride         ☐ the groom       ☑ the relatives

**B** Answer each question in your **own** way.   Answers will vary.

1. What's the most important holiday in your country?
   What kind of a holiday is it (seasonal, historical, religious)?
   **YOU** _____

2. What's the longest holiday in your country?  How long is it?
   **YOU** _____

3. What's the most interesting wedding tradition in your country?
   **YOU** _____

🎧 *TOP NOTCH* SONG
"Endless Holiday"
Lyrics on last book page.

*TOP NOTCH* PROJECT
Use the library or the Internet to research a holiday or wedding customs from another country. Tell your classmates about it.

*TOP NOTCH* WEBSITE
For Unit 5 online activities, visit the *Top Notch* Companion Website at www.longman.com/topnotch

**C** Complete each statement.  Then write the name of a holiday or celebration for each one.   Answers may vary. Possible answers include:

**Holiday or celebration**

1. Name a holiday when people __set off__ fireworks.              _New Year's_
2. Name a holiday when people __march__ in parades.              _Carnaval_
3. Name a holiday when people __have__ picnics.                   _Independence Day_
4. Name a holiday when people __spend__ time with their families. _Eid ul-Fitr_
5. Name a holiday when people __wear__ costumes.                  _Mardi Gras_
6. Name a holiday when people give __each other__ gifts.          _Christmas_
7. Name a holiday when people wish __each other__ well.           _Ramadan_

**D** Complete each sentence with an adjective clause.   Answers may vary. Possible answers include:

1. A groom is a man _who has just gotten married_____.
2. Ramadan is a religious observance _that takes place during the ninth month of the Islamic calendar_.
3. A honeymoon is a vacation _that people take after they get married_____.
4. A hanbok is a traditional dress _that Korean people wear during the Harvest celebration_.
5. Songkran is a holiday _that marks the Buddhist New Year in Thailand_____.
6. Simon Bolivar was a Venezuelan _leader who led the armies that freed Venezuela and other countries from Spain_.

**E** **WRITING.**  Describe a holiday or a tradition in your country.  When does it take place?  What do people do?  What are the origins of these customs / traditions?

# UNIT 5
# CHECKPOINT

## A 🎧 LISTENING COMPREHENSION
**(CD3, Track 15)**

| | |
|---|---|
| Suggested teaching time: | 10 minutes |
| Your actual teaching time: | _____ |

- To review the vocabulary, you may want to call on volunteers to give a brief definition or even a description of each word—*engagement, reception, honeymoon, bride, groom,* and *relatives.*

- Pause after each conversation to allow students time to write the check marks.

- Review as a class.

**Option:** Have students listen to the recording again and make notes that support their answers. (1. The man is showing the pictures he took in Tahiti, and he says they took off right after the reception. 2. The woman congratulates the man and asks him about the date he has decided to get married. 3. The woman says that she caught the bouquet the bride threw to her—a tradition at wedding receptions. 4. They are talking about the newlyweds' relatives, who paid a lot for the reception. The man also says weddings are for the family.) **[+5 minutes]**

**Language note:** *Tie the knot* is an informal expression meaning to get married.

### AUDIOSCRIPT

CONVERSATION 1
**M:** Check out these pictures we took in Tahiti.
**F:** Oh, these are really nice! Is that your wife?
**M:** Yes. We took off right after the reception.
**F:** How romantic! How long were you there?
**M:** Ten days.

CONVERSATION 2
**F:** Hey, congratulations! I heard the news!
**M:** Thanks. I guess everyone knows now.
**F:** That's great! So when's the date?
**M:** In September. We've got a lot of planning to do.
**F:** Well, the great thing is that you've decided to tie the knot. Congratulations!

CONVERSATION 3
**M:** Is it true what I hear—that you caught the bouquet?
**F:** Uh-huh. She threw it right to me.
**M:** Well, you've been great friends since childhood, right?
**F:** Yeah, we have. I'm so happy for her!

CONVERSATION 4
**F:** Can you believe how much money they paid for this reception?
**M:** I know. It's unbelievable! It must have cost a fortune.
**F:** I heard the parents and the grandparents all wanted a really big wedding. They must have a lot of money!
**M:** Well, you know what they say. Weddings are really for the family.
**F:** I guess so. Everyone does seem to be having a wonderful time.

## B  Answer each question . . .

| | |
|---|---|
| Suggested teaching time: | 5 minutes |
| Your actual teaching time: | _____ |

- Have students compare answers with a partner.
- To review, have students read the complete sentence and their example.

## C  Complete each statement . . .

| | |
|---|---|
| Suggested teaching time: | 5–10 minutes |
| Your actual teaching time: | _____ |

- Do the first item with the class.
- Have students compare answers with a partner. Then review as a class.

## D  Complete each sentence . . .

| | |
|---|---|
| Suggested teaching time: | 5 minutes |
| Your actual teaching time: | _____ |

- Review the example first.
- Review answers by having students read their complete sentences out loud. Make necessary corrections.

## E WRITING

| | |
|---|---|
| Suggested teaching time: | 5–10 minutes |
| Your actual teaching time: | _____ |

- Pre-writing: To help students organize their writing, you may want to write the following on the board. Then ask students to write notes for each item.

    *Name of holiday*    *Customs and traditions*
    *When it takes place*    *Food*
    *What I like about*    *Clothing*
       *this holiday*    *Events*
                     *Other*:

- Encourage students to use the vocabulary and grammar of this and previous units.

 **Writing Process Worksheets**

 ***Top Notch Pop* Song Activities**
**(CD3, Track 16)**

***TOP NOTCH* PROJECT**

**Idea:** Group work. Form groups of three or four. Ask each group to choose a topic. Encourage group members to do research individually or in pairs. The group should combine the information they find and develop a presentation for the class.

# UNIT WRAP-UP

| Suggested teaching time: | 15–20 minutes |
|---|---|
| Your actual teaching time: | _____ |

## Vocabulary

- Pair work. Encourage students to write a list of the different ways in which people are celebrating this event.

- Review as a class.

**┌─ Your students can say . . . ─┐**
having a picnic, setting off fireworks, wishing each other well, marching in a parade, watching a parade, wearing [hot pepper] costumes, remembering [the dead], throwing [peppers] at a wedding

## Social Language

- Tell students to first identify who the two people are; for example, do they both live in this town or is one of them visiting? etc.

- Pair work. Ask students to write conversations.

**Option: Who are you?** Ask various pairs to identify their roles and to perform their role plays for the class.
**[+10 minutes]**

**Culture note:** The Annual Hot Pepper Festival is an imaginary celebration created by the authors for *Top Notch.*

**┌─ Your students can say . . . ─┐**
**A:** I love watching parades. **B:** Me, too. This holiday is one of my favorites. **A:** It's great those people are getting married [at the Hot Pepper Festival]. **B:** It's really starting to be a tradition! **A:** Look! They're throwing hot peppers at the newlyweds! **B:** Now that's a new custom!

**A:** This is an important holiday here, isn't it? **B:** That's right. **A:** What kind of holiday is it? **B:** It's a seasonal holiday that takes places in [month]. People [march in parades] and [have picnics].

**A:** Do you mind if I ask you something? **B:** Of course not. What's up? **A:** I'm not sure of the customs here. Why aren't they throwing [rice] at those newlyweds? **B:** Well, we throw [hot peppers] at weddings.

## Grammar

- Review the example first.

- You may want to form pairs.

- Ask students to write as many statements using adjective clauses as they can about the picture.

- Ask various students to say one of their statements. Make necessary corrections.

**┌─ Your students can say . . . ─┐**
The parade we're watching is great! People are remembering those who fought for the country's independence. The fireworks the children are setting off look like peppers. I see a couple that / who just got married. There are relatives that / who are throwing hot peppers at the newlyweds. The people that / who are having a picnic are enjoying the parade. There are children that are wearing hot pepper costumes. The couple that / who is waving has a daughter in the parade. Some people are wearing caps that look like hot peppers. There is a girl who is carrying a flag. There is someone who is carrying a plate with a big hot pepper. There are lots of people who are having fun.

**Challenge: Hot Pepper Memory.** Pair work. Ask students to write on a sheet of paper eight statements about the picture, some of which should be false. Books closed. Students exchange sheets of paper with another pair and mark the statements true or false. **[+10 minutes]**

**┌─ Individual oral progress check (optional) ─┐**

- Use the illustration on page 61. Encourage the student to use material (vocabulary, grammar, rhythm and intonation) practiced in this unit.

- Evaluate the student on correctness and intelligibility.

- Tell the student to describe the ways the people are celebrating the Hot Pepper Festival using adjective clauses. Encourage the student to use the vocabulary for commemorating a holiday and getting married that he/she learned in this unit. Examples: *There are three people who are having a picnic. There are some boys who are setting off fireworks. There are some people marching in a parade.*

- Point to the two people with empty speech balloons, and tell the student that together you are going to role-play a conversation. Point out that the man is the visitor and the woman lives there. Ask the student to take the role of the resident and answer the visitor's questions about the Hot Pepper Festival. Example: T: *What are the people celebrating?* S: *The Hot Pepper Festival. It's a seasonal holiday that we celebrate in [month].* T: *What are some of the traditions for this festival?* S: *People [march in parades] and [have picnics]. Some people [wear hot pepper costumes].* T: *Well, I hope you enjoy yourself during the festival!* S: *Thanks! Same to you!*

 **Cumulative Vocabulary Activities**

 You may wish to use the video and activity worksheets for Unit 5 at this point.

 **Complete Assessment Package**
**Unit 5 Achievement Test**
**Review Test 1, Speaking Test 1**

## Unit Wrap-Up

- **Vocabulary.** Name the ways people are celebrating the holiday.
- **Social language.** Create a conversation for the man and woman.
- **Grammar.** Describe what is happening on this holiday, using adjective clauses.
  *There are people who are wearing costumes in the parade.*

ANNUAL HOT PEPPER FESTIVAL

HOT PEPPER QUEEN!

✓ **Now I can ...**
- ☐ find out about a holiday.
- ☐ ask about the customs of another culture.
- ☐ describe a holiday or celebration.
- ☐ explain wedding traditions.

# Disasters and Emergencies

 **TOPIC PREVIEW.** Look at three historic news events. Which of these famous disasters are you familiar with?

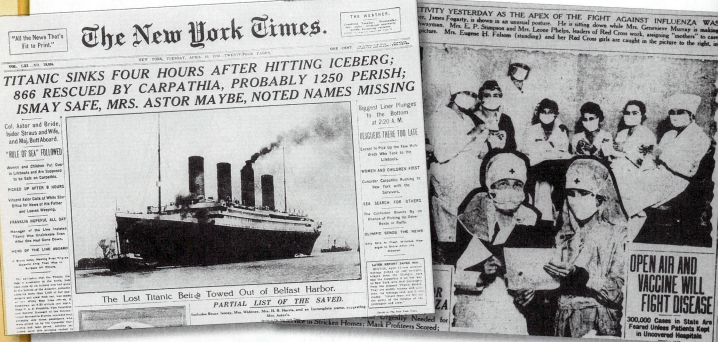

On April 10, 1912, the British ocean liner Titanic sinks with a loss of over 1,500 people.

The influenza epidemic of 1918-19 leaves an estimated 25 million people dead worldwide.

On December 26, 2004, a 9.0-magnitude earthquake created a tsunami that killed over 250,000 people in Indonesia, Sri Lanka, India, Thailand, and other countries.

 **DISCUSSION.** Why do you think the news is often about disasters? What other kinds of news stories make headlines? What happens to the "good news"?

# UNIT

# Disasters and Emergencies

 **TOPIC PREVIEW**

Suggested teaching time: 10–15 minutes
Your actual teaching time: _____

- Write on the board:
  1. *He's sick with* <u>*influenza.*</u>  a. *strong winds*
  2. *Boats can* <u>*sink*</u> *during a storm.*  *moving in a circle*
  3. *Vaccinations prevent* <u>*epidemics.*</u>  b. *the flu*
  4. *The* <u>*cyclone*</u> *destroyed houses.*  c. *lots of people*
     *infected by*
     *diseases*
     d. *not float any more*

- Pre-reading: Have students match the underlined words with the definitions.

- Review as a class. (1. b  2. d  3. c  4. a)

- Then have students look at the pictures and scan the text in the newspapers and say what three events they see. (the sinking of the *Titanic*, a worldwide influenza epidemic, an earthquake and tsunami that killed over 250,000 people)

- Ask students what they know about each disaster.

**Culture note:** The ***Titanic,*** famous for being the largest vessel ever built (260 m), was also believed to be unsinkable. On its maiden voyage from England to the U.S., it hit an iceberg on the night of April 14, 1912, and sank within three hours at 2:20 A.M. on April 15. Over 1,500 of the 2,200 passengers and crew died due to the shortage of lifeboats. The **influenza epidemic of 1918** infected approximately one-fifth of the world's population, killing 25 million people. The epidemic broke out at the end of World War I. With the majority of doctors working with troops, the U.S. Red Cross had to recruit thousands of volunteers. The 2004 **Indian Ocean earthquake** generated a tsunami that by a final count may have killed over 250,000 people. Nations all over the world rushed to provide over (U.S.) $3 billion to help rebuild infrastructure, provide food aid, and assist in economic recovery.

**Language note:** Students may need help with the following words: *call* (request); *aid* (help); *perish* (die); *missing* (someone who is missing has disappeared).

## DISCUSSION

Suggested teaching time: 10 minutes
Your actual teaching time: _____

- Point out that *to make (the) headlines* is an expression that means that a news story is widely reported in newspapers, on television, and on the radio.

- Group work. Form small groups of three. Ask students to make two lists: one list of news that makes the headlines and one list of news or situations that rarely make headlines. (Possible answers: List 1: wars, crimes, plane accidents, scandals; List 2: success stories, peaceful or environmental campaigns, personal achievements)

- Walk around the room and help students with vocabulary.

- Ask students for their ideas and make two lists on the board.

- Ask the class to say why they think the news is often about disasters and what happens to the "good news." Examples: *TV channels provide shocking news so more people watch their programs. Newspapers know this is what people want to read about. Good news is not as exciting as bad news.*

**Language note:** *News* is an uncountable noun and needs a singular verb or demonstrative pronoun. *The news* <u>*is*</u> *often about disasters. Look at* <u>*this*</u> *news.* You may want to point out that *the news* refers to a regular radio or television program that gives reports of recent events. *I saw it on the news. I watched the news last night.*

## SOUND BITES

(CD3, Track 18)

| Suggested teaching time: | 10–15 minutes |
|---|---|
| Your actual teaching time: | _____ |

- Pair work. Ask students to make a list of adjectives that could describe the facial expressions and emotions of the two people. (Students may say: *worried, concerned, upset, angry, confused,* etc.)

- Point out that the Richter scale is used to rate the intensity of earthquakes. Other devastating earthquakes were a 9.5 in Chile in 1960 and a 9.2 in Alaska in 1964.

- Write the following questions on the board:
  1. *Is the news "old" or "new"?*
  2. *What do we know so far about the situation?*

- Books closed. Ask students to listen for the answers and the information that supports the answers. (1. new: It happened yesterday. 2. It was a big earthquake—8.6. A lot of things were destroyed [property: houses, buildings, cars, land, etc.]. We don't know how many people got hurt or died.

**Language note:** Encourage students to use the information in the text to figure out the meaning of *breaking news* (news that is happening right now); *Richter scale* (a scale that shows how strong an earthquake is, 1 = very weak to 10 = the strongest); *damage* (physical harm).

## UNDERSTANDING FROM CONTEXT

| Suggested teaching time: | 5 minutes |
|---|---|
| Your actual teaching time: | _____ |

- Do the first item with the class.

- To practice the reading skill of understanding vocabulary from context, encourage students to use the information in the text to help them figure out the meaning of words or expressions.

- Have students compare answers with a partner. Then review as a class.

**Language note:** You may want to tell students that some words in the conversation are typically used to talk about disasters. Point out *strike* (to happen suddenly and unexpectedly), *casualty* (people who are either injured or killed in a disaster), *damage* (physical harm), and *injury* (physical harm to a person). Examples: *The town was struck by a terrible storm. There were no casualties. There was a lot of damage. / Many buildings were damaged. There were some injuries. / Some people were injured.*

## WHAT ABOUT **YOU?**

| Suggested teaching time: | 10–15 minutes |
|---|---|
| Your actual teaching time: | _____ |

- Point out that there are two tasks: First fill out the chart with individual information and then discuss the questions and use the notes in the chart.

- Walk around and provide help as needed.

- Group work. Encourage students to ask each other follow-up questions to find out the reasons. Examples: Student A: *I get most of my news on the Internet.* Student B: *Really? Do you like it better than reading a newspaper?* Student A: *Yes. I can get the news easily from my computer all day. What about you?* Student B: *I like to read a newspaper while I have breakfast. It's relaxing.* Student A: *What newspaper do you read?* Student B: *"Daily News."*

- Take a poll to find out what sources students use for each type of news.

## EXTRAS (optional)

**Workbook:** Exercises 1, 2

**C** 🎧 **SOUND BITES.** Read along silently as you listen to a natural conversation.

**RACHEL:** Oh, my goodness! **CN1**
Look at this breaking news from Romania. **CN2**
**TOM:** What happened?
**RACHEL:** It says there was a huge earthquake there yesterday. It was 8.6 on the Richter scale. What a disaster!
**TOM:** 8.6? That's gigantic! Any word on casualties?

**CN1** **Corpus Notes:** The three most common words to follow *oh my* in spoken English are *God, gosh,* and *goodness,* in that order.

**RACHEL:** They say there's a lot of property damage, but luckily it struck during the day. So far no reports of deaths or injuries.
**TOM:** Well, let's hope for the best.
**RACHEL:** I wonder if 8.6 is a record.
**TOM:** Believe it or not, no. There was once a 9.5 near Chile.

**CN2** **Corpus Notes:** The collocation *breaking news* is used most frequently to describe TV and radio news broadcasts. It is rarely used for other kinds of news.

**D**  **UNDERSTANDING FROM CONTEXT.** Find a word or expression in the conversation that means …

1. news that's happening right now. breaking news

2. any terrible event where many people are hurt or killed. a disaster

3. very, very large. gigantic

4. deaths and injuries. casualties

5. the largest in history. a record

6. it's unbelievable but true. Believe it or not

## WHAT ABOUT **YOU?**

**Check the places you get the news. Then write the name of the newspaper, magazine, TV station, etc.**

| | Source | Name |
|---|---|---|
| ☐ | a daily newspaper | |
| ☐ | a weekly news magazine | |
| ☐ | TV | |
| ☐ | the radio | |
| ☐ | the Internet | |
| ☐ | word of mouth | |

**DISCUSSION.** Which news sources do you think are the best for breaking news? Weather forecasts? Emergency information? Explain your reasons and give examples.

**LESSON**

# 1 Convey a Message

 CONVERSATION **MODEL** Read and listen.

**A:** I'm on the line with your parents. **CN1** Would you like to say hello?

**B:** I would, but I'm running late. **CN2**

**A:** Anything you'd like me to tell them?

**B:** Yes. Please tell them to watch the news. There's a storm on its way.

**A:** Will do.

🎧 **Rhythm and intonation practice**

**A** **GRAMMAR. Indirect speech: imperatives**

When you report what someone said, but without quoting the <u>exact</u> words, use indirect speech. Don't use quotation marks when you write indirect speech.

> direct speech: Peter said, "Come for dinner on Sunday."
> indirect speech: Peter said to come for dinner on Sunday.

In indirect speech, an imperative becomes an infinitive.

> They said, "**Read** the weather forecast." They said **to read** the weather forecast.
> She says, "**Don't go** without a full tank of gas." She says **not to go** without a full tank of gas.

Make changes in pronouns and time expressions in indirect speech to preserve the speaker's original meaning.

> She told Dan, "Call **me tomorrow**." She told Dan to call **her the next day**.

GRAMMAR BOOSTER

**PAGE G10**
For more …

**B** **PAIR WORK. With a partner, say what you think the speaker's original words were.**

1. He told them to call him at three. ❝(Please) call me at three.❞

2. The police said to leave a window or door open when there's going to be a severe storm.
   "Leave a window or door open when there's going to be a severe storm."

3. She told his parents to read the emergency instructions in the newspaper.
   "Read the emergency instructions in the newspaper."

4. They told her to get vaccinated before her trip to Tanzania.
   "Get vaccinated before your trip to Tanzania."

5. She asked him to pick up some supplies for her on the way home.
   "Please pick up some supplies for me on your way home."

6. They told me not to call them after nine.
   "Please don't call us after nine."

**CN1** **Corpus Notes:**
*On the line* has the same meaning as *on the phone*.
*On the phone* is more frequent in spoken English.

**CN2** **Corpus Notes:**
To *be late* is more frequently used than *running late*, but *running late* is more informal.

## LESSON

# 1 *Convey a Message*

## 🎧 CONVERSATION **MODEL**

**(CD3, Track 19)**

| Suggested teaching time: | 5 minutes |
|---|---|
| Your actual teaching time: | _____ |

- After students read and listen, ask *Why doesn't the man talk to his parents?* (because he's in a hurry / he's late) *What advice does he give?* (His parents should watch the news because there's going to be a storm.)

- Point out that other ways to say *Will do* are *I will, Sure,* or *OK.*

**Language note:** You may want to clarify the following expressions: *I'm on the line with . . .* (I'm on the phone with . . . ); *I'm running late* (I'm not on schedule). You may also want to point out the difference between *on the line* (on the phone) and *online* (connected to other computers through the Internet / available through the Internet).

## 🎧 **Rhythm and intonation practice**

**(CD3, Track 20)**

| Suggested teaching time: | 5 minutes |
|---|---|
| Your actual teaching time: | _____ |

- Have students repeat each line chorally.
- Make sure students:
  ○ use rising intonation for *Would you like to say hello?*
  ○ pause after *would* in *I would, but I'm running late.*
  ○ use rising intonation for *Anything you'd like me to tell them?*
  ○ stress <u>will</u> and use falling intonation in *Will do.*
  ○ use the following stress pattern:

**STRESS PATTERN**

**A:** I'm on the line with your parents. Would you like to say hello?

**B:** I would, but I'm running late.

**A:** Anything you'd like me to tell them?

**B:** Yes. Please tell them to watch the news. There's a storm on its way.

**A:** Will do.

## GRAMMAR

| Suggested teaching time: | 15–20 minutes |
|---|---|
| Your actual teaching time: | _____ |

- Note: Indirect speech with *say* and *tell* and tense changes is covered on page 66.
- Direct attention to the box and have students read the first explanation and study the examples.
- Write on the board:
  1. Steve said, "Ask Carol."
  2. Steve said <u>to ask</u> Carol.
- To help clarify, say *Direct speech uses the exact words someone says. Indirect speech doesn't use the exact words.*
- Point out the quotation marks in written direct speech. Point out that they are placed at the beginning of the quoted information and after the period (punctuation) at the end.
- Have students read the second explanation and study the examples.
- Point out *ask* and *to ask* in the examples on the board.
- To check comprehension, do a substitution drill. Tell students to change the sentences into indirect speech starting with *The teacher said . . . Do your homework.* (The teacher said to do your homework.) *Come to class on time.* (The teacher said to come to class on time.) *Have fun learning English!* (The teacher said to have fun learning English!)
- Write on the board:
  3. The guide said, "Don't touch it."
  4. The guide said <u>not to</u> touch it.
- Point out that the negative imperative—*Don't touch*—becomes a negative infinitive—*not to touch.*
- Have students read the last explanation and study the examples.
- To help clarify, point out the change from *me* to *her* and from *tomorrow* to *the next day.*

**Language note:** You may want to point out other words that often change. For example, *here* changes to *there*, and *this* changes to *that*. Example: *Art said, "Leave this book here." Art said to leave that book there.*

 Grammar Self-Checks

## PAIR WORK

| Suggested teaching time: | 5–10 minutes |
|---|---|
| Your actual teaching time: | _____ |

- Review the example first. Point out the change in the pronoun from *him* to *me.*
- Ask students why *please* is included but in parentheses. (It's possible the speaker said the sentence either way because it's a request.)
- Have students compare answers with a partner. Then review as a class.

**T64**

**C** **Rewrite each statement . . .**

| Suggested teaching time: | 5 minutes |
| --- | --- |
| Your actual teaching time: | _____ |

- Review the example first.
- Remind students to change time expressions if necessary.
- Review answers by having students read their new sentences out loud. Make necessary corrections.

**Option:** Group work. Form groups of three. To provide more practice, ask students to talk about the instructions or commands their parents tell / used to tell them. Examples: Student A: *My mother always told me not to be home late.* Student B: *My mother tells me to be home before 10:00.* Student C: *When my father lent me his car, he told me not to drive fast.* Student A: *My father never lends me his car. He tells me to use the bus.* **[+5 minutes]**

###  **D** 🎧 **PRONUNCIATION**
**(CD3, Track 21)**

| Suggested teaching time: | 5 minutes |
| --- | --- |
| Your actual teaching time: | _____ |

- First listening: Have students listen and study the examples.
- Point out that in direct speech the pause tells the listener they're going to hear the exact words. Point out that there is no pause in indirect speech.
- Second listening: Have students listen and repeat chorally.
- You may want to point out that in written direct speech the pause is indicated by a comma. Point out the comma after *said* and *parents* in the examples. Then point out that there is no comma in written indirect speech.

 **Pronunciation Activities**

## CONVERSATION **PAIR WORK**

| Suggested teaching time: | 5–10 minutes |
| --- | --- |
| Your actual teaching time: | _____ |

- To get students ready for the activity, have students read the conversation model on page 64 again. You may also want to have students listen to the model.
- Tell students they can say *I'm on the line with . . .* or *I'm on the phone with . . .*
- Review the possible excuses and possible messages. Encourage students to write down their own message.
- Point out / remind students that they should use indirect speech. Students can refer to Exercise C for help with the grammar, if necessary.
- Choose a more confident student and role-play a conversation. Encourage students to ask follow-up questions.
- Walk around the room and provide help as needed. Encourage students to use the correct rhythm and intonation.
- Make sure each student plays both roles.

 **Pair Work Cards**

## EXTRAS (optional)

**Grammar Booster**
**Workbook: Exercises 3–7**
**Copy & Go: Activity 21**

**Pronunciation Supplements**

**Rewrite each statement in indirect speech, making necessary changes.**

1. Martha told me, "Be home before the storm."
   <u>*Martha told me to be home before the storm.*</u>

2. Everyone says, "Get ready for a big storm tomorrow."
   Everyone said to get ready for a big storm the next day.

3. The radio says, "Get supplies of food and water in case the roads are closed."
   The radio said to get supplies of food and water in case the roads were closed.

4. They told her, "Don't be home too late."
   They told her not to be home too late.

5. Maria always tells him, "Don't leave your doors open."
   Maria always tells him not to leave his doors open.

 🎧 **PRONUNCIATION. Direct and indirect speech: rhythm.** Listen to the rhythm of sentences in direct and indirect speech. Then repeat.

He said, [pause] "Be home before midnight."
He said to be home before midnight.

I told your parents, [pause] "Get a flu shot at the clinic."
I told your parents to get a flu shot at the clinic.

## CONVERSATION
## PAIR WORK

**Role-play conveying a message. Use the guide, the possible excuses, and the possible messages, or create a new conversation.** Answers will vary.

**A:** I'm on the line with _____ . Would you like to say hello?

**B:** I would, but _____ .

**A:** Anything you'd like me to tell _____?

**B:** Yes. Please _____ .

**A:** _____ .

**Possible messages**

Watch the news. There's a story about _____.
Turn on the TV. There's bad weather on its way.
Call me at the office.
Your <u>own</u> message: _____.

**Possible excuses**

I'm running late.
I have an appointment.
I don't have time right now.

### ⌒ CONVERSATION MODEL  Read and listen.

**A:** What's going on in the news today?
**B:** Well, there was a terrible storm in the south.
**A:** Really?
**B:** Yes. It says lots of houses were destroyed.
**A:** What a shame.
**B:** But there were no deaths.
**A:** Thank goodness for that.

⌒ **Rhythm and intonation practice**

**A ▷ GRAMMAR.  Indirect speech: <u>say</u> and <u>tell</u>; tense changes**

> **Use <u>tell</u> when you mention the listener(s). Use <u>say</u> when you don't.**
> Maggie **told her parents** to stay home. (listeners mentioned)
> Maggie **said** to stay home. (listener not mentioned)

> **When <u>say</u> or <u>tell</u> are in the past tense, the verbs in the indirect speech statement often change. Present becomes past. Past becomes past perfect.**
> They **said**, "The weather **is** awful."  They **said** (that) the weather **was** awful.
> Dan **said**, "We all **had** the flu."  Dan **said** (that) they **had** all **had** the flu.

GRAMMAR BOOSTER

**PAGES G10–G11**
**For more ...**

> **CN  Corpus Notes:**  A common learner error is to use *say* when the reporting verb *tell* is correct. (*I said her that I didn't want to see her again.*) Be sure students understand the difference.

**B ▷ Circle the correct verbs for indirect speech.**

## My Great-Grandmother Meets Hurricane Cleo

Hurricane Cleo struck the United States in August, 1964. My great-grandmother, Ana, was traveling in Miami when the hurricane struck. She (1. said / **told**) me that she still remembers how scared everyone was. She (2. said / **told**) me that one morning the hotel (3. calls / **called**) her room and (4. said / **told**) her that a big storm (5. is / **was**) on its way. They (6. **said** / told) that all hotel guests (7. have to / **had to**) stay in the hotel until the weather service (8. tell / **said**) that it (9. is / **was**) safe to leave. She stayed in her room and she didn't know what happened until the storm was over. When she turned on the TV, the reports (10. **said** / told) that a lot of people (11. have been / **had been**) injured and that all the roads (12. are / **were**) flooded. She always (13. **says** / said) that she still (14. **feels** / felt) lucky to have survived Hurricane Cleo.

# LESSON 2 ▶ *Report News*

## 🎧 CONVERSATION **MODEL**
**(CD3, Track 22)**

| Suggested teaching time: | 5 minutes |
|---|---|
| Your actual teaching time: | _____ |

- After students read and listen, ask students to summarize what happened in the south. (There was a terrible storm. A lot of houses were destroyed. No one died.)
- Tell students another way to say *What a shame* is *That's too bad.*
- Point out that *Thank goodness for that* means *I'm glad* or *That's good news.*

## 🎧 **Rhythm and intonation practice**
**(CD3, Track 23)**

| Suggested teaching time: | 5 minutes |
|---|---|
| Your actual teaching time: | _____ |

- Have students repeat each line chorally.
- Make sure students:
  - use falling intonation for *What's going on in the news today?*
  - stress new information, such as <u>terrible</u>, <u>storm</u> and <u>south</u> in *Well, there was a terrible storm in the south.*
  - use rising intonation for *Really?*
  - stress <u>what</u> and <u>shame</u> in *What a shame.*
  - stress <u>no</u> in *But there were no deaths.*
  - use the following stress pattern:

**STRESS PATTERN**

A: What's going on in the news today?
B: Well, there was a terrible storm in the south.
A: Really?
B: Yes. It says lots of houses were destroyed.
A: What a shame.
B: But there were no deaths.
A: Thank goodness for that.

## 🔺A GRAMMAR

| Suggested teaching time: | 5–10 minutes |
|---|---|
| Your actual teaching time: | _____ |

- Direct attention to the box and have students read the first explanation and study the examples.
- Write on the board:
  1. She _____ to use her computer.
  2. He _____ us to listen to the news.
  3. They _____ John to buy the newspaper.
  4. Pete _____ to get the best tickets for the game.
- To check comprehension, ask students to complete the sentences with *said* or *told*. Encourage students to identify a listener. (1. said 2. told 3. told 4. said)
- Have students read the second explanation and study the examples.
- Note: The Grammar Booster, page G10, provides students with the three situations when the backshift of tense in indirect speech is not necessary.
- To help clarify, model some examples. Tell students to answer your questions with complete sentences. Examples: Indicate a student and ask *What kind of music do you like?* S: *I like [pop music].* Tell the class *[Carol] said that she <u>liked</u> [pop music].* Indicate another student and ask *What did you do last Saturday?* S: *I [visited some friends].* Tell the class *[John] said that he <u>had</u> [visited some friends].*
- Point out that *that* can be omitted. Say *John said he had visited some friends.*
- To point out the different tense changes, you may want to write on the board:

| Direct speech | | Indirect speech | |
|---|---|---|---|
| "I | work." → | He said that he | worked. |
| | worked." → | | had worked. |
| | have worked." → | | had worked. |
| | am working." → | | was working. |

- Point out that both the simple past and the present perfect change to the past perfect in indirect speech.

🔵 **Grammar Self-Checks**

## 🔺B Circle the correct . . .

| Suggested teaching time: | 5 minutes |
|---|---|
| Your actual teaching time: | _____ |

- Do the first item with the class.
- Have students identify the tense(s) in each sentence.
- Have students compare answers with a partner. Then review as a class.
- Note: In items 2 and 3 there is no backshift because the change is not necessary. If students bring this up, have them look at the Grammar Booster, page G10, which provides students with the three situations when the backshift of tense in indirect speech is not necessary.

**T66**

 **VOCABULARY**
(CD3, Track 24)

| Suggested teaching time: | 5 minutes |
|---|---|
| Your actual teaching time: | _____ |

- Have students listen and study the words. Then have students listen and repeat chorally.
- Books closed. Write on the board:
    1. *strong winds and heavy rain*
    2. *a long period with no rain*
    3. *a lot of water covering an area*
    4. *earth and rocks falling down a mountain*
    5. *strong winds moving fast in a circle*
- To check comprehension, have students work in pairs. Student A has the book open and says each vocabulary word (not in order). Student B says which definition on the board matches each word. (1. hurricane, etc. 2. drought 3. flood 4. landslide 5. tornado)
- Walk around the room and provide help as needed.

> **Language note:** Hurricanes, typhoons, and cyclones are all the same severe weather event, but what they are called depends on where they are formed. *Hurricanes*: Atlantic and East Pacific Oceans; *typhoons*: West Pacific Ocean; *cyclones*: Indian Ocean and the South Pacific.

 **Vocabulary Cards**

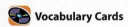 **Change each statement . . .**

| Suggested teaching time: | 5 minutes |
|---|---|
| Your actual teaching time: | _____ |

- Do the first item with the class.
- Note: The Grammar Booster (page G10) offers three situations where the backshift in tense is necessary.
- Make sure students change the verb tense in each item for this exercise.
- Have students compare answers with a partner. Then review as a class.

**Option:** After students complete the corresponding Grammar Booster exercises, ask them to review the items in Exercise D and say which ones must use a backshift in tense. **[+5 minutes]**

 **LISTENING COMPREHENSION**
(CD3, Track 25)

| Suggested teaching time: | 5–10 minutes |
|---|---|
| Your actual teaching time: | _____ |

- Encourage students to listen for the details describing each weather event. They may want to make notes.
- Have students compare answers with a partner. Then review as a class.

**Audioscript for Exercise E is on page T69.**

**T67**

 **PAIR WORK**
(CD3, Track 26)

| Suggested teaching time: | 5 minutes |
|---|---|
| Your actual teaching time: | _____ |

- Have students listen to the first report and review the model.
- Encourage students to write notes as they listen.
- Stop after each report and have students do the activity. To review, ask one group to say their answers.
- (Possible answers: Report 1: She said that Brazilian farmers had reported damage to cattle. He said that the land couldn't feed the animals. Report 2: He said that the rain hadn't stopped in a week. He said that the people were moving out of their houses. Report 3: She said that the winds had reached a record of 150 kilometers per hour. She said that trees were down, and the beaches were heavily damaged. Report 4: He said the dark, funnel-shaped cloud was knocking down trees. He said roofs had been blown off.)

## CONVERSATION **PAIR WORK**

| Suggested teaching time: | 5–10 minutes |
|---|---|
| Your actual teaching time: | _____ |

- To get students ready for the activity, have students read the conversation model on page 66 again. You may also want to have students listen to the model.
- Review the events and vocabulary in the headlines. If necessary, clarify the meaning of *avian influenza* (an infectious disease of birds, which can also infect pigs and humans); *elderly* (older people); *flee* (escape); *famine* (a situation in which a large number of people have little or no food for a long time and many people die).
- Point out that if students use a reporting verb in the present, it is not necessary to change the verb tense in reported speech. Example: *The Mercury headline says that influenza is causing many deaths.*
- Point out that headlines often use the simple present to refer to past actions. Students will need to change the verb to the past tense in reported speech. Examples: *The Morning Herald says that 20,000 died. The Dar Post says that people fled the river valley. The National News says the drought caused severe famine.*
- Encourage students to react to the news and ask follow-up questions.
- Choose a more confident student and role-play a conversation. Encourage students to ask follow-up questions.
- Walk around the room and provide help as needed. Encourage students to use the correct rhythm and intonation.
- Make sure each student plays both roles.

 **Pair Work Cards**

 **Learning Strategies**

## EXTRAS (optional)

**Grammar Booster**
**Workbook: Exercises 8–14**
**Copy & Go: Activity 22**

**VOCABULARY.** **Severe weather events.** **Listen and practice.**

| a tornado | a hurricane / a typhoon / a monsoon | a flood | a landslide | a drought |

D **Change each statement from direct speech to indirect speech, changing the verb tense in the indirect speech statement.**

1. The TV reporter said, "The landslide is one of the worst in history."
   The TV reporter said (that) the landslide was one of the worst in history.
2. He also said, "It caused the destruction of half the houses in the town."
   He said (that) it had caused the destruction of half the houses in town.
3. My sister called and said, "There is no electricity because of the hurricane."
   My sister called and said (that) there was no electricity because of the hurricane.
4. The newspaper said, "There was a tornado in the central part of the country."
   The newspapers said (that) there had been a tornado in the central part of the country.
5. The paper said, "The drought of 1999 was the worst natural disaster of the century."
   The paper said (that) the drought of 1999 had been the worst natural disaster of the century.

E **LISTENING COMPREHENSION.** **Listen to the news.** **Write each weather event.**

1. a drought
2. a flood
3. a hurricane / a typhoon / a monsoon
4. a tornado

F **PAIR WORK.** **Listen to each report again. After each report, tell your partner what the reporter said. Use indirect speech and make necessary changes.**

> "She said it hadn't rained in months."

## CONVERSATION
## PAIR WORK

**Report what it says in the news. Use the headlines here or use real headlines from your newspaper. Start like this:** Answers will vary.

**A:** What's going on in the news today?
**B:** Well, _____ …

**Continue the conversation in your own way.**

### Morning Herald
20,000 killed in earthquake in Iran

### DAR Post
People flee flooded river valley

### National News
**Drought causes severe famine**
**Thousands die of hunger**

### Mercury
**Avian influenza epidemic causes record deaths in Indonesia**
Doctors urge children and elderly to receive vaccinations

### Village Times
**Severe dust storm hits Kabul suburbs**
**Extreme damage to cars, buildings**

## 3 ▷ *Prepare for an Emergency*

 **A ▷** 🎧 **VOCABULARY. Emergency preparations and supplies. Listen and practice.**

**an emergency**   a very dangerous situation that requires immediate action

**a flashlight**   a portable, battery-operated light

**an evacuation**   the removal of all people from an area or neighborhood that is too dangerous

**a power outage**   an interruption in the flow of electricity over a large area

A battery-operated flashlight is a must in many emergencies.

**a first-aid kit**   a small box containing supplies to treat minor illnesses and injuries

**non-perishable food**   food that doesn't need refrigeration, such as canned foods and dried foods

**a shelter**   a safe place where people may go when the area they live in has been evacuated

**B ▷** 🎧 **LISTENING COMPREHENSION. Listen to an emergency radio broadcast. What's the emergency? Then listen again. Correct each of the following statements, using indirect speech.**

> **❝** No. He said not to stand near windows during the storm. **❞**

**Example:** He said you should stand near windows during the storm.

1. He said you should turn your refrigerator and freezer ~~off~~. *to very cold*

2. He said that if there is a flood, you should put valuable papers on the ~~lowest~~ floor of your home. *highest*

3. He said you should ~~read the newspapers~~ *listen to the radio* for the location of shelters.

 **C ▷ PAIR WORK. What did the radio announcer say in the emergency radio broadcast? Together, complete each statement in indirect speech. Listen again if necessary.**

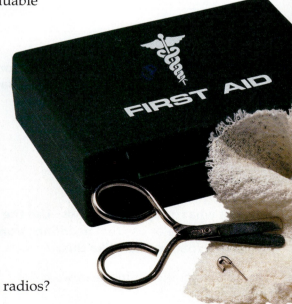

1. According to the speaker, what should you do to get your car ready for evacuation?

   He said to ___fill your car with gas now___ .

2. What should you do with outdoor furniture?

   He said to ___bring it inside___ .

3. What should you buy for flashlights and portable radios?

   He said to ___buy extra batteries___ .

So is a first-aid kit with scissors and bandages.

4. How should you get official instructions in case of an evacuation?

   He said to ___listen to the radio___ .

5. How should you prepare to have food and water, in case you have to stay indoors for several days?

   He said to ___get a supply of non-perishable food and water___

**LESSON**

# 3 ► *Prepare for an Emergency*

 **VOCABULARY**
**(CD3, Track 27)**

| Suggested teaching time: | 10 minutes |
|---|---|
| Your actual teaching time: | _____ |

- Have students listen and study the words and the definitions. Then have students listen and repeat chorally.
- Write on the board:
  1. *a portable light*
  2. *a small box with things to treat injuries*
  3. *a safe building*
  4. *a period with no electricity*
  5. *a dangerous situation*
  6. *things to eat that need no refrigeration*
  7. *the act of leaving a dangerous place*
- Books closed. Ask students to listen again to each word and match it with the correct definition.
- Have students compare answers with a partner. Then ask students to open their books and check their words. (1. flashlight 2. first-aid kit 3. shelter 4. power outage 5. emergency 6. non-perishable food 7. evacuation)

 **Vocabulary Cards**

 **LISTENING COMPREHENSION**
**(CD3, Track 28)**

| Suggested teaching time: | 10–15 minutes |
|---|---|
| Your actual teaching time: | _____ |

- If necessary, clarify the meaning of *radio broadcast* (a program on the radio).
- First listening: Have students listen to the first part and say the kind of emergency it is. (A tropical storm with high winds and heavy rain is coming. Flooding is expected.)
- Then have students read the statements.
- Second listening: Stop after the correct answer to the first statement is given and go over the model / answer.
- Have students listen to the rest of the program and make corrections as they listen.
- Have students compare answers and then review as a class.
- You may want students to listen again to review their corrected statements.

 **Learning Strategies**

**AUDIOSCRIPT**

[M = U.S. Regional, Southern]

**M:** Today is Monday, October 11. This is a Government Weather Service update on Tropical Storm Maria, which is approaching our area. The storm is expected to arrive between 9 and 11 A.M. tomorrow. This is an extremely dangerous storm with high winds and heavy rain. Flooding is expected, and evacuation may be necessary. The following are emergency procedures that all area residents should follow:

1. Fill your car with gas now, in case evacuation is necessary.
2. Bring outdoor furniture, tools, and other objects inside. They can be dangerous in high winds.
3. Close all windows and cover windows with wooden boards. When the storm hits, don't go near windows in case the wind causes the glass to break.
4. Turn your refrigerator and freezer to very cold and only open when necessary to preserve perishable food in the event of a power outage.
5. Buy extra batteries for flashlights in case there is a power outage or an evacuation.
6. If you don't have a portable, battery-operated radio, buy one today, and have a good supply of extra batteries for the radio. Listen to the radio for official instructions in case evacuation is necessary.
7. Check your first-aid kit. Be sure it contains bandages, painkillers, and antiseptic in case of minor injuries.
8. Put valuable papers in a waterproof container on the highest floor of your home in case of flooding.
9. Get a supply of non-perishable food and water. You may have to stay indoors for several days, and local water supplies may be contaminated by flooding.

If evacuation becomes necessary:
1. Leave as soon as possible. Avoid flooded roads. Follow radio instructions for the best and safest evacuation route.
2. Listen to the radio for the location of shelters serving your neighborhood.
3. Take all emergency supplies and warm clothing and blankets to the shelter.
4. Lock your home and leave.

 **PAIR WORK**
**(CD3, Track 28)**

| Suggested teaching time: | 5–10 minutes |
|---|---|
| Your actual teaching time: | _____ |

- Have students look at the questions.
- Encourage students to try to complete the statements with the information they remember from the emergency broadcast in Exercise B.
- Have students listen again and complete any unfinished items.
- Review as a class.
- You may want the students to listen again to review the corrected statements.

# TOP NOTCH **INTERACTION**

| Suggested teaching time: | 20–25 minutes |
|---|---|
| Your actual teaching time: | _____ |

## STEP 1. GROUP WORK.

• Review the list of emergencies. Students can choose an emergency not on the list.

• Review the example on the notepad.

• Review the ideas to consider when planning for an emergency. Brainstorm and write on the board other supplies. Examples: *a flashlight, a first-aid kit, wooden boards, warm clothing, blankets, a battery-operated radio, matches,* etc.

• Ask students to write at least six items in the supplies column.

• Encourage students to include details about their plan; for example, if the planning is for a long-term or short-term emergency.

• Walk around the room and provide help as needed.

## STEP 2. Present your plan . . .

• Review the model first.

• As the groups present their plan, ask the class to take notes. The notes will help the class compare the plans. You may want to draw the following chart on the board for students to organize their notes.

| Group number | Type of emergency | Supplies | Other information |
|---|---|---|---|
| 1 | | | |
| 2 | | | |
| 3 | | | |
| 4 | | | |
| 5 | | | |
| 6 | | | |

 **Graphic Organizers**

## EXTRAS (optional)

**Workbook: Exercises 15–19**
**Copy & Go: Activity 23**

**AUDIOSCRIPT for Exercise E, page T67**

REPORT 1
**F:** Brazil farmers report the loss of dairy and beef cattle. There has been no measurable rainfall in three months, and the dry land cannot feed their animals.

REPORT 2
**M:** The rain hasn't stopped in a week, and people nearest the river are moving out of their houses because the roads are covered in water.

REPORT 3
**F:** The storm's winds reached a record 150 kilometers per hour, and the torrential rains are expected to continue for at least six more hours. Trees are down, and areas nearest the beaches are heavily damaged.

REPORT 4
**M:** A fast-moving, dark, funnel-shaped cloud is making its way across the eastern side of town, knocking down trees. Roofs on many houses have blown off. Residents are urged to immediately go underground and take cover until the danger has passed.

**STEP 1. GROUP WORK.** Divide into groups. Each group chooses an emergency to plan for. Then, write plans for your emergency on your notepads. Use the ideas to help you plan.

**Emergencies**
a flood
a volcanic eruption
an earthquake
a tornado
a typhoon
other _____

**Ideas to consider in your planning**
- food, water, batteries, cell phones, and other supplies
- relatives that live in other places
- emergency telephone numbers
- family pets
- shelter

**Emergency supplies**
2 liters of water per person per day

**Goal**
have enough water

**Reason**
in case water is unsafe

**Type of emergency:**

| Emergency supplies | Goal | Reason |
|---|---|---|
| | | |

matches

bottled water

batteries

> 66 Our group prepared for a storm. We said to be sure cell phones were working. A power outage might occur. 99

**STEP 2.** Present your plan to the class. Compare your plans.

# 4 Describe Natural Disasters

## A 🎧 VOCABULARY. Discussing disasters. Listen and practice.

**natural disaster**  a disaster caused by nature, not people

**death toll**  the number of people killed

**destruction**  loss of buildings, roads, trees, and plants caused by disasters

**casualties / victims**  people who are either injured or killed in a disaster **CN**

**survivors**  people who are not killed when a disaster occurs

**missing**  people who can't be found after a disaster

**homeless**  people who have no place to live after a disaster

| 🎧 Adjectives for describing disasters | |
|---|---|
| mild | ! |
| moderate | !! |
| severe | !!! |
| deadly | !!!! |
| catastrophic | !!!!! |

**CN** **Corpus Notes:** The most frequent collocation with *casualties* is *heavy casualties* meaning *a large number of casualties*. *Casualty* is used much more frequently in written English than in spoken English. In spoken English, *victim* is many times more likely to be used than *casualty*.

## B Have you or someone you know experienced a natural disaster? What happened? Use the vocabulary. Answers will vary.

## C 🎧 READING. Read about earthquakes. Why are earthquakes so frightening?

# Earthquakes

Damage to road in 1995 earthquake in Kobe, Japan

Earthquakes are among the deadliest natural disasters, causing the largest number of casualties, the highest death tolls, and the greatest destruction. In 1556 in China, the deadliest earthquake in history killed 830,000 people. But many other earthquakes have caused the deaths of more than 100,000 people, and it is not unusual, even in modern times, for an earthquake death toll to reach 20,000 to 30,000 people with hundreds of thousands left homeless.

There are four factors that affect the casualty rate and economic impact of earthquakes: magnitude, location, quality of construction of buildings, and timing.

### Magnitude

The magnitude, or strength, of an earthquake is measured on the Richter scale, ranging from 1 to 10, with 10 being the greatest. Earthquakes over 6 on the Richter scale are often deadly, and those over 8 are generally catastrophic, causing terrible damage.

### Location

However, a severe earthquake that is located far from population centers does not cause the same damage as a less severe one that occurs in the middle of a city. As an example, in 1960, the strongest earthquake ever recorded, 9.5 magnitude on the Richter scale, struck in the Pacific Ocean near the Chilean coastline, killing over 2,000 people and injuring another 3,000. If this quake had struck a city, it would have been catastrophic, and hundreds of thousands might have been killed. Similarly, in Alaska, in 1964, a magnitude 9.2 quake hit an area with few people, and the death toll was 117.

### Quality of Construction

Furthermore, modern building construction techniques can lessen the death toll and economic impact of a moderate earthquake that would otherwise cause severe destruction of older-style buildings. In 2003, a terrible earthquake in the historic city of Bam in Iran caused the destruction of over 90% of the buildings, mostly due to old construction.

### Timing

Finally, the time of occurrence of an earthquake can affect the number of deaths and casualties. Earthquakes that occur in the night, when people are indoors, usually cause a greater death toll than ones that occur when people are outdoors.

**SOURCE:** www.worldbookonline.com

## LESSON 4 *Describe Natural Disasters*

### A 🎧 VOCABULARY
**(CD3, Tracks 29,30)**

| | |
|---|---|
| Suggested teaching time: | 5–10 minutes |
| Your actual teaching time: | _____ |

- Have students listen and study the words and the definitions. Then have students listen and repeat.
- Have students listen to the adjectives in the small box. Then have students listen and repeat chorally. Point out that the words are graded from least damaging to most damaging.
- Books closed. Draw the following diagram on the board:

🔘 **Graphic Organizers**

- Have students listen again and write the word that matches the definition in each box.
- Review as a class. (a. destruction  b. survivors  c. missing  d. homeless  e. casualties / victims  f. death toll)

> **Language note:** *Casualties, victims,* and *survivors* are nouns. *Missing* and *homeless* are adjectives. Write on the board:
> *There were 100 casualties / survivors / victims.*
> *100 people are missing / homeless.*
> *100 people were reported missing.*
> *100 people were left homeless.*

🔘 **Vocabulary Cards**

### B Have you or someone you know ...

| | |
|---|---|
| Suggested teaching time: | 5 minutes |
| Your actual teaching time: | _____ |

- Help students organize ideas. Write on the board:
  *Type of natural disaster: Where? When?*
  *How serious was it?*
  *moderate, severe, deadly, catastrophic*
  *What happened to buildings? To people?*

- Note: If neither students nor the people they know have experienced a natural disaster, you can ask them to complete the outline with information about a disaster they know about.
- Group work. Form groups of four. Encourage students to use the vocabulary to describe their event.

### C 🎧 READING
**(CD3, Track 31)**

| | |
|---|---|
| Suggested teaching time: | 10–15 minutes |
| Your actual teaching time: | _____ |

- Write on the board:
  1. *The deadliest earthquakes in history*
  2. *The factors that affect the consequences of an earthquake*

- To practice the reading strategy of scanning, have students scan the text to decide which topic from the board best describes what the text is about. Encourage students to support their choice by underlining in the text the four factors (magnitude or strength, location, quality of construction, timing). (Answer 2)
- Group work. Form groups of three. Have students discuss why they think earthquakes are frightening.

**Option:** Use this option if you want to do a listening activity. Books closed. Draw the following chart (without the answers) on the board. Have students complete each sentence for each of the factors affecting the consequences of an earthquake. Then have students read the text to confirm their answers. **[+10 minutes]**

| | An earthquake will cause more damage if . . . | An earthquake will cause less damage if . . . |
|---|---|---|
| **Magnitude** | *it measures low / below 6 (on the Richter scale).* | *it measures over 6.* |
| **Location** | *strikes a city.* | *strikes far from a city / in the ocean.* |
| **Quality of construction** | *buildings are old.* | *buildings are modern.* |
| **Timing** | *it strikes at night.* | *it strikes during the day.* |

🔘 **Extra Reading Comprehension Activities**

🔘 **Graphic Organizers**

🔘 **Learning Strategies**

> **Language note:** Another type of disaster, where people are the cause, is called a *man-made disaster*. For example, oil spills, forest fires started by people, air pollution, etc.

> **Language note:** Make sure students understand the following words: *magnitude* (strength); *location* (place where the disaster takes place); *quality of construction* (materials and design used for building); *timing* (moment when the disaster takes place).

**T70**

**Answer the questions . . .**

| Suggested teaching time: | 5 minutes |
| Your actual teaching time: | _____ |

• Review the example first.

• To review with the class, have students use complete sentences to say their answers.

 **Extra Reading Comprehension Activities**

 **DISCUSSION**

| Suggested teaching time: | 5 minutes |
| Your actual teaching time: | _____ |

• If you used the graphic organizer in Exercise C, ask students to use their notes. If not, you may want to use the graphic organizer for Exercise C on the Teacher's Resource Disk.

• Group work. Form groups of four. Encourage students to support their views with examples from the article.

• Ask various students for their answers and opinions and write them on the board.

## TOP NOTCH **INTERACTION**

| Suggested teaching time: | 15–20 minutes |
| Your actual teaching time: | _____ |

### STEP 1. PAIR WORK.

• Have students decide who is reading which news report.

• Review the model.

• Walk around the room and provide help as needed. Encourage students to use indirect speech.

### STEP 2. GROUP WORK.

• Review the list of historical disasters.

• Point out that students can also choose another disaster they know about.

• Ask groups to present in front of the class. Encourage the class to ask follow-up questions.

**Culture note:** On April 18, 1906, an earthquake measuring 7.9 on the Richter scale struck San Francisco, United States. More than 3,000 people died, and there was a lot of damage to buildings and roads. More than half the population of 400,000 were left homeless. A three-day fire followed the earthquake and caused more damage than the earthquake itself.

Mount Saint Helens is located in southwestern Washington, United States. The volcano—dormant since 1857—suddenly began to erupt on March 18, 1980. The eruption sent a huge cloud of gas and ashes into the air and turned day into night. The eruption also caused an earthquake that measured 5.1 on the Richter scale. Fifty people died and more than 150 square miles of forest were destroyed.

An earthquake struck the city of Bam, Iran, at dawn on December 26, 2003. Over 26,000 people died, and tens of thousands of people were injured and left homeless. Tents were set up on the outskirts of the city to provide water, food, and shelter for survivors. Bam is a historic city, and many of its buildings are made of mud brick. This is the main reason why the earthquake caused so much property damage—it destroyed 70 percent of the city's buildings.

An undersea earthquake in the Indian Ocean on December 26, 2004, generated a tsunami. The result was one of the deadliest disasters in modern history. Scientists now believe the earthquake registered 9.3 on the Richter Scale. The death toll will most likely reach 300,000 people. Southeast Asia and nine other countries were the most directly impacted, but countries around the world were affected as many tourists and international travelers were in the region during the holiday season.

### STEP 3. WRITING.

• Ask students to use the notes on their notepad as a guide.

• Remind students to use the vocabulary in this unit.

• Encourage students to expand their information by drawing conclusions about the effects of the magnitude and timing.

• Walk around the room as students write and provide help as needed.

 **Writing Process Worksheets**

### EXTRAS (optional)

**Workbook:** Exercises 20–24
**Copy & Go:** Activity 24

**D** **Answer the questions, according to the information in the article.**

> The article said the earthquake in 1556 in China was the deadliest in history.

1. Which earthquake was the deadliest in history?
   The article said (that) the deadliest earthquake in history was in 1556 in China. It killed 830,000 people.
2. Which earthquake had the highest recorded Richter scale reading?
   The article said (that) the strongest earthquake ever recorded struck near the Chilean coastline in 1960.
   It was a 9.5 on the Richter scale.
3. How can location affect the death toll of an earthquake?
   The article said (that) if an earthquake strikes far from population centers it causes less damage.
4. How can building techniques lessen the destruction and economic impact of an earthquake? The article said (that) modern building construction techniques can lesson the death toll and economic impact of an earthquake that might otherwise cause severe destruction of older buildings.

**E** **DISCUSSION.** How do magnitude and timing affect the casualty rate and economic impact of earthquakes?

## TOP NOTCH
### INTERACTION • *What a disaster!*

**Partner B**
**from Apex News**

**Date:** September 14
**Place:** Italy
**Event:** earthquake, magnitude 5.5
**Property damage:** slight in newer buildings; moderate in older ones
**Casualties:** 12 injuries, none severe or life-threatening

**STEP 1. PAIR WORK. Prepare a news report about fictional disasters and present it to your partner.** Answers will vary.

**Partner A**
**from Star News Agency**

**Date:** September 20
**Place:** Port-au-Prince, Haiti
**Event:** hurricane
**Property damage:** many houses damaged by wind, rain, flooding, and landslides
**Casualties:** hundreds homeless and missing

> There was a 5.5 magnitude earthquake in Italy.

**STEP 2. GROUP WORK. Choose one of the following historic disasters. Find information about it on the Internet, at a library, or in a bookstore. Write the information on your notepad. Then present the information to the class.**

The San Francisco earthquake of 1906 (U.S.)
The Mount Saint Helens volcanic eruption in 1980 (U.S.)
The Bam earthquake of 2003 (Iran)
The tsunami of 2004 (Indian Ocean)
One of <u>your</u> choice: _____

place and date:

event:

casualties:

destruction:

**STEP 3. WRITING. On a separate sheet of paper, write about the disaster you researched.**

**A** 🎧 **LISTENING COMPREHENSION.** **Listen to the report. Then check the eight disasters mentioned. Listen again if necessary.**

| | | Place | Year | Disaster | Killed |
|---|---|---|---|---|---|
| ☑ | 1 | worldwide | 1917 | epidemic | 20,000,000 |
| ☐ | 2 | Soviet Union | 1932 | famine | 5,000,000 |
| ☑ | 3 | China | 1931 | flood | 3,700,000 |
| ☑ | 4 | China | 1928 | drought | 3,000,000 |
| ☑ | 5 | worldwide | 1914 | epidemic | 3,000,000 |
| ☑ | 6 | Soviet Union | 1917 | epidemic | 2,500,000 |
| ☑ | 7 | China | 1959 | flood | 2,000,000 |
| ☑ | 8 | India | 1920 | epidemic | 2,000,000 |
| ☐ | 9 | Bangladesh | 1943 | famine | 1,900,000 |
| ☑ | 10 | China | 1909 | epidemic | 1,500,000 |

**The 10 Most Deadly Natural Disasters of the 20TH Century**

**SOURCE:** CRED (Center for Research on the Epidemiology of Disasters)

*TOP NOTCH* SONG
"Lucky to Be Alive"
Lyrics on last book page.

*TOP NOTCH* PROJECT
Check the global weather report in the newspaper or on the Internet. Report storms and other weather. emergencies around the globe.

*TOP NOTCH* WEBSITE
For Unit 6 online activities, visit the *Top Notch* Companion Website at www.longman.com/topnotch.

**B** **Complete each statement with the name of the event.**

drought
flood
landslide
epidemic
hurricane

1. In a <u>landslide</u>, mud and soil cover the houses and can bury whole towns.

2. A widespread event in which many people become sick with the same illness is an <u>epidemic</u>.

3. A <u>flood</u> occurs when water from a river enters houses and roads.

4. A storm with high winds and rain is a <u>hurricane</u>.

5. When there is no rain for a long period of time, a <u>drought</u> is said to occur.

**C** **Complete each indirect statement or question. Use <u>said</u> or <u>told</u>.**

1. They <u>told</u> me to call the office in the morning.

2. He <u>said</u> the storm was awful.

3. The students <u>said</u> the test had been very difficult.

4. Who <u>told</u> us to get a flu shot?

5. We <u>told</u> the children to prepare for the storm.

**D** **WRITING.** **On a separate sheet of paper, write about one of the following subjects:**

1. How to prepare for an emergency

2. What to do when an emergency occurs

3. How location, magnitude, timing, and building construction affect the amount of destruction caused by an earthquake

# UNIT 6
# CHECKPOINT

## A  LISTENING COMPREHENSION
### (CD3, Track 32)

| Suggested teaching time: | 5–10 minutes |
|---|---|
| Your actual teaching time: | _____ |

- Tell students they will listen to a general report and that specific disasters are not mentioned. Students need to listen for the vocabulary that identifies the type of disaster.
- First listening: Students listen to the report and check the disasters.
- Second listen: Students compare answers with a partner and listen again to confirm their answers.
- Review with the class.

### AUDIOSCRIPT

[F = British]

**F:** Good morning, listeners. Today we'll be discussing some of the worst natural disasters of the last century. It's hard to imagine events with death tolls over a million, but, believe it or not, they're surprisingly common. Once in the last century, a lack of rainfall killed over a million people. And twice, too much water has done the same thing.
　　But the worst disasters by far are episodes of sickness that affect millions. Five were situations where over a million people died.

## B  Complete each statement . . .

| Suggested teaching time: | 5 minutes |
|---|---|
| Your actual teaching time: | _____ |

- Do the first item with the class.
- Have students compare answers with a partner and then review as a class.

**Option:** Books closed. Pair work. To provide more practice, students take turns saying a statement that describes a disaster and guessing the kind of disaster. Example: Student A: *It's a period with no rain.* Student B: *A drought.* Students cannot repeat the disaster, and they should continue until they each guess four disasters. (Students learned ten types of disaster in this unit: cyclone, tornado, hurricane, typhoon, monsoon, flood, landslide, drought, earthquake, volcanic eruption.) **[+5 minutes]**

## C  Complete each indirect . . .

| Suggested teaching time: | 5 minutes |
|---|---|
| Your actual teaching time: | _____ |

- Do the first item with the class.
- Have students compare answers with a partner. Then review as a class.

## D  WRITING

| Suggested teaching time: | 15–20 minutes |
|---|---|
| Your actual teaching time: | _____ |

- Brainstorm different types of emergencies students might experience in their areaß or city.
- If students need to review information / vocabulary, have them look at Lesson 3 for preparing for emergencies and Lesson 4 about earthquakes.
- Review with students ideas about how to organize their writing. For example, remind them to introduce the topic, give concrete examples and supporting information, and to write some concluding remarks to finish their paper.
- Walk around the room and provide help as needed.

 **Writing Process Worksheets**

 ***Top Notch Pop* Song Activities**
　　**(CD3, Track 33)**

### *TOP NOTCH* PROJECT

**Idea:** Encourage students to find information about severe weather events, and to write notes about the information they find. Be sure to ask students to use indirect speech to report the information they found.

# UNIT WRAP-UP

| | |
|---|---|
| Suggested teaching time: | 15–20 minutes |
| Your actual teaching time: | _____ |

## Narration

- Ask students to interpret the pictures and write notes for each question to help prepare their stories.

- Pair work. Students take turns telling their story. Encourage students to use the language they learned.

- As students tell the stories, walk around the room and provide help as needed.

**Option: Get ready!** Pair work. Have students identify everything they see in the picture. Examples: *weather report, evacuation, high winds, boarded windows, supplies,* etc. **[+5 minutes]**

**Option: What's the story?** Ask volunteers to tell their stories in front of the class. **[+5 minutes]**

## Social Language

- Encourage students to use the language they learned in this unit to create the conversation(s).

┌─ **Your students can say . . .** ──────────

**A:** What's going on in the news today? **B:** Well, a tropical storm is expected today. **A:** Really? **B:** Yes. The report said winds will be strong. It also said to prepare food and water. **A:** I'll go to the store right away.

**A:** What did the report say about the weather? **B:** There's a storm on its way. **A:** What kind of storm? **B:** A tropical storm with high winds. The report said to prepare for a power outage. **A:** I'll have to get batteries and a flashlight.

**A:** Did you hear the weather report? **B:** No. What's up? **A:** A tropical storm is on its way. **B:** Really? **A:** Yes. Floods are expected in coastal areas. **B:** Did they say to prepare for an emergency? **A:** Yes. They said to get your car ready for evacuation.

└────────────────────────────────────

**Challenge: The day after . . .** Pair work. Ask students to write a paragraph describing the consequences of the storm. Encourage students to include the vocabulary they learned in Lesson 4 to describe natural disasters. **[+10 minutes]**

┌─ **Individual oral progress check (optional)** ──

- Use the illustration on page 73. Encourage the student to use material (vocabulary, grammar, rhythm and intonation) practiced in this unit.

- Evaluate the student on correctness and intelligibility.

- Tell the student to answer your questions using indirect speech. Point out he / she can invent the information. Examples: T: *What did the report say about the weather?* S: *They said there was going to be a tropical storm.* / *They said a tropical storm was expected / on its way.* T: *What did they say about winds?* S: *They said that winds were strong.* T: *What instructions did they give?* S: *They said to prepare for an emergency. They said to buy [emergency supplies].*

- Point to the top picture (the two men speaking on the phone) and tell the student that together you are going to role-play a conversation. Tell the student to use reported speech. Ask the student to take the role of the younger man. Start the conversation. Example: T: *What's going on in the news today?* S: *There's a tropical storm on its way.* T: *Really?* S: *Yes. They said to prepare for an emergency . . .*

└────────────────────────────────────

 **Cumulative Vocabulary Activities**

 You may wish to use the video and activity worksheets for Unit 6 at this point.

 **Complete Assessment Package Unit 6 Achievement Test**

# TUESDAY

## UNIT WRAP-UP

- **Narration.** Tell the story in the pictures. Who do you think the people are? What does the report say about the weather?

- **Social Language.** Create a conversation between the two men on Tuesday.

TOMORROW'S WEATHER...

TROPICAL STORM EXPECTED, WITH HIGH WINDS, DAMAGING RAIN, POSSIBLE FLOODING NEAR COASTAL AREAS

# WEDNESDAY

THE SHELTER IS NOW OPEN AND ACCEPTING PEOPLE FROM AREAS NEAR THE BEACH

✓ **Now I can ...**

☐ convey a message.
☐ report news.
☐ prepare for an emergency.
☐ describe natural disasters.

73

# Books and Magazines

## UNIT GOALS

1 Recommend a book
2 Explain where you learned something
3 Discuss the quality of reading material
4 Describe your reading habits

**A** ▷ **TOPIC PREVIEW.** Look at the bookstore website. Which books look the most interesting to you? Why?

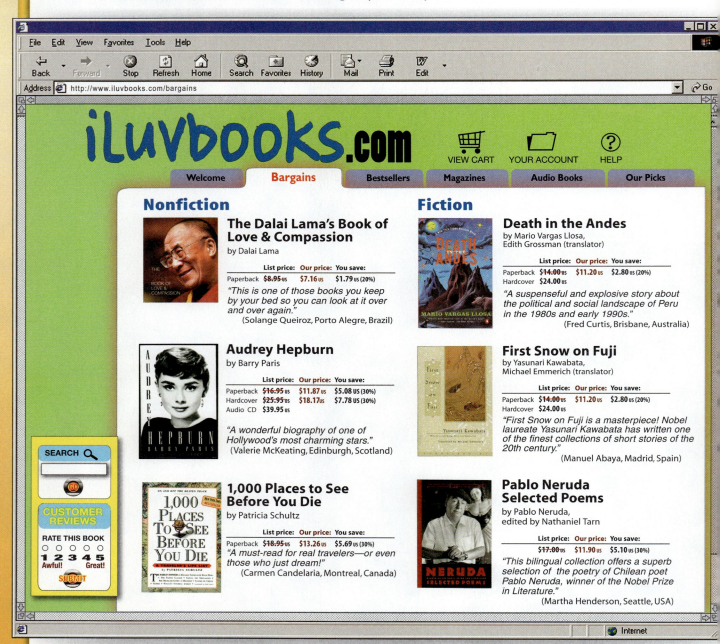

iLuvbooks.com

VIEW CART    YOUR ACCOUNT    HELP

Welcome    **Bargains**    Bestsellers    Magazines    Audio Books    Our Picks

## Nonfiction

**The Dalai Lama's Book of Love & Compassion**
by Dalai Lama

| List price: | Our price: | You save: |
|---|---|---|
| Paperback $8.95 US | $7.16 US | $1.79 US (20%) |

"This is one of those books you keep by your bed so you can look at it over and over again."
(Solange Queiroz, Porto Alegre, Brazil)

**Audrey Hepburn**
by Barry Paris

| List price: | Our price: | You save: |
|---|---|---|
| Paperback $16.95 US | $11.87 US | $5.08 US (30%) |
| Hardcover $25.95 US | $18.17 US | $7.78 US (30%) |
| Audio CD $39.95 US | | |

"A wonderful biography of one of Hollywood's most charming stars."
(Valerie McKeating, Edinburgh, Scotland)

**1,000 Places to See Before You Die**
by Patricia Schultz

| List price: | Our price: | You save: |
|---|---|---|
| Paperback $18.95 US | $13.26 US | $5.69 US (30%) |

"A must-read for real travelers—or even those who just dream!"
(Carmen Candelaria, Montreal, Canada)

## Fiction

**Death in the Andes**
by Mario Vargas Llosa,
Edith Grossman (translator)

| List price: | Our price: | You save: |
|---|---|---|
| Paperback $14.00 US | $11.20 US | $2.80 US (20%) |
| Hardcover $24.00 US | | |

"A suspenseful and explosive story about the political and social landscape of Peru in the 1980s and early 1990s."
(Fred Curtis, Brisbane, Australia)

**First Snow on Fuji**
by Yasunari Kawabata,
Michael Emmerich (translator)

| List price: | Our price: | You save: |
|---|---|---|
| Paperback $14.00 US | $11.20 US | $2.80 US (20%) |
| Hardcover $24.00 US | | |

"First Snow on Fuji is a masterpiece! Nobel laureate Yasunari Kawabata has written one of the finest collections of short stories of the 20th century."
(Manuel Abaya, Madrid, Spain)

**Pablo Neruda Selected Poems**
by Pablo Neruda,
edited by Nathaniel Tarn

| List price: | Our price: | You save: |
|---|---|---|
| $17.00 US | $11.90 US | $5.10 US (30%) |

"This bilingual collection offers a superb selection of the poetry of Chilean poet Pablo Neruda, winner of the Nobel Prize in Literature."
(Martha Henderson, Seattle, USA)

SEARCH

GO

CUSTOMER REVIEWS

RATE THIS BOOK
○ ○ ○ ○ ○
1 2 3 4 5
Awful!    Great!
SUBMIT

**B** ▷ **DISCUSSION.** Do you prefer fiction or nonfiction? Have you ever read a book in English? A magazine? A newspaper? If not, would you like to?

# UNIT 7

# Books and Magazines

## A TOPIC PREVIEW

| | |
|---|---|
| Suggested teaching time: | 10–15 minutes |
| Your actual teaching time: | _____ |

- To practice the reading strategy of scanning, ask students to read the text (quickly) and answer the following questions: *What is the name of the bookstore?* (Iluvbooks) *Which two types of reading or literature are offered on this page?* (fiction and nonfiction)

- Point out that *luv* is an informal way of writing *love*.

- You may want to point out that this web page offers *bargains* (something bought for less than its usual price). Ask students to notice the two prices and then the amount of money saved.

- Ask students to review the books listed and decide which ones they are most interested in. Encourage students to write some reasons for their choices.

- Group work. Form groups of three. Students take turns talking about which books they chose. Encourage students to give reasons and ask each other follow-up questions. Example: Student A: *I'd like to read the Dalai Lama's book. I'm interested in his beliefs.* Student B: *Have you read any other books by him?* Student B: *No. But I've heard his writing is inspiring.*

- Take a poll to find out which book on this list is the most popular in the class.

**Culture note:** **The Dalai Lama** is the spiritual leader of the Tibetan people. Currently, Tenzin Gyatso, the 14th Dalai Lama, lives in exile in India. He received the Nobel Peace Prize in 1989. **Audrey Hepburn** (1929–1993), born in Belgium, won a U.S. Academy Award in 1953 for the romantic comedy *Roman Holiday*. After she left Hollywood, she spent time working with the United Nations International Children's Fund and other organizations helping children around the world. **Patricia Schultz**, a veteran guide writer, made the *New York Times* bestseller list with *1,000 Places to See*. It offers an around-the-world list of places to visit, both on and off the beaten track. **Mario Vargas Llosa**, a Peruvian novelist, playwright, and essayist, writes about social change and political corruption in Peru. **Yasunari Kawabata**, the first Japanese novelist to win a Nobel Prize for Literature (1968), used his narrative mastery to express the "Japanese mind." Kawabata and other young writers formed the neosensationist movement in the 1920s by using lyricism and impressionism in their writing instead of social realism. **Pablo Neruda**, considered one of the best poets of the 20th century, was born in Chile in 1904 (died 1973). In 1924, his novel *Twenty Love Poems and a Song of Despair* became a bestseller. He won the Nobel Prize in Literature in 1971.

**Language note:** Students may need help with the following words: *paperback* (a book that has a soft paper cover); *hardcover* (a book that has a strong stiff cover); *biography* (a book about a person's life, written by someone else); *must-read* (a piece of writing that is so interesting everyone should read it); *masterpiece* (a work of art, piece of writing, or music etc. that is of very high quality); *laureate* /ˈlɔriɪt/ (someone who has been given an important prize).

## B DISCUSSION

| | |
|---|---|
| Suggested teaching time: | 10–15 minutes |
| Your actual teaching time: | _____ |

- Have students look at the books listed in each category, and ask students *What is the difference between fiction and nonfiction?* (fiction: books and stories about imaginary people and events; nonfiction: books and stories about real people and actual events)

- To prepare for the discussion, ask students to write two lists. List 1: Students should write the titles of some favorite books and label them fiction or nonfiction. These could be in any language. List 2: Write the titles (or even types) of books, magazines, and newspapers they have read or tried to read in English.

- If students don't read a lot of books or magazines in English, but do a lot of reading in English on the computer / on websites, they should include this information.

- Group work. Form small groups. Encourage students to give reasons for their choices and to ask each other follow-up questions. Example: Student A: *I try to read the newspaper* The International Herald Tribune *at least once a week.* Student B: *Why only once a week?* Student A: *A lot of the vocabulary is difficult for me so I use my dictionary when I read it. I almost need the whole week to finish it!*

- To review, ask students what books, magazines, or newspapers in English they have read or plan to read. You may want to write a list on the board.

**Option:** Take a poll to find out if students prefer fiction or nonfiction. **[+5 minutes]**

 **SOUND BITES**

(CD4, Track 2)

| Suggested teaching time: | 5 minutes |
|---|---|
| Your actual teaching time: | _____ |

- After students read and listen, ask *What is Janet shopping for?* (gardening magazines for her mom) *What does Lucy say she's reading lately?* (poetry) *What does Janet recommend?* (a new book by John Grisham)

- Point out that *till the end* means *until the end*.

- If students have questions regarding vocabulary, let them know that the next exercise will help clarify their questions.

> **Culture note:** U.S. writer John Grisham is considered the master of the legal thriller. Graduating from law school and practicing law inspired him to write his first novel, *A Time to Kill*, in 1988. Grisham's books have been translated into 29 languages, and seven have been turned into Hollywood movies.

 **UNDERSTANDING FROM CONTEXT**

| Suggested teaching time: | 10 minutes |
|---|---|
| Your actual teaching time: | _____ |

- Point out that *I can't get into it* is similiar to *I'm (not) really into it*.

- Have students compare answers with a partner. Then review as a class.

- Pair work. Students take turns briefly telling their partners about books or materials they have read or are reading and using the expressions in the activity.

> **Language note:** If necessary, clarify the meaning of the expressions: *I can't put it down.* / *It's a real page-turner.* (I find it extremely interesting. I can't stop reading it.) *I'm really into it.* (I'm very interested in it.) *I can't get into it.* / *It doesn't turn me on.* (I can't get interested in it.) *I can't get enough of it.* (I like it so much that I want a lot of it.)

**E** **IN OTHER WORDS**

| Suggested teaching time: | 5 minutes |
|---|---|
| Your actual teaching time: | _____ |

- Encourage students to identify who says each phrase and to use the context of the conversation to help work out the meaning.

- Have students compare answers with a partner. Then review as a class.

- Students may use words or expressions that are different from the Answer Key. (Students may say: 1. I just want to look around. 2. Thanks for the (helpful) information. 3. You can borrow it.)

## WHAT ABOUT **YOU?**

| Suggested teaching time: | 5–10 minutes |
|---|---|
| Your actual teaching time: | _____ |

- Group work. Form groups of three or four.

- Walk around the room and provide help as needed.

- To finish the activity, take a poll. Ask each student to say which reading material they assigned the highest percentage.

## EXTRAS (optional)

**Workbook: Exercises 1–5**

 🎧 **SOUND BITES.** **Read along silently as you listen to a natural conversation.**

**JANET:** Hey, Lucy! Looking for anything special?

**LUCY:** Janet! No, I'm just browsing. What are <u>you</u> up to?

**JANET:** I'm picking up some gardening magazines for my mom. She can't get enough of them. So are you reading anything good these days?

**LUCY:** Well, I've got a book of poetry on my night table, but I just can't seem to get into it. I guess poetry just doesn't turn me on.

**JANET:** Have you read the new John Grisham?

**LUCY:** No, actually, I haven't. I didn't know he had a new book out.

**JANET:** Well, I can't put it down. It's a real page-turner.

**LUCY:** Thanks for the tip. I think I'll get that.

**JANET:** Don't bother. I'm just about finished. If you can wait till the end of the week, I'll lend it to you. **CN**

 **UNDERSTANDING FROM CONTEXT.** **Classify each of the following expressions by its meaning. Explain your choices.**

| | | |
|---|---|---|
| I can't put it down. | I can't get into it. | I can't get enough of it. |
| I'm really into it. | It doesn't turn me on. | It's a real page-turner. |

**CN** **Corpus Notes:** *Just about* and *almost* mean the same thing but *almost* is used much more frequently, especially in written English. *Just about* occurs in speech much more frequently than in writing.

| I like it. | I don't like it. |
|---|---|
| I can't put it down.<br>I'm really into it.<br>I can't get enough of it.<br>It's a real page-turner. | I can't get into it.<br>It doesn't turn me on. |

 **IN OTHER WORDS.** **Explain the meaning of the following expressions from the conversation.**

1. "I'm just browsing."
2. "Thanks for the tip."
3. "I'll lend it to you."

1. I don't need anything specific. I'm just looking.
2. Thanks for the advice.
3. I'll let you borrow it.

**WHAT ABOUT YOU?**

**What percentage of your reading time do you spend on the following materials? (Make sure it adds up to 100%!)** Answers will vary.

| | % |
|---|---|
| magazines | _____ |
| newspapers | _____ |
| websites | _____ |
| fiction | _____ |
| nonfiction | _____ |
| other | _____ |

**1** ▶ ## Recommend a Book

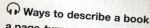

### ⌒ CONVERSATION
### MODEL  Read and listen.

**A:** What's that you're reading?

**B:** It's a Hemingway novel, *The Old Man and the Sea*.

**A:** I've always wanted to read that!  Is it any good?

**B:** Oh, I'd highly recommend it.  It's a real page-turner. **CN1**

**A:** Do you mind if I borrow it when you're done?

**B:** Not at all.

⌒ **Rhythm and intonation practice**

> ⌒ **Ways to describe a book**
> **a page-turner:** makes you want to keep reading it
> **a cliffhanger:** exciting; you don't know what will happen next
> **hard to follow:** difficult to understand
> **a bestseller:** very popular; lots of copies have been sold
> **a fast read:** not very challenging, but enjoyable
> **trash:** very poor quality

**A** ▶ **GRAMMAR.  Noun clauses:  embedded questions**

You can "embed" a question in a larger statement.
Begin embedded <u>yes</u> / <u>no</u> questions with <u>if</u> or <u>whether</u>.

| Yes / no questions | Embedded yes / no questions |
|---|---|
| Is it any good? | I don't know **if** (or **whether**) **it's any good**. |
| Did he like the novel? | I wonder **if** (or **whether**) **he liked the novel**. |
| Have you finished the book? | Could you tell me **if** (or **whether**) **you've finished the book**? |
| Can I borrow John's magazine? | Would you mind asking John **if** (or **whether**) **I could borrow his magazine**? |

Use a question word to begin embedded information questions.

| Information questions | Embedded information questions |
|---|---|
| What's the book about? | Tell me **what the book's about**. |
| Why did you decide to read it? | Tell me **why you decided to read it**. |
| Who's the author? | I wonder **who the author is**. |
| Who is it written for? | I wonder **who it's written for**. |
| Whose book is this? | I'd like to know **whose book this is**. |
| When was it written? | Do you know **when it was written**? |
| Where does it take place? | Do you know **where it takes place**? |

> **BE CAREFUL! CN2**
> Use normal (not inverted) word order in embedded questions.
> Do you know **who** the author **is**?
> **NOT** Do you know ~~who is~~ the author?

**GRAMMAR BOOSTER**
**PAGES G11–G12**
**For more …**

**CN1 Corpus Notes:** *Highly recommend* and *strongly recommend* have the same meaning but *strongly recommend* is slightly more common.

**B** ▶ **Use each question to complete the embedded questions.**

1. Does she like to read?  I wonder <u>if she likes to read</u> .

2. Where did you get this magazine?  Can you tell me <u>where you got this magazine</u> ?

3. Is he a Garcia Marquez fan?  I've been wondering <u>if he's a Garcia Marquez fan</u>

4. Why do you never read fiction?  I'm curious <u>why you never read fiction</u>

5. Who told you about this author?  I was wondering <u>who told you about this author</u>

6. When did you first hear about that website?  I'd really like to know <u>when you first heard about that website</u> .

**CN2 Corpus Notes:** Learners commonly make errors with word order in embedded questions, for example: *Do you know ~~what are~~ the advantages of studying English?* Be sure students are aware of correct word order.

# LESSON

## 1 Recommend a Book

### 🎧 CONVERSATION **MODEL**
**(CD4, Tracks 3, 5)**

| Suggested teaching time: | 5 minutes |
|---|---|
| Your actual teaching time: | _____ |

- After students read and listen, ask *What kind of book is the woman reading?* (a novel, fiction) *Is it a good book?* (Yes, it's a page-turner.) *What does the man want to do?* (borrow the book / read the book)
- Have students listen and study the information in the small box. Then have them listen and repeat.

**Culture note:** Ernest Hemingway (1899–1961) was a U.S. novelist and short-story writer. *The Old Man and the Sea* earned him the Pulitzer Prize in fiction in 1953.

### 🎧 Rhythm and intonation practice
**(CD4, Track 4)**

| Suggested teaching time: | 5 minutes |
|---|---|
| Your actual teaching time: | _____ |

- Have students repeat each line chorally.
- Make sure students:
  - use falling intonation for *What's that you're reading?*
  - stress <u>Old</u>, <u>Man</u>, and <u>Sea</u> in the title *The Old Man and the Sea.*
  - use rising intonation for *Do you mind if I borrow it when you're done?*
  - Link *Not* with *at* in *Not at all.*
  - use the following stress pattern:

**STRESS PATTERN**

**A:** What's that you're reading?

**B:** It's a Hemingway novel, *The Old Man and the Sea.*

**A:** I've always wanted to read that! Is it any good?

**B:** Oh, I'd highly recommend it. It's a real page-turner.

**A:** Do you mind if I borrow it when you're done?

**B:** Not at all.

### 🔺A GRAMMAR

| Suggested teaching time: | 15 minutes |
|---|---|
| Your actual teaching time: | _____ |

- Tips for organizing information on the board: Write the sample sentences on one side of the board. This creates a resource for students as they do the practice activities.

- Direct attention to the box and have students read the first explanation and study the examples.
- Write on the board:
  1. Is it a bestseller?
  2. I don't know <u>if it is a bestseller</u>.
- To help clarify, point out the underlined information in item 2 and say *An embedded question is part of a larger sentence. It's another way to express information that is not known.*
- Then point to item 1 on the board and ask *Is this question a <u>yes</u> / <u>no</u> question or an information question?* (a <u>yes</u> / <u>no</u> question) Then point to item 2 and say *Embedded <u>yes</u> / <u>no</u> questions can start with <u>if</u> or <u>whether</u>.*
- Ask students to rewrite item 2 using *whether.* (I don't know <u>whether it is a bestseller</u>.)
- Write on the board:
  3. <u>Does</u> he like the book?
  4. I don't know <u>if he likes the book</u>.
- Point out that auxiliary verbs are not used in embedded questions and point out the verb form in item 4.
- Have students read the second explanation and study the examples.
- Write on the board:
  5. Where did you buy it?
  6. Can you tell me <u>where you bought it</u>?
- Point to item 5 and ask *Is this question a <u>yes</u> / <u>no</u> question or an information question?* (an information question)
- Say *Embedded information questions start with a Wh-question word.* Point out the underlined information in item 6.
- Have students look at the embedded information questions in the Grammar box and underline the question words. (what, why, who, whose, when, where)
- Review the Be careful! box. You can point out items 2, 4, 6 on the board. As a comparison, point out that inverted word order is used in regular <u>yes</u>/<u>no</u> or information questions.
- Write on the board:
  Could you tell me _____?          I wonder _____.
  Do you know if we _____?
- To check comprehension, have students make embedded <u>yes</u>/<u>no</u> and information questions using the prompts. Examples: *Could you tell me what time it is? Could you tell me if my taxi is here? Do you know when the party starts? Do you know if we have a test next week? I wonder where my jacket is. I wonder whether she got the flowers.*

 Grammar Self-Checks

###  B Use each question . . .

| Suggested teaching time: | 5 minutes |
|---|---|
| Your actual teaching time: | _____ |

- Do the first item with the class. Make sure students use the correct verb form (*likes*) and not the auxiliary verb *does* in the embedded question.
- Have students compare answers with a partner. Then review as a class.

**T76**

 **VOCABULARY**

(CD4, Track 6)

| | |
|---|---|
| Suggested teaching time: | 5–10 minutes |
| Your actual teaching time: | _____ |

- Review the difference between *fiction* and *nonfiction*. (fiction: books and stories about imaginary people and events; nonfiction: books and stories about real people and actual events)

- Have students listen and study the types of books. Then have students listen and repeat chorally.

**Option:** To check comprehension, write the following words and definitions on the board and have students match them. (1. d, 2. b, 3. e, 4. c, 5. a) **[+10 minutes]**

| | |
|---|---|
| 1. a mystery | a. the life of a person |
| 2. an autobiography | b. the life of the writer of the book |
| 3. a thriller | c. some personal experiences of the author |
| 4. a memoir | d. a story in which events are not explained until the end |
| 5. a biography | e. an exciting story about a murder, spies, or dangerous situations |

**Option:** To provide practice, write the following words on the board: *a memoir, a travel book, a thriller, an autobiography, a mystery, science fiction, short stories, a romance novel, a novel, a self-help book, a biography.*

Then use the following information to describe a type of book and have students say the type of book. Say *This book is about life on another planet.* (science fiction) *This book is about tips to stay healthy.* (a self-help book) *This book is about a detective who solves a murder case.* (a mystery) *This book doesn't have just one story but many.* (short stories) *This book is about a love story.* (a romance novel) *I wrote a book about my life.* (an autobiography) *I wrote a book about the life of an important person.* (a biography) *I wrote a book about the life of an imaginary person.* (a novel) *This book is about visiting a foreign country.* (a travel book) *This book is about spies and has a lot of suspense.* (a thriller) *This book is about the personal experiences of a soldier.* (a memoir). **[+10 minutes]**

**Language note:** The word *book* is used with category words, for example, a *travel book*, a *self-help book*, etc. Do not say: a *novel book*. To describe more in detail what kind of novel it is, use the topic word; for example, a *romance novel*, a *historical novel*, an *autobiographical novel*, etc.

 **Vocabulary Cards**

 **GUESSING GAME**

| | |
|---|---|
| Suggested teaching time: | 5–10 minutes |
| Your actual teaching time: | _____ |

- Role-play the models with a student.

- Write on the board:

  **To say you don't know something**
  *I don't know . . .*
  *I'm not sure . . .*
  *I wonder . . .*

  **To ask (politely) for information**
  *Can / Could you tell me. . . ?  Do you know. . . ?*
  *Can you remember. . . ?  I'd like to know . . .*
  *Would you mind. . . ?  Tell me . . .*

- Ask students to use the phrases on the board and embedded questions to make their guesses. If necessary, review the Grammar box on page 76.

- Walk around the room and provide help as needed.

## CONVERSATION **PAIR WORK**

| | |
|---|---|
| Suggested teaching time: | 5–10 minutes |
| Your actual teaching time: | _____ |

- To get students ready for the activity, have students read the conversation model on page 76 again. You may also want to have students listen to the model.

- Review things you can ask about the book in the Ideas box to the right.

- Point out that if students are not reading a book right now, they can talk about a book they read in the past or choose a type from Exercise C.

- Choose a more confident student and role-play a conversation. Encourage students to ask follow-up questions.

- Walk around the room and provide help as needed. Encourage students to use the correct rhythm and intonation.

 **Pair Work Cards**

 **Learning Strategies**

## EXTRAS (optional)

**Grammar Booster**
**Workbook:  Exercises 6–15**
**Copy & Go:  Activity 25**

**VOCABULARY.** **Types of books.** Listen and practice.

## FICTION

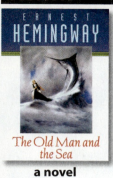
**a novel**

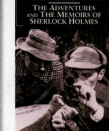
**a mystery**

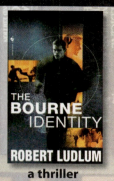
**a thriller**

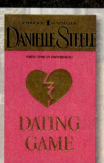
**a romance novel**

**science fiction**

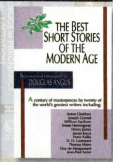
**short stories**

## NONFICTION

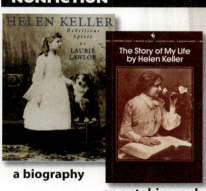
**a biography**

**an autobiography** CN

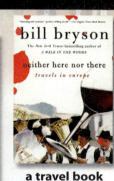
**a travel book**

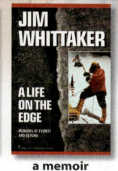
**a memoir**

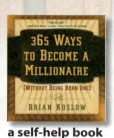
**a self-help book**

CN **Corpus Notes:** *Biography* and *autobiography* are frequently followed by the preposition *of* (a biography of Tiger Woods, *The Autobiography of Malcolm X*).

**D** ▷ **GUESSING GAME.** Choose a well-known book title. Your classmates use embedded questions to guess the title of the book.

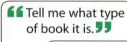
❝Tell me what type of book it is.❞

❝It's a novel.❞

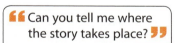
❝Can you tell me where the story takes place?❞

❝Colombia.❞

## CONVERSATION
### PAIR WORK

**Have a conversation about a book. Ask and answer embedded questions about the author, the characters, etc.** Answers will vary.

**Use the conversation on page 76 as a guide, or start like this:**

**A:** What are you reading these days?

**B:** _____ …

**Ideas**

Ask:
- who wrote it
- what it's about
- where it takes place
- who it's written for
- when it was written
- if it's any good

## 2

# Explain Where You Learned Something

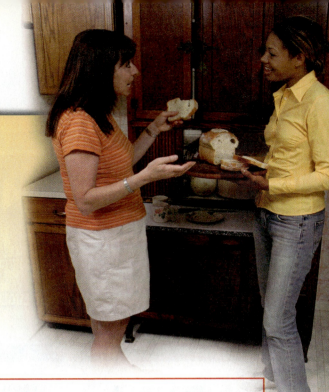

### ∩ CONVERSATION MODEL Read and listen.

**A:** What incredible bread! Did you make it?

**B:** Yes, thanks! I learned how in the latest issue of *Home* magazine.

**A:** I didn't know they had recipes.

**B:** Would you like to borrow a copy?

**A:** I don't think so. I'm all thumbs!

∩ **Rhythm and intonation practice**

---

**A** ▸ **GRAMMAR.** **Noun clauses as direct objects**

**A noun clause can be the direct object of a verb of mental activity.**

                     noun clause

I didn't know    **that *Home* magazine had recipes**.

I think           **that they have great recipes**.

**When the noun clause is a direct object, the word <u>that</u> is often omitted. There is no change in meaning.**

I didn't know ~~that~~ you read *Home* magazine.

I hope ~~that~~ the store has the latest issue.

**As in reported speech, the tense in the noun clause often changes to support meaning.**

I hope we aren't too late. I **hoped** we **weren't** too late.

I think she finished the book. I **thought** she **had finished** the book.

**In short answers, use <u>so</u> to replace the noun clause after the verbs <u>think</u>, <u>believe</u>, <u>guess</u>, and <u>hope</u>.**

    A: Do you have the latest issue of *Car* magazine?

    B: I think **so**. / I don't think **so**.

         I believe **so**. / I don't believe **so**.

  (so = that I have the latest issue.)

**PAGES G12–G13**
**For more …**

**BE CAREFUL!**

I hope so. / I hope **not**.
**NOT** ~~I don't hope so.~~

I guess so. / I guess **not**.
**NOT** ~~I don't guess so.~~

---

**B** ▸ ∩ **PRONUNCIATION.** **Sentence stress in short answers with <u>think</u>, <u>hope</u>, <u>guess</u>, or <u>believe</u>. Listen and repeat.**

1. Does your husband like reading mysteries?    I **THINK** so.

2. Has Jack finished that travel book yet?    I don't **THINK** so.

3. Do you think that novel will be good?    I **HOPE** so.

4. Did your sister enjoy that romance novel?    I **GUESS** so.

5. Is the ending of that story interesting?    I be**LIEVE** so.

 **Corpus Notes:**
A common learner error with noun clauses is using an incorrect tense when the main verb is in the past tense, for example: *I thought he ~~is~~ crazy.* Make sure students don't make this error.

# LESSON 2
## *Explain Where You Learned Something*

## 🎧 CONVERSATION **MODEL**
**(CD4, Track 7)**

| | |
|---|---|
| Suggested teaching time: | 5 minutes |
| Your actual teaching time: | _____ |

- After students read and listen, ask *What's special about the bread?* (It tastes so good / wonderful. It's homemade. The woman in the yellow shirt made it herself.) *Why isn't the woman in the orange shirt interested in learning how to make it?* (Because she thinks she's not good at baking. She thinks she is clumsy.)
- Point out the expression *I'm all thumbs.* Ask students for different ways to say this. Examples: *I'm clumsy. I'm not good at ___ ing. I can't seem to do it.*
- Tell students that *they* in "I didn't know they had recipes" refers to the (writers of the) magazine. *They* is used as an impersonal pronoun in spoken English.

**Language note:** Use *What + (a / an) + adjective + noun!* to show you are impressed with something. Examples: *What incredible bread! What a nice chair!*

## 🎧 **Rhythm and intonation practice**
**(CD4, Track 8)**

| | |
|---|---|
| Suggested teaching time: | 5 minutes |
| Your actual teaching time: | _____ |

- Have students repeat each line chorally.
- Make sure students:
  ○ use falling intonation for *What incredible bread!*
  ○ use rising intonation for *Did you make it?*
  ○ stress new information in a sentence, like <u>Home</u> *magazine.*
  ○ use rising intonation for *Would you like to borrow a copy?*
  ○ use the following stress pattern:

---STRESS PATTERN---

**A:** What incredible bread! Did you make it?

**B:** Yes, thanks! I learned how in the latest issue of
*Home* magazine.

**A:** I didn't know they had recipes.

**B:** Would you like to borrow a copy?

**A:** I don't think so. I'm all thumbs!

## Ⓐ GRAMMAR

| | |
|---|---|
| Suggested teaching time: | 15 minutes |
| Your actual teaching time: | _____ |

- Direct attention to the box and have students read the first explanation and study the examples.

- Write on the board:

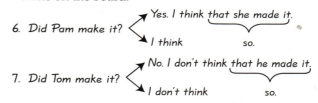

- Say *These are verbs of mental activity.*
- Tell students the underlined noun clause is the direct object of the verb. It expresses the information you "know," "believe," "think," etc.
- To check comprehension, ask various students to make sentences with verbs of mental activity and noun clauses. Examples: *I know he passed the test. I believe that we're going to the mall. I guess she left.*
- Have students read the second explanation and study the examples.
- Tell students the *that* in parentheses can be omitted when the noun clause is the direct object of the verb. Point out that the omission of *that* is very common, especially in spoken English.
- Have students read the third explanation and study the examples.
- Write on the board:

1. It *is* a thriller.   3. I *thought* that it *was* a thriller.
2. I *think* that it *is* a thriller.

- To help clarify, point out that the verb tenses change to match "when" we are talking about.
- Write on the board:

4. I / believe / it / easy.     5. I / believed / it / easy.

- To check comprehension, have students use the cues to write sentences with noun clauses. Review as a class. (4. I believe (that) it is easy. 5. I believed (that) it was easy.)
- Have students read the last explanation and study the examples.
- Write on the board:

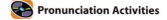
6. Did Pam make it? → Yes. I think *that she made it.*
    → I think   so.

7. Did Tom make it? → No. I don't think *that he made it.*
    → I don't think   so.

- To help clarify, say *Noun clauses can be replaced by* so *in short answers.*
- Review the Be careful! box.

💿 **Grammar Self-Checks**

## Ⓑ 🎧 PRONUNCIATION
**(CD4, Track 9)**

| | |
|---|---|
| Suggested teaching time: | 5–10 minutes |
| Your actual teaching time: | _____ |

- Have students listen and study the examples. Then have them listen and repeat.
- To provide more practice, ask students to take turns asking and answering the questions in Exercise B. Use rising intonation.

💿 **Pronunciation Activities**

 **Change each statement . . .**

| | |
|---|---|
| Suggested teaching time: | 5 minutes |
| Your actual teaching time: | _____ |

- Review the example first. Point out that *has* does not change because *think* is in the present tense. When the main verb is in the present tense, the verb in the noun clause does not change.

- You may want to point out that item 6 requires a change to the past perfect.

- Have students compare answers with a partner and review as a class.

 **PAIR WORK**

| | |
|---|---|
| Suggested teaching time: | 5–10 minutes |
| Your actual teaching time: | _____ |

- Role-play the model with a student.

- Brainstorm and write on the board topics students might ask each other about. Examples: *weekend activities, trips, jobs, studies, plans for the next day*

- Remind students of negative answers. Examples: *I don't think / believe so. I hope / guess not.*

- Walk around the room and provide help as needed.

## CONVERSATION **PAIR WORK**

| | |
|---|---|
| Suggested teaching time: | 5–10 minutes |
| Your actual teaching time: | _____ |

- To get students ready for the activity, have students read the conversation model on page 78 again. You may also want to have students listen to the model.

- Have students look at the magazine covers. Ask what kind of things each magazine teaches you to make. Examples: *Into Knitting:* scarves, sweaters, mittens, cardigans; *Home Workshop:* bookshelves, chairs, tables, stools; *Electronics Today:* speakers, radios, repairs; *Happy Home:* curtains, cushions, bed covers.

- Point out the two models to start the conversation and have students repeat chorally.

- Choose a more confident student and role-play a conversation. Encourage students to ask follow-up questions.

- Make sure each student plays both roles.

- Walk around the room and provide help as needed. Encourage students to use the correct rhythm and intonation.

 **Pair Work Cards**

## EXTRAS (optional)

**Grammar Booster**
**Workbook: Exercises 16–20**
**Copy & Go: Activity 26**

**Pronunciation Supplements**

C **Change each statement to a direct object noun clause, changing verb tenses if necessary.**

1. The latest issue of *Car* magazine has information on hybrid cars.
   I think _the latest issue of Car has information on hybrid cars_ .

2. That article on knitting sweaters in *Home* magazine is great.
   She thought _that article on knitting sweaters in Home magazine was great_ .

3. *PC Magazine* is pretty inexpensive.
   Most people believe _PC Magazine is pretty inexpensive_ .

4. There aren't any articles about fixing furniture in *Handy* magazine this month.
   I guess _there aren't any articles about fixing furniture in Handy magazine this month_ .

5. There's an article about Nelson Mandela in this week's *Weekly News*.
   We hope _there's an article about Nelson Mandela in this week's Weekly News_ .

6. Nancy bought last week's issue of *World Affairs* before the new one came out.
   Frank thought _Nancy had bought last week's issue of World Affairs before the new one came out._

D **PAIR WORK. Ask and answer yes / no questions about your partner's future plans. Respond with short answers, using think, believe, hope, or guess.** Answers will vary.

> 66 Are you going to go out of town this weekend? 99

> 66 I think so! 99

## CONVERSATION
## PAIR WORK

**Role-play a conversation about where you learned to do something. Use the photos and magazine covers here and the conversation model on page 78 as a guide.**

> 66 What a beautiful scarf! 99

> 66 What amazing speakers! 99

curtains

a scarf

a bookshelf

speakers

CONTROLLED PRACTICE

79

# Discuss the Quality of Reading Materials

 **READING WARM-UP.** Do you read comics? Does anyone in your family read them? Do you think they're good reading material?

 🎧 **READING.** Read the article. In what country are comics the most popular?

# COMICS
## trash or treasure?

In Japan, they call them *manga*; in Latin America, *historietas*; in Italy, *fumetti*; in Brazil, *historia em quadrinhos*; and in the U.S., comics. But no matter what you call them, comics are a favorite source of reading pleasure in many parts of the world.

In case you're wondering how popular comics are, the bestselling comic title in the U.S. sells about 4.5 million copies a year. All of Mexico's comic titles together sell over 7 million copies a week. But Japan is by far the leading publisher of comics in the world. *Manga* account for nearly 40 percent of all the books and magazines published in Japan each year. And few magazines of any kind in the world can match this number: *Shonen Jump*, the leading comic title, has a circulation of 6.5 million copies per week!

Ever since comics first appeared, there have been people who have criticized them. In the 1940s and 50s, many people believed that comics were immoral and that they caused bad behavior among young people. Even today, many question whether young people should read them at all. They argue that reading comics encourages bad reading habits.

But some educators see comics as a way to get teenagers to choose reading instead of television and video games. And because of the art, a number of educators have argued

that comics are a great way to get children to think creatively. More recent research has suggested that the combination of visuals and text in comics may be one reason young people handle computers and related software so easily.

In many places, comics have been a convenient way to communicate social or political information. For example, in the 1990s, comics were used by the Brazilian health ministry to communicate information about AIDS.

In Japan, the Education Ministry calls comics "a part of Japan's national culture, recognized and highly regarded abroad." Comics are increasingly being used for educational purposes, and many publishers there see them as a useful way of teaching history and other subjects.

No matter how you view them, comics remain a guilty pleasure for millions worldwide.

▲ Spider-Man® is one of the world's most recognizable and celebrated comic superheroes. Fifteen million Spider-Man comics are sold each year in 75 countries and in 22 languages, and he appears in 500 newspapers worldwide.

◀ In Japan, train station newsstands do a booming business selling *manga* during rush hour. And for those addicts who must have their *manga* in the middle of the night, automatic vending machines are everywhere.

◀ More comic books are consumed per capita in Mexico than in any other Latin American country.

**SOURCES:** Associated Press, Ananova News Service, PRNewswire

## LESSON
# 3
## *Discuss the Quality of Reading Materials*

### A  READING WARM-UP

| Suggested teaching time: | 5 minutes |
|---|---|
| Your actual teaching time: | _____ |

- Take polls to see who reads comics in the class and which family members read them.

- Then write on the board:

  *Reasons comics are or are not good reading material*

- Ask students to brainstorm reasons. Examples: *At least younger people are reading instead of watching TV. They are creative. It's good practice if the comic is in a foreign language. Comics can teach what's right and wrong (in society).* OR *They are not intelligent reading material. They are childish. Some are very sexist and violent.*

### B  🎧 READING
#### (CD4, Track 10)

| Suggested teaching time: | 10–15 minutes |
|---|---|
| Your actual teaching time: | _____ |

- To activate schema (students' prior knowledge), have students look at the pictures and say what they already know about comics in their country and in other countries. Students may say *The Japanese are famous for their comics. Spider-Man is a superhero and famous around the world. Romantic comics are very popular in Mexico.*

- Have students read the title of the article. Ask students for the meanings of *trash* (garbage or something that is of very poor quality) and *treasure* (a very valuable or important object).

- After students read, ask for the answer to the question in the direction line. (Japan: see paragraph 2)

**Option:** Use this option if you want to do a listening activity. Books closed. Write the following questions on the board:

  *1. Which country sells more comics a year?*

  *2. How many copies of Shonen Jump are sold per week in Japan?*

  *3. What opinion did many people have of comics when they first appeared?*

  *4. What is one way comics can help young people?*

Have students write the answers. Tell students that question 4 has at least four answers. Then have students read the text to confirm their answers. (1. Japan  2. 6.5 million  3. negative / not good 4. Comics get children to think creatively. They help teenagers use computers and software easily. Comics can give social or political information (AIDS). They can teach history (and other subjects). **[+10 minutes]**

**Challenge:** Pair work. Draw the following diagram (without the answers) on the board. Ask students to skim the text and complete the diagram with notes about the positive effects of comics for each area. After students complete the diagram, you may want to ask pairs to combine to compare answers. Then review answers as a class. **[+15 minutes]**

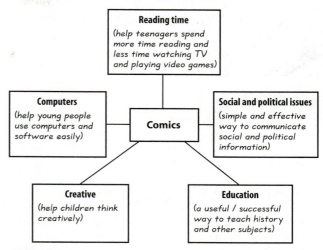

🔵 **Graphic Organizers**

**Language note:** Students may need help with the following words: *publisher* (a person or company whose business is to print and sell books); *account for* (to make up an amount of something); *circulation* (the average number of copies sold over a period of time); *visuals* (drawings, diagrams, and other artwork), *AIDS* (Acquired Immune Deficiency Syndrome); a *guilty pleasure* (something you enjoy doing that you feel a bit ashamed for enjoying).

🔵 **Learning Strategies**

**Answer the questions ...**

| Suggested teaching time: | 5–10 minutes |
|---|---|
| Your actual teaching time: | _____ |

- Encourage students to underline the information that supports their answer to each question.
- Have students compare answers with a partner. Then review as a class.

 **Extra Reading Comprehension Activities**

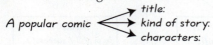 **DISCUSSION**

| Suggested teaching time: | 10 minutes |
|---|---|
| Your actual teaching time: | _____ |

- Write the following on the board:

  *A popular comic* → *title:*
  → *kind of story:*
  → *characters:*

- Before students discuss, ask them to write some notes about a popular comic or comics they know. Students can write about comics for adults, teenagers, or children.
- Group work. Form small groups. Encourage students to use their notes as they discuss and to give their own opinion of comics.
- Walk around the room and provide help as needed.

## TOP NOTCH **INTERACTION**

| Suggested teaching time: | 15–20 minutes |
|---|---|
| Your actual teaching time: | _____ |

### STEP 1. PAIR WORK.

- Review the model first.
- You may want to brainstorm other words and phrases to describe reading materials. Encourage students to use vocabulary from this and other units. Write them in two columns, *Treasure* and *Trash,* on the board. Examples: Treasure: *fun, interesting, exciting, useful, informative, a cliffhanger, a page-turner, a fast read.* Trash: *boring, immoral, too conservative/radical, useless, silly, causes bad behavior, sets bad examples.*
- Encourage students to ask each other questions. Example: Student A: *What do you think of comics?* Student B: *I think they're trash. The stories are so silly. Do you like them?* Student A: *No, not really.*

### STEP 2. DISCUSSION.

- Point out the NEED HELP? section and review the words and expressions. Encourage students to use embedded noun clauses (page 76) and verbs of belief + noun clauses (page 78) to express their reasons. Examples: *I wonder if people think comics are trash because they've actually never read any! I think that the stories are silly.*
- Group work. Form groups of four. Encourage students to ask each other follow-up questions, and use as much vocabulary and grammar from the unit as they can.
- Walk around the room and provide help as needed.

**Option:** Students write a short paragraph about the reading material they like best. **[+10 minutes]**

### EXTRAS (optional)

**Workbook:** Exercises 21, 22
**Copy & Go:** Activity 27

**C**  **Answer the questions, according to the information in the article.**

1. What are the reasons some people criticize comics?
2. What are some of the possible benefits of comics?
3. Why do some people feel guilty or bad about reading comics?

1. Some people think comics are immoral and cause bad behavior. Others argue that comics encourage bad reading habits.
2. Teenagers are reading instead of watching television or playing video games. Also, comics get children to think creatively.
3. Some people feel guilty about reading comics because ever since they first appeared there have been people who criticize them.

**D**  **DISCUSSION.** Who reads comics in your country?  What kinds of stories and characters can you find in comics?  What do you think of comics?

## TOP NOTCH
### INTERACTION • *Trash or treasure?*

**STEP 1. PAIR WORK.** Complete your notepad with your opinions about different reading materials.  Discuss your answers with your partner.  Answers will vary.

| | trash or treasure? | | reasons... |
|---|---|---|---|
| comics | ☑ | ☐ | I think they are violent and sexist. |

| | trash | or | treasure? | reasons... |
|---|---|---|---|---|
| comics | ☐ | | ☐ | |
| teen magazines | ☐ | | ☐ | |
| fashion magazines | ☐ | | ☐ | |
| sports magazines | ☐ | | ☐ | |
| movie magazines | ☐ | | ☐ | |
| romance novels | ☐ | | ☐ | |
| thrillers | ☐ | | ☐ | |
| mysteries | ☐ | | ☐ | |
| other _____ | ☐ | | ☐ | |

**STEP 2. DISCUSSION.** Choose one type of reading material that you think is trash and one that you think is treasure.  Explain your opinions, using specific titles of books, magazines, etc.

**NEED HELP?** Here's language you already know:

**Expression of opinion**
I think (that)…
In my opinion…
Could you explain why you think (that)… ?
I guess you're saying (that)…

**Describing reading materials**
I can't put [them] down.
I'm really into [them].
I can't get enough of [them].
They're a fast read.
I can't get into [them].
[They] don't turn me on.

**Other types of reading materials**
science fiction
biographies
autobiographies
self-help books
novels
travel books
memoirs
short stories

**FREE PRACTICE**

## Describe Your Reading Habits

**A** 🎧 **VOCABULARY.** Some ways to enjoy books, magazines, and newspapers.
**Listen and practice.**

**curl up with a book**

**read aloud to someone**

**collect clippings**

**do puzzles**

**skim through a newspaper**

**listen to books on tape**

**B** Complete the sentences. Use the new vocabulary in the correct form.

1. Jerry has a lot of great recipes. He loves to ___collect clippings___ from newspaper cooking articles.

2. Martin enjoys grabbing a pencil and _doing puzzles_. It helps him learn new words and pass the time.

3. Nancy finds it really convenient to ___listen to books on tape___ rather than reading them. She can do it while she's driving.

4. It gives Tom great pleasure to _read aloud_ to his kids before they go to bed.

5. When it's late at night, Beatrice likes nothing more than to _curl up with_ a fashion magazine and a cup of tea before she goes to sleep.

6. Kate is so busy she doesn't really have a lot of time to read. She just _skims through_ things, never reading anything from start to finish.

**C** 🎧 **LISTENING COMPREHENSION.** Listen to each person talk about reading habits.
Then read the chart and listen again. Check the reading habits of each person.

☑ enjoys reading newspapers
☐ prefers reading in the park
☑ likes to curl up in bed with a newspaper
☑ reads in the bathroom
☑ is into historical novels
☐ collects magazine clippings
☑ enjoys skimming through magazines

**Ignacio Saralegui**
Buenos Aires, Argentina

☑ likes to curl up with a good book
☐ reads in the kitchen
☐ likes to read in coffee shops
☑ enjoys skimming through magazines
☑ enjoys doing puzzles
☐ is into movie magazines
☐ collects newspaper clippings

**Su Yomei**
Taipei, Taiwan

**SOURCE:** authentic *Top Notch* interviews

# LESSON 4
## *Describe Your Reading Habits*

 **VOCABULARY**
(CD4, Track 11)

| | |
|---|---|
| Suggested teaching time: | 10 minutes |
| Your actual teaching time: | _____ |

• Have students listen and study the phrases. Then have students listen and repeat chorally.

• To clarify the meaning of *curl up with a book,* direct attention to the way the woman is relaxing on the sofa. To clarify the meaning of *skim,* direct attention to the way the woman is using her finger to read through a text quickly for the main ideas.

• Write on the board:
*Someone who . . .*
*1. likes word games probably likes to ___ .*
*2. is very busy but wants to be informed probably ___ the newspaper.*
*3. has little children probably ___ to them.*
*4. loves reading probably ___ a book at night.*
*5. spends a long time commuting might ___ .*
*6. likes to cook probably ___ .*

• To provide more practice, ask students to use the words in bold in Exercise A to identify the situations. Point out that they should use the correct verb form.

• Have students compare answers with a partner and review as a class. (1. do puzzles 2. skims through 3. reads aloud 4. curls up with 5. listen to books on tape 6. collects clippings)

 **Vocabulary Cards**

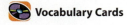 **Complete the sentences . . .**

| | |
|---|---|
| Suggested teaching time: | 5–10 minutes |
| Your actual teaching time: | _____ |

• You may want to do the first item with the class.

• Have students compare answers with a partner. Then review as a class.

 **LISTENING COMPREHENSION**
(CD4, Track 12)

| | |
|---|---|
| Suggested teaching time: | 10–15 minutes |
| Your actual teaching time: | _____ |

• You may want to ask students to write notes about these people's reading habits.

• Then have students listen again and check the information that is true.

• Have students compare answers with a partner. Then review as a class.

• You may want students to listen again to confirm the correct answers.

 **Learning Strategies**

**AUDIOSCRIPT**

[M = Spanish, F = Chinese]

**M:** I really like to keep up with the news. I get the paper delivered on weekends, so that's when I enjoy reading it most. Pretty much from the first to the last page. During the week I enjoy skimming through the newspaper in a café. But the weekend is the best time. There's nothing like lying in bed with the paper, a good cup of coffee, and some croissants or toast. Or when the weather is nice, sitting in the garden and reading about what's going on in the world. And, well, I have to admit, one of my favorite places to read it is in the, um, well, bathroom . . . I can spend a good half hour there reading the paper.

Aside from newspapers, I really enjoy stopping at newsstands and spending about five or ten minutes browsing through magazines. And, of course, I also enjoy going to bookshops and checking out the latest novels. Particularly historical novels. I just can't seem to read enough of those.

**F:** There is nothing I like more than curling up with a good book. I like all kinds of literature—novels, general fiction, short stories . . . I also read a lot of books written by Japanese authors, translated into Chinese. My favorite author, though, is Chang Ailing. She's a very famous author from China. Her work has inspired women for many generations.

I like to read whenever I have a bit of quiet time— like early in the morning, or during lunch hour—and at night when I'm lying in bed. I usually read in a small room next to my living room. It's like a small library with good natural sunlight. I really don't enjoy reading in coffee shops or other public places. I need a quiet space to read. Besides books, I often skim through magazines and newspapers, and I enjoy doing the puzzles. They are fun and interesting to do. I used to collect articles from the newspaper—you know, for useful information or recipes—but I really don't do that anymore.

For me, reading is a spiritual experience that gives me great personal satisfaction. Television and movies can't do that. I can't understand why anyone doesn't enjoy reading. I can't think of any better way to relax, to forget the pressure of each day.

# TOP NOTCH **INTERACTION**

| | |
|---|---|
| Suggested teaching time: | 20–25 minutes |
| Your actual teaching time: | _____ |

## STEP 1. PAIR WORK.

- Before students begin the interviews, have them read the questions individually and think of their own answers to each of the questions. They may want to write some notes on a separate piece of paper.

- During the interview, encourage students to look back into the unit if they need help with vocabulary or grammar.

- Encourage students to ask follow-up questions during the interview. Example: Student A: *When do you like to read?* Student B: *At night.* Student A: *Why?* Student B: *Because it helps me relax and go to sleep.*

- Walk around the room and provide help as needed.

- Then have students compare their reading habits. Example: Student A: *We both enjoy reading at night.* Student B: *Yes, but you like to read thrillers, and I like to read romance novels!*

**Option:** Ask students to interview another student and then compare the reading habits of the two people interviewed. **[+10 minutes]**

## STEP 2. Tell your class . . .

- Note: To give everyone a chance to speak, have students choose only two of their partners' answers to share with the class.

- Review the model.

- Ask students to share their information with the class.

**Option:** As students talk about their partners, write notes to help create questions to ask about the reading habits in the class. Examples: *1. Who hates reading aloud? 2. Who always skims newspapers and never reads them? 3. Who collects newspaper clippings about impressive works of architecture?* After the presentations are over read the questions out loud and ask students to say the answers. **[+10 minutes]**

## STEP 3. WRITING.

- Draw the following graphic organizer on the board and include the example information:

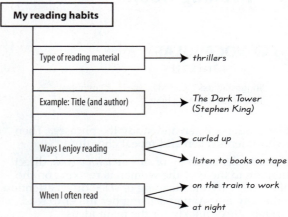

 **Graphic Organizers**

- Before students write, have students complete a graphic organizer with their own information. Point out that students can draw more arrows for each section.

- Walk around the room and provide help as needed.

**Option:** Read some of the descriptions of the students' reading habits out loud, but don't say the student's name. The class guesses whose habits you're describing. **[+10 minutes]**

 **Writing Process Worksheets**

## EXTRAS (optional)

**Workbook: Exercises 23–25**
**Copy & Go: Activity 28**

# INTERACTION • *What are your reading habits?*

**STEP 1. PAIR WORK.** Interview your partner. Write your partner's answers. Answers will vary.

 **1.** Tell me where you like to do most of your reading.

 **2.** When do you like to read?

 **3.** Do you enjoy skimming through magazines, books, or other reading materials? (Explain.)

 **4.** Do you like collecting newspaper or magazine clippings? (From where? What do you do with them?)

 **5.** Do you like to read aloud to other people or have other people read aloud to you?

 **6.** Do you ever listen to books on tape? (Why or why not?)

 **7.** What types of books do you like to read?

 **8.** What are your favorite books of all time?

 **9.** Tell me who your favorite authors are.

**STEP 2.** Tell your class about your partner's reading habits.

**STEP 3. WRITING.** Describe your <u>own</u> reading habits.

> " Ellen told me that she prefers to read in bed before she goes to sleep. "

**A**  **LISTENING COMPREHENSION.** **Listen carefully to the conversations and write the type of book each person is discussing. Then listen again and check how the person feels about the book.**

| | type of book | likes it | doesn't like it |
|---|---|---|---|
| **Conversation 1** | mystery | ☑ | ☐ |
| **Conversation 2** | travel | ☐ | ☑ |
| **Conversation 3** | romance | ☑ | ☐ |
| **Conversation 4** | autobiography | ☐ | ☑ |

**B** **Complete each statement with a type of book.**

1. A novel about people falling in love is usually called a <u>romance novel</u>.

2. A book about a famous person is called a <u>biography</u>.

3. A book that a famous person writes about his or her own life is called an <u>autobiography</u>.

4. A very exciting novel about a dangerous situation can be called a <u>thriller</u>.

5. Books that are about factual information are called <u>nonfiction</u>.

6. A strange fictional story about the future is called <u>science fiction</u>.

**C** **Use each question to complete the embedded question.**

1. Where does the story take place?
   Could you tell me <u>where the story takes place</u>?

2. Who is the main character in the novel?
   I was wondering <u>who the main character in the novel is</u>.

3. How much was that German newspaper?
   I can't remember <u>how much that German newspaper was</u>.

4. How do you say this in English?
   I was wondering <u>how you say this in English</u>.

5. What does this word mean?
   Could you explain <u>what this word means</u>?

**D** **WRITING.** **Write a review about a book you've read. Say who the author is. Describe where it takes place, who the characters are, and what it's about. Recommend it or warn the reader to avoid it.**

*TOP NOTCH* **WEBSITE**
For Unit 7 online activities, visit the *Top Notch* Companion Website at www.longman.com/topnotch.

*TOP NOTCH* **PROJECT**
Create a literary review journal. Include reviews students have written about different types of reading material.

# UNIT 7
# CHECKPOINT

## A 🎧 LISTENING COMPREHENSION
**(CD4, Track 13)**

| Suggested teaching time: | 10–15 minutes |
|---|---|
| Your actual teaching time: | _____ |

- First have students listen for the type of book. Then have them listen again for the adjectives that describe if the person likes the book or not. You may want to ask them to write the words they hear.

- Pause after each conversation to allow students time to write.

- Have students compare answers with a partner. Encourage students to use *I think* to discuss the answers. Example: Student A: *The speaker doesn't like the book.* Student B: *I checked that he likes it. I think he said he can't wait to get to the ending.* Student A: *I thought he said he didn't like the ending.*

- Review as a class.

### AUDIOSCRIPT

CONVERSATION 1
**M:** I'm reading a new mystery by Smithson.
**F:** Really? Is it any good?
**M:** Oh, it's a real cliffhanger. I can't wait to get to the ending!
**F:** Then don't tell me how it ends. I might want to read it, too.
**M:** I'll let you borrow it.
**F:** Thanks!

CONVERSATION 2
**F:** How's that travel book you're reading?
**M:** Well, apparently it's a bestseller.
**F:** Oh yeah? Must be good.
**M:** Actually, I can't get into it. It's not a fast read—at all.
**F:** Oh.

CONVERSATION 3
**M:** When are you going to finish that romance novel?
**F:** Pretty soon. To tell the truth, it's really trash. But you know something, I just can't put it down.
**M:** I don't get it. Why are you reading it if it's trash?
**F:** I can't help it. It's a page-turner. I've really been getting into it.

CONVERSATION 4
**F:** I'm reading an autobiography by a famous Italian artist.
**F:** Wow. That must be interesting.
**M:** I guess it should be. But I'm just not really into it.
**F:** Don't you like autobiographies?
**M:** Sure! I love them. Just not this one.

## B Complete each statement . . .

| Suggested teaching time: | 5 minutes |
|---|---|
| Your actual teaching time: | _____ |

- You may want to do the first item with the class.

- Have students compare answers with a partner. Then review as a class.

## C Use each question . . .

| Suggested teaching time: | 5 minutes |
|---|---|
| Your actual teaching time: | _____ |

- Have students do the first item and then review as a class. Remind students that embedded questions use normal word order.

- Have students compare answers with a partner. Then review as a class.

## D WRITING

| Suggested teaching time: | 10–15 minutes |
|---|---|
| Your actual teaching time: | _____ |

- Encourage students to review vocabulary and grammar presented in this unit.

- You may want to write the following sentence starters on the board to help students organize their ideas:

  *[title of the book] is a [type of book] by [writer's name].*
  *The book is about ___.*
  *The story takes place in ___.*
  *The main characters are ___.*
  *I'd highly recommend it because ___.*
  *I think it's a must-read because ___.*
  *I would recommend it to those who ___.*

- Walk around the room and provide help as needed.

**Option:** Group work. Form groups of three. Students read their reviews aloud. Encourage students to ask each other follow-up questions. Have students say if they would like to read any of the books or not and give reasons. **[+10 minutes]**

🔵 **Writing Process Worksheets**

### *TOP NOTCH* PROJECT

**Idea:** Explain that a literary review journal is a magazine containing reviews of books, magazines, newspapers, and other reading materials. Group work. Form groups of four. Ask students to create a name for their journal. Encourage students to include their reviews from Exercise D. Students can also add other reviews.

**Idea:** Students may want to design a cover for their journal (include the name of the journal, their names, and some decorative art).

**T84**

# UNIT WRAP-UP

Suggested teaching time: 15–20 minutes
Your actual teaching time: _____

## Grammar

- Role-play the model with a student.

- Pair work. Have one student ask questions and then change roles. Remind students who answer the questions to keep their books closed.

- Encourage students to use the vocabulary from the unit. Review affirmative and negative short answers with *think, believe,* and *guess: I think / believe / guess so. I don't think / believe so. I guess not.*

- Walk around the room and provide help as needed.

### Your students can say ...
Is someone sitting and reading a book? Is someone choosing a self-help book? Are there any children reading books? Is someone listening to a book on tape? Is there a mother reading aloud to her child? Is someone doing a puzzle? Is someone choosing a fiction book? Is there a girl curled up with a book? Is someone choosing a business book? Is someone skimming through a cookbook?

**Option: What are you reading?** Pair work. Students take turns pointing to the picture and describing what they think is happening. Examples: Student A: *I think this woman is choosing a romance novel.* Student B: *I believe this woman is going on vacation.* Student A: *This woman is a cook in a restaurant.* Student B: *I guess this man wants to buy a thriller.* **[+5 minutes]**

## Social Language

- Role-play the model with a student.

- Direct attention to the circle on the right. Ask *What does the woman in green like?* (the other woman's sweater)

- Direct attention to the circle in the bottom left-hand corner. Ask *What do you think the woman wants to know?* (what type of book the man is reading; where he found that book)

- Encourage students to use the language presented in this and previous units to create the conversations.

### Your students can say ...
**A:** What a great sweater. **B:** Thanks. I made it. **A:** Really? How? **B:** I read [name of magazine] every week and they always give you great projects to do. **A:** I wish I could knit, but I'm all thumbs!

**A:** What a nice sweater! Did you make it? **B:** Yes, thanks! I learned how in the latest issue of [name of magazine]. **A:** Can I borrow a copy? **B:** Sure. I have a lot of issues. You can choose one.

**A:** What's that you're reading? **B:** It's a [type of book]. **A:** Oh, I've heard about it. Is it any good? **B:** Oh, I'd highly recommend it. It's a [page-turner]. **A:** Do you mind if I borrow it when you're done? **B:** Not at all.

**A:** What are you reading? **B:** [Name of book] by [author's name]. **A:** Really? Is it interesting? **B:** Well, it's really [trash]. **A:** Why are you reading it then? **B:** I'm really into it because I want to know the ending now!

**Challenge: Let's get ...** Pair work. Students imagine they are in the bookshop in the picture and role-play a conversation in which they decide what books to buy for different people they know. Examples: Student A: *Let's buy a sports book for Tom. He loves sports.* Student B: *I think he likes travel best.* Student A: *OK. Let's buy him a travel book then.* Student B: *And for Sarah?* Student A: *She said she's good at cooking. Why don't we buy her a cookbook?* **[+10 minutes]**

### Individual oral progress check (optional)

- Use the illustration on page 85. Encourage the student to use material (vocabulary, grammar, rhythm and intonation) practiced in this unit.

- Evaluate the student on correctness and intelligibility.

- Tell the student to answer your questions giving his / her opinion using *I think, I believe,* and *I guess.* Point to the people in the picture and ask the questions. Example: T: (point to the woman in red) *What do you think this woman wants to buy?* S: *I think she wants to buy a thriller.* T: (point to the man sitting on the floor) *What is this man reading?* S: *I believe he's reading a sports magazine.* T: (point to the man choosing a self-help book) *What kind of books does this man like?* S: *I guess he likes improving his life.* T: (point to the woman looking at a business book) *What's this woman doing?* S: *I think she's skimming through a business book.*

- Tell the student to answer your questions using short answers with *think, believe,* and *guess.* Example: *I think so.* Point to the people in the picture and ask the questions. T: (point to the woman dressed as a cook) *Is this woman buying a gift?* S: *I don't think so.* T: (point to the woman carrying camera) *Is this woman a tourist?* S: *I guess so.* T: (point to the man in sports clothes) *Does this man want to buy a travel book?* S: *I don't think so.* T: (point to the woman skimming through a nonfiction book) *Does this woman like fiction?* S: *I believe so.*

 **Cumulative Vocabulary Activities**

 You may wish to use the video and activity worksheets for Unit 7 at this point.

 **Complete Assessment Package**
**Unit 7 Achievement Test**

## UNIT WRAP-UP

- **Grammar.** Look at the picture for a minute; then close your book. Answer your partner's questions with short answers, using <u>think</u>, <u>believe</u>, or <u>guess</u>.

  A: Is someone skimming through magazines?
  B: I think so.

- **Social Language.** Create conversations for the people.

  A: What a great sweater.
  B: Thanks...

CHILDREN'S LITERATURE

FICTION

BUSINESS

TRAVEL

COMPUTER

SPORTS & FITNESS

SELF-HELP

NON-FICTION

GENERAL

COOK BOOKS

### ✓ Now I can ...

- ☐ recommend a book.
- ☐ explain where I learned something.
- ☐ discuss the quality of reading materials.
- ☐ describe my reading habits.

85

# UNIT 8

# Inventions and Technology

## UNIT GOALS

1 Discuss a new product
2 Accept responsibility for a mistake
3 Evaluate inventions
4 Discuss the impact of key inventions in history

**A** **TOPIC PREVIEW.** Do you consider the wheel to be the most important mechanical invention in history? What other modern uses of the wheel can you name?

a wooden wagon wheel

logs used as wheels

two-wheeled carts

a horse-drawn chariot

a potter's wheel

an automobile

**B** **DISCUSSION.**

1. What difficulties did people have before the invention of the wheel?
2. How did the wheel change the lives of people?

# UNIT

# Inventions and Technology

 **TOPIC PREVIEW**

| Suggested teaching time: | 10 minutes |
|---|---|
| Your actual teaching time: | _____ |

- Have students look at the pictures and read the captions.
- Ask students what they think the pictures represent. Students may say *transportation, movement, advancement, old and new technologies, the history of the wheel.*
- Have students make a list of old and modern objects that need wheels. Encourage students to include things they use every day. Examples: *carts, windmills, cars, bicycles, trains, watches, electrical generators, cassettes, jet engines, computer disk drives,* etc.
- Take a poll to find out how many students think the wheel is the most important mechanical invention in history.

**Option:** Ask students to put the pictures in chronological order. Review as a class. (Note: The dates of the earliest uses of the wheel depend on the historical source. A possible order is: 1. The potter's wheel is invented. 2. Men use logs to transport stones. 3. Egyptian chariots use the first wheels with spokes. 4. Carts that have two wheels with spokes are used around the world to transport people and things. 5. The car is invented. **[+5 minutes]**

**Culture note:** One of the first potter's wheels was probably used in China between 5000 and 4000 B.C. Originally, people transported heavy objects by placing logs under them and pulling. The oldest wheel, discovered in Mesopotamia, is from around 4000–3500 B.C. Spoked wheels were first used around 2000 B.C. on Egyptian chariots. The first motorcar was a three-wheeled car built in 1886 by Karl Benz. Benz also built the first four-wheeled motorcar in 1891.

**B** **DISCUSSION**

| Suggested teaching time: | 10–15 minutes |
|---|---|
| Your actual teaching time: | _____ |

- Before students begin their discussions, ask them to think about the questions and write some notes.
- If necessary, offer some example answers: Before the invention of the wheel: *It took a long time to travel short or long distances. People used animals to carry and move things. People carried things on their back,* etc. After the invention of the wheel: *People could travel long distances more quickly. Carts, cars, trucks transported things. Trade expanded. All types of tasks became easier and were accomplished faster,* etc.
- Group work. Form small groups.
- To finish the activity, ask various students to express some of their group's ideas for each question.

## C  SOUND BITES
(CD4, Track 14)

| Suggested teaching time: | 5 minutes |
|---|---|
| Your actual teaching time: | _____ |

- First ask students to look at the pictures and say what they think the women are talking about.
- After students read and listen, ask *What happened during Marian's camping trip?* (She was bitten by mosquitoes. / She got a lot of mosquito bites.) *What product does Lilian tell Marian about?* (something you put on your wrist to stop mosquitoes from biting you)

**Language note:** *Bug* is an informal word to refer to any kind of small insect. *To bug someone* means to bother someone.

## D UNDERSTANDING FROM CONTEXT

| Suggested teaching time: | 5 minutes |
|---|---|
| Your actual teaching time: | _____ |

- Review the matching words and expressions from the dialogue as a class.
- Write on the board:
   *Stop bugging me. I'll clean my room later.*
   *It really bugs me when you talk so loud.*
- Review different ways to use *bug* as *bother / annoy.* Ask students to turn to a partner and say one sentence with *bug.*
- Point out that *I got eaten alive* is often used to describe having a lot of bug bites.

## E  PAIR WORK

| Suggested teaching time: | 5–10 minutes |
|---|---|
| Your actual teaching time: | _____ |

- Encourage students to use the context of the conversation to help work out the meaning of the expressions.
- Tell students that the you in *Where have you been?* is underlined because it is stressed / emphasized.
- Review answers by asking students for their explanations.
- Clarify that you is emphasized because Lillian thinks that everyone knows about this wristband except Marian.

## WHAT ABOUT **YOU?**

| Suggested teaching time: | 10–15 minutes |
|---|---|
| Your actual teaching time: | _____ |

- Have students write some notes about how they decided to rank the inventions.
- Group work. Form small groups. Encourage students to use their notes to explain their decisions and to ask each other follow-up questions.
- Walk around the room and provide help as needed.
- Take a poll to find out which inventions students consider the most and the least important.

**Culture note:** Although the first four-wheeled motorcar was built by Karl Benz in 1891 and the telephone was originally patented by Alexander Graham Bell in the 1870s, both inventions became popular in the twentieth century.

**Teacher's note:** To prepare for the activity in the Conversation Pair Work in Lesson 1, page 89, ask students to bring in advertisements for technology products; for example, laptops, camcorders, scanners, cell phones. If possible, the advertisements should be in English.

## EXTRAS (optional)
**Workbook: Exercises 1–4**

**C** 🎧 **SOUND BITES.** Read along silently as you listen to a natural conversation.

**LILIAN:** Where did you get all those mosquito bites?

**MARIAN:** On our camping trip. The bugs were horrendous. I tried everything, but I still got eaten alive! Don't you wish someone would invent something for mosquitoes that works?

**LILIAN:** Where have <u>you</u> been? They have!

**MARIAN:** No way! **CN**

**LILIAN:** Yeah. It's this thing you put on your wrist, and mosquitoes quit bugging you. It really works.

**MARIAN:** I don't believe it. If I'd known that, I would have gotten one before I left.

**CN** **Corpus Notes:** The expression *No way!* is frequent in spoken English, but not in written English.

**D** **UNDERSTANDING FROM CONTEXT.** Find words and expressions in the conversation. Then use each one in a sentence.

1. Find a word that means "terrible." _____horrendous_____

2. Find an expression that means "The bugs bit me a lot." _I got eaten alive._

3. Find a word that means "bothering" or "annoying." _____bugging_____

an early television, 1950

**E** **PAIR WORK.** With a partner, answer the questions. Explain your answers.

1. What does Lilian mean when she asks Marian, "Where have <u>you</u> been?" She's surprised Marian doesn't know about the bracelet.

2. What does Marian mean when she says, "No way!" I can't believe it!

## WHAT ABOUT **YOU?**

**The following machines were invented in the twentieth century. Rank them in order of importance from 1 to 5, with 1 being the most important:**

☐ the computer  ☐ the airplane  ☐ the automobile  ☐ the telephone  ☐ the television

**DISCUSSION.** Explain your rankings.

# 1 ▶ Discuss a New Product

🎧 **CONVERSATION MODEL** Read and listen.

**A:** I need a new coffee maker. Do you think I should get the Brew Rite? It's on sale at TechnoMart.

**B:** That depends. How much are they selling it for?

**A:** $75.

**B:** Definitely. That's a great price. If I needed a coffee maker, I'd buy one too. It's top of the line.

🎧 **Rhythm and intonation practice**

**A** 🎧 **VOCABULARY.** Describing manufactured products. Listen and practice.

| Uses new technology | Offers high quality | Uses new ideas |
|---|---|---|
| high-tech | high-end | innovative |
| state-of-the-art | top-of-the-line | revolutionary |
| cutting-edge | first-rate | novel **CN** |

**CN** **Corpus Notes:** The adjective *novel* usually comes before the noun it describes (for example, *a novel approach*) much more frequently than it does after the verb *(an approach that is novel).*

**B** **GRAMMAR.** Factual and unreal conditional sentences: review

**Present factual conditionals: Use the simple present tense in both clauses.**
    If you **make** a lot of coffee, you **need** a good coffee maker.

**Future factual conditionals: Use the simple present tense in the <u>if</u> clause. Use the future with <u>will</u> or <u>be going to</u> in the result clause.**
    If they **sell** the Brew Rite for as low a price as the Coffee King, they**'ll sell** a lot of them.

**Present unreal conditionals: Use the simple past tense or <u>were</u> in the <u>if</u> clause. Use <u>would</u> in the result clause.**
    If I **were** you, I **wouldn't buy** it. (unreal condition: I am not you.)
    If Teletex **had** a cutting-edge digital camera phone, they **would sell** more.
    (unreal condition: Teletex doesn't have one.)

**BE CAREFUL!** Don't use a future form in the **if** clause.
    If I buy it, I'll be happy.
    **NOT** If I ~~will buy~~ it, I'll be happy.

Don't use <u>would</u> in the **if** clause.
    If they knew the best brand, they would get it.
    **NOT** If they ~~would know~~ the best brand, they would get it.

GRAMMAR BOOSTER

**PAGES G13–G14**
For more ...

**C** **Practice distinguishing between factual and unreal conditions. Check the statements that describe <u>unreal</u> conditions.**

☐ **1.** If they see something first-rate, they buy it.

☐ **2.** If we take the bus to TechnoMart, we save a lot of time.

☑ **3.** If you walked to the theater, you would get there late.

☐ **4.** They won't get any phone calls if they don't have their cell phones.

☑ **5.** If she were a photographer, she would sell her old camera and buy a new one.

## LESSON

# 1 ▶ *Discuss a New Product*

## ♩ CONVERSATION **MODEL**
**(CD4, Track 15)**

| Suggested teaching time: | 5 minutes |
|---|---|
| Your actual teaching time: | _____ |

• After students read and listen, ask *Why does the first speaker want to buy the coffee maker at TechnoMart?* (because it's on sale there) *Why does her friend think it's a good choice?* (it's a very good brand)

• *It's top of the line* means it's one of the best.

> **Language note:** Point out the definite article *the* used in *Do you think I should get the Brew Rite?* Both speakers understand what is being referred to.

## ♩ Rhythm and intonation practice
**(CD4, Track 16)**

| Suggested teaching time: | 5 minutes |
|---|---|
| Your actual teaching time: | _____ |

• Have students repeat each line chorally.
• Make sure students:
  ○ use rising intonation for *Do you think I should get the Brew Rite?*
  ○ use falling intonation for *How much are they selling it for?*
  ○ pause after <u>maker</u> in *If I needed a coffee maker.*
  ○ use the following stress pattern:

┌─ **STRESS PATTERN** ──────────────────┐

**A:** I need a new coffee maker. Do you think I should get

the Brew Rite? It's on sale at TechnoMart.

**B:** That depends. How much are they selling it for?

**A:** Seventy-five dollars.

**B:** Definitely. That's a great price. If I needed a coffee

maker, I'd buy one too. It's top of the line.

└──────────────────────────────────────┘

## A ♩ VOCABULARY
**(CD4, Track 17)**

| Suggested teaching time: | 5 minutes |
|---|---|
| Your actual teaching time: | _____ |

• Tell students that *manufactured products* are goods or items made in large numbers in factories; for example, cameras, cars. Ask for more examples.

• Have students listen and study the words and phrases. Then have students listen and repeat.

• Point out that the words are all adjectives (to describe nouns). Examples: *a cutting-edge monitor, a revolutionary camera, a novel invention.*

---

> **Language note:** Compound adjectives are hyphenated when they precede nouns. *I want a top-of-the-line computer.* vs. *My computer is top of the line.*

 **Vocabulary Cards**

## B GRAMMAR

| Suggested teaching time: | 5–10 minutes |
|---|---|
| Your actual teaching time: | _____ |

• Write on the board:
  IF CLAUSE        RESULT CLAUSE
  1. If I get up early, I make breakfast for my family.

• To review conditional sentences, point out the *if* clause and the result clause. Point out the comma. If the *if* clause is second, do not use a comma.

• Direct attention to the box and have students read the first explanation and study the examples.

• Tell students that the present factual conditional is used to talk about a habitual action, and the simple present is needed in both clauses.

• To check comprehension, ask various students to say what they usually do *if* they get up early. Example: *If I get up early, I go running.*

• Have students read the second explanation and study the example.

• Write on the board:
  2. If I <u>buy</u> the Brew Rite, I'<u>ll save</u> $10.
  I'<u>m going to</u> save $10.

• Review the future factual conditional by asking students *What is the condition here?* (buying the Brew Rite) *What will the result be?* (the person will save $10).

• Point out that the *if* clause / condition needs the simple present tense, and the result needs *will* + base form or *be going to* + base form.

• To check comprehension, ask students to say what they will do this weekend *if* it rains. Examples: *If it rains, I'll stay at home. If it rains, I'm going to go shopping.*

• Have students read the third explanation and study the example.

• Write on the board:
  3. If I <u>needed</u> a new car, I'<u>d buy</u> a high-end model.

• Point out that present unreal conditionals express an imagined condition (needing a new car) and its imagined result (buying one).

• Point out that the *if* clause / condition needs the simple past tense and the result needs *would* + base form. Point out the contraction *I'd* for *I would.*

• Have students read the Be careful! box. Point out that these are common errors (even for native speakers).

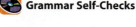 **Grammar Self-Checks**

## C  Practice distinguishing . . .

| Suggested teaching time: | 5 minutes |
|---|---|
| Your actual teaching time: | _____ |

• Do the first item with the class.

• Have students compare answers with a partner. Then review as a class.

**T88**

**Complete each ...**

| Suggested teaching time: | 5 minutes |
|---|---|
| Your actual teaching time: | _____ |

- Do the first item with the class. Review the correct answer by pointing out that for the present factual conditional both the *if* clause and the result clause need the simple present tense.

- Have students compare answers with a partner and then review as a class.

**Culture note:** 100 degrees is the boiling point of water on the Celsius scale. The Fahrenheit equivalent is 212 degrees.

 **Choose the correct ...**

| Suggested teaching time: | 5 minutes |
|---|---|
| Your actual teaching time: | _____ |

- Do the first item with the class and review the answer. Students can use contractions.

- Have students compare answers with a partner. Then review as a class.

**F** **PAIR WORK**

| Suggested teaching time: | 5–10 minutes |
|---|---|
| Your actual teaching time: | _____ |

- Point out that *could* in the sentence starter in item 2 is the past tense for *can*.

- Provide models for the students. Examples: *If I were an inventor, I would invent something that prepares my meals before I get home! If I could go anywhere in the world, I would go to Alaska. If I needed a car, I would buy a small one.*

- Ask students to write down sentences. Encourage them to make necessary corrections and give each other feedback.

- Walk around the room and provide help as needed.

- Ask various students to say one of their sentences out loud.

**Option:** After completing the activity, form new pairs. Students take turns saying their sentences and asking follow-up questions. Example: Student A: *If I could go anywhere in the world, I would go to Greece.* Student B: *Really? Why would you go there?* Student A: *Because it's full of history and it's warm! Where would you go?* Student B: *If I could go anywhere in the world, I would go to Africa. I'd love to explore the geography.* **[+5 minutes]**

## CONVERSATION **PAIR WORK**

| Suggested teaching time: | 5–10 minutes |
|---|---|
| Your actual teaching time: | _____ |

- To get students ready for the activity, have students read the conversation model on page 88 again. You may also want to have students listen to the model.

- Have students read the advertisements on this page or the ads brought to class. You may want to change the prices to reflect local currency.

- Review the names of the items in the ads (on this page): *a digital camera, a scanner, a telephone, a computer monitor, a palm pilot*

- Choose a more confident student and role-play a conversation.

- Encourage students to give advice using the present unreal conditional. Examples: *If I were you, I wouldn't buy it. If I needed a monitor, I'd buy the Teknicon, too.* Encourage students to use contractions.

- Make sure students play both roles.

- Walk around the room and provide help as needed. Encourage students to use the correct rhythm and intonation.

 **Pair Work Cards**

## EXTRAS (optional)

**Grammar Booster**
**Workbook:** Exercises 5–12
**Copy & Go:** Activity 29

**D** **Complete each present factual conditional sentence.**

1. Water ____boils____ if you ____raise____ its temperature to 100 degrees.
   boil                raise

2. If I ____see____ something that's really cutting edge, I ____want____ it.
   see                                                      want

3. She ____grinds____ her own beans if she ____wants____ really great coffee.
   grind                                       want

4. He always ____uses____ state-of-the-art equipment if it ____is____ available.
   use                                                       be

 **E** **Choose the correct form to complete each future factual conditional sentence.**

1. If they ____want____ to get there fast, they ____will take____ the express train.
   want / will want                                take / will take

2. If he ____buys____ the product, the mosquitoes ____won't bite____.
   buys / will buy                                 don't bite / won't bite

3. If they ____see____ her tomorrow, they ____will show____ her their new camera phone.
   see / will see                            show / will show

4. ____Are you going to get____ the camera phone if they ____offer____ it on sale?
   Are you going to get / Do you get                      offer / will offer

 **F** **PAIR WORK.** **Take turns completing each present unreal conditional in your <u>own</u> way.**

Answers will vary.

1. If I were an inventor, I …

2. If I could go anywhere in the world, …

3. If I needed a car, …

## CONVERSATION PAIR WORK

**Bring in advertisements for products from a newspaper, or use these ads. Use the vocabulary on page 88 to describe the products. Discuss whether or not to buy them.** Answers will vary.

**Start like this:**

**A:** I need a new _____.
Do you think I should get the _____? …

**B:** _____ …

**Digicon B1X**
- cutting-edge technology
- 5.44 megapixel

us **$3899**

**Micro Scanner**
- state-of-the-art

us **$199**

**Digi-Phone**
- 2-line digital phone system

us **$79**

**Save $50**
us **$379**

**17" LCD Monitor**
*Teknicon*

**Strawberry Palmtop** SPECIAL BUY
- handheld
- Internet capable
- secure digital
- media card slot

us **$99**
super special

**CONTROLLED PRACTICE**

89

# 2 Accept Responsibility for a Mistake

## 🎧 CONVERSATION MODEL  Read and listen.

**A:** Sorry we're late. We got lost.

**B:** That's OK. It can happen to anyone.

**A:** Well, it was entirely my fault. If I had stopped to ask for directions, we would have been on time.

**B:** Well, better late than never. Please come in. And let me get you something to drink.

🎧 **Rhythm and intonation practice**

---

**A** **GRAMMAR.** The past unreal conditional

**Use the past unreal conditional to describe unreal or untrue conditions and results.**
If I **had had** a cell phone, I **could have called** for directions. (But I didn't, so I couldn't call.)
She **wouldn't have been** late if she **had checked** the map. (But she didn't, so she was late.)

**BE CAREFUL!** Don't use <u>would</u> or <u>could</u> in the <u>if</u> clause in the past unreal conditional.
If I ~~would have had~~ a cell phone, I could have called for directions.

**Questions and answers**
Could they have arrived on time if they had left earlier?   Yes, they could have. / No, they couldn't have.
When would you have arrived if you had taken the train?   At four o'clock.

**PAGES G14–G15**
**For more …**

---

**CN** **Corpus Notes:** Many learners make the error of saying *would had* instead of *would have*, and *had have* instead of *had had*. Make sure students are aware of these common errors.

**B** **Choose the meaning of each past unreal conditional sentence.**

1. They wouldn't have gone if they hadn't gotten a ticket on the Bullet Train.
   (**a.**) They went.          **b.** They didn't go.

2. If we had been there, we would have chosen another kind of transportation.
   **a.** We were there.          (**b.**) We weren't there.

3. If you hadn't told them about it, they never would have known.
   (**a.**) You told them about it.          **b.** You didn't tell them about it.

4. If someone had explained the directions better, we wouldn't have gotten lost.
   (**a.**) We got lost.          **b.** We didn't get lost.

**C** **Choose the correct forms to complete each past unreal conditional sentence.**

1. What would you have done if you ____hadn't had____ a phone in your car?
   wouldn't have had / hadn't had

2. If you ____had known____ about the storm, would you have tried to evacuate?
   would have known / had known

3. If the airplane had not been invented, people ____would have found____ a way to travel more quickly by land.
   would find / would have found

4. If the flood ____had occurred____ during the night, many more people
   would have occurred / had occurred
   ____would have been injured____ .
   would have been injured / would be injured

---

# LESSON 2
# Accept Responsibility for a Mistake

## 🎧 CONVERSATION **MODEL**
### (CD4, Track 18)

| Suggested teaching time: | 5 minutes |
|---|---|
| Your actual teaching time: | _____ |

- After students read and listen, ask *Why weren't the man and the woman on time?* (because they got lost) *What is the host's reaction?* (She's happy they finally made it / arrived.)
- If necessary, clarify that *Better late than never* means that even if something happens late or someone arrives late, this is better than it not happening at all.
- You may want to point out that it is common to say *Sorry I'm late* instead of *I'm sorry I'm late.*

**Language note:** Students may need help with the following words: *entirely* (completely); *my fault* (I am responsible).

## 🎧 Rhythm and intonation practice
### (CD4, Track 19)

| Suggested teaching time: | 5 minutes |
|---|---|
| Your actual teaching time: | _____ |

- Have students repeat each line chorally.
- Make sure students:
  - pause after *Please come in.*
  - stress <u>late</u> and <u>never</u> in *Well, better late than never.*
  - use the following stress pattern:

**STRESS PATTERN**

— · · — · ·
**A:** Sorry we're late. We got lost.

— · · · · — ·
**B:** That's okay. It can happen to anyone.

· · — · · — · · · — ·
**A:** Well, it was entirely my fault. If I had stopped to ask

· · — · · — · ·
for directions, we would have been on time.

· · — · · — · — · ·
**B:** Well, better late than never. Please come in. And let

· · · · · · —
me get you something to drink.

## 🅐 GRAMMAR

| Suggested teaching time: | 5–10 minutes |
|---|---|
| Your actual teaching time: | _____ |

- Direct attention to the box and have students read the first explanation and study the examples.
- Write on the board:
    *If they <u>had known</u> the way,*
        *they <u>would have arrived</u> on time.*
- Point out that both the *if* clause (condition) and the result clause talk about an unreal or untrue situation.

- Review the verb tenses: the *if* clause needs the past perfect and the result clause needs *would have +* past participle.
- Write on the board:
    *If I had gotten lost ___ .*
- To check comprehension, ask various students to say what they would have done if they had been invited to dinner and they had gotten lost on the way. Examples: . . . *I would have called for directions / I would have used a public phone / I would have checked a map / I would have stopped at a gas station.*
- Direct attention to the Be careful! note. Point out that this is a common mistake.
- Have students read the questions and answers.
- Pair work. Students take turns asking each other how they would have reacted if they had been the host in the conversation model. Examples: Student A: *Would you have gotten upset if you had been the host?* Student B: *No, I wouldn't have. But I would have been worried. And you? Would you have gotten angry?* Student A: *Maybe. But I wouldn't have let them know!*

**Option:** To provide more practice, write the following sentences on the board and ask students to correct the mistakes in the past unreal conditional. Review as a class. (1. <u>have called</u> 2. <u>had had</u> 3. <u>had known</u>)
**[+5 minutes]**
1. If I had remembered it was her birthday, I would call her.
2. If I would have had my credit card, I would have bought it.
3. What would you have done if you knew the truth?

 **Grammar Self-Checks**

## 🅑 Choose the meaning . . .

| Suggested teaching time: | 5 minutes |
|---|---|
| Your actual teaching time: | _____ |

- Do the first item with the class. Review the correct answer by pointing out that both parts of the sentence are unreal or not true. You may want to ask *Why were they able to go?* (Because they had a ticket on the Bullet Train.)
- Have students compare answers with a partner. Then review as a class.

## 🅒 Choose the correct forms . . .

| Suggested teaching time: | 5–10 minutes |
|---|---|
| Your actual teaching time: | _____ |

- If necessary, remind students that *would* or *could* is not used in the *if* clause.
- Review answers with the class.
- Pair work. Students imagine unreal conditions and take turns saying how their life would have been different. Examples: *If I had gone to another school, I wouldn't have learned any English. If I had bought that new sports car, I would have made a big mistake.*

 **PAIR WORK**

| Suggested teaching time: | 10 minutes |
|---|---|
| Your actual teaching time: | _____ |

- Note: Students learned the verb *strike* (to happen suddenly and unexpectedly) in Unit 6 Disasters and Emergencies. Point out *strike* as a verb in the first headline but *strike* as a noun in the second headline. *Strike* as a noun means a period of time when a group of people stop working because they are not happy with payment, working conditions, etc.

- Ask students to complete the statements on their own first.

- Encourage students to give reasons for the actions they would have taken as they discuss.

- Walk around the room to make sure students are using the past unreal conditional correctly.

- (Possible answers: 1. I would have left the town. I would have bought some supplies. I wouldn't have gone out. 2. I would have used my bicycle. I would have left home earlier. I would have stayed at home 3. I would have gone to the stores. I would have bought more things. I would have told my friends.)

 **PRONUNCIATION**
**(CD4, Track 20)**

| Suggested teaching time: | 5 minutes |
|---|---|
| Your actual teaching time: | _____ |

- First listening: Have students listen and study the examples.

- Have students notice the additional syllable in *It'd* /ɪtəd/.

- Second listening: Have students listen and repeat chorally.

**Language note:** *Where'd, Who'd,* and *It'd* are used in spoken English and are not used in writing.

 **Pronunciation Activities**

## CONVERSATION **PAIR WORK**

| Suggested teaching time: | 5–10 minutes |
|---|---|
| Your actual teaching time: | _____ |

- To get students ready for the activity, have students read the conversation model on page 90 again. You may also want to have students listen to the model.

- Review the ideas in the box to the right. Students may want to add ideas.

- To help students prepare for their conversations, ask students to use the unreal conditional to explain how things could have been different for each idea in the box. Examples: You were late: *If I had gotten up earlier, I wouldn't have been late.* You forgot someone's birthday: *If I had looked at the calendar, I would have remembered.* You didn't pay a bill on time: *If I were more organized, I wouldn't have forgotten to pay it.* You forgot to call someone: *If I had written it down in my planner, I wouldn't have forgotten.*

- You may want to brainstorm ways to respond to an apology. Examples: *It can happen to anyone. Don't worry. It's not a problem. It's OK.*

- Choose a more confident student and role-play a conversation. Encourage students to ask follow-up questions.

- Make sure each student plays both roles.

- Walk around the room and provide help as needed. Encourage students to use the correct rhythm and intonation.

 **Pair Work Cards**

## EXTRAS (optional)

**Grammar Booster**
**Workbook: Exercises 13–17**
**Copy & Go: Activity 30**

 **Pronunciation Supplements**

**PAIR WORK.** Take turns completing the statements about each headline.
Then discuss the actions you would have taken if you had read the headlines. Answers will vary.

### Hurricane to Strike Tonight
### Floods Expected

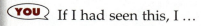 **YOU** If I had seen this, I …

### Massive Transportation Strike
#### Taxis, Buses, Trains Out of Service
#### Huge Traffic Jams Expected

**YOU** If I had seen this, I …

### Stores Announce Protest Against Taxes
### Half-price Sales Begin Today

**YOU** If I had seen this, I …

 🎧 **PRONUNCIATION.** Contractions with **'d** in spoken English. Notice the reduction
of **had**, **would**, and **did**. Read and listen. Then repeat.

1. If we had had time, we
would have stayed.
→ /wid/
If **we'd** had time, we would have stayed.

2. Where did you go?
→ /wɛrd/
**Where'd** you go?

3. Who did you see?
→ /hud/
**Who'd** you see?

4. It would be OK.
→ /ɪtəd/
**It'd** be OK.

 ## CONVERSATION
## PAIR WORK

**Role-play accepting responsibility for a mistake. Use the past
unreal conditional to explain how things could have been different.
Accept your partner's apology.** Answers will vary.

**A:** Sorry _____ .

**B:** That's OK. _____ .

**A:** Well, it was entirely my fault. If _____ …

**Continue the conversation in your own way.**

💡 **Ideas...**

- You were late.
- You forgot someone's birthday.
- You didn't pay a bill on time.
- You forgot to call someone.
- Your own idea:
  _____

# 3 ▸ *Evaluate Inventions*

**CN1** Corpus Notes:
The adjectives *high-tech* and *low-tech* come before the nouns they describe (*a high-tech invention / a low-tech solution*) much more frequently than they do after a verb (*It was really high-tech. / The idea seems very low-tech.*)

## A ▸ 🎧 VOCABULARY. Descriptive adjectives. Listen and practice.

**low-tech / high-tech** **CN1**          **wacky**          **unique** **CN2**          **efficient / inefficient**

## B ▸ 🎧 LISTENING COMPREHENSION. Listen carefully to people discussing their problems. Write the number of the conversation next to the invention each person should have had.

4  The Robo-Tiller

3  The All-Body Umbrella

1  The Pet Exit

2  The Vac Bot

## C ▸ DISCUSSION. Describe each invention with one or more of the adjectives from the vocabulary.

> ❝ It's not a novel idea, but the Pet Exit is both low-tech and efficient. It doesn't need electronics or machinery. ❞

**CN2** Corpus Notes:
The adjective *unique* is frequently modified by adverbs such as *very* and *really* in spoken English, even though many consider this to be grammatically incorrect.

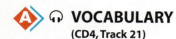

## LESSON

# 3 ▶ *Evaluate Inventions*

## A 🎧 VOCABULARY
### (CD4, Track 21)

| | |
|---|---|
| Suggested teaching time: | 10 minutes |
| Your actual teaching time: | _____ |

- Have students listen and study the phrases.
- Then have students listen and repeat chorally.
- You may want to point out that *wacky* (silly and exciting in an amusing way) is an informal word mainly used in spoken English.

**Option:** Books closed. Write on the board:
1. *the only one of its kind*
2. *doesn't use modern methods or machines*
3. *doesn't waste time, money, or energy*
4. *silly and exciting*
5. *wastes time, money, or energy*
6. *uses modern methods or machines*

Ask students to listen and write the words. Say *wacky, low-tech, high-tech, efficient, unique, inefficient.* Then have them match the correct definition with each word. Then write the words next to the correct definitions on the board so students can check their answers and spelling. (1. unique 2. low-tech 3. efficient 4. wacky 5. inefficient 6. high-tech )
[+5 minutes]

 **Vocabulary Cards**

 **Learning Strategies**

## B 🎧 LISTENING COMPREHENSION
### (CD4, Track 22)

| | |
|---|---|
| Suggested teaching time: | 10–15 minutes |
| Your actual teaching time: | _____ |

- Before listening, have students look at the pictures and say what they think each invention does. Students may say: The Robo-Tiller: *It gets the soil / ground / earth ready for planting. / a garden tool*; The All-Body Umbrella: *It protects your whole body from the rain because it reaches the floor*; The Pet Exit: *It's a small door for pets to come in and go out alone.* The Vac Bot: *It cleans the floor.*
- Ask students to listen and write the number of the matching invention.
- Then have students listen again and write the information that supports their answers. (Possible answers: Conversation 1: The woman should have had the Pet Exit because the cats woke her up three times last night. Conversation 2: They should have had the Vac Bot because the floor was dusty / dirty, and they had just one hour to clean up. 3. The woman should have had the All-Body Umbrella because cars had splashed water on her skirt. 4. The man should have had the Robo-Tiller because he had to get the soil ready for tomatoes, and he had a lot of work to do in the home.)
- Review as a class.

**CONVERSATION 1**
**F1:** I'm going crazy. I didn't sleep a wink last night.
**F2:** How come?
**F1:** It's my cats again. If they're out, they want to come in. And if they're in, they want to go out. Like T.S. Eliot said: "They're on the wrong side of every door." Last night they woke me up three times.

**CONVERSATION 2**
**F:** Oh, no! Look at the time! It's already six o'clock and your mother is coming at seven!
**M:** This place is a mess. Look at the dust on the floor! What'll we do?
**F:** Relax. I'll clean up while you make dinner.
**M:** We'll never be ready in time. Maybe she won't notice the dust.

**CONVERSATION 3 [F2 = French]**
**F1:** Georgette! What happened to your skirt? You look like you fell in the river.
**F2:** I might as well have. I had to wait a long time for the bus, and every car that passed by splashed water on me.
**F1:** Yeah! The puddles from the rain are enormous.
**F2:** And filthy!

**CONVERSATION 4**
**M:** Thanks so much for the tomato plants! I love homegrown tomatoes.
**F:** You're welcome. Just be sure to plant them within a couple of days. They're getting a little too big for their pots.
**M:** I will. See you soon!
**F:** Bye now.
**M:** Oh, my gosh. I don't have time to get the soil ready for so many plants! I have a lot of work to do in the house this weekend.

## C 🔺 DISCUSSION

| | |
|---|---|
| Suggested teaching time: | 10–15 minutes |
| Your actual teaching time: | _____ |

- Review the model first.
- You may want to clarify that *novel* means *unique.*
- Pair work. Students may say *The Robo-tech is high-tech. It looks fast and efficient. The All-Body Umbrella is really wacky. It's also low-tech and efficient. The Vac Bot is unique. It looks very efficient!*
- You may want to do this as a whole-class activity or form small groups. To provide more practice, ask students to say which inventions they would like to have. Students can also say why they wouldn't be interested in some of the inventions. Examples: Student A: *I'd love to have the All-Body Umbrella because I hate getting wet when it rains. I'd also like to have the Vac Bot because I don't have much time to work in the house.* Student B: *I wouldn't be interested in the Robo-Tiller because my garden is very small.* Student C: *I don't have a pet, so I wouldn't be interested in the Pet Exit.*

# TOP NOTCH **INTERACTION**

| Suggested teaching time: | 15–20 minutes |
|---|---|
| Your actual teaching time: | _____ |

## STEP 1. Check the boxes . . .

- Review the example first. Point out the impersonal use of *you*, which students might also want to use to describe their new inventions. *So you don't fall asleep while driving* means the same as *so people don't / someone doesn't fall asleep while driving*, etc.

- Encourage students to check at least one box for each category and to use a dictionary for words they may need help with.

- Walk around the room and provide help as needed.

**Language note:** *Eureka*—from Greek meaning *I have found it!*—is an interjection used to show how happy you are that you have finally discovered the answer to a problem, found something, etc.

## STEP 2. PAIR WORK.

- Students can use an idea from Step 1.
- Draw the following graphic organizer on the board:

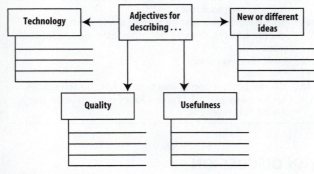

**Graphic Organizers**

- Review vocabulary students can use to fill in their organizers as a class. Examples: Technology: *high-tech, state-of-the-art, cutting-edge, low-tech.* Quality: *top-of-the-line, high-end, first-rate.* Usefulness: *efficient, inefficient, practical.* New or different ideas: *innovative, wacky, unique, novel, revolutionary.*

- To prepare students to describe their inventions in Step 3, review the descriptive adjectives in the NEED HELP? section. Ask students to work in pairs and write one adjective on each line in their organizers.

- Encourage students to use adjectives from their graphic organizer as they write or draw their invention.

## STEP 3. DISCUSSION.

- Students will need to use conditionals to explain what would happen if they had their invention now. Review the factual and unreal conditionals in the NEED HELP? section.

- Provide a model. Example: *I once fell asleep while I was driving. Now I never drive at night because I'm afraid it might happen again. If I had a wake-up alarm in my car, I would be able to drive at night. If I had had a wake-up alarm, I wouldn't have crashed.*

- Remind students to use the vocabulary in this and previous units, and encourage students to ask follow-up questions.

## EXTRAS (optional)

**Workbook:** Exercises 18, 19
**Copy & Go:** Activity 31

**STEP 1.** **Check the boxes to show where you think new inventions are needed.**
**Then complete the chart with more information about each invention.** Answers will vary.

| | New invention | Why people would want it |
|---|---|---|
| **home and car** | | |
| ☑ for the car | a wake-up alarm | so you don't fall asleep while driving |
| ☐ for organizing | | |
| ☐ for cooking | | |
| ☐ for raising children | | |
| ☐ for pets | | |
| ☐ for cleaning | | |
| ☐ for relaxing | | |
| **office** | | |
| ☐ for writing | | |
| ☐ for organizing papers | | |
| ☐ for training staff | | |
| ☐ for communicating | | |
| ☐ for eating lunch or snacking | | |
| **English class** | | |
| ☐ for learning new words and grammar | | |
| ☐ for getting more speaking practice | | |
| ☐ for preparing to take tests | | |
| ☐ for reading faster | | |

**STEP 2.** **PAIR WORK.** **Choose one area and invent something. It can be wacky, low-tech, high-tech, or even impossible! Name your invention. On a separate sheet of paper, draw a picture of it or write a description of it.** Answers will vary.

**STEP 3.** **DISCUSSION.** **Tell the class about your invention. Explain what would happen if you had one now. Explain what you could have done if you'd had one in the past.**

NEED HELP? **Here's language you already know:**

**Descriptive adjectives**

| top-of-the-line | wacky |
|---|---|
| high-tech | practical |
| high-end | unique |
| state-of-the-art | efficient |
| cutting-edge | inefficient |
| low-tech | novel |
| first-rate | revolutionary |
| innovative | |

**Factual and unreal conditionals**

Don't you wish someone would invent
    something for ___?
If I had a ___, I would be able to ___ .
If I had had a ___, I would have been
    able to ___ .

93

**FREE PRACTICE**

## Discuss the Impact of Key Inventions in History

 **READING WARM-UP.** In what ways did people communicate words and ideas to each other before the invention of the telegraph, the telephone, the radio, and the computer?

 🎧 **READING.** Read about the invention of printing. How do you think this invention changed the world?

# The Printing Press

Until the 6th or 7th century, all books had to be written by hand.

ladle for pouring hot metal

**I**f you asked a large number of people what the most important invention has been, many would say the printing press. Others might say the wheel. But even though it's debatable whether the appearance of the printing press affected the course of history more than the wheel, the printing press ranks within the top two or three inventions in history.

Long before the telephone, the television, the radio, and the computer, the written word was the only way to communicate ideas to people too far away to talk with. Until the sixth or seventh century, all books had to be written

by hand. Creating a book was difficult, and in comparison with today, very few books existed. Therefore, very few people read books.

In the sixth and seventh centuries, the Japanese and Chinese invented a way to print pages by carving characters and pictures on wooden, ivory, or clay blocks. They would put ink on the blocks and then press paper onto the ink, printing a page from the block. This process is called letterpress printing. The invention of letterpress printing was a great advance in communication because each block could be inked many times and many copies of each page could be made. Many books could now be made. Therefore, many people

could read the same book.

Later, in the 11th century, another great advance occurred. The Chinese invented "movable" type. Each character was made as a separate block which could be used many times in many texts. This meant that pages could be created by putting together individual characters rather than having to have whole pages carved. Movable type was much more efficient than the earlier Japanese and Chinese print blocks because books could be created much more quickly by people with less skill.

In Europe, movable type was used for the first time in the 15th century. And there, Johannes Gutenberg invented typecasting, a way to make movable type much more quickly, by melting metal and pouring it into the forms of the letters. This greatly increased the speed of printing, and eventually made books available to many more people.

carved print blocks

**SOURCE:** Eyewitness Books: *Invention.* By Lionel Bender, Alfred A. Knopf, New York, © 1991.

# 4 Discuss the Impact of Key Inventions in History

## A  READING WARM-UP

| Suggested teaching time: | 5–10 minutes |
|---|---|
| Your actual teaching time: | _____ |

• Ask students for their ideas and make a list on the board. (Students may say: smoke signals, drum beating, sign language, talking, using messengers, pigeons that carried a message attached to one of their legs, flashing lights at sea, mail or postal services.)

## B ∩ READING

### (CD4, Track 23)

| Suggested teaching time: | 10–15 minutes |
|---|---|
| Your actual teaching time: | _____ |

• Before students read, have students look at the title and the pictures and ask questions. Examples: *What is the text about?* (the printing press) *What is the printing press?* (a machine that prints newspapers, books, etc. used before computers were common) *What do you think the three pictures illustrate?* (three steps that led to the invention of the printing press)

• After students read, ask for their ideas about how the printing press affected / changed the world.

**Option:** Ask students to match each picture with a paragraph from the text. Encourage students to underline in the text the sentence that supports their choice. Have students compare answers with a partner and then review as class. (Man writing a book by hand: second paragraph—Until the sixth or seventh century, all books had to be written by hand. Carved print blocks: third paragraph—. . . the Japanese and Chinese invented a way to print pages by carving characters on wooden, ivory, or clay blocks. Ladle: Last paragraph—. . . Johannes Gutenberg invented typecasting, a way to make movable type much more quickly, by melting metal and pouring it into the forms of letters). **[+10 minutes]**

**Challenge:** Use this option if you want to do a listening activity. Books closed. Draw the following event chain and write the events on the board.

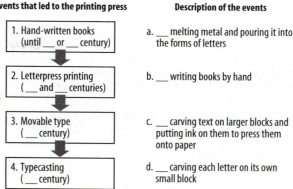

**Events that led to the printing press**

1. Hand-written books (until ___ or ___ century)
2. Letterpress printing ( ___ and ___ centuries)
3. Movable type ( ___ century)
4. Typecasting ( ___ century)

**Description of the events**

a. ___ melting metal and pouring it into the forms of letters

b. ___ writing books by hand

c. ___ carving text on larger blocks and putting ink on them to press them onto paper

d. ___ carving each letter on its own small block

Point out that each event in the chain was a step toward the invention of the printing press. Have students listen and fill in the centuries. Then have them listen again match each event with the corresponding description by writing the correct number before each description. Then have students read the text to confirm their answers. (1. 6th / 7th 2. 6th / 3. 11th 4. 15th) (a, 4 b. 1 c. 2 d. 3) **[+15 minutes]**

 **Graphic Organizers**

**Language note:** Students may need help with the following words: *carve* (to cut a letter on the surface of something); *ivory* (the hard, smooth yellowish-white substance from the tusks of an elephant); *melt* (heat a hard substance at a high temperature to make it become liquid).

**Extra Reading Comprehension Activities**

**Learning Strategies**

 **DISCUSSION**

| Suggested teaching time: | 10 minutes |
|---|---|
| Your actual teaching time: | _____ |

- Group work. Form small groups.

- Encourage students to use the past unreal conditional to discuss question 1. Provide a model. Example: *If the printing press hadn't been invented, people would have passed stories from one generation to the next only verbally / orally.*

- (Students may say: If books didn't exist, we wouldn't know much about the past. If we didn't have newspapers, we wouldn't know about events in different places.)

- Encourage students to use the correct verb for the different ways to communicate in writing. Examples: *writing: letters, notes, memos; sending: faxes, postcards, e-mails, text messages.*

- Have various groups state their choices for the top inventions. Encourage them to explain their choices.

## TOP NOTCH **INTERACTION**

| Suggested teaching time: | 20–25 minutes |
|---|---|
| Your actual teaching time: | _____ |

### STEP 1. PAIR WORK.

- Have students read the captions. If necessary, clarify vocabulary: *crop* (rice, wheat or corn); *steam* (point out the white vapor / steam coming out of the chimney in picture 2); *the steam locomotive* (a vehicle used for pulling trains; the first vehicle faster than the horse)

- If necessary, review what each invention does by asking questions. Encourage students to answer in their own words. Examples: *What was the plow used for?* (getting the soil / land ready for planting crops) *What was the steam locomotive used for?* (carrying / moving things over long distances) *Why would people prefer zippers to buttons?* (because they are easy and practical) *What did people do to keep things cool or cold before the refrigerator was invented?* (used boxes / containers filled with ice; put things outside in cold weather)

- Write the following on the board:
  *How did it improve the quality of (daily) life?*
  *Did it lead to other inventions? Which ones?*
  *Did it create economic growth? How?*
  *What other positive outcomes did the invention create?*

- To help students analyze the importance of each invention and decide which ranking they want to assign, ask students to think about the questions on the board as they discuss.

- Students may write on their notepads:
  ○ the plow: (life before) people had to dig by hand using a simple tool; (life after) people could dig more fields and faster
  ○ the train: (life before) products were carried in carts pulled by horses, people transported a few things from one place to the other; (life after) products reached their destination much faster, people started transporting more products from one place to another
  ○ the zipper: (life before) people took longer to do and undo their clothes, it took longer to make clothes because they had to sew on lots of buttons; (life after) the zipper is so practical that its use became widespread, it took less time to make clothes because zippers are easier to sew on
  ○ the refrigerator: (life before) people bought food more often, people couldn't store some foods the way we do today, there was less food variety; (life after) people don't need to shop for food so often, people store foods in refrigerators and freezers, there is more food variety

- Take a poll to find out which inventions students rated the most and the least important.

### STEP 2. GROUP WORK.

- Form small groups. You may want to make sure all of the inventions are chosen.

- If students choose an invention not on this page, encourage them to go through the same process as in Step 1 to analyze it. Examples of other inventions: *Velcro, duct tape, computers, the Internet, cars, cell phones.*

- Point out that "the impact" the invention had includes how life would have been both with or without that specific invention.

- Tell students to refer back to the Grammar box on page 90 for help with the past unreal conditional. Example: *If the plow hadn't been invented, farms would have remained small.*

- Point out that students will use also use the past unreal conditional *if* clause with information about the present. Example: *If the plow hadn't been invented, farmers would still need a lot of time to prepare the fields.*

- Encourage each group to assign part of the presentation to each student.

### EXTRAS (optional)

**Workbook:** Exercises 20–22
**Copy & Go:** Activity 32

1. How would life have been different if printing hadn't been invented?

2. In what ways do we communicate "in writing" today?

3. What makes an invention important? What do you think are the top two or three inventions in history?

---

TOP NOTCH
**INTERACTION** • *It's the greatest invention since the wheel!*

**STEP 1. PAIR WORK.** On your notepads, write your own ideas about how life changed as a result of each of these inventions. Then rank the four inventions in order of importance.

Answers will vary.

2000 B.C.: The plow loosens and turns the soil so crops can be planted efficiently.

1802: The steam locomotive permits transportation of products over long distances by train.

1914: The modern zipper permits the opening and closing of clothes without buttons and buttonholes.

1920s: The electric refrigerator keeps food fresh.

|  | Life before | Life after |
|---|---|---|
| the plow: |  |  |
| the train: |  |  |
| the zipper: |  |  |
| the refrigerator: |  |  |

**"** After the plow was invented, farmers could plant large areas in a short time. Then they could plant enough food to sell to other people. **"**

**STEP 2. GROUP WORK.** Choose one of the inventions above or another invention. Present a report to your classmates about the impact the invention had in history.

# UNIT 8
# CHECKPOINT

 **LISTENING COMPREHENSION.** Listen to the people talking about new products. Match the name of the product and the adjective that best describes it.

| Products | Adjectives |
|---|---|
| _a_ 1. The Ultraphone | a. cutting-edge |
| _b_ 2. Dinner-from-a-distance | b. efficient |
| _c_ 3. Kinder-TV | c. unique |
| _d_ 4. Ten Years Off | d. top-of-the-line |

**B** Check the statement that is true for each situation.

1. We wouldn't have gotten lost if we had called in advance for directions.
   - ☐ We called and we got lost.
   - ☑ We didn't call and we got lost.
   - ☐ We called and we didn't get lost.
   - ☐ We didn't call and we didn't get lost.

2. If the salesman were here, he would explain how the Omni works.
   - ☐ The salesman is here, so he can explain how the Omni works.
   - ☐ The salesman is here, so he can't explain how the Omni works.
   - ☐ The salesman isn't here, but he can explain how the Omni works.
   - ☑ The salesman isn't here, so he can't explain how the Omni works.

3. If Laura had bought the Ultraphone, she would have already sent those e-mails.
   - ☐ Laura bought the Ultraphone and she has already sent those e-mails.
   - ☑ Laura didn't buy the Ultraphone and she hasn't sent those e-mails yet.
   - ☐ Laura bought the Ultraphone and she hasn't sent those e-mails yet.
   - ☐ Laura didn't buy the Ultraphone and she has already sent those e-mails.

**C** Complete each conditional sentence. Answers may vary. Possible answers include:

1. If I had a very fast car, __I'd enjoy driving more__ .

2. Most people would look better if __they got more sleep__ .

3. Will you buy a new car next year if __you have the money__ ?

4. If I had been born before there were cars, __I would've had to walk everywhere__ .

**D** **WRITING.** Choose one of the following inventions. Write about how it changed life and what would have happened if it had not been invented.

- the telephone
- the washing machine
- the microwave oven
- the computer

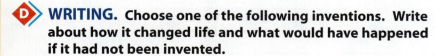

**TOP NOTCH SONG**
"Reinvent the Wheel"
Lyrics on last book page.

*TOP NOTCH* **PROJECT**
Choose an invention appearing during your own lifetime that has changed your life. Make a presentation to the class about the invention.

*TOP NOTCH* **WEBSITE**
For Unit 8 online activities, visit the *Top Notch* Companion Website at www.longman.com/topnotch.

# UNIT 8
# CHECKPOINT

 ⌕ **LISTENING COMPREHENSION**
**(CD4, Track 24)**

| Suggested teaching time: | 10–15 minutes |
|---|---|
| Your actual teaching time: | _____ |

- Pause after each conversation to allow students time to match the products and the adjectives.

- Have students listen again to write information that supports their answers. Example: *Ten Years Off is top of the line because it is the best one Lake makes.* Ask them to compare answers and reasons with a partner.

- Review as a class.

- To provide more practice, have students listen again and identify what each product is and does. (1. a phone that can read your lips and permits you to create documents in your office 2. a machine operated by a remote (control) that keeps the food cold and also cooks it 3. a special TV that permits you to remove the programs you don't want your children to watch 4. a face cream that makes you look younger.)

**AUDIOSCRIPT**

CONVERSATION 1
**M:** I want one of those phones that does everything: takes pictures, does e-mail, pays bills … I'm tired of my old-fashioned phone. All you can do is call people and talk!
**F:** Well, have you seen the Ultraphone? It's got the latest technology. You just talk into it, and it can create documents at your office.
**M:** How does it do that?
**F:** It can read your lips. You just speak into the lens of the camera so it can see your lips.
**M:** You're pulling my leg. That sounds impossible!
**F:** No. Just step this way. I'll show you how it works.
**M:** Wow! The Ultraphone …

CONVERSATION 2
**F1:** I need a faster way to get dinner ready. It takes too long to start after I get home from work.
**F2:** Well, let me show you something better—remote-controlled cookware. You combine the ingredients the night before and just plug it in. The cookware keeps everything cold until you press the button on this remote. Then the cookware heats up and cooks everything. When you get home, dinner is ready!
**F1:** "Dinner-from-a-Distance" sounds like a lot less work in a lot less time!

CONVERSATION 3
**M1:** We're worried about what our children are watching on TV. There are so many terrible programs. What can we do?
**M2:** Well, have you heard about Kinder-TV? It takes the worry out of TV for parents.
**M1:** No. What's that?
**M2:** Well, you buy this special TV and then you register by e-mail. Once a week, you receive an e-mail describing daytime TV programs for that week. You just check off the programs you don't want and Kinder-TV simply removes them.
**M1:** Unbelievable. I've never heard of anything like that.
**M2:** It's absolutely the only one that exists.

**AUDIOSCRIPT continues on page T97.**

 **Check the statement . . .**

| Suggested teaching time: | 5 minutes |
|---|---|
| Your actual teaching time: | _____ |

- Remind students that the present and past unreal conditionals express imagined conditions and results—things that do / did not actually happened.

- Have students compare answers with a partner.
- Review as a class.

 **Complete each . . .**

| Suggested teaching time: | 5 minutes |
|---|---|
| Your actual teaching time: | _____ |

- Model item 1 by saying a sentence about yourself. Example: *If I had a very fast car, I would probably get a speeding ticket!*

- Pair work. Students take turns saying their sentences. Encourage students to make necessary corrections.

 **WRITING**

| Suggested teaching time: | 10–15 minutes |
|---|---|
| Your actual teaching time: | _____ |

- Encourage students to create two paragraphs—one about how the invention changed life and the other about what would have happened if it hadn't been invented.

- If necessary, have students review the grammar for conditionals on pages 88 and 90.

- You may want to ask students to finish their piece of writing with a third paragraph about their own use of the invention.

- Walk around the room and provide help as needed.

 **Writing Process Worksheets**

 *Top Notch Pop* **Song Activities**
**(CD4, Track 25)**

***TOP NOTCH* PROJECT**

**Idea:** Encourage students to make notes about the following:

- Name of the invention
- How old they were when it appeared
- Why it changed their lives / Why it is important for them
- How their life would be different if it hadn't appeared

Point out that the invention doesn't need to be revolutionary. It can be a small and simple product that affected any part of life.

# UNIT WRAP-UP

| | |
|---|---|
| Suggested teaching time: | 15–20 minutes |
| Your actual teaching time: | _____ |

## Vocabulary

- Have students identify the manufactured items. (a washing machine; a television; a hair dryer; a walkman; a CD player; a combined refrigerator, oven, and microwave; a stereo / CD player)

- Pair work. Students take turns describing the machines and how they work.

**┌─ Your students can say ... ─┐**

The Airpro 4000 is top of the line / first-rate. The Presto is efficient and fast. It looks practical. The Super Sonic uses cutting-edge technology. The Super Sonic looks high-end. The Drago 4 is unique. The Drago 4 looks wacky. The All-in-One Cooker-Fridge is revolutionary. The All-in-One Cooker-Fridge looks high-tech and efficient. Dan's walkman is low-tech. Dan's walkman is not state of the art, but it is practical. The top-of-the-line CD player is not very practical.

## Grammar

- As a class create an example for each sentence starter.
- If necessary, ask students to review the conditionals in this unit (pages 88 and 90).

**┌─ Your students can say ... ─┐**

If she buys the Super Sonic, she'll be able to dry her hair quickly each morning. If she buys the Cooker-Fridge, her life is going to be easier. If they bought the Cooker-Fridge, they would eat right when they get home after work. If they bought the CD player on sale, they would save a lot of money. If Dan hadn't bought the hand-held CD player, he would have money to invite the girl for coffee. If the hair dryer wasn't so powerful, it wouldn't have knocked her glasses off. If the TVs aren't on sale, we can't buy one.

## Social Language

- To check comprehension, ask *What's special about the Cooker-Fridge?* (It cools, freezes, defrosts, microwaves, and cooks.) *Why do you think the woman on the left turned the hair dryer on?* (to see how it worked) *What happened to the other woman's glasses?* (They blew off.)

- Encourage students to use the grammar and the vocabulary from this and previous units.

**┌─ Your students can say ... ─┐**
**The man and woman**
A: This is a [high-tech] cooker-fridge. Do you think we should buy it? B: That depends. How much are they selling it for? A: It's on sale for [$300] B: Yes, definitely! That's a great price.

**The two women**
A: Sorry! B: That's OK. A: If I had known this hairdryer was so strong, I wouldn't have turned it on. B: Please don't worry. If I go now, I can get them fixed.

**Option: If I could ...** Pair work. Students take turns saying which products from the store they would like to buy and why. **[+5 minutes]**

**Challenge: "First-rate" salesperson.** Pair work. Ask students to role-play a conversation between a persuasive salesperson and a customer. The salesperson should persuade the customer to buy an item from the store. The salesperson should use as many adjectives as possible to describe the items and the conditionals (page 88) to describe how the customer's life would change if he /she had the items. **[+5 minutes]**

**┌─ Individual oral progress check (optional) ─┐**

- Use the illustration on page 97. Encourage the student to use material (vocabulary, grammar, rhythm and intonation) practiced in this unit.

- Evaluate the student on correctness and intelligibility.

- Tell the student to answer your questions and give reasons using descriptive adjectives. Ask: *If you needed a hair dryer, which one would you buy?* (I'd buy the Airpro 4000 because it's top of the line.) *Why wouldn't you buy the [Drago]?* (I wouldn't buy the Drago because I don't like its unique design!) *If a friend offered you Dan's walkman or the other boy's CD player, which one would you choose?* (I'd choose the CD player. I think it's first-rate.) *Why wouldn't you choose the (item student did not choose)?* (It's practical, but it looks low-tech.)

- Point to the man and woman looking at the All-in-One Cooker-Fridge. Tell the student that together you are going to role-play a conversation. Start the conversation. Example: T: *Do you think we should buy this Cooker-Fridge?* S: *Well, it's revolutionary! It cools, freezes, defrosts, microwaves, and cooks!* T: *It looks kind of high-end. Is it very expensive?* S: *I don't think so. It's on sale. And remember, cutting-edge technology usually makes people's lives easier!*

 **Cumulative Vocabulary Activities**

 You may wish to use the video and activity worksheets for Unit 8 at this point.

 **Complete Assessment Package Unit 8 Achievement Test**

**◀ AUDIOSCRIPT ▶**

**AUDIOSCRIPT continued from Exercise A, page T96.**

CONVERSATION 4
F1: This face cream is great. It makes me look ten years younger.
F2: You DO look great. What's it called?
F1: "Ten Years Off."
F2: Who makes it?
F1: Lake.
F2: Well Lake is the best brand, so I'm not surprised that "Ten Years Off" is great.
F1: They make a lot of creams, but they told me "Ten Years Off" is absolutely the best one they make.

UNIT WRAP-UP

- **Vocabulary.** Talk about the items in the store, using adjectives to describe them.
- **Grammar.** Complete the statements, using the factual and unreal conditional. Then make more statements.
  *If she buys the . . .*
  *If they bought the . . .*
  *If Dan hadn't bought the . . .*
- **Social Language.** Create conversations for the people.

**Now I can . . .**

- ☐ describe an innovation.
- ☐ accept responsibility for a mistake.
- ☐ evaluate inventions.
- ☐ discuss the impact of key inventions in history.

# UNIT 9

# Controversial Issues

UNIT GOALS
1 Ask if it's OK to discuss a topic
2 Discuss controversial issues politely
3 Propose solutions to global problems
4 Debate the pros and cons of issues

 **A** 🎧 **TOPIC PREVIEW.** Read the dictionary definitions of some political terms. Then listen and practice.

**con·sti·tu·tion** /ˌkɑnstəˈtuʃən/ *n.* a set of basic laws and principles that a democratic country is governed by, which cannot easily be changed by the political party in power

**de·moc·ra·cy** /dɪˈmɑkrəsi/ *n.* **1** a system of government in which every citizen in the country can vote to elect its government officials **2** a country that allows its people to elect its government officials

**dic·ta·tor·ship** /dɪkˈteɪtəˌʃɪp/ *n.* government by a ruler who has complete power

**e·lec·tion** /ɪˈlɛkʃən/ *n.* an occasion when people vote to choose someone for an official position

**gov·ern·ment** /ˈgʌvəmənt, ˈgʌvənmənt/ *n.* the group of people who govern a country or state: *the French government*

**mon·ar·chy** /ˈmɑnəki/ *n.* **1** the system in which a country is ruled by a king or queen **2** a country that is ruled by a king or queen

**pol·i·tics** /ˈpɑləˌtɪks/ *n.* **1** ideas and activities that are concerned with gaining or using power in a country: *Brock's been involved in city politics since college.* | *Politics doesn't interest me much.* **2** the profession of being a politician: *Flynn retired from politics in 1986.* **3** [plural] the activities of people who are concerned with gaining personal advantage within a group: *I'm tired of dealing with all the office politics.* **4** [plural] someone's political beliefs and opinions: *I don't agree with Michael's politics, but he's sure a nice guy.*

**vote** /voʊt/ *v.* to show by marking a paper, raising your hand, etc. which person you want to elect or whether you support a particular plan: *Greg says he has never voted.* | *Who did you vote for in the last election?*

**SOURCE:** *Longman Advanced American Dictionary*

**B** **DISCUSSION.** Should every country have the same form of government? Why don't all countries have the same form of government? In your opinion, which is the best form of government?

# UNIT 9

# Controversial Issues

## A  TOPIC PREVIEW
### (CD5, Track 2)

| Suggested teaching time: | 10–15 minutes |
|---|---|
| Your actual teaching time: | _____ |

- Direct students' attention to the unit title. Elicit or explain that *controversial issues* are problems or topics that can cause a lot of disagreement because people have strong personal opinions about them.

- Ask students to say topics they feel are controversial. Examples: *politics or politicians, family traditions, values, sex on TV, religious beliefs, environmental problems, smoking in public places,* etc.

- Ask students to listen and study the words.

- Point out that *democracy, dictatorship,* and *monarchy* can be used to describe both a form of government and a country having that form of government. Give examples: *Some countries are slowly moving toward democracy. Argentina is a democracy.*

- Then ask students to listen and repeat chorally.

- Write the vocabulary words on the board. Pair work. Students take turns reading definitions aloud and saying the matching words. Each student should read three definitions. The student who is identifying the words keeps his / her book closed. Point out that students don't need to read the complete definition. Example: Student A: *A set of laws and principles that a democratic country is governed by.* Student B: *Constitution.* Student A: *A country that is ruled by a king.* Student B: *Monarchy.*

 **Vocabulary Cards**

## B DISCUSSION

| Suggested teaching time: | 10–15 minutes |
|---|---|
| Your actual teaching time: | _____ |

- Draw the following graphic organizer on the board:

```
          ┌─────────────────────┐
          │ Forms of government │
          └─────────────────────┘
         ┌──────────┼──────────┐
  ┌───────────┬──────────────┬──────────┐
  │ Democracy │ Dictatorship │ Monarchy │
  ├───────────┼──────────────┼──────────┤
(+)│           │              │          │
  ├───────────┼──────────────┼──────────┤
(−)│           │              │          │
  └───────────┴──────────────┴──────────┘
```

 **Graphic Organizers**

- Have students think of some advantages and disadvantages for each form of government and write notes in the chart.

- Group work. Form small groups.

- You may want to remind students they might not / don't have to agree as they discuss the questions. Walk around the room and provide help as needed.

- Ask students for their opinions. Students may say: *Every country couldn't have the same form of government because people's values and beliefs condition the way in which they want to be governed. All countries don't have the same form of government because they all have a different history.*

- Ask various students to say which form of government they think is best and to give one of their reasons. Examples: *In my opinion, a democracy is the best form of government because each person has a chance to express their opinions when they vote.*

 **SOUND BITES**

(CD5, Track 3)

| Suggested teaching time: | 5 minutes |
|---|---|
| Your actual teaching time: | _____ |

- After students read and listen, ask *What situation does Sam need help with?* (He wants to know if politics are too controversial to discuss at the dinner table with a Taiwanese family.) *What is San-Chi's advice?* (He suggests that Sam talk about something else, because Sam has strong opinions about politics. It would not be polite to argue with the parents.)
- Point out that *bring up* means start a conversation about / to talk about a topic.

> **Language note:** *It would not be cool* means it wouldn't be a good idea; *what a coincidence* means someone is surprised to run into / see someone; *mm-hmm* is a common way to indicate *yes* in spoken English; *opinionated* means expressing very strong opinions and thinking that your ideas are always right.

 **IN OTHER WORDS**

| Suggested teaching time: | 10 minutes |
|---|---|
| Your actual teaching time: | _____ |

- Have students read the expressions. To practice the reading skill of understanding vocabulary from context, encourage students to use the information in the text to help them figure out the meaning of words or expressions.
- Do the first item with the class. Review other ways to ask about someone's life: *What's new? How's everything? What's new and interesting in your life?*
- Have students compare answers with a partner and then review as a class.
- Review other ways to say each item. 1. *So what's new?* 2. *Yup.* (very informal) 3. *Should I not bring that up?* 4. *That wouldn't be a good idea.* 5. *I'm pushy sometimes.*

## WHAT ABOUT **YOU?**

| Suggested teaching time: | 10–15 minutes |
|---|---|
| Your actual teaching time: | _____ |

- Group work. Form small groups.
- (Students may say: democracies: the United States, Argentina, Mexico, Brazil, India, Israel, Turkey, France, Germany; monarchies: Japan, United Kingdom, Spain, Saudi Arabia, Belgium, Morocco, Malaysia; dictatorships: Cuba, Sudan, Nigeria, North Korea, Turkmenistan, Zimbabwe)
- Encourage students to give reasons for their answers and ask each other follow-up questions. Examples: Student A: *I don't like to talk about politics.* Student B: *Really? Why not?* Student C: *Because I usually end up arguing.* Student B: *Are you very opinionated?* A: *I'm not . . . but other people are!*
- To finish the activity, ask various students to say what they would tell a visitor to their country about talking politics at the dinner table.

## EXTRAS (optional)

**Workbook: Exercises 1–3**

**C** 🎧 **SOUND BITES.** Read along silently as you listen to a conversation in the United States.

**SAN-CHI:** So what are you up to these days, Sam?

**SAM:** Hi, San-Chi! What a coincidence. I've been meaning to give you a call. I need some cultural advice. **CN1**

**SAN-CHI:** What about?

**CN1** **Corpus Notes:** While *call someone* and *give (someone) a call* mean the same thing, *give (someone) a call* is used much more frequently in spoken English.

**SAM:** Well, I'm having dinner at Mei-Li's house tonight, and her parents are in from Taiwan.

**SAN-CHI:** Really?

**SAM:** Mm-hmm. And you know how much I love to talk politics. Would it be rude to bring that up at the dinner table?

**SAN-CHI:** Uh . . . Well, not really. Most people from Taiwan like to talk about politics too. But it would <u>not</u> be cool to argue with them if you don't agree with what they say!

**SAM:** How well you know me! I do tend to be a little opinionated. **CN2**

**SAN-CHI:** Well, in that case, I'd advise you to talk about something else!

**D** **IN OTHER WORDS.** Find a word or expression in the conversation that is similar in meaning to each of the following words and expressions.

1. What have you been doing lately?
   What are you up to these days?
2. Yes.
   Mm-hmm.
3. Would it be impolite to talk about that?
   Would it be rude to bring that up?
4. It wouldn't be OK.
   . . . it would not be cool to . . .
5. I express my beliefs strongly.
   I do tend to be a little opinionated.

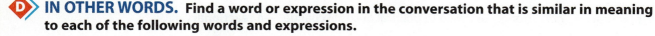

**WHAT ABOUT YOU?**

**CN2** **Corpus Notes:** *Do* can be used before a verb or verb phrase to emphasize it, especially when what is being said is surprising. *Do* is used most frequently this way before the verbs *have, need,* and *know.*

How much do you know about governments around the world? Write the names of countries on the chart. Then compare your chart with your classmates' charts. Answers will vary.

| a democracy | a monarchy | a dictatorship |
|---|---|---|
|  |  |  |

**DISCUSSION.** Do you like to talk about politics? Do you think politics is a good topic for discussion when you are invited to someone's home?

# 1

## Ask If It's OK to Discuss a Topic

🎧 **CONVERSATION MODEL** Read and listen.

**A:** In general, is it acceptable here to ask people about politics?

**B:** That depends. If you know someone well, it's OK.

**A:** Well, would it be OK to ask you?

**B:** Sure! What would you like to know?

**A:** Who do you think will win the election?

**B:** That's a good question!

🎧 **Rhythm and intonation practice**

 🎧 **VOCABULARY. A continuum of political and social beliefs.** Listen and practice.

**radical** *adj.* supporting complete political or social change —**a radical** *n.*

**liberal** *adj.* supporting changes in political, social, or religious systems that allow more people to do what they want —**a liberal** *n.*

**moderate** *adj.* having opinions or beliefs, especially about politics, that are not extreme and that most people consider reasonable or sensible —**a moderate** *n.*

**conservative** *adj.* preferring to continue to do things as they have been done in the past rather than risking changes —**a conservative** *n.*

**reactionary** *adj.* strongly opposed to political or social change —**a reactionary** *n.*

 🎧 **LISTENING COMPREHENSION.** Listen to each conversation about political and social opinions. Then, with a partner, decide where you think each person belongs on the continuum of political and social thought. Explain your answers. Listen again if necessary to check your work. *Answers may vary. Possible answers include:*

| Conversation | radical | liberal | moderate | conservative | reactionary |
|---|---|---|---|---|---|
| 1. He's | ✓ | ○ | ○ | ○ | ○ |
| 2. She's | ○ | ○ | ○ | ✓ | ○ |
| 3. He's | ○ | ○ | ✓ | ○ | ○ |
| 4. She's | ○ | ○ | ○ | ○ | ✓ |
| 5. He's | ○ | ○ | ✓ | ○ | ○ |

**LESSON**

# LESSON 1
## *Ask If It's OK to Discuss a Topic*

## CONVERSATION **MODEL**
**(CD5, Track 4)**

| | |
|---|---|
| Suggested teaching time: | 5 minutes |
| Your actual teaching time: | _____ |

- After students read and listen, ask *What cultural advice is the first speaker asking for?* (If it's OK to talk to people about politics.) *What does the second speaker suggest?* (It's OK when you know the other person well.)
- Tell students *That's a good question!* in this situation means *I don't know.*
- Point out that the two men are probably in a work setting. Ask students if it makes a difference or not where you are when you want to talk politics, for example, at work vs. in a social setting.

> **Language note:** To decline or avoid an embarrassing, inappropriate, or very personal question, you can say *Actually, I'd rather not say* or *Can we talk about something else?* A common answer to an embarrassing or personal question from the media is *No comment.*

### Rhythm and intonation practice
**(CD5, Track 5)**

| | |
|---|---|
| Suggested teaching time: | 5 minutes |
| Your actual teaching time: | _____ |

- Have students repeat each line chorally.
- Make sure students:
  ○ use rising intonation for *is it acceptable here to ask people about politics?*
  ○ pause after *well* in *If you know someone well, it's OK.*
  ○ use rising intonation for *would it be OK to ask you?*
  ○ use falling intonation for *What would you like to know?*
  ○ use falling intonation for *Who do you think will win the election?*
  ○ use the following stress pattern:

```
┌─STRESS PATTERN──────────────────────────────────
       •  —  • •  • •  — •  • •  — •  •  • • •
   A:  In general, is it acceptable here to ask people about
       — • •
       politics?
       —  • — •  • •  •  • — • •—
   B:  That depends. If you know someone well, it's okay.
       —   •  • •  •—  — •  —
   A:  Well, would it be okay to ask you?
       —   • •  • •  • •
   B:  Sure!  What would you like to know?
       —  — • •  •  • •  •—  •
   A:  Who do you think will win the election?
       —  • — •  —
   B:  That's a good question!
```

## A  VOCABULARY
**(CD5, Track 6)**

| | |
|---|---|
| Suggested teaching time: | 5–10 minutes |
| Your actual teaching time: | _____ |

- Draw the following on the board:

Strong support          Strong opposition
of change                    to change
←——————————————————→

- To help clarify, tell students that a continuum shows different degrees of something.
- Have students listen and study the vocabulary. Then have students listen and repeat chorally.
- Ask students to say which words match the definitions on the board. (on the left: radical; on the right: reactionary)
- To provide more practice, have students study the words and close their books. Say the vocabulary words and have students write them on a continuum: *conservative, liberal, radical, moderate, reactionary.* (starting from the left: radical, liberal, moderate, conservative, reactionary)

> **Language note:** The words are both adjectives and nouns. If necessary, review that adjectives are words that modify nouns. *She has radical views. She's a radical.*

 **Vocabulary Cards**

## B  LISTENING COMPREHENSION
**(CD5, Track 7)**

| | |
|---|---|
| Suggested teaching time: | 10 minutes |
| Your actual teaching time: | _____ |

- Write on the board:

  *Topic?  Change: How much change / No change?*

- Ask students to listen for each topic and to what degree the speaker wants things to change or stay the same.
- Pay attention to *He's* and *She's* in the first column to focus on whose opinions students are evaluating.
- Review as a class. Ask students to give reasons. Refer them to the definitions when necessary.
- Possible reasons: 1. He's a radical because he wants to end the institution of marriage. 2. She's conservative because she wants to vote for a political party that doesn't make any changes. 3. He's liberal because he thinks change that helps people is good. 4. Her views are reactionary because she thinks the old laws should be brought back. 5. His views are moderate because he's not going to vote for a liberal but for someone who is not so extreme.
- Note: Answers may vary depending on personal judgment.

**AUDIOSCRIPT for Exercise B is on page T107.**

> **Language note:** You may also want to point out that *left-wing, centrist,* and *right-wing* are also common ways to describe a continuum of political beliefs.

**T100**

## C  GRAMMAR

| Suggested teaching time: | 5–10 minutes |
|---|---|
| Your actual teaching time: | _____ |

- Direct attention to the Grammar box and have students read the first explanation and study the nouns in the box.
- Point out non-count nouns that students already know. Examples: *butter, money, bread, love.*
- Have students read the second explanation and study the examples.
- To make sure students understand why the incorrect examples are wrong, ask *Why is "the" wrong in the first example?* (because non-count nouns cannot be preceded by *a, an,* or *the*) *Why is "Educations" and "are" wrong in the second example?* (because non-count nouns have no plural form and need a singular verb)

**Option:**  To check comprehension, write the following sentences on the board and ask students to correct the mistakes.  Have students compare answers with a partner. Then review as a class.  (1. <u>is</u> good news  2. are making <u>progress</u>  3. <u>peace</u> might be)  **[+5 minutes]**

 1. *There are good news in the newspaper today.*

 2. *Negotiators are making progresses in reaching an*

 3. *agreement, and the peace might be restored soon.*

 **Grammar Self-Checks**

## D  Complete each statement . . .

| Suggested teaching time: | 5 minutes |
|---|---|
| Your actual teaching time: | _____ |

- Do the first item with the class.
- Have students compare answers with a partner. Then review as a class.

## E  🎧 PRONUNCIATION
**(CD5, Track 8)**

| Suggested teaching time: | 5 minutes |
|---|---|
| Your actual teaching time: | _____ |

- First listening:  Have students listen and study the examples.
- Review the information in parentheses and point out how changing the stress in a sentence affects the meaning.
- Second listening:  Have students listen and repeat chorally.
- Pair work.  Tell students that the focus of this activity is to develop the skill of listening for meaning. Students should listen for and identify the information that is stressed.

**Challenge:**  To provide more practice, write on the board:

 1. *Did TOM buy a car?*   2. *Did Tom BUY a car?*

 3. *Did Tom buy a CAR?*   4. *Did Tom buy a SPORTS car?*

Pair work.  Ask students to write answers (in capital letters) for each of the questions based on the stressed information.  Do the first item with the class.  Point out the stress is on TOM, which means the speaker is surprised or clarifying that it was Tom who bought a car.  Write on the board: *No, ROD bought a car.* (Possible answers: 2. No, he RENTED a car. 3. No, he bought a CAT. 4. No, he bought a SMALL car.)
**[+10 minutes]**

 **Pronunciation Activities**

## CONVERSATION **PAIR WORK**

| Suggested teaching time: | 5–10 minutes |
|---|---|
| Your actual teaching time: | _____ |

- As students compare their answers, encourage them to give reasons why.  Examples: Student A:  *I think the first question is OK if you're not in a work situation.*  Student B:  *I think the second question is very personal. I think it's only OK to ask if you know someone well.*
- To get students ready for the role play, have students read the conversation model on page 100 again.  You may also want to have students listen to the model.
- Choose a more confident student and role-play a conversation.  Encourage students to ask follow-up questions.
- Make sure students play both roles.
- Walk around the room and provide help as needed. Encourage students to use the correct rhythm and intonation.

 **Pair Work Cards**

 **Learning Strategies**

## EXTRAS (optional)

**Grammar Booster**
**Workbook:** Exercises 4–9
**Copy & Go:**  Activity 33

 **Pronunciation Supplements**

**GRAMMAR.** **Non-count nouns for abstract ideas**

Nouns that represent abstract ideas are non-count nouns.

Remember: non-count nouns are neither singular nor plural.
They have no plural form, and they are not preceded by <u>the</u>, <u>a</u>,
or <u>an</u>. When a non-count noun is the subject of a sentence, use a singular verb.

> **Education is** an important issue.
> NOT ~~The~~ education is an important issue. NOT ~~Educations are~~ an important issue.

| Nouns for abstract ideas | | |
|---|---|---|
| advice | information | progress |
| education | justice | proof |
| health | news | time |
| help | peace | work |
| importance | poverty | |

**GRAMMAR BOOSTER**
**PAGE G15**
**For more ...**

 Complete each statement with the correct form of the nouns and verbs.

1. Our ____**advice**____ to you ____**is**____ to avoid discussing politics.
   <sub>advice / advices</sub>   <sub>is / are</sub>

2. ____**Poverty**____ ____**was**____ the topic of the international conference.
   <sub>Poverty / The poverty</sub>   <sub>was / were</sub>

3. Both candidates have programs for ____**health**____ and ____**education**____.
   <sub>the health / health</sub>   <sub>educations / education</sub>

4. There is no ____**proof**____ they've made ____**progress**____ in fighting ____**injustice**____.
   <sub>proof / proofs</sub>   <sub>a progress / progress</sub>   <sub>injustice / the injustice</sub>

5. Making ____**peace**____ takes a lot of ____**work**____ and a long time.
   <sub>peace / the peace</sub>   <sub>works / work</sub>

6. Good news ____**is**____ hard to find in the newspaper these days.
   <sub>is / are</sub>

🎧 **PRONUNCIATION.** **Stress to emphasize meaning.** **Listen and practice
the different intonations of this sentence.**

1. Are you in favor of censorship?        (normal stress)

2. **ARE** you in favor of censorship?        (I need to know whether you are or you aren't.)

3. Are **YOU** in favor of censorship?        (I'm surprised <u>you</u> would have that opinion.)

4. Are you in **FA**vor of censorship?        (I thought you were against it.)

5. Are you in favor of **CEN**sorship?        (Are you in favor of <u>that</u>?)

**Now, with a partner, take turns saying a sentence out loud. Your partner points to
the sentence you read and reads the meaning of that stress pattern.**

## CONVERSATION
## PAIR WORK

**Check the questions that you think are OK to ask someone you don't know well.
Compare your answers with a partner's. Do you agree?** Answers will vary.

☐ Are most people here liberal or conservative?      ☐ Who are you voting for?

☐ Are you liberal or conservative?      ☐ What do you think of the president /
                                               prime minister / king / queen?

☐ Who's going to win the election?

**Now role-play a conversation with someone visiting from another
country. Use the conversation model on page 100 as a guide.**

**CONTROLLED PRACTICE**

# Discuss Controversial Issues Politely

## 🎧 CONVERSATION MODEL Read and listen.

**A:** Are you in favor of capital punishment? **CN1**

**B:** Yes, I am. I believe if you kill someone you deserve to be killed. What about you?

**A:** Actually, I'm against the death penalty. I think it's wrong to take a life, no matter what.

**B:** Well, I guess we'll have to agree to disagree!

## 🎧 Rhythm and intonation practice

🎧 **Disagreement**
Really? I have to disagree with you there.
Do you think so? I'm not sure I agree.
Well, I'm afraid I don't agree.

🎧 **Agreement**
I agree with you on that one.
I couldn't agree more.
I couldn't have said it better myself.
That's exactly what I think.

**A** 🎧 **VOCABULARY. Some controversial issues.** Listen and practice. **CN2**

**CN1 Corpus Notes:** *Death penalty* is almost always preceded by *the* (the death penalty) but *capital punishment* stands alone. A common student error is to say or write *the capital punishment.*

**censorship of books and movies**

compulsory military service

**lowering the driving age**

**raising the voting age**

**prohibiting smoking indoors**

your own controversial issue:
_____

**B** 🎧 **LISTENING COMPREHENSION.** Listen to people's opinions about controversial issues. **Then listen again and complete each statement with <u>for</u> or <u>against</u>.**

1. She's ___for___ prohibiting smoking indoors.
2. He's ___against___ compulsory military service.
3. She's ___for___ raising the driving age.
4. He's ___for___ lowering the voting age.
5. She's ___for___ censorship of TV programs.

**C** **DISCUSSION.** Which of the people's opinions do you agree or disagree with? Give reasons.

**CN2 Corpus Notes:** *Prohibit* and *compulsory* are formal words that are used more frequently in writing than in speech. It is more common to say that something is *not allowed* or that someone *can't (do something)* than that something is *prohibited.* And it is more common to say that someone *has to (do something)* than that something is *compulsory.*

## LESSON 2 — *Discuss Controversial Issues Politely*

### 🎧 CONVERSATION **MODEL**
(CD5, Tracks 9, 11, 12)

| Suggested teaching time: | 5 minutes |
|---|---|
| Your actual teaching time: | _____ |

• After students read and listen, ask students to summarize how each woman defends her opinion. (Possible answer: Speaker A thinks there is never a good reason for killing someone. Speaker B believes the death penalty is a fair way / the right way to punish someone for killing another.)
• Point out that the expression *no matter what* means *in any or all circumstances or situations.*
• Have students listen and read the ways to agree and disagree in the small boxes. Then have them repeat.

**Language note:** Point out that *death penalty* (the legal punishment of being killed) and *capital punishment* are synonyms.

### 🎧 Rhythm and intonation practice
(CD5, Track 10)

| Suggested teaching time: | 5 minutes |
|---|---|
| Your actual teaching time: | _____ |

• Have students repeat each line chorally.
• Make sure students:
  ○ use rising intonation for *Are you in favor of capital punishment?*
  ○ use falling intonation for *What about you?*
  ○ stress *against*, to show their opinion in *I'm against the death penalty.*
  ○ use the following stress pattern:

**STRESS PATTERN**

**A:** Are you in favor of capital punishment?

**B:** Yes, I am. I believe if you kill someone you deserve to be killed. What about you?

**A:** Actually, I'm against the death penalty. I think it's wrong to take a life, no matter what.

**B:** Well, I guess we'll have to agree to disagree!

### 🅐 🎧 VOCABULARY
(CD5, Track 13)

| Suggested teaching time: | 5–10 minutes |
|---|---|
| Your actual teaching time: | _____ |

• Have students listen and study the phrases. Then have students listen and repeat chorally.

• To check comprehension, ask a question about each issue. Examples: *Do you know of any books or movies that were censored? Give an example of a country where military service is compulsory. What's the driving age in this country? When can people vote in this country? When did smoking become a controversial issue in this country?*
• Write the following in two columns on the board:
  *Personal and social problems   Environmental problems*
• Ask students to brainstorm (controversial) topics and write them in the correct column. Point out that students can mention issues in their own country or in other places. Help students with words they might not know in English. (Students may say: personal and social problems: divorce, abortion, euthanasia, drug addiction, discrimination, cloning, genetic manipulation; environmental problems: pollution, global warming, hunting, forest destruction, animal testing, nuclear waste)
• Take a poll and ask each student to say which (controversial) issue concerns him/her the most.

**Option:** Pair work. Student A makes a "position statement" for a controversial issue. Student B agrees or disagrees using the sentences and expressions from the boxes in the conversation model activity. Students shouldn't continue the conversation. Then switch roles. Examples: Student A: *I believe monarchies are the best form of government.* Student B: *Really? I have to disagree with you there.* Student C: *I think this country needs a radical change.* Student D: *I couldn't agree more.* **[+5 minutes]**

 **Vocabulary Cards**

### 🅑 🎧 LISTENING COMPREHENSION
(CD5, Track 14)

| Suggested teaching time: | 5–10 minutes |
|---|---|
| Your actual teaching time: | _____ |

• First have students listen and read the sentences.
• Then students listen again and complete each statement with *for* or *against.* You may want to stop after each conversation to allow students to write.
• Review as a class.

**Option:** Books closed. Have students listen to the conversations and write down the controversial issues people are talking about. Then have students open their books and check their answers by reading the issue in each item. **[+5 minutes]**

**AUDIOSCRIPT for Exercise B is on page T103.**

### 🅒 DISCUSSION

| Suggested teaching time: | 5 minutes |
|---|---|
| Your actual teaching time: | _____ |

• Group work. Form groups of three or four.
• Point out that students can give the same reasons the speakers in the conversations used.
• Take a poll of the class to find out what which issue is the most difficult to agree on.

**T102**

 **GRAMMAR**

| Suggested teaching time: | 10 minutes |
|---|---|
| Your actual teaching time: | _____ |

- Direct attention to the box and have students read the explanation and study the examples.

- Review that the infinitive form is *to* + the base form of the verb.

- Then have students study the lists of verbs in the small boxes. Encourage students to use the dictionary if necessary.

- Write on the board:
    1. I agreed <u>to plan</u> the party.
    2. I advised (him) <u>to stay</u> home.
    3. I pretended not <u>to see</u> her.
    4. I reminded (them) not <u>to be</u> late.

- Point out the objects (circled) in sentences 2 and 4.

- Point out that the negative is formed by adding *not* before the infinitive.

**Option:** Write on the board:
    1. I decided _____ the train.
    2. I reminded _____ the invitations.
    3. I can't afford _____ that car.
    4. I warned _____ to strangers.
    5. I convinced _____ on holiday with us.

To check comprehension, ask students to complete the statements. (Answers may vary.) Students should decide whether to use an infinitive or an object + infinitive. Have students compare answers with a partner and review as a class. (Possible answers: I decided (not) to take the train. 2. I reminded him to send the invitations. 3. I can't afford to buy that car. 4. I warned her not to talk to strangers. 5. I convinced them to come on holiday with us.) **[+5 minutes]**

> **Language note:** Some verbs are followed by an infinitive or an object and an infinitive, such as *ask, choose, expect, help, promise, would like,* etc. Examples: *I want to study medicine. I want her to study medicine.* See page 130 in the Appendix.

 **Grammar Self-Checks**

 **PAIR WORK**

| Suggested teaching time: | 5 minutes |
|---|---|
| Your actual teaching time: | _____ |

- Review the example first.
- Have students compare answers with a partner. Then review as a class.

## CONVERSATION **PAIR WORK**

| Suggested teaching time: | 5–10 minutes |
|---|---|
| Your actual teaching time: | _____ |

- To get students ready for the activity, have students read the conversation model on page 102 again. You may also want to have students listen to the model and the ways to agree and disagree.

- Review the issues in the box. Students may also want to review the issue they added in Exercise A on page 102.

- Review the ways to express opinions. You may want to ask students to repeat chorally.

- Choose a more confident student and role-play a conversation. Encourage students to ask follow-up questions.

- Make sure each student plays both roles.

- Walk around the room and provide help as needed. Encourage students to use the correct rhythm and intonation.

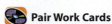 **Pair Work Cards**

## EXTRAS (optional)

**Grammar Booster**
**Workbook: Exercises 10–14**
**Copy & Go: Activity 34**

---

**AUDIOSCRIPT**

**AUDIOSCRIPT for Exercise B, page T102.**

[M1 = French, F3 = Indian]

**F1:** Oh, no! I can't believe how inconsiderate people are. My eyes are burning, and I can't taste the food. I really think smoking should be outlawed in restaurants.

**M1:** I'm a pacifist. I am against all wars, no matter what. I really think governments would be less likely to go to war if there weren't so many soldiers to send! Let's change the law so the government doesn't have such a large military force.

**F2:** Look at this article in the newspaper. It says research has proved that sixteen-year-olds are not mature enough to drive cars. People shouldn't be permitted to drive until they're at least eighteen. I think we should change the driving age.

**M2:** I think it's ridiculous that people can go in the army at eighteen but they can't vote until they're twenty-one. Eighteen-year-olds are smart enough to vote.

**F3:** Some of the things you see on TV these days are horrible. I don't want my children watching so much violence and immoral behavior. Can't we stop the TV stations from showing such terrible stuff?

## D ▸ GRAMMAR. Verbs followed by objects and infinitives

**Certain verbs can be followed by infinitives, but some verbs must be followed by an object before the infinitive.**

The newspaper reminded **all 18-year-olds** to vote.

We urged **them** to write letters against the death penalty.

The law requires **everyone** to wear a seatbelt.

**Verbs followed directly by an infinitive**

| | | | |
|---|---|---|---|
| agree | decide | manage | pretend |
| appear | deserve. | need | refuse |
| can't afford | hope | offer | seem |
| can't wait | learn | plan | |

**Verbs followed by an object before an infinitive**

| | | | | |
|---|---|---|---|---|
| advise | convince | permit | request | urge |
| allow | encourage | persuade | require | warn |
| cause | invite | remind | tell | |

More complete lists can be found on page 130.

GRAMMAR BOOSTER

**PAGE G16**
**For more …**

## E ▸ PAIR WORK. Using an object before the infinitive, change each sentence from the passive voice to the active voice. Use the phrase in parentheses as the subject of the sentence.

> **"** The teachers **persuaded the school administration to vote** against the new rules. **"**

1. The school administration was persuaded (by the teachers) to vote against the new rules.

2. We were reminded (by our friends) to vote early.
   *Our friends reminded us to vote early.*

3. I was invited (by the town) to give a speech about violence in movies.
   *The town invited me to give a speech about violence in movies.*

4. The voters were convinced (by accident statistics) to change the driving age. *Accident statistics convinced voters to change the driving age.*

5. Citizens are expected (by the government) to register for military service at age 18. *The government expects citizens to register for military service at age 18.*

6. People are not permitted (by the city) to smoke in public buildings.
   *The city does not permit people to smoke in public buildings.*

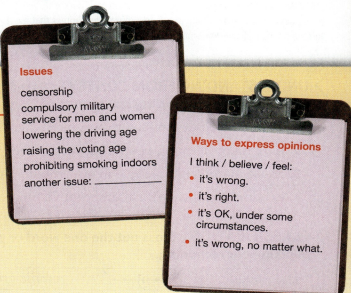

## CONVERSATION ▸ PAIR WORK

**Express your opinion about a controversial issue. Agree or disagree politely. Use these issues or another controversial issue you have an opinion about.** *Answers will vary.*
**Start like this:**

**A:** Are you in favor of _____?

**B:** _____ …

**Continue the conversation in your own way.**

**Issues**

censorship
compulsory military service for men and women
lowering the driving age
raising the voting age
prohibiting smoking indoors
another issue: _____

**Ways to express opinions**

I think / believe / feel:
- it's wrong.
- it's right.
- it's OK, under some circumstances.
- it's wrong, no matter what.

**CN Corpus Notes:** Of the verbs on this list, learners make the most errors with *permit, allow,* and *advise.* Be sure to remind students that these verbs are immediately followed by an object, not the infinitive.

CONTROLLED PRACTICE

# 3 Propose Solutions to Global Problems

**A** **READING WARM-UP.** What do you think are the most serious problems in the world today?

**B** 🎧 **READING.** Read about some issues people are talking about. Are these problems growing or decreasing in the world today?

## The following issues were most frequently mentioned in a global survey about current world problems.

### Poverty

Approximately one-fifth of the world's population, over one billion people, earns less than US$ 1.00 a day. Each day, over a billion people in the world lack basic food supplies. And each day, 35,000 children under the age of five die of starvation or preventable infectious disease.

### Corruption

People all over the world complain about the corruption of police, government officials, and business leaders. Three examples of corruption are:

> a police officer takes money [a bribe] from a driver so he doesn't give the driver a ticket for speeding

> a public official gives a government contract to a company in which he or she has a financial interest

> a company that wants to do business with a government agency offers a public official money or a gift to choose that company for the job

Some people feel that power promotes corruption and that corruption is just an unavoidable part of human nature. But everyone agrees that it is a terrible problem all over the world.

### Terrorism

Every day we see or hear about terrorism and terrible violent acts committed against innocent people for religious or political reasons. Many ask why terrorism is on the rise.

Some social scientists believe that television and movies may contribute to growing anger. They claim that some people may feel frustrated and powerless when they measure their lives against the lives of extremely wealthy people they see in the media.

### Racism and ethnic discrimination

Racism and ethnic discrimination exist in many places. These two terrible problems cause human rights violations all over the world. But what causes racism and ethnic discrimination?

At the core, both result from the belief that genetic or cultural differences produce the superiority or inferiority of one group over another. When taken to the extreme, some racists justify the domination and destruction of groups they consider to be either superior or inferior. Although we like to believe that humans have progressed away from such discredited ideas, the history of the last hundred years has seen some of the worst examples of racism and ethnic discrimination in history: the European Holocaust, South African apartheid, and massacres in Eastern Europe and the Sudan are only a few of the tragic events of recent times.

**C** **UNDERSTANDING FROM CONTEXT.** Based on the reading, write the problems described by the following statements.

1. lack of necessary money to survive: _____poverty_____
2. judging or harming people because of their genetic heritage: _racism / ethnic discrimination_
3. abuse of power by people in government or business: _____corruption_____
4. extreme violence toward innocent victims: _____terrorism_____

**D** **CLASSIFICATION.** Cross out the one word or phrase that is unrelated to the others. Explain your reasoning.

| | | | | |
|---|---|---|---|---|
| 1. | people | ~~politics~~ | ethnic groups | races |
| 2. | money | property | income | ~~racism~~ |
| 3. | bribe | corruption | discrimination | ~~money~~ |
| 4. | hunger | starvation | ~~domination~~ | lack of food |
| 5. | racism | ~~business~~ | discrimination | prejudice |

**LESSON**

# 3 Propose Solutions to Global Problems

## A READING WARM-UP

| Suggested teaching time: | 5 minutes |
|---|---|
| Your actual teaching time: | _____ |

• Ask students to brainstorm problems they consider serious in today's world and make a list on the board. Examples: *wars, drug abuse, global warming, pollution, overpopulation, nuclear weapons, destruction of natural resources, hunger, infectious diseases, endangered species,* etc.

## B 🎧 READING

**(CD5, Track 15)**

| Suggested teaching time: | 10–15 minutes |
|---|---|
| Your actual teaching time: | _____ |

• Ask students to scan the text and name the four problems discussed in the article. (poverty, corruption, terrorism, racism and ethnic discrimination)

• As students read the article, encourage them to underline important information that describes each problem.

• Group work. Form small groups. Encourage students to also talk about the information they undelined and the information they didn't know.

**Challenge:** Use this option if you want to do a listening activity. Books closed. Draw the following chart without the answers on the board. Ask students to complete the chart with as much information as they can. Then have students read the text to check their information. **[+10 minutes]**

| Causes | World Problems | Results |
|---|---|---|
| earning very little money | Poverty | lack of basic food supplies; starvation; disease |
| abusing / misusing power | Corruption | people in power act in their own interests |
| political or religious beliefs; rising anger | Terrorism | violent acts against innocent people |
| believing someone is inferior or superior | Racism and ethnic discrimination | human rights are violated |

 **Graphic Organizers**

**Language note:** Students may need help with the following words: *starvation* (suffering or death because of lack of food); *unavoidable* (impossible to prevent); *powerless* (unable to stop or control something because you do not have the power or strength to do it); *ethnic discrimination* (treating the people of a particular race, nation, or tribe differently from other people or in an unfair way); *discredited* (ideas that people don't believe in anymore)

**Culture note:** European Holocaust: murder of six million Jews and others by the Nazis in World War II; South African apartheid: system of discrimination in which whites ran the government and controlled all the wealth; massacres in Easter Europe: killings of ethnic groups in Bosnia, Kosovo, Serbia, Croatia; massacres in Sudan: killings of indigenous African populations.

 **Learning Strategies**

## C UNDERSTANDING FROM CONTEXT

| Suggested teaching time: | 5 minutes |
|---|---|
| Your actual teaching time: | _____ |

• Encourage students to do the items they know first.

• Have students compare answers with a partner. Then review as a class.

 **Extra Reading Comprehension Activities**

## D CLASSIFICATION

| Suggested teaching time: | 5–10 minutes |
|---|---|
| Your actual teaching time: | _____ |

• Review the example first. Elicit or explain that *politics* does not refer to people.

• Have students compare answers with a partner.

• To review, ask students to give the reason for each answer. (Possible reasons: 2. other words are related to money 3. other words are things that are illegal 4. other words are related to not having food 5. other words refer to negative attitudes / actions against people)

**Language note:** If necessary, clarify the meanings of *domination* (power or control over someone or something); *prejudice* (an unreasonable dislike and distrust of people who are different from you in some way, especially because of their race, sex, religion, etc.)

# TOP NOTCH **INTERACTION**

| Suggested teaching time: | 20–25 minutes |
|---|---|
| Your actual teaching time: | _____ |

## STEP 1. Which world issues . . . ?

• Walk around the room and provide help as needed.

• Take a poll to find out which issue ranked highest for importance and which for difficulty to accomplish.

## STEP 2. PAIR WORK.

• Review the example first.

• Point out that students can include solutions for local or global problems.

• (Students may say: reducing poverty and hunger: help poor countries grow, raise money for the poor, teach the poor how to utilize their land; preventing terrorism: change foreign policy, reduce poverty, promote freedom in all countries, guarantee human rights in all countries; avoiding war: promote peace, respect others; ending or reducing corruption: promote moral values, enforce stricter legal punishments; wiping out racism and ethnic discrimination: teach children to respect others, teach children to value diversity; protecting human rights: teach democratic values, help international organizations that protect them.)

• Walk around the room and provide help as needed.

## STEP 3. DISCUSSION.

• Before students begin, ask them to review the ways to agree and disagree on page 102 (conversation model). You may want to ask them to review the non-count nouns for abstract ideas in the Grammar box on page 101.

• Pair work. Remind students to acknowledge their partner's opinion (agree / disagree), give their reasons, and state their own opinion and reason(s). Examples: Student A: *I'm very concerned about poverty and hunger. I can't believe people are dying of starvation and others throw away food.* Student B: *I agree with you on that one. Governments could spend less money on wars and use that money to help reduce this problem.* OR Student C: *To me, the most important issue is preventing terrorism.* Student D: *Really? I'm afraid I don't agree. Many more people die because of hunger and even ethnic discrimination!* Student C: *That may be true, but . . .*

• Encourage students to use their notes from Step 2 to compare their suggestions for solutions.

**Option:** Choose problems from the list in Step 1 and ask various groups for solutions they discussed. Make a list on the board. **[+5 minutes]**

## STEP 4. WRITING.

• Write the following on the board:

  *I'm deeply concerned about . . .*
  *The world problem that worries me the most is . . .*
  *In my opinion, _____ is an important issue that needs the world's immediate attention.*
  *People have strong opinions about _____.*
  *Personally, I believe . . .*

• Encourage students to use the sentence starters.

• Walk around the room and provide help as needed.

**Challenge:** Student project. Ask students to do research, for example, on the Internet, to find out what an international organization—for example, the United Nations or the World Bank—is doing to try to solve one of the world problems they discussed. Ask them to write notes so that they can then report to the class about their findings. Encourage them to explain whether they agree or disagree with what the organization is doing and give supporting reasons. **[times will vary]**

🔘 **Writing Process Worksheets**

## EXTRAS (optional)

**Workbook:** Exercises 15, 16
**Copy & Go:** Activity 35

**STEP 1.** **Which world issues concern you the most? Put this list in order of importance for you, from 1 to 6, with 1 being the most important. Then rank them in order of difficulty to accomplish from 1 to 6, with 1 being the most difficult.** Answers will vary.

**Order of importance**

**Order of difficulty to accomplish**

○ reducing poverty and hunger ○

○ preventing terrorism ○

○ avoiding war ○

○ ending or reducing corruption ○

○ wiping out racism and ethnic discrimination ○

○ protecting human rights ○

**STEP 2.** **PAIR WORK.** **On your notepads, write some approaches you think would be effective for each problem. If you know a place that has that problem, write the name of the place.** Answers will vary.

| problem | place | possible approaches |
|---------|-------|---------------------|
| reducing hunger/poverty | Haiti | collect packages of food to send |

| problem | place | possible approaches |
|---------|-------|---------------------|
| | | |
| | | |
| | | |
| | | |
| | | |

**STEP 3.** **DISCUSSION.** **Discuss world or local problems with your classmates. Do you all have the same concerns? Do you agree on the solutions?**

**STEP 4.** **WRITING.** **Write about one of the problems you discussed. In the first paragraph, identify the problem. Talk about the place, giving as many details as you can. In the second paragraph, write about the solution. Use your notepad and your discussion notes for support.**

FREE PRACTICE

# Debate the Pros and Cons of Issues

**A** 🎧 **VOCABULARY. Ways to disagree politely. Listen and practice.**

1. "I think smoking is a disgusting habit."

"**That may be true, but** if you only smoke in your own house, you're not hurting anyone but yourself."

2. "I think more people should be active in politics. That way we would have better governments."

"**I see what you mean, but** it's not realistic to expect everyone to care."

3. "Our president is doing an excellent job."

"**Well, on the one hand,** he's not corrupt. **But on the other hand,** he hasn't done much to improve the country."

4. "I think we should just vote against everyone who's in office now. That's a good way to get change."

"**That's one way to look at it, but** how do we know inexperienced candidates will be any better than what we already have?"

**B** **PAIR WORK. Take turns saying and responding to each opinion below. Use the phrases in the vocabulary above and the expressions from page 102 to agree or disagree.** Answers will vary.

1. "Actually, in some countries, dictatorship has helped stop corruption."

"I couldn't agree with you more. Countries with dictatorships are better off." **OR** "That may be true, but no one should have to live under a dictatorship."

2. "There is no real democracy. All governments are controlled by a few powerful people."

3. "I think moderates are the only people you can trust in government."

4. "I'm not going to vote. All the candidates are corrupt."

**C** 🎧 **LISTENING COMPREHENSION. Listen to three conversations about politics. Then listen again and work in pairs. Partner A: Summarize the argument in favor. Partner B: Summarize the argument against.** Answers may vary. Possible answers include:

1. **about dictatorship**
   Partner A (pro): Some countries need dictatorships. They're effective, efficient, and they make people live in peace.
   Partner B (con): They are morally wrong; people have no rights and they cannot replace the government if it does something terrible.

2. **about democracy**
   Partner A (pro): People have the power to vote for who they like.
   Partner B (con): One of the disadvantages of a democracy is that we can get a president who only has a small percentage of the votes; that is minority rule. Majority rule is better.

3. **about monarchy**
   Partner A (pro): Without it, you'd lose your tradition and your history.
   Partner B (con): Monarchs aren't the real government; they cost a lot of money that could be used to help people.

# LESSON 4
# *Debate the Pros and Cons of Issues*

## A 🎧 VOCABULARY
**(CD5, Track 16)**

| | |
|---|---|
| Suggested teaching time: | 5–10 minutes |
| Your actual teaching time: | _____ |

- Have students listen and study the bolded phrases. Then have students listen and repeat chorally.

- Point out that the listener uses these phrases to tell the speaker he / she is disagreeing with the speaker's opinion.

- Pair work. Students take turns making a statement and disagreeing politely.

**Language note:** Point out that *on the one hand* is always used together with *on the other hand*.

## B PAIR WORK

| | |
|---|---|
| Suggested teaching time: | 10 minutes |
| Your actual teaching time: | _____ |

- Review the example answers first. Point out that students can agree or disagree.

- You may want to ask students to review ways to agree and disagree on page 102.

## C 🎧 LISTENING COMPREHENSION
**(CD5, Track 17)**

| | |
|---|---|
| Suggested teaching time: | 10–15 minutes |
| Your actual teaching time: | _____ |

- Pre-listening. Books closed. Ask students to listen for the main idea. Have them write down which form of government is discussed in each conversation. Then have students compare their answers with the items in Exercise C.

- Form pairs. Make sure students know which letter they are—A or B.

- Point out that students will hear arguments for and against, but they will only write notes for their assigned view (pro or con). You may want to point out that the speakers sometimes mention a good point for the opposing view even as they are making the opposite argument.

- Stop the recording after each conversation to allow students time to write.

- To review, combine two pairs and have them compare information.

- Then ask various students to state their information. Encourage the class to add anything that was not included.

- You may want to write the information on the board.

🔵 **Learning Strategies**

---

**AUDIOSCRIPT**

CONVERSATION 1
**M:** You know: I feel that some countries don't deserve democracy. The citizens are just incapable of living in peace.
**F:** Well, what form of government would be best for them?
**M:** I hate to say it, but some places need dictatorships. Even military dictatorships. They're effective. They're efficient. They make people live in peace.
**F:** I totally disagree. I believe dictatorships are morally wrong. The people have no rights in a dictatorship. If the government does something terrible, the people can't replace it.

CONVERSATION 2 [F = Australian]
**F:** Which party are you going to vote for in the election?
**M:** The Liberal Party.
**F:** Why?
**M:** Because they want to change the election laws so there can be only two candidates for president.
**F:** But that's not democratic. This is a democracy. The people have the power. They can vote for who they like. That's what's good about democracy.
**M:** That's one way to look at it. But one of the disadvantages of democracy is that we can get a president who only has a small percentage of the votes. We're supposed to have majority rule, not minority rule.

CONVERSATION 3 [F = Dutch]
**M:** How do you feel about the royal family?
**F:** Me? Well, on the one hand, I like the royals as people—they do a lot of important charity work, like visiting sick children and raising money for hospitals. But on the other hand, I believe that in this day and age, monarchy is wrong. The monarchs aren't the real government and they cost us a lot of money.
**M:** That's true, but if you didn't have the monarchy, you'd lose your tradition and your history.
**F:** I see what you mean, but with all the problems we have, we should use all that money to help people with their problems.

# TOP NOTCH **INTERACTION**

| Suggested teaching time: | 20–25 minutes |
|---|---|
| Your actual teaching time: | _____ |

## STEP 1. As a class . . .

- Ask students for suggestions on local political issues or other issues to add to the choices.
- Take a poll to see which issue will be debated.
- Note: If you think your students will find it difficult to debate, use Steps 1 and 2 to prepare students for role plays using the same topics.

## STEP 2. PAIR WORK.

- Encourage students to use the vocabulary and grammar from this unit to write reasons. Tell students to include some specific examples to support their views.
- As students write, walk around the room and provide help as needed.

## STEP 3. DEBATE.

- Before dividing the class in half, point out that students will be supporting one of the arguments regardless of their personal opinion.
- Encourage a friendly and polite debate.
- Review the language in the NEED HELP? section.
- After a student expresses his / her views, you may want to ask students who want to agree or disagree to first put up their hands and then speak.
- Note: If students are doing role plays, have them work in groups of two or three. Ask them to do a role play for each topic. Then ask various groups to perform one of their role plays in front of the class.

## EXTRAS (optional)

**Workbook:** Exercises 17, 18
**Copy & Go:** Activity 36

### AUDIOSCRIPT for Exercise B, page T100

CONVERSATION 1
**M:** I'm completely against marriage. I don't think a piece of paper means anything!
**F:** What piece of paper are you talking about?
**M:** A marriage license. What good is it? Everyone today is getting divorced anyway. I think we should simply end the institution of marriage! Marriage is a thing of the past.
**F:** Those are pretty extreme ideas.

CONVERSATION 2
**M:** Well, you're finally old enough to vote, Marianne. Who are you going to vote for?
**F:** I'm going to vote for the Constitution Party.
**M:** The Constitution Party. Wow, is that a surprise! You're so young. Don't you want to see change? The Constitution Party just has the same old ideas election after election.
**F:** So? What's wrong with the same ideas? They're better than some of the new ones! I think it's safer to stick with policies that have been successful. If it isn't broke, don't fix it.

CONVERSATION 3
**M:** You know—I used to be afraid of change. I thought there was only one way to look at things. That the way we did things when I was young was the only way.
**F:** How have you changed?
**M:** Well, for instance, I used to think there should be certain roles for men and certain roles for women. Now I've come to think I was silly.
**F:** You mean you're turning out to be a radical in your old age?
**M:** Come on. I'm no radical, just more thoughtful. I'm not in favor of big changes, but a little change is good. Especially when it makes people more free.
**F:** That sounds reasonable.

CONVERSATION 4
**F:** I can't imagine bringing children into this 21st–century world.
**M:** What do you mean?
**F:** Well, there are no rules anymore. You can buy anything . . . anywhere. You can see all kinds of disgusting stuff on TV and in the movies: violence, sex, whatever! Anything goes. There's no respect.
**M:** I can't believe anyone so young can have such old ideas!
**F:** I think we should bring back some of the old laws.

CONVERSATION 5
**F:** Who are you going to vote for?
**M:** I think I'm going to vote for Bartlett Nardone.
**F:** I thought you liked Al Smith.
**M:** No. He's too liberal for me. But Nardone, he's not so extreme. He's a pretty sensible guy.

# TOP NOTCH
## INTERACTION • *That's one way to look at it!*

**STEP 1.** As a class, choose an issue that you'd like to debate.

Democracy

Censorship

Capital Punishment

Your <u>own</u> local political issue: _____

**STEP 2. PAIR WORK.** On your notepads, write arguments for and against. Answers will vary.

arguments in favor:
_____
_____
_____

arguments against:
_____
_____
_____

**STEP 3. DEBATE.** Divide the class in half, with one side in favor and the other side against. Take turns presenting your views. Sit or stand with the people who have the same argument as you. Take turns and disagree politely.

NEED HELP? **Here's language you already know:**

**Discuss controversies politely**

Are you in favor of ____?
That's a good question!
It's not cool to ____.

I tend to be a little opinionated.

I'm opposed to ____ / in favor of ____.
I think / believe / feel
  • it's wrong.
  • it's right.
  • it's OK under some circumstances.
    • it's wrong no matter what.

**Express agreement**

I agree with you on that one.
I couldn't agree more.
I couldn't have said it better myself.
That's exactly what I think.

**Express disagreement**

We'll have to agree to disagree!
I have to disagree with you there.
I'm not sure I agree.
I'm afraid I don't agree.

107

FREE PRACTICE

# UNIT 9
# CHECKPOINT

**A** 🎧 **LISTENING COMPREHENSION.** Listen to the excerpts from a radio news program. Write the four problems being reported.

1. fighting on the border between the Sorindian and Ramay provinces

2. a package of explosives was left at the central post office

3. large numbers of homeless poor

4. a police captain accused of taking bribes from engineers

**B** Using an object before the infinitive, change each sentence from the passive voice to the active voice. Use the phrase in parentheses as the subject of the sentence.

1. The president is not allowed (by the law) to change the Constitution.

   The law doesn't allow the president to change the Constitution.

2. Presidents are required (by the Constitution) to leave office after two terms.

   The Constitution prohibits presidents from serving more than eight years.

3. The candidates were invited (by the election committee) to speak about their policies.

   The election committee invited the candidates to speak about their policies.

4. We were advised (by all our friends) not to be disappointed about the election.

   All our friends advised us not to be disappointed about the election.

**C** Complete the paragraph about an election.

Many _____candidates_____ running for election make _____promises_____ about
     1. candidate / candidates                      2. promise / promises
_____education_____. But _____progress_____ comes slowly, and _____information_____
3. education / the education   4. progress / the progress        5. information / informations
_____is_____ hard to get. Voters would like to see _____proof_____ that their _____advice_____
6. is / are                                    7. proof / the proof              8. advice / advices
_____is_____ being followed. For instance, we are just now receiving _____news_____ of
9. is /are                                                            10. the news / news
education statistics and _____it's_____ not very good. _____Help_____ is needed, and
                          11. it's / they're                 12. Help / The help
_____time_____ is necessary to improve our schools.
13. the time / time

**D** **WRITING.** Write about one of the following issues: compulsory military service, capital punishment, censorship of books and movies. Include both the pros and cons of the issue.

**TOP NOTCH PROJECT**
Find articles in the newspaper about world problems. Describe the problem and suggest solutions. Post your solutions on a bulletin board.

**TOP NOTCH WEBSITE**
For Unit 9 online activities, visit the *Top Notch* Companion Website at www.longman.com/topnotch.

# UNIT 9 CHECKPOINT

## A  LISTENING COMPREHENSION
**(CD5, Track 18)**

| | |
|---|---|
| Suggested teaching time: | 10 minutes |
| Your actual teaching time: | _____ |

- Pre-listening: To review, ask students to give examples of world problems. Examples: *wars, corruption, terrorism, nuclear weapons, poverty, pollution, drug abuse, ethnic discrimination.* (pages 102, 104, and 105)

- Point out that in the listening, students will hear descriptions of several problems. Students are listening to understand meaning from context. Encourage them to make notes.

- You may want to pause to allow students time to write.

- Have students compare answers with a partner.

- Review as a class.

### AUDIOSCRIPT

**F:** Good evening. Fighting has broken out again tonight on the border between the Sorindian and Ramay provinces. Ethnic Sorindians say they are not permitted to observe their dietary laws and that their children are not permitted to wear traditional dress at school.

On another note, a package containing a large amount of explosive material was discovered at the central post office today. Authorities are searching for the person or persons who left it in the men's restroom.

In the central city, volunteers are opening soup kitchens to feed the large numbers of homeless poor who have recently arrived from the countryside. The government is making funds available to help this growing population.

And finally, a police captain in Spartock has been accused of taking bribes to permit engineers to build buildings that don't conform to safe construction laws. A report will be issued tomorrow.

## B  Using an object ...

| | |
|---|---|
| Suggested teaching time: | 5–10 minutes |
| Your actual teaching time: | _____ |

- Review the example first.

- Have students compare answers with a partner.

- To review, have various students read their sentences out loud. Make necessary corrections.

## C  Complete the paragraph ...

| | |
|---|---|
| Suggested teaching time: | 5 minutes |
| Your actual teaching time: | _____ |

- You may want to do the first item with the class.

- Have students compare answers with a partner. Then review as a class.

## D WRITING

| | |
|---|---|
| Suggested teaching time: | 10–15 minutes |
| Your actual teaching time: | _____ |

- Draw the following diagram of scales on the board:

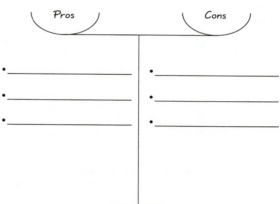

###  Graphic Organizers

- As a pre-writing activity, have students choose an issue and use the scales to write notes about the pros and cons.

- Encourage students to finish their paragraph with their opinion of whether they are for or against it.

### Writing Process Worksheets

### *TOP NOTCH* PROJECT

**Idea:** Ask students to bring in interesting articles about world problems. If students don't have access to English newspapers, tell them to visit the BBC or CNN websites on the Internet. Group work. Form groups of four. Ask the members of each group to scan the articles and then choose one for their project. Ask students to write a short report that includes a brief description of the problem and some solutions.

# UNIT WRAP-UP

| | |
|---|---|
| Suggested teaching time: | 15–20 minutes |
| Your actual teaching time: | _____ |

## Vocabulary

- Pair work. Encourage students to make a list of issues.

- Review as class.

**Your students can say . . .**

People at the top right-hand corner: corruption; Woman pointing to the newspaper: terrorism, poverty, ethnic discrimination, capital punishment, compulsory military service, censorship, raising the voting age, lowering the voting age, prohibiting smoking indoors. People watching TV: election candidates, political parties

## Social Language

- Pair work. Ask students to create one conversation. Then students should change roles and create another conversation.

**Your students can say . . .**

**A:** Do you mind if I ask you something? **B:** Of course not. What's up? **A:** Are you in favor of democracy? **B:** Yes, I am. I believe it's the best form of government. What about you? **A:** I'm not sure. I think people may need an authoritative government. Otherwise, they abuse the freedom they have. **A:** Really? I have to disagree with you there.

**A:** Are you in favor of capital punishment? **B:** No, I'm not. I think it's wrong to take a life. What about you? **A:** Actually, I think it's OK, under some circumstances. If the crime was very serious, the criminal deserves to be killed. **A:** Well, I guess we'll have to agree to disagree.

**A:** Which party are you going to vote for in the next election? **B:** The Conservative Party. **A:** Why? **B:** I don't want to risk changes. Things are not so bad after all. **A:** Well, that's one way to look at it, but if we don't take risks, things will never get better.

**A:** I'm concerned about so much corruption. I think we need stricter laws to reduce it. **B:** I see what you mean, but we also need to go back to the old moral values. People seem to have forgotten about them. **A:** I couldn't agree more.

**Challenge: This candidate cares.** Pair work. Ask students to role-play a conversation between the election candidate and the TV reporter. The TV reporter asks the candidate how his party is planning to approach different world issues. Encourage students to use the vocabulary and grammar for this unit. **[+10 minutes]**

**Individual oral progress check (optional)**

- Use the illustration on page 109. Encourage the student to use material (vocabulary, grammar, rhythm and intonation) practiced in this unit.

- Evaluate the student on correctness and intelligibility.

- Tell the student to point to the picture and say the world issues the people might be talking about. Examples: *corruption, democracy, political parties, terrorism.*

- Point to the two women talking to each other. Tell the student that they are discussing a controversial issue and that together you are going to role-play a conversation between them. Start the conversation. Example: T: *Are you in favor of compulsory military service.* S: *Yes, I am. I think we need to protect ourselves, and we should have soldiers to defend ourselves. What about you?* T: *Actually, I'm against it. I think there shouldn't be any wars. If countries wouldn't fight wars, they wouldn't need soldiers.* S: *Well, I guess we'll have to agree to disagree.*

- Open your book to page 103 and point to the boxes of verbs in Exercise D. Tell the student to look at the picture on this page (109) and say what the people are doing, using objects and / or infinitives. Tell the student to use at least two verbs from each list. Encourage the student to use his / her imagination. Examples: *She's warning her not to vote for the Blue Party. He's advising her not to take a bribe. He's planning to return to Senegal after the elections.*

 **Cumulative Vocabulary Activities**

 You may wish to use the video and activity worksheets for Unit 9 at this point.

 **Complete Assessment Package**
**Unit 9 Achievement Test**

## UNIT WRAP-UP

- **Vocabulary.** What do you think the people are talking about in each conversation?

- **Social Language.** Role-play polite political discussions for the people. Agree and disagree.

**Now I can ...**

☐ ask if it's OK to discuss a topic.
☐ discuss controversial issues politely.
☐ propose solutions to global problems.
☐ debate the pros and cons of issues.

# UNIT 10

# Enjoying the World

**UNIT GOALS**

1 Warn about a possible risk
2 Describe where a place is located
3 Describe a natural setting
4 Debate about development

 **TOPIC PREVIEW.** Are you good at reading maps? Study the map.

COSTA RICA

**Mountain Ranges**
1 Guanacaste Range
2 Central Volcanic Range
3 Talamanca Range
▲ = Volcano
● = City
★ = Capital City

**National Parks**
4 La Amistad
5 Chirripó
6 Corcovado
7 Braulio Carrillo
8 Santa Rosa
9 Tortuguero

```
0        50        100 kilometers
0        31        62 miles
```

 Use the map to answer the questions about Costa Rica.

1. What's the capital city? San José
2. What two bodies of water are on either coast of Costa Rica?
   The Caribbean Sea and the Pacific Ocean
3. What two countries share a border with Costa Rica? Nicaragua and Panama
4. What's the largest national park? La Amistad
5. What's the largest lake in Costa Rica? Lake Arenal
6. Approximately how far is Puntarenas from San José? About 80 km, or about 48 miles
7. In which mountain range is San José located? Central Volcanic Range

# UNIT 10

# Enjoying the World

##  TOPIC PREVIEW

| Suggested teaching time: | 10–15 minutes |
|---|---|
| Your actual teaching time: | _____ |

- Ask *Which countries are shown on the (larger) map?* (Nicaragua, Costa Rica, Panama) *Where is Costa Rica?* (in Central America) Note: If necessary, direct students' attention to the smaller map at the top right-hand corner.

- As students study the map and the reference box, encourage them to use the pictures to work out the meaning of unknown words.

- To check comprehension, say *Name some cities on this map.* (Liberia, La Fortuna, Puntarenas, Puerto Limón, San José) *What does a small star indicate?* (the capital city) *What symbol do volcanoes have?* (a triangle) *What's a mountain range?* (a group of mountains) *What can you say about the national parks?* (They cover large areas. They are mostly in the mountains.)

- Direct students' attention to the compass above the box of symbols. Have students repeat chorally *North, South, East, West*.

- Point out the scale for distance under the box of symbols.

> **Culture note:** If your students are not familiar with Costa Rica, you may want to share the following information. Costa Rica, "Rich Coast," is a tropical country with an incredible variety of habitats and microclimates. Many of the habitats are under protective status; more than 24 national parks cover 21% of the country. The economy is based on agriculture (coffee and bananas), electronics exports, and tourism. Over a million people visit Costa Rica annually. It is a popular spot for eco-tourists, who come to see the diverse flora and fauna—mountains, rainforests, volcanoes, 850 species of birds, and 200 mammal species!

##  Use the map . . .

| Suggested teaching time: | 10–15 minutes |
|---|---|
| Your actual teaching time: | _____ |

- Have students compare answers with a partner.

- For question 6, point out students should work out the approximate distance using the scale.

- Review as a class.

- Pair work. Student A describes a location on the map using points on the compass, distance from the scale, etc. Student B guesses. Example: Student A: *This city is south of Braulio Carrillo.* Student B: *The capital city, San José.* Student B: *It's a large area and there probably aren't buildings and roads. It's between Coronado Bay and the Gulf of Dulce.* Student A: *The national park, Corcovado.*

 **Learning Strategies**

## C  SOUND BITES

(CD5, Track 19)

| Suggested teaching time: | 10 minutes |
|---|---|
| Your actual teaching time: | _____ |

- After students read and listen, ask *What's the coincidence?* (David just visited the same place that Carlo wants to go visit.) *What's David's opinion about Carlo visiting both places in the same day?* (David doesn't think it's a problem.)

- Point out the word *warning* and ask students to give you examples of warning symbols or information they see or hear in everyday life. Examples: *Walk / Don't walk* signs, red traffic lights, stop signs, etc.

- Write on the board:
  *You wouldn't happen to know anything about _____, would you?*

- Pair work. Have students take turns asking each other about different places and events. Example: Student A: *. . . about nice places to go hiking . . .* Student B: *Actually, I just went hiking last Saturday. I went to . . .*

## D IN OTHER WORDS

| Suggested teaching time: | 5 minutes |
|---|---|
| Your actual teaching time: | _____ |

- Encourage students to identify who says the phrases and to use the context of the conversation to help work out their meaning.

- Have students compare answers with a partner. Then review as a class.

- Other possible answers: 1. Is it really beautiful / very interesting? 2. The whole setting is really impressive / unbelievable. 3. But pay attention on your way down. 4. Be sure to come down slowly / not to hurry. 5. What if I want to go to the Arenal Volcano, too? 6. Do you think we can do it all / visit both places in two days? 7. I'm sure you could visit / go to both.)

**Option:** Pair work. Students talk about whether they would like to go to any of the places on the map on page 110. Encourage them to give supporting reasons. Point out they can also talk about other waterfalls or volcanoes they have seen. Example: Student A: *I'd love to go to these places.* Student B: *Really? Why?* Student A: *I really like natural places. I visited Iguazu Falls in Argentina last year, and they are really breathtaking!* Student B: *Well, I'd rather visit a busy city. There's usually so much worth seeing and doing, like going to museums, parks, and eating at nice restaurants!*
**[+5 minutes]**

## WHAT ABOUT YOU?

| Suggested teaching time: | 10–15 minutes |
|---|---|
| Your actual teaching time: | _____ |

- You may want students to work in pairs or small groups.

- Point out that students can write the names of places in different countries.

- Encourage students to include the English names of places they identify.

- To review, draw the following on the board. Draw lines from each circle and write the names of places students identify.

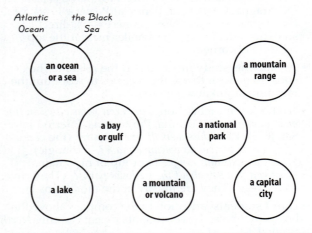

**Language note:** *Sea* (a large area of salty water that is smaller than an ocean or that is enclosed by land), *gulf* (a large area of ocean partly enclosed by land), *bay* (a part of the ocean that is enclosed by a curve in the land).

## EXTRAS (optional)

**Workbook:** Exercises 1–4

**C** 🎧 **SOUND BITES.** **Read along silently as you listen to a conversation in Costa Rica between Carlo, from Italy, and David, from Hong Kong.**

**CARLO:** You wouldn't happen to know anything about the waterfall at La Fortuna, would you? We've been planning to rent a car and drive up there this weekend. **CN1**

**DAVID:** Actually, we just got back from there yesterday.

**CARLO:** What a coincidence! Is it worth seeing? **CN2**

**DAVID:** You definitely don't want to miss it. The whole setting is really breathtaking.

**CARLO:** Good. I can't wait.

**DAVID:** But watch out on your way down. The path can get pretty wet, so be sure to take it slow.

**CARLO:** Thanks for the warning. What if we want to get a look at the Arenal Volcano, too? Do you think that's all doable in two days? **CN3**

**DAVID:** It's only about twenty minutes west of La Fortuna. I'm sure you could handle both.

La Fortuna waterfall

**D** ▷ **IN OTHER WORDS.** **Read the conversation again and restate the following underlined words and phrases in your own way.** Answers may vary. Possible answers include:

1. "Is it <u>worth seeing</u>?" worth the trouble of visiting
2. "The whole setting is really <u>breathtaking</u>." beautiful
3. "But <u>watch out</u> on your way down." be careful
4. "Be sure to <u>take it slow</u>." go slow

5. "What if we want to <u>get a look at</u> the Arenal Volcano, too?" see
6. "Do you think <u>that's all doable</u> in two days?" able to be done
7. "I'm sure you <u>could handle</u> both." can do

**CN1 Corpus Notes:** *Do you know* is a much more common way to begin a question than *You wouldn't happen to know.* However, *You wouldn't happen to know . . . , would you?* is used to make the question seem less direct, and therefore more polite.

**WHAT ABOUT YOU?**

**CN2 Corpus Notes:** A common learner error is to follow the preposition *worth* with the infinitive form of the verb (*There are many other facts worth ~~to mention~~ . . .*). Be sure students do not make this error.

**Write the name of places you know for each of the following geographical features.**

| | |
|---|---|
| an ocean or a sea: | a lake: |
| a bay or gulf: | a mountain or volcano: |
| a mountain range: | a capital city: |
| a national park: | |

**CN3 Corpus Notes:** You can *get a look, take a look,* and *have a look* at something. They mean the same thing, but *take a look* is the most common.

# Warn about a Possible Risk

## 🎧 CONVERSATION MODEL   Read and listen.

**A:** Excuse me. Can you tell me the way to the beach?

**B:** That way. It's not very far.

**A:** Thanks. Do you think the water's too cold to go swimming?

**B:** Not at all. But you should be careful. The undertow can be quite dangerous.

**A:** Thanks for the warning.

🎧 **Rhythm and intonation practice**

undertow

---

**A** 🎧 **VOCABULARY. Describe possible risks. Listen and practice.**

It can be quite **dangerous**.

It can be very **rocky**.

It can be extremely **steep**.

It can be really **foggy**.

It can be quite **slippery**.

It can be pretty **dark**.

It can be terribly **exhausting**.

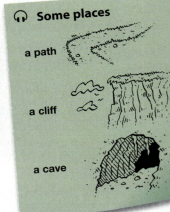

🎧 **Some places**

a path

a cliff

a cave

---

**B** 🎧 **LISTENING COMPREHENSION. Listen to the conversations. Check if the speaker thinks the place is safe or dangerous.**

|  | is completely safe. | could be dangerous. |
|---|---|---|
| 1. She thinks that swimming in the bay … | ☑ | ☐ |
| 2. He thinks that hiking around the waterfall … | ☐ | ☑ |
| 3. She thinks climbing the mountain … | ☐ | ☑ |
| 4. He thinks swimming in the river … | ☐ | ☑ |

**CN** **Corpus Notes:**
The verbs *tell*, *show*, and *know* are frequently used with the noun *way*. You can *tell/show (someone) the way* to a place, or you can ask someone if he or she *knows the way (to a place)*.

# LESSON

# 1

## Warn about a Possible Risk

## 🎧 CONVERSATION **MODEL**
**(CD5, Track 20)**

| Suggested teaching time: | 5 minutes |
|---|---|
| Your actual teaching time: | _____ |

- After students read and listen, ask *What are the two things the speakers are concerned about?* (1. the temperature of the water [Is the water too cold?] 2. if it's safe to swim [Be careful of the undertow.])
- Point out that *Excuse me* in this situation is used to get someone's attention.
- Direct students' attention to the illustration of the undertow. If necessary, explain that *the undertow* is the water current under the surface that pulls back to the ocean strongly after a wave comes up to the shore.

**Language note:** You may want to point out that the contraction of a noun + *is* (*water's*) is common in spoken English, but not in formal written English.

## 🎧 Rhythm and intonation practice
**(CD5, Track 21)**

| Suggested teaching time: | 5 minutes |
|---|---|
| Your actual teaching time: | _____ |

- Have students repeat each line chorally.
- Make sure students:
  - use rising intonation for *Can you tell me the way to the beach?*
  - use rising intonation for *Do you think the water's too cold to go swimming?*
  - stress important information like <u>should</u> and <u>careful</u> in *But you should be careful,* and <u>undertow</u> and <u>dangerous</u> in *The undertow can be quite dangerous.*
  - use the following stress pattern:

┌─**STRESS PATTERN**─────────────────────

**A:** Excuse me. Can you tell me the way to the beach?

**B:** That way. It's not very far.

**A:** Thanks. Do you think the water's too cold to go swimming?

**B:** Not at all. But you should be careful. The undertow can be quite dangerous.

**A:** Thanks for the warning.

## 🅐 🎧 VOCABULARY
**(CD5, Tracks 22, 23)**

| Suggested teaching time: | 5–10 minutes |
|---|---|
| Your actual teaching time: | _____ |

- Have students listen and study the words. Then have students listen and repeat chorally.
- Write the following continuum on the board and tell students that the adverbs express different degrees of intensity.

(+)                                  (++)

←────────────────────────────────────────→

*pretty    quite    very / really    extremely / terribly*

- Have students listen and study the words in the box at the bottom right. Then have students listen and repeat chorally.
- To check comprehension, have students make different combinations using the vocabulary of risks and places. Students can also include the adverbs of intensity. Examples: *a rocky path, a steep cliff, an extremely exhausting path, a very slippery path, a terribly dark cave*

**Option:** Group work. Form groups of three. Ask students to take turns describing places and experiences using the vocabulary in Exercise A. Encourage students to ask follow-up questions or make comments. Example: Student A: *Last year I went to Machu Picchu. The path up the mountain was extremely steep.* Student B: *Was it also dangerous?* Student A: *No. But it's a high altitude, so it's not so easy to breathe.* Student C: *Yesterday my aerobics class was pretty exhausting.* Student A: *Why?* Student C: *I haven't been to the gym in a month!*
**[+10 minutes]**

🔵 **Vocabulary Cards**

## 🅑 🎧 LISTENING COMPREHENSION
**(CD5, Track 24)**

| Suggested teaching time: | 10 minutes |
|---|---|
| Your actual teaching time: | _____ |

- You may want to stop after each conversation to check answers.
- Have students listen again if necessary.
- Review as a class.

┌─  ───
**AUDIOSCRIPT**

CONVERSATION 1 [F = Australian]
**M:** I've heard that the bay is really nice.
**F:** Oh, it's beautiful. The water is great.
**M:** I heard there's quite an undertow though.
**F:** In the bay? I don't think so.
**M:** Are you sure it's OK? Someone told me it wasn't safe.
**F:** Who told you that? We go swimming there all the time.
**AUDIOSCRIPT continues on page T113.**

## GRAMMAR

| Suggested teaching time: | 10–15 minutes |
| --- | --- |
| Your actual teaching time: | _____ |

- Direct attention to the box and have students read the first explanation and study the examples.
- Write on the board:

  1. *It's too foggy to drive fast.*

- Point out *too + adjective + infinitive* is used to give an explanation, reason, or warning.
- Write on the board:

  *climb Mt. Everest*
  *swim across the English Channel (England to France)*
  *hike in the mountains at night*

- To check comprehension, ask students to give reasons for not doing these activities. Examples: *Mt. Everest is too steep to climb. It's too far to swim across the channel. It's too dangerous to hike at night.*
- Have students read the second explanation and study the examples.
- Clarify for students that using *for + a person* specifies who the explanation or warning is for.
- Direct students' attention to the Be careful! box.
- Point out that students shouldn't repeat the subject. *Cliffs* and *them* refer to the same thing.
- To check comprehension, write the following on the board:

  1. *It's too exhausting finish in one day.*
  2. *It's too foggy for he to go hiking.*
  3. *It's too cold to you to go swimming today.*

- Pair work. Students make corrections and discuss them. Review as a class. (1. It's too exhausting <u>to</u> finish in one day. (An infinitive, not a base from, is needed after the adjective.) 2. It's too foggy for ~~he~~ <u>him</u> to go hiking. (An object pronoun, not a subject pronoun, is needed after *for*.) 3. It's too cold ~~to~~ <u>for</u> you to go swimming today. (*For*, not *to*, is needed before the person.)

 **Grammar Self-Checks**

## Write sentences . . .

| Suggested teaching time: | 5 minutes |
| --- | --- |
| Your actual teaching time: | _____ |

- Do the first item with the class.
- Have students compare answers with a partner. Then review as a class.

## CONVERSATION **PAIR WORK**

| Suggested teaching time: | 5–10 minutes |
| --- | --- |
| Your actual teaching time: | _____ |

- To get students ready for the activity, have students read the conversation model on page 112 again. You may also want to have students listen to the model.

---

- Have students review the places to go and the pictures of the animals.
- Write the following verbs on the board: *sting   bite*
- Pair work. Have students match the animals with the verbs. (sting: a scorpion, a jellyfish, a mosquito; bite: a snake, a shark, a mosquito)
- Tell students to use adverb + adjective or infinitive + *too* to create warnings and explanations. Examples: *The scorpions are extremely dangerous. It's too dangerous to go swimming because of the sharks.*
- Choose a more confident student and role-play a conversation. Encourage students to ask follow-up questions.
- Walk around the room and provide help as needed. Encourage students to use the correct rhythm and intonation.
- Make sure each student role plays both roles.

**Language note:** The plural of *jellyfish* is *jellyfish*. (NOT ~~jellyfishes~~)

 **Pair Work Cards**

## EXTRAS (optional)

**Grammar Booster**
**Workbook: Exercises 5–9**
**Copy & Go: Activity 37**

### AUDIOSCRIPT

**AUDIOSCRIPT continued from Exercise B, page T112.**

CONVERSATION 2
F: I can't wait to see the waterfall. I've heard it's spectacular.
M: It is. It's just unbelievable.
F: I'd like to hike around and take lots of pictures.
M: Well, just be careful. The path can be very slippery.
F: Don't worry. I'll watch out.

CONVERSATION 3 [F = Chinese]
M: Well, I'll be heading off for Sorak Mountain tomorrow morning.
F: Wow! That's great. First time?
M: Uh-huh.
F: Are you going alone?
M: Uh-huh.
F: Well, be careful. They say the climb can be pretty steep and the path can be quite rocky.
M: OK. I'll be careful. Thanks.
F: Really. I'm not joking around.
M: OK.

CONVERSATION 4
F: Well, I'm off for a swim.
M: In the hotel pool? Maybe I'll join you.
F: No, in the river. I didn't come halfway across the world to swim in a swimming pool!
M: In the river? I wouldn't recommend that.
F: Why not?
M: Who knows what's in the river? I don't think that's a good idea.

## C GRANMAR. Infinitives with too

**Use an infinitive after <u>too</u> and an adjective to give a warning or an explanation.**

It's **too dangerous to go** swimming at that beach. = Don't go swimming there because it's dangerous.

It's **too dark to go** hiking. = Don't go hiking now because it's too dark.

Those cliffs are **too steep to climb**. = Don't climb them because they're very steep.

**You can clarify with a <u>for</u> phrase.**

Those cliffs are too steep **for you** to climb.

It's too dangerous **for children** to go swimming at that beach.

GRAMMAR BOOSTER

**PAGES G16–G17
For more ...**

> **BE CAREFUL!**
> Don't say:
> Those cliffs are too steep
> to climb ~~them~~.

## D Write sentences using <u>too</u> + an infinitive and a <u>for</u> phrase.

1. It's _____too dangerous for you to go_____ to that neighborhood alone.
   <small>dangerous / you / go</small>

2. This map of the national park is _too confusing for me to understand_.
   <small>confusing / me / understand</small>

3. The ancient monuments you want to see aren't _too steep for you to climb_.
   <small>steep / you / climb</small>

4. It's not _too late for you to catch_ the 6:00 train to the capital.
   <small>late / you / catch</small>

5. The path is _too rocky for your children to walk_ on safely.
   <small>rocky / your children / walk</small>

6. It's really _too hot for us to go hiking_ to the waterfall today.
   <small>hot / us / go hiking</small>

## CONVERSATION PAIR WORK

> **Places to go**
> the waterfall
> the path
> the cave
> the beach
> the cliffs

**Role-play asking for directions to a place. Warn about possible risks or dangerous animals or insects. Use the pictures and the guide, or create a new conversation.** Answers will vary.

**A:** Excuse me. Can you tell me the way to _____?

**B:** _____ .

**A:** Thanks.

**B:** But you should be careful. The _____ can be quite _____ .

**A:** _____ ...

a jellyfish

a snake

a scorpion

a mosquito

a shark

**CONTROLLED PRACTICE**

## Describe Where a Place is Located

**CONVERSATION MODEL** Read and listen.

**A** Where exactly is Miyajima Island located?

**B:** About an hour west of Osaka by train. Are you planning on going?

**A:** I've been thinking about it.

**B:** It's a must-see. Be sure to take pictures!

**Rhythm and intonation practice**

**Positive comments**
It's a must-see.
You don't want to miss it.

**Negative comments**
It's overrated.
It's a waste of time.

**A** **GRAMMAR. Prepositions of place** CN

Cobán is **in** the central part **of** Guatemala.

Tikal is **in** the North.

Belize is northeast **of** Guatemala.

Quetzaltenango is about 100 kilometers west **of** Guatemala City.

Champerico is **on** the west coast **of** Guatemala.

Flores is **on** the south shore **of** Lake Petén Itzá.

El Rancho is located **on** the Motagua River.

GRAMMAR BOOSTER
PAGES G17–G19
For more …

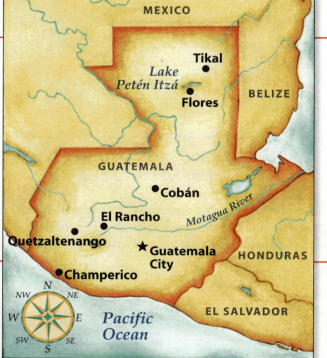

**B** Complete the sentences with the correct prepositions.

1. Vladivostok is __on__ the eastern coast __of__ Russia.

2. Barranquilla is __in__ the northern part __of__ Colombia.

3. Haikou is __on__ the northern coast __of__ Hainan Island in China.

4. Machu Picchu is located about 100 kilometers northwest __of__ Cuzco.

5. Vietnam is south __of__ China.

6. Kota Kinabalu is __on__ the north coast of Borneo, a part of Malaysia.

7. Manaus is located __on__ the Amazon River in Brazil.

8. Canada is north __of__ the United States.

CN **Corpus Notes:**
Be sure students know to use *of* with directions.
A common learner error is to use *from* instead
(*It is a small city west ~~from~~ Munich.*).

# LESSON 2

## Describe Where a Place Is Located

### 🎧 CONVERSATION **MODEL**
**(CD5, Tracks 25, 27, 28)**

| Suggested teaching time: | 5–10 minutes |
|---|---|
| Your actual teaching time: | _____ |

• After students read and listen, ask them to summarize what they read / heard about Miyajima. (It's an island. You can get there by train. It's an hour west of Osaka. It's a beautiful place.)

• Point out that *plan* _on_ doing something has the same meaning as *plan* _to_ do something.

• Have students listen and study the positive and negative comments. Then have students repeat.

• To provide practice, ask students to use the positive and negative comments to describe things they have seen and places they have visited. Examples: *The new movie is overrated—I fell asleep watching it!*

**Language note:** *It's a must-see.* (something that is so exciting, interesting, etc. that you think people should see it or visit it); *You don't want to miss it.* (something that is so good that you think people should not fail to see it); *It's overrated.* (not as good or important as some people think); *It's a waste of time.* (not worth the time that you spend)

**Culture note:** Miyajima (also called Itsukushima) is an island in the Seto Sea. It is located just off the mainland near the city of Hiroshima. It is considered one of the most beautiful and sacred places in Japan. Miyajima is also famous for its frequent and varied festivals, from the colorful Walking on Fire Ceremony to the simple Memorial Service for Kitchen Knives.

### 🎧 Rhythm and intonation practice
**(CD5, Track 25)**

| Suggested teaching time: | 5 minutes |
|---|---|
| Your actual teaching time: | _____ |

• Have students repeat each line chorally.

• Make sure students:

  ○ use falling intonation for *Where exactly is Miyajima Island located?*

  ○ stress important information like <u>hour</u>, <u>west</u>, O<u>sa</u>ka, and <u>train</u> in *About an hour west of Osaka by train.*

  ○ use rising intonation for *Are you planning on going?*

  ○ stress both <u>must</u> and <u>see</u> in *It's a must-see.*

○ use the following stress pattern:

┌─ **STRESS PATTERN** ─────────────────────────┐

**A:** Where exactly is Miyajima Island located?

**B:** About an hour west of Osaka by train. Are you planning on going?

**A:** I've been thinking about it.

**B:** It's a must-see. Be sure to take pictures!

└──────────────────────────────────────────────┘

### 🅐 GRAMMAR

| Suggested teaching time: | 5–10 minutes |
|---|---|
| Your actual teaching time: | _____ |

• Direct attention to the Grammar box. Have students study the examples and find the places on the map.

• Write on the board:

  *Northeast  Southeast  Southwest  Northwest*

• Direct students' attention to the compass. Have students repeat the directions chorally.

• Point out the different prepositions for *It's* _in the North_. / *It's* _on the north coast_.

• You may want to write the following on the board to summarize the prepositions of location:

| **in** | the [North] | **on** | the coast |
|---|---|---|---|
| | the central part of | | the shore |
| | | | a river |

| [west] | the central part | **of a place** |
|---|---|---|
| [southeast] | the coast | |

 **Grammar Self-Checks**

### 🅑 Complete the sentences ...

| Suggested teaching time: | 5 minutes |
|---|---|
| Your actual teaching time: | _____ |

• Do the first item with the class.

• Have students compare answers with a partner. Then review as a class.

• You may want to ask students to review the items they answered incorrectly and review the corresponding grammar information in the Grammar box.

• To provide more practice, ask students to make sentences describing the location of cities, coasts, etc. in their country or in another country. Use the prepositions of place in Exercise A. Examples: *Cancun is located on the east coast of Mexico. New York is north of Washington D.C. Mt. Fuji is located about 200 kilometers west of Tokyo.*

## C 🎧 PRONUNCIATION
### (CD5, Track 29)

| Suggested teaching time: | 10 minutes |
|---|---|
| Your actual teaching time: | _____ |

- Have students listen and study the examples.

- Point out that if a sound is voiceless, there is no vibration (in the throat). If a sound is voiced, there is vibration. You may want to have students put their hand on their throat to compare the vibration with the voiced *th–* (the) and no vibration with the voiceless *th–* (north). (See Language note.)

- Have students listen again and repeat chorally.

- Before students do the exercise, ask them to study the words and check the columns they predict are correct. Have students compare answers.

- Then have students listen and confirm their answers or make corrections.

- Review as a class.

- Pair work. Ask students to write down six words containing *th–*. Students can look in their Student's Book for words. Then ask students to decide whether the words they found are pronounced with the voiced or voiceless *th–*. To review, write the words students say in two columns on the board.

**Language note:** Students often have difficulty pronouncing the sound /ð/, as in *there,* and substitute a sound like /z/ or /d/. Demonstrate the position of the tongue: The tongue is placed loosely between the upper and lower teeth. The tip of the tongue lightly touches the upper teeth and vibrates. The sound /ð/ is voiced, which means the vocal cords vibrate, and the voice is used to produce the sound. Also difficult for many students is the voiceless *th–* sound /θ/, as in *thin.* They often substitute a sound like /s/ or /t/. To pronounce the sound /θ/, the tongue is placed between the upper and lower teeth. The tip of the tongue very lightly touches the upper teeth (and doesn't vibrate). The sound /θ/ is voiceless; the vocal cords do not vibrate and the voice is not used.

 **Pronunciation Activities**

## CONVERSATION **PAIR WORK**

| Suggested teaching time: | 15–20 minutes |
|---|---|
| Your actual teaching time: | _____ |

- You may want to draw on students' schema (prior knowledge) and ask students what they already know about Alaska and Australia. Students may say *There are many mountains and glaciers in Alaska. There are polar bears and penguins in Alaska. Australia is a continent. There are kangaroos in Australia.*

- To get students ready for the activity, have students read the conversation model on page 114 again. You may also want to have students listen to the model.

- Review the expressions for positive and negative descriptions on page 114.

- Have students study the maps and find cities, islands, national parks, mountains, deserts, and capital cities.

- If students would like to know more about the places on the maps, briefly give them some information about the places before role-playing the conversation. (See Culture notes.)

- Choose a more confident student and role-play a conversation. Encourage students to ask follow-up questions.

- Walk around the room and provide help as needed. Encourage students to use the correct rhythm and intonation.

- Make sure each student role-plays both roles.

- Ask various pairs to perform one of these conversations in front of the class.

**Challenge:** Student project. Ask students to visit the official websites of the Denali National Park or the Kodiak National Wildlife Refuge and find interesting information about them. Ask students to report to the class the most interesting piece of information they found. **[times will vary]**

**Culture note: Alaska** Anchorage, the largest city in Alaska, is a modern city, but you'll still see wild animals, such as moose, wandering around town! Fairbanks, the second largest city, is ideal for tourists who like adventure. Popular activities include hunting, fishing, camping, rafting, boating, skiing, and dog races. The state capital, Juneau, includes a beautiful glacier only thirteen miles from the city center. Denali National Park, covering over six million acres, is the most visited national park in Alaska. The tallest mountain in North America, Mt. McKinley, is located in Denali Park. Katmai National Park is located 290 miles southwest of Anchorage. Tourists arrive on ships to visit Glacier Bay National Park.

**Culture note: Australia** Sydney, the largest city, is known as an important seaport and commercial center. Melbourne, the second largest city, is the cultural center of the country. Canberra is the nation's capital. Alice Springs is a popular access point to many of the surrounding parks. Ayers Rock, the world's largest monolith, is a sacred place for the aboriginal people. Kakadu National Park has been home to animals and people for over 50,000 years. Tasmania is part of the Commonwealth of Australia.

 **Pair Work Cards**

 **Learning Strategies**

## EXTRAS (optional)

**Grammar Booster**
**Workbook: Exercises 10–14**
**Copy & Go: Activity 38**

 **Pronunciation Supplements**

🎧 **PRONUNCIATION.** Voiced and voiceless <u>th</u>.
Listen and repeat.

**voiceless <u>th</u>**

1. nor**th**
2. nor**th**eastern
3. sou**th**
4. sou**th**western

**voiced <u>th</u>**

5. **th**e West
6. **th**is way
7. nor**th**ern
8. sou**th**ern

Now listen to the words. Check if the <u>th</u> is
voiceless or voiced.

| | voiceless <u>th</u> | voiced <u>th</u> |
|---|:---:|:---:|
| 1. thanks | ☑ | ☐ |
| 2. breathtaking | ☑ | ☐ |
| 3. though | ☐ | ☑ |
| 4. path | ☑ | ☐ |
| 5. breathe | ☐ | ☑ |

Miyajima Island, Japan

# CONVERSATION
## PAIR WORK

Role-play a conversation about the location
of an interesting place. Use the maps or your
<u>own</u> map. Start like this: Answers will vary.

**A:** Where exactly is _____ located?

**B:** _____ …

Continue the conversation in your <u>own</u> way.

**CONTROLLED PRACTICE**

# Describe a Natural Setting

**Positive adjectives to describe the beauty of nature**
The scenery was **breathtaking**.
The views were **spectacular**.
The sights were **extraordinary**.

**A** ▶ 🎧 **VOCABULARY.** Describing the natural world.
**Listen and practice.**

## GEOGRAPHIC ADJECTIVES

**mountainous**  **hilly**  **flat**  **lush** CN  **arid**

## GEOGRAPHIC NOUNS

**a forest**  **a jungle**  **a canyon**  **an island**  **a valley**

**CN** Corpus Notes:
The adjective *lush* frequently collates with the adjective *green* (*lush green valleys / lawns / hills*).

**B** ▶ 🎧 **LISTENING COMPREHENSION.** Listen to Kenji Ozaki describe a trip he took several years ago. Check the natural features he saw.

- ☐ super-high waterfall
- ☑ super-high cliffs
- ☐ an ancient valley
- ☑ an ancient forest

- ☑ extraordinary trees
- ☐ extraordinary jungles
- ☐ fresh water
- ☑ fresh air

**SOURCE:** Authentic *Top Notch* interview

Kenji Ozaki
Tokyo, Japan

**Listen again. Answer the questions.**

1. What country did Kenji Ozaki visit? The United States

2. What kind of a place did he visit? A National Park—Yosemite

3. What do you think he liked best about it? Why? He liked the size of it and the natural beauty. He felt like he was part of nature.

# LESSON

## 3 ▸ *Describe a Natural Setting*

### A ⌾ **VOCABULARY**
(CD5, Tracks 30, 31)

| Suggested teaching time: | 10–15 minutes |
|---|---|
| Your actual teaching time: | _____ |

- Have students listen and study the words. Then have students listen and repeat chorally.
- Review the positive adjectives in the small box.
- Point out that these adjectives have a similar meaning. They mean very impressive or exciting.
- Small groups. Have students describe different places they know or have heard about using adjectives and nouns. Students should also use the positive adjectives.
- You may want to teach more geographic adjectives: *rural* (relating to the country, not the city); *desolate* (empty and sad-looking because there are no people and there is not much activity); *touristy* (full of tourists and things that attract tourists); *developed* (having buildings, industries, and comfortable living for most people); *untouched* (not affected or damaged). Examples: *Sheep are raised in rural areas. We flew over a desolate canyon. Paris is too touristy for me. The area directly around New York City has been over-developed. Most national parks remain untouched.*

**Language note:** If necessary, clarify the meaning of the following nouns: *scenery* (the natural features of a place such as mountains, forest, and deserts); *view* (the area that you can see from a place); *sights* (something that you can see, especially something unusual or beautiful). *Scenery* is always used to describe nature. *Views* and *sights* can also be used when describing places built by man.

 **Vocabulary Cards**

### B ▸ ⌾ **LISTENING COMPREHENSION**
(CD5, Track 32)

| Suggested teaching time: | 10–15 minutes |
|---|---|
| Your actual teaching time: | _____ |

- Before listening, have students read the answer choices for the first exercise.
- Ask students to listen and mark their answers.
- Then have students listen again to write notes that support their answer choices. Examples: *He said he saw a waterfall, but he didn't say it was high. He said the cliffs were high. / He said he saw a forest with giant trees. The trees are so tall because they are very old.*
- Review the first exercise as a class.
- Then have students read the questions in the second exercise and listen one more time.
- Review answers as a class.

 **Learning Strategies**

---

**AUDIOSCRIPT** ▸

**Kenji Ozaki** [Japanese]

About two years ago, I went to the United States on vacation with friends. We drove everywhere. About 190 miles east from San Francisco to Yosemite National Park. I'd say it took about six hours to get there.

Yosemite National Park was huge!!! I mean REALLY huge. I was so excited to be there surrounded by those beautiful mountains—with so many things to see. In Yosemite Valley, there were these super-high cliffs . . . and spectacular waterfalls. There's this one spot called the Mariposa Grove—it's an ancient forest with literally hundreds of giant sequoias—the sequoia's one of the biggest and most extraordinary trees there is. We also visited Glacier Point, which has breathtaking views of Yosemite Valley and all the mountains around it.

What I can't forget is the fresh air . . . the smell . . . it was so clean. Everything was just so great. And I was really surprised when I saw some people way up high on the cliffs—they were actually climbing—they looked so small to me. Someone told me that it would actually take them more than a couple of days to get to the top.

What I liked best about Yosemite National Park was the size of it. And the natural beauty. I had never ever seen a park that big and so . . . well . . . untouched. At least it seemed that way to me. Since I grew up in Japan, I had never imagined there could be such a place. I felt like I was a part of nature.

# TOP NOTCH **INTERACTION**

| Suggested teaching time: | 25–30 minutes |
|---|---|
| Your actual teaching time: | _____ |

## STEP 1. On your notepad . . .

- If there is a world map in the classroom, ask volunteers to point out the places.
- To help students organize the information on their notepad, write on the board:

  *Name and location of place:*
  *Description: Natural features:*
       *Wildlife:*
       *Places to visit:*
       *Any advice or warnings?*

- Remind students to use geographic adjectives and nouns in their descriptions.

**Culture note:** **The Galapagos Islands,** a group of volcanic islands in the Pacific Ocean, are located about 1,050 kilometers (650 miles) to the west of Ecuador (South America). Some wildlife species, such as giant tortoises and lizards, are found only on these islands. **Tahiti,** an island in the southern Pacific Ocean, is a popular tourist destination. Mountains, waterfalls, and lush vegetation cover the island. **Zambia** is a republic in the south central part of Africa. Many tourists go on safaris here because of the abundant wildlife. Also popular are the breathtaking views of Victoria Falls, the biggest waterfall in the world. **Alaska,** the largest state in the U.S., has spectacular scenery, with mountains, glaciers, volcanoes, and forests. **Tibet,** an autonomous region in China, is considered the highest region on earth, with an average height of 4,000 meters (12,000 feet) above sea level. Mount Everest, the highest mountain in the world (8,848 meters or 29,028 feet), is also located there. Potala (shown in the picture), was built in the 17th century. It is located in Llasa, the capital.

## STEP 2. PAIR WORK.

- Review the language in the NEED HELP? section.
- Encourage students to use the language they learned in this unit.
- Point out that students should ask follow-up questions. Examples: Student A: *Last year I went to Patagonia.* Student B: *Where's that?* Student A: *In the south of Argentina.* Student B: *Is it beautiful?* Student A: *Yes. Many areas remain untouched.* Student B: *And what did you do?* Student B: *We cycled along a lonely road in the mountains. The cliffs were quite steep, so we had to be careful. It was terribly exhausting, but it was too beautiful to miss. The views from the road were spectacular.*
- Walk around the room and provide help as needed.

## STEP 3. WRITING.

- Write on the board:

  *The most spectacular place I've ever visited*
  *is _____.*
  *If I could go anywhere in the world, I'd go*
  *to _____.*

- Tell students they can start their paragraph with one of the sentence beginnings on the board.
- Encourage students to give reasons why the place is spectacular and use as much vocabulary from the unit as they can.
- Walk around the room and provide help as needed.

**Option:** Have students read their paragraphs out loud in small groups or in front of the class. **[+10 minutes]**

 **Writing Process Worksheets**

## EXTRAS (optional)

  **Workbook:** Exercises 15–18
  **Copy & Go:** Activity 39

# TOP NOTCH
## INTERACTION • *It's spectacular!*

**STEP 1.** On your notepad, write about a spectacular place. Write about a place you've visited or research the places in the pictures. What does it look like? What can you do there?
Answers will vary.

the Galapagos Islands

Tahiti

Zambia

Alaska

Tibet

**?**
Your idea

| | |
|---|---|
| Name of place: | |
| Description: | |

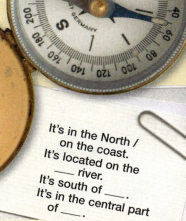

**STEP 2. PAIR WORK.** Tell your partner about the place you wrote about on your notepad.

**NEED HELP?** Here's language you already know:

It's in the North / on the coast.
It's located on the ___ river.
It's south of ___.
It's in the central part of ___.

**STEP 3. WRITING.** Write about the most spectacular place you've ever visited or someplace you'd like to go. Include pictures if you can.

# 4 ▷ Debate the Pros and Cons of Development

**A** ▷ **READING WARM-UP.** Are there any places in the world where you think tourism would be a danger to the environment? Why?

**B** ▷ 🎧 **READING.** Read the article. Does ecotourism sound like an interesting way to take a vacation? Why or why not?

## ECOTOURISM: the Promise and Perils

Farming, mining, logging, and hunting are traditional approaches to economic development.

**W**orldwide, tourism generates annual revenues of nearly 3 trillion US dollars—nearly 11% of all global revenues—making it the world's largest industry. In recent years, ecotourism—or environmentally friendly tourism—has grown in popularity, uniting the interests of both environmentalists and developers. However, finding a compromise between the environment and development is often challenging, and ecotourism can actually cause additional problems for the very regions it is supposed to protect.

Practically speaking, ecotourism includes activities in which visitors enjoy hands-on experiences, such as bird-watching in the Brazilian rainforest, hiking in the mountains of Nepal, participating in a traditional village celebration, or taking a canoe trip down a river. Local guides usually accompany small groups of tourists, teaching them all about local plants and animals and the culture of the region. Tourists typically stay with local families, or at small, environmentally friendly hotels. The cross-cultural exchange that is part of the experience adds greatly to its value for many people. Ecotourism also encourages the development of native handicrafts

and artwork for souvenirs, and thus contributes to the preservation of cultural heritage.

Ecotourism presents an alternative to traditional approaches to economic development, such as farming, logging, mining, or hunting. It offers local people the chance to escape a cycle of poverty and, by sharing their knowledge of the local terrain and ecology with visitors, to develop a stronger sense of community pride.

However, ecotourism is not always beneficial to local people and the ecology. Any increase in population, however temporary, produces larger amounts of waste and pollution and can require more development. Tourist overcrowding is causing severe environmental damage to the Galapagos Islands, for example. Tourists who go to view wildlife can scare animals away from their feeding and nesting sites. Tourism may even encourage the development of markets in wildlife souvenirs (skins, bones, etc.) which further damages the environment.

### Glossary
**the environment** the air, water, and land in which people, animals, and plants live

**ecology** the way in which plants, animals, and people are related to each other and to their environment

**development** planning and building new houses, streets, etc. on land

**SOURCE:** Cambridge Scientific Abstracts (*Hot Topics* series), www.csc.com

**C** ▷ **PAIR WORK.** Find these expressions in the article. Explain what they mean. Answers may vary. Possible answers include:

1. **environmentally friendly** not harmful to the environment
2. **cross-cultural exchange** communication about customs and traditions between people from different cultures
3. **preservation of cultural heritage** valuing and keeping customs and traditions
4. **environmental damage** harm to the environment

## LESSON

# 4 Debate the Pros and Cons of Development

## A ▸ READING WARM-UP

| | |
|---|---|
| Suggested teaching time: | 5 minutes |
| Your actual teaching time: | _____ |

- Group work. Form groups of three or four.
- To review, call on students from different groups to say their ideas and give reasons. Encourage students to give the names of specific places.
- (Students may say: Tourism could be a negative influence in places where endangered species live. Tourism would destroy their habitat. For example, in the Galapagos, Argentina. OR Tourism could damage places that still remain untouched. OR Tourists produce a lot of waste and pollution.)

## B ▸ 🎧 READING
### (CD5, Track 33)

| | |
|---|---|
| Suggested teaching time: | 10 minutes |
| Your actual teaching time: | _____ |

- Have students read the title of the article and the words in the glossary (bottom right in article).
- Ask students what they know or have heard about ecotourism. Examples: *Tourism that protects the land. Trips to places that are not built up. Hiking with a guide to see areas that have not been visited a lot.*, etc.
- Ask students for synonyms for *promise* and *perils*. (pros and cons, positive and negative effects, advantages and disadvantages)
- Have students underline positive and negative aspects of ecotourism as they read.
- Group work. Form groups of three.
- Encourage students to use grammar and vocabulary from this unit.
- Walk around the room and provide help as needed.

**Option:** Use this option if you want to do a listening activity. Books closed. Draw the following graphic organizer on the board. Have students listen for the three positive effects and the three negative effects and write them in the chart. Then have students read the text to confirm their answers. (The promise: brings economic development, preserves the local culture, develops a sense of community pride; The perils: produces waste and pollution, affects animals, develops a market in wildlife souvenirs) **[+15 minutes]**

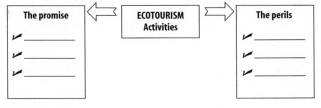

 Graphic Organizers

Learning Strategies

## C ▸ PAIR WORK

| | |
|---|---|
| Suggested teaching time: | 5–10 minutes |
| Your actual teaching time: | _____ |

- Encourage students to use information in the text to help them figure out the meanings of the expressions.
- Review as a class.

**Language note:** To practice the reading skill of understanding vocabulary from context, encourage students to use information in the text to help them figure out the meanings of words they don't know. Make sure students understand the following: *trillion* (1,000,000,000,000); *environmentalist* (someone who is concerned about protecting the environment); *developer* (someone involved in building up an area); *hands-on experience* (providing practical experience by letting people do it themselves); *terrain* (land); *overcrowding* (the condition of living too close together, with too many people in a small place).

 Extra Reading Comprehension Activities

**T118**

 **DISCUSSION**

| Suggested teaching time: | 5–10 minutes |
|---|---|
| Your actual teaching time: | _____ |

• Group work. Form small groups.

• Encourage students to give reasons for their answers. Examples: 1. *I think the article makes a stronger argument in favor of ecotourism because it only introduces disadvantages in the last paragraph.* 2. *People want something new—an alternative to the more traditional ways of taking a vacation. Many tourists live in cities, so they want contact with nature during their vacation.*

• Ask volunteers from different groups to report their conclusions to the class.

## TOP NOTCH **INTERACTION**

| Suggested teaching time: | 20–25 minutes |
|---|---|
| Your actual teaching time: | _____ |

## STEP 1. GROUP WORK.

• Encourage students who are developers to make a list of things that can be done to develop the economy. Examples: *build small hotels, improve the airport facilities, set up restaurants that serve authentic French cuisine, develop a market in local souvenirs, organize activities for adventurers, rent boats for people to get nearer whales, rent horses for people to go horse riding, build a garbage dump, develop the hunting industry in the low forests.*

• Encourage students who are environmentalists to write a list of things that can be done to protect the environment during development. Examples: *build environmentally-friendly cottages for tourists, create national parks to protect the animals, restrict tourists to small parts of the island, plant trees, forbid the sale of wildlife souvenirs, forbid hunting on the island.*

• Walk around the room and provide help as needed.

## STEP 2. DISCUSSION.

• Review the language in the NEED HELP? section.

• Form groups of four or six students. Make sure half are developers and half are environmentalists.

• Encourage students to give concrete reasons and examples during their debate.

• To finish the activity, ask each group to briefly say if the other group was able to convince them or not.

## EXTRAS (optional)

**Workbook: Exercises 19–21**
**Copy & Go: Activity 40**

**DISCUSSION.**

1. Do you think the article makes a stronger argument for or against ecotourism?

2. Why do you think ecotourism has become so popular in recent years?

## TOP NOTCH
### INTERACTION • *That's one way to look at it...*

**STEP 1. GROUP WORK.** Divide the class into groups of developers and groups of environmentalists. Decide what can be done to develop Miquelon's economy while protecting its beautiful environment.

**Developers:**
You want to develop the economy.

**Environmentalists:**
You want to protect the environment.

### Miquelon

The fishing village of Miquelon is "off the beaten path"— on a rocky but very scenic island with little tourism and no industry to speak of.

**Population:** 1,000
**Location:** Off the coast of Newfoundland, Canada
**Language:** French
**Food:** Excellent authentic French cuisine!

**Attractions:**
- a small fishing village with colorful houses and friendly people
- a bay where thousands of seals come to give birth to baby seals
- beautiful beaches, good for swimming in summer. Low forests, good for hunting
- hiking: spectacular views of the ocean and cliffs, beautiful wildflowers, wild horses
- interesting history
- whale-watching: breathtaking views of whales in their natural habitat

**Problems:**
- small population and no real hotels (But foreign students have stayed in homes to learn French.)
- pollution: garbage thrown off a cliff on the western coast
- no industry or farming, no tall trees for logging
- decline in fishing jobs: too much fishing led to a decline in fish

**STEP 2. DISCUSSION.** Present the ideas from each group. Try to convince the other side that your plan is a good one.

**NEED HELP?** Here's language you already know:

| | | |
|---|---|---|
| Are you in favor of ____ ?<br>I think it's wrong to ____ .<br>I think it's a good idea to ____ .<br>I'm against ____ . | It isn't acceptable to ____ .<br>That's true, but ____ .<br>I see what you mean, but ____ . | On the one hand, ____ . But on the other hand, ____ .<br>That's one way to look at it, but ____ .<br>That depends. |

**A** 🎧 **LISTENING COMPREHENSION. Listen to the conversations. Check the type of place each person is talking about. Check whether or not the person recommends going there.**

| | type of place? | | | recommends going? | |
|---|---|---|---|---|---|
| **1.** | ☑ a canyon | ☐ a waterfall | ☐ cliffs | ☐ yes | ☑ no |
| **2.** | ☐ a cave | ☐ a canyon | ☑ a waterfall | ☑ yes | ☐ no |
| **3.** | ☐ a volcano | ☑ an island | ☐ a canyon | ☑ yes | ☐ no |
| **4.** | ☐ a volcano | ☑ a valley | ☐ a canyon | ☐ yes | ☑ no |

**B** **Look at the pictures. Complete the warnings about each danger, using _too_.**

1.    2.    3.    4.

1. ____It's too dangerous to____ go swimming in the bay.

2. Those steps _____are too slippery to_____ climb.

3. _____It's too dark to_____ go in the cave without a flashlight.

4. That road _____is too rocky for_____ for us to use.

**C** **Write the exact locations of the following places. Use the map.**

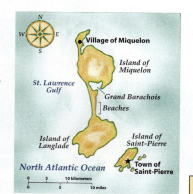

1. The village of Miquelon __is on__ the island of Miquelon.

2. The island of Langlade __is south of__ the island of Miquelon.

3. The island of Saint-Pierre __is southeast of__ Langlade.

4. The village of Miquelon ____is____ about __22 miles__ from the town of Saint-Pierre.

5. The beaches __are on__ the __eastern__ coast.

**TOP NOTCH PROJECT**
Use the Internet to get information about the places in STEP 1 on page 117. Tell your classmates why they should go there.

**TOP NOTCH WEBSITE**
For Unit 10 online activities, visit the *Top Notch* Companion Website at www.longman.com/topnotch.

**D** **WRITING. Write about a natural setting you would like to visit. Say as much as you can. OR Write about your plan for Miquelon. Explain the problem and suggest solutions.**

# UNIT 10
# CHECKPOINT

 **A** 🎧 **LISTENING COMPREHENSION**

(CD5, Track 34)

| | |
|---|---|
| Suggested teaching time: | 5–10 minutes |
| Your actual teaching time: | _____ |

- Pause after each conversation to allow students time to answer.
- Have students compare answers with a partner.
- Have students listen again to confirm answers or make changes.
- Review as a class.

**Option:** Have students listen to the recording and write the speakers' negative or positive comments about each place. Encourage students to listen for the expressions they learned in this unit. (1. It's a little overrated. 2. It's a must-see. 3. You don't want to miss it. 4. It's a waste of time.) **[+5 minutes]**

**AUDIOSCRIPT**

CONVERSATION 1
F: Have you ever gone to Morton's Pass?
M: Oh, yeah.
F: I heard it's a pretty nice canyon to visit. How far is it?
M: Oh, I'd say about fifty miles south of the city.
F: Would you recommend it?
M: Well, if you ask me, it's a little overrated. I'd pick something else to see, instead.
F: Thanks for letting me know.

CONVERSATION 2
M: Terry tells me that you've been to Bash Bish Falls.
F: Did she tell you that?
M: Yeah. I'm thinking of going next week. I love waterfalls. So what do you think? Is it worth it?
F: In my opinion, it's a must-see. You'd be crazy not to go.
M: Really!

CONVERSATION 3
F: Have you ever been to Treasure Island?
M: A bunch of times. Why?
F: Well, I'm wondering if it's worth a trip. I'm not sure if I'd like being on an island.
M: In my opinion?
F: Yes, I'd love to hear your opinion.
M: You don't want to miss it.
F: That's all you have to say?
M: That's all I have to say.

CONVERSATION 4
M: So in the last days of my vacation I'm thinking of spending some time in Pipo Valley. Tom told me it was spectacular.
F: Oh, yeah?
M: What do you mean, "Oh, yeah?"
F: Well, if you ask me, I'd say it was a waste of time.
M: You've been there?
F: I've been there. There's Mount Pi on one side. And Mount Po on the other side.
M: And?
F: I still don't think it's worth it. But to each his own.

 **B** **Look at the pictures . . .**

| | |
|---|---|
| Suggested teaching time: | 5 minutes |
| Your actual teaching time: | _____ |

- Have students do the first item. Review the answer with the class by pointing out the grammar needed: *too* + adjective + infinitive
- Have students compare answers with a partner. Then review as a class.

 **C** **Write the exact locations . . .**

| | |
|---|---|
| Suggested teaching time: | 5 minutes |
| Your actual teaching time: | _____ |

- Point out that students need to write the correct verb forms also.
- Have students compare answers with a partner. Then review as a class.

**D** **WRITING**

| | |
|---|---|
| Suggested teaching time: | 10–15 minutes |
| Your actual teaching time: | _____ |

- Encourage students to refer to the grammar and vocabulary from the unit as they write: page 114, prepositions of place; page 116, describing natural settings; page 119, Miquelon and approaches to economic development.
- Walk around the room and provide help as needed.

***TOP NOTCH* PROJECT**

**Idea:** Group work. Form groups of three or four students and have them choose a place. Ask them to research individually and write notes. Then ask them to share the information with their group's members and prepare an opinion summary for the class. Encourage them to include reasons why their classmates should plan a trip to that particular place.

**T120**

# UNIT WRAP-UP

| | |
|---|---|
| Suggested teaching time: | 20–25 minutes |
| Your actual teaching time: | _____ |

## Vocabulary

- Pair work. Ask students to take turns pointing to the picture and naming the geographical features.
- Review as class. You may want to write a list on the board as you get feedback from students.

**Your students can say ...**

island, sea, volcano, river, waterfall, sea, path, cliff, cave, beach

## Conversation

- Pair work. Ask students to create at least two conversations.

**Your students can say ...**

**A:** Where exactly is [Myrobi]? **B:** About an hour northeast of this island by boat. Are you planning on going? **A:** I've been thinking about it. **A:** You don't want to miss it. Be sure to take pictures!

**A:** Where exactly is [Pakasoto Island] located? **B:** To the south of this island. **A:** I'm thinking of going tomorrow. Is it worth it? **A:** If you ask me, it's a waste of time. It's a flat piece of land covered by a forest.

**Option: Look, honey ...** Direct attention to the couple who are having a photograph taken. Ask students to write down the ways in which they could describe the view from up there. (The view is spectacular / extraordinary / breathtaking.) **[+5 minutes]**

## Grammar

- Ask students to write as many warning statements as they can. Point out the compass on the illustration of the map.
- Have students compare answers with a partner and make necessary corrections.
- Ask various students to say a sentence each.

**Your students can say ...**

It's too dangerous to go swimming on the northwest coast. The undertow is very strong. It's too dangerous to go surfing on the northwest coast. There are sharks. The volcano is too steep to climb. The path is too slippery to walk on safely. The cave is too dark to go in without a flashlight. It's too dangerous to go swimming on the south coast. There are jellyfish. The beach is too dangerous for anyone to go barefoot. There are scorpions.

**Challenge: Spotting Honi Honi differences.** Have students look at the island for one minute. Closed books. Then ask students to draw a map of the island with as many details as they remember. Make sure students understand that the quality of their drawings is not important. Pair work. Students take turns looking at each others' pictures and analyzing the differences with the Student's Book picture. Examples: *In your picture there aren't any jellyfish. You didn't draw the cave. Smoke is not coming out of your volcano. You didn't draw the man looking down the cliff.* **[+10 minutes]**

## Writing

- Students can work alone or in groups.
- Encourage students to refer back to the unit for grammar and vocabulary.
- Ask students to hang their advertisements up on the walls. Have students circulate around the room to read each other's ads.

**Option: And the winner is ...** Take a poll to see which ad is voted the best, the funniest, the most original. **[+5 minutes]**

**Individual oral progress check (optional)**

- Use the illustration on page 121. Encourage the student to use material (vocabulary, grammar, rhythm and intonation) practiced in this unit.
- Evaluate the student on correctness and intelligibility.
- Tell the student to point to the picture and say the geographical features he / she can see. Examples: *island, sea, volcano, river, waterfall, sea, cliff.*
- Tell the student to look at the picture and give at least three warnings about the risks on the island. Ask the student to use *too.* Examples: *The volcano is too steep to climb. The sea is too dangerous to go swimming. The cave is too dark to go in without a flashlight.*

 **Cumulative Vocabulary Activities**

 You may wish to use the video and activity worksheets for Unit 10 at this point.

 **Complete Assessment Package**
**Unit 10 Achievement Test**
**Review Test 2, Speaking Test 2**

Welcome to

# Honi Honi Island

## Unit Wrap-Up

- **Vocabulary.** Name all the natural and geographical features in the picture.
- **Conversation.** Create conversations for the people on the beach.
- **Grammar.** Write statements warning about risks on the island.
- **Writing.** Write an advertisement to get people to visit Honi Honi Island.

MYROBI

HONI HONI-ISLAND

HONI CITY

MOO MOO VOLCANO

PAKASOTO

WARNING! DANGEROUS UNDERTOW

NO SWIMMING

BICYCLE REPAIR

Beach Eats

✔ *Now I can ...*

☐ warn about a possible risk.
☐ describe where a place is located.
☐ describe a natural setting.
☐ debate about development.

# Alphabetical word list

This is an alphabetical list of all productive vocabulary in the **Top Notch 3** units. The numbers refer to the page on which the word first appears or is defined. When a word has two meanings, both are in the list.

## A
abdomen  18
ability  44
absolutely  3
accept  90
acceptable  100
acupuncture  20
address (someone)  4
advice  99
advise against  99
agree  99
aloud  82
antacid  22
antibiotic  22
antihistamine  22
appointment  15
appreciate  15
appropriate  54
argue  99
arid  116
artistic ability  44
arts  38
a.s.a.p.  27
assign  34
athletic ability  44
author  76
autobiography  77
auto repair shop  31
autumn  52

## B
bandage  68
battery  69
battery-operated  68
bay  110
beach  112
behavior  8
believe  102
benefit  81
bestseller  76
binding  26
biography  77
blood test  18
book on tape  82
bookshelf  79
border  110
borrow  76
bother  18
bottled water  69
bouquet  58
break (a tooth)  16
breaking news  63
breathtaking  111
bribe  104
bride  58
bridge (dental)  16
bring up  99

browse  75
budget  34
bug (n)  87
bug (v)  87
business  38
business card  26
business day  30
business school  39
button  27

## C
camping trip  87
cancellation  15
canyon  116
capital city  110
capital
    punishment  102
card  52
careful  112
cashmere  32
casualty  63
catastrophic  70
caterer  34
cave  112
celebration  51
censorship  102
ceremony  58
chameleon  11
change (one's)
    mind  40
checkup  19
chest  18
chiropractic  20
chrysanthemum  12
circumstances  103
clerk  15
cliff  112
cliffhanger  76
clipping  82
coffee maker  88
coincidence  99
cold tablet  22
collect  82
come out  16
comic book  80
commemorate  52
common sense  44
compassion  44
compulsory  102
conservative  100
constitution  98
construction  70
controversial  102
conventional
    medicine  20
copy  28
copying  26

corruption  104
costume  52
cotton  32
cough  18
cough medicine  22
count on  39
courier service  30
crafts  38
criticize  80
cross-cultural
    exchange  118
crown (dental)  16
cultural heritage  118
cultural literacy  8
curl up  82
curtain  79
custom  3
custom-made  32
customary  8
cutting-edge  88

## D
damage  63
danger  118
dangerous  112
dark  112
dead  52
deadly  70
death  63
death penalty  102
death toll  70
decongestant  22
decorate  34
definitely  88
deliver  28
democracy  98
dental care  14
dental emergency  16
dental school  40
dentist  15
deserve  102
destroy  66
destruction  70
develop (film)  28
developer  118
development  118
dictatorship  98
dinosaur  11
directions  90
disagree  102
disaster  62
discrimination  104
disease  39
dizzy  18
DJ  34
doable  111
document design  26

do's and don'ts  9
dosage  22
dream  39
driving age  102
drought  67
dry-clean  28
dry cleaner  30

## E
earthquake  63
ecology  118
economic impact  70
ecotourism  118
education  44
efficient  30
EKG  19
election  98
emergency  15
emergency
    broadcast  68
engagement  58
enlarge  28
entirely  90
environment  118
environmental  118
environmentalist  118
environmentally
    friendly  118
epidemic  62
ethnic
    discrimination  104
etiquette  8
evacuation  68
exactly  114
examination  19
exhausting  112
experience  44
extraordinary  116
extremely  112
eye drops  22
eyewear  14

## F
factory-made  32
familiar  6
family name  3
famine  67
fast read  76
fault  90
fiction  74
field (occupation)  38
filling  16
film  28
fireworks  52
first-aid kit  68
first name  3
first-name basis  3

first-rate  88
fit in  15
flashlight  68
flat  116
flood  67
foggy  112
forest  116
form of address  11
frame (v)  28

## G
garment  32
geographic  116
get engaged  58
get into  75
get lost  90
get married  58
get together  51
gift  52
gigantic  63
government  98
groom  58
guest  15
guest list  34
guilty  80
gulf  110
gums  16

## H
handle (v)  111
handmade  32
hard to follow  76
helpful  30
herbal therapy  20
high-end  88
high-tech  88
hilly  116
hip  18
hire  34
historical  52
holiday  51
homeless  62
homeopathy  20
honest  30
honeymoon  58
horrendous  87
host  54
huge  63
humanitarian  44
human rights  105
hunger  105
hurricane  67
hurry  27
hurt  16

## I
immoral  80
impact  94

## Social language list

This is a unit-by-unit list of the productive social language from *Top Notch 3*.

### Unit 1

Allow me to introduce myself.
Everyone calls me [Surat].
Beautiful day, isn't it?
It really is.
By the way, I'm [Jane].

Do you mind my asking you the custom here?
Do you mind if I call you [Rob]?
Would it be rude to call you [Magda]?
Absolutely not.
Please do.

What would you like to be called?
How do you prefer to be addressed?
Do you use Ms. or Mrs.?
You know, you look familiar.

### Unit 2

I was wondering if you might be able to recommend [a doctor].
So I hear you're from overseas.
I'm here on business.
Thanks for fitting me in.
This [tooth] is killing me.
Glad to be of help.
I really appreciate it.

Thought I'd better see someone right away.
Well, let's have a look.
I wonder if I might be able to [see the dentist].
Oh, that must hurt.
Are you in a lot of pain?

Well, let me check.
Could you be here by [3:00]?
That would be fine.
You must be [Mr. Brown].
Is anything bothering you today?
Why don't you have a seat?
I'll see if the doctor can see you.

### Unit 3

You look like you're in a hurry!
I sure hope so.
But that's not all.
What else?
First thing [Monday morning]
I won't keep you, then.

Do you think I could [get this dry-cleaned by Thursday]?
That might be difficult.
I'm sorry, but it's pretty urgent.
Well, in that case, I'll see what I can do.

I have to get this to [Chicago] a.s.a.p.
Can you recommend a [courier service]?
Why don't you have [Aero Flash] take care of it?
They're really reliable.

### Unit 4

I wish I'd [gone to medical school].
Since when have you been [interested in medicine]?
I could have [made a difference].
Maybe it's not too late.
Think so?
Sorry about that.
You can count on me.
Long time no see.
How have you been?

Not bad, thanks.
So what are you doing these days?
No kidding!
How come?
It's hard to make a living [as a painter].
My tastes changed.
My family talked me out of it.
I just changed my mind.
Why do you think that?
Could be. But you never know.

Please tell me something about your [skills].
Do you have knowledge of [Arabic]?
What kind of [talents] do you have?
What [work] experience do you have?
I have experience in [teaching].
I don't have much experience.
I'm good at [math].
I have three years of [French].

### Unit 5

[That dress is] spectacular!
What was the occasion?
It takes place [in September].
Oh yeah?
We get together with our [relatives].
[The roads are] impossible.
It takes hours to get anywhere.

I heard there's going to be [a holiday].
What kind of [holiday] is that?
People spend time with their [families].
Have a great [holiday]!
Same to you!
Do you mind if I ask you something?

Of course not.
What's up?
I'm not sure of [the customs here].
Would [flowers] be appropriate?
Absolutely perfect!
It's a good thing I asked.

## Unit 6

Oh, my goodness!
What happened?
What a disaster!
That's gigantic!
Any word on [casualties]?
Let's hope for the best.

I wonder if [8.6 is a record].
Believe it or not.
I'm on the line with [your parents].
Would you like to say hello?
I'm running late.
Anything you'd like me to tell them?

There's a storm on its way.
Will do.
What's going on [in the news today]?
What a shame.
Thank goodness [for that].

## Unit 7

Looking for anything special?
I'm just browsing.
What are you up to?
I'm picking up [some gardening magazines].
She can't get enough of [them].
Are you reading anything good these days?
Not really.
I just can't seem to get into it.

I guess [poetry] just doesn't turn me on.
I can't put it down.
It's a real page-turner.
Thanks for the tip.
Don't bother.
What's that you're reading?
I've always wanted to read that!
Is it any good?
It's hard to follow.
It's a fast read.

I'd highly recommend it.
Do you mind if I borrow it when you're done?
Not at all.
What incredible [bread]!
I learned how [in the latest issue of Home magazine].
I didn't know they had [recipes].
I'm all thumbs!

## Unit 8

[The bugs were] horrendous.
I got eaten alive.
Don't you wish someone would [invent something that works]?
Where have you been?
No way!
I don't believe it.

Do you think I should get the [Brew Rite]?
It's on sale.
That depends.
How much are they selling it for?
Definitely.
That's a great price.
It's top of the line.

Sorry we're late.
We got lost.
That's OK.
It can happen to anyone.
It was entirely my fault.
Better late than never.
Let me get you something to [drink].

## Unit 9

So what are you up to these days?
What a coincidence.
I've been meaning to [give you a call].
Would it be rude to [bring that up at the dinner table]?
It would not be cool to [argue with them].
How well you know me!
I do tend to be [a little opinionated].
In general, is it acceptable here to [ask people about politics]?
Would it be OK to [ask you]?

What would you like to know?
That's a good question!
Are you in favor of [capital punishment]?
What about you?
Actually, I'm against [the death penalty].
I think it's wrong to [take a life], no matter what.
I'm opposed to [censorship].
I guess we'll have to agree to disagree.
I have to disagree with you there.
I'm not sure I agree.
I'm afraid I don't agree.

I agree with you on that one.
I couldn't agree more.
I couldn't have said it better myself.
That's exactly what I think.
It's OK, under some circumstances.
That may be true, but ___.
I see what you mean, but ___.
Well, on one hand ___. But on the other hand, ___.
That's one way to look at it.

## Unit 10

You wouldn't happen to know anything about [La Fortuna], would you?
Is it worth seeing?
You definitely don't want to miss it.
The whole setting is really [breathtaking].
I can't wait.
Watch out on the way down.
Be sure to take it slow.

Thanks for the warning.
Do you think that's all doable in [two days]?
I'm sure you could handle both.
Can you tell me the way to [the beach].
That way.
Not at all.
[The undertow] can be quite [dangerous].

Where exactly is [Miyajima] located?
About [an hour west of Osaka by train].
Are you planning on going?
I've been thinking about it.
It's a must see.
Be sure to [take pictures]!
You don't want to miss it.
It's overrated.
It's a waste of time.

# Pronunciation table

These are the pronunciation symbols used in *Top Notch 3*.

## Vowels

| symbol | key word | symbol | key word |
|--------|----------|--------|----------|
| i | beat, feed | ə | banana, among |
| ɪ | bit, did | ɚ | shirt, murder |
| eɪ | date, paid | aɪ | bite, cry, buy, eye |
| ɛ | bet, bed | aʊ | about, how |
| æ | bat, bad | ɔɪ | voice, boy |
| ɑ | box, odd, father | ɪr | deer |
| ɔ | bought, dog | ɛr | bare |
| oʊ | boat, road | ɑr | bar |
| ʊ | book, good | ɔr | door |
| u | boot, food, flu | ʊr | tour |
| ʌ | but, mud, mother | | |

## Consonants

| symbol | key word | symbol | key word |
|--------|----------|--------|----------|
| p | pack, happy | z | zip, please, goes |
| b | back, rubber | ʃ | ship, machine, station, special, discussion |
| t | tie | | |
| d | die | | |
| k | came, key, quick | ʒ | measure, vision |
| g | game, guest | h | hot, who |
| tʃ | church, nature, watch | m | men |
| | | n | sun, know, pneumonia |
| ʤ | judge, general, major | ŋ | sung, ringing |
| f | fan, photograph | w | wet, white |
| v | van | l | light, long |
| θ | thing, breath | r | right, wrong |
| ð | then, breathe | y | yes |
| s | sip, city, psychology | t̬ | butter, bottle |
| | | t̚ | button |

# Irregular verbs

| base form | simple past | past participle | base form | simple past | past participle |
|-----------|-------------|-----------------|-----------|-------------|-----------------|
| be | was / were | been | lend | lent | lent |
| become | became | become | let | let | let |
| begin | began | begun | lose | lost | lost |
| bite | bit | bit / bitten | make | made | made |
| bleed | bled | bled | mean | meant | meant |
| break | broke | broken | meet | met | met |
| bring | brought | brought | pay | paid | paid |
| build | built | built | put | put | put |
| burn | burned / burnt | burned / burnt | quit | quit | quit |
| buy | bought | bought | read /rid/ | read /rɛd/ | read /rɛd/ |
| catch | caught | caught | ride | rode | ridden |
| choose | chose | chosen | ring | rang | rung |
| come | came | come | rise | rose | risen |
| cost | cost | cost | run | ran | run |
| cut | cut | cut | say | said | said |
| do | did | done | see | saw | seen |
| draw | drew | drawn | sell | sold | sold |
| dream | dreamed / dreamt | dreamed / dreamt | send | sent | sent |
| drink | drank | drunk | sew | sewed | sewn |
| drive | drove | driven | shake | shook | shaken |
| eat | ate | eaten | sing | sang | sung |
| fall | fell | fallen | sit | sat | sat |
| feed | fed | fed | sleep | slept | slept |
| feel | felt | felt | speak | spoke | spoken |
| fight | fought | fought | spend | spent | spent |
| find | found | found | spread | spread | spread |
| fit | fit | fit | stand | stood | stood |
| flee | fled | fled | steal | stole | stolen |
| fly | flew | flown | stick | stuck | stuck |
| forbid | forbade / forbid | forbidden | sting | stung | stung |
| forget | forgot | forgotten | strike | struck | struck |
| get | got | gotten | swim | swam | swum |
| give | gave | given | take | took | taken |
| go | went | gone | teach | taught | taught |
| grow | grew | grown | tell | told | told |
| have | had | had | think | thought | thought |
| hear | heard | heard | throw | threw | thrown |
| hit | hit | hit | understand | understood | understood |
| hold | held | held | wake up | woke up | woken up |
| hurt | hurt | hurt | wear | wore | worn |
| keep | kept | kept | win | won | won |
| know | knew | known | write | wrote | written |
| leave | left | left | | | |

# Verb tense review: present, past, and future

 **THE PRESENT OF BE**

### Statements

| | | |
|---|---|---|
| I | am | |
| You We They | are | late. |
| He She It | is | |

 **THE SIMPLE PRESENT TENSE**

### Statements

| | |
|---|---|
| I You We They | speak English. |
| He She | speaks English. |

### Yes / no questions

| | | |
|---|---|---|
| Do | I you we they | know them? |
| Does | he she | eat meat? |

### Short answers

| | | |
|---|---|---|
| Yes, | I you we they | do. |
| | he she it | does. |

| | | |
|---|---|---|
| No, | I you we they | don't. |
| | he she it | doesn't. |

### Information questions

| | | |
|---|---|---|
| What do | you we they | need? |
| When does | he she it | start? |
| Who | wants needs likes | this book? |

 **THE PRESENT CONTINUOUS**

### Statements

| | | |
|---|---|---|
| I | am | watching TV. |
| You We They | are | studying English. |
| He She It | is | arriving now. |

### Yes / no questions

| | | |
|---|---|---|
| Am | I | |
| Are | you we they | going too fast? |
| Is | he she it | |

### Short answers

| | | |
|---|---|---|
| Yes, | I | am. |
| | you | are. |
| | he she it | is. |
| | we they | are. |

| | |
|---|---|
| No, | I'm not. |
| | you aren't / you're not. |
| | he isn't / he's not. |
| | she isn't / she's not. |
| | it isn't / it's not. |
| | we aren't / we're not. |
| | they aren't / they're not. |

### Information questions

| | | | |
|---|---|---|---|
| What | are | you we they | doing? |
| When | is | he she it | leaving? |
| Where | am | I | staying tonight? |
| Who | is | | driving? |

 **THE PAST CONTINUOUS**

### Statements

| | | |
|---|---|---|
| I | was | singing that song. |
| You We They | were | playing the piano. |
| He She It | was | leaving from Central Station. |

### Yes / no questions

| | | |
|---|---|---|
| Was | I he she it | landing in Sydney when the storm began? |
| Were | we you they | |

### Short answers

| | | |
|---|---|---|
| Yes, | I he she it | was. |
| | we you they | were. |

| | | |
|---|---|---|
| No, | I he she it | wasn't. |
| | we you they | weren't. |

**Information questions**

| When | was | I<br>he<br>she<br>it | speeding? |
|---|---|---|---|
| Where | were | we<br>you<br>they | going? |
| Who | was | | arriving? |

## 5 THE PAST OF <u>BE</u>

**Statements**

| I<br>He<br>She<br>It | was late. |
|---|---|
| We<br>You<br>They | were early. |

**<u>Yes</u> / <u>no</u> questions**

| Was | I<br>he<br>she<br>it | on time? |
|---|---|---|
| Were | we<br>you<br>they | in the same class? |

**Short answers**

| Yes, | I<br>he<br>she<br>it | was. |
|---|---|---|
| | we<br>you<br>they | were. |

| No, | I<br>he<br>she<br>it | wasn't. |
|---|---|---|
| | we<br>you<br>they | weren't. |

**Information questions**

| Where | were | we?<br>you?<br>they? |
|---|---|---|
| When | was | he<br>she<br>it | here? |
| Who | were | they? |
| Who | was | he?<br>she?<br>it? |

## 6 THE SIMPLE PAST TENSE

Many verbs are irregular in the simple past tense.
See the list of irregular verbs on page 126.

**Statements**

| I<br>You<br>He<br>She<br>It<br>We<br>They | stopped working. |
|---|---|

| I<br>You<br>He<br>She<br>It<br>We<br>They | didn't start again. |
|---|---|

**<u>Yes</u> / <u>no</u> questions**

| Did | I<br>you<br>he<br>she<br>it<br>we<br>they | make a good dinner? |
|---|---|---|

**Short answers**

| Yes, | I<br>you<br>he<br>she<br>it<br>we<br>they | did. |
|---|---|---|

| No, | I<br>you<br>he<br>she<br>it<br>we<br>they | didn't. |
|---|---|---|

**Information questions**

| When did | I<br>you<br>he<br>she<br>it<br>we<br>they | read that? |
|---|---|---|
| Who | | called? |

## 7 THE FUTURE WITH <u>WILL</u>

**Affirmative and negative statements**

| I<br>You<br>He<br>She<br>It<br>We<br>They | will<br>won't | stop at five o'clock. |
|---|---|---|

**<u>Yes</u> / <u>no</u> questions**

| Will | I<br>you<br>he<br>she<br>it<br>we<br>they | be on time? |
|---|---|---|

### Affirmative and negative short answers

| Yes, | I you he | will. |
|------|---------|-------|
| No, | she it we they | won't. |

### Information questions

| What will | I you he she it we they | do? |
|-----------|------------------------|-----|
| Who will | | be there? |

 ## THE FUTURE WITH <u>BE GOING TO</u>

### Statements

| I'm You're He's She's It's We're They're | going to | be here soon. |
|------------------------------------------|----------|---------------|

| I'm You're He's She's It's We're They're | not going to | be here soon. |
|------------------------------------------|--------------|---------------|

### Yes / <u>no</u> questions

| Are | you we they | going to want coffee? |
|-----|-------------|------------------------|
| Am | I | going to be late? |
| Is | he she it | going to arrive on time? |

### Short answers

| Yes, | I | am. | No, | I'm not. |
|------|-----|------|------|-----------|
| | you | are. | | you aren't / you're not. |
| | he she it | is. | | he isn't / he's not. she isn't / she's not. it isn't / it's not. |
| | we they | are. | | we aren't / we're not. they aren't / they're not. |

### Information questions

| What | are | you / we / they | going to see? |
|------|-----|------------------|----------------|
| When | is | he / she / it | going to shop? |
| Where | am | I | going to stay tomorrow? |
| Who | is | | going to call? |

 ## THE PRESENT PERFECT

### Affirmative and negative statements

| I You We They | have haven't | left yet. |
|---------------|--------------|-----------|
| He She It | has hasn't | |

### Yes / <u>no</u> questions

| Have | I you we they | said enough? |
|------|---------------|--------------|
| Has | he she it | already started? |

### Affirmative and negative short answers

| Yes, No, | I you we they | have. haven't. |
|----------|---------------|----------------|
| Yes, No, | he she it | has. hasn't. |

### Information questions

| Where | have | I you we they | seen that book? |
|-------|------|---------------|------------------|
| How | has | he she it | been? |
| Who | has | | read it? |

 ## THE PASSIVE VOICE

| Form the passive voice with a form of <u>be</u> and the past participle of the verb | | |
|---|---|---|
| | **ACTIVE VOICE** | **PASSIVE VOICE** |
| simple present | Art collectors **buy** famous paintings. | Famous paintings **are bought by** art collectors. |
| present continuous | The Cineplex **is showing** that film. | That film **is being shown** by the Cineplex. |
| present perfect | All the critics **have reviewed** that book. | That book **has been reviewed** by all the critics. |
| simple past | Vera Wang **designed** this dress. | This dress **was designed** by Vera Wang. |
| past continuous | Last year, World Air **was** still **selling** tours to the Ivory Coast. | Last year, tours to the Ivory coast **were** still **being sold**. |
| future with <u>will</u> | The children **will return** the books tomorrow. | The books **will be returned** tomorrow. |
| <u>be going to</u> | Bart's Garage **is going to repair** my car this afternoon. | My car is **going to be repaired** by Bart's Garage this afternoon. |

## Verbs followed by a gerund

| | | | | | |
|---|---|---|---|---|---|
| acknowledge | delay | escape | keep | prohibit | resent |
| admit | deny | explain | mention | propose | resist |
| advise | detest | feel like | mind | quit | risk |
| appreciate | discontinue | finish | miss | recall | suggest |
| avoid | discuss | forgive | postpone | recommend | support |
| can't help | dislike | give up | practice | regret | tolerate |
| celebrate | endure | imagine | prevent | report | understand |
| consider | enjoy | justify | | | |

## Verbs followed directly by an infinitive

| | | | | | |
|---|---|---|---|---|---|
| afford | choose | help | mean | pretend | volunteer |
| agree | consent | hesitate | need | promise | wait |
| appear | decide | hope | neglect | refuse | want |
| arrange | deserve | hurry | offer | request | wish |
| ask | expect | intend | pay | seem | would like |
| attempt | fail | learn | plan | struggle | yearn |
| can't wait | grow | manage | prepare | swear | |

## Verbs followed by an object before an infinitive*

| | | | | | |
|---|---|---|---|---|---|
| advise | convince | get | order | remind | urge |
| allow | enable | help | pay | request | want |
| ask | encourage | hire | permit | require | warn |
| cause | expect | invite | persuade | teach | wish |
| challenge | forbid | need | promise* | tell | would like |
| choose | force | | | | |

* These verbs can also be followed by the infinitive without an object (example: *want to speak* or *want someone to speak*).

## Verbs followed by either a gerund or an infinitive

| | | |
|---|---|---|
| begin | hate | remember* |
| can't stand | like | start |
| continue | love | stop* |
| forget* | prefer | try |

* There is a big difference in meaning when these verbs are followed by a gerund or an infinitive.

## Adjectives followed by an infinitive*

| | | | | | |
|---|---|---|---|---|---|
| afraid | curious | disturbed | fortunate | pleased | shocked |
| alarmed | delighted | eager | glad | proud | sorry |
| amazed | depressed | easy | happy | ready | surprised |
| angry | determined | embarrassed | hesitant | relieved | touched |
| anxious | disappointed | encouraged | likely | reluctant | upset |
| ashamed | distressed | excited | lucky | sad | willing |

* EXAMPLE: I'm willing to accept that.

# Grammar Booster

### Note about the Grammar Booster

Many will elect to do the Grammar Booster as self-study. If you choose to use the Grammar Booster as a classroom activity instead, included in these pages are some suggestions similar to those found in the teaching notes from the corresponding units. Before students begin an exercise, you may want to do a review with the class. Teaching notes are provided for the grammar charts on the Grammar Booster pages.

## UNIT 1 **LESSON 1**

 **Correct the error . . .**

- Write on the board:
  1. *Sam isn't here, is he?*  3. *I'm too early, aren't I?*
  2. *They speak English, don't they?*
- Review how tag questions are formed by pointing out that the tense of the verb or auxiliary verb in the tag question should match the verb tense in the statement.
- Point out *Sam* in the statement and *he* in the tag question. Remind students that names or nouns are not used in tag questions, but pronouns are.
- Check comprehension by asking *What kind of tag question is needed when the statement is affirmative?* (negative) *What kind of tag question is needed when the statement is negative?* (affirmative)
- Remind students that affirmative statements with *I am* require negative tag questions with *aren't.* (#3)
- As students work on the exercise, encourage them to underline the verb or verb phrase (auxiliary plus main verb) in each statement to help them decide what the correct tag question should be. (1. 'd like; 2. 's; 3. met; 4. made; 5. were; 6. don't know; 7. isn't; 8. 's; 9. can travel; 10. 'm)
- Then review as a class.

## UNIT 1 **LESSON 2**

 **Review: verb usage in the present and past**

### The simple present tense (and NOT the present continuous)

- Have students study the first use and the three examples.
- To review, ask *Which example expresses a scientific fact?* (Water boils at 100°.) *What do the other two examples express?* (things that happen regularly or regular occurrences)

- To check comprehension, ask students to work in pairs to write two examples of facts and two examples of regular occurrences.
- Then ask various groups to read their sentences out loud. Make necessary corrections.
- Have students study the second use and the example sentence.
- Ask students to say the frequency adverb in the example. (never) Remind students that a frequency adverb expresses how often something happens. Give or elicit other examples: *usually, often, sometimes, occasionally, rarely.*
- Have students find the two time expressions in the statement. (before 6:00 / on weekdays) Then elicit other time expressions. Examples: *at night, in the morning, after lunch, at weekends, on Saturdays.*
- Have students study the third use and the list of verbs in the box.
- Remind students that stative verbs express emotions: *love, hate;* mental states: *think, understand;* possession: *have, own;* and perception: *see, hear.*
- Have students study the last use and the example sentence.
- Write on the board: *1. flight / 2:00  2. meeting / 6:00*
- Have pairs make sentences using the simple present tense for future actions. Examples: *The flight leaves at 2:00 tomorrow. The meeting starts at 6:00 tonight.*

### The present continuous (and NOT the simple present tense)

- Have students study the three uses and example sentences.
- Write on the board: *1. this Friday / next weekend  2. this week / month / year  3. now / right now*
- To check comprehension, have students match each set of time expressions on the board with the three uses of the present continuous presented here. (1. future actions; 2. actions occurring during this period of time; 3. actions happening now)

### The present perfect or the present perfect continuous

- Have students study the information and examples.
- Point out that with *for* or *since* there is no difference in meaning between the present perfect and the present perfect continuous.
- Write on the board: *since I was born    for a long time*
- To check comprehension, have pairs take turns using the phrases on the board and the present perfect or the present perfect continuous to make true statements about themselves. Examples: *I've lived / I've been living in the same house since I was born. I've studied / I've been studying English for a long time.*

# GRAMMAR BOOSTER

The *Grammar Booster* is optional.  It provides more explanation and practice, as well as additional grammar concepts.

 **UNIT 1   Lesson 1**

**A**  **Correct the error in each item.**

1. They'd both like to study abroad, ~~would~~ they?  *wouldn't*
2. It's only a six-month course, ~~is~~ it?  *isn't,*
3. Clark met his wife on a rafting trip, didn't ~~Clark~~?  *he*
4. Marian made three trips to Japan last year, ~~hasn't~~ she?  *didn't,*
5. There were a lot of English-speaking people on the tour, wasn't ~~it~~?  *there*
6. The students don't know anything about that, ~~don't~~ they?  *do*
7. There isn't any problem with my student visa, ~~isn't~~ there?  *is*
8. It's always interesting to travel with people from other countries, ~~aren't they~~?  *isn't it*
9. With English, you can travel to most parts of the world, ~~can~~ you?  *can't*
10. I'm next, ~~are~~ I?  *aren't*

**UNIT 1   Lesson 2**

┌─ **Review:  verb usage in the present and past** ──────────────────

**The simple present tense (and NOT the present continuous)**

  **for facts and regular occurrences**
    I **study** English. Class **meets** every day. Water **boils** at 100°.

  **with frequency adverbs and time expressions**
    They never **eat** before 6:00 on weekdays.

  **with stative (non-action) verbs**
    I **remember** her now.

  **for future actions, especially those indicating schedules**
    Flight 100 usually **leaves** at 2:00, but tomorrow it leaves at 1:30.

**The present continuous (and NOT the simple present tense)**

  **for actions happening now (but NOT with stative verbs)**
    They**'re talking** on the phone.

  **for actions occurring during a time period in the present**
    This year I**'m studying** English.

  **for some future actions, especially those already planned**
    Thursday I**'m going** to the theater.

**The present perfect or the present perfect continuous**

  **for unfinished or continuous actions**
    I**'ve lived** here since 2001. OR I**'ve been living** here since 2001.
    I**'ve lived** here for five years. OR I**'ve been living** here for five years.

└─────────────────────────────────────────────────────────────

**Stative (non-action) verbs**

| | | | |
|---|---|---|---|
| appear | have | own | suppose |
| be | hear | possess | taste |
| believe | know | prefer | think |
| belong | like | remember | understand |
| contain | look | see | want |
| cost | love | seem | weigh |
| feel | need | smell | |
| hate | notice | sound | |

┌─────────────────────────────────────────────────────────────────┐
**Review: verb usage in the present and past (continued)**

**The present perfect (but NOT the present perfect continuous)**

    **for completed or non-continuing actions**

        I**'ve eaten** there three times.

        I**'ve** never **read** that book.

        I**'ve** already **seen** him.

**The simple past tense**

    **for actions completed at a specified time in the past**

        I **ate** there in 2003. NOT I̶'̶v̶e̶ ̶e̶a̶t̶e̶n̶ there in 2003.

**The past continuous**

    **for one or more actions in progress at a time in the past**

        At 7:00, we **were eating** dinner.

        They **were swimming** and we **were sitting** on the beach.

**The past continuous and the simple past**

    **for an action that interrrupted a continuing action in the past**

        I **was eating** when my sister **called**.

**<u>Used to</u>**

    **for past situations and habits that no longer exist**

        I **used to smoke**, but I stopped.

        They **didn't use to require** a visa, but now they do.

**The past perfect**

    **to indicate that one past action preceded another past action**

        When I arrived, they **had finished** lunch.
└─────────────────────────────────────────────────────────────────┘

 **Correct the verbs in the following sentences.**

                  *am talking*
1. I t̶a̶l̶k̶ on the phone with my fiancé right now.
              *avoids*
2. She's usually a̶v̶o̶i̶d̶i̶n̶g̶ sweets.
      *are eating*
3. They e̶a̶t̶ dinner now and can't talk on the phone.
              *I go*
4. Every Friday I̶'̶m̶ ̶g̶o̶i̶n̶g̶ to the gym at 7:00.
        *wants*
5. Burt i̶s̶ ̶w̶a̶n̶t̶i̶n̶g̶ to go home early.
             *studied*
6. This year we all s̶t̶u̶d̶y̶ English.
             *leaves*
7. The train i̶s̶ never l̶e̶a̶v̶i̶n̶g̶ before 8:00.
        *freezes*
8. Water i̶s̶ ̶f̶r̶e̶e̶z̶i̶n̶g̶ when the temperature goes down.
      *We like*
9. W̶e̶'̶r̶e̶ ̶l̶i̶k̶i̶n̶g̶ coffee.
              *I stay*
10. On most days I̶'̶m̶ ̶s̶t̶a̶y̶i̶n̶g̶ home.

 **Complete each sentence with the present perfect continuous.**

1. We _____*'ve been coming*_____ to this spa for two years.
          *come*

2. *Lost in Translation* _____*has been playing*_____ at the Classic Cinema since last Saturday.
                     *play*

3. Robert _____*has been waiting*_____ for an admissions letter from the language school for a week.
               *wait*

4. The tour operators *have been worrying about* weather conditions for the rafting trip.
                    *worry about*

5. I _____*'ve been talking about*_____ that tour with everyone.
      *talk about*

## The present perfect (but NOT the present perfect continuous)

- Have students study the information and the examples.
- Point out that the action includes the time up to the present.

## The simple past tense

- Have students study the information and the examples.
- Review with students that the simple past is used with an action that happened and finished in the past.
- Point out that past time expressions help make it clear when that action happened. Examples: *We went to Tokyo last year. We were at the game on Sunday.*
- Write on the board: *What did you do _____?*
- Pair work. Students take turns asking the question and answering using the simple past. Example: A: *What did you do last June?* B: *Last June I took a trip to Paris.* B: *What did you do for your birthday last year?* A: *I had a big party on the beach!*

## The past continuous

- Have students study the information and the example sentences.
- To review, ask *How do we form the past continuous?* (*was* or *were* plus the present participle)
- To check comprehension, say *At 8:00 this morning I was eating breakfast.* Then ask several students *What were you doing at 8:00 this morning?* You may want to change the time and even the day each time you ask a new question.

## The past continuous and the simple past

- Have students study the information and the example sentence.
- Point out that the action in the simple past tense interrupts the action in the past continuous.
- To check comprehension, ask various students to say what they were doing when you—or another person—arrived earlier today. Examples: *I was talking with Sarah when you walked into the classroom. I was taking out my books when you came in. I was hanging up my jacket when you opened the door.*

## <u>Used to</u>

- Have students study the information and the example sentences.
- Point out the affirmative *used to* + base form of the verb (*smoke*). Then point out the negative form *didn't* + *use to* and make sure students notice the change in spelling: *used* to vs. *didn't use* to.
- To check comprehension, ask various students to say something they did in the past but no longer do now. Also ask for things that didn't happen in the past, but do now. Examples: *I used to go to work by bus. Now I go by train. I didn't used to want to get married, but now I do!*

## The past perfect

- Have students study the use of the information and the example.
- To check comprehension, ask *What happened first: they had finished lunch or I arrived?* (they finished lunch)
- Point out that the past perfect is used for the event that happened / finished first.
- To review how to form the past perfect, ask *How do we form the past perfect?* You may want to write on the board: *had + past participle*
- Have students share with the class what they had done by _____ (fill in different times) on _____ (which day). Examples: *By ten o'clock this morning I had walked the dog and read the newspaper. By noon today I had worked five hours and had lunch. By nine o'clock last night I had gone to bed.*

**Option:** Pair work. To provide more practice, ask students to take turns talking about the things they achieved up to a given moment in their lives. Examples: *By June last year I had passed my final exams and found a job. By the time I turned 25, I had graduated, bought a new car, and gotten married.*

 **Correct the verbs . . .**

- This exercise provides practice with the simple present and present continuous tenses.
- As students start the exercise, have them think about what each statement expresses—a fact, a regular occurrence, an action happening now, a description of a schedule, OR a future action—to help them decide on the correct tense needed.
- Encourage students to notice key words—frequency adverbs, time expressions, stative verbs.
- Have students compare answers with a partner and then review as a class.

**Option:** To provide more practice, write on the board:
| | |
|---|---|
| *1. Right now we* | *4. Winter* |
| *2. She always* | *5. The morning bus* |
| *3. This Saturday* | *6. This month* |

Pair work. Students complete the sentences using the simple present tense or the present continuous. (Possible answers: 1. Right now we are doing an exercise. 2. She always arrives first. 3. This Saturday we are going to the movies. 4. Winter starts in December. 5. The morning bus leaves at 8:00. 6. This month he is living in France.)

**B** **Complete each sentence . . .**

- This exercise provides practice with the present perfect continuous.
- After students complete the exercise, have them compare answers. Then review as a class.

**Option:** To provide more practice, ask students to change phrases with *for* to *since* and phrases with *since* to *for* in items 1, 2, and 3. (Possible answers: 1. We have been coming to this spa since [2003]. 2. *Lost in Translation* has been playing at the Classic Cinema for [one week]. 3. Robert has been waiting for an admissions letter from the language school since [last month].)

**Check the sentences . . .**

- Review the direction lines with the class to make sure students understand there are two tasks: 1. identifying items with actions that are unfinished / continuing and 2. changing the tense in the identified sentences.

- Do items 1 and 2 with the class and review the answers.

- Item 1: Point out that *have lived* and *since* tells us that the Averys are still living in New York. (an unfinished / continuing action) Point out that the present perfect continuous tells us that an action started in the past and is still happening now. (have been living)

- Item 2: Point out that *already* tells us that the call was made and it's finished. Point out that the present perfect continuous is not used for finished actions.

- Have students compare answers with a partner. Then review as a class.

 **Complete each sentence . . .**

- This exercise reviews the simple past and the past continuous.

- Have students compare answers and then review as a class.

**Option:** To provide more practice, have students choose their own verbs to complete the sentences in the exercise. Examples: 1. *I was talking on the phone when I heard (the crash of) the accident.* 2. *They were changing the channels of the TV when they saw the news.*

## UNIT 2 **LESSON 1**

## <u>May</u>, <u>might</u> and <u>must</u>: degrees of certainty

- Have students study the examples and their degrees of certainty.

- Review with the class that *may, might*, and *must* let you know the degree of certainty the speaker (or writer) feels about a situation and how much he / she probably knows about the situation. Make sure students notice that the simple present is used to state something that is true / a fact.

- Point out the structure: *may / might / must* + base form of the verb.

- Write the following situation on the board:

   *Sally changed her mind and she's not going to marry Steven.*

- To check comprehension, ask students to work in pairs to make sentences using *may, might,* or *must* about the situation. Examples: *She may have met someone else. She might be in love with another man. She may not want to marry so young. She might not want to lose her independence. She must like to live on her own. Steven must be very upset. He must be brokenhearted.*

- Ask various pairs for one or two of their sentences. Make corrections as necessary.

 **Write a statement . . .**

- As students start the exercise, have them look at the pictures and say the two ailments and the occupation. (backache, headache, chef)

- To review, have different students read one of their sentences out loud. Make necessary corrections.

**Option:** To provide more practice, ask students to write five true (general) statements about themselves. Pair work. Student A says a sentence and Student B responds using *may, might,* and *must*. Examples: Student A: *I always walk to work.* Student B: *You must live near your office.* Student A: *Yes, I live just a few blocks away.* Student B: *My throat really hurts today.* Student A: *You may need to see a doctor.*

**C** Check the sentences and questions that express unfinished or continuing actions. Change the verb phrase in those sentences to the present perfect continuous.

☑ 1. The Averys have ~~lived~~ in New York since the late nineties.
　　　*been living*

☐ 2. Their relatives have already called them.

☑ 3. We have ~~waited~~ to see them for six months.
　　　*been waiting*

☐ 4. I haven't seen the Berlin Philharmonic yet.

☐ 5. This is the first time I've visited Dubai.

☑ 6. We have ~~eaten~~ in that old Peruvian restaurant for years.
　　　*been eating*

☐ 7. Has he ever met your father?

☑ 8. How long have they ~~studied~~ Arabic?
　　　*been studying*

☐ 9. My husband still hasn't bought a car.

☐ 10. The kids have just come back from the race.

**D** Complete each sentence using the past continuous in one blank and the simple past tense in the other.

1. I ___*was speeding*___ when I ___*had*___ the accident.
　　　*speed*　　　　　　*have*

2. They ___*were watching*___ TV when they ___*heard*___ the news.
　　　*watch*　　　　　　　　　*hear*

3. What ___*were you doing*___ when I ___*called*___?
　　　*you / do*　　　　　　　*call*

4. People ___*were waiting*___ for the theater to open when the fire ___*started*___.
　　　*wait*　　　　　　　　　　　　　　　　　*start*

5. Who ___*was using*___ the computer when the electricity ___*went*___ off?
　　　*use*　　　　　　　　　　　　　　　　　　　*go*

## UNIT 2　*Lesson 1*

---
### May, might, and must: degrees of certainty

| | |
|---|---|
| He's carrying a violin. | certainty (a fact) |
| He **must** be a musician. | probability (probably true) |
| He **might (may)** play very well. | possibility (could be true) |
---

**A** Write a statement of certainty, possibility, and probability about the person in each picture.

Answers will vary. Possible answers include:

1. certainty ___*He's in a lot of pain.*___
   possibility ___He might need to go to the doctor.___
   probability ___He must have a backache.___

2. certainty ___He's not feeling well.___
   possibility ___He may need to take a painkiller.___
   probability ___He must have a headache.___

3. certainty ___She's cooking a meal.___
   possibility ___She might work in a restaurant.___
   probability ___She must be a cook.___

## UNIT 3  Lesson 1

---
**The passive causative:  the <u>by</u> phrase**

**Use a <u>by</u> phrase if knowing who performed the action is important.**

   I had my shoes repaired **by a young man** at the train station.

**If knowing who performed the action is <u>not</u> important, you don't need to include a <u>by</u> phrase.**

   I had my shoes repaired ~~by someone~~ at the train station.
---

 **Use the cues to write advice about services with the passive causative.**

1. shoe / repair / Mr. Gil / Boot Stop  *Get your shoes repaired by Mr. Gil at the Boot Stop.*

2. picture / framed / Lydia / Austin Custom Framing  Get that picture framed by Lydia at Austin Custom Framing.

3. hair / cut / Eva / Bella Gente Hair Salon  Get your hair cut by Eva at Bella Gentle Hair Salon.

4. photos / process / mall  Get your photos processed at the mall.

5. custom suit / make / Luigi  Get a custom suit made by Luigi.

6. dry cleaning / do/ Midtown Dry Cleaners  Get your dry cleaning done at Midtown Dry Cleaners.

## UNIT 3  Lesson 2

**A** **Complete each sentence with an infinitive, a base form, or a past participle.**

1. They got the dry cleaner _____to clean_____ the suit again.
   <small>clean</small>

2. He had the photographer _____take_____ pictures of everyone in the family.
   <small>take</small>

3. I missed class, so I got my classmates _____to tell_____ me what happened that day
   in class. <small>tell</small>

4. Are you going to have those pants _____shortened_____?
   <small>shorten</small>

5. She made her son _____stay_____ in bed because he wasn't feeling well.
   <small>stay</small>

6. I'd better get to the bank before it closes if I want to get that check _____cashed_____.
   <small>cash</small>

7. Our teacher had us _____write_____ about what we did during the vacation.
   <small>write</small>

8. You'd better get the travel agent _____to change_____ your flight right away.
   <small>change</small>

9. Are you going to get your paintings _____framed_____ for the art exhibit?
   <small>frame</small>

10. If you need to know when the next train leaves, you can have my assistant _____call_____
    the station. <small>call</small>

---
**Let**

**Use <u>let</u> to show that someone permits someone to do something.**

   I **don't let** my children **stay** out after 9:00.    Why don't you **let** me **help** you?

**<u>Let</u> is followed by an object and the base form of a verb.**

|  | object | base form |  |
| --- | --- | --- | --- |
| She **let** | her sister | **wear** | her skirt. |

   NOT  She let her sister ~~to wear~~ her skirt.
---

G4

## UNIT 3 **LESSON 1**

### The passive causative: the <u>by</u> phrase

• Write on the board:

| I | had | the document copied. |
|---|-----|----------------------|
|   | got |                      |

• Before students study the Grammar box, have them look at the examples on the board. Review the passive causative by asking *How do we form the passive causative?* (*have* or *get* + object + the past participle)

• Review the use of the passive causative by brainstorming everyday services the students use. Examples: *have a document copied, get a sweater dry-cleaned, have your house cleaned,* etc.

• Then have students study the first explanation and the example sentence.

• Point out that the *by* phrase in the example sentence (*by a young man*) adds important / necessary information. The listener learns who performed the action.

• Point out that if students want to say the location where a service is received, they need to use *at*. Examples: *at the garage, at the bank, at the hair salon*

• To review the structure, ask *Where do we place the <u>by</u> (or <u>at</u>) phrase in the sentence?* (after the past participle)

• Write on the board:

| film developed | car repaired |
|----------------|--------------|
| documents copied | hair colored |
| clothes dry-cleaned | checks cashed |

• To check comprehension, ask students to say who performs these services or where they receive these services. You may want to point out they can use *by* plus a person or *at* plus a place. Examples: *I have my film developed by my brother. I have my photos developed at the drugstore.*

• Have students study the second explanation and the example sentence.

• Point out that the *by* phrase in the example (*by someone*) does not add any specific or helpful information, so it is not necessary.

###  Use the cues . . .

• Review the example with the class. Point out that the example includes *at* plus a place.

• To review, ask various students for their sentences. Make necessary corrections.

**Challenge:** Group work. Groups of three. Have students share bad or good experiences they have had arranging a service. Example: *I once had a package sent by a local company, and the package never arrived. They said it would reach its destination in just three days, but it got lost on its way!* To finish the activity, you may want to have a few volunteers share one of their experiences with the class.

## UNIT 3 **LESSON 2**

### Complete each sentence . . .

• You may first want to do the following review of the causative and passive causative before students do this exercise.

• Write on the board:

| | | | | |
|---|---|---|---|---|
| 1. Sue | HAD | her carpet | CLEANED | last week. |
| 2. Sue | GOT | her brother | TO CLEAN | her carpet. |
| 3. Bill | GOT | his car | REPAIRED | at my garage. |
| 4. Bill | HAD | the new guy | REPAIR | his car. |

• Review the use of the passive causative and causative by pointing out that both grammar points use *get* and *have*, but for different reasons. Say *The causative tells us that someone caused another person to do something. Use the passive causative to show that the action or service was arranged.*

• To check comprehension, ask *Which sentences on the board are examples of the causative?* (2, 4) *Which sentences are examples of the passive causative?* (1, 3)

• Ask students to study the structures used. Ask students to point out the structure for each sentence. You may want to write them on the board. (Sentences 1, 3: *get / have* + object + participle; Sentence 2: *get / have* + object + infinitive; Sentence 4: *get / have* + object + base form)

• Have students compare answers with a partner. Then review as a class.

**Option:** To provide more practice, divide the class into two teams—A and B. Read one sentence starter per team. A student from team A repeats the starter and completes the sentence with the passive causative or causative. If the sentence is correct, team A scores a point. If it's incorrect, team B has the chance to correct it and get a point. The team with the most points wins. Make sure students on each team take turns. Example: Team A: *I got my brother to give me some money.* T: *Correct!* Team B: *She had her jacket a long time.* T: *I'm sorry, that's not correct.* Team A? Team A: *She had her jacket dry-cleaned.* T: *Correct!*

| | |
|---|---|
| I got my brother . . . | They had the package . . . |
| She had her jacket . . . | We had the car . . . |
| He got the teacher to . . . | He had the waiter . . . |
| I got the photos . . . | We got the bank . . . |

### <u>Let</u>

• Have students study the explanations and the examples.

• Point out that *let* is used to talk about giving or asking for permission. Ask students to study the structure and say which verb form is used with *let*. (base form of the verb)

• To check comprehension, ask various students *What did your parents let you do when you were a child? What didn't they let you do?* (Students may say: My parents let me walk to school by myself. They let me go to bed late on Saturday nights. They didn't let me ride my bike in the street. They didn't let me stay out late at night.)

### B On a separate sheet of paper . . .

- You may want to review the information in the Grammar box on the previous page (and the teaching notes) before students begin this exercise.

- As students work on the exercise, remind them to pay attention to necessary changes in verb forms.

- Have students compare answers with a partner. Then review as a class.

**Challenge:** Write various topics on the board: *go on vacations with friends, pierce their bodies, dye their hair, smoke, go out on weeknights, get a part-time job, quit school to work full time,* etc. Form small groups. Ask students to imagine they are parents of teenagers—and some of your students may be! Have them discuss what they let / don't let AND / OR what they are going to let / not going to let their teens do. Example: Student A: *I'm not going to let my son pierce his body!* Student B: *I let my son and daughter go to discos, but they have to be home my midnight.*

**Answers to Unit 3, Lesson 2—Exercise B**

1. Don't let your little brother open the oven door.
2. You should let your little sister go to the store with you.
3. Actually, we don't let our daughter eat a lot of candy.
4. I wouldn't let my youngest son go to the mall alone.
5. Why won't you let him see that movie?
6. You should let the tailor do what he thinks is best.
7. We always let him stay out late.

## Causative <u>have</u> and past perfect auxiliary <u>have</u>

- Write on the board: *I <u>have</u> them fix it.*

- Review with students that the causative can occur in different tenses. Ask *What tense is the statement on the board in?* (simple present)

- Have students change the statement on the board to the simple past (I had them fix it.) and then to the future. (I will have them fix it.)

- Have students study the explanation and examples in the Grammar box.

- Have students look at the examples again. To check comprehension, ask *In the first example, who called before 10:00?* (they / the other people) *In the second example, who called before 10:00?* (the speaker / I) *Which example uses the simple past tense causative?* (the first) *Which example uses the past perfect?* (the second)

- Write on the board:
  1. *Steven had the air conditioner repaired before the party.*
  2. *Steven had repaired the air conditioner before the party.*

- To provide more practice, ask students to explain the difference between the two examples on the board. (1. Someone else repaired the air conditioner for Steven. 2. Steven himself repaired the air conditioner.)

### C  Who did what? Read . . .

- Go over the example with the class. Ask *Did the people fix the car themselves, or did someone else to do it?* (someone else)

- Review that *had* is causative in the first sentence because it is followed by an object and a base form.

- Have students compare answers with a partner. Then review as a class.

**Option:** Write on the board (or make copies for the class):
  1. *She had her assistant to mail the letter.*
  2. *Her assistant had mail the letter the day before.*
  3. *Michael had his brother fixed his bicycle.*
  4. *Michael have already fixed his bicycle when his brother arrived.*
  5. *The teacher had edit the students their work.*
  6. *The students had finish their work before the bell rang.*

To provide more practice, have students correct the error in each sentence. Review as a class. (1. She had her assistant mail the letter. 2. Her assistant had mailed the letter the day before. 3. Michael had his brother fix his bicycle. 4. Michael had already fixed his bicycle when his brother arrived. 5. The teacher had the students edit their work. 6. The students had finished their work before the bell rang.)

## UNIT 4 **LESSON 1**

### Review: Expressing the future

- Have students read the first explanation and study the four examples.

- Point out that the example for the simple present needs more context.

  Example: *When I see her tomorrow, I'll tell her you said hello.*

- To review, ask students to use any of the four structures to say what their plans are for the upcoming weekend. Examples: *I'll go to my mother's house on Sunday. I'm going to visit an old college professor. I'm playing soccer with friends. I need to pick up my new car on Saturday.*

- Have students read the second explanation and study the examples.

- Review that *may* and *might* mean that something is possible in the future. Ask students to use a future tense to restate the first two examples. (Possible answers: Maybe I'll see her tomorrow. I'm probably going to see her tomorrow.)

- Review that *can* means someone is able to do something and *tomorrow* indicates that it will be in the future.

- To provide practice, ask pairs to role-play the following situation: Student A asks Student B if he or she *can* do an activity in the future. Student B says no and explains why using *may* or *might*. Examples: Student A: *Can we meet on Thursday?* Student B: *I'm sorry. I may work from home on that day. How about Friday?* Student B: *Can I see you on Monday?* Student A: *I'm sorry. I might have a meeting on Monday.*

**On a separate sheet of paper, rewrite each sentence using let.**

1. Don't permit your little brother to open the oven door.
2. You should permit your little sister to go to the store with you.
3. Actually, we don't permit our daughter to eat a lot of candy.
4. I wouldn't permit my youngest son to go to the mall alone.
5. Why won't you permit him to see that movie?
6. You should permit the tailor to do what he thinks is best.
7. We always permit him to stay out late.

---

**Causative have and the past perfect auxiliary have**

**BE CAREFUL!** Don't confuse the simple past tense causative <u>have</u> with <u>have</u> used in the past perfect.

    I **had them call** me before 10:00.    (They called me.)

    I **had called** them before 10:00.    (I called them.)

---

 **Who did what? Read the sentence. Complete the statement.**

1. We had them fix the car before our trip.    _They_ fixed _the car_ .
   We had fixed the car before our trip.    _We_ fixed _the car_ .

2. Janet had already called her mother.    _Janet_ called _her mother_ .
   Janet had her mother call the train station.    _Her mother_ called _the train station_ .

3. Mark had his classmate help him with it.    _His classmates_ helped _Mark_ .
   Mark had helped his classmate with it.    _Mark_ helped _his classmates_ .

4. My father had signed the check for his boss.    _My father_ signed _the check_ .
   My father had his boss sign the check.    _His boss_ signed _the check_ .

5. Mr. Gates had them open the bank early.    _They_ opened _the bank_ .
   Mr. Gates had opened the bank early.    _Mr. Gates_ opened _the bank_ .

---

# UNIT 4 *Lesson 1*

**REVIEW: Expressing the future**

**The future can be expressed in all the following ways:**

| | |
|---|---|
| <u>will</u> + base form | **I'll see** |
| <u>be going to</u> + base form | **I'm going to see** |
| the simple present tense | **I see** |
| the present continuous | **I'm seeing** |

} her tomorrow.

**Modals can also be used to talk about the future.**

| | |
|---|---|
| modal + base form | I **might see** |
| | I **may see** |
| | I **can see** |

} her tomorrow.

**A** ▷ **Complete the conversations using <u>will</u> or <u>be going to</u>.**

1. **A:** Would you like to go running in the park? I __'m going to leave__ in about half an hour.
   <br>                                                                              _leave_

   **B:** That sounds great. I __'ll meet__ you there.
   <br>_meet_

2. **A:** It's midnight. Why are you still reading?

   **B:** We __'re going to have__ a test tomorrow.
   <br>_have_

3. **A:** Do you have plans for tomorrow?

   **B:** Yes. I __'m going to see__ a chiropractor for the first time.
   <br>_see_

4. **A:** I hope you can come tomorrow night. We'd really like you to be there.

   **B:** OK. I __'ll come__ .
   <br>_come_

5. **A:** I'm thinking about getting a new laptop.

   **B:** Really? Well, I __'ll show__ you mine. I love it.
   <br>_show_

**B** ▷ **Read each sentence. Check the sentences that have future meaning.**

☐ **1.** Hannah is studying English this month.

☑ **2.** Max is studying French next month.

☐ **3.** Nancy studies English in the evening.

☑ **4.** I'm taking my daughter out for dinner tonight.

☑ **5.** You should call me tomorrow.

☑ **6.** He might have time to see you later.

☑ **7.** My parents are arriving at 10:00.

## REVIEW: Future with <u>will</u> and <u>be going to</u>

- Have students study the explanations and the examples.
- To review, ask students to work in pairs and make an example for each use of *will* and *be going to*. Encourage students to give feedback to each other.
- Walk around and provide help as needed.

###  A  Complete the conversations . . .

- Do the first item with the class. Review the correct answers by clarifying: 1. *I am going to leave:* The person has a plan. 2. *will meet:* The person shows willingness to do something.
- Have students compare answers with a partner. Then review as a class.

**Option:** Write on the board:
1. A: Are you free this Friday?
   B: No, I _____ .
2. A: Did you hear the weather report for tomorrow?
   B: Yes, it _____ .
3. A: I don't know how to use this copier. Can you give me a hand?
   B: Sure. I _____ .

Pair work. Ask students to complete the conversations using *will* or *be going to*. To review, ask various pairs to perform one of their conversations. Make sure students use 1. *be going to*—prior plan; 2. *will / be going to*—prediction; 3. *will*—willingness.

## REVIEW: The present continuous, the simple present tense, and modals with future meaning

- Have students study the first explanation and the examples.
- Point out that including time words when using present continuous for the future helps make the future meaning more clear.
- Have students find and say the time word in the example. (tomorrow)
- To provide practice, say statements and have students restate them using the present continuous for future. Students should add a time word each time. Examples: *I'm going to travel to Spain.* (I'm traveling to Spain [next week].) *I'm going to see Sue.* (I'm seeing Sue tomorrow [at 3:00].) *He's going to leave.* (He's leaving [after supper].)

- Have students study the second explanation and the example.
- To check comprehension, write on the board:
   1. *Our Friday meetings usually <u>start</u> at 10:00.*
   2. *This Friday our meeting <u>starts</u> at 11:00.*
- Ask *Which example shows the simple present used with future meaning?* (2) *How do you know?* (because it says *This Friday*)
- Have students study the third explanation and the example.
- To clarify further, write on the board:
   1. *You should call the doctor.*
   2. *You should call the doctor tomorrow.*
- Point out that there are no time words in the first example and it has present meaning. The second example has future meaning because of the word *tomorrow.*
- To provide practice, say the modals one by one and ask various students to make a sentence and include time words to give it future meaning. Examples: *You should see her tomorrow. Maybe we could go to Canada next summer. He may be late to class on Monday. She might find a surprise when she gets home. You have to finish this by Friday. I can help you with your homework after dinner.*

### B  Read each sentence . . .

- Ask students to underline the time words that give the statements future meaning. (2. next month; 4. tonight; 5. tomorrow; 6. later; 7. at 10:00; 8. today)
- If necessary, point out that in item 1, *this month* refers to an action occurring during a present period of time.
- Ask students to find a statement in which the future meaning is given by the context only. (10)
- Have students compare answers with a partner. Then review as a class.

## UNIT 4 **LESSON 2**

### Regrets about the past: <u>wish</u> + the past perfect; <u>should have</u> and <u>ought to have</u>

- Write on the board: *I wish I <u>had</u> a car.*
- To review expressing a present regret with *wish* + simple past, ask *Does this sentence express something I want to have now or something I wanted to have in the past?* (something you want to have now)
- Point out that the simple past tense follows *wish* to express a present regret.
- To check comprehension, ask various students to say things they wish they had. Examples: *I wish I had a bigger apartment. I wish I had an interesting job.*
- Have students study the first explanation and the example sentence.
- Ask students *What are the two regrets the person has in the first example?* (1. It was mistake to marry so young. 2. It was a mistake to marry Celine.)
- Point out that the past perfect follows *wish* to express regret about something already done or decided.
- To check comprehension, ask various students to make sentences using *I wish* about past actions or decisions they regret. Examples: *I wish I had never moved to the city. I wish I had married my first boyfriend.*
- Have students study the second explanation and the examples.
- Point out that both *should have* and *ought to have* express regret.
- To check comprehension, ask students to work in pairs. Student A uses *I wish* to express a past regret. Then Student B says the same sentence using *I should have* or *I ought to have*. Example: Student A: *I wish I had listened to my parents about studying.* Student B: *I should have listened to my parents about studying.*
- Make sure to point out the Note. Using *should have* instead of *ought to have* in negative statements and questions is more common in American English.

####  Restate the statements . . .

- Go over the example with the class.
- Have students compare answers with a partner. Then review as a class.

**Challenge:** Write on the board:

   *studies    trips    work/job*

Pair work. Ask students to take turns using *wish, should have* or *ought to have* to talk about past decisions they regret about the topics on the board. Students may say *I wish I had gone to college. I should have finished my studies. I ought to have gone on vacation when I had the chance. I wish I hadn't spent so much money on a trip to London. I should have accepted the first job I was offered. I ought to have taken a part-time job while I was at college.*

## UNIT 5 **LESSON 1**

####  On a separate sheet of paper . . .

- To review adjective clauses, write on the board:
    *I just took a trip that I will never forget.*
- Ask students to find and say the adjective clause in the statement on the board. (that I will never forget)
- Then ask *What do adjective clauses give additional information about?* (a noun / a person or thing) *What does the clause on the board give additional information about?* (a trip) *What relative pronoun introduces it?* (that) *Would it also be correct to use <u>who</u>?* (no, *who* is used for people)
- Have students compare answers with a partner. Review as a class.

**Challenge:** Groups of three. Ask students to use adjective clauses to make sentences about different people they saw or talked to recently and various things they did this past week. Examples: *The friend who / that I saw yesterday used to be my neighbor. The movie that opened on Saturday was not very good. Our weekly meeting which begins at 9:00 on Mondays is usually interesting.*

#### Answers to Unit 5, Lesson 1—Exercise A

2. My cousin who lives in New Zealand called today.
3. We have a meeting that begins at 9:30 every morning.
4. The celebration that takes place in the spring is spectacular.
5. The teacher who teaches the grammar class is not very formal.
6. Patients who want to avoid strong medication might prefer homeopathy.
7. The copy shop that offers express service is closed on weekends.
8. The hotel that has a swimming pool is very expensive.
9. Do you like the teacher who teaches the grammar class?

☑ **8.** The class finishes at 3:00 today.

☐ **9.** The class always starts at 2:00 and finishes at 4:00.

☑ **10.** We may stay another week in Paris.

 ## UNIT 4 Lesson 2

> **Regrets about the past:** <u>wish</u> + **the past perfect;** <u>should have</u>
> **and** <u>ought to have</u>
>
> <u>wish</u> + **the past perfect**
>
> **You can express a regret about the past with** <u>wish</u> + **the past perfect.**
>
> I **wish** I **had married** later. And I **wish** I **hadn't married** Celine!
>
> Do you **wish** you **had bought** that car when it was available?
>
> <u>should have</u> **and** <u>ought to have</u>
>
> <u>**Ought to have**</u> **has the same meaning as** <u>should have</u>. <u>**Should have**</u> **is much more common in spoken English.**
>
> I **should have married** later. = I **ought to have married** later.
>
> I **shouldn't have married** Celine. = I **ought not to have** married Celine.
>
> **Should** he **have married** Celine? = **Ought** he **to have** married Celine?
>
> **Note: American English speakers use** <u>should have</u> **instead of** <u>ought to have</u> **in negative statements and in questions.**

**A** ▷ **Restate the statements and questions with** <u>wish</u> + **the past perfect to statements and questions with** <u>should have</u> **or** <u>ought to have</u>.

**1.** I wish I had studied law. (should) _I should have studied law._

**2.** She wishes she had had children. (ought to) _She ought to have had children._

**3.** Do you wish you had studied Chinese? (should) _Should you have studied Chinese?_

**4.** I wish I had gone to Chile instead of Australia. (ought to) _I ought to have gone to Chile instead of Australia._

**5.** Do you wish you had taken the job at the embassy? (should) _Should you have taken the job at the embassy?_

 ## UNIT 5 Lesson 1

**A** ▷ **On a separate sheet of paper, combine the two sentences into one sentence, making the second sentence an adjective clause. Use** <u>who</u> **or** <u>that</u>.

**1.** The hotel clerk was very helpful. / He recommended the restaurant.

   _The hotel clerk who recommended the restaurant was very helpful._

**2.** My cousin called today. / He lives in New Zealand.

**3.** We have a meeting every morning. / It begins at 9:30.

**4.** The celebration is spectacular. / It takes place in spring.

**5.** The teacher is not very formal. / She teaches the grammar class.

**6.** Patients might prefer homeopathy. / They want to avoid strong medication.

**7.** The copy shop is closed on weekends. / It offers express service.

**8.** The hotel is very expensive. / It has a swimming pool.

**9.** Do you like the teacher? / He teaches the grammar class.

---
**Reciprocal pronouns: each other and one another**

**Each other** and **one another** have the same meaning, but **one another** is more formal.

People give **each other** (or **one another**) gifts.        Friends send **each other** (or **one another**) cards.

**BE CAREFUL!** Reciprocal pronouns have a different meaning from reflexive pronouns.

They looked at **themselves**. (Each person looked in a mirror.)

They looked at **each other**. (Each person looked at the other person.)

---

**B** **On a separate sheet of paper, rewrite each underlined phrase using a reciprocal pronoun.**

1. On Christmas, in many places in the world, people <u>give and receive presents</u>.

   *On Christmas, in many places in the world, people give each other presents.*

2. On New Year's Eve in New York City, people wait in Times Square for midnight to come so they can <u>kiss other people</u> and <u>wish other people</u> a happy new year.

3. During the Thai holiday Songkran, people <u>throw water at other people</u> on the street.

4. During the Tomato Festival in Bunol, Spain, people have a lot of fun <u>throwing tomatoes at other people</u> for about two hours.

5. After a day of fasting during Ramadan, Muslims around the world <u>invite other people to eat</u> in their homes in the evening.

---

**Reflexive pronouns**

A reflexive pronoun should always agree with the subject of the verb.

**People** really enjoy **themselves** during Carnaval.

**My sister** made **herself** sick from eating so much!

**Common expressions with reflexive pronouns**

| | |
|---|---|
| **believe in oneself** | If you **believe in yourself**, you can do anything. |
| **enjoy oneself** | We **enjoyed ourselves** very much on our vacation. |
| **feel sorry for oneself** | Don't sit around **feeling sorry for yourself**. |
| **help oneself to** (something) | Please **help yourselves** to dessert! |
| **hurt oneself** | Paul **hurt himself** when he tried to move the refrigerator. |
| **give oneself** (something) | I wanted to **give myself** a gift, so I bought a watch. |
| **introduce oneself** | Why don't you **introduce yourself** to your new neighbor? |
| **be proud of oneself** | Jackie **was** really **proud of herself** when she got that job. |
| **take care of oneself** | You should **take** better **care of yourself**. OK? |
| **talk to oneself** | I sometimes **talk to myself** when I'm feeling nervous. |
| **teach oneself** (to do something) | Niki **taught herself** to use a computer. |
| **tell oneself** (something) | I always **tell myself** I'm not going to eat dessert, and then I do anyway. |
| **work for oneself** | Oscar left the company last year. He now **works for himself**. |

**Reflexive pronouns**

| me | → | myself |
|---|---|---|
| you | → | yourself |
| him | → | himself |
| her | → | herself |
| it | → | itself |
| us | → | ourselves |
| them | → | themselves |

---

**C** **Complete the sentences with reflexive pronouns.**

1. My brother and his wife really enjoyed <u>themselves</u> on their vacation.

2. My uncle has been teaching <u>himself</u> how to cook.

3. The food was so terrific that I helped <u>myself</u> to some more!

4. Don't sit around feeling sorry for <u>yourself</u>.

5. I hope your sister's been taking good care of <u>herself</u>.

6. I didn't know anyone at the party, and I was too shy to introduce <u>myself</u> to anyone.

7. Mr. Yu hurt <u>himself</u> while lighting firecrackers for the Chinese New Year.

# Reciprocal pronouns: <u>each other</u> and <u>one another</u>

- Have students study the first explanation and the examples.

- Write on the board:

    <u>Friend</u>s send <u>each other</u> cards.
    <u>Friend</u>s send <u>one another</u> cards.

- Point out that the subject *Friends* and the reciprocal pronouns *each other* and *one another* refer to the same people. Tell students that using reciprocal pronouns shows that everyone is doing the same action.

- To check comprehension, ask students *When do people give each other gifts in your family and circle of friends? When do we send one another cards / write letters?*

- Encourage students to say full sentences and use reciprocal pronouns. Examples: *In our family, we give each other gifts on our birthdays, etc. My friends and I send one another postcards when we go on vacation.*

- You may want to tell students that some native speakers use *one another* for more than two people and *each other* for two people. In everyday use they are considered interchangeable.

- Have students study the Be Careful! note and the examples.

- To help clarify, write on the board:

    *1. They looked at themselves in the mirror.*
    A ⟶ A      B ⟶ B

    *2. They looked at each other.*
    A ⟵ B

- Say *In item 1 A looked at A and B looked at B. In item 2 A looked at B and B looked at A.*

- You may want to have students stand up and demonstrate the examples on the board. You can draw a picture of a mirror on the board.

##  On a separate sheet of paper . . .

- Go over the example with the class.

- Have students compare answers with a partner. Then review as a class.

**Option:** To provide more practice, have students think about someone they know; for example, someone who lives far away from them or someone very important to them. Pair work. Students take turns asking each other questions about their partner's person. Students should use reflexive pronouns in their questions and answers. Write some example questions on the board to guide the students.

    *1. Where did you meet each other?*
    *2. How do you keep in touch with each other?*
    *3. What do you usually tell each other about?*
    *4. Do you send each other cards or gifts?*
    *5. Do you ever see each other?*

## Reflexive pronouns

- Have students study the explanation and the examples.

- Have students read the object pronouns and reflexive pronouns in the box to the right.

- Write on the board:

    _____ *looked at* _____ *in the mirror.*

- Say subject pronouns at random order and have volunteers use each pronoun you say plus a reflexive pronoun to complete the sentence on the board. Examples: T: *He.* S1: *He looked at himself in the mirror.* T: *We.* S2: *We looked at ourselves in the mirror.*

- Have students study the common expressions and the examples.

- Answer any questions they may have. Students will practice these expressions in Exercise D (on the next page). You may also want to use the option following Exercise D to provide more practice.

##  Complete the sentences . . .

- Do the first item with the class. Make sure students know that the correct answer is *themselves* because *My brother and his wife* can be replaced by *They.*

- Have students compare answers with a partner and review as a class.

**Complete each sentence . . .**

- Do the first item with the class. Remind students that after they choose the correct expression based on meaning, they need to make sure to use the correct form of the verb plus the correct reflexive pronoun.

- Have students compare answers with a partner and review as a class.

**Option:** Ask various students questions using the expressions with reflexive pronouns in the Grammar box on page G8. Point out that students should use the expressions in their answers. Examples: *Have you ever hurt yourself badly?  How can we help children feel good about themselves?  Have you ever taught yourself to do something?  Do you ever talk to yourself?  Would you like to work for yourself?  Do you ever give yourself gifts?*

## **by** + reflexive pronouns

- Have students study the explanation and the examples.

- To check comprehension, ask students if they can think of other things they or others can and can't do by themselves. Examples: *Babies can't feed themselves. I can't drive by myself yet; I'm still taking driving lessons.  My grandparents can't live by themselves anymore as they need help now.*

 **Complete each sentence . . .**

- Do the first item with the class.

- Have students compare answers with a partner. Then review as a class.

---

## Adjective clauses: <u>who</u> and <u>whom</u> in formal English

- Have students study the explanation and the examples.

- Point out that many native speakers use *who* instead of *whom*.

- Write on the board:

    *1. The woman who wanted to see you is here.*
    *2. The woman whom you wanted to see is here.*

- To review, ask students to make two sentences out of each example.  (1. The woman is here.  She wanted to see you.  2. The woman is here.  You wanted to see her.)

- Make sure students see the differences in meaning in the two examples.

- To check comprehension, ask students to finish these sentence starters:

    *The man / woman who . . .*
    *The man / woman whom . . .*

- (Students may say: *The man whom you met is my brother.  The woman whom you wanted to talk to is on vacation.  The man who really influenced me in life was my grandfather.  The woman who just called is my mother!*)

**A** **Complete the sentences**

- Do the first item with the class.

- Remind students to use *whom* for object relative pronouns (not *who*).

- Have students compare answers with a partner.

- Review as a class.

**D** Complete each sentence with one of the common expressions with reflexive pronouns.

1. When did your brother _____teach himself_____ how to play the guitar?

2. You'd better tell your daughter to stop playing near that stove or she'll _____hurt herself_____.

3. I really hope you _____enjoy yourself_____ when you're on vacation!

4. To practice greetings and introductions, I ask my students to _____introduce themselves_____ to each other on the first day of class.

> **by + reflexive pronouns**
>
> **Use by with a reflexive pronoun to mean "alone."**
> You cannot put on a kimono **by yourself**. You need help.
> Students cannot learn to speak in English **by themselves**. They need to practice with each other.

**E** Complete each sentence with **by** and a reflexive pronoun.

1. Very young children shouldn't be allowed to play outside _____by themselves_____.

2. Did your father go to the store _____by himself_____?

3. When did you learn to fix a computer _____by yourself_____?

4. We got tired of waiting, so we found a table _____by ourselves_____.

# UNIT 5 Lesson 2

> **Adjective clauses: who and whom in formal English**
>
> **In formal written or spoken English, use who for subject relative pronouns and whom for object relative pronouns.**
> The singer was terrible. + **He** sang in the restaurant.
>     subject relative pronoun
> The singer **who** sang in the restaurant was terrible.
>
> The singer was terrible. + We heard **him** last night.
>     object relative pronoun
> The singer **whom** we heard last night was terrible.

**A** Complete the sentences with **who** or **whom**.

1. The manager _____who_____ works at that hotel is very helpful.

2. The man _____whom_____ I met at the meeting has invited us to lunch.

3. The sales representative _____who_____ lives in Hong Kong may apply for that job.

4. I am very satisfied with the hair stylist _____whom_____ you recommended.

5. The guests _____whom_____ we invited to the event were three hours late.

6. The dentist _____whom_____ you'll see tomorrow speaks English.

7. The DJ _____whom_____ you requested is performing at the club tonight.

8. The tailor _____whom_____ I'm recommending is very reasonable.

9. My friend _____who_____ works at the embassy will help you.

10. Is your colleague someone _____whom_____ I can really trust?

## UNIT 6   Lesson 1

 **On a separate sheet of paper, write and punctuate each of the following statements in direct speech.**

1. They said tell us when you will be home   *They said, "Tell us when you will be home."*
2. Martin told me don't get a flu shot
3. My daughter said please pick me up after school
4. The English teacher said read the newspaper tonight and bring in a story about the weather
5. We said please don't forget to buy batteries
6. They said don't buy milk
7. We told them please call us in the morning
8. She said please tell your parents I'm sorry I can't talk right now

 **Look at each statement in indirect speech. Then complete each statement, making the indirect speech statement a direct speech statement. Use correct punctuation.**

1. They told us to be home before midnight.  They told us _____, "Be home before midnight."_____

2. The sign downtown said to pack emergency supplies before the storm.
   The sign downtown said _____, "Pack emergency supplies before the storm."_____

3. Your daughter called and told me to turn on the radio and listen to the news
   about the earthquake.  Your daughter told me _____, "Turn on the radio and listen to the news about the earthquake."_____

4. Your parents said not to call them before nine A.M.
   Your parents said _____, "Don't call us before nine A.M."_____

5. Mr. Rossi phoned to tell me not to go downtown this afternoon.
   Mr. Rossi told me _____, "Don't go downtown this afternoon."_____

## UNIT 6   Lesson 2

# UNIT 6 **LESSON 1**

## Punctuation rules for direct speech

- Have students study the explanations and the examples.
- Review with students that direct speech means we are quoting the exact words someone said.
- Write various incorrect direct speech sentences on the board. Examples:
    1. *Sandra "said don't call me before six".*
    2. *He said, I have a meeting next Monday.*
- Pair work. Have students identify the errors and rewrite the sentences correctly. (1. Sandra said, "Don't call me before 6:00." 2. He said, "I have a meeting next Monday.")
- Review as a class.

 **On a separate sheet of paper . . .**

- Before students do the exercise write on the board:
    1. *Brandon said, "I'm hungry."*
    2. *Brandon said he was hungry.*
- Ask *Do the two sentences on the board have the same meaning?* (yes) *What's the difference between them?* (Item 1 uses direct speech—the exact words the speaker said; item 2 uses indirect speech.)
- Have students compare answers with a partner and the review as a class.

**Answers to Unit 6, Lesson 1—Exercise A**
2. Martin told me, "Don't get a flu shot."
3. My daughter said, "Please pick me up after school."
4. The English teacher said, "Read the newspaper tonight and bring in a story about the weather."
5. We said, "Please don't forget to buy batteries."
6. They said, "Don't buy milk."
7. We told them, "Please call us in the morning."
8. She said, "Please tell your parents I'm sorry I can't talk right now."

 **Look at each statement . . .**

- Do the first item with the class.
- Have students compare answers with a partner and then review as a class.

**Option:** Ask students to think about instructions they heard today or on a previous day. Encourage students to write three or four statements using direct speech. Pair work. Have students read each others' sentences and make any necessary corrections. Examples: *This morning my father said, "Don't forget your umbrella." My boss told Sarah, "I need the report right now."*

# UNIT 6 **LESSON 2**

## Indirect speech: optional tense changes

- Have students study the first explanation and the three examples.
- Review that the change in verb tense is optional. Point out that students should be able to understand and even produce both forms.
- Point out that the tense of the reporting verb "controls" the verb form in the reported information.
- Have students study the Be Careful! note.
- Point out that a reporting verb in the present tense is appropriate if the information is recent or it still true.
- To check comprehension, say various sentences and have students work in pairs to make sentences in reported speech. Encourage students to use both *say* and *tell*, as well as *teacher, she / he*, and *just*. Examples:
1. *School is closed tomorrow.* (The teacher said the school was closed tomorrow. OR The teacher said the school is closed tomorrow.)
2. *The weather report says rain tomorrow.* (She said that the weather report said rain tomorrow. OR She said that the weather report says rain tomorrow.)
3. *You need to work on increasing your active vocabulary.* (The teacher told us we needed to work on . . . OR The teacher told us we need to work on . . .)

**On a separate sheet of paper . . .**

- Do the first item with the class. Review with students that the verb tense needs to change because it doesn't meet the three criteria in the Grammar box on page G10.

- Have students compare answers with a partner. Encourage them to discuss why the verb tense changes or not and to check the Grammar box.

- Then review as a class.

**Answers to Unit 6, Lesson 2—Exercise A**
1. Last Friday my husband said he was going to pick up some supplies before the storm.
2. Last year my parents said they were going to go to Spain on vacation.
3. She told them this year's flu shot was not entirely protective against the flu.
4. He just said the danger of a flood is over.
5. We always say it's always easier to take the train than drive.
6. When I was a child, my parents told me it's really important to get a good education.
7. The National Weather Service is saying that tonight's weather is terrible.
8. Your parents just told me they want to leave for the shelter immediately.

## UNIT 7 **LESSON 1**

### Embedded questions: usage

- Have students study the first explanation and the examples.

- To review embedded questions, ask students to underline the embedded question in each statement. (what time it is, why it's not working, where the bathroom is, how to get to Main Street)

- Then have students study the Be Careful! note to the right.

- Write on the board:
    1. *I know where <u>he is</u>.*
    2. *I know where <u>is he</u>.*
    3. *I don't know what <u>did he buy</u>.*
    4. *I don't know what <u>he bought</u>.*

- Ask students to say which statements on the board are correct. (1 and 4) Review with students that embedded questions require normal word order— no inversion and no auxiliaries.

- Have students study the phrases often followed by embedded questions.

- Point out that embedded questions are more polite than direct questions. They are often used when we're asking for a favor, for information, or when we are talking to people we don't know.

- To check comprehension, ask various students to make statements using a phrase plus an embedded question. Examples: *I don't know when they are coming. I wonder where I put my jacket. Can you tell me what time it is?*

**Option:** To provide more practice with embedded questions, write on the board:
  *I remember (who, what, where, when, why) _____.*
  *I don't remember (who, what, where, when, why) _____.*

Have students think about their childhood. Ask them to say things they remember / don't remember using embedded questions. Examples: *I remember where we used to go on vacation. It was on the beach . . . I remember what my first grade classroom was like. It was sunny and . . . I don't remember who my first teacher was.*

**Option:** To provide more practice, have students take turns role playing a tourist visiting this city or country and someone who lives here. Encourage the tourist to use embedded questions. Example: Student A: *Hello. Can you tell me how to get to the train station from here?* Student B: *Sure. Walk up this street two blocks and . . .*

### Embedded questions: punctuation

- Have students study the explanations and the examples.

- Write on the board:
    1. *Do you know why she's not here*
    2. *I wonder why she's not here*

- To check comprehension, ask students to say which punctuation is needed for each item. (1. a question mark; 2. a period)

 **On a separate sheet of paper . . .**

- Go over the example with the class.

- Tell students they can refer to the Grammar box for phrases. Also point out that more than one phrase can be correct for each item.

- Review as a class by having various students say their questions. Make necessary corrections.

**Answers to Unit 7, Lesson 1—Exercise A**
2. Would you mind telling me what time the concert starts?
3. Could you explain how this CD player works?
4. Do you know why the train is late?
5. Can you tell me where the nearest bathroom is?
6. I wonder if they speak English at this hotel.

 **On a separate sheet of paper . . .**

- Do the first item with the class.

- Have students compare their answers. Then review as a class.

**On a separate sheet of paper, write each direct speech statement in indirect speech. Change the verb in the indirect speech only if necessary.**

1. Last Friday my husband said, "I'm going to pick up some supplies before the storm."
2. Last year my parents said, "We're going to Spain on vacation this year."
3. She told them, "This year's flu shot is not entirely protective against the flu."
4. He just said, "The danger of a flood is over."
5. We always say, "It's always easier to take the train than drive."
6. When I was a child, my parents told me, "It's really important to get a good education."
7. The National Weather Service is saying, "Tonight's weather is terrible."
8. Your parents just told me, "We want to leave for the shelter immediately."

## UNIT 7   Lesson 1

### Embedded questions: usage

**Use embedded questions to ask politely for information.**

Can you tell me what time it is?

Could you explain why it's not working?

Do you know where the bathroom is?

Would you mind telling me how to get to Main Street?

**Phrases that are often followed by embedded questions:**

I don't know…

I'd like to know…

Let me know…

Do you know…?

Can you tell me…?

I can't remember…

Can you remember…?

Let's ask…

I wonder…

I'm not sure…

Could you explain…?

Would you mind telling me…?

> **BE CAREFUL!** Do not use question form in embedded questions.
>
> Do you know **why** she won't read science fiction novels?
>
> NOT   Do you know ~~why won't she read science fiction novels~~?
>
> Can you tell me **if** this bus **stops** in Guatemala City?
>
> NOT  Can you tell me ~~does this bus stop~~ in Guatemala City?

### Embedded questions: punctuation

**Sentences with embedded questions are punctuated according to the meaning of the whole sentence.**

**If an embedded question is in a sentence, end the sentence with a period.**

I don't know (something). → I don't know **who she is.**

**If an embedded question is in a question, end the question with a question mark.**

Can you tell me (something)? → Can you tell me **who she is?**

 **On a separate sheet of paper, write polite questions using noun clauses with embedded questions. Begin each question differently.**

1. You need directions to the airport.   *Could you tell me how to get to the airport?*
2. You want to find out what time the concert starts.
3. You don't understand how your new CD player works.
4. You'd like to know why the train is late.
5. You need to find out where the nearest bathroom is.
6. You'd like to know something: Do they speak English at the hotel?

 **On a separate sheet of paper, complete each sentence with an embedded question using the question in parentheses. Punctuate each sentence correctly.**

1. Please let me know (When does the movie start?) when the movie starts.
2. I wonder (Where is the subway station?) where the subway station is.
3. Can you tell me (How do you get to King Street?) how to get to King Street.
4. We're not sure (What should we bring for dinner?) what we should bring for dinner.

5. They'd like to understand (Why doesn't Pat want to come to the meeting?) *why Pat doesn't want to come to the meeting.*

6. Please tell the class (Who painted this picture?) *who painted this picture.*

 **Correct the errors in each item.**

1. Could you please tell me ~~does~~ *whether* this train ~~go~~ *goes* to Nagoya~~.~~ **?**

2. I was wondering ~~can~~ *if* I get your phone number~~?~~ **.**

3. I'd like to know what time ~~does~~ Flight 82 arrive**s**.

4. Can you tell me how much ~~does~~ this magazine cost**s**?

5. Do you remember where ~~did~~ he use**d** to live~~.~~ **?**

6. I'm not sure why ~~do~~ they keep calling me~~?~~ **.**

7. I wonder ~~will~~ *if,* she ~~come~~ *will* come on time~~?~~ **.**

---

### Embedded questions with infinitives

In embedded questions, an infinitive can be used to express possibility (**<u>can</u>** or **<u>could</u>**) or advice (**<u>should</u>**). You can use an infinitive after the question words <u>when</u>, <u>where</u>, <u>how</u>, <u>who</u>, <u>whom</u>, <u>what</u>, <u>which</u>, or <u>whose</u>.

> I don't know where I can get that magazine. = I don't know **where to get** that magazine.
> I'm not sure when I should call them. = I'm not sure **when to call** them.
> She'd like to know which train she should take. = She'd like to know **which train to take**.

You can use an infinitive after <u>whether</u>.

> I don't know whether I should read that book next. = I don't know **whether to read** that book next.

**BE CAREFUL!** Don't use an infinitive after <u>if</u>.

> I'd like to know if I should read that book next. = I'd like to know **whether to read** that book next.
> NOT  I'd like to know ~~if to read~~ that book next.

---

 **On a separate sheet of paper, rewrite each sentence with an infinitive.**

1. Could you tell me whose novel I should read next?
   *Could you tell me whose novel to read next?*

2. I'd like to know where I can buy Toni Morrison's latest book.

3. Can you remember whom I should call to get that information?

4. I'd like to know which train I can take there.

5. Let me know if I should give her the magazine when I'm done.

6. I wasn't sure when I could get the new edition of her book.

7. Let's ask how we should get to the train station.

## UNIT 7   Lesson 2

### Noun clauses with <u>that</u>:  after mental activity verbs

The following verbs often have noun clauses as their direct objects. Notice that they are all a kind of mental activity. It is optional to include <u>that</u>.

| | | | |
|---|---|---|---|
| **agree** | We agree (that) he should work harder. | **doubt** | I doubt (that) they really understand the problem. |
| **assume** | I assume (that) you made a reservation. Right? | **dream** | She dreamed (that) she was a movie star. |
| **believe** | She believes (that) all people are created equal. | **feel** | We feel (that) everyone needs to try harder. |
| **decide** | We decided (that) we should stay another night. | **find out** | I found out (that) the bill had already been paid. |
| **discover** | He discovered (that) the work hadn't been done yet. | **forget** | She forgot (that) she had been there once before. |

## 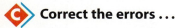 Correct the errors . . .

- Point out that the example could also be *Could you please tell me if . . .*
- Have students compare answers. Then review as a class.

## Embedded questions with infinitives

- Have students study the first explanation and the examples.
- Point out that the infinitive can be used to express possibility (examples 1 and 2) and to express advice (example 3).
- Have students study the second explanation and the example.
- Then have students read the Be Careful! note.
- To check comprehension, say the following sentences and ask students to restate them using infinitives. *Let me know where I can find that information.* (Let me know where to find that information.) *I'm not sure who I should talk to.* (I'm not sure who to talk to.) *I'd like to know how I can repair it.* (I'd like to know how to repair it.) *I don't know whether I should ask for my money back.* (I don't know whether to ask for my money back.) *I don't know if I can watch that horror movie.* (I don't know whether to watch that horror movie.)
- You may want to write the sentences on the board and have students write their answers.

## On a separate sheet of paper . . .

- Go over the example with the class.
- Review as a class by having students read their sentences out loud or write them on the board.
- Make necessary corrections.

**Option:** To provide more practice, ask students to work in pairs or small groups and choose a place to go on vacation. Write on the board:

   *We should find out _____.*

Then have students write at least four sentences about what they should find out before they go. Examples: *We should find out where to stay. We should find out interesting things to do there. We should ask where to go for the best local food. We should find out whether to bring warm clothes.* Combine pairs / groups and ask them to share their information. Encourage students to make necessary corrections.

**Answers to Unit 7, Lesson 1—Exercise D**

2. I'd like to know where to buy Toni Morrison's latest book.
3. Can you remember whom to call to get that information?
4. I'd like to know which train to take there.
5. Let me know whether to give her the magazine when I'm done.
6. I wasn't sure when to get the new edition of her book.
7. Let's ask how to get to the train station.

## UNIT 7 LESSON 2

## Noun clauses with <u>that</u>: after mental activity verbs

- Have students study the explanation and the examples.
- Write on the board:

   *I dreamed that I was sailing round the world.*

- Have students identify the noun clause and underline it. (<u>that I was sailing round the world</u>)
- Ask students to identify the verb of mental activity in the example (dream). You may want to remind students that the noun clause functions as the direct object of the verb of mental activity.
- Ask students *Can <u>that</u> be omitted?* (yes) Write parentheses ( ) around *that* on the board.
- To check comprehension, say or write verbs from the list one by one and have various students make sentences with the verb and a noun clause. Make necessary corrections.
- You may prefer to have students do this activity in pairs or small groups.

## Noun clauses with <u>that</u>: after other expressions

• Have students study the explanation, the list of expressions, and the examples.

• Review which expressions are <u>be</u> + adjective (afraid, angry, sad, sorry, sure) and which are <u>be</u> + past participle (ashamed, disappointed, surprised, worried).

• Write on the board:
  1. *They were sure that they would miss the plane.*
  2. *I'm sorry to hear that you didn't get the job.*

• Have students identify the noun clause in both examples. (1. [that] they would miss the plane 2. [that] you didn't get the job)

**Option:** If students need more controlled practice before starting Exercise A, ask various students to make sentences using the expressions and noun clauses. Encourage students to make corrections and give each other feedback. You may want to write the correct sentences on the board.

 **On a separate sheet of paper . . .**

• Have students compare their answers.

• Review as a class by having various students read one of their sentences. Make necessary corrections.

**Option:** To provide more practice, ask students to work in pairs and small groups and think about important moments and first-time experiences in their lives. For example, the first day of school or college, the interview for their first job, the first day at work, the first time on an airplane, etc. Write on the board:

  I was _____ that _____.
  My parents were _____ that _____.

Ask students to take turns expressing their feelings about those different moments or experiences by completing the sentences on the board. Encourage students to use the expressions in the Grammar box and noun clauses. Give students these examples: *When I started my new job, I was afraid that I would make mistakes. My parents were disappointed that I didn't want to play sports in school.* Walk around and provide help as needed.

## UNIT 8 **LESSON 1**

## <u>Unless</u> in conditional sentences

• Have students study the explanation and the examples.

• Point out that *unless* has the same meaning as *if . . . not*.

• Write on the board:
  1. *If you don't hurry, you'll be late.*
  2. *Unless _____, you'll be late.*
  3. *He won't buy it, if it's not on sale.*
  4. *He won't buy it, unless _____.*

• To check comprehension, ask students to complete items 2 and 4. (2. you hurry 4. it's on sale)

| | | | |
|---|---|---|---|
| **guess** | I guess (that) we'll just have to do it ourselves. | **notice** | Did you notice (that) they didn't call us back? |
| **hear** | He heard (that) they were planning another meeting. | **realize** | Do you realize (that) tomorrow is her birthday? |
| **hope** | I hope (that) everyone is OK. | **remember** | He remembered (that) he forgot to call home. |
| **know** | They know (that) we asked everyone to come at 8:00. | **see** | I see (that) you've finished everything. |
| **learn** | She learned (that) the book was written in 1933. | **suppose** | I suppose (that) you're hungry. Right? |
| | | **think** | She thinks (that) everyone should help. |
| | | **understand** | We understand (that) you're from Brazil. Is that right? |

---

**Noun clauses with <u>that</u>: after other expressions**

Use noun clauses after these expressions with <u>be</u> + adjective or <u>be</u> + past participle.

| | |
|---|---|
| **be afraid that** | I'm afraid (that) we'll have to leave early. |
| **be angry that** | She's angry (that) he never called. |
| **be ashamed that** | He's ashamed (that) he never called. |
| **be disappointed that** | We're disappointed (that) you couldn't come. |
| **be happy that** | They're happy (that) they passed the test. |
| **be sad that** | I'm sad (that) you're leaving. |
| **be sorry that** | We're sorry (that) we missed you. |
| **be sure that** | Are you sure (that) he's the man who did it? |
| **be surprised that** | She was surprised (that) she won. |
| **be worried that** | They're worried (that) he may be angry. |

**A** ▶ **On a separate sheet of paper, complete the sentences in your own way. Use noun clauses with <u>that</u>.** Answers will vary. Possible answers include:

1. When I was young, I couldn't believe . . .
   that I would be tall one day.
2. Last year, I decided . . .
   that I would go back to school.
3. Recently, I dreamed . . .
   that I was a famous musician.
4. This year, I was surprised to discover . . .
   that I had won the lottery.
5. Last week, I forgot . . .
   that I had a doctor's appointment.
6. Recently, I heard . . .
   that they were planning a trip.

7. In the future, I hope . . .
   that we go on an exciting vacation.
8. Now that I study English, I know . . .
   that I enjoy learning new languages.
9. In the last year, I learned . . .
   that I like to cook.
10. Not long ago, I remembered . . .
    that I used to ride horses.
11. (Your own idea) . . .
    Answers will vary.
12. (Your own idea) . . .
    Answers will vary.

# UNIT 8   *Lesson 1*

**<u>Unless</u> in conditional sentences**

You can use <u>unless</u>, instead of <u>if not</u>, in conditional sentences.

**Unless they buy** a freezer, they'll have to cook every night. = If they don't buy a freezer, …

She wouldn't drive a car **unless she had** a cell phone. = … if she didn't have a cell phone.

Martin doesn't buy electronics **unless they're** state of the art. = … if they're not state of the art.

**A** On a separate sheet of paper, rewrite the sentences, changing <u>if not</u> statements to <u>unless</u> and making any necessary changes.

1. If you don't buy the Brew Rite coffee maker, you'll be sorry.
   *Unless you buy the Brew Rite coffee maker, you'll be sorry.*
2. If you aren't in a hurry, you should take the train.
3. If I didn't need to drive long distances, I wouldn't consider the top-of-the-line model.
4. She won't go running in the park if her friends don't go with her.
5. Claire won't buy a high-tech car if it doesn't have a good sound system.
6. I wouldn't get the one with cutting-edge technology if I weren't rich.

---

**Clauses after <u>wish</u>**

Use <u>were</u> or the simple past tense after <u>wish</u> to express a regret about something that's not true now.

 I **wish** my laptop **were** top of the line.

 We **wish** we **had** a Brew Rite coffee maker.

Use the past perfect after <u>wish</u> or <u>wished</u> to express a regret about something that was not true in the past.

 Sean **wishes** he **hadn't sold** his car.

 Sean **wished** he **hadn't sold** his car.

Use <u>would</u> and a base form after <u>wish</u> to express a desire that something will occur in the future or on a regular basis.

 I **wish** it **would rain**.  (present desire for a future occurrence)

 I **wish** you **would help** with the housework more often.  (desire for something to occur regularly)

Use <u>would</u> and a base form after <u>wished</u> to express a wish one had in the past for a future occurrence.

 Yesterday I **wished** it **would rain**, but it didn't.  (a wish for the future one had in the past)

---

**B** Complete each statement or question with the correct form of the verb.

1. I wish my favorite author _____would write_____ a new book.  I've read all of his old books so many times.
   <sub>write</sub>
2. Pat wished she _____had spent_____ more time test-driving cars before she bought that SUV.
   <sub>spend</sub>
3. Most people wish they _____were_____ rich.
   <sub>be</sub>
4. I wish it _____had been_____ possible for me to get a better camera last time.
   <sub>be</sub>
5. They wished they _____had known_____ sooner that the computer couldn't be fixed.
   <sub>know</sub>
6. When I was a child, my parents wished I _____would become_____ a doctor.
   <sub>become</sub>
7. Do you wish you _____had_____ a more comfortable car for the trip tomorrow?
   <sub>have</sub>
8. Don't they wish they _____had studied_____ German?
   <sub>study</sub>
9. I wish I _____were_____ married to a mechanic.  My car keeps breaking down!
   <sub>be</sub>

## UNIT 8  Lesson 2

**The unreal conditional:  variety of forms**

Unreal conditional sentences can have a variety of active and passive forms in either clause.

 If he had worn a seat belt, he **wouldn't have been hurt**.

 If the car **had been totaled**, she could have bought a new one.

 If the computer hadn't been invented, we **would** still **be using** typewriters.

 If the typewriter **were still being used**, fewer people would have computers.

**On a separate sheet of paper . . .**

- Go over the example with the class.

- Point out the comma in the example. Remind students to include a comma after the *if* clause or *unless* clause when they come at the beginning of the sentence.

- Have students compare answers with a partner. Then review as a class.

**Answers to Unit 8, Lesson 1—Exercise A**

2. Unless you're in a hurry, you should take the train.
3. Unless I need to drive long distances, I wouldn't consider the top-of-the-line model.
4. She won't go running in the park unless her friends go with her.
5. Claire won't buy a high-tech car unless it has a good sound system.
6. I wouldn't get the one with cutting-edge technology unless I were rich.

## Clauses after <u>wish</u>

- Have students study the first explanation and the examples.

- Remind students that *were* is used for all persons. Example: *I wish I were rich.* (NOT ~~I wish I was rich.~~)

- To check comprehension, ask various students to make (simple) sentences with *I wish + were.* Examples: *I wish I were on vacation. I wish my car were faster. I wish laptops were cheaper.*

- Have students study the second explanation and the examples.

- Write on the board:
  *I wish I had (not) _____.*
  *I wished I had (not) _____.*

- To check comprehension, ask various students to complete the sentences. Check to make sure they use the past participle. Examples: *I wish I had studied more for the test today! John wished he hadn't spent all his money on a new car. I wish I had tried to make my hotel reservations earlier.*

- Have students study the third explanation and the examples.

- Write on the board:
  *I wish _____ would _____.*

- To check comprehension, ask various students to complete the sentence. They can make sentences about themselves or about someone they know. Tell students they should say two sentences: their wish plus the reason or information why they wish it. Examples: *I wish it would be hot and sunny today. I want to go to the beach. I wish he would come home earlier. I get worried when he's out so late.*

- Have students study the fourth explanation and the example.

- Ask volunteers to say wishes they had in the past for the future. Examples: *When I was on vacation last summer, I wished the week would never end. When I was in college, I wished I would find a girlfriend!*

 **Complete each statement . . .**

- Encourage students to figure out "when" the speaker is making the wish.

- Have students compare answers with a partner and review as a class.

**Challenge:** Write on the board:
  *1. something you have but you wish you didn't have*
  *2. something you don't have but you wish you had*
  *3. something you did but you wish you hadn't done*
  *4. something you didn't do but you wish you had done*
  *5. something you have to do but you wish you wouldn't have to do*

Ask students to think about each situation and write brief notes for each one. Form small groups. Students take turns talking about their wishes and regrets using their notes as a guide. Walk around and help as needed.

## UNIT 8 **LESSON 2**

## The unreal conditional: variety of forms

- Have students study the first explanation and the examples.

- Write on the board:
  *1. <u>If they had advertised the job</u>, he would have applied for it.*
  *2. If he had applied for the job, <u>they would have hired him</u>.*

- To check comprehension, ask pairs to rewrite the sentences changing the verbs in the underlined clauses into the passive.

- Review as a class. (If the job had been advertised, he would have applied for it. 2. If he had applied for the job, he would have been hired.)

- Have students study the second explanation and the examples.

- Write on the board:
  *1. If the car hadn't broken down, we would have been _____.*
  *2. If we had been _____, we would have heard the news.*

- As a class, complete the sentences with continuous verb forms and add any other necessary information. (Possible answers: 1. dancing right now OR swimming at the beach OR playing golf; 2. watching TV OR listening to the radio OR paying attention)

**Complete the following . . .**

• Have students share their answers with a partner.

• Then review as a class by having various students read their sentences out loud.

## UNIT 9 **LESSON 1**

### Count and non-count nouns

• Have students study the first explanation and the examples.

• Ask the class to give examples of other count nouns. Have students give the singular form using *a* or *an* and then the plural form. Examples: *a book—books, an umbrella—umbrellas, a season—seasons, etc.*

• Have students study the second explanation and the examples.

• Point out that abstract ideas are also non-count nouns. Examples: *progress, help, importance, health, education*

• Point out that fields of study, foods, and materials are also non-count nouns. Examples: *law, biology, chocolate, juice, wood, cotton, plastic*

• Write on the board:
    1. _____ paper       3. _____ water
    2. _____ bread       4. _____ furniture

• Ask students to say or write unit expressions for each item. (Possible answers: 1. a piece of; 2. a loaf of, a piece of; 3. a glass of, a pitcher of, a bottle of; 4. a piece of, a truck full of)

• Have students study the third explanation and the examples.

• Write on the board:
    1. *I don't like <u>coffee</u>.*
    2. *I had a <u>coffee</u>.*
    3. *I saw a <u>chicken</u>.*
    4. *I ate <u>chicken</u>.*
    5. *Turn on <u>the light</u>.*
    6. *There's very little <u>light</u> in this room.*

• Pair work. Ask students to discuss how the meaning of the underlined words is different in each pair of sentences. Ask students to say if an item is count or non-count.

• Review as a class. (1. non-count; 2. count; 3. count; 4. non-count; 5. count; 6. non-count)

 **Complete each sentence . . .**

• Point out that students might need to include an article or the plural form of the noun.

• Have students compare answers with a partner. Then review as a class.

**Option:** If you feel your students need more practice, have them make sentences with the words in the Grammar box, as well as any words you may have written on the board during the presentation.

**A** Complete the following unreal conditional sentences in your <u>own</u> way, using active and passive forms. *Answers will vary. Possible answers include:*

1. If I were elected president, I wouldn't raise taxes .
2. The car would have been invented earlier if people had had more free time .
3. If I were driving and another driver cut me off, I would slow down .
4. If they had been selling this phone when I was looking for one, I would have bought it .
5. If I didn't want to travel , I wouldn't be studying English now.
6. If she were getting married today, she would be very excited .

## ▶ UNIT 9 Lesson 1

### Count and non-count nouns

**Count nouns name things that can be counted individually. They have singular and plural forms.**

| | |
|---|---|
| a president | presidents |
| a government | governments |
| a liberal | liberals |
| an election | elections |
| an official | officials |

**Non-count nouns name things that are not counted individually. They don't have singular or plural forms and they are not preceded by <u>a</u> or <u>an</u>. To express a specific quantity of an uncountable noun, use unit expressions.**

| | |
|---|---|
| a piece of news | a time of peace |
| a cup of tea | an act of justice |
| a kilo of rice | |

**Many nouns can be used as count or non-count nouns, but the meaning is different.**

She studied **government** at the university. (= academic subject)
That country has had four **governments** in ten years. (= group of people who rule the country)

I love **cheese**. (in general)
I bought a **cheese**. (the whole manufactured product, such as a "wheel of cheese.")

She has blond **hair**. (in general = all of her hair)
She got a **hair** in her eye. (= one individual hair)

**A** Complete each sentence with the correct form of each noun.

1. The government has made ___progress___ in the economy.
   <small>progress</small>
2. They've given a lot of ___importance___ to making the banks stable.
   <small>importance</small>
3. Unfortunately, ___radicals___ changed the law.
   <small>radical</small>
4. ___Peace___ can only come if people stop making war.
   <small>peace</small>
5. ___Moderates___ don't favor extreme change.
   <small>moderate</small>
6. He's ___a reactionary___ who would like to outlaw freedom of speech.
   <small>reactionary</small>
7. If I could give you one piece of ___advice___, it would be to vote.
   <small>advice</small>
8. Some ___governments___ are more liberal than others.
   <small>government</small>
9. If more people don't find ___work___, people will elect a different president.
   <small>work</small>
10. It's impossible to end all ___poverty___.
    <small>poverty</small>

## UNIT 9   Lesson 2

### Gerunds and infinitives: form

A gerund (the base form of a verb + -ing) functions as a noun.  Gerunds can be subjects, objects, and subject complements.

**Discussing** politics is my favorite activity.  (subject)

I love **reading** about government.  (direct object)

I read a book about **voting**.  (object of preposition <u>about</u>)

My favorite activity is **watching** TV news.  (subject complement after <u>be</u>)

An infinitive (<u>to</u> + the base form of a verb) also functions as a noun.

**To lie** around on a beach all day would be my ideal vacation.  (subject)

I love **to guess** who's going to win the election.  (object)

My greatest dream for the summer is **to swim** every day.  (subject complement after <u>be</u>)

 **A** Using the sentences in the box above as a model, write sentences on a separate sheet of paper using the gerunds and infinitives in the form shown.  Answers will vary. Possible answers include:

1.  (as the subject of a sentence) Swimming     Swimming is my favorite activity.
2.  (as a direct object) driving   I hate driving in the rain.
3.  (as the object of the preposition <u>of</u>) studying   I'm tired of studying.
4.  (as the subject of a sentence) To travel   To travel to Africa would be my ideal vacation.
5.  (as a direct object) to eat   I love to eat Italian food.

### Review: Gerunds and infinitives after certain verbs

Certain verbs are followed by gerunds:  <u>avoid</u>, <u>can't stand</u>, <u>discuss</u>, <u>dislike</u>, <u>enjoy</u>, <u>feel like</u>, <u>(don't) mind</u>, <u>practice</u>, <u>quit</u>, <u>suggest</u>.

Other verbs are followed by infinitives:  <u>agree</u>, <u>choose</u>, <u>decide</u>, <u>expect</u>, <u>hope</u>, <u>learn</u>, <u>need</u>, <u>plan</u>, <u>seem</u>, <u>want</u>, <u>wish</u>, <u>would like</u>.

Other verbs can be followed by either a gerund or an infinitive:  <u>begin</u>, <u>continue</u>, <u>hate</u>, <u>like</u>, <u>love</u>, <u>prefer</u>.

For a more complete list, see Appendix on page 130.

**B** Complete the paragraph with gerunds or infinitives.

I hope _____**to make**_____ some positive changes in my life, and I would like
       (make)

_____**to start**_____ right away.  I have observed that a lot of people enjoy _____**complaining**_____ about
      (start)                                                                                    (complain)

the political situation, but they don't like _____**to do/doing**_____ anything about it.  They love
                                                    (do)

_____**to watch**_____ the news and say they care about all the poor people who don't have enough
      (watch)

to eat, but they don't feel like _____**doing**_____ anything about it.  They worry about poverty but
                                      (do)

they don't mind _____**wasting**_____ money on stupid things they don't need _____**to have**_____.  Well,
                      (waste)                                                          (have)

I'm sick of _____**reading**_____ about how people are suffering, and I've agreed _____**to join**_____ a
                 (read)                                                                  (join)

political action group.  I simply hate _____**not doing**_____ anything!
                                             (not do)

## UNIT 10   Lesson 1

 **A** Choose ten adjectives from the box.  On a separate sheet of paper, write a sentence for each adjective.  Use <u>too</u> and an infinitive to give an explanation or a warning.

| | | | |
|---|---|---|---|
| afraid | down in the dumps | high | sad |
| busy | early | important | sick |
| conservative | expensive | loud | self-critical |
| depressing | heavy | old | young |

**EXAMPLE:**   difficult   *This homework is too difficult to finish in one hour.*

# UNIT 9 **LESSON 2**

## Gerunds and infinitives: form

- Have students study the first explanation and the examples.
- Clarify any doubts students might have about the grammatical functions. For example, subjects precede verbs in statements, direct objects follow verbs, objects of prepositions follow prepositions, subject complements follow *be*, etc.
- Write on the board:
  *1. You should avoid talking to strangers.*
  *2. Skiing is his passion.*
  *3. I'm not interested in discussing politics.*
  *4. Her favorite pastime is sailing.*
- To check comprehension, ask students to underline the gerunds and identify their function. Ask students to compare their answers with a partner.
- Review as a class. (1. *talking:* direct object; 2. *skiing:* subject; 3. *discussing:* object of preposition of preposition *in;* 4. *sailing:* subject complement)
- Have students study the second explanation and the examples.
- Write on the board:
  *1. I hope to see her this weekend.*
  *2. My plan is to go on vacation in July.*
  *3. To be informed is important.*
- Pair work. Ask students to underline the infinitives and identify their function.
- Review as a class. (1. *to see:* direct object; 2. *to go:* subject complement; 3. *to be:* subject)

### A Using the sentences in the box . . .

- Encourage students to refer to the Grammar box if they need help.
- To review, you can have students compare answers or you may want students to do peer correction. Students should exchange papers and focus on checking for the correct usage of gerunds and infinitives as nouns.

## Review: Gerunds and infinitives after certain verbs

- Have students read the first explanation and the list of verbs.
- If students do not know the meaning of a verb, you may want to give an example along with the explanation.
- Pair work or small groups. Ask students to take turns making sentences using the verbs and gerunds. Encourage students to give each other feedback focusing on gerund forms.
- Have students read the second explanation and the list of verbs.
- Answer questions about vocabulary.

- Pair work or small groups. Ask students to find new partners and take turns making sentences with infinitives and giving feedback.
- Have students read the third explanation and the list of verbs.
- You may want to give examples: *Yesterday I began crying for no reason! Yesterday I began to cry for no reason!*
- Make sure students find new partners. Pair work or small groups. Encourage students to give two sentences, one with the gerund and the other with an infinitive. Example: *I felt really sick, but I continued working. Even though I was sick, I continued to work.*

### B Complete the paragraph . . .

- Point out students can refer to the list in the Grammer box or in the Appendix.
- Have students compare answers with a partner. Then review as a class.

# UNIT 10 **LESSON 1**

### A Choose ten adjectives . . .

- To review the use of <u>too</u> + infinitive, write on the board:
  <u>too</u> + adjective + infinitive
  <u>too</u> + adjective + <u>for</u> + person + infinitive
- Go over the example with the class.
- Ask students to add *for* + a person. (This homework is too difficult for John to finish in one hour.)
- To review, have students exchange papers and do peer correction.
- You may want to collect the papers and make a list of the most common errors to review with the class.

**Answers to Unit 10, Lesson 1—Exercise A**
Answers will vary. Possible answers include:
I am too afraid to go out at night.
He's too busy to go to the movies today.
My sister is too young to vote.
They're too sick to come with us.
This stereo is too expensive to buy now.
It's too early to eat lunch.
We're too conservative to wear wacky clothes.
The meeting is too important to miss.
That car is too old to drive.
The refrigerator is too heavy to lift by myself.

## Infinitives with <u>enough</u>

- Have students study the explanation, the examples, and the Be Careful! note.
- Write on the board:

  1. strong   →   *lift that suitcase*
  2. tall   →   *reach the shelf*
  3. sick   →   *stay home*
  4. old   →   *drive on his / her own*

- To check comprehension, ask students to work in pairs to write statements using *enough* + an infinitive.
- Ask various pairs for their answers. Make necessary corrections. (Possible answers: 1. He's not strong enough to lift that suitcase. 2. She's tall enough to reach that shelf. 3. I'm sick enough to stay home. 4. She's not old enough to drive on her own.)

 **On a separate sheet of paper . . .**

- Review any words students don't know.
- If you feel you won't have enough time in class to review each student's work, assign one word to a pair.
- To review, ask each pair to say their sentence. Encourage the class to make necessary corrections.
- You may want to write the correct sentences on the board.

**Option:** To provide more practice, ask the class to say sentences describing people in their family, friends, or other people they know using *too* or *enough* plus an infinitive. Examples: *My sister is beautiful enough to be a model. My brother is too lazy to get a job!*

## UNIT 10 **LESSON 2**

## Prepositions of place more usage

- Have students read the examples with *on*.
- Give other examples: *Cairo is on the Nile River. I spent my vacation on an island in the Caribbean.*
- Ask the class to create more examples.
- Have students read the examples with *in*.
- Give other examples: *The Galapagos Islands are in the Pacific Ocean. There are many active volcanoes in Ethiopia.*
- Ask the class to create more examples.
- Have students read the examples with *of*.
- Give other examples: *Chile is west of Argentina. Mongolia is north of China.*
- Ask the class to create more examples.

**A** **Write the correct . . .**

- Do the first item with the class.
- Have students compare answers with a partner and review as a class.

**Option:** To provide more practice, have students choose a place they know well and use the prepositions to describe that place. Student can work in pairs or small groups. Encourage the class to focus on prepositions and give each other feedback.

**Answers to Unit 10, Lesson 1—Exercise B**
Answers will vary. Possible answers include:
She's not old enough to drive.
Marco is smart enough to study law.
This chair isn't strong enough to sit on.
I'm hungry enough to eat now.
They're not calm enough to take the test.
We're polite enough to offer our help.
I'm thirsty enough to drink three glasses of water.
You're not responsible enough to watch your sister.
He's not successful enough to buy an expensive car.
This party's not exciting enough to stay at.
I'm happy enough to finish this book instead of going out.

## Infinitives with enough

**Use an infinitive after an adjective or adverb and <u>enough</u> to give an explanation.**

She's **old enough** to vote.    They drove **fast enough** to get there on time.

He's not **busy enough** to complain.    It isn't **warm enough to go** hiking today.

**BE CAREFUL! <u>Enough</u> comes after an adjective or an adverb, not before.**

It's **too far** to walk.  It isn't **close enough** to walk.  NOT ~~It isn't enough close to walk.~~

 **B** On a separate sheet of paper, write a sentence with <u>enough</u> and an infinitive for each adjective in the box.

| | | | |
|---|---|---|---|
| not old | smart | not strong | hungry |
| all | not calm | polite | thirsty |
| not responsible | not successful | not exciting | happy |

## UNIT 10   Lesson 2

### Prepositions of place: more usage

It's **on**
- the Nicoya Peninsula.
- Easter Island.
- the Hudson River.  (also: **along** the Hudson River.)
- Coronado Bay.
- the coast.
- Lake Placid.
- the Gulf of Aqaba.

It's **in**
- Cheju Province.
- the Rocky Mountains.
- the Central Valley.
- the Sahara Desert.
- the Atlantic Ocean.
- the state of Jalisco.

It's in the central part
It's southwest       } **of** Madrid.
It's about 50 km north

 **A** Write the correct prepositions of place.

1. Pisco is __on__ the Pacific coast of Peru.

2. Tianjin, in China, is __in__ Hebei Province.

3. Desaguadero is __on__ Lake Titicaca in Bolivia.

4. The island of Bahrain is __in__ the Persian Gulf.

5. Cabimas is __on__ Lake Maracaibo in Venezuela.

6. Sapporo is __on__ Hokkaido Island in Japan.

7. Riobamba is __on__ the Pastaza River in Ecuador.

8. Taiwan's Jade Mountain National Park is east __of__ the city of Alishan.

9. Fengkang is __in__ the southern part __of__ Taiwan.

10. The city of Budapest, Hungary is __on__ the Danube River.

11. Denmark is north __of__ Germany.

12. The capital of Chile, Santiago, is located __in__ the Central Valley.

## Proper nouns: capitalization

When words like <u>east</u> or <u>southeast</u> are used as the name of a place, they should be capitalized.

It's in **the South**.      It's in **the Northeast**.      It's in the **Middle East**.

When they are just used to describe a place, the words are not capitalized.

It's **south of** Taipei.      It's a **northeastern** city.      It's on the **eastern** shore of Lake Superior.

Capitalize names of:

| | | | |
|---|---|---|---|
| people (and their titles) | Mary | Mary Smith | Dr. Mary Smith |
| places | Bolivia | the United Kingdom | Kyoto |
| buildings and public places | the Golden Gate Bridge | the Paramount Theater | the Tower of London |
| organizations | the U.N. | the World Bank | Amnesty International |
| religions | Christianity | Judaism | Islam |
| holidays | New Year's Day | the Moon Festival | Carnaval |
| historic times or events | the Cold War | the Middle Ages | the Edo Period |
| languages / nationalities | French | English | Arabic |
| the days of the week | Monday | Wednesday | Sunday |
| the months of the year | January | October | December |

When a proper noun has more than one word, each word is capitalized except for articles (<u>the</u>) and prepositions (<u>of</u>).

Panama City                the Gulf of Aqaba                the City of Chicago

the University of Buenos Aires        Niagara Falls                the Bay of Biscayne

Capitalize all the words of a title, except for articles and prepositions that have fewer than four letters. If an article or a preposition is the first word of a title, capitalize it.

The Story of English                Looking Back on My Life

The International Herald Tribune        I Know Why the Caged Bird Sings

 **B** **Correct the capitalization.**

1. I'm reading one hundred years of solitude. [O H Y S]
2. My cousins are studying french. [F]
3. The leaning tower of pisa is in northern italy. [L T P I]
4. It's on the southern coast of australia. [A]
5. I visit the city museum of art every monday. [C M A M]
6. My uncle works for the united nations. [U N]
7. The channel tunnel (chunnel) between england and france was completed in 1994. [C T C E F]
8. She just graduated from the university of washington. [U W]
9. We enjoyed the movie about the great wall of china. [G W C]
10. My son goes to the college of sciences. [C S]
11. His father speaks korean and japanese fluently. [K J]
12. Their grandson was born last march. [M]

G18

## Proper nouns: capitalization

- Have students read the first two explanations and the examples.
- Write on the board:
  1. It's in the <u>north</u>.
  2. It's in the <u>north</u> of Japan.
  3. It's on the <u>southwestern</u> shore of Costa Rica.
  4. It's in the <u>southwest</u>.
- Pair work. Ask students to decide which underlined words should be capitalized.
- Review as a class. (1. It's in the North. 4. It's in the Southwest.)
- Have students study the list of names that need capitalization. Say each category out loud and ask for more examples. Make necessary corrections.
- Have students study the information about proper nouns and the examples.
- Ask the class for any examples they know of proper nouns with more than one word. Examples: *the Eiffel Tower, Times Square, the Great Wall, Ipanema Beach,* etc.
- Have students study the last explanation and the examples.
- Write on the board:
  1. the story of my life
  2. six legends to remember
  3. adventures in the mountains
  4. tales from the jungle
- Tell students to imagine the phrases on the board are titles of books. Ask students to say which words should be capitalized. (1. The Story of My Life; 2. Six Legends to Remember; 3. Adventures in the Mountains; 4. Tales From the Jungle)

 **Correct the capitalization.**

- Do the first item with the class.
- Have students compare answers with a partner. Encourage students to refer to the Grammar box if necessary.
- Review as a class.

## Proper nouns: use of <u>the</u>

- Have students study the explanations and the examples.

- If necessary, point out the last use of <u>the</u> in the box and explain that an *acronym* is a word made up from the first letters of the names of something.

- Write on the board (without the answers):
    1. *the Indian Ocean*  (4)
    2. *the World Meteorological Organization*  (6)
    3. *South Korea*  (5)
    4. *the Czech Republic*  (2)
    5. *the Pyrenees*  (3)
    6. *the Bay of Biscay*  (1)
    7. *NASA*  (7)

- Pair work.  Ask students to number the explanations in the Grammar box from 1 to 7.  Then have them match the examples with the explanations.

- Review as a class.

 **Correct the sentences.**

- Do the first item with the class.

- Have students compare answers with a partner. Encourage students to refer to the Grammar box if necessary.

- Review as a class.

**Challenge:**  Groups of three or four.  Bring in newspapers in English.  (If the Internet is available, students can visit the CNN or BBC websites.) Student A scans the newspaper to find three names of countries, organizations, or geographical areas. Then he / she writes them on a slip of paper with no capitalization.  If the names include *the*, they can be written with or without *the*.  Then he / she gives the slip of paper to Students B and C, who capitalize the names and add *the* wherever necessary.  Student A corrects his / her partners' work.  Then students change roles.

## Proper nouns: use of the

**When a proper noun includes the word of, use the.**

| with the | without the |
|---|---|
| the Republic of Korea | Korea |
| the Gulf of Mexico | Mexico City |
| the Kingdom of Thailand | Thailand |

**When a proper noun uses a political word such as republic, empire, or kingdom, use the.**

the United Kingdom    the British Empire    the Malagasy Republic

**When a proper noun is plural, use the.**

| | |
|---|---|
| the Philippines | the United States |
| the Netherlands | the Andes Mountains |

**When a proper noun includes a geographical word such as ocean, desert, or river, use the. Do not use the with the following geographical words: lake, bay, mountain, island, park.**

| with the | without the |
|---|---|
| the Atlantic Ocean | Hudson Bay |
| the Atacama Desert | Crystal Lake |
| the Yangtze River | Hainan Island |
| the Iberian Peninsula | Ueno Park |
| the Persian Gulf | Yellow Mountain |

**When words like east or southwest are used as the name of a geographical area, use the. Do not use the when they are used as adjectives.**

| with the | without the |
|---|---|
| the Middle East | Western Europe |
| the Far East | East Timor |
| the West | Northern Ireland |

**When a proper noun includes a word that is a kind of organization or educational group, use the. Do not use the with a university or college (unless the name uses of).**

| with the | without the |
|---|---|
| the International Language Institute | Columbia College |
| the United Nations | Chubu University |
| the World Health Organization | |
| the University of Adelaide | |

**Do not use the with acronyms.**

U.C.L.A. (the University of California, Los Angeles)

NATO (the North Atlantic Treaty Organization)

OPEC (the Organization of Petroleum Exporting Countries)

---

**C ▷ Correct the sentences.**

1. When she went to ~~the~~ Malaysia, she brought her husband with her.
2. A lot of people from _the_ United States teach English here.
3. ~~The~~ Haiti is the closest neighbor to _the_ Dominican Republic.
4. When we arrived in ~~the~~ Berlin, I was very excited.
5. Yemen is a country in _the_ Middle East.
6. I introduced our visitors to _the_ University of Riyadh.
7. I lived in _the_ People's Republic of China for about two years.
8. Yan is a student at _the_ College of Arts and Sciences.
9. She is the director of _the_ English Language Institute.
10. She's the most famous actress in _the_ Netherlands.
11. He's interested in cultures in _the_ Near East.
12. Poland was one of the first countries in ~~the~~ Eastern Europe to change to a democracy.

# 🎵 TOP NOTCH POP LYRICS 🎵

## It's a Great Day for Love [Unit 1]

Wherever you go,
there are things you should know,
so be aware
of the customs and views—
all the do's and taboos—
of people there.
You were just a stranger in a sea of new
faces.
Now we're making small talk on a
first-name basis.
(CHORUS)
**It's a great day for love, isn't it?**
**Aren't you the one I was hoping to find?**
**It's a great day for love, isn't it?**
**By the time you said hello,**
**I had already made up my mind.**
Wherever you stay
be sure to obey
the golden rules,
and before you relax,
brush up on the facts
you learned at school.
Try to be polite and always be sure to get
some friendly advice on proper etiquette.
(CHORUS)
and when you smiled at me
and I fell in love,
the sun had just appeared
in the sky above.
You know how much I care, don't you?
And you'll always be there, won't you?
(CHORUS)

## I'll Get Back to You [Unit 3]

Your camera isn't working right.
It needs a few repairs.
You make me ship it overnight.
Nothing else compares.
You had to lengthen your new skirt,
and now you want to get
someone to wash your fancy shirts
and dry them when they're wet.
Come a little closer—
let me whisper in your ear.
Is my message getting across
to you loud and clear?
(CHORUS)
**You're always making plans.**
**I'll tell you what I'll do:**
**let me think it over and**
**I'll get back to you.**
You want to get your suit dry-cleaned.
You want to get someone
to shorten your new pair of jeans
and call you when they're done.
I guess I'll have them print a sign
and hang it on your shelf,
with four small words in one big line:
"Just do it yourself."
Let me tell you what this song
is really all about.
I'm getting tired of waiting while you
figure it out.
I've heard all your demands,

but I have a life too.
Let me think it over and
I'll get back to you.
I'm really reliable,
incredibly fast,
extremely helpful
from first to last.
Let me see what I can do.
Day after day,
everybody knows
I always do what I say.
(CHORUS)

## Endless Holiday [Unit 5]

Day after day,
all my thoughts drift away
before they've begun.
I sit in my room
in the darkness and gloom
just waiting for someone
to take me to a tourist town,
with parties in the street and people
dancing to a joyful sound.
(CHORUS)
**It's a song that people sing.**
**It's the laughter that you bring**
**on an endless holiday.**
**It's the happiness inside.**
**It's a roller coaster ride**
**on an endless holiday.**
I try and I try
to work hard, but I
get lost in a daze,
and I think about
how sad life is without
a few good holidays.
I close my eyes, pull down the shade,
and in my imagination I am dancing in a
big parade,
and the music is loud.
I get lost in the crowd
on an endless holiday.
It's a picnic at noon.
It's a trip to the moon
on an endless holiday,
with flags and confetti,
wild costumes and a great big marching
band,
as we wish each other well
in a language we all understand.
The sky above fills with the light
of fireworks exploding, as we dance along
the street tonight.
(CHORUS)

## Lucky to Be Alive [Unit 6]

(CHORUS)
**Thank you for helping me to survive.**
**I'm really lucky to be alive.**
When I was caught in a freezing
snowstorm,
you taught me how to stay warm.
When I was running from a landslide
with no place to hide,
you protected me from injury.
Even the world's biggest tsunami

has got nothing on me,
because you can go faster.
You keep me safe from disaster.
You're like some kind of hero—
you're the best friend that I know.
(CHORUS)
When the big flood came with
the pouring rain,
they were saying that a natural
disaster loomed.
You just opened your umbrella.
You were the only fellow who kept calm
and prepared.
You found us shelter.
I never felt like anybody cared
the way that you did when you said,
"I will always be there—
you can bet your life on it."
And when the cyclone turned the day into
night,
you held a flashlight and showed me the
safe way home.
You called for help on your cell phone.
You said you'd never leave me.
You said, "Believe me,
in times of trouble you will never be alone."
They said it wasn't such a bad situation.
It was beyond imagination.
I'm just glad to be alive—
and that is no exaggeration.
(CHORUS)

## Reinvent the Wheel [Unit 8]

You've got your digi camera with the
Powershot,
four mega pixels and a memory slot.
You've got your e-mail and your Internet.
You send me pictures of your digi pet.
I got the digi dog and the digi cat,
the digi this and the digi that.
I hate to be the one to break the news,
but you're giving me the digi blues.
(CHORUS)
**And you don't know**
**the way I really feel.**
**Why'd you have to go and**
**reinvent the wheel?**
You've got your cordless phone and your
microwave,
and your Reflex Plus for the perfect shave.
It's super special, top of the line,
with the latest new, cutting-edge design.
You've got your SLR and your LCD,
your PS2 and your USB.
I've seen the future and it's pretty grim:
they've used up all the acronyms.
(CHORUS)
I keep waiting for a breakthrough
innovation:
something to help our poor communication.
Hey, where'd you get all of that high-tech
taste?
Your faith in progress is such a waste.
Your life may be state of the art,
but you don't understand the human heart.
(CHORUS)

# Workbook Answer Key

**Note:** In communicative exercises where several answers are possible, this answer key contains some examples of correct answers, not all possible answers. Any valid answer in this type of exercise should be considered acceptable.

## UNIT 1

### Exercise 1

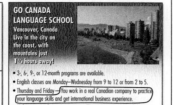

1. English Exchange [through DCU] (in Dublin, Ireland)
2. Go Canada Language School (in Vancouver, Canada)
3. Study Chicago English Program (in Chicago, USA)
4. Lingua Tech English Language School (in Melbourne, Australia)

### Exercise 2
Answers will vary.

### Exercise 3
1. yes  2. Mr. Vernon  3. Todd  4. no

### Exercise 4
1. c  2. d  3. b  4. a

### Exercise 5
Answers will vary.

### Exercise 6
_1_  Hi! It's a great day, isn't it?
_4_  Thanks. You too. Would it be rude to call you Joe?
_2_  It really is. Allow me to introduce myself. I'm Amanda Decker.
_5_  Absolutely not. Please do.
_6_  Great. And call me Amanda.
_3_  I'm Joe Hanson. It's nice to meet you.

### Exercise 7
1. d  2. b  3. f  4. a  5. c  6. e

### Exercise 8
2. No, it isn't.  3. Yes, it is.  4. No, there isn't.  5. No, it wasn't.  6. No, they haven't.  7. No, they aren't.
8. Yes, he does.  9. Yes, she is.

### Exercise 9
3. 'll be; won't you OR 're going to be; aren't you  4. hasn't gotten; has she OR isn't; is she  5. wasn't; was he
6. doesn't like; does she

### Exercise 10
Answers will vary, but must include a correct tag question. Following are some examples of what students may write:
2. You prefer *Ms.*, don't you?  3. You were born on October 27, 1985, weren't you?  4. You were born in Hong Kong, weren't you?  5. You live in Canada, don't you?
6. You're a student, aren't you?

### Exercise 11
Answers will vary.

### Exercise 12
1. b  2. a  3. b

### Exercise 13
2. had already composed  3. had already written
4. hadn't yet received  5. had already won  6. hadn't yet won  7. had already made  8. hadn't yet led

### Exercise 14
1. a  2. b  3. b  4. a  5. a

### Exercise 15
2. had already given; hadn't yet taken  3. had already read
4. hadn't yet had  5. had already exercised  6. hadn't yet gone

### Exercise 16
Answers will vary.

### Exercise 17
1. offensive      very rude      ~~polite~~
2. ~~customary~~   not allowed    taboo
3. impolite       ~~nice~~        rude
4. ~~not usual~~   traditional    customary
5. etiquette      ~~punctuality~~ manners

### Exercise 18
1. false  2. false  3. true  4. true  5. no information
6. false

### Exercise 19
Answers will vary.

### Exercise 20
1. a  2. b  3. a  4. b  5. c

### Exercise 21
Answers will vary.

### Exercise 22
Answers will vary.

### GRAMMAR BOOSTER
### Exercise A
1. haven't  2. was  3. aren't  4. aren't  5. has
6. don't

## Exercise B

**2.** have   **3.** am / 'm making   **4.** leaves   **5.** tells
**6.** is going   **7.** are; doing

## Exercise C

**2.** has / 's been shining   **3.** have / 've been   **4.** have / 've met   **5.** have / 've been traveling   **6.** have / 've been asking

## Exercise D

**1.** Answers will vary, but must include correct use of the present perfect or present perfect continuous and <u>for</u> or <u>since</u>.

**2–4.** Answers will vary, but must include correct use of the present perfect and <u>for</u> or <u>since</u>.

## Exercise E

**2.** My family ~~was going~~ *went* to Cairo last summer. It was a great trip!

**3.** I *'ve* already seen that movie.

**4.** They have know*n* her since 2003.

**5.** He didn't use~~d~~ to work there, but now he does.

**6.** I ~~watched~~ *was watching* a movie when he called, but I didn't mind the interruption.

## JUST FOR FUN

**1.** greetings   **2.** taboo   **3.** study abroad   **4.** called
**5.** early   **6.** small talk   **7.** titles   **8.** quiet   **9.** customary
**10.** Table manners   **11.** first   **12.** impolite   **13.** Offensive

### UNIT 2

## Exercise 1

**1.** dental care   **2.** medication   **3.** a vaccination
**4.** eyewear

## Exercise 2

Answers will vary.

## Exercise 3

**1.** b   **2.** c   **3.** c   **4.** a   **5.** b

## Exercise 4

**1.** an appointment   **2.** a toothache   **3.** pain
**4.** appreciate

## Exercise 5

**1.** no   **2.** yes   **3.** no information   **4.** yes

## Exercise 6

**1.** a   **2.** b   **3.** a   **4.** a   **5.** b

## Exercise 7

**1.** may   **2.** must   **3.** must   **4.** might   **5.** must
**6.** might   **7.** may

## Exercise 8

**1.** must   **2.** must   **3.** must not   **4.** must   **5.** must not

## Exercise 9

**2.** may / might not be able to   **3.** may / might have to
**4.** may / might be able to   **5.** must not have to

## Exercise 10

| I have a pain in my ... | I feel ... | I've been ... |
| --- | --- | --- |
| chest | weak | coughing |
| hip | short of breath | sneezing |
| ribs | nauseous | vomiting |
| abdomen | dizzy | wheezing |

## Exercise 11

**1.** chest   **2.** weak   **3.** nauseous   **4.** sneezing
**5.** coughing   **6.** abdomen

## Exercise 12

**1.** a blood test   **2.** a shot   **3.** an X-ray   **4.** An EKG
**5.** a checkup

## Exercise 13

**1.** receptionist   **2.** patient   **3.** patient   **4.** receptionist
**5.** patient   **6.** doctor / receptionist   **7.** doctor / receptionist   **8.** patient   **9.** doctor

## Exercise 14

Answers will vary.

## Exercise 15

**1.** c   **2.** a   **3.** e   **4.** f   **5.** b   **6.** d

## Exercise 16

Answers will vary. Following is an example of what students may write:

| | pros | cons |
| --- | --- | --- |
| acupuncture | It can help you quit smoking. It's 5,000 years old, so it must work. | I don't like needles! |
| chiropractic | good for people who play sports and get injuries | mostly for pain, not illnesses; only effective for certain pains |
| conventional medicine | I trust doctors and health care based on scientific study. | Sometimes people depend too much on drugs to fix their problems. |
| herbal therapy | probably inexpensive | I think that sometimes herbs don't work as well as prescription medication. |
| homeopathy | low cost; everything is natural, so you don't put chemicals in your body | Remedies sometimes aren't as effective as prescription medication. |
| spiritual healing | can be used together with other kinds of treatments | If you don't believe in it, then it doesn't really work. |

## Exercise 17

Answers will vary.

## Exercise 18

**1.** a   **2.** b   **3.** a   **4.** b   **5.** d

## Exercise 19

Answers will vary. Following is an example of what students may write:

| Type of treatment | How it's similar to reflexology | How it's different from reflexology |
| --- | --- | --- |
| homeopathy | Both treatments try to get the body to heal itself. | Reflexology doesn't involve any remedies or medicines. |
| chiropractic | Both can be combined with other treatments. Neither use any medications. Both are used to relieve pain. | Chiropractic is a very new treatment; Reflexology is from ancient times. |
| acupuncture | Both treatments focus on certain parts of the body to relieve pain and problems in other parts. Both began in ancient times. | Reflexology only uses hands, no needles. |

## Exercise 20
Answers will vary.

## Exercise 21
Answers will vary, but may include the following:

| symptom | medication | reason |
|---------|-----------|--------|
| 1. sneezing | *cold tablets, nasal spray, antihistamine* | *They can all help reduce sneezing.* |
| 2. a toothache | *pain killers* | *They relieve pain.* |
| 3. weakness, exhaustion | *vitamins* | *They can give you more energy.* |
| 4. coughing | *cough medicine cold tablets* | *They can help quiet a cough.* |
| 5. stomach problems | *antacid* | *It can help relieve discomfort.* |
| 6. a burn from hot oil | *ointment, pain killers* | *They prevent infection and relieve pain.* |
| 7. red eyes | *eye drops, antihistamine* | *They reduce redness and itching, and can help if allergies are causing the problem.* |
| 8. an infection | *antibiotic* | *It kills infections.* |

## Exercise 22
Answers will vary.

## Exercise 23
Answers will vary.

## GRAMMAR BOOSTER
### Exercise A
1. may  2. must  3. must  4. might  5. must  6. may

### Exercise B
Answers will vary but may include the following:
2. She might need to see the doctor. ; She must have a cold.
3. Someone may have had bad table manners. ; Someone must have done something offensive.
4. This person might be traveling for business. ; This person must be speaking with someone from another country.
5. This person may need medication. ; This person must not be able to walk.

## JUST FOR FUN
### Exercise 1
1. Answers will vary. Following is an example of what students may write:

| | | | | |
|---|---|---|---|---|
| men | let | green | end | male |
| real | net | cent | metal | age |
| man | cry | great | dry | name |

### Exercise 2
1. homeopathy  2. cold tablets  3. blood tests
4. crown

 **UNIT 3**

## Exercise 1
Answers will vary.

## Exercise 2
1. tailoring  2. courier service  3. copying  4. printing
5. housecleaning

## Exercise 3
2. b  3. a  4. c

## Exercise 4
1. enlarge  2. express  3. urgent  4. appreciate

## Exercise 5
1. a  2. b  3. b

## Exercise 6
2. process film  3. dry-clean a dress  4. enlarge a picture
5. deliver a package  6. print a report  7. print a sign

## Exercise 7
2. have your film processed  3. get these pages copied
4. had my blouse dry-cleaned  5. have this package delivered  6. get the photo enlarged  7. had them shortened  8. 's getting her shoes repaired OR is going to get her shoes repaired OR will get her shoes repaired

## Exercise 8
3. You can have your shoes repair~~.~~ for much less than it costs to buy a new pair. *(ed)*
4. We're having signs ~~to print~~ to announce the big event next week. *(printed)*
5. Where did you ~~get~~ your film from vacation processed? *(get)*
6. You should get your skirt shorten~~.~~ so it fits perfectly. *(ed)*
7. I'd like to have ~~framed~~ this picture so I can hang it up. *(framed)*
8. They didn't ~~had~~ the house cleaned yesterday. *(have)*

## Exercise 9
Answers will vary but should include the correct use of the passive causative.

## Exercise 10
3  Have you taken your shoes there before?
1  Can you recommend a good shoe repair place to fix these shoes?
5  Thanks.
4  Of course. They do a great job.
2  Why don't you have Sam's Shoe Repair do it?

## Exercise 11
1. do  2. sign  3. to clean  4. to help  5. do  6. take

## Exercise 12
1. to help  2. do  3. clean  4. stop  5. to cook
6. share

## Exercise 13
1. ≠  2. =  3. ≠  4. ≠  5. =  6. ≠  7. =

## Exercise 14
1. professional  2. helpful  3. efficient  4. reliable
5. honest  6. reasonable  7. fast

## Exercise 15
Answers will vary.

## Exercise 16
1. false  2. false  3. false  4. true  5. true  6. true
7. false

## Exercise 17
Answers will vary but may include the following:
1. People usually wash their clothes at home with soap and water, but there's no water used in dry cleaning.
2. People used kerosene and gasoline for dry cleaning in the late 1800s.
3. People started using perc because it's safer than kerosene or gasoline.

## Exercise 18
1. yes  2. yes  3. no  4. yes  5. yes  6. yes
7. no information

## Exercise 19
Answer will vary.

## Exercise 20
1. Kayla  2. Samantha  3. Mike  4. Alan  5. Carrie
6. Abby  7. Page  8. Ryan

## Exercise 21
Answer will vary.

## Exercise 22
1. a  2. c  3. b  4. c

## Exercise 23
Answers will vary.

## GRAMMAR BOOSTER
### Exercise A
2. The gallery always gets things framed by Colin's Frames.
3. We get our holiday cookies made by a professional bakery down the street.
4. They're having the package sent by Zipp's Delivery Service.
5. She got the kids' pictures taken by ~~the person with the camera~~.

### Exercise B
2. I; I got the salesperson ∧to get me a different sweater from the back.
3. C
4. I; Please get these pictures ~~copying~~ *copied* for me.
5. C
6. I; I'd love to get someone ∧to watch the children for a few hours a week.

### Exercise C
1. don't let her go; let her eat; let her stay
2. lets him go; doesn't let him eat; doesn't let him stay
3. let them go; let them eat; don't let them stay

### Exercise D
Answers will vary, but may include the following:
2. Don't let her eat candy.  3. Let your family help you clean.
4. Don't let her watch any TV.

### Exercise E
Answers will vary.

### Exercise F
2. Lisa's parents  3. their friends  4. Brian
5. us / We did.  6. Steve

## JUST FOR FUN
### Exercise 1
a. right away  b. hurry up

### Exercise 2
Across
1. budget  4. delivered  7. reliable  8. hand
9. copy  10. framed  12. fast  13. caterer  15. repair
19. professional  20. processed  21. invitations  22. DJ
Down
2. decorate  3. helpful  5. lengthened  6. dry cleaned
11. efficient  14. enlarge  16. printed  17. honest
18. custom

## UNIT 4

### Exercise 1
business: manager, business owner
science: doctor, dentist, scientist
social work: family therapist, marriage counselor
arts: painter, designer, song writer
crafts: builder, tailor

### Exercise 2
1. false  2. true  3. true  4. false  5. true  6. false

### Exercise 3
Answers will vary.

### Exercise 4
Answers will vary.

### Exercise 5
1. a  2. a  3. a  4. b

### Exercise 6
6  No kidding! I thought you wanted to be a police officer.
4  What are you up to?
3  Great, thanks.
7  That's right. I was going to, but then I changed my mind.
1  Gerry! Long time no see!
8  Really? Why?
5  Well, I'm a lawyer now.
9  Well, my tastes changed.
2  Pat! How have you been?

### Exercise 7
1. a  2. a  3. b  4. c  5. b  6. a  7. b

### Exercise 8
1. weren't going to  2. was going to  3. weren't going to
4. Was; going to  5. was going to  6. was going to
7. Weren't; going to  8. were going to  9. wasn't going to  10. were going to

### Exercise 9
1. a  2. c  3. b  4. c  5. c

### Exercise 10
Answers will vary.

### Exercise 11
1. c  2. a  3. b  4. e  5. d

### Exercise 12
1. no  2. yes  3. no  4. no

### Exercise 13
I can't believe what I did! Everyone **may** /(**must**)have laughed so hard when they heard about it—I'm sure of it. I(**should**)/ **must** have taken Jason's good advice. If I had listened to him, I **would** /(**wouldn't**)have made such a fool of myself! And I (**shouldn't**)/ **must** have left immediately, either. I(**might**)/ **must** have made the situation better by staying there for a little while. I(**must not**)/ **should not** have been thinking clearly. But I just had to leave. Everyone **should** /(**must**)have talked about it afterwards. I'm so embarrassed!

### Exercise 14
1. no  2. yes  3. yes  4. probably

### Exercise 15
Answers will vary.

### Exercise 16
2. no  3. no  4. probably  5. yes  6. maybe

**Exercise 17**

**2.** should have taken   **3.** may / might / may not / might not
have talked   **4.** must have gotten   **5.** shouldn't have sold
**6.** might / may have gotten   **7.** couldn't have done

**Exercise 18**

**1.** A talent   **2.** A skill   **3.** Experience   **4.** Knowledge

**Exercise 19**

|  | Simon Clark | Clayton Boyer | Christina Nelson |
|---|---|---|---|
| **1.** good leadership skills |  |  | ✔ |
| **2.** common sense |  |  | ✔ |
| **3.** experience in sales | ✔ |  |  |
| **4.** good language skills |  | ✔ |  |
| **5.** artistic ability |  | ✔ |  |
| **6.** logical thinking ability | ✔ |  |  |

**Exercise 20**

☐ artistic talent          ☑ computer skills
☑ management skills        ☐ mathematical ability
☑ good communication skills ☐ compassion
☑ experience in a similar position ☑ common sense
☑ organizational ability   ☐ manual dexterity

**Exercise 21**

Answers will vary.

**Exercise 22**

**1.** a  **2.** a  **3.** b  **4.** c  **5.** a

**Exercise 23**

Answers will vary but may include the following:
**1.** You should talk to all of your family members.
**2.** You might have less money for a house and a car if you
quit your job.
**3.** Some alternatives are working from home a few days
per week, working part-time, and starting a business in
your home.

**Exercise 24**

Answers will vary.

**Exercise 25**

**1.** b  **2.** a  **3.** a  **4.** a  **5.** b

**GRAMMAR BOOSTER**

**Exercise A**

Answers will vary.

**Exercise B**

**2.** A: My car broke down!  How will I get to work?  I guess
     I **could take / have to take /** ~~take~~ the bus.
   B: Don't worry.  I ~~am going to take~~ **/ will take / can take**
     you.
**3.** A: Do you want to go to the movies tomorrow night?
   B: I can't.  I am **seeing /** ~~will see~~ **/ am going to see** a play.
     You **could come / should come /** ~~are going to come~~
     with me.
**4.** A: Let's go to Bloomfield's this weekend.  I need a new pair
     of shoes.
   B: I don't know…  Bloomfield's **is having /** ~~can have~~ **/**
     **will have** their big sale tomorrow.  There ~~is~~ **/ will be /**
     **might be** too many people there!
**5.** A: The cable's out again!  That's it!  I **am calling /** ~~call~~ **/**
     **am going to call** a repairman!
   B: Go ahead, but it **will take / takes /** ~~is taking~~ hours for
     him to get here on the weekend.

**6.** A: We need one hundred copies of this report by the
     end of the week.  **Will you make / Can you make /**
     ~~Do you make~~ them tomorrow, Frank?
   B: I'm sorry.  I **will be / am /** ~~can be~~ busy all day tomorrow.

**Exercise C**

**2.** I shouldn't have ordered steak.   **3.** He ought to have
borrowed more books [from the library].   **4.** They wish they
hadn't gone skiing for their honeymoon.   **5.** Katie shouldn't
have eaten so many cookies.

**JUST FOR FUN**
**Exercise 1**

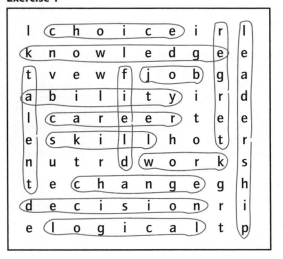

Message: Live without regret.

**UNIT 5**

**Exercise 1**

**1.** true   **2.** false   **3.** true   **4.** false   **5.** false

**Exercise 2**

Answers will vary.

**Exercise 3**

**1.** mobbed   **2.** takes place   **3.** get together
**4.** spectacular

**Exercise 4**

Answers will vary but may include the following:
Visitor: Tell me about a holiday that you celebrate in
        your country.
YOU    Well, one holiday is _Easter_.
Visitor: What kind of holiday is it?
YOU    It's a(n) _religious_ holiday that takes place in
        _the spring_.
Visitor: How do you celebrate it?
YOU    Well, in my family we usually _eat a large meal_
        _together_.
Visitor: That sounds great!

**Exercise 5**

**1.** seasonal   **2.** historical   **3.** seasonal   **4.** religious

**Exercise 6**

Answers for the second column will vary.
**2.** costumes   **3.** in a parade   **4.** fireworks   **5.** the dead
**6.** cards   **7.** a picnic

**Exercise 7**

1. a gift   2. a parade   3. a costume   4. fireworks
5. the dead   6. a picnic   7. a card

**Exercise 8**

1. who / that   2. that   3. that   4. who acts   5. that
6. that/ who

**Exercise 9**

1. who enjoy being outside
2. that are celebrated with the whole family
3. that is celebrated in Latin America
4. who is invited to someone's home
5. that people send to one another
6. who David can't stop talking about

**Exercise 10**

Mitch:     Do you mind if I ask you something?
Vanessa: **Yes, of course.** /(**Of course not.**)
Mitch:     I'm not sure about the appropriate behavior here. When you go to someone's house for dinner, what should you bring?
Vanessa: (**You should bring a small gift.**)/ **You should bring the host.**
Mitch:     **Absolutely perfect.** (**Thanks.**) It's a good thing I asked.

**Exercise 11**

Answers will vary.

**Exercise 12**

3. The woman ~~that~~ you were talking with is a professional party planner.
4. The couple ~~who~~ we saw at the movies last night used to live in our building.
5. Ella is someone (who) always makes people feel good about themselves.
6. On Valentine's Day, I think about the people ~~that~~ I love.
7. It's great to meet someone (who) goes out of their way to help you.
8. What should a person (who) is invited to dinner take?

**Exercise 13**

1. Korea   2. Japan   3. Turkey   4. India; Turkey
5. Japan; Korea

**Exercise 14**

Answers will vary.

**Exercise 15**

1 engagement
3 reception
4 honeymoon
2 wedding ceremony

**Exercise 16**

1. got engaged   2. engagement   3. wedding
4. ceremony   5. reception   6. bride   7. groom
8. newlyweds   9. honeymoon

**Exercise 17**

1. b   2. b   3. c   4. b   5. c

**Exercise 18**

Answers will vary.

**GRAMMAR BOOSTER**
**Exercise A**

1. f   2. e   3. d   4. a   5. b   6. c

**Exercise B**

Answers will vary but may include the following:
2. Ms. Heidle and Ms. Cook waved at each other.
3. Gerry and Trish meet each other for lunch every day.
4. James, Erica, and Jessie tried to find one another.
5. The employees buy one another gifts.

**Exercise C**

1. myself; (answers will vary)   2. ourselves; (answers will vary)   3. myself; (answers will vary)   4. yourself; (answers will vary)   5. himself; (answers will vary)   6. herself; (answers will vary)

**Exercise D**

A. 1. c   2. b   3. d   4. a
B. 1. c   2. a   3. d   4. b

**Exercise E**

1. by himself   2. by yourself   3. by themselves   4. one another / each other   5. by himself   6. by ourselves
7. each other / one another   8. by herself

**Exercise F**

2. who; (answers will vary)   3. who; (answers will vary)
4. whom; (answers will vary)   5. (answers will vary); whom
6. (answers will vary); whom

**JUST FOR FUN**
**Exercise 1**

Answers will vary.

**Exercise 2**

Answers will vary.

**UNIT 6**

**Exercise 1**

1. true   2. false   3. no information   4. no information
5. true   6. false

**Exercise 2**

1. gigantic   2. an earthquake   3. casualties
4. property damage

**Exercise 3**

Rob:     I'm talking to Judy. (**Would you like to say hello?**)/ **I'd like to say hello.**
Lillie:   I would, but **I have extra time** /(**I have an appointment.**)
Rob:     Is there anything you'd like me to tell (**her**)/ **them**?
Lillie:   Yes, **will do** /(**tell her to call me later.**)
Rob:     Sure, no problem.

**Exercise 4**

2. to get a new house   3. not to spend it all at one time
4. to save it for his kids   5. to give some to her   6. to put it in the bank   7. not to buy a lot of expensive things

**Exercise 5**

2. not to make a mess in the kitchen.   3. to eat all her vegetables.   4. not to touch her stuff.   5. to put away their things.

**Exercise 6**

Answers will vary, but may include the following:
2. *Open your mouth.* ; The dentist told the patient *to open his mouth.*
3. *Clean the floor.* ; She said *to clean the floor.*
4. *Be careful!* ; Her dad said *to be careful.*

## Exercise 7
Answers will vary.

## Exercise 8
*1*  What's going on in the news today?
*5*  Thank goodness for that.
*6*  Yes, but several buildings were destroyed downtown.
*2*  I heard about a bad storm in Nagoya.
*4*  They said that no one was hurt.
*3*  Are people okay?
*7*  What a shame.

## Exercise 9
**Jonathan:** I just talked to Gary Feldman on the phone.
**Barbara:** Oh, what did he **tell** / (**say**)?
**Jonathan:** He **said** / (**told**) me **don't go** / (**not to go**) to work today. He **told** / (**said**) that he **tries** / (**tried**) to go, but he **has to** / (**had to**) turn around.
**Barbara:** Why? What happened?
**Jonathan:** He (**said**) / **told** that the storm last night **is** / (**was**) really awful. The roads are covered in ice.
**Barbara:** Really? I listened to the weather report last night, and they **told** / (**said**) it **isn't** / (**wasn't**) going to be too bad.

\*         \*         \*         \*         \*

**Nicole:** Did Nancy **say** / (**tell**) you anything about yesterday's meeting?
**Jenna:** She didn't **tell** / (**say**) too much. Why?
**Nicole:** Well, she (**told**) / **said** me that it **goes** / (**went**) OK and (**not to**) / **doesn't** worry. But she (**told**) / **said** Charlie that it (**was**) / **is** a disaster!
**Jenna:** It sounds like she didn't (**tell**) / **say** someone the truth.

## Exercise 10
1. flood  2. drought  3. landslide  4. hurricane
5. tornado

## Exercise 11
Answers will vary but may include the following:
2. The radio announcer said the cyclone was coming in our direction.
3. Alexa said the weather in the islands was horrible.
4. Howard Denton told me that the storm was strong.
5. Peter and Sam said that a flood covered the road.

## Exercise 12
3. Ryan told Debbie (that) there was a problem with the car.
4. Valerie said (that) they had called her late.
5. Kathy told Colleen (that) she was ready to go any time.
6. Paul said (that) everyone had gotten sick.

## Exercise 13
2. The *Morning Sun* said (that) a flood left thousands of people homeless.
3. The *Daily News* said (that) a police officer saved 13 children.
4. The *Evening Edition* said (that) President John Westin delivered his last speech.

## Exercise 14
Answers will vary but may include the following:
2. Chris said (that) he'd just gotten back from Machu Picchu in Peru. Theresa told him to show her the pictures.
3. The little girl told her father to tell her the story about the princess. Her father said (that) she'd already heard that story a thousand times.
4. Joey said (that) he'd gotten the fruits and vegetables at a farmer's market. Brooke told him that they were very fresh and delicious.

5. Janet told Brandon not to tell anyone her news yet. Brandon said (that) he wasn't going to say anything to anyone.
6. The customer said (that) she was looking for a brown leather belt for her husband. The salesperson told her that they had several great styles available.

## Exercise 15
☐ monsoon   ☐ flood   ☑ non-perishable food
☑ first-aid kit   ☐ power outage   ☐ other: _____
☐ evacuation   ☑ flashlight

## Exercise 16
2. g  3. e  4. a  5. c  6. i  7. d

## Exercise 17
☑ Have a plan in case there is an emergency or disaster.
☑ Write down emergency telephone numbers.
☑ Gather together some things you might need in an emergency.
☐ Show young children how to turn on and off the water, gas, and electricity.
☑ Know how to use the items in a first aid kit.
☐ Decide when to evacuate.
☑ Find a place for everyone in your family to go if you aren't together.
☐ Practice your plans one time.

## Exercise 18
2. to make   3. to review   4. to decide   5. to choose

## Exercise 19
Answers will vary.

## Exercise 20
1. natural disaster  2. missing  3. survivors  4. death toll
5. victims  6. destruction  7. homeless

## Exercise 21
*3*  severe
*5*  mild
*2*  deadly
*1*  catastrophic
*4*  moderate

## Exercise 22
1. false  2. true  3. false  4. false  5. no information
6. true

## Exercise 23
Answers will vary but may include the following:
1. the ship; the boat; on *Endurance*
2. because there were no supplies
3. none

## Exercise 24
Answers will vary. Following is one example of what students may produce:

What a disaster! I think there was a terrible storm in this town. Some buildings were destroyed and the roads are closed. I think a tornado passed through, and then there was a flood. It looks like there were no deaths.

## GRAMMAR BOOSTER
### Exercise A
2. **I**; The child said "Please read me a story."
3. **C**
4. **C**

**5.** I; The travel guide tells visitors ~~to~~ "Try to take a tour of the island."

**6.** I; The woman told her son ~~to~~ "Don't play with your food."

### Exercise B
1. "Have a good weekend."
2. "Put the mail on the desk."
3. "Try the salmon."
4. "Don't believe everything on television."
5. "Don't come home too late."
6. "Get the package ready to mail."

### Exercise C
2. to make sure our homework is done for tomorrow.
3. not to leave without him.
4. him to bring me a glass of water.
5. me to pick up his shirts from the dry cleaners.

### Exercise D
Answers will vary but may include the following:
2. I'm *surprised by the results of your tests.*; Yesterday, the doctor said *he was surprised by the results of the patient's tests.*
3. He *took my doll!*; Kimmy told her mother *that he had taken her doll.*
4. We're *going to win the game!*; The coach said *that they are going to win the game.*

### JUST FOR FUN
### Exercise 1
1. Answers will vary, but might include the following words:

| | | | | |
|---|---|---|---|---|
| sea | lean | net | nail | dear |
| turtle | tea | real | side | tear |
| neat | nut | ties | dial | near |

 **UNIT 7**

### Exercise 1
1. *Hatchepsut: The Female Pharaoh*
2. *The 7 Habits of Highly Effective People*
3. *The DaVinci Code; The Interpreter of Maladies*
4. *Hatchepsut: The Female Pharaoh; The 7 Habits of Highly Effective People*
5. *The Interpreter of Maladies*

### Exercise 2
Answers will vary.

### Exercise 3
2. = 3. = 4. ≠ 5. =

### Exercise 4
1. What are you up to? 2. Are you looking for anything specific? 3. it didn't really turn me on 4. it's a real page-turner 5. thanks for the tip 6. I'll lend it to you

### Exercise 5
Answers will vary.

### Exercise 6
1. c 2. a 3. d 4. b

### Exercise 7
1. true 2. false 3. true 4. false 5. true

### Exercise 8
Answers will vary.

### Exercise 9
1. a 2. a 3. a 4. b 5. b 6. a

### Exercise 10
1. whether 2. if 3. when 4. what 5. if

### Exercise 11
1. a travel book 2. a mystery 3. a biography 4. science fiction 5. an autobiography 6. a romance novel

### Exercise 12
Answers will vary.

### Exercise 13
2. what the magazine is about
3. if / whether there are any other books by Vanessa Heart
4. why the book is so popular

### Exercise 14
Answers will vary but may include the following:
2. Tell me whether this is a bestseller.
3. I was wondering why you didn't finish reading this.
4. Can you tell me when she wrote her memoir?
5. I'm curious who this present is for.
6. I'd really like to know whether you like to read nonfiction.
7. I wonder if we are ready to go to the library.

### Exercise 15
Answers will vary.

### Exercise 16
6 Would you like to go with me sometime?
1 What a beautiful painting!
7 No thanks. I'm all thumbs.
4 Yes, I learned how at the art supplies store on First Avenue.
2 Thanks.
5 I didn't know they had art classes there.
3 Did you make it?

### Exercise 17
Answers will vary.

### Exercise 18
1. so 2. so 3. not 4. not 5. so

### Exercise 19
2. C
3. I; I didn't think that they ~~have~~ <sup>had</sup> any extra time.
4. I; I don't ~~guess~~ <sup>think / believe</sup> so. OR I ~~don't~~ guess so.
5. I; I hoped we ~~aren't~~ <sup>weren't</sup> the last people to arrive.
6. C

### Exercise 20
Answers will vary.

### Exercise 21
1. true 2. true 3. false 4. true 5. false

### Exercise 22
1. e 2. d 3. c 4. a 5. b

### Exercise 23
1. skimmed through 2. collected clippings 3. listened to a book on tape 4. did puzzles 5. read aloud 6. curled up with

### Exercise 24
a. did puzzles; 4 b. collected clippings; 2 c. listened to a book on tape; 3 d. curled up with; 6 e. read aloud; 5 f. skimmed through; 1

### Exercise 25
Answers will vary.

**GRAMMAR BOOSTER**

**Exercise A**

**2.** b  **3.** c  **4.** c  **5.** a  **6.** b

**Exercise B**

**2.** Can you tell me *where everyone went?*
**3.** I don't know *when the movie starts.*
**4.** We wonder *if the product is available online.*
**5.** Would you mind telling me *why the flight is arriving late?*
**6.** I can't remember *what she looks like.*

**Exercise C**

**2.** ☑ We're wondering if the baby is a boy or a girl.

☐ We're wondering whether is it going to rain.

**3.** ☐ Can you tell me what is the time?

☑ Could you explain what the problem is?

**4.** ☑ Do you know where they're going?

☐ Did they tell you when are they eating dinner?

**5.** ☐ I'm not sure when did they arrive.

☑ I want to know when their plane left.

**6.** ☐ Can you tell me *if / whether* the book is a page-turner?

☑ Can you tell me if the book is based on a true story?

**Exercise D**

Answers will vary but may include the following:
**2.** to cook  **3.** to move  **4.** to buy  **5.** to arrive
**6.** to call

**Exercise E**

Answers will vary.

**JUST FOR FUN**

**Exercise 1**

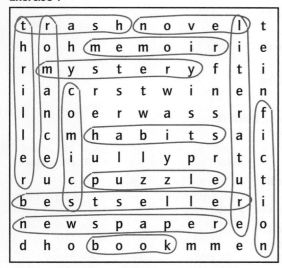

Answer: The first winner was Sully Prudhomme.

**Exercise 2**

**1.** cliffhanger  **2.** autobiography  **3.** magazines  **4.** titles
**5.** authors  **6.** review  **7.** borrow  **8.** guess  **9.** issue
**10.** believe  **11.** clippings  **12.** hope  **13.** book
**14.** think

**UNIT 8**

**Exercise 1**

Answers will vary.

**Exercise 2**

Answers will vary.

**Exercise 3**

Answers will vary.

**Exercise 4**

**1.** a  **2.** b  **3.** b  **4.** b

**Exercise 5**

**2.** offering high quality    ~~novel~~    top-of-the-line
**3.** innovative    ~~high-end~~    revolutionary
**4.** state-of-the-art    cutting-edge    ~~unique~~
**5.** top-of-the-line    high-end    ~~fast~~
**6.** new    revolutionary    ~~high-tech~~
**7.** ~~innovative~~    first-rate    high-end

**Exercise 6**

Answers will vary.

**Exercise 7**

**1.** maybe  **2.** no  **3.** no  **4.** maybe  **5.** no  **6.** yes
**7.** no  **8.** no

**Exercise 8**

**1.** take  **2.** are  **3.** get

**Exercise 9**

**1.** 'll lose  **2.** won't have  **3.** will have

**Exercise 10**

**1.** didn't think  **2.** weren't  **3.** cost

**Exercise 11**

**2.** is  **3.** don't want  **4.** wouldn't do  **5.** knew  **6.** will
have to  **7.** don't change  **8.** won't have  **9.** want
**10.** weren't

**Exercise 12**

Answers will vary.

**Exercise 13**

A: *I'm sorry I spilled coffee on the rug.*
B: No problem. It can happen to anyone.
A: *Well, it was my fault.*
B: Why do you say that?
A: *If I had paid attention to where I was going, I would
have seen that table.*
B: That's OK. *Don't worry about it.*

**Exercise 14**

**1.** yes  **2.** no  **3.** yes  **4.** no  **5.** yes  **6.** yes  **7.** yes

**Exercise 15**

**1.** hadn't been  **2.** would have had  **3.** wouldn't
have bought  **4.** wouldn't have gone  **5.** had known
**6.** had trained

**Exercise 16**

**1.** had made  **2.** hadn't talked to  **3.** would have chosen
**4.** would have had  **5.** wouldn't have eaten

**Exercise 17**

Answers will vary.

**Exercise 18**

**1.** c  **2.** b  **3.** f  **4.** f  **5.** c  **6.** d  **7.** g  **8.** e  **9.** g
**10.** g  **11.** c  **12.** f  **13.** h  **14.** a

**Exercise 19**

Answers for explanations will vary. Following the correct
adjective is an example of what students may produce.
**1.** low-tech; *It doesn't have any parts or use any technology.*
**2.** efficient; *It's a quick way to produce your address many times.*

3. high-tech; *The invention uses new technology.*
4. wacky; *The instrument is silly and crazy. It's fun, but it probably doesn't make very beautiful music.*
5. innovative; *Nothing like this exists!*
6. low-tech; *The product doesn't use energy or electricity.*

**Exercise 20**
1. true  2. false  3. false  4. false  5. false  6. true

**Exercise 21**
Answers will vary but may include the following:
1. Ella didn't like how uncomfortable high heels were.
2. Ella's shoes are comfortable. / The high-heel on Ella's shoes can be changed to make a flat shoe.
3. Answers will vary.

**Exercise 22**
Answers will vary.

**GRAMMAR BOOSTER**
**Exercise A**
1. if  2. if  3. If  4. unless  5. if  6. Unless  7. Unless

**Exercise B**
2. wish you would come  3. wishes he had  4. wish I had invented  5. wishes the patient would eat  6. wish I hadn't eaten  7. wishes her mother would take

**Exercise C**
2. had been damaged  3. would (still) be dancing
4. would (still) be looking for  5. had been given
6. would (still) be working

**JUST FOR FUN**
**Exercise 1**
Across
1. would  3. invention  7. cutting edge  9. high end
12. innovative  13. fault
Down
2. unique  4. efficient  5. wacky  6. technology
8. had  10. novel  11. were

**UNIT 9**

**Exercise 1**
Across
1. dictatorship  3. government  5. constitution
7. election
Down
1. democracy  2. politics  4. monarchy  6. vote

**Exercise 2**
1. =  2. ≠  3. ≠  4. =  5. =

**Exercise 3**
Answers will vary.

**Exercise 4**
5  The election. Who do you think is going to win?
3  Well, would you mind if I asked you a question?
6  That's a good question!
1  In general, is it acceptable to discuss politics here at work?
4  Not at all. What would you like to know?
2  That depends on how well you know someone.

**Exercise 5**
Answers will vary.

**Exercise 6**

← radical   liberal   moderate   conservative   reactionary →

**Exercise 7**
1. moderate  2. reactionary  3. liberal  4. radical
5. conservative

**Exercise 8**
Answers will vary.

**Exercise 9**
3. I; There *is* a lot of news to tell you about!
4. I; Do you have time~~s~~ to help us?
5. C
6. I; Good help *is* hard to find.
7. I; Government officials from both sides are meeting to discuss ~~a~~ peace.
8. C
9. I; Money is collected to help families living in ~~the~~ poverty.
10. I; Without proof~~s~~, the police can't arrest him.

**Exercise 10**
1. e  2. b  3. d  4. a  5. c

**Exercise 11**
1. true  2. false  3. true  4. false  5. true  6. false

**Exercise 12**
1. a.  2. b  3. a  4. b  5. a  6. a

**Exercise 13**
Objects will vary but may include the following:  3. his friends  4. parents  5. people  6. X  7. X  8. him
9. X  10. X

**Exercise 14**
Answers will vary.

**Exercise 15**
1. c  2. b  3. c  4. b  5. a  6. b

**Exercise 16**
Answers will vary.

**Exercise 17**
Answers will vary.

**Exercise 18**
Answers will vary.

**GRAMMAR BOOSTER**
**Exercise A**
1. justice is  2. law  3. hair  4. much sugar  5. peace
6. light  7. Medicine is  8. coffee is; tea  9. cheeses are

**Exercise B**
Answers will vary, but must include correct use of a gerund or an infinitive as a noun.

**Exercise C**
Answers will vary
1. [gerund]  2. [infinitive]  3. [gerund]  4. [gerund]
5. [infinitive]  6. [gerund]  7. [infinitive]  8. [infinitive or gerund]

**JUST FOR FUN**
**Exercise 1**
"Be the change you want to see in the world."

**Exercise 2**
1. issue  2. vote  3. wrong  4. age  5. election

## UNIT 10

### Exercise 1
**1.** Colombia  **2.** Caracas  **3.** Brasilia  **4.** Rio de Janeiro
**5.** Atlantic Ocean  **6.** Lake Titicaca

### Exercise 2
**1.** Chile; Ecuador  **2.** Santa Cruz  **3.** Montevideo  **4.** the Andes Mountains  **5.** Argentina  **6.** Bolivia; Paraguay

### Exercise 3
Answers will vary.

### Exercise 4
**1.** a  **2.** b  **3.** a  **4.** b  **5.** a

### Exercise 5
**1.** Yes, it's that way  **2.** can be  **3.** dangerous  **4.** warning

### Exercise 6

**Attention All Hikers:** Hiking is great exercise, and it can be a lot of fun. But hiking can also be __dangerous__. Follow these rules to stay safe.

• Take plenty of food and water. This is a long hike, and it can be __exhausting__. You'll need food to give you energy.
• Don't ever go into a __cave__. Animals might be living there, and they'll fight to protect their territory.
• Be careful if you hike early in the morning. Sometimes it's __foggy__, and it can be difficult to see.

• If you hike in the evening, take a flashlight. If you're not back before it gets __dark__, you'll need it to find your way back.
• Be careful in the winter. The paths can get icy, and then they're really __slippery__.

### Exercise 7
**1.** Wow! This is steep!  **2.** It's really dark.  **3.** This path is exhausting.  **4.** It can be really rocky.

### Exercise 8
Answers will vary but may include the following:
**2.** The book is too long to read in one day.
**3.** It's too big (for her) to wear.
**4.** It's too late (for them) to see that movie.
**5.** It's too noisy (for him) to sleep.
**6.** They're too tired to keep walking

### Exercise 9
**2.** That sweater is too expensive for her to buy.
**3.** It's not too late for you to call Matt.
**4.** It's too hot for me to drink coffee.
**5.** That movie is too violent for Beverly to see.

### Exercise 10
**1.** no  **2.** yes  **3.** yes  **4.** no  **5.** yes

### Exercise 11
Answers will vary.

### Exercise 12

**PORTUGAL**

Portugal is a nation __in__ southwestern Europe, and is __on__ the western coast __of__ the Iberian Peninsula. Spain is both north and west __of__ Portugal, which is on the Atlantic Ocean.

There are many mountain ranges __in__ the North, but the largest and highest mountain range in the country, Serra da Estrela, is located __in__ the central region of the country.

The capital city, Lisbon, is __on__ the west coast __of__ Portugal. It is also located __on__ the Tajo River, which is the longest river in Portugal.

The city of Porto is located __on__ the Douro River, which is __in__ the North.

### Exercise 13
Answers will vary but may include the following:
**1.** _Vladivostock_ is in _the southeast of Russia_.
**2.** _Kazakstan_ is southwest of _Russia_.
**3.** _Murmansk_ is on _the north coast of Russia_.
**4.** _Astana_ is in _Kazakhstan_.
**5.** _Volgograd_ is north of _Groznyy_.

### Exercise 14
Answers will vary.

### Exercise 15
**1.** mountainous  **2.** valley  **3.** flat  **4.** hilly  **5.** island
**6.** forest

### Exercise 16
**1.** c  **2.** h  **3.** f  **4.** i  **5.** b  **6.** d  **7.** e  **8.** a  **9.** g

### Exercise 17
Answers will vary.

### Exercise 18
Answers will vary.

### Exercise 19
**1.** d  **2.** c  **3.** a  **4.** b

### Exercise 20
**1.** c  **2.** c  **3.** b  **4.** a  **5.** c

### Exercise 21
**1.** over 7.5 km  **2.** tour guides  **3.** call or visit them online

## GRAMMAR BOOSTER
### Exercise A
Answers will vary but may include the following:
**2.** expensive to buy all the time  **3.** young to leave alone  **4.** steep to climb  **5.** high to go swimming
**6.** uncomfortable to wear all day

### Exercise B
Answers will vary but may include the following:
**2.** _Charlie's Angels_ is a movie that's not good enough _to see twice_.
**3.** _My mother_ is pretty enough _to be a model_.
**4.** In my opinion, _10_ years old isn't old enough _to stay home alone_.
**5.** _Donald Trump_ is a person who is rich enough _to buy whatever he wants_.
**6.** _Our dog_ isn't big enough _to scare anyone_.

### Exercise C
**2.** on; in  **3.** of  **4.** in  **5.** in; of  **6.** on  **7.** of

### Exercise D
**2.** $\overset{T}{t}$he novel $\overset{D}{d}$racula by $\overset{I}{i}$rish author $\overset{B}{b}$ram $\overset{S}{s}$toker was first published in $\overset{G}{g}$reat $\overset{B}{b}$ritain in 1897.
**3.** $\overset{I}{i}$n $\overset{C}{c}$anada, $\overset{T}{t}$hanksgiving is celebrated on the second $\overset{M}{m}$onday in $\overset{O}{o}$ctober. $\overset{B}{b}$ut in the $\overset{U}{u}$nited $\overset{S}{s}$tates, the holiday is celebrated on the fourth $\overset{T}{t}$hursday of $\overset{N}{n}$ovember.
**4.** $\overset{T}{t}$he beginning of the $\overset{M}{m}$iddle $\overset{A}{a}$ges is often called the $\overset{D}{d}$ark $\overset{A}{a}$ges. $\overset{B}{b}$y this time the $\overset{G}{g}$reat $\overset{C}{c}$ivilizations of $\overset{G}{g}$reece and $\overset{R}{r}$ome had fallen, and life in $\overset{E}{e}$urope was very hard.

5. $\overset{C}{\cancel{C}}$ity of $\overset{G}{g}$od" is a $\overset{B}{b}$razilian movie about life in one part of $\overset{R}{r}$io de $\overset{J}{j}$aneiro. The movie is in $\overset{P}{p}$ortuguese.

6. $\overset{H}{h}$induism is one of the oldest religions in the world. $\overset{T}{t}$oday it is practiced primarily in $\overset{I}{i}$ndia, $\overset{N}{n}$epal, and a few other countries.

**Exercise E**
Answers will vary.

**Exercise F**
2. _The_ Roman Empire reached its most powerful point in the year 116. At this time, much of __X__ Europe, __X__ Asia, and parts of __X__ Africa were under Rome's control.

3. The Caspian Sea is the largest lake in the world. It is a saltwater lake that is surrounded by __X__ Kazakhstan, __X__ Turkmenistan, __X__ Iran, __X__ Azerbaijan, and __X__ Russia. The largest freshwater lake is __X__ Lake Superior, which is located on the border between __X__ Canada and _the_ United States.

4. The explorer Marco Polo is often credited with introducing pasta from __X__ China to his native country, __X__ Italy. Although this fact is debatable, it is known that Marco Polo did travel to _the_ Far East and is responsible for some of the first introductions of eastern culture to _the_ West.

5. Can you name the tallest mountain in the world? You've probably learned that it's __X__ Mount Everest (8,850 meters tall) in _the_ Himalaya Mountains. The top of this mountain is the highest point on earth. But did you know that there is another mountain that is actually taller? Its name is __X__ Mauna Kea, and it's located in _the_ Pacific Ocean. This mountain is 9,750 meters tall from its bottom to its top. But since the bottom of this mountain is on the ocean floor, it doesn't reach as high as __X__ Mount Everest.

6. _The_ Gulf of Aqaba is in _the_ Middle East. It separates _the_ Sinai Peninsula, which is part of __X__ Egypt, from _the_ Kingdom of Saudi Arabia.

**JUST FOR FUN**
**Exercise 1**
Answers will vary, but might include the following words:

| take | great | near | break |
|------|-------|------|-------|
| beat | treat | eat | bake |
| tear | ring | hike | bike |

**Exercise 2**
Answers will vary.